Science, Students, and Schools:

A GUIDE FOR THE MIDDLE AND SECONDARY SCHOOL TEACHER

Science, Students, and Schools:

A GUIDE FOR THE MIDDLE AND SECONDARY SCHOOL TEACHER

Ronald D. Simpson
Norman D. Anderson
NORTH CAROLINA STATE UNIVERSITY AT RALEIGH

To Dock & Lee:

Best wishes to the two individuals responsible for rearing my wife, and hence, making my life richer and happier. I don't expect you to read all of this but you might enjoy some of the boxed chapter openers.

Ron Simpson
march 27, 1981

John Wiley & Sons
NEW YORK • CHICHESTER • BRISBANE • TORONTO

Library of Congress Cataloging in Publication Data

Simpson, Ronald D.
  Science, students, and schools.

  Includes bibliographies and index.
  1. Science—Study and teaching (Secondary)—
United States. 2. Science—Teacher training—
United States. I. Anderson, Norman D., joint
author. II. Title.
Q183.3.A1S53   507'.12   80-23124
ISBN 0-471-02477-5

Printed in the United States of America

10 9 8 7 6 5 4 3 2 1

PREFACE

The preface is the place where authors can discuss some of the general principles that guided the writing of their book and where they can express their gratitude to all those who have helped them turn a dream into a reality. This is what we would like to do here. If this discussion were given a title, it would be "In These Things We Believe."

We believe that science and technology have played a major role in the movement of humankind from a primitive, harsh existence to a world of knowledge, understanding, and increased comfort. We also believe that with this giant step has come freedom, which means more choices and options for individuals in our society. With freedom, of course, comes responsibility. It is the need for worldwide responsibility that breeds a need for scientific and technological literacy. As Thomas Jefferson pointed out, any democracy depends on an informed and educated citizenry. We believe few challenges are more urgent and compelling than that of educating our young people in science.

We believe that young people are our country's most precious resource and that they come in all shapes, sizes, and temperaments. Regardless of background, culture, and personality, each of these young people is important, both as an individual and as a potentially productive member of our society.

We believe that many of the societal issues of our times are related to science and should be examined in the science curriculum. At a time when per capita resources are diminishing, when energy is limited, and when social and moral values are changing, science education holds a very special place in the curriculum of our schools. As a student of ours recently remarked, "Many of our problems are science-caused and will have to be science-solved." Indeed, our survival as a country and as a planet depends on how harmoniously we can live within our environment and how well we can relate to others. Our ultimate success, we believe, will depend in large measure on how the people of the world use science and technology.

Finally, we are aware that there are many ways to organize and conduct science instruction and to evaluate students. The mark of professional science teachers is the repertoire of skills they use in the classroom and the ways they interact with students. Effective teaching embodies many skills that can be learned and improved upon over time. We have drawn from many years of our own experience, from the experience of others, and from a broad range of literature and research in an effort to describe the state of the art of science teaching and to offer practical suggestions for ways science teachers can continue to improve instruction. It is our hope that readers of this book, many of whom will be college students preparing to teach science, will find our ideas and suggestions useful.

We wish to thank those who reviewed parts or all of the manuscript. Professor Frank Crawley, University of Texas at Austin; Professor Jerome DeBruin, University of Toledo; Professor John Shrum, University of Georgia; Professor Irwin Slesnick, Western Washington University; and Professor A. Paul Wishart, University of Tennessee, reviewed the manuscript and made many useful suggestions. Professor Dean Brown of Colorado State University, one of the great teachers of prospective science educators, used preliminary copies of the manuscript with his students and gave us valuable feedback. Mr. Bill Spooner of the Science Education Division of the North Carolina State Department of Public Instruction provided many useful materials and good ideas on school science safety.

We also wish to acknowledge the valuable contributions of those who helped with the typing and dozens of other tasks involved in writing a book. Without the assistance of Ms. Vicki Price, Mrs. Margie Miller, Ms. Betsy Council, and Mrs. Trish Sanford, this task would have been impossible and would have been abandoned long ago. We deeply appreciate their expertise, loyalty, and patience.

Ronald D. Simpson
Norman D. Anderson

Raleigh, North Carolina
July, 1980

CONTENTS

CHAPTER 1

Why Study Science?

AS JUNIOR SCIENTISTS SEE IT...

Mark Twain once observed that the most interesting information comes from children, for "they tell all they know and then stop." During the 14 years that I've taught youngsters, I've found that their remarks on scientific subjects can be not only interesting, but hilarious. Here's what I mean:

"A scientific fact was only a theory as a child."

"The axis is just a make-believe line, but the earth still manages to turn on it somehow."

"Naughtical miles tell how far it is to places we should not go."

"Newton noticed that anything at rest tended to remain at rest. For this he grew famous."

"One way to tell for sure if a sweater is made of wool is to hold it over a flame. If it burnt slowly it was wool."

"Climate is with us all the time, while weather comes and goes."

"There is nothing to keep a liquid from changing to another state. The Mississippi River, as we all know, does not have to stay in that state alone."

"As a puddle dries up the water goes into the air. Chemically, we say that the puddle evacuates."

"In looking at a drop of water under a microscope, they found that there are twice as many Hs as Os."

"Heavy water is with ships in it."

"The water cycle is a thing on which a person can ride on the water by pedaling along. I don't think it has been invented yet."

"The Nebulus Theory of how the earth got started is still pretty hazy."

"Many things about chemistry that were once thought to be science fiction now actually are."

"After chemists went to all the trouble to learn how to mix iron and oxygen, they only came up with rust."

"Glycerin is sociable with almost everything except nitrogen."

"To most people solutions mean finding the answer, but to chemists solutions are things that are still all mixed up."

"We say the cause of perfume disappearing is evaporation. Evaporation gets blamed for many things people forget to put the top on."

"While molecules in gases and liquids bounce around from place to place, in solids they just lay there and vibrate."

"Some oxygen molecules help fires to burn while others choose to help make water, so sometimes it is brother against brother."

"Rocks are gradually softened through aging. The first hundred years of a rock's life are the hardest."

From Carl Davis, "As Junior Scientists See It," *Catholic School Journal*, December 1969, pp. 16–17. Reprinted with permission of the publisher. Copyright © 1969 by Macmillan Professional Magazines, Inc. All rights reserved.

Have you noticed how short, straightforward questions are often the most difficult ones to answer satisfactorily? So it is with the question of "why *study* science?," or its companion question stated in the terms usually employed by teachers and schools, "why *teach* science?" Let's consider these questions from two perspectives.

First, what do students see as the benefits of studying science? Comments were solicited from several hundred students ranging in age from ten to eighteen. Several of these student statements, selected to show the range of opinions and ideas, are reported below under WHAT STUDENTS SAY. Because student ideas and opinions are an important part of science education, student views are reported on a variety of other topics throughout this book.

Second, what do educators, scientists, parents, and society in general see as the goals or purposes of teaching science in our middle and secondary schools? A partial answer can be obtained by checking the headlines in newspapers and news magazines or by catching the news on radio or television (see Figure 1.1). Every day there are dozens of news stories that illustrate how science permeates every "nook and cranny" of our daily lives. For most adults, a major goal of science teaching is to prepare our young people for happy and productive lives in this age of science.

WHAT STUDENTS SAY

How Can I Benefit From Studying Science?

- Because it will help me get a better job when I get out of school.
- I don't get anything out of science—it is my worst subject!
- My teacher says it will help make me a better thinker.
- Understand myself better.
- In the ninth grade I *really* dreaded biology. I guess it was the thoughts of dissecting a frog that scared me most. During the tenth grade biology became my favorite subject, and I overcame my fears of a lot of animals.
- Our counselor says that taking lots of science in high school helps you in college.
- The more I study science the more I appreciate everything around me.
- A good question—I wish someone would explain to me why I have to take science to graduate.
- I guess it will help me in college.

Why study life science in junior high school?

We live in an age of science. Without some knowledge of life science, there are many things happening everyday you would not be able to understand. Would you be able to read the newspaper with much understanding? Would you be able to understand what the news commentators are talking about on the news programs on the radio and television? Probably not.

EPIDEMIC FORECAST

The State Department of Public Health today warned that a new strain of flu virus may strike this winter. Health officials advised that babies and older people should be vaccinated.

Local doctors indicated an adequate supply of vaccine is on hand. The vaccinations can be obtained from most doctors and at the City Health Clinic.

Studying life science should help you to ask questions and to be a better thinker. The questioning mind is an important characteristic of scientists. In studying science you should feel free to ask lots of questions. You will learn that we don't have answers to many of these questions—at least not yet.

Don't be afraid of asking questions and trying to solve them. It is good preparation for solving the many problems you will face throughout life.

HOT CITY COUNCIL MEETING

City officials this morning were at a loss about what to do about the city's mosquito problem. Of the 200 citizens who attended last night's city council meeting, about half wanted the spraying continued and about half wanted it stopped.

Mr. Oliver Cole, who spoke for those opposed to the spraying, raised several important questions.

"How does the chemical spray affect other living things, such as humans, pets, and birds?"

"Is there any danger if the poisonous spray gets into the city's drinking water?"

"What other ways can the mosquitoes be controlled besides by the use of sprays?"

Many jobs require a knowledge of life science. The number of scientists increases each year. It is estimated that over ninety percent of the scientists that have ever lived are alive today! But perhaps more important is the fact that workers in many fields need a knowledge of life science.

Secretary, Doctor's Office. Must know medical terms, shorthand, and be able to type. 40 hours per week, no Saturday work. Circle Employment Agency. 499-6103.

Farm Help. Owner ill. Need help to care for livestock and harvest crops. Good pay. Mrs. Bill Goodman. 737-0964.

Landscape Foreman. Must know local trees, shrubs, and flowers. Capable of supervising nursery crews. Prefer college graduate. Write Box 93A in care of this paper.

Medical Technologist. Small hospital. Good working conditions, paid health insurance. Also need nurses, full and part-time. Call 787-9642.

Hobbies and recreation often involve life science. Your great-grandparents probably didn't have as much time for hobbies and recreation as you do. Because of the advances made by science and technology, we now work fewer hours each week. And science is involved in many of the ways we spend our increased amounts of leisure time.

**WHAT'S GOING ON
AROUND THE CITY**
Want some new ideas for Christmas presents? Attend the demonstration on making terrariums at the Craft Shop in City Park at 8:00 PM Tuesday.

* * * * * *

Judges for the Capital City Dog Show will meet at 12:30 PM on Wednesday at Red's Cafeteria.

* * * * * *

The Annual Fall Bird Watch will be held next Sunday beginning at 6:00 AM. Those interested should meet at the Lodge in Big Lake State Park. Bring field glasses, warm clothes, and a sack lunch. Free drinks will be provided.

FIGURE 1.1 This section from a junior high school science textbook discusses some of the ways students can benefit from studying science. Reprinted by permission of Harper & Row, Publishers, Inc., New York. From Walter R. Brown and Norman D. Anderson, *Life Science: A Search for Understanding,* pp. 9–10. Copyright © 1977, 1971 by J. B. Lippincott Company.

Science in our Lives

We live in a world of rapid change. Ours is a world of electronic calculators, stereophonic sound, and colored television pictures via satellite from all parts of the earth and beyond. In contrast, people only a generation or two ago added columns of figures on the back of grocery lists, listened to warped records on spring-driven phonographs, and were thrilled by their first "talking" motion picture.

Not all of the changes have brought us happiness and a better way of life. Rivers and streams that once meandered across a tranquil landscape too often are now open sewage ditches stretched across a horizon of junked automobiles, strip mines, and decaying cities. The open fields and peaceful woods of Henry David Thoreau, Daniel Boone, and Buffalo Bill Cody are crisscrossed, bisected, and punctuated by highways, power-lines, and settlements large and small. It is little wonder that older citizens talk so much of the "good old days," and many of us find ourselves saying, "There is no such thing as a free lunch!"

Most of the changes of this century have been fueled by the partnership of science and technology. To the parents of a child whose life has been saved by open-heart surgery, the fruits of science and technology represent what is good about living in the twentieth century. To those whose parents or grandparents are dying of brown lung disease or pesticide poisoning, what is considered by some to be our salvation is instead

How many ways do you see science and technology illustrated in this picture?

perceived as the villain of modern civilization. What should the ledger sheet show for science and technology—the black ink of accomplishment or the red ink of failure?

In addition to the materialistic products, any assessment should include the other ways science has changed our lives. The attitudes and thought processes of modern science color our perceptions and greatly influence our decisions. Those knowledgeable of science reject superstition and treasure the demonstration of "cause-and-effect." The practices of modern medicine are readily accepted, and little thought is given to witches and demons. As Bertrand Russell has pointed out in *The Impact of Science on Society*,[1] it was diffusion of the scientific outlook in the seventeenth century that brought an end to any widespread belief in witchcraft.

There is no doubt about it—our time is an age of science. Science affects every aspect of our lives: what we eat and what we wear; what we do as work and what we do as play; what we think and what we feel; even how we are born and how we die. Few moments in our lives are untouched by the products and processes of science.

---

[1] Bertrand, Russell, *The Impact of Science on Society*, New York: Columbia University Press, 1951.

The Central Goal of Science Education

Because of the scientific nature of our society and the individual needs of its members, every person in order to function effectively must be *scientifically literate.* Scientific literacy must be one of the major goals of the education received by each new generation. And for those whose formal schooling has ended, ways must be found to enable them to continue to learn about the achievements and advancements of science.

Scientific literacy is the central goal for teaching science in elementary and secondary schools. Like Polaris, the North Star, which gives us a fixed point for steering a course, the goal of scientific literacy can give direction to what we do and how we do it. And science programs designed to help all our students become scientifically literate must be greatly different from those limited to preparing a selected few for careers in science.

Although the goal of scientific literacy can give direction to a science program, its components must be described before instruction can take place. Teachers must know if they are to teach about atoms, or ants, or attitudes. They also must know if factual information is to be taught by rote or thinking skills emphasized through investigative laboratory work.

What is Scientific Literacy?

National groups and individuals have made numerous attempts to define scientific literacy. The reports of several of these are cited in the references listed at the end of this chapter. A major portion of one report is reproduced as part of one of the application and analysis questions at the end of this chapter. In addition, the first Research Report, a feature that appears throughout this book, tells of two studies directed toward the formulation of a definition. Based on these reports and studies, and our own experience and thought, we believe that scientific literacy can best be defined by describing seven major components in the behavior desired of a scientifically literate person.

The scientifically literate person:

- Has knowledge of the major concepts, principles, laws, and theories of science and applies these in appropriate ways.
- Uses the processes of science in solving problems, making decisions, and other suitable ways.
- Understands the nature of science and the scientific enterprise.
- Understands the partnership of science and technology and its interaction with society.
- Has developed science-related skills that enable him or her to function effectively in careers, leisure activities, and other roles.
- Possesses attitudes and values that are in harmony with those of science and a free society.

**RESEARCH
REPORT**

Defining
Scientific Literacy

Determining the knowledge needed to read science-type stories in newspapers and magazines is one approach that has been used to define scientific literacy. Koelsche[2] at the University of Georgia found that a total of 2,999 science-related news items appeared in the twenty-two major newspapers and nine widely read magazines that were analyzed over a six-month period, extending from November, 1963 through April, 1964. One hundred and seventy-five scientific principles and 693 vocabulary words were identified that appeared one or more times in these news items. Examples of the principles identified are "All living things respond to stimuli" and "Radioactive emission involves nuclear changes."

A team composed of Pella, O'Hearn, and Gale[3] at the Scientific Literacy Research Center of the University of Wisconsin at Madison analyzed one hundred documents (books, articles in professional journals, etc.) that included one or more references to scientific literacy or closely related topics such as science and general education, and the interrelationships among science, technology, and society. It was concluded that the scientifically literate person is characterized as one with an understanding of:

1. Interrelationships of science and society (67)
2. Ethics that control the scientist in his or her work (58)
3. Nature of science (51)
4. Basic concepts in science (51)
5. Differences between science and technology (21)
6. Interrelationships of science and the humanities (21)

The numbers in the parentheses indicate the number of documents out of the one hundred analyzed that contained one or more references to that particular referent of scientific literacy.

---

[2] Charles L., Koelsche, "Scientific Literacy as Related to the Mass Media of Communication," *School Science and Mathematics*, 65 (November, 1965):719–725.
[3] Milton O. Pella, George T. O'Hearn, and Calvin W. Gale, "Scientific Literacy—Its Referents," *The Science Teacher*, 33 (May, 1966):44.

- Has developed interests that will lead to a richer and more satisfying life and a life that will include science and life-long learning.

**Translating Goals
into Objectives**

The seven major components comprising scientific literacy must be further reduced to smaller parts before instruction can take place. This is done by identifying instructional objectives that are members of the seven component subsets of scientific literacy. For example, an objective is for students to know how to calculate the resistance in an electrical circuit when the amperage and voltage are known. Knowledge of Ohm's Law and the ability to apply it is but one of the hundreds of objectives making up the first component listed above. Figure 1.2 shows the relationships among the general goals of education, scientific literacy, and the objectives it encompasses.

While goals are usually stated in general terms, represent long-range outcomes, and give overall direction, objectives are stated in more specific terms. They represent more immediately obtainable outcomes and give direction to the day-to-day activities in the classroom.

Objectives stated in terms of the behavior desired of students at the end of instruction are called *behavioral objectives* or, in some cases, *performance objectives*. These terms rise out of the fact that the behavior or performance expected of the student is stated in advance of instruction. Instructional objectives written in this format are useful in terms both of how the subject will be taught and how the students will be evaluated.

Behavioral objectives are often written so that the following three conditions are satisfied:

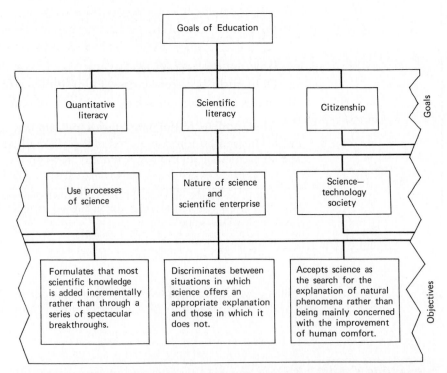

FIGURE 1.2 The diagram shows the relationship of science objectives to scientific literacy and the other general goals of education. Just as a food chain fails to show the complex relationships existing in a food web, the network of interrelationships between science objectives and the objectives in other subjects is not shown.

RESEARCH REPORT

Goals of Education

Numerous groups during this century have identified what they believe the goals of education should be. Unlike experimental studies in which empirical data are analyzed, these studies rely heavily on philosophical analysis and the weighing of judgments made by authorities in various fields. As might be expected, the evolution of the goals of education reflect changes in our society and recognize that elementary and secondary schools enroll a large majority of the nation's youth in contrast to the elitism of many schools at the turn of the century.

One of the most widely cited reports is that of the Commission on the Reorganization of Secondary Education, which in 1918 stated the goals of education as the seven cardinal principles: health, command of fundamental processes, worthy home membership, vocation, citizenship, worthy use of leisure, and ethical conduct.[4] Although neither science nor any of the other school subjects was included as one of the seven "principles," the role and importance of science in achieving the seven cardinal principles is obvious.

The *Imperative Needs of Youth* were formulated by the Educational Policies Commission at the midcentury mark. One of the ten imperative needs identified dealt specifically with science: "All youth need to understand the methods of science, the influence of science on human life, and the main scientific facts concerning the nature of the world and man."[5]

In the mid-1960s, the Educational Policies Commission released another report on the goals of education. Entitled *Education and the Spirit of Science,* this document has been widely quoted in the development of a definition of scientific literacy. The first paragraph of the recommendations section of the report illustrates the emphasis given to science.

> The schools should help to realize the great opportunities which the development of science has made apparent in the world. They can do this by promoting understanding of the values on which science is everywhere based. Although no particular scientist may fully exemplify all these values, they characterize the enterprise of science as a whole. We believe that the following values underlie science:
>
> 1. Longing to know and to understand
> 2. Questioning of all things
> 3. Search for data and their meaning
> 4. Demand for verification
> 5. Respect for logic
> 6. Consideration of premises
> 7. Consideration of consequences[6]

---

[4] Commission on the Reorganization of Secondary Education, *Cardinal Principles of Secondary Education,* U.S. Office of Education; Bulletin, 1918, No. 35, Washington, D.C.: U.S. Government Printing Office, 1918.

[5] *Education of All American Youth—A Further Look,* Washington, D.C.: Educational Policies Commission, 1952, p. 216.

[6] *Education and the Spirit of Science,* Washington, D.C.: Educational Policies Commission, 1962, p. 15.

1. The behavior desired, or what students should be able to do at the end of instruction, is clearly identified.

2. The conditions under which the expected behavior is to occur are identified.

3. The level of acceptable performance is indicated.

Examples of behavioral objectives that meet all three of these conditions are:

• Allowed to view onion cells through a microscope, the student can correctly identify at least four out of five of the following structures: cell wall, cell membrane, cytoplasm, vacuoles, and nucleus.

• Placed outside away from city lights on a clear night or placed in a planetarium, the student can use the Big Dipper and/or other stars to find north within 30°.

• Given the names of the first twenty elements in the Periodic Table of the Elements, the student can correctly write the symbols for at least eighteen out of the twenty.

Compare these behavioral objectives with the following examples of science objectives stated in a different manner:

• To know important structures of plant cells.

• To determine direction using the positions of stars.

• To know chemical symbols.

A comparison of the two sets of objectives shows how behavioral objectives clarify what is to be taught and often imply strategies or methods for doing so. If a student is to find North using the stars, then it is obvious that the student must learn how this is done and practice doing it. Behavioral objectives also usually imply ways to evaluate whether or not the student has achieved the desired outcome. Another advantage of stating objectives in behavioral terms is that they can be used to inform students what it is they are expected to learn.

As with other educational practices, the use of behavioral objectives has its limitations as well as its advantages. Perhaps the most serious is the danger of overemphasizing trivial outcomes because these objectives are often easier to state in behavioral terms than those dealing with applications, interests, and attitudes. Moreover, instructors teaching for the attainment of a rigid set of prespecified behavioral objectives may fail to capitalize on "teachable moments"—the day a beautiful butterfly flies in an open window or the morning after a big earthquake. Since behavioral objectives and evaluation are so closely related, some educators fear that testing and grades will become the "tail that wags the dog" and that the use of behavioral objectives will foster the practice of teaching for the test.

The controversy surrounding the use of behavioral objectives has raged for more than two decades, and the claims and counterclaims continue. As in the case of many other controversial practices, the wisest course of action seems to be that of using behavioral objectives in situations where the advantages outweigh the disadvantages. Teachers also must watch for any undesirable side-effects incurred by using any particular practice. For example, if giving students a list of behavioral objectives at the beginning of a unit or chapter in any way results in less student achievement, then the practice should be modified or perhaps discontinued.

In actual practice, many teachers have found that students become discouraged when too many objectives are "unveiled" at one time. Consequently, some teachers prefer to share their objectives a few at a time—preferably at the beginning of each class period. Other teachers have found it cumbersome in stating objectives to always include the condition under which a student should perform each objective. Likewise, it may not be necessary to include a criterion level with each objective since students are often graded on an overall percentage of correct responses. An objective such as "the student will be able to compare the amount of gravity on Earth with the amount of gravity on the moon" need not be stated in terms of a condition or criterion levels in order to be useful and clear to a student.

Classifying Objectives

Classification is a tool used by scientists in their study of most objects and events—atoms, stars, and plants as well as storms, earthquakes, and chemical reactions. Many advantages accrue from the use of classification. It is much easier to work with groups of atoms or plants having common characteristics than to deal with the much larger number of individuals making up each group. Classification also aids in the search for the relationships that exist among groups and individuals. A major thrust of science is to discover order in the universe, and classification is a valuable tool in doing so.

Systems for classifying objectives have been developed for the same reasons scientists use classification. Instead of dealing with thousands or even millions of individual objectives, it is much easier to work with a small number of groups. And, as in the case of scientific classification, the relationships among groups are of much importance.

The most widely used system of classification places objectives into three domains: *cognitive, affective,* and *psychomotor.* Cognitive objectives are those involving intellectual processes; affective objectives include feelings, attitudes, and interests; and the manual skills are classified as psychomotor objectives. As is usually the case in classification, each of these domains is divided into smaller categories. Figure 1.3, shows the relationships among the six major categories of objectives in the cognitive domain.

Highest

Levels of Cognition

Lowest

6.0 *Evaluation*—to make quantitative and qualitative judgments using certain criteria or standards of appraisal.

5.0 *Synthesis*—to put together elements or parts so as to form a whole, such as in hypothesis formulation and problem-solving.

4.0 *Analysis*—to break down information into its elements or parts.

3.0 *Application*—to supply or use abstracts in concrete situations.

2.0 *Comprehension*—to know what is being communicated and to be able to make use of the ideas without necessarily relating the knowledge to other material.

1.0 *Knowledge.*— to be able to recall information, such as specifics, methods, processes, patterns, or settings.

FIGURE 1.3   Categories of objectives in the cognitive domain.

The six categories in Figure 1.3 are arranged as a *hierarchy*. Notice that the lowest level, knowledge objective, is on the bottom and that the highest levels, evaluation and synthesis objectives, are on the top. While "low-level" objectives can often be achieved by memorization, the "high-level" objectives require more complex forms of learning. The idea of hierarchies of objectives is discussed further in Chapter 3.

Each of these six categories is further divided. For example, the *Taxonomy of Educational Objectives in the Cognitive Domain*[7] lists three groups under knowledge (1.0):

1.10   Knowledge of specifics
1.20   Knowledge of ways and means of dealing with specifics
1.30   Knowledge of the universals and abstractions in a field

These three groups of objectives under knowledge are further subdivided, as are all the other groups in the cognitive domain. Although the details of this taxonomy are useful to curriculum planners and test writers, most classroom teachers prefer to use just the major categories specified in Figure 1.3. In fact, many teachers group the three higher categories together to make four functional categories instead of six:

1. Knowledge—to know

2. Comprehension—to understand

3. Application—to apply

4. Higher-order objectives—to analyze, synthesize, and evaluate

---

[7] Benjamin S. Bloom, (Ed.), *Taxonomy of Educational Objectives: The Classification of Educational Goals. Handbook 1: Cognitive Domain,* New York: Longmans, Green and Company, 1956.

The *Taxonomy of Educational Objectives in the Affective Domain* contains five categories, which are also arranged in a hierarchy: receiving stimuli; responding; valuing; organization; and characterization of a value or value complex.[8] Another way of classifying objectives in the affective domain is by using categories such as interests, attitudes, and values. Although these three categories do not possess a hierarchical relationship as do the five in the Taxonomy of the Affective Domain, they often are more useful in classroom situations.

Objectives in the psychomotor domain have also been divided into five categories representing a hierarchy of behavior: perception; set (a preparatory adjustment or readiness); guided response; mechanism; and complex overt response.[9] While these five categories may be useful in courses that primarily emphasize manipulative skills, the skill objectives in science teaching placed in the psychomotor domain are not usually subdivided. In writing behavioral objectives, science teachers find it useful to have a list of action verbs, such as is shown in Figure 1.4, that correspond to the behaviors in each of the domains. These action verbs also serve as examples of the kind of behaviors included in the three domains.

Relating Goals and Objectives to the Content of Science

Scientists frequently use models to show relationships among the various components of a system, to test a system, and to communicate their ideas. Models can take various forms. Wave tanks and wind tunnels are physical models that can be used to collect empirical data. Equations ($E = mc^2$), computer programs, and diagrams are but a few of the symbolic models used in science.

Models are also used in education to show the relationships among various components. Figure 1.5 is a model that shows the relationships among the components of scientific literacy, the various categories of objectives, and some of the important content areas of science. This model can also be used to classify objectives in a three-dimensional way. Take for example, the following objective:

> When asked on an examination, a student can correctly identify a rabbit as a primary consumer.

This objective falls in the first component of scientific literacy (concepts, principles, laws, and theories), the recall level of cognition, and comes

---

[8] David R. Krathwohl, Benjamin S. Bloom, and Bertram B. Masia, *Taxonomy of Educational Objectives. Handbook II: Affective Domain*, New York: David McKay Company, Inc., 1964.
[9] Elizabeth J. Simpson, "The Classification of Educational Objectives. Psychomotor Domain," *Illinois Teacher of Home Economics*, 10, 4 (1966):100–144.

COGNITIVE DOMAIN

Knowledge

Chooses, defines, describes, identifies, labels, lists, matches, names, selects, states

Comprehension

Distinguishes, estimates, explains, extends, generalizes, gives examples, infers, predicts, rewrites, summarizes

Application

Computes, demonstrates, discovers, manipulates, modifies, operates, predicts, produces, solves, uses

Analysis

Differentiates, discriminates, distinguishes, illustrates, infers, outlines, relates, selects, separates, subdivides

Synthesis

Combines, compiles, composes, designs, generates, plans, rearranges, reorganizes, revises, summarizes

Evaluation

Appraises, compares, concludes, contrasts, criticizes, discriminates, explains, justifies, interprets, summarizes

AFFECTIVE DOMAIN

Receiving

Asks, describes, follows, gives, holds, identifies, locates, names, selects, replies

Responding

Assists, discusses, helps, labels, performs, practices, presents, recites, selects

Valuing

Completes, differentiates, explains, initiates, invites, joins, justifies, proposes, reports, selects

Organization

Adheres, combines, completes, defends, explains, integrates, modifies, orders, organizes, relates

Characterization of a Value or Value Complex

Displays, influences, performs, practices, proposes, qualifies, questions, revises, serves, verifies

PSYCHOMOTOR DOMAIN

Adjusts, builds, calibrates, constructs, dismantles, displays, dissects, fastens, fixes, focuses, grinds, heats, manipulates, measures, mends, mixes, organizes, prepares, sketches, works

FIGURE 1.4   Action verbs corresponding to behaviors in the cognitive, affective, and psychomotor domains.

from the content area of ecology. Perhaps the most important fact illustrated by this model is that objectives have a content dimension.

Let's take our rabbit example to see what this means. In some cases, teachers may want students to know specifically about rabbits as primary consumers. This might be the case in Australia where rabbits have greatly damaged much of the rangelands. Students are expected to "know"

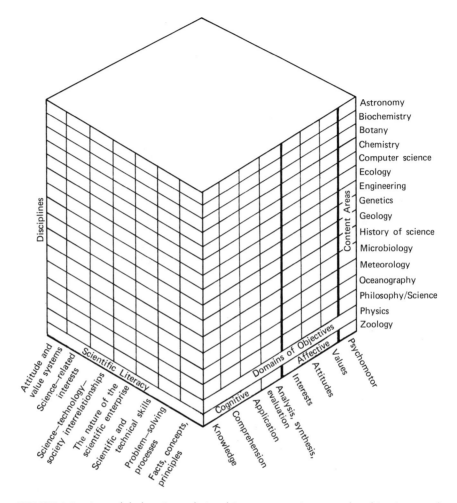

FIGURE 1.5   A model showing relationships among science goals, objectives, and content.

about rabbits, and not necessarily about other primary consumers. Thus, the specific content "rabbits are primary consumers" is the objective or the *end* being sought.

In other situations, specific content can be a means to an end. For example, we must want to teach about the energy flow in an ecosystem. To do so means we introduce ideas like food chains, webs, and pyramids. To talk about these ideas means talking about producers, consumers, and decomposers. What organisms will be used *as an example* of a primary consumer? Why not rabbits? In this case, the specific content (rabbits are primary consumers) is a means to an end (energy flow in an ecosystem) or perhaps even a broad idea (management of our environment depends on an understanding of ecosystems and other ecological ideas).

In still another type of situation, we may want to use some of the

Good science teaching is the art of assisting
discovery.

processes of science, such as recognize, classify, and predict. Once again,
we use the content of science to achieve these objectives. We teach students about pendulums as a means of giving them experience with the
processes of science. Five or ten years from now, what they learned about
predicting may be far more important than what they remember about
pendulums.

In like manner, science content may be used to teach interest, attitudes, and values. A lesson on ham radio may help a physical science
class see both career and leisure-time possibilities in modern electronics.
A debate on the future of nuclear energy provides an opportunity for
students to reexamine their attitudes and values.

Regardless of the nature of science objectives, they all involve the
facts, concepts, and principles of some phase of science. They also involve
student behaviors in the various domains of learning as shown in Figure
1.4. Finally, if they are appropriate objectives for today's science students,
they will in some way be related to the areas of scientific literacy that have
been discussed in this chapter.

**Relating Goals
and Objectives to
Instruction and
Evaluation**

Constructing objectives is an integral part of science teaching. Additional
ideas on the identification of objectives and their use in planning are
developed in Chapter 3. Chapters 4 and 5 describe strategies used to
achieve science objectives. In fact, once an objective is clearly defined, it is

much easier to select an effective strategy with which to accomplish the objective.

The third major part of the educational process, evaluation, is examined in Chapter 6. When objectives are stated as observable student outcomes, evaluation is made easier. If both the teacher and student know what is expected, evaluation follows as a natural activity. To paraphrase Robert Mager, who helped popularize the importance of educational objectives, we need to know *where* we are going (objectives), *how* we are going to get there (instructional strategies), and how we will know we have arrived (evaluation).

To talk about science teaching is to talk about objectives. This will be a major theme throughout this book. Without objectives, teaching has no purpose. Without objectives, the most appropriate teaching methods cannot be selected. And, without objectives to serve as benchmarks, evaluation has neither direction nor meaning. Remember: "To talk about science teaching is to talk about objectives."

In Perspective

A first reaction may be that the goal of scientific literacy for all students is too ambitious, too idealistic, and impossible to achieve. The thought of providing so much may leave us with the same feeling we have when an inspirational speaker calls for more than we think we can deliver. However, time for reflection often makes the task seem more attainable. Besides, what choice do we have? Bring up a generation illiterate in the accomplishments and ways of science?

In reflecting on what is involved in assisting *every* student to become scientifically literate, it may be helpful to consider the following:

1. No one is expected to become scientifically literate in an hour, day, or month nor in a single lesson, unit, or course. What is desired is that each student in each science experience make progress toward becoming more scientifically literate. And, as we expect some people to be healthier than others, some to be better at mathematics than others, so we must be willing to accept the fact that some students will become more scientifically literate than others. What is of utmost importance is that each student have the opportunities and that all those who teach science give their best in assisting students to make progress across the continuum of scientific literacy.

2. No one teacher has to do the whole job. Many of the objectives encompassed by the goal of scientific literacy are also important objectives of mathematics, English, social studies, industrial arts, and the other school subjects. Nor should what students learn outside of school be overlooked. Students learn many things from parents and other family members—especially in the areas of attitudes and values. Television, which is educational as well as entertaining, is another powerful force. The 150 to 200 hours a student spends in a year-long science course is

only one small part of a student's experiences that leads to scientific literacy.

3. In discussing the reasonableness of goals, John Richardson, who taught science education for many years at The Ohio State University, was quick to quote Robert Browning:

> Oh, but a man's reach should exceed his grasp,
> Or what is a heaven for?

Schools and science teachers should welcome the challenge to do a bit more than that which can be easily achieved. After all, our future in large part is what is happening to our youth today. And to quote the teacher pictured below at the end of a long and tiring day, "Nobody said it was going to be easy."

Review Questions

1. List as many reasons as possible for students studying science in elementary and secondary schools.

2. Briefly discuss some of the ways science and technology have affected our lives. Which of these are primarily the results of the products of science (knowledge and its applications)? Which are the results of the processes of science (the methods of science)?

"Nobody said it was going to be easy."

3. What are the major components of scientific literacy?

4. What approaches were used by Koelsche and by a team headed by Pella to define scientific literacy?

5. Briefly describe how the goals of education formulated by each of the following groups relate to the reasons for teaching science:
a. Commission on Reorganization of Secondary Education—"Seven Cardinal Principles"
b. Educational Policies Commission—*Ten Imperative Needs of Youth*
c. Educational Policies Commission—*Education and the Spirit of Science*

6. What three conditions must be satisfied in writing objectives in behavioral terms? What are some of the advantages and limitations to stating objectives behaviorally?

7. Define in your own words *cognitive, affective* and *psychomotor.* Explain how objectives in each domain can be arranged in the form of a hierarchy.

8. Describe how the components of scientific literacy, objectives in the cognitive, affective, and psychomotor domains, and the various content areas of science are related. Give at least two examples of how objectives for science teaching fit into the above three categories.

For Application and Analysis

1. Interview several people to determine what they think are the major benefits of studying science in elementary and secondary schools. If possible, include students, scientist, science teachers, college science educators, and parents. You may also wish to ask what science means to them and how they feel about the impact of science on their lives.

2. Philip Johnson, a long-time science educator at Cornell University, was fond of saying that the goals of science teaching are represented by the acronym ASK. Not only does the word symbolize the questioning spirit of science, but it also is an easy way of remembering *attitudes, skills,* and *knowledge.* Develop your own definition of scientific literacy. Can you arrange your answer in such a way that it is easy to remember and thus, perhaps, more usable?

3. Herbert Spencer, the British sociologist, philosopher, and scientist, published an essay in 1860 entitled "What Knowledge Is of Most Worth?" In answering the question, Spencer identified five categories of activities and placed them in a hierarchical order:

1. Activities which directly minister to self-preservation;
2. Activities which, by securing the necessaries of life, indirectly minister to self-preservation;
3. Activities which have for their end the rearing and disciplining of offspring;
4. Activities which are involved in the maintenance of proper social and political relations;

5. Activities which make up the leisure part of life devoted to the gratification of the tastes and feelings.

Spencer went on to say:

Thus to the question with which we set out—What knowledge is of most worth?—the uniform reply is—Science. This is the verdict on all counts. For direct self-preservation, or the maintenance of life and health, the all-important knowledge is—Science. For that indirect self-preservation which we call gaining a livelihood, the knowledge of greatest value is—Science. For the due discharge of parental functions, the proper guidance is to be found only in—Science. For that interpretation of national life, past and present, without which the citizen cannot rightly regulate his conduct, the indispensable key is—Science. Alike for the most perfect production and highest enjoyment of art in all its forms, the needful preparation is still—Science. And for the purposes of discipline—intellectual, moral, religious—the most efficient study is, once more—Science. [10]

How do Spencer's ideas on the goals of education apply today, some 120 years later? Which of the five categories of activities are adequately provided for in today's schools and which ones do you feel should receive more attention? To which ones does science contribute the most and what additional contributions do you believe should be made by science?

4. Compare the following statement on levels of performance with the description of the cognitive domain presented in Figure 1.3 on page 12. What do you see as the advantages and disadvantages of using levels of performance instead of using Bloom's taxonomy to classify objectives in the cognitive domain?

Levels   *Performance*

I.   Imitating, duplicating, repeating.
       This is the level of initial contact. Students can repeat or duplicate what has just been said, done, or read. Indicates that students are at least conscious or aware of contact with a particular concept or process.

II.   Level I, plus recognizing, identifying, remembering, recalling, classifying.
       To perform on this level, students must be able to recognize or identify the concept or process when encountered later, or to remember or recall the essential features of the concept or process.

III.   Levels I and II, plus comparing, relating, discriminating, reformulating, illustrating.
       Here the students can compare and relate this concept or process with other concepts or processes and make discrimina-

[10] Herbert Spencer, *Education: Intellectual, Moral, and Physical*, New York: D. Appleton and Company, 1860, pp. 11–16.

tions. They can formulate in their own words a definition, and they can illustrate or give examples.

IV.   Levels, I, II, and III, plus explaining, justifying, predicting, estimating, interpreting, making critical judgments, drawing inferences.

On the basis of their understanding of a concept or process, they can make explanations, give reasons, make predictions, interpret, estimate, or make critical judgments. This performance represents a high level of understanding.

V.   Levels, I, II, III, and IV, plus creating, discovering, reorganizing, formulating new hypotheses, new questions, and problems.

This is the level of original and productive thinking. The students' understanding has developed to such a point that they can make discoveries that are new to them and can restructure and reorganize their knowledge on the basis of their new discoveries and new insights.[11]

5. Reproduced below is the major part of a statement on scientific literacy developed by Victor Showalter and his collaborators at the Center for Unified Science Education in Columbus, Ohio. As a means of reacting to the statement, try one or more of the following:

(a) Identify one or more examples of content or activities from a textbook used in middle or secondary school that relates to each of the dimensions of scientific literacy and, if possible, to each of the factors listed under the various dimensions.

(b) Write a behavioral objective in science that relates to each of the dimensions of scientific literacy and, if possible, to each of the factors listed under the various dimensions.

(c) Classify behavioral objectives in science obtained from sources such as those described in Chapter 3 according to which of the dimensions of scientific literacy they are most closely associated.

The Dimensions of Scientific Literacy

I. The scientifically literate person understands the nature of scientific knowledge.
II. The scientifically literate person accurately applies appropriate science concepts, principles, laws, and theories in interacting with his universe.
III. The scientifically literate person uses processes of science in solving

---

[11] James M. Bradfield and H. Stewart Moredock, *Measurement and Evaluation in Education,* New York: The Macmillan Company, 1957, p. 204.

problems, making decisions, and furthering his own understanding of the universe.
IV. The scientifically literate person interacts with the various aspects of his universe in a way that is consistent with the values that underlie science.
V. The scientifically literate person understands and appreciates the joint enterprise of science and technology and the interrelationships of these with each other and with other aspects of society.
VI. The scientifically literate person has developed a richer, more satisfying, and more exciting view of the universe as a result of his science education and continues to extend this education throughout his life.
VII. The scientifically literate person has developed numerous manipulative skills associated with science and technology.

Nature of Science

I. The scientifically literate person understands the nature of scientific knowledge.

Probably the only characteristic of scientific knowledge that is permanent is the nature of that knowledge as contrasted to the knowledge itself. There is no doubt that scientific knowledge, as such, is in a continuous state of change. Some scholars have concluded that not only is change in scientific knowledge inevitable but that the rate of change is increasing.
The nature of scientific knowledge is such that it is:

1. *tentative.* It is subject to change and therefore does not purport to be "truth" in an absolute and final sense. This characteristic does not diminish the value of the knowledge in the eyes of the scientifically literate person.
2. *public.* It is based on evidence that is public as opposed to personal. It is assumed that other individuals would arrive at similar conclusions when confronted with the same evidence.
3. *replicable.* It is based on evidence which, at least in theory, could be obtained by other investigators working in a different place and at a different time given similar conditions.
4. *probabilistic.* It enables probabilistic, as opposed to absolute, predictions and explanations when applied to real situations.
5. *humanistic.* It is a product of mankind resulting from an effort to impose order on nature or find patterns in nature and involves creative imagination. The knowledge itself is shaped by and from elements (i.e., concepts) that are a product of the culture.
6. *historic.* Scientific knowledge of the past has provided the basis for today's knowledge which in turn will provide the basis for tomorrow's knowledge. Science knowledge of the past should be viewed in its historical context and not be degraded on the basis of our present knowledge.

7. *unique.* Scientific knowledge is one of several "realms of meaning" or ways of knowing that man has developed. It is distinguished from other realms by virtue of the nature of its knowledge and its procedures for generating new knowledge. Conflict may occur when the same thing or event is explained by science and some other way of knowing.

8. *holistic.* Scientific knowledge produced by the various specialized sciences contributes to an overall conceptual scheme which is internally consistent. The differences among the specialized sciences are differences of degree rather than of kind.

9. *empirical.* Scientific knowledge is based ultimately on and/or derived from observation or experiment even though theory may be a useful guide to further work. It has its origin in the real world and is dependent on sense experience.

II. The scientifically literate person accurately applies appropriate science concepts, principles, laws, and theories in interacting with his universe.

Concepts in Science

There has been a persistent problem of identifying a minimal conceptual core of science knowledge ever since science courses have been established in schools. The problem has been intensified since the mid-1950s when the concept of scientific literacy became popular. To be functional, the resulting list of content items should be comprehensive without being so long as to be unwieldy.

It follows that it is not appropriate to speak of one's having attained a key concept or not. Each of these concepts represents a continuum which extends from complete naivete to increasing levels of sophistication with no upper limit. It is, therefore, appropriate to speak of an individual's level of development regarding a particular concept. Thus, a given person may have a highly developed concept of "equilibrium" but a very elementary concept of "population."

The key concepts of science are:

1. *cause-effect.* A relationship of events that substantiates the belief that "nature is not capricious." Once established, it enables predictions to be made.

2. *change.* Everything is in the process of becoming different or something else. The rate at which it happens varies from very fast to very slow so that it may be unnoticed in these extreme cases. May involve several stages or mechanisms.

3. *cycle.* The apparent pattern in which certain events or conditions seem to be repeated at regular intervals or periods.

4. *energy-matter.* Interchangeable manifestations of substance and that which enables something to be moved or changed.

5. *entropy.* An expression of the randomness, disorder, or chaos in a collection of things. Always increases in a closed system.

6. *equilibrium.* That state of affairs in which changes or tendencies to change occur in opposite directions, exist, or happen at equal rates or are of the same magnitude.

7. *evolution.* A series of slow changes that can be used to explain how something got to be the way it is or what it might become in the future. Generally regarded as going from simple to complex.

8. *field.* A region or space in which something influences or affects something else, often without direct physical contact.

9. *force.* A push or a pull.

10. *fundamental entities.* Those units which are useful in explaining certain phenomena. Units of structure and function.

11. *gradient.* A situation in which the intensity of something varies in a more or less regular pattern.

12. *interaction.* A situation in which two or more things influence or affect each other.

13. *invariance.* A characteristic of an object or a situation which stays constant even though other characteristics may change.

14. *model.* A more or less tentative scheme or structure which seems to correspond to a real structure, event, or class of events and which has explanatory value.

15. *orderliness.* The belief that there is either order in nature or that man is able to impose order on nature. Includes the various schemes or patterns that are used to express this order such as the periodic table of the elements.

16. *organism.* An open dynamic system which is characterized by the processes of life. May be used as an analog to explain certain non-life events or things.

17. *perception.* The interaction between the human mind and the external world.

18. *probability.* The relative certainty (or lack of it) that can be assigned to certain events happening in a specified time interval or sequence of other events.

19. *population.* A group of fundamental entities that have certain similarities or common characteristics.

20. *quantification.* An expression containing a numerical component resulting from measurement and associated with a concrete or abstract attribute of a thing, situation, or event.

21. *replication.* A belief that doing the same things will produce the same results if all other conditions are the same. A necessary characteristic of scientific experiments.

22. *resonance.* An action within one system which causes a similar action within another system.

23. *scale.* A consideration that other characteristics of or relationships within a system may or may not stay the same as its dimensions are increased or decreased.

24. *significance.* The belief that certain differences which exist or which follow certain actions exceed those that would be expected to be caused by chance alone.

25. *symmetry.* The belief that most, if not all, patterns in nature are structurally or functionally independent of direction.

26. *system.* A group of things or events which can be defined, at least in part, by boundaries that one person can communicate to another and which enable it to be discussed and studied more effectively.

27. *theory.* A connected and internally consistent group of sentences, equations, models, or a combination of these which serves to explain a relatively large and diverse group of things and events.

28. *time-space.* A dimension of the real world which separates things and events.

29. *validation.* A belief that similar relationships obtained by two or more different methods reflect an accurate representation of the situation being investigated.

Processes of Science

III. The scientifically literate person uses processes of science in solving problems, making decisions, and furthering his own understanding of the universe.

In recent years, the intellectual processes of science have attained the status of legitimate content for science learning. Much of this new status is due to the impetus provided by the Commission on Science Education of the American Association for the Advancement of Science (AAAS). One very persuasive argument in favor of these processes of science as basic content for science learning is that the processes are much less likely to change in time than is the traditional knowledge-based content.

The processes of science marked with "*" were designated by AAAS as "integrated processes" and were viewed as subsuming the other "basic" processes. By listing the processes alphabetically, it is intended that each process be given an "open-ended" status. That is, the basic processes are viewed as being worthy of development even after a learner has made progress with one or more of the integrated processes.

The processes of science are:

1. *classifying.* A systematic procedure used by a person to impose order on collections of objects or events.

2. *communicating.* Any one of several procedures involving various media and which carries information from one person to another.

3. *controlling variables.* Identifying and managing the factors that may in-

fluence a situation or event so that the effect of a given factor may be learned.

4. *defining operationally.* * Producing definitions of a thing or event in terms that give a physical description and/or that which results from conducting a given procedure.

5. *designing experiments.* Planning a series of data-gathering operations which will provide a basis for testing a hypothesis or answering a question.

6. *formulating models.* Devising a mechanism, scheme, or structure which will act or perform as if it were a specific real object or event.

7. *hypothesizing.* * Stating a tentative generalization that may be used to explain a relatively large number of events but which is subject to immediate or eventual testing by one or more experiments.

8. *inferring.* Explaining an observation in terms of one's previous experience.

9. *interpreting data.* * To find a pattern or other meaning inherent in a collection of data. Leads to stating a generalization.

10. *measuring.* A procedure by which one uses an instrument to estimate a quantitative value associated with some characteristic of an object or an event.

11. *observing.* The most basic process of science in which a person uses his senses to obtain information about himself or the world around him.

12. *predicting.* Predicting what future observations will be on the basis of previous information which distinguishes it from "guessing."

13. *questioning.* To raise an uncertainty, doubt, or unsettled issue which may be based on the perception of a discrepancy between what is observed and what is known by the questioner.

14. *using numbers.* The technique of using number systems to express ideas, observations, relationships, etc., often as a complement to the use of words.

15. *using space-time relationships.* The description of spatial relationships and their change with time.

Values

IV. *The scientifically literate person interacts with the various aspects of his universe in a way that is consistent with the values that underlie science.*

This dimension of scientific literacy is based on a definition of "value" as "a principle, standard, or quality considered worthwhile or desirable." Thus, this dimension implies that some values which many or most learners bring to school will need to be modified, even though it may be argued that schools should not seek to impress a given set of values on learners. Nevertheless, it is impossible to imagine any scientifically literate person who does not act in a way that is consistent with these values in situations that are amenable to scientific thought and action. The more consistently the individual shows this behavior in appropriate situations, the more scientifically literate the person is.

In 1966, *Education and the Spirit of Science* was published by the National Education Association as a principal product of the Educational Policies Commission consisting of teachers, scientists, and school administrators. This book assesses the modern impact of science and technology and describes the potential value of the scientific and technological "revolution" for all people. It suggests that the "... values and associated modes of thought may in the long run be more important to mankind and to education than the visible fruits of scientific and technological pursuits."

The values that underlie science as identified in *Education and the Spirit of Science* are:

1. *longing to know and understand.* A conviction that knowledge is desirable and that inquiry directed toward its generation is a worthy investment of time and other resources.

2. *questioning of all things.* A belief that all things, including authoritarian statements and "self-evident" truths are open to question. All questions are prized although some are of greater value than others because they lead to further understanding through scientific inquiry.

3. *search for data and their meaning.* Prizing of the acquisition and ordering of data because they are the basis for theories which, in turn, are worthwhile because they can be used to explain many things and events. In some cases these data have immediate practical applications of value to mankind, as in cases in which data enables one to assess accurately the severity of a problem in society and/or the effects of policies directed to improve such situations.

4. *demand for verification.* A high regard for requests that supporting data be made public and that new empirical tests be invented and/or conducted to assess the validity or accuracy of a finding or assertion.

5. *respect for logic.* An esteem for those chains of inference that lead from raw data to conclusion according to some logical scheme and an insistence that conclusions or actions not based on such chains be subject to doubt.

6. *consideration of premises.* A prizing of frequent review of the basic external and internal assumptions from which a line of inquiry has arisen, especially when they are used as a basis for determining further action.

7. *consideration of consequence.* A belief that frequent and thoughtful review of both the direct and indirect effects resulting from pursuing a given line of inquiry or action is worthwhile and that a decision to continue or abort the inquiry or action will be made in terms of the consequences.

V. The scientifically literate person understands and appreciates the joint   **Science-Society**
enterprise of science and technology and the interrelationships of these with
each other and with other aspects of society.

The distinctions between science and technology are relatively subtle as
each depends on the other for its continued pursuit. Technology is generally
regarded as the application of scientific knowledge to producing real products
or to the treatment of specific problems. Thus, new technology may occur
either when an "old" bit of scientific knowledge is applied in a new way or
when a "new" bit of scientific knowledge generates technological "spin-off."

Some of the factors involved in the interrelationships among science,
technology, and other aspects of society are:

1. *science/technology.* There is a distinction between science and technology, although they often overlap and each depends on the other for
   continued progress. Science deals with generating and ordering conceptual knowledge. Technology deals with applying scientific knowledge to
   achieve full or partial solution of problem situations.

2. *variable positions.* Scientific thought and knowledge can be used to
   support different positions in response to specific problems (e.g., population control, water fluoridation, etc.). Thus, it is "normal" for scientists/
   technologists to disagree among themselves, even though they may in-
   voke the same scientific theories and data.

3. *social influence on science/technology.* The selection of problems investigated by scientific and technological research is influenced by the
   needs, interests, and financial support of the larger society.

4. *ultimate value of science knowledge.* Although scientists often pursue
   what, on the surface, seem socially irrelevant phenomena or investigate
   apparently trivial phenomena, history shows a significant proportion of
   these studies eventually have broad application value in various and
   sometimes unexpected technologies. A viable bank of scientific knowledge is required to ensure the future success of technology.

5. *impact of science/technology.* Scientific and technological developments have real and direct effects on each person's life. Not all effects are
   desirable, nor are any effects completely free of some undesirable side-
   effects. In essence, there seems to be a "trade-off" principle working in
   which each gain is matched by one or more "losses" in terms of what has
   been. The "trade-off" principle involves items of knowledge, belief, and
   social structure as well as those of a material nature.

6. *science requires "openness."* Science thrives best when there is a free
   flow of questions, ideas, and results that is not restricted by personal
   boundaries or external authority.

7. *technology controlled by society.* Although science requires freedom to
   inquire if it is to function fully, applications of scientific knowledge and of
   technological products and practices are ultimately determined by the
   whole of society including scientists and technologists. These groups

have a special responsibility to inform the public and other decision makers of both the possible consequences of such applications and the need to search for such consequences.

8. *public understanding gap*. A considerable gap between scientific/technological knowledge and public understanding of it has existed in the past, continues to exist in the present, and will exist in the future. Constant effort is required by scientists, technologists, educators, and the public to minimize this gap.

9. *resources for science/technology*. The conduct of modern science and technology requires considerable resources in the form of talent, time, money, etc. Many of these resources such as that of talent require long-term preparation and allocation.

10. *limitations of science/technology*. Science/technology cannot guarantee a solution to any specific problem. In fact, ultimate solution of any problem is usually impossible, and a partial or temporary solution is all that is ever possible at a given point in time. Solutions to problems cannot be legislated, bought, or guaranteed by extreme allocation of resources. Some problems and areas of human concern are not amenable to the approaches of science/technology.

11. *scientists/technologists are human*. Scientists and technologists are "people." In fact, outside of their special field, they may not exhibit strong development of all or even most of the dimensions of scientific literacy. All people, not just an elite few, are capable of "doing" science/technology at their own level of sophistication. By the same token, vocations in some aspect of science/technology are open to practically all people.

12. *science/technology and natural resources*. Society has the ability and responsibility through science/technology to regulate environmental quality and the usage rate of natural resources to ensure a good quality of life for this and succeeding generations.

13. *science/technology and other realms*. Although there are distinctive characteristics of the knowledge and processes that characterize science/technology, there are many connections to and overlaps with the other realms of human knowledge and understanding.

Interest

VI. *The scientifically literate person has developed a richer, more satisfying, and more exciting view of the universe as a result of his science education and continues to extend this education throughout his life.*

This is a very personal dimension of scientific literacy and involves a general and abiding interest in science and a favorable attitude toward all aspects of science and technology. This does not mean that the scientifically literate person automatically endorses anything and everything that appears or occurs in the name of science/technology. It does mean that the person has enthusiasm for reading, listening, watching, talking about, and getting involved in science-related things and events.

The following factors contribute to this dimension of scientific literacy:

1. *interest*. The individual feels and expresses a satisfactory level of interest in science. At the very least, the person does not "hate" science.

2. *confidence*. The individual believes he can participate in the doing of science and can understand scientific things at his own level of sophistication. He also believes he will attain a measure of self-satisfaction by doing so.

3. *media preference*. The individual chooses to become involved (reading, watching, visiting, etc.) in a significantly high proportion of science-related television programs, newspaper articles, books, public displays (e.g., museums), etc.

4. *explanation preference*. The individual shows a significant preference for scientific explanations of a given event or thing compared to non-scientific explanations for the same event or thing, assuming that the scientific explanation is at an appropriate level of sophistication.

5. *avocation*. The individual pursues, has pursued, or would like to pursue a science-related hobby such as shell collecting, photography, bird watching, etc.

6. *vocation*. The individual either is considering entering a science-related job or career or has seriously considered entering such a field.

7. *continuous learner*. The individual has gained some scientific knowledge within the very recent past no matter what age he happens to be. He frequently pursues some line of scientific inquiry of his own volition. This may take the form of enrolling in a science course which is not required by any formal program of study to which the person is committed.

8. *response preference*. The person gives a high proportion of science-based responses when questioned about events and things in an informal situation. This is especially significant when the questioner is *not* a teacher or other authority figure.

9. *"hero" perception*. The person has a relatively high esteem for the role of the scientist/technologist in today's world and acknowledges several specific scientists/technologists as having made significant contributions in the past.

VII. The scientifically literate person has developed numerous manipulative **Skills**
skills associated with science and technology.

The instruments and other hardware typical of science/technology seem to be a forbidding aspect of science and technology that precludes certain individual's achievement of a high degree of scientific literacy. Many individuals are very reluctant to get involved in the active operation of unfamiliar scientific instruments or machines for one reason or another.

The list of instruments that follows is intended to represent manipulative skills important to the achievement of scientific literacy:

1. *microscope*
2. *thermometer*
3. *meter stick*
4. *balance*
5. *graduated cylinder*
6. *timing device*
7. *camera*
8. *calculator*
9. *tape recorder*
10. *computer terminal*
11. *syphgmomanometer*
12. *oscilloscope*
13. *polygraph (or some other instrument that records data as a function of time)*
14. *ammeter*
15. *pH meter (or some other electronic instrument that measures current as a function of some other physical variable)*[12]

References

Eiss, Albert F. and Mary B. Harbeck. *Behavioral Objectives in the Affective Domain.* Washington, D.C.: National Science Supervisors Association, 1969.

This book discusses the importance of objectives in the affective domain, gives examples of such objectives, and describes a means of evaluating the achievement of affective objectives.

Hurd, Paul DeHart. "Scientific Enlightenment for an Age of Science," *The Science Teacher,* January, 1970 (37, 1), pp. 13–15.

After discussing the scientific enlightenment as a point of view about the purposes for teaching science, the author identifies twelve areas of knowledge and attitude in which a scientifically enlightened person should have an operational understanding.

---

[12] Victor Showalter, and others, "Program Objectives and Scientific Literacy, Parts 5 and 6." *Prism* (Newsletter of the Center for Unified Science Education), 2, 3–4 (Spring and Summer, 1974).

Mager, Robert F. *Preparing Instructional Objectives*, Second Edition, Palo Alto, Calif.: Fearon Publishers, 1975.

This is a classic on instructional, or behavioral, objectives—a programmed learning format that describes the distinguishing features and major advantages of stating objectives in this manner.

Robinson, James T. *The Nature of Science and Science Teaching.* Belmont, Calif.: Wadsworth Publishing Company, Inc., 1968.

The writings of six scholars, all working scientists, are examined, and from this analysis is synthesized a description of the various components of scientific literacy.

CIPHER IN THE SNOW

It started with tragedy on a biting cold February morning. I was driving behind the Milford Corners bus as I did most snowy mornings on my way to school. It veered and stopped short at the hotel, which it had no business doing, and I was annoyed as I had to come to an unexpected stop. A boy lurched out of the bus, reeled, stumbled, and collapsed on the snowbank at the curb. The bus driver and I reached him at the same moment. His thin, hollow face was white even against the snow.

"He's dead," the driver whispered.

It didn't register for a minute. I glanced quickly at the scared young faces staring down at us from the school bus. "A doctor! Quick! I'll phone from the hotel. . . ."

"No use. I tell you he's dead." The driver looked down at the boy's still form. "He never even said he felt bad," he muttered, "just tapped me on the shoulder and said, real quiet, 'I'm sorry. I have to get off at the hotel.' That's all. Polite and apologizing like."

At school, the giggling, shuffling morning noise quieted as the news went down the halls. I passed a huddle of girls. "Who was it? Who dropped dead on the way to school?" I heard one of them half whisper.

"Don't know his name; some kid from Milford Corners," was the reply.

It was like that in the faculty room and the principal's office. "I'd appreciate your going out to tell the parents," the principal told me. "They haven't a phone, and anyway, somebody from school should go there in person. I'll cover your classes."

"Why me?" I asked. "Wouldn't it be better if you did it?"

"I didn't know the boy," the principal admitted levelly. "And in last year's sophomore personalities column I noted that you were listed as his favorite teacher."

I drove through the snow and cold down the bad canyon road to the Evans place and thought about the boy, Cliff Evans. His favorite teacher! Why, he hasn't spoken two words to me in two years! I could see him in my mind's eye all right, sitting back there in the last seat in my afternoon literature class. He came in the room by himself and left by himself. "Cliff Evans," I muttered to myself, "a boy who never talked." I thought a minute. "A boy who never smiled. I never saw him smile once."

The big ranch kitchen was clean and warm. I blurted out my news somehow. Mrs. Evans reached blindly toward a chair. "He never said anything about bein' ailing."

His stepfather snorted. "He ain't said nothin' about anything since I moved in here."

Mrs. Evans got up, pushed a pan to the back of the stove, and began to untie her apron. "Now hold on," her husband snapped. "I got to have breakfast before I go to town. Nothin' we can do now anyway. If Cliff hadn't been so dumb, he'd have told us he didn't feel good."

After school I sat in the office and stared bleakly at the records spread out before me. I was to close the boy's file and write his obituary for the school paper. The almost bare sheets mocked the effort. "Cliff Evans, white, never legally adopted by stepfather, five half brothers and sisters." These meager strands of information and the list of D grades were about all the records had to offer.

How do you go about making a boy into a zero? The grade school records showed me much of the answer. The first and second grade teachers' annotation read "sweet, shy child"; timid but eager." Then the third grade note had opened the attack. Some teacher had written in a good, firm hand, "Cliff won't talk. Uncooperative. Slow learner." The other academic sheep had followed with "dull"; "slow-witted"; "low IQ." They became correct. The boy's IQ score in the ninth grade was listed at 83.

Cliff Evans had silently come in the school door in the mornings and gone out the school door in the evenings, and that was all. He had never belonged to a club. He had never played on a team. He had never held an office. As far as I could tell, he had never done one happy, noisy kid thing. He had never been anybody at all.

But his IQ in the third grade had been 106. The score didn't go under 100 until the seventh grade. Even timid, sweet children have resilience. It takes time to break them.

I stomped to the typewriter and wrote a savage report pointing out what education had done to Cliff Evans. I slapped a copy on the principal's desk and another in the sad, dog-eared file; slammed the file; and crashed the office door shut as I left for home. But I didn't feel much better. A little boy kept walking after me, a boy with a peaked face, a skinny body in faded jeans, and big eyes that had searched for a long time and then had become veiled.

I could guess how many times he'd been chosen last to be on a team, how many whispered child conversations had excluded him. I could see the faces and hear the voices that said over and over, "You're dumb. You're dumb. You're just a nothing, Cliff Evans."

A child is a believing creature. Cliff undoubtedly believed them. Suddenly it seemed clear to me: When finally there was nothing left at all for Cliff Evans, he collapsed on a snowbank and went away. The doctor might list "heart failure" as the cause of death, but that wouldn't change my mind.

We couldn't find 10 students in the school who had known Cliff well enough to attend the funeral as his friends. So the student body officers and a committee from the junior class went as a group to the church, looking politely sad. I attended the service with them and sat through it with a lump of cold lead in my chest and a big resolve growing in me.

I've never forgotten Cliff Evans or that resolve. He has been my challenge year after year, class after class. Each September, I look up and down the rows carefully at the unfamiliar faces. I look for veiled eyes or bodies scrouged into a seat in an alien world. "Look, kids," I say silently, "I may not do anything else for you this year, but not one of you is going out of here a nobody. I'll work or fight to the bitter end doing battle with society and the school board, but I won't have one of you leaving here thinking yourself into a zero."

Most of the time—not always, but most of the time—I've succeeded.

Reprinted by permission of the author and *Today's Education,* the National Education Association. Todhunter, Jean Mizer, "Cipher in the Snow," Vol. 64, No. 2, pp. 66-67, 1975.

"Will I be able to relate to my students?" "Will they like me?" "What will students expect of me as a person?" "What will they expect of me as their science teacher?" These are questions that run through the minds of beginning teachers; in fact, these are among the most important concerns during the first year or two of teaching.

Secondary school students give a variety of responses when asked to describe an effective teacher. Although student commentaries vary widely, research data indicate that common characteristics associated with good teaching do exist. Students expect their teachers to be competent in their subject field. Students show a high preference for teachers

WHAT STUDENTS SAY

About Teachers

- I love teachers who listen to me—I mean listen carefully.
- Somehow my science teacher has a way of making me feel embarrassed if I don't know an answer.
- The best teachers are those with a good sense of humor.
- I don't mind a teacher who makes you work hard, as long as she (or he) is fair.
- One of the worst things teachers do is pick their favorites. I'll tell you, if you don't get on their good side fast you might as well forget it.
- You can tell my teacher just loves biology. I think it's kind of catching.
- I seem to relate better to my younger teachers. Sometimes older teachers don't seem to understand teenagers.
- I hate it when a teacher says, "Back in my day we did it this way."
- Students want teachers to respect them as people. I'd say that's the most important thing of all.
- Once teachers label you as dumb, it seems that they are never willing to change their minds.
- Most people my age will work hard for a teacher who cares. That seems to make all the difference in the world.

who care about them as individuals. Students prefer teachers who listen to their problems and understand their needs. They like teachers who afford them respect and trust. They also prefer teachers who can explain things to them in a patient, clear, and interesting fashion, and who can display a sense of humor when appropriate.

Since all of us have been students at one time, we all have definite ideas about what distinguishes a "good teacher" from a "poor teacher." While we all have notions about these qualities, we do not necessarily possess the human relations skills and other characteristics needed for effective teaching. In this chapter, we will deal with the nature of students in secondary schools and a few well-known models for improving interpersonal relations and for dealing with common discipline problems.

Focusing on Students

Most beginning science teachers have completed four or more years of study at a college or university and have taken about half of their course work in science or closely related subjects. Many hours have been spent in lectures and laboratories, and, for the most part, much of what has been learned in science has been from college professors who are experts in their respective fields. The college environment, unlike the typical American community, is filled with scholars and researchers who are preoccupied most of the time with "their subject" and "their research." Classes are often large, and knowledge is frequently transmitted by way of lectures to attentive, disciplined, and experienced students. Upon finishing college, the new graduate leaves the environment of the campus to enter "the real world." For those entering secondary school teaching, the real world consists of homerooms, tardy bells, noisy cafeterias and classrooms filled with students less mature and less disciplined than those on college campuses.

It is quite natural for the beginning science teacher to want to share the many exciting things in science that he or she learned in college. It is a proud feeling to view oneself as an expert in chemistry or biology, ready to share with the world all that you know. The secondary school environment and the secondary school student, however, are quite different from the climate and people found at the college level. Adolescent students, in particular, have many unique needs and motives. While it is important that science teachers be well versed in science, the teacher's primary professional responsibility is to promote learning among students. Rather than being scientists, secondary school science teachers are *communicators of science*. In order to effectively communicate science to students, the teacher must have a sound understanding of what adolescents are like, how to motivate them, and what the most effective methods are for meeting their needs. For these and other reasons, science teachers must learn not only to *teach science* but also to *teach students*.

COMMON
CHARACTERISTICS
OF ADOLESCENTS

Adolescence is a crucial and often stormy period of time for young people in our society. Students entering middle or junior high schools are changing physically, emotionally, and mentally more rapidly than at any other period in their lives, with the exception perhaps of their first two or three years of life. Those in high school are preparing to enter an adult world and to make decisions that will have life-long effects. Going to college, deciding upon a career, getting married, and having children are just around the corner for most of these young people; yet, only yesterday they were in elementary school where they depended almost entirely on their parents and teachers.

It is extremely important for secondary school teachers to understand adolescents. By being aware of the developmental changes that are occurring and by being able to understand the feelings of teenagers, teachers can foster a more effective climate for the mental and emotional growth of students. Some of the most important characteristics to remember about secondary school students are:

- Physical changes are occurring rapidly. Girls develop breasts and wider hips and begin menstruation. Boys become increasingly muscular, begin shaving, and often go through an embarrassing voice change. Girls usually develop faster than boys during early adolescence.
- Rapid growth and change in physical qualities are often accompanied by an "identity crisis." Girls who mature faster often become the object of increased male interest, and boys frequently aspire to athletic accomplishments. Hence, the "cheerleader" and the "star athlete" often become the role-model during this period.
- Adolescence is marked by a shift from adult orientation to peer group orientation. Friendships become increasingly important, and "being popular" with the same and opposite sex is highly valued.
- Cliques are common, and conforming to current behavioral and dress codes is often mandatory. Becoming "part of the crowd" or a member of the "in-group" is a common goal.
- Teenagers are often self-conscious, usually considered socially awkward by adult standards, and frequently worry about what others think of them. They generally spend inordinate amounts of time showering, grooming their hair, and talking on the telephone.
- To conceal lack of self-confidence, adolescents often behave unpredictably, boisterously, and emotionally. Boys are particularly competitive with each other at this age and delight in teasing girls. Both boys and girls behave in ways calculated to attract attention from others in the group.
- The most pervasive preoccupation for many students is the opposite sex. Talk about dating and going steady dominate their conversation.

Many students during this time become sexually active and by high
school talk freely about marriage and having families of their own.

• While teenagers are usually healthy, their eating and sleeping habits are
often atrocious. Nutrition and health are important topics that need to
be dealt with during this time.

• Though students at this age tend to be independent, opinionated, and
dogmatic, they are at an age where logical and abstract reasoning is
possible. Young people during this time, however, are very impres-
sionable. From an educational and cultural standpoint, this period of
time represents one of the most malleable and formative stages of life.

• It is common for adolescents to be in constant conflict with their parents. During this time, students often turn to their teachers for arbitra-
tion and sometimes as new role-models.

• From a learning standpoint, it is generally agreed that students reach
close to maximum intellectual efficiency during late adolescence. Although the potential is high, students at this age characteristically "fail
to apply themselves" and often do not reach peak mental performance
until they enter college or a career.

• Young people at this age spend considerable time daydreaming, thinking about their future, planning careers, and developing their
"philosophies of life." Political, ethical, and religious matters are often
frustrating to them and by late adolescence most young people begin
questioning many of the traditional values they have learned at home,
school, and church. Students during this period often reject many
views held by the adult generation, holding tightly, instead, to counter-
views popular among those in their age group.

While students of this age group possess, by adult standards, many
awkward behaviors, they also possess many desirable characteristics.
They are active, enthusiastic, sincere, and usually quite serious about
many things relevant to their lives and their future. For these and other
reasons, most secondary school teachers find working with adolescents
not only challenging, but also extremely rewarding.

THE IMPORTANCE
OF SCIENCE FOR
ADOLESCENT
STUDENTS

In general, science is not emphasized in the elementary schools of this
country; reading, writing, arithmetic, and art occupy much more of the
daily schedule of children in the earlier grades. For many students, middle school or junior high school represents their first formal exposure to
science. Since adolescence is such a critical period, and since this is when
students devote the most time to the study of science, the quality of the
science program offered is extremely crucial.

The teacher is the single most important influence on student commitment to and achievement in science. Science teachers who can com-

RESEARCH REPORT

Teachers Who Care

"Why is knowing that a teacher cares about you so important?" This is a question Dr. Mary Budd Rowe asked dozens of students as she visited several school systems during one of her research studies. "If teachers don't care why should we?" the students responded.

In a review of several research reports, Rowe concluded that students consistently ranked "caring" on the part of teachers as the most important aspect of the school environment. Time and time again, she noted that teachers' attitudes toward students seemed to be a major factor in the success or failure of a particular program. "Though most course evaluations focus on content or organization," she wrote, "I consistently found that teacher personality overrode these other factors in importance."[1]

While Rowe noted that more research needs to be done in this area, she stated that there already is convincing evidence that students of those who care do achieve more than students of those who do not.

What can teachers do about their attitudes toward students? What is really meant by the concept of caring? Are there ways they can demonstrate more clearly to students that they care? Are there methods that can be used to prepare teachers for today's classroom? These and other compelling questions are currently being addressed by researchers in education, psychology, sociology, and other fields.

[1] M. B. Rowe, "Teachers Who Care," *The Science Teacher*, 44, 5 (1977):37.

municate skillfully with adolescent students are likely to produce students who appreciate science and feel as though they can be successful. In order to accomplish this, science teachers need to possess interpersonal skills that are appropriate to use with young people this age. Teachers capable of creating lasting impressions toward science are those who encourage questioning, who portray science as a search for knowledge, and who communicate to students that they care about them.

There is evidence that many young people in our schools turn away from science during the junior high school years. Many students see science as difficult, boring, or a subject to be taken only by those who plan to go to college. Unfortunately, science has been portrayed all too often in our society and in our schools as a subject appropriate only for bright people. When this attitude is perpetuated, many adolescent students end up disliking science, hence, selecting other courses over science in high school and college. Or students may decide that science is not very important in their lives and grow up feeling negative or uncomfortable with scientific and technological phenomena. Instructional strategies designed to increase interest in science and to promote positive attitudes and values associated with science are described in Chapter 7.

RESEARCH
REPORT

Science for Early
Adolescents

The National Science Foundation in 1978 heard from a special panel that had been established to review science education for early adolescents. The committee was headed by Paul DeHart Hurd of Stanford University.[2] Through careful and systematic analysis, this group sought to identify ways for improving the science instruction received by this age group.

The panel expressed general dissatisfaction with many current practices in science teaching in middle and junior high schools. The panel criticized these practices as:

1. Lacking social and cultural validity.

2. Being insensitive to student characteristics and needs.

3. Not providing for a wide diversity of learning experiences in various contexts.

4. Being unrelated to the real world, often trivial, overly structured, and often meaningless.

5. Failing to attract the interest of students.

6. Using a linear organization that may be an obstacle to effective learning.

7. Neglecting considerations of values, ethics, or morals underlying the resolution of major science/social problems.

8. Being discipline based and neglecting the social interaction of the subject matter and its relevance to life and living.

9. Not accommodating the subcultures within a classroom, such as race, sex, and background.

10. Failing to respond to the full range of educational goals—career awareness, health management, assuming responsibility, uses of leisure time and others.

The panel, in their report to the National Science Foundation, made several recommendations for improving science education for adolescent students, including the following:

Science should relate to the real world of the student—both as an individual and as a member of society.

The science curriculum should provide for the great diversity among adolescents by options in subject matter, learning styles, and levels of cognitive ability.

Minority students should be encouraged to take regular science programs.

---

[2] Paul DeHart Hurd, Final Report of the National Science Foundation Early Adolescence Panel Meeting, Washington, D.C., May, 1978.

A variety of out-of-school activities are essential for the best possible education for adolescents. Agencies such as museums, zoos, parks, scouts, and 4-H can contribute effectively to desirable educational goals in science. Often, through such activities adolescents have greater access to adult role-models.

Adolescents should be allowed to explore the work places of adults to become aware of career possibilities and meaning of work. Science should be analyzed for potential careers that are relevant to the lives of young people.

Teaching strategies used with adolescents should allow for students to be actively involved in the learning process.

Science programs should be integrated when possible with mathematics and social studies. Students should be helped to see the many interconnections between science and other subjects they study.

Adolescents should be given maximum opportunities to relate interpersonal and social problems to what they study in school. Opportunities for problem-solving and social interaction should be encouraged. Students should be allowed to express opinions freely and be given opportunities to develop values based on rational thinking and scientific evidence.

Both internal and external conditions which promote learning among adolescents should be explored carefully by science teachers. Internal influences such as self-esteem, alienation, health, and motivation are particularly important among adolescents. External influences such as family, peers, classroom climate, and teacher-student relationships are equally important.

This report underscores the notion that adolescence is a critical period in the lives of people in our society. Adolescents are neither children nor adults; therefore, educators who work with this age group need to be aware of the many unique needs and characteristics of students this age. The report suggests that science in the past has been taught from a discipline-centered perspective without giving students this age enough time to make the much needed transition from the child-centered elementary school curriculum to the adult-focused world of high school.

FOSTERING POSITIVE ATTITUDES TOWARD SCIENCE AMONG FEMALES

A chemist, Kay Shearin, describes the way many females feel about entering science.

Equal pay for equal work is not the main issue, and neither is the reluctance of many employers to hire women. Rather it is the ubiquitous social pressure to conform to the traditional model which prevents women a free choice of profession. This pressure is so pervasive, and at times so subtle, that no amount of consciousness-raising could even identify all of it. It comes from people but also from television, books and magazines, from churches and civic groups, and from virtually every source of education or information. . . . In schools it causes teachers and counselors to turn girls away from shop or engineering and into home economics, education or secretarial classes.[3]

Traditionally, girls have not been encouraged to take advanced science courses and pursue careers in science to the same extent boys have. Many parents, counselors, and teachers have been guilty of subtly encouraging girls to enter fields other than science, while at the same time persuading boys to consider the sciences, medicine, engineering, and other science-related fields. As a result, we have an adult female population that has taken less science and thus has less formal preparation for making decisions about nutrition, health care, and the hundreds of other science-related problems and issues in today's world. Many researchers have concluded that different levels of interest in science between males and females is largely cultural. More recently, it has been recognized that many textbooks and other instructional materials contain sex biases and perpetuate stereotyping of male and female roles in science. For example, in older books boys are often pictured manipulating science equipment while girls serve as onlookers, posed and passive. Likewise, the majority of pictures depicting adults in scientific roles were of males.

All science teachers should attempt to create a classroom climate that will encourage *all* students to participate in science. By being aware of the many cultural influences still operating today, science teachers can avoid making many of the mistakes that have been made in the past. By distributing equal numbers of roles and activities to females and males, by calling on girls to answer problem-solving questions, and by using female examples as role-models, science teachers can help establish a learning climate that does not discriminate against females. In addition, by talking with parents, other teachers, guidance counselors, and school administrators, science teachers can help dispel any notion that females are less fit for science than males.

SCIENCE AND
STUDENTS FROM
MINORITY
GROUPS

The United States has been called the "melting pot" of the world. In addition to Anglo-Americans and other groups from Eastern and Western European countries, our country is comprised of Afro-Americans (11 percent), Mexican Americans (2 percent), Puerto Rican Americans (.7 percent) American Indians (.4 percent), Japanese Americans (.3 percent),

---

[3] K. Kay Shearin, "Women's Lib Is Human Lib," *Chemical and Engineering News*, 51, 1 (August 6, 1973).

Filipino Americans (.2 percent), and many other ethnic groups.[4] Early in our history, English immigrants gained control over most of our economic, social, and political institutions. During the late 1800s and early 1900s, "Americanization" was interpreted as "Anglicization." In other words, customs, values, and attitudes, particularly those fostered in schools, were largely from the Anglo-American heritage.

Today there is an emphasis on *multicultural* education. The great diversity of backgrounds among students is being recognized, and ways of studying and appreciating the contributions of all ethnic groups in the country are being incorporated in the science program. Instructional strategies are being used that allow students of different races and ethnic backgrounds to share their differing customs for music, food, and entertainment.

Kluckhohn, in discussing value orientations, has suggested that human beings relate to nature in three basic ways: "Man Subjugated to Nature," "Man in Nature," and "Man Over Nature."[5] The philosophy of "Man Subjugated to Nature" implies a fatalistic attitude and is held by many of Spanish-American ancestry. "If it is the Lord's Will that I die, then I shall die" represents this position. The "Man in Nature" philosophy regards all natural elements, including humans, as parts of one harmonious whole; this attitude has been dominant in China and other parts of the Far East in past centuries. "Man Over Nature" is characteristic of many Americans. In this view, natural forces are to be overcome and used for human purposes. In many Western civilizations, science and technology have been the primary tools for enacting this philosophy. It is obvious that science instruction for students from different cultural backgrounds needs to be planned with these different perspectives in mind.[6]

As has been the case with females, few students from minority groups have been attracted to science. For example, relatively few Afro-Americans and American Indians in the past have entered fields of science. Recently, several studies have shown that teacher expectations for black students differ from those for white students. In many schools, for example, a smaller percentage of black than white students are encouraged to take advanced mathematics and science courses. Despite recruitment programs, there are still inordinately small numbers of minority groups entering engineering, chemistry, physics, and scientific areas of agriculture.

---

[4] Percentages based on data reported in Bureau of the Census, *Subject Reports: Ethnic Groups*, 7 vols., Washington, D.C.: U.S. Government Printing Office, 1973.

[5] F. R. Kluckhohn, "Dominant and Variant Value Orientations," *In Nature, Society and Culture*, Chapter 21, Edited by F. R. Kluckhohn and H. A. Murray, Alfred A. Knopf, Inc., New York, 1956.

[6] R. D. Simpson, "Relating Student Feelings to Achievement in Science," National Science Teachers Association, 1978. Reprinted by permission of the National Science Teachers Association from Rowe, Mary Budd. *What Research Says to the Science Teacher*, Vol. 1. Washington, D.C.: National Science Teachers Association, 1978, p. 44.

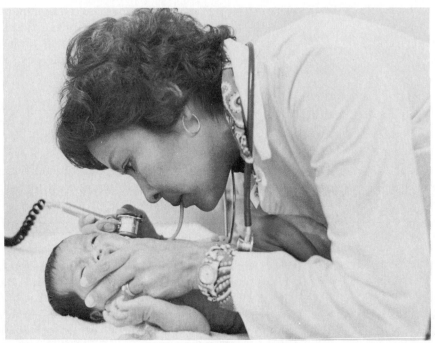

Women and minorities in science, medicine, and engineering serve as strong role-models for young students.

Today's teacher needs to be prepared to teach science in a multicultural school environment. This begins with the teacher being sensitive to the different backgrounds of students. In a study by Spilka,[7] for instance, it was found that many values being forwarded by a secondary school comprised of 753 Sioux Indians and 455 whites were in direct opposition to those taught in the homes of the Indian students. As a result of value conflicts, many Indian students were being alienated, either at home or school. Teachers at this school had to learn that many things taught in school were conflicting with attitudes and beliefs taught at home. In this particular situation, it was found that the longer the Sioux students stayed in school and the more they learned, the lower their alienation scores became. This change was at least in part effected by the teachers coming to understand that many of their values were conflicting with those of their students and that tolerance and flexibility were necessary. If formal science instruction is not in harmony with the values of a given cultural group, students may reject science.

---

[7] B. Spilka, "Alienation and Achievement Among Oglala Sioux Secondary School Students," A final report to the National Institute of Mental Health, Bethesda, Md., ERIC Report No. ED 045225, *Resources in Education*, April, 1971.

ATTRACTING
MINORITY
STUDENTS TO
SCIENCE

Several studies have shown that students from many ethnic and racial groups, and particularly blacks, do not enter science in the same proportion as do white and Oriental students. The following suggestions are ways in which science teachers can encourage black as well as other minority students to develop interest in and positive attitudes toward science.

The science teacher should treat all students, regardless of race, creed, or color, as individuals potentially capable of achieving in science and of entering science-related fields.

Students should have contact with minority group members who are practicing scientists, engineers, mathematicians, or actively engaged in some area of science or technology. These individuals serve as powerful role-models for minority students.

Classrooms should contain pictures or displays that will make minority students feel "at home" in science. Pictures of black scientists, or of minority students doing science projects, for example, communicate to all students that science is for *everyone.*

Provisions should be made for minority students to learn more about various careers in science. Since minority students often do not have access to science-related role-models at an early age, it is important to allow them to explore these roles in their science courses. They should be encouraged to discuss these at home and be given opportunities to express their feelings in class.

Minority students should be encouraged to do projects or reports that focus on the work and accomplishments of scientists of ethnic backgrounds similar to their own.

Attempts should be made to cultivate positive self-concepts among minority students with regards to science. When students experience success in science and receive positive reinforcement from their science teachers, their confidence is increased and they come to realize that through efforts of their own they can be successful in science.

Teachers should communicate the same levels of expectation to all students. It should be made clear that each student, regardless of race, sex, or national origin, is expected to achieve in science. This can begin with teachers listening carefully to all students and giving equal attention to all responses.

Science teachers should realize that some minority students upon entering secondary school science may be lacking some of the early concrete experiences commonly afforded a larger proportion of our students. For example, these students may not have taken care of a pet, participated in youth activities, such as Scouts or summer camp, or traveled far from their home. In such cases, it is important to provide students with ample concrete, activity-based experiences that they may have missed. For students from culturally deprived backgrounds (both white and black), formal instruction in science may be abstract and esoteric; therefore, the curriculum should be modified so it begins at a level commensurate with student backgrounds and achievement levels.

Models for Working with Students

During the past two decades, several approaches have emerged from the fields of psychology and counseling that can be used by teachers as guides when working with students. Some of these new approaches are based on ideas that, when pieced together, form what we call "models." Models usually explain phenomena and events within a particular

---

RESEARCH REPORT

The Influence of Teacher Expectations on Student Achievement

One of the most widely cited research studies ever done in education was conducted by Rosenthal and Jacobson.[8] These researchers *randomly* selected 20 percent of a large group of sixth graders who had recently taken an IQ test, and they then told teachers that these students had high IQs. The teachers were instructed to watch these students closely, since they were likely to "bloom" intellectually. Eight months later, the entire group of sixth graders was retested, and it was found that those students who had been (randomly) labeled "very bright" demonstrated significantly higher IQs than did other students. Rosenthal and Jacobson concluded that the teachers had apparently communicated their high expectations to the "bright" students and that the students obliged their teachers by better achievement. Although Cronback and Snow have challenged the statistical analysis,[9] other studies reviewed by Rosenthal and Jacobson show similar results and raise the question of how much teacher expectation affects student achievement.

Recent studies by Adenkia and Berry[10] and Altman and Snyder[11] present evidence that teacher expectations are lower for minority students than for whites, which may influence the kind of instruction minority students receive and, ultimately, their self-concepts. Other studies have shown that our society's expectations for female students are lower than for males.

---

[8] R. Rosenthal and L. Jacobson, *Pygmalion in the Classroom: Teacher Expectations and Pupils' Intellectual Development*, New York: Holt, Rinehart and Winston, Inc., 1968.

[9] L. J. Cronback and R. E. Snow, *Aptitudes and Instructional Strategies: A Handbook for Research on Interactions*, New York: Irvington Publishers, Inc. 1977.

[10] T. J. Adenkia and G. L. Berry, "Teacher's Attitude Toward the Education of the Black Child," *Education* 97, (1976):102–114.

[11] R. A. Altman and P. O. Snyder, *The Minority Student on the Campus: Expectations and Possibilities*, Boulder, Colo.: Western Interstate Commission for Higher Education, 1971.

framework of orientation, like the Bohr Model helps us to conceptualize atoms and the kinetic-molecular theory aids us in understanding energy.

Two of the most promising human relations models are the Carkhuff Model and Transactional Analysis. With a basic understanding of these models, a teacher can deal more effectively with many of the day-to-day interactions with students and help them solve their problems.

THE CARKHUFF MODEL

Teachers and counselors have many things in common. Both interact with large numbers of young people each day, and both are faced with students who have problems. Many techniques that have been developed for counselors are appropriate for use by teachers in the classroom.

Working with Carl Rogers at the University of Wisconsin, Robert Carkhuff and other investigators have studied major characteristics of the helping process and how counselors and their clients successfully solve problems. George Gazda and coworkers at the University of Georgia have slightly modified this model so that it can be easily used by teachers. Essentially, this model represents a series of stages through which a helper (a teacher) and a helpee (a student) must progress in order for a successful relationship to develop and for successful problem-solving to occur. As a teacher proceeds with a student in a helping relationship, three dimensions must be experienced before a meaningful result can occur.

The three helping dimensions have been identified as *helpee self-*

Many ideas of the famous counselor Carl Rogers have influenced the way teachers view and treat students today.

exploration, helpee understanding, and *helpee action*. During the *helpee self-exploration* phase, the helper tries to put himself or herself in "the helpee's shoes." By carefully exploring together the helpee's problem, both parties begin to better understand the nature and magnitude of the problem. For example, is the helpee's problem a result of not understanding the homework assignment? Or is it a case of not possessing the mathematical skills required to do the problems assigned? Frequently, an unskilled helper quickly begins giving advice or offering solutions "off the top of the head." Responses of this type usually are based on such sparse information and are of little value to the helpee. In fact, they are usually a "put-down," as the potential helper is actually implying to the helpee "Your problem is so obvious and simple that I already found a solution." As will be explained in greater detail later, the first thing an effective teacher should do while in a helping role is be a good listener.

As a teacher and student progress to the *helpee understanding* phase, the student's problem is explored in greater depth and the teacher tries to help the student fit pieces of the puzzle together. Sometimes the person needing help has already figured out the problem but needs reinforcement in finding an appropriate solution. For example, a student may already know that it is the influence of the "group" that sits next to her in biology class that is creating the problem. The student may need only a small amount of reinforcement from the teacher in order to clarify this situation.

During the *helpee-action* phase, the teacher encourages the student to devise a plan of action. Often, alternative plans are discussed, various consequences considered, and ultimately the most promising option selected. By helping the person "come up with his or her own plan," the teacher increases the chances that the student will follow through with the plan. There are times when a teacher may not be successful in working through this phase with a student. There are other times when additional helpers with special skills are needed in order for the helpee to resolve a complex problem.

The Carkhuff Model seeks to form an effective cycle of helping. During the three phases, students and teachers and helpees and helpers attempt to explore, understand, and select appropriate actions for resolving student problems. To use the approach embodied in the Carkhuff Model effectively, several basic skills are needed.

FACILITATING SELF-EXPLORATION.   A teacher's primary role during the self-exploration phase, using the Carkhuff Model as a guide, is to establish rapport with the student. The following skills are especially important in this phase of teacher-student interaction.

Empathy.   The initial role of the helper is to communicate quickly to the helpee an attitude of "I understand how you feel." Although empathy alone cannot solve problems, it is a powerful source of comfort to one who has a problem. Once a student is convinced the teacher understands his or her feelings and frustrations, a new relationship is possible. Conversely, students who are not convinced teachers understand their feelings usually block attempts to develop helpful relationships. To be able to "stand in someone else's shoes" is an important attribute for a teacher to possess.

Gazda has developed a four-point scale on which to measure empathetic responses. A response level of 1 is an irrelevant or hurtful response that disregards the feelings of a helpee. Suppose a female student says to her teacher after class, "I know the reason boys never call me is because I'm so tall." According to Gazda's scale, an example of Level I response would be, "Since you know what the problem is, why don't you just stop worrying about it." This response does not address the feelings of the student and is somewhat hurtful. The response "Cheer up, who was that tall fellow I saw you with last Saturday," while not as hurtful, is irrelevant and still fails to attend to the feelings of the student. Gazda would score this approximately a 2. A response such as "It must be frustrating to feel that your height keeps you from having dates with boys" would be scored by Gazda as a 3 or 4. This response exhibits empathy and conveys to the girl the idea that one understands her problem.

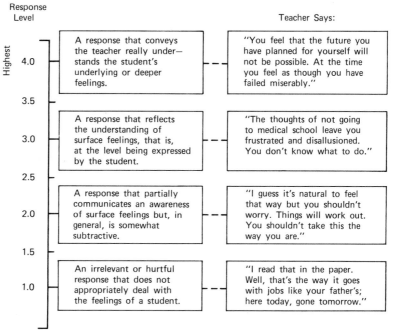

FIGURE 2.1   Key portions of Gazda's Empathy Scale with examples.

A modified copy of Gazda's four-point empathy scale with example responses is presented in Figure 2.1. Key words are presented which typify the general tone of response at the various levels. Teachers who respond to students with three- and four-level responses are perceived by students as being more "caring" and possessing more warmth. Being able to *listen* carefully and communicating in return that one understands how another person feels is a powerful tool, one that has a direct relationship to effective teaching.

Respect.   Within this model, "respect" refers specifically to helpers communicating their belief in the helpee's ability to deal with a problem. Respect is the opposite of pity. When a teacher communicates to a student "I believe you have the ability to solve your problem," the relationship between teacher and student deepens, and a second step in the facilitative process occurs.

Warmth.   Out of empathy and respect comes care. By now, if a teacher and student have progressed this far in a problem-solving relationship, rapport has been established. Nonverbally, the teacher is communicating to the student, "I accept you as an individual and I want to share your joys as well as your troubles." Instead of disapproving facial expressions and subtle signs of disinterest, the teacher with "warmth" is intensely attentive, and his or her expressions portray complete acceptance.

TRANSITION SKILLS.   During the *helpee self-exploration* phase, the teacher concentrates on establishing rapport with the student and helping the student examine his or her feelings. This is facilitated by the teacher's empathetic listening, the respect paid the student, and displays of warmth and concern. If the relationship progresses to this point, the student and teacher are ready to deal with a problem in more specific terms. It is important to remember, as Gazda has said, that teachers must first "earn the right" to help a student. During the *helpee understanding* phase, the teacher facilitates the transition from exploration to action. There are three dimensions in this phase: concreteness, genuineness, and the action phase.

Concreteness.   Concreteness is the ability to pinpoint feelings and experiences accurately. Here the teacher encourages the student to be more specific and to look beneath the surface of the problem. At this point, the teacher and student attempt to label important feelings as well as recognize concrete aspects of the problem. The teacher might ask, "Can you think of specific reasons why you are having difficulty learning chemistry?" If the student initially gives vague answers like "I seem to have difficulty studying" or "I just can't get with chemistry," the teacher's role becomes one of guiding the student toward more specific responses. As the discussion continues, the student may gradually begin to bring up problems from home, the fact that four hours a day are spent in a part-time job or that some previously studied major concept in chemistry is still unclear. When this happens, the teacher and student are in a position to understand the problem more clearly and to start acting upon it.

Genuineness.   If a teacher and student are to move toward a deeper understanding of a problem, they both must exercise honesty. They must be willing to be authentic, and elements of phoniness or role-playing must be eliminated. As can be seen in Figure 2.2, this kind of relationship is called *genuineness*.

Teachers who are genuine in their approach to problem-solving encourage students to stop hiding their feelings. In addition, teachers and students who behave in a genuine way toward each other are better able to say what they feel and to feel what they say. They can be both honest and natural. When a person's verbal actions are in line with what is actually felt, congruency is reached. According to Carkhuff, when a relationship between teacher and student reaches a point where specific parts of the problem can be discussed and these verbal accounts are congruent with the true feelings of the people involved, the problem is more likely to be understood and solved. A genuine teacher is one who is perceived by students as "human," "understanding," and "fair," and according to the Carkhuff Model, the capacity to be genuine is an important component of the helping relationship.

ACTION PHASE.   As we have seen, the first two phases of the Carkhuff Model deal with exploring and understanding problems. During the first phase, emphasis is placed on developing a warm and genuine relationship between teacher and student. During the exploration phase, the teacher exhibits empathy and respect toward the student. During the understanding phase, the teacher becomes more concrete with the student as they attempt to deal specifically with the problem. The final phase of this model involves *confrontation*; the teacher has "earned the right" to assist the student in confronting the problem. It is now the proper time for the teacher to encourage the student to take action.

As was stated earlier, it is often tempting for a teacher to respond quickly to student problems and to give what Gazda calls "cheap advice." But advice, no matter how brilliant, is usually ineffective if it is not internalized by students or other helpees. The major role of the teacher during

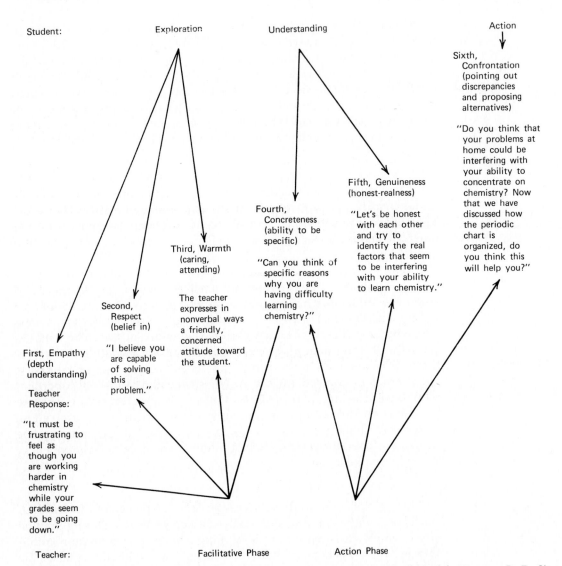

Student:

Exploration   Understanding   Action

Sixth,
Confrontation
(pointing out
discrepancies
and proposing
alternatives)

"Do you think that
your problems at
home could be
interfering with
your ability to
concentrate on
chemistry? Now
that we have
discussed how
the periodic
chart is
organized, do
you think this
will help you?"

Fifth, Genuineness
(honest-realness)

"Let's be honest
with each other
and try to
identify the real
factors that seem
to be interfering
with your ability
to learn chemistry."

Fourth,
Concreteness
(ability to be
specific)

"Can you think of
specific reasons
why you are
having difficulty
learning
chemistry?"

Third, Warmth
(caring,
attending)

The teacher
expresses in
nonverbal ways
a friendly,
concerned
attitude toward
the student.

Second,
Respect
(belief in)

"I believe you
are capable
of solving
this
problem."

First, Empathy
(depth
understanding)

Teacher
Response:

"It must be
frustrating to
feel as
though you
are working
harder in
chemistry
while your
grades seem
to be going
down."

Teacher: Facilitative Phase   Action Phase

FIGURE 2.2   A modification of the helping process outlined in the Carkhuff Model. (*Source:* R. D. Simpson, "Relating Student Feelings to Achievement in Science," National Science Teachers Association, 1978. Reprinted by permission of the National Science Teachers Association, from Rowe, Mary Budd. *What Research Says to the Science Teacher,* Vol. I. Washington, D.C.: National Science Teachers Association, 1978, p. 49.)

this phase, then, is to help students generate alternative solutions. As the student and teacher discuss these options, the teacher can help point out discrepancies. Ultimately, the student is encouraged to focus on the most promising alternative(s) and to make a strong commitment in this direction. In other words, at this time the student is encouraged to make a plan and to take action. "I'll set aside at least 45 minutes *every* evening to study chemistry," or "I'll stop listening to my sister's stereo while I'm studying chemistry." More serious actions may include "I'll go to my parents and ask them to stop arguing so much," "I'll ask my boss at work if I can work less during the week so I'll have more time for studying," or "I'll stop running around with Harry and Sue so I don't keep getting into trouble with the police."

It is important in this phase that the student be willing to take *action*. For a solution to have a lasting effect, the student must believe in the plan, have internalized the consequences of the actions, and be committed to the plan. These all come from the ability to confront specific aspects of the problem honestly and openly and to deal concretely with alternatives and discrepancies.

TRANSACTIONAL ANALYSIS

Transactional Analysis (TA) has been widely used in programs for the improvement of human relations in recent years. As the name suggests, it is an analysis of the transactions that take place between people. You possibly have heard of Eric Berne's *The Games People Play*[12] and Thomas Harris's *I'm OK, You're OK.*[13] Transactional Analysis theory, as depicted in these two books, is based on the premise that all our behavior is influenced by three distinct ego states—parent, child, and adult.

THE THREE EGO STATES. In the parent ego state, people tend to behave the way they remember their mother or father behaving. Here people act in a protective, critical, helpful, and even "bossy" manner. While playing the parent role a person carries with him rules, regulations, and "how-to" data. Each acts as a judge, jury, and authority.

The child ego state is the emotion-filled, carefree, and uncensored part of life. Here the impulsive, fun-loving side of a person protrudes. A person often exhibits the child when reacting to authority or to criticism in a "sheepish" or "guilty" fashion. An "I'm not OK" attitude often accompanies the child ego state.

As people mature and learn to find answers for themselves, the adult begins to emerge. In the adult ego state, people behave on the basis of their set of experiences. Objective and rational decision-making takes place. The adult is free to take the position "I'm OK—You're OK."

---

[12] Eric Berne, *The Games People Play: The Psychology of Human Relations,* New York: Ballantine Books, 1964.
[13] Thomas Harris, *I'm Ok, You're Ok: A Practical Guide to Transactional Analysis,* New York: Harper and Row, Publishers, 1969.

None of these positions is tied directly to age. Grownups frequently behave in the child state, and children are capable of responding in the adult or parent states. All three ego states are important, and all are appropriate at given times for people of all ages.

TRANSACTIONAL THEORY.   Transactional Analysis deals with the way people interact using the various ego states. Let's look at a hypothetical situation and observe how TA applies. Assume it is Friday and Thomas Jefferson High School is playing in a championship football game this evening. Students have just returned to their chemistry lab and from an emotional pep rally. As Ms. Jackson enters the noise-filled room, she yells frantically, "Sit down, shut up, and get your lab manuals out!" A hush moves over the room as one student sheepishly replies, "Gosh, Ms. Jackson, we were just having fun—we're sorry you are mad at us." From what ego state was Ms. Jackson operating? From what ego state were the students operating?

Let's look at another way this situation could have been handled and see if you can detect a difference. Suppose as the teacher enters the noisy room she remarks, "Pep rallies really get you folks excited. Do you think they really help the team play better?" Gradually, the class joins in on a short discussion concerning the advantages and disadvantages of pep rallies after one student replies: "Yes, I think so. Athletes are influenced by school spirit." Soon Ms. Jackson shifts to the chemistry investigation for the day. The students, while more talkative than usual, get out their equipment and begin work. In the first episode, the transaction would fit the following description:

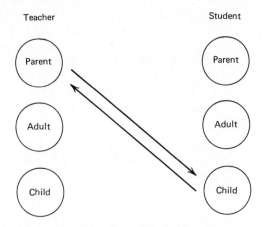

Teacher: *Sit down, shut up, and get your lab manuals out!*
Student: *Gosh, Ms. Jackson, we were just having fun—we're sorry you are mad at us.*

In the second episode, the transaction took a different form, coming from the following ego states:

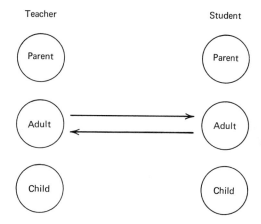

Teacher: *Pep rallies really get you folks excited. Do you think they really help the team play better?*

Student: *Yes, I think so. Athletes are influenced by school spirit.*

An application of TA to teaching is the notion that adult-adult interactions are more productive than parent-child transactions. Students respond more positively when the teacher shows trust and respect. Rapport is difficult to establish as demonstrated by our first example.

Another application of TA demonstrates why communication is sometimes "shut-off" between two people. When two students shout at each other, turn their backs on each other, and are unable to communicate any more, it is likely they have just experienced a *crossed transaction*. This transaction can be demonstrated as follows:

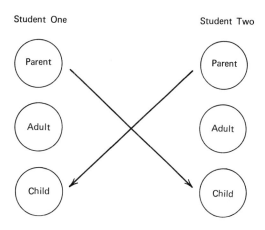

Student One: *I'm sick and tired of you always borrowing notebook
paper from me.*

Student Two: *Well excuse me! I'm sick and tired of your complaining
to me all the time.*

In this transaction, the Student One stimulus was parent. Since Student Two did not respond in the adult or child, a *crossed* response occurred. When a person fails to respond as expected, lines between ego states cross and communications usually break down. When misunderstandings have arisen, it is likely that crossed transactions were involved.

Another example of a crossed transaction between a teacher and a student is:

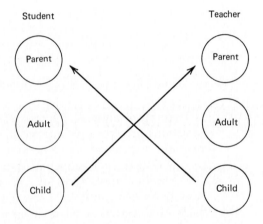

Student: *Where's the hydrochloric acid? I can never find anything in
this lab.*

Teacher: *Why are you always asking me to find things for you? I'm not
your servant.*

In this transaction, again, lines between ego states crossed. The student was expecting a response from the teacher different from the one received. Had the teacher responded in the adult or parent the lines would not have crossed, and communication would likely have continued longer.

HARRIS'S FOUR LIFE POSITIONS. In *I'm OK—You're OK*, Harris places human attitudes and behaviors into four "life positions": I'm OK—You're OK, I'm Not OK—You're OK, I'm OK—You're Not OK, and I'm Not

OK—You're Not OK. Figure 2.3 shows some common traits associated with these four positions.

Transactional Analysis theory deals with attempts to move people from negative positions to the "I'm OK—You're OK" position. Many students in schools today have "I'm Not OK" attitudes. Effective teachers are those who are skillful in building up the ego of students. "Stroking" is a term used in TA to describe how one responds to another. In classrooms where abundant *positive strokes* are received from the teacher, students appear happier and learn more. By being sensitive to the ego states of students and using TA, teachers can help students develop better feelings about themselves and others.

PSYCHOLOGICAL GAMES IN THE CLASSROOM.   Transactional Analysis is also used to describe many of the psychological games that commonly are played in the classroom. The participants play-act various roles based on parent or child scripts they have learned during childhood. *Victims,* for example, are students and others who falsify their reasons for failure in order to reexperience "I'm Not OK" feelings from their child ego state. *Rescuers* are those who, by being helpful, keep others dependent upon them. In fact, Rescuers may only appear to be helpful while actually hindering success or reinforcing their own "You're Not OK" feelings. Another player is the *Persecutor.* The Persecutor who sets unnecessarily strict limits and often enforces rules with brutality is another example of a person with "You're Not OK" feelings.

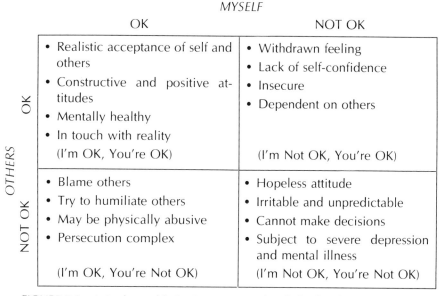

MYSELF

		OK	NOT OK
OTHERS	OK	• Realistic acceptance of self and others • Constructive and positive attitudes • Mentally healthy • In touch with reality (I'm OK, You're OK)	• Withdrawn feeling • Lack of self-confidence • Insecure • Dependent on others (I'm Not OK, You're OK)
	NOT OK	• Blame others • Try to humiliate others • May be physically abusive • Persecution complex (I'm OK, You're Not OK)	• Hopeless attitude • Irritable and unpredictable • Cannot make decisions • Subject to severe depression and mental illness (I'm Not OK, You're Not OK)

FIGURE 2.3   Attitudes and behaviors associated with the four life positions.

Victims, rescuers, and persecutors comprise what is often called the *psychodynamic triangle*. An example of how this game is played is described by the following incident. Susan Barrett drops in to see her biology teacher after class. She complains bitterly to Mr. Martin, that Mr. Langston, her English teacher, is out to "fail her." "I know he's out to get me," she says. The stage is set: Susan is the victim, Mr. Langston is the Persecutor, and Mr. Martin, the biology teacher, is supposed to be the Rescuer (see Figure 2.4). In cases involving the psychodynamic triangle, if one does not choose to play the game, the player will often attempt to shift roles. For example, if the biology teacher in this case chooses not to be the Rescuer, the student might change roles and try to make him the Persecutor or even the Victim. By recognizing these roles, teachers and students can often avoid being caught in games where child and parent ego states are "play-acted."

Psychological games involve "ulterior transactions" where the hidden motive may lead to a payoff. Students play illegitimate or phony roles in order to play-act childhood experiences. Moreover, students play games merely to reinforce their "I'm Not OK" or "You're Not OK" feelings. Teachers who recognize these games can help structure events that will produce more "I'm OK—You're OK" feelings.

In playing status games, and this is perhaps more prevalent in colleges and universities, students and teachers may seek reinforcement of child and parent behaviors. A student, for example, may attempt repeatedly to elicit

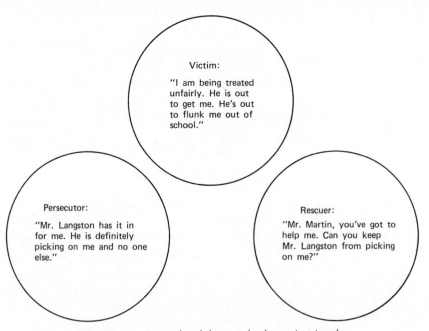

FIGURE 2.4   Example of the psychodynamic triangle.

strokes from a teacher such as "Yes Johnny, you are very smart" or "Jane, you are a lovely person with a brilliant future." Teachers, on the other hand, are often tempted to elicit praise from their students that reinforces their position as an "authority" or "person in charge" ("go ahead, tell me how impressed you are with my vast knowledge of science"). In both cases, participants are play-acting child or parent ego states in hopes of receiving needed strokes.

By understanding fundamental aspects of the TA model, teachers can help guide students to more positive and fruitful interactions by helping them discover and avoid some of the common psychological games that occur in classrooms. Further, by engaging in adult transactions, students and teachers are more apt to resist some of the common settings that lead to games.

FAMILY SCRIPTS.   One final aspect of TA that teachers can apply is the understanding of *scripts*. A script contains the rules and roles one learns to go by. Scripts are usually family or cultural in origin, containing the expectations of parents and the traditions of one's culture. Some scripts are helpful and some are hurtful. Students who are taught to be honest, obedient, and responsive are likely to follow these scripts in school and to be rewarded in return. Other scripts are less helpful. Students with extremely aggressive or demanding parents are likely to exhibit similar behaviors at school. Students who are "put-down" or criticized a lot at home are likely to have I'm Not OK feelings. Hence they may behave in the child ego state while seeking to reinforce these feelings. Scripts are passed down from generation to generation by members of some families or cultures. Frequently, people play these scripts in the parent ego state without being aware they are doing so.

The inappropriate classroom behavior of a student that is annoying to the teacher and others is often the result of scripting we have just discussed. Again, when people act out their scripts they are usually behaving in either the parent or child ego state. Teachers who recognize common scripts and can identify some of their sources are in a better position to understand their students. It is much easier to tolerate "different" behaviors if we understand their origins and accept the fact that our society is made up of a great diversity of family and cultural backgrounds.

While many scripts are helpful and many others must be tolerated, some are hurtful. In situations where the well-being of others is affected, teachers have a responsibility to intervene. In cases particularly where students are acting out I'm Not OK and You're Not OK feelings, attempts to change student behavior are in order. By helping students overcome dominant parent or child ego states, teachers are in a position to help others in the "de-scripting" process. For example, by helping the withdrawn, insecure student accept the fact that he or she can be successful in science, a teacher can help the student overcome I'm Not OK child feelings. In the case where a student is frequently trying to boss or humiliate other students, the principles of TA can also be used. By dealing with the You're Not OK feelings of the student and by encouraging the student to exhibit more behavior in the adult ego state, the teacher may be able to help individuals of this type become more positive toward others.

While parent and child are an integral part of each person's behavior and should not be assumed as always "bad" or "wrong," it is true that much of the inappropriate behavior of students in classrooms comes from these two ego states. According to the TA model, adult-adult transactions are generally the most productive. Teachers who themselves operate from the adult and encourage students to do the same are in a position to affect transaction levels in their classrooms. By helping students recognize their parent, adult, and child ego states, many inappropriate behaviors can be corrected. By increasing adult-adult communication in the classroom, students are encouraged to mature and the classroom climate is improved.

Dealing with Discipline Problems

Dealing with discipline problems is one of the major concerns of most teachers, especially beginning teachers. The following section deals with some of the fundamental causes of misbehavior in the classroom as well as some of the most promising techniques for dealing with common discipline problems.

MAJOR CAUSES OF DISCIPLINE PROBLEMS

In dealing with problems of any kind, it is important first to identify causes. Most classroom discipline problems have recognizable causes which can be identified if efforts are made to do so. Many of these discipline problems are partially the result of actions taken by teachers and parents. Others are almost entirely the result of actions by students. In most cases, however, discipline problems are related to the actions of several of these groups.

TEACHER-RELATED CAUSES. Most of us can probably cite several examples in our own education of an incident erupting because of something a teacher did or said. Sarcastic remarks, singling out one student "to make an example out of him," or treating one student different from another, are examples of how a teacher can prompt inappropriate behavior in students. In most cases, teacher-caused problems occur when teachers, accidentally or intentionally, infringe upon the dignity of their students. When this happens, or students are "forced into a corner," the only way out for the students is to strike back. While it may be proper at times for a teacher to display anger, express disappointment, or "blow off steam," few situations warrant ridicule or attack on a student's character or dignity. Even flagrant violations of conduct by students should be dealt with by focusing on the act instead of the student's character or personality.

Other types of teacher behavior can elicit inappropriate student responses. Trying to be humorous at the wrong time, for example, may lead to the teacher losing temporary control of the class. Failing to plan properly for a given class period, failing to start a class on time, or boring students with irrelevant matters are but other examples of how teachers generate, or at least increase, the probability of misbehavior.

In order to eliminate or reduce as many discipline problems as possible, teachers must ask themselves each time a discipline problem arises if anything they did was the cause.

ADMINISTRATOR-RELATED CAUSES.   A common scene in a typical secondary school is that of the teacher and students engaged in a serious discussion about an important topic. All of a sudden, a voice over the intercom system shrieks, "All members of the Student Council report to the gymnasium for pictures for the yearbook." As six students leave the classroom and the other students begin talking to each other, the train of thought is lost. The frustrated teacher stands at the front of the classroom searching for something to say and finally yells, "Get Quiet"! This is an administrator-caused problem. Had proper planning occurred, all seventy-six classrooms in the school would have been spared this unwelcomed intrusion.

One of the most important variables in any school is the attitude of the principal and his or her assistants toward students and teachers. Students are not likely, for example, to misbehave at a school where the firm, consistent enforcement of a common set of rules is practiced. On the other hand, school administrators who proliferate unrealistic rules and regulations are likely to produce a system that encourages student defiance and unnecessary misbehavior. Strict dress codes, frequent lectures over the intercom about misconduct, schedules with no opportunities for rest periods, harsh penalties for minor infractions, and frequent schedule changes that disrupt all classes are examples of administrator-related causes of misbehavior.

HOME-RELATED CAUSES.   Students are products of their home environment when they enroll in school and are likely to behave accordingly. Parent, child, and sibling relationships in the home have a bearing on why certain students behave the way they do. Most discipline problems do not appear suddenly at school. Many are extensions of problems that exist in the home and with parents. Furthermore, the manner in which a student reacts to parental authority influences how the pupil reacts to other adults, including teachers. Students with strict parents usually respond differently to authority figures than students with permissive parents. Thus, teachers often have to deal with students in different ways depending on how they are disciplined at home.

The attitudes of parents toward school play an important role in how students behave in school. Students under great pressure from parents to make high grades sometimes exhibit aggressive or hostile behavior. Students from homes where negative attitudes toward school are expressed often bring these attitudes to the classroom. Students who think learning is unimportant respond negatively in class. In other cases, students may work long hours on a job in order to help alleviate financial problems at home. When one of these students falls asleep in class, it is probably because of fatigue and not because of boredom or disrespect for the teacher or subject. One of the most difficult aspects of developing good human relations between students and teachers is to learn that problems that start in the morning at home and that are sometimes brought to the classroom are not the failure of the teacher or of teaching techniques. By understanding this source of discipline problems, both students and teachers increase their chances for dealing with them more effectively.

STUDENT-RELATED CAUSES.   We always run the risk of becoming too simplistic when searching for the "cause" of any event. Most of the time there is multiple causality—acts or events perpetuated by several factors. While teachers, administrators, and parents cause many problems, it should be remembered that any problem involves more than one person. Many discipline problems can be attributed to the fact that adolescent students often lack maturity, self-control, and the ability to use good judgment. For many students, school is a place where they *have to go,* a place they perceive as boring and meaningless to their lives.

A general lack of motivation is no doubt the cause of most discipline problems in secondary schools. In addition, at the heart of many discipline problems is a lack of security or self-esteem on the part of students. Many students misbehave simply to get attention; for these attention-starved youngsters, even negative attention is better than none at all. Psychologist William Glasser points out that people behave as they do in search of rewards. When Johnny throws a piece of chalk across the room, his reward may be the much-needed attention he gets from this inappropriate act. Most adolescents are searching for new identity and recognition. Talking in class, passing notes, making wisecracks, and other aggressive behaviors are means by which young people frequently attempt to get attention. This, in turn, helps satisfy strong needs for acceptance, particularly by peers.

Of course, some discipline problems are more serious than others. Many problems relating to immaturity and lack of a sense of responsibility center on such things as failure to do homework, failure to follow directions, failure to bring proper materials to class, and talking instead of listening. Other problems have more serious causes as well as consequences. Stealing, lying, cheating, truancy, destroying property, and chronic hyperactivity or aggressiveness may at first appear as despicable student-caused problems, but beneath the surface there are usually more deeply rooted problems. In instances where serious problems are evident, the teacher should move quickly to help the student get proper help. Guidance counselors, school administrators, and parents represent sources of additional help for students who endanger themselves or the well-being of others. By understanding the nature of adolescent students, teachers can understand more clearly the wide range of causes associated with these problems.

Techniques for Dealing with Discipline Problems

In many ways discipline problems are like disease. Just as disease represents an absence of good health, discipline problems represent behaviors undesirable in a classroom. The two are alike in another way: "An ounce of prevention is worth a pound of cure." In the case of teaching, this means establishing the best learning environment possible and developing an *esprit de corps* among students and teachers. Unfortunately, achieving this goal is not as easy as it may sound and may even be impossible. Thus, other ways for dealing with discipline problems are required.

Teachers are *decision-makers*. During the course of a day, each teacher faces many situations in which a problem has to be analyzed, alternatives weighed, and prompt action taken. Experienced teachers usually anticipate most of these problems and know how they will respond ahead of time.

There is no list, nor should there be, that prescribes how to deal with such problems. However, a few fundamental considerations and techniques do exist that have been found worthwhile and helpful.

TEACHER SELF-CONTROL

There are few situations that justify a teacher's loss of self-control or dignity, regardless of how large or small a discipline problem may be. The calm, firm countenance of the teacher is the best insurance against loss of self-control in any classroom or educational setting. A loss of self-control by a teacher not only is an admission of inadequacy, but also signals to students that things, at least temporarily, are out of control. This invites further irrational behavior from students and makes it more difficult in the future for the teacher to influence student behavior. The watchword of all teachers is "Maintain self-control at all times." As long as a teacher keeps his or her presence, a situation will be perceived by students as "under control."

USE OF SIGNALS

As one of the authors of this book likes to tell students, "There is no need to kill a gnat with a two-by-four." Frequently, the teacher can control minor misconduct merely by maintaining strong eye contact with the students involved. If this is not enough, the teacher can usually stop talking and stare long enough for the participants to get the message. Sometimes clearing the throat or expressing a mild gesture such as a frown will signal students of a teacher's displeasure. If this subtle approach works, then there is no need to make a larger issue of it or use a more severe measure. Additional signals may include shaking one's head, pointing a finger, or saying "Someone is making it difficult for the rest of us to think." Even better, the use of *positive* verbal and nonverbal signals is effective. Smiling or listening intently communicates approval to students and encourages them to repeat desired behaviors.

PROXIMITY
CONTROL

Most "discipline problems" that erupt during the day are minor ones. In many instances, the presence or closeness of the teacher will be enough to control the situation. Oftentimes, for example, when two students are talking or "horsing around," movement of the teacher in that direction will decrease the inappropriate activity. If the students are perceptive and reasonably cooperative, this measure may be enough to correct he situation. If the students do not eventually respond to it, of course, the teacher should then separate them. One particularly effective solution to habitual "wandering eyes" during tests is merely to ask one of the culprits to take another seat. Here, the teacher does not accuse the students, yet everyone gets the message. And, by being physically separated, the sharing of information cannot continue. Experience has shown that students will usually follow this suggestion to move in a very conforming manner.

HUMOR AS A
CONTROL
MEASURE

One of the smoothest ways to avert a potentially tense moment or to keep a small incident from growing needlessly into a major one is for the teacher to inject humor into the situation. Take, for example, a startling, and probably unfounded, accusation made by a student in front of the entire class, "Mr. Smith, why do you always pick on me?" This might best be handled by quickly responding in a friendly tone of voice "Because I like you so much" or "You should be so lucky to get all that attention." By seriously denying the student's charge in front of all the students, a teacher might only make matters worse. Care should be taken, however, to avoid sarcasm. Later, in private, the teacher might wish to follow up on the incident if it appears serious.

One important thing most effective teachers develop, and one thing students like, is a healthy sense of humor. Teachers who can laugh at themselves and at their mistakes demonstrate a flexibility that is both refreshing and often necessary in maintaining an equilibrium in the classroom. A round of laughter is often just the remedy needed to soften an anxious moment.

Humor can also be used to suggest to students that they change minor yet annoying habits. For instance, a student in the back of the room, tapping a pencil repeatedly, might be reminded of this annoyance by the teacher saying in a friendly manner, "I don't think this scientific discussion needs an accompanying drum section." While the right blend of humor can be appropriate at times, a teacher should be careful not to overdo the humor to the extent of becoming sarcastic or "corny."

ISOLATION

More stringent measures must be taken for chronic misbehavior. When a student continually fails to respond to other control measures, it may be necessary to isolate the individual from the other students. Psychiatrist William Glasser suggests that, when students participate in serious acts of misbehavior, they be isolated until they can freely admit what they did, are ready to accept responsibility for the act, and are willing to offer a plan to correct the situation. He states that it may take a student several days, or in severe cases a week or more, to complete this process. If there is room, a teacher may be able to isolate students within the classroom or laboratory area. In some schools, there are places such as in-school suspension rooms where students can be sent for this purpose.

DIRECT APPEAL

One of the most effective methods for dealing with misbehavior is simply to appeal directly to a student or group of students for cooperation. Looking her firmly in the eye and asking "Susan, will you please cooperate with us on this activity?" is often an effective method for communicating to a student that the teacher is aware of her disruptive behavior and wants her to change. When students know the teacher is serious and the teacher is willing to ask for cooperation in a firm, yet decent manner, students will generally respond positively.

PRIVATE
CONFERENCE

During class a discipline problem may erupt while the teacher is busy helping another student or is explaining an important idea. When it is not convenient to deal with a problem on the spot, or when a student persists in an annoying habit, it is appropriate to say "Please see me after class." Private conferences, while sparing embarrassment to both student and teacher, also allow teachers an opportunity to find out specific problems behind student misbehavior. In a one-to-one confrontation, students are usually more serious and are more impressed with the teacher's intentions. During private conferences, both student and teacher can look more carefully at the problem and often are able to agree on a way of improving the situation.

**Glasser on
Discipline**

From his work in psychiatry, Dr. William Glasser has developed several techniques for dealing with discipline problems in the schools. Through working with several schools, he has applied one of his most widely known counseling techniques, Reality Therapy, as a positive way of changing the inappropriate behaviors of students. In the popular book *Schools Without Failure*, Glasser discusses how Reality Therapy, classroom meetings, and other techniques can be used to produce more positive student behavior in schools.

REALITY THERAPY

Why are some students always involved in fighting? Why do certain students talk back to teachers? Why do others miss school frequently? Glasser believes that the students exhibiting each of these behavior patterns are denying the reality of the world around them. Basic among the needs of all people is to love and be loved. When students feel they are not loved by others or they have not themselves learned to love, they lose touch with reality. This uncomfortable, often miserable condition frequently leads to misbehavior.

Methods that lead people toward reality, toward grappling successfully with the tangible and intangible aspects of life, have been labeled by Glasser as Reality Therapy. Reality Therapy encourages involvement with other people as well as being a means for fulfilling the basic human need of feeling worthwhile. To feel worthwhile one must maintain a satisfactory standard of conduct, and to do this a student must learn to make corrections when he or she does something wrong. Self-discipline can come only after the student learns responsibility. Reality Therapy, therefore, deals with helping students fulfill basic needs through the development of *responsibility* and *commitment*.

PRACTICING
REALITY THERAPY
IN THE
CLASSROOM

In *Schools Without Failure*, Glasser describes how teachers can use Reality Therapy to reduce failure among students. Consider the following scene: During a science lab, Paul, one of the major sources of discipline problems in the class, throws a chalkboard eraser across the room, which glances off Nancy's head and breaks a glass beaker. Glasser suggests that Reality Therapy can be used in dealing with the situation through the following actions.

1. Make a Value
Judgment

An essential element in Reality Therapy is for the *student* to make a value judgment concerning what has been or is being done at the time of misbehavior. In cases like Paul's, Glasser recommends asking the question "What did you do?" The question "Why did you do it?" may be a more natural response, but it is not nearly as effective, according to Glasser. Asking "What" encourages a student to examine the behavior and to think about the direct consequences of the behavior in question.

Many students have difficulty answering the question "What did you do?" In fact, some students may require considerable time before being able to answer. In more serious cases, Glasser recommends isolating misbehaving students from the rest of the class in order for them to think about "What did you do?" While "Why" asks for abstract motives that the student may or may not understand, "What" requires that a student recount the behavior just exercised, and this is usually more difficult to do and reveals more about why the student did what he or she did. In most cases, an opportunity for a value judgment follows a student telling the teacher *what* he or she has done. In Paul's case, if he does not elaborate further after saying "I threw an eraser at Nancy and broke a beaker," the teacher should ask him to describe the consequences of his act. Regardless of how Paul finally answers the "What" question, he should be encouraged ultimately to relate to the teacher that his stunt was inappropriate. Acceptable responses might be "I could have really hurt Nancy," and "I broke a piece of equipment that costs money."

2. Assume Responsibility

After a student admits what he or she has done and has made a value judgment concerning the inappropriate behavior, the individual is then in a position to accept responsibility for the act. At this point, Glasser suggests that students be encouraged to *make a plan* to correct the misbehavior. For instance, in Paul's case, the teacher might ask "Can you think of a plan that will help correct what you just did?" One of the important facets of Reality Therapy is to allow students to assume responsibility. Instead of going into Paul's past, embarrassing him in front of the entire class, or administering some type of arbitrary punishment, the teacher using Reality Therapy would encourage Paul to take responsibility for his actions and to do something to correct them. After Paul admits what he did and expresses remorse over his actions, he will be in a better position to outline positive steps needed to make amends. He might say to his teacher "First, I should find out if Nancy is hurt and apologize to her. Second, I will sweep up the glass so no one else gets hurt. Finally, I will pay for the beaker out of my own money."

3. Make a Commitment

A commitment to correct misbehavior should be based on a judgment that what was done is wrong and it will not be repeated. In using Reality Therapy, it is not enough to encourage a student to admit wrongdoing and to make a plan. The student must also be encouraged to make a formal commitment to the plan. Glasser suggests that this act be formalized by shaking hands, having the student write down what is to be accomplished or outline the plan on a tape recorder for future reference.

In Paul's case, a genuine handshake would probably be enough. In cases where the plan includes long-range commitments like "I will turn in my homework on time" or "I will stop talking to Charlie during class," documentation of the plan is suggested.

4. Following Through

Seeing to it that students follow through with their plans and commitments is often the hardest part of using Reality Therapy. This is especially true in cases where students attempt to correct chronic problems that require long-range commitments. The keystone to improving self-discipline using Reality Therapy and, hence, changing the behavior of students is to let individuals know that no excuse will be acceptable for not following through. Students learn responsibility and self-discipline, Glasser says, only when they realize they must follow through on commitments. When students are allowed to break their promises or renege on their commitments, Reality Therapy is reduced to lip service and students do not learn the meaning of responsibility.

In some cases, students will propose plans that are too idealistic. Teachers should accordingly encourage a more realistic plan. In other cases, students will not possess ample maturity and persistence to follow through with every detail of a plan. Such students may therefore need to be allowed to modify their plan temporarily in order to have more time to successfully complete the plan. Bill, for instance, may find it almost impossible to refrain from talking to Charlie, and, thus, he will have to make a new plan which includes moving to a new seat.

CLASSROOM MEETINGS

An additional technique described by Glasser for improving classroom discipline is the "classroom meeting." Using this technique, the teacher asks students to sit in a tight circle and to discuss problems that face the class or school. For example, if absenteeism is high, the teacher may ask questions like "How many people are absent today?," "Why do you think so many students at this school are absent?," "Have any of you here today missed school for reasons other than sickness?," and "Do any of you have suggestions for dealing with this problem?" During the class meeting, the teacher tries to remain nonjudgmental while encouraging students to be open and honest.

Class meetings allow students opportunities to express their feelings and to hear the opinions of others. Glasser has found that this technique often has a great impact on students. In one class he asked the question "Is everyone in this class a kind person?" Two members of the class who had been treating their classmates unkindly were surprised and shocked to learn that their peers did not consider them kind persons.

Class meetings should be relatively short for younger students but can be as long as an entire class period for high school students. Class meetings should be called whenever the teacher or students feel there is an important problem to discuss. In many cases, it may be appropriate for the teacher to ask the class to "make a plan" concerning a persistent problem. Relative to the problem of absenteeism, Glasser has asked students to sign a paper pledging to do something about the problem. Although one or two class meetings will not usually solve a problem, Glasser has found that when this technique is used regularly, discipline problems are gradually reduced.

GLASSER'S SUGGESTIONS FOR IMPROVING DISCIPLINE

In addition to his ideas on Reality Therapy and class meetings, Glasser offers five suggestions for improving the classroom climate. The five points are:

1. School Should Be a Good Place

Many students dread coming to school or attending certain classes. The first thing a teacher should attempt to provide is an environment perceived by students as "a good place." When students look forward to coming to their science class, they are going to be more receptive to learning.

2. Students Should Know the Rules

Sometimes students break rules because they do not know what the rules are. Glasser suggests that teachers should take ample time to go over important rules. In some cases, it may be helpful to read the rules, discuss them, and then have students sign a sheet acknowledging that they understand the rules.

3. Students Should Agree with the Rules

According to Glasser, the major reason people break rules is that they do not agree with them. In classes where the majority of the students agree with the rules, rules will generally be followed. When there is a lack of acceptance of a particular rule, usually the rule should be questioned, discussed, and perhaps altered.

4. Students Should Have Some Say in Making and Helping Change the Rules

One way to improve both the quality and acceptance of rules is to allow students opportunities to help make them. When students feel they have had a part in making rules, they will work harder to enforce them. In addition, students will consider rules more valid and reasonable when they know that there is a potential for helping to change or modify existing rules. As rules become outdated or irrelevant, students should also be allowed to help change them.

5. Students Should Know What Will Happen if They Break the Rules

As Glasser has stated, there is no use having rules if they are not enforced. Students should know what will happen when violations occur. It is imperative that teachers enforce rules in a consistent fashion; otherwise, rules serve no real purpose. Ideally, there should be as few rules as possible, but those few should be consistently enforced.

In Perspective

As with all good ideas in teaching, there are many precautions one should consider in using the various techniques and models described in this chapter. Science teachers are trained professionally to teach science, not to be counseling psychologists. Many of the techniques require experience and practice before they can be used effectively. In addition, in the busy world of teaching, one may not always have ample time to invest in changing certain student behaviors. Furthermore, many students exhibit rather deeply ingrained patterns of behavior by the time they reach the secondary schools, and these are not likely to change overnight.

This is not to suggest that science teachers should ignore problems of student behavior whether they be disruptive or like that of the student described in "Cipher in the Snow." Students bring these problems to the classroom, and teachers, working individually or with counselors, as well as administrators and others *must do their best* to help students achieve success in science and school.

The difficulties of beginning teachers in mastering the details of Transactional Analysis, the Carkhuff Model, Reality Therapy, and other approaches should not be allowed to overshadow several important themes that are incorporated by all of them. For example, it is important that teachers care about the welfare of students and let these feelings show. Students want to be liked, respected, and successful. This is the minimum students can expect of teachers.

Review Questions

1. Describe your feelings after you read *Cipher in the Snow* by Jean Mizer Todhunter. What would you do if a Cliff Evans were in your class?
2. What are the major characteristics of teachers that students like best?
3. Make a list of several common or unique behaviors of adolescents. In another column, explain *why* these behaviors may occur.
4. Why is the quality of science instruction especially important during the middle and junior high school grades?
5. Describe at least five things science teachers can do that might encourage more females and minorities to consider science-related careers.
6. Describe the major dimensions of the Carkhuff Model.
7. Describe briefly the major premise on which Transactional Analysis (TA) is based.
8. List at least three common causes of discipline problems and at least five general techniques for dealing with such problems.
9. Discuss briefly three techniques Dr. William Glasser has suggested for improving discipline in the classroom.
10. In what important ways are Transactional Analysis, the Carkhuff

Model, and Reality Therapy similar? What, if any, are the major differences among the three approaches?

For Application and Analysis

1. A science class is characterized by an absentee rate of approximately 25 percent each day. By using ideas from this chapter, how would you attempt to correct this situation in a positive manner?

2. Two girls in your sixth period science class, Belinda and Lillian, continue to whisper back and forth during class. You have asked them to stop talking, but this has been to no avail. Explain how you might use Reality Therapy to correct this situation.

3. You are taking over the seventh grade life science class at Jefferson Junior High School at midyear. You have heard that the teacher you are replacing has had some discipline problems and that the teacher was quite "slack" in handling them. What would you do during your first week to establish a new "tone" in the class?

4. The following episodes are examples of discipline problems that commonly occur in secondary school classrooms. Read the problem carefully, then examine each of the alternative actions that can be taken. Indicate the option you feel is most appropriate for each situation. Feel free to list additional alternatives that you think are appropriate.

    A. During a test you notice that John periodically looks in the direction of Bill's paper. After you see this happen several times, which of the following courses of action would you take:
       a. Ignore it since you cannot prove that John is actually cheating.
       b. Announce to the entire class that you know that some students are cheating.
       c. Go back and stand next to John's desk.
       d. Move promptly to John's desk, take up his paper, and inform him he will receive a zero on this test.
       e. Quietly ask John to take another seat.

    Additional Options

    B. On the first day of class you are making some general announcements when a student in the back of the room makes a wisecrack. Since you want to get off to a good start, you should do what?
       a. Ignore the comment and keep on talking
       b. Make an example of the student by sending him to the office.
       c. Ask the student to see you after school.
       d. Take this opportunity to talk to the class about basic rules and regulations.
       e. Say something humorous back to the student.

Additional Options

C. You notice that Susan has been missing your science class with increasing frequency. How would you approach her about this problem?
   a. Tell her if she misses any more classes you will be forced to give her an "F" for this grading period.
   b. Give her extra makeup work every time she misses.
   c. Talk to her casually and try to find out why she is missing so often.
   d. Call her parents and discuss the situation openly with them.
   e. Talk to the principal and guidance counselor about Susan.

Additional Options

D. For the last two days, Pedro has fallen asleep in your class. What is your immediate reaction for correcting this situation?
   a. Ask him to sit on a stool in the front of the room in order to stay awake.
   b. Tap him on the head with a meter stick each time you catch him sleeping until he stops.
   c. Let him sleep since you do not know if he is sick or upset about something.
   d. Start asking him questions early in the class period so he will not have an opportunity to fall asleep.
   e. Talk to Pedro after class to see if you can find out why he is falling asleep so much.

Additional Options

5. Directions: Given below are three student comments directed toward their teacher. After each student comment are several potential responses the teacher could make. Using Gazda's empathy scale (Figure 2.1), rate each of the responses. Responses may be rated 1, 1.5, 2, 2.5, 3, 3.5, or 4. After you have rated the responses under each problem, you may wish to compare your responses to those of others.
   A. *Student:* "Sometimes I feel physics is a waste of time. Since I've decided not to go to college, it seems silly to waste my time in a course like that."

RESPONSES

1. "I would be glad to sit down and discuss this with you sometime."
2. "If you do decide to go to college, physics will really look good on your record."
3. "You sound frustrated. Is it that you aren't quite sure in what direction you want to go and you are having difficulty deciding what is important to you?"

4. "You are making a big mistake selling physics short. It is the most basic of all subjects."

5. "It's always confusing when you can't make up your mind about something."

    B. *Student:* "I can't stand working with Charlie in chemistry lab! He's the most clumsy and inconsiderate lab partner I've ever had."

RESPONSES

1. "I doubt that it's all Charlies fault. Why don't you examine your own behavior."

2. "Would you like to change partners?"

3. "You and Charlie are having difficulty working together. It appears that he goes ahead and does things without consulting you first."

4. "Why don't you try to work things out with Charlie."

5. "It sounds like you and Charlie aren't communicating. Can't you think of anything you could do that would improve this situation?"

    C. *Student:* "That last biology test really sank my ship. I thought sure I'd make an "A," but instead I just barely got a "C.""

RESPONSES

1. "You felt you were well prepared for the test, and now you are disappointed that you didn't do as well as you'd expected too."

2. "Don't sweat it. There will be many other tests to take."

3. "Actually, this demonstrates one thing: you don't know the material as well as you think you do."

4. "It is really disappointing to think you're going to do well on a test and things do not work out that way."

5. "Several other students did well on the test. You'll just have to try harder next time."

References

Bassin, Alexander, Thomas E. Bratter, and Richard L. Rachin (Eds.). *The Reality Therapy Reader.* New York: Harper & Row Publishers, 1976.

This book contains a survey of the work of William Glasser. Articles are grouped into six categories: Glasser the Man; Theory; Practice; Education; Corrections; and Role Playing. This volume is a comprehensive, up-to-date compilation on how to implement the ideas of William Glasser in a variety of settings.

Berne, Eric. *Beyond Games and Scripts.* New York: Grover Press, Inc., 1976.

This book edited by Claude M. Steiner and Carmen Kerr is based on selections by Eric Berne, the originator of Transactional Analysis. Many of Berne's major ideas are contained in this volume which serves as an excellent summary of TA.

Gazda, George M., Frank R. Asbury, Fred J. Balzer, William C. Childers, R. Erick Desselle, and Richard P. Walters. *Human Relations Development: A Manual for Educators.* Boston: Allyn and Bacon, Inc., 1978.

For additional reading on the Carkhuff Model, this paperback is an excellent resource. Each component of the model is dealt with separately, and skills associated with each phase of development are presented. There are many opportunities for the reader to practice various skills and to work toward higher levels of proficiency.

Glasser, William. *Reality Therapy.* New York: Harper & Row Publishers, 1965.

This earlier work of Glasser demonstrates how the technique Reality Therapy can be used in a number of settings. The book also discusses in depth how Reality Therapy differs from traditional psychotherapy.

Glasser, William. *Schools Without Failure.* New York: Harper & Row Publishers, 1969.

Working with several school systems in California, Glasser demonstrates how educators can use basic elements of Reality Therapy to turn failure into success in our schools. This book contains many ideas for teachers who want to learn how to implement positive and innovative methods for improving discipline in schools.

Jenkins, Edward S., Gossie H. Hudson, W. Sherman Jackson, and Exyie C. Ryder. *American Black Scientists and Inventors.* Washington, D.C.: National Science Teachers Association, 1975.

This work presents interesting stories of twelve black scientists and inventors who have made great but, in some cases, little-known contributions to science and technology in the United States.

Smith, Walter S., and Kala M. Stroup. *Science Career Exploration for Women.* Washington, D.C.: National Science Teachers Association, 1978.

This book contains activity modules designed to assist talented women students explore science-related professional careers that require university training and that have been historically underrepresented by women.

LETTER TO GENERAL B. McCLELLAN

CHAPTER 3

Planning
for Science
Instruction

Executive Mansion
Washington, Feb. 3, 1862.

Major General McClellan

My Dear Sir:

You and I have distinct, and different plans for a movement of the Army of the Potomac—yours to be down the Chesapeake, up the Rappahannock to Urbana, and across land to the terminus of the Railroad on the York River—, mine to move directly to a point on the Railroad South West of Manassas.

If you will give me satisfactory answers to the following questions, I shall gladly yield my plan to yours.

1st. Does not your plan involve a greatly larger expenditure of time, and money than mine?

2nd. Wherein is a victory *more certain* by your plan than mine?

3rd. Wherein is a victory *more valuable* by your plan than mine?

4th. In fact, would it not be *less* valuable, in this, that it would break no great line of the enemy's communications while mine would?

5th. In case of disaster, would not a safe retreat be more difficult by your plan than by mine?

Yours truly,

A. LINCOLN

Planning is an important part of most human activities—conducting a military campaign, building a house, taking a vacation, or preparing a dinner for guests. In fact, it is difficult to name any phase of our lives that does not involve at least some planning. And, in some instances, if we fail to plan properly, the results can be disastrous!

Planning plays a key role in effective science teaching. In general, planning for science teaching, like other kinds of planning, involves asking questions, identifying alternative answers, and deciding on courses of action. President Lincoln's letter to General McClellan illustrates well the spirit of planning—identifying problems and weighing alternative solutions.

President Lincoln's letter also illustrates the importance of anticipating contingencies. What should the general do if the battle goes badly? What does the science teacher do when the filmstrip projector breaks, if it rains on the day an outdoor activity is planned, of if the living materials do not arrive on the date requested in the order?

Most science teachers find that planning is a complex and time-consuming process. And like other creative processes, there are no simple formulas or sets of rules for planning. However, there are techniques and approaches that can be helpful.

Guidelines for Planning Science Instruction

Planning consists of identifying objectives, selecting content, choosing materials, deciding upon appropriate teaching strategies, and structuring ways to evaluate what students have learned. What do I want my students to know about magnets? Do I use a film, demonstration, or laboratory investigation to teach what happens during cell division? What have the students learned about the solar system during their study of astronomy?

Although in many ways this is an oversimplification of the planning process, it does provide a framework for use in considering the various aspects of planning. But, in doing so, it is important to remember that in actual practice planning often does not take place in this exact order. The teacher may decide to do the lab on bright line and dark line spectra and then ask what objectives are to be achieved. Or some of the objectives are not clearly identified until it comes time to write the exam questions. Regardless of the order of the steps taken in the planning process, however, the following important questions should be considered:

1. What is expected of the learner at the end of instruction?

2. Is that which is expected of the learner reasonable on the basis of physical and mental maturity, knowledge possessed, previous experience, and other factors?

3. What is the most effective manner of organizing the concepts, skills, and other things to be learned?

4. What are the available strategies and materials that can be used in teaching for the outcomes desired, and what factors should be considered in selecting these strategies and materials?

5. How can achievement be evaluated during and following instruction?

IDENTIFYING
OBJECTIVES

Curriculum developers and designers of instructional materials often use models in identifying what is to be expected of the learner at the end of instruction. One such model was developed by Ralph Tyler over thirty years ago and is still widely used today.[1] The Tyler Model has three sources of objectives:

1. the discipline (biology, chemistry, physics, etc.)

2. the nature of the learner (adolescent, male or female, etc.)

3. the nature of the society in which the school exists (democratic, rapidly changing, technological, etc.)

From these three sources, the objectives for a science course, unit, or lesson can be derived.

These three sources can also be used in judging the importance of objectives once they have been identified. For example, do students need to know the steps in mitosis in order to understand the big ideas of biological science? Are adolescents more interested in human reproduction or plant reproduction? In light of the rapid changes taking place in our society, which of the sciences that students learn today will be most useful in the year 2000?

Another model used by science educators is one developed by Mauritz Johnson at Cornell University.[2] In the Johnson Model, the source of objectives is the "available teachable cultural content." Basically, this includes everything that can be learned and that is available for teaching (as opposed to secret knowledge or "classified" information). The use of the Johnson Model in science teaching is briefly described in a book on science programs and facilities published by the National Science Teachers Association (NSTA)[3] and in greater detail in *A Theory of Education*.[4]

---

[1] Ralph W. Tyler, *Basic Principles of Curriculum and Instruction*, Chicago: University of Chicago Press, 1949.

[2] Mauritz, Johnson, Jr., "Definitions and Models in Curriculum Theory," *Educational Theory*, 17, 2 (April, 1967): 127–140.

[3] Joseph D. Novak, *Facilities for Secondary School Science Teaching: Evolving Patterns in Facilities and Programs*, Washington, D.C.: National Science Teachers Association, 1972.

[4] Joseph D. Novak, *A Theory of Education*, Ithaca, N.Y.: Cornell University Press, 1977.

In practice, few science teachers ever have the time to use the models such as those developed by Tyler or Johnson to systematically identify the objectives for a course or unit. Instead, they rely on other sources such as those listed below. When using such sources, the teacher's job becomes mainly one of accepting or rejecting the objectives being proposed.

Sources useful in assembling lists of objectives include:

Objectives proposed in a course guide or syllabus prepared by a state department of public instruction or a local school unit.

Objectives that were prepared by the writers of a science program or textbook; these may appear in the teacher's guide or at the beginning of each chapter or module in the student materials.

Objectives or lists of concepts that have been identified by various curriculum researchers. For example, the work of Roth,[5] Geens and Stegner[6] and Mid-Continent Regional Educational Laboratory[7] would be very useful in preparing for teaching in the respective areas covered by these lists.

Objectives in data banks. One such collection was developed by the Instructional Objectives Exchange at the University of Southern California and includes hundreds of science objectives contributed by science teachers from across the United States.[8]

The objectives prepared for purposes of constructing science achievement tests and other evaluation instruments. For example, a booklet containing examples of science objectives was issued prior to each of the national assessments in science.[9]

Commercially prepared lists or books of objectives. For example, *Science Behavioral Objectives*[10] contains approximately 1,000 objectives, many of which are appropriate for secondary school science.

---

[5] Robert E. Roth, "Fundamental Concepts of Environmental Management Education (K–16)," *Environmental Education*, 1, 3 (Spring, 1970); 69–73.

[6] Maura Geens and Robert W. Stegner, "A Conceptual Scheme for Marine and Coastal Environmental Studies," *Coastal/Oceanic Awareness Studies*. Newark, Del.: Marine Environment Curriculum Study, University of Delaware, no date.

[7] Richard M. Bingman. (Ed.), Inquiry Objectives in the Teaching of Biology, Kansas City, MO.: Mid-Continent Regional Educational Laboratory and Biological Sciences Curriculum Study, 1969.

[8] As an example of these collections, see *Biology 10–12*. Los Angeles, Calif.: The Instructional Objectives Exchange of the University of Southern California Center for the Study of Evaluation, 1970.

[9] *National Assessment of Educational Progress: Science Objectives*, Ann Arbor, Mich.: Committee on Assessing the Progress of Education, 1969.

[10] John C. Flanagan and others, *Behavioral Objectives: A Guide to Individualized Learning, Science*, Palo Alto, Calif.: Westinghouse Learning Press, 1971.

SELECTING
OBJECTIVES IN
TERMS OF
LEARNERS'
CHARACTERISTICS
AND OTHER
FACTORS

Frequently, more objectives are identified than can be achieved in the time available for instruction. The problem then becomes one of selection. It already has been illustrated how three aspects of the Tyler Model can be used in selecting objectives as well as identifying them. The Tyler Model also contains two other ways of screening objectives or eliminating those judged to be unacceptable. (See Figure 3.1.)

The first screen is that of philosophy. This may be the teacher's philosophy of science, the school's philosophy of education, or the views of some other group, such as a school board or state legislature. By philosophy, we mean a set of mutually supportive statements about education. Specifically, a philosophy of science teaching probably would include statements about the importance of science instruction for all students, the use of science in careers and leisure time, and some of our ideas about how students best learn science.

What are some examples of objectives that might be screened out by a teacher or a school's philosophy? The following objectives are related to one or more of Tyler's three sources, but might not be included in the science curriculum in some schools:

1. To be able to discuss the cause and prevention of two common kinds of venereal disease.

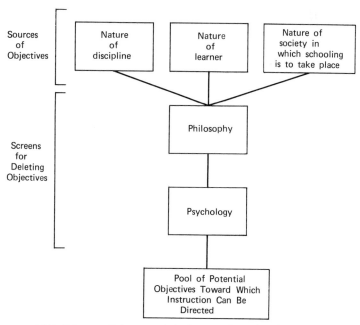

FIGURE 3.1   Tyler's model of curriculum development.

2. To compare and contrast the theory of evolution with other theories dealing with the origin and development of life.

3. To describe at least five ways of controlling population.

4. To identify the harmful effects of using tobacco, alcohol, and selected drugs.

The second screen is that of psychology. Psychology, which helps us understand *how* we learn, can also assist us in deciding *what* is to be learned. Some objectives that are identified may represent behaviors that are not readily obtained by all students. For example, a lack of physical development may make it difficult for some students to master certain psychomotor skills such as manipulating the riders on an analytical balance or holding glass tubing properly when attempting to bend it.

Psychologists have long been concerned with the concept of readiness. When is a child ready to learn to read or to do mathematics? Recently, science educators have become concerned with a form of readiness in science, particularly with the work of the Swiss psychologist Jean Piaget. Piaget and his coworkers have identified specific stages of cognitive development through which they believe each child normally passes before being capable of abstract or formal thought. These stages, with examples of behaviors associated with each stage, are:

Approximate Age	Stage	Behaviors
0 to 2 years	Sensory-motor	Awareness of permanent objects
2 to 7 years	Preoperational	Ability to form mental symbols to represent things and events
7 to 12 years	Concrete operational	Classifying and ordering Inductive reasoning
12 years and up	Formal operational	Control of variables Vertification of statements Proportionality

On first thought, it may seem that the significance of Piaget's work is mainly for students in the elementary schools. However, it has been found that 50 percent or more of the students in some high schools have not reached the formal operational stage. An examination of high school textbooks suggests that these students are not capable of achieving many of the objectives included in these courses. This is even more the case for students and courses in middle and junior high school.

In addition to the student's level of cognitive development, other student characteristics can be used in selecting objectives. One of these is

This student in the formal operations period can reason about and manipulate abstract or hypothetical concepts.

the quantity and quality of previous experience that the students have had. We believe that the best science program is one that provides opportunity for many kinds of "hands-on" experience. If the students did not learn how to use a Bunsen burner in previous science courses, then an objective dealing with this important piece of lab equipment should be on the list. If the students come mainly from urban environments and have never planted a garden, then an objective dealing with various kinds of plant reproduction may be judged worthy of instructional time. As these examples illustrate, selecting objectives also frequently involves deciding whether or not certain experiences will be included in a particular science course at a particular time.

In addition to the general discussion above, the following are some of the questions that can be used in selecting objectives and accompanying experiences:

- Does the objective represent an important part of science?
- Will achievement of the objective contribute to the student becoming more scientifically literate?
- Does the objective represent a student need, or is it a topic of interest to secondary school students?
- Is the objective worthy of the time and effort required for its achievement?
- Is the objective consistent with the teacher's and/or school's philosophy of education?
- Can students with the mental maturity of those being taught achieve the objective or is it beyond their grasp?
- Will students have the background or experience required to achieve the objective, and, if not, will it be possible to provide them with these prerequisites?

- Is the objective also a part of other science courses and/or other subjects in the curriculum?
- Does the objective build on what the students have already been taught, and does it lead to what they will study later in science?

ORGANIZING OBJECTIVES, CONTENT, AND EXPERIENCES

Most science objectives imply the content involved and the experiences by which students can achieve these objectives. As an example, let's consider the objective "Given ten common minerals, the student will be able to correctly name eight of them." It is obvious that students involved in instruction aimed toward this objective will be dealing with content such as Mho's Scale of Hardness, specific gravity, luster, and cleavage planes. In addition, it would be expected that the experiences provided students would include their using these characteristics to identify unknown minerals. Because of this close interrelationship among objectives, content, and experience, it is appropriate and functional to include all three in discussing the organizational aspects of planning.

The structure of the discipline represents one way of organizing a science course. The approach was widely used by curriculum innovators in the 1960s and was described by Bruner[11] and illustrated by a NSTA publication on curriculum.[12] According to those advocating this position, grasping the structure of science involves understanding the big ideas in such a way that many other related things fit together meaningfully. For example, a student grasping the meaning of "ecosystem" will be able to see more clearly the relationships existing among producers, consumers, and decomposers than if these three ideas are presented without the framework provided by "ecosystem"—one of the central ideas of the discipline of ecology.

Although organizing science instruction around the structure of discipline is often done and has definite advantages, there are unresolved problems in doing so and other approaches can be used. Let's consider the other approaches first. A biological science course organized around the discipline might include unit titles such as "Nature of Life," "Animals," "Plants," "Diversity," and "Genetics." An alternative approach is to organize the course around societal needs or the needs and interests of students. Units in such a course might be titled "Keeping Healthy," "Improving Our Community's Environment," "Making Wise Choices as a Living Organism," and "Debating the Issues in Biological Science." A word of caution: the titles of these units can mislead one into believing that the students are not learning any "good" biology. Quite the opposite

---

[11] Jerome S. Bruner, *The Process of Education*, Cambridge, Mass.: Harvard University Press, 1960.

[12] *Theory into Action in Science Curriculum Development*, Washington, D.C.: National Science Teachers Association, 1964.

is usually the case; the students are still studying much of the same content, but the purposes for learning it differ, as does the overall organization of the course.

A major problem unresolved by organizing a course around the structure of the discipline involves the learner. Students do not necessarily learn things in the order implied by the discipline's structure, nor does the structure suggest all the things they need to know to grasp a big idea of science. Perhaps another illustration is in order.

In an earlier example, the teacher wants students to be able to identify eight out of ten common minerals. One of the things they should be able to do is to find the specific gravity of a mineral. This in turn suggests that they understand that specific gravity is a ratio between the density of a mineral and the density of water. To find the density of an object, students must be able to determine its mass and its volume. In the case of irregularly shaped objects like mineral specimens, finding the volume means using the water displacement method. There are other subtasks, such as using the metric system and finding mass on a balance, that the student must be able to do in order to use specific gravity in identifying a mineral.

Robert Gagne[13] suggests that learning can be facilitated by properly arranging these subtasks into a learning hierarchy. As Figure 3.2 illustrates, being able to perform the terminal task (writing a balanced equation for a chemical reaction) requires the student to be able to do several subtasks, which in turn requires that the student be able to do other subtasks. In using Gagne's ideas on learning hierarchies in planning instruction, the key is to identify the subtasks required to complete the terminal task and to arrange them in the order that best fosters learning.

Another psychologist whose ideas have influenced science teaching is David Ausubel.[14] One of his ideas, that of the advance organizer, has received the most attention. According to Ausubel, meaningful learning occurs when new knowledge is linked to what the student already knows. This is referred to as cognitive structure. When planning, therefore, it is important to identify in advance ways to relate new knowledge to some broad concept or generalization already familiar to students—hence, the term *advance organizer.*

Advance organizers can take many forms. Diagrams, such as the one of the Tyler Model in Figure 3.1, can be used to relate various ideas on curriculum development to some bigger picture. Sometimes a question at the beginning of instruction can serve the same purpose. "If photosynthesis in green plants produces carbohydrates, how can the synthesis of

---

[13] Robert M. Gagne, *The Conditions of Learning,* **Second Edition.** New York: Holt, Rinehart and Winston, Inc., 1970.

[14] David P. Ausubel, *Educational Psychology: A Cognitive View,* New York: Holt, Rinehart, and Winston, Inc., 1968.

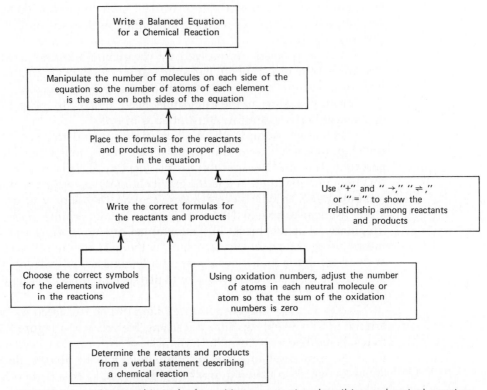

FIGURE 3.2   A learning hierarchy for writing an equation describing a chemical reaction.

proteins in a plant be explained?" In other cases, the structure of the discipline can be used to relate the parts to a whole. Fission, fusion, and breeder reactions can be more meaningfully considered once the student grasps the idea of conservation of mass and energy.

In actual practice, few science teachers make extensive use of any one approach to organizing objectives, content, and experiences. Rather, they are eclectic, or they select what appears to be the best of various psychological theories along with their consideration of a host of other factors. Should I teach a unit on plants in the fall, winter, or spring? How can I so arrange a chemistry course that there are no long periods without laboratory work? Should an earth science course start as near as possible to where the students live, or would it be better to start in space? Should I follow the order of topics suggested in the textbook? What are the students' preferences concerning the order in which the topics will be studied?

SELECTION OF STRATEGIES AND MATERIALS

What strategies, or teaching methods as they are often called, and materials are available for use in a course, unit, or lesson? Knowledge of the available strategies and materials and the ability to use them effectively is

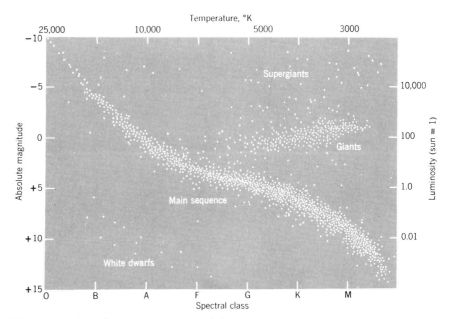

Diagrams such as the Hertzspring-Russel diagram can serve as an advanced organizer in presenting a topic such as star types and stellar evolution.

one of the major factors that distinguishes master science teachers from those who are less capable. Because of their importance, a major portion of the following chapters are devoted to descriptions of these strategies and materials and their use. See Figure 3.3 for a list of the major strategies and materials and a cross-reference to where they are discussed in this book.

Many factors should be considered in deciding whether or not to use a particular strategy or type of material. The following illustrate the questions science teachers ask in making these decisions:

• How will the strategy contribute to the achievement of the various components of scientific literacy? For example, will its use result only in students learning facts, concepts, and principles, or will students also be able to develop attitudes, interests, and values?

• Is the strategy appropriate for the students being instructed? For example, lack of laboratory skills or class management problems may dictate a demonstration rather than individual laboratory work at the beginning of a course.

• Is the strategy the most efficient method of instruction? For example, a film may be a more efficient way of introducing a topic than a class discussion or a reading assignment.

• Are materials or the necessary financial resources available for using a strategy? For example, once again, using a film may be a better strategy

Strategies and materials	Chapter
Computer-assisted instruction	8
Demonstrations	5
Field trips	5
Films, filmstrip, overhead transparencies	9
Games	5
Laboratory investigations	4
Library and reference books	9
Panel discussions, debates, and other group activities	5
Periodicals	9
Research projects and other independent work	4, 8, 10
Science facilities and equipment	4
Tests and other evaluation instruments and techniques	6
Textbooks	9
Videotapes and other forms of television	9

FIGURE 3.3   Major strategies and materials for science teaching.

in situations where expensive equipment such as oil-immersion micro-scopes and VanderGraff generators are not available.

- Is the strategy safe to use in the particular situation for which it is being prepared? For example, the safety hazards associated with typing blood and generating hydrogen gas may suggest that alternative approaches be considered.
- Is the strategy being considered the most appropriate way of handling controversial topics? For example, the use of simulation activities and games may be better than lectures and visiting speakers in considering environmental problems and other subjects on which each student is entitled to his or her own opinion.
- What strategies have been used in recent lessons? For example, students like variety and will become tired of even highly stimulating strategies such as laboratory work and demonstrations if one strategy is used continuously.

EVALUATION OF ACHIEVEMENT

Evaluation of achievement requires planning from the beginning and is not something that can be put off to near the end of the instructional period. There are two major reasons why it cannot be delayed. First, evidence of student achievement should be collected throughout the period of instruction and should consist of more than the grade on a final exam. How well students do on laboratory reports, homework assignments, and individual projects and how they participate in the class discussions are examples of the many things that should be considered in evaluating student achievement. Often, immediate feedback to students serves to stimulate further thinking or may help students who are having difficulty understanding a major point.

Second, student achievement is evaluated for many important reasons in addition to the need to assign grades. Do the students possess the necessary knowledge and skills to undertake a unit of work or a particular topic? When are they ready to move on to the next topic? Evaluation helps the teacher diagnose student performance at a given point and make important adjustments when necessary. These are but a few of the reasons why evaluation should take place throughout and why plans must provide for its proper role in the teaching process.

These important ideas on evaluation are developed in greater detail and many useful evaluation techniques are described in Chapter 6.

Long-Range Planning

There are many ways to go about long-range planning. A useful and frequently used approach is to prepare a calendar that indicates the nature and order of the units or major topics to be studied, an approximate time allocation for each, and the proposed date for starting and completing each unit. The following table illustrates such a calendar:

Yearly Calendar for Physical Science

Unit		Number of Days Allotted to Unit	Approximate Dates for Starting and Finishing Unit
I	Introduction to Physical Science	10	Sept. 2–15
II	Matter, Molecules, and Heat Energy	20	Sept. 16–Oct. 13
III	Chemistry	40	Oct. 14–Dec. 19
IV	Nuclear Energy	15	Jan. 3–Jan. 25
V	Mechanics	35	Feb. 5–March 22
VI	Magnetism, Electricity, and Electronics	30	March 25–May 2
VII	Sound and Light	25	May 6–June 7
VIII	Careers in Physical Science	5	June 10–June 14
		180	

Several factors were considered in preparing the above calendar. First, the order of the topics was established. Next, the time was allocated to each on the basis of its importance and the amount of content it includes. Although most schools have about 180 days of classes per year, time should be allowed for assemblies, standardized tests, fire drills, bomb scares, and all the other things that interrupt instruction. In the case of the above calendar, the teacher using it probably will have a day or so less for the actual teaching of each unit than is indicated. However, by setting the dates for each unit, films can be ordered, laboratory materials can be prepared, long-range assignments and major examinations scheduled, and numerous other tasks completed before the unit is taught.

By making slight adjustments in time or by arranging the units in a certain order, the dates for initiating and completing a unit coincide with breaks in the school calendar. Notice how the chemistry unit is scheduled to be completed before Christmas vacation begins. The unit on nuclear energy is scheduled between the end of Christmas vacation and the end of the first semester in late January. In scheduling certain units in biology and earth science, the weather and seasons of the year should be taken into consideration if outdoor activities are planned.

THE RESOURCE UNIT

Many science teachers assemble a resource unit for each of the major topics included in a course. As the name implies, a resource unit is a collection of resources that can be used in teaching a unit of instruction. A resource can take many forms—a recipe box containing cards on which ideas for teaching the unit have been noted, a shoe box or grocery box in which all the resources on chemistry or mechanics have been assembled, or a file cabinet containing folders on various topics. The file cabinet or a grocery box substitute has many advantages. Chief among these is the ease with which things can be found when they are needed.

Although there are many ways to organize a resource unit, the following example illustrates the major categories and typical items found in each. This particular resource unit was set up on a group of file folders with an individual folder for each category. This makes it easy to add new resources as they are found and, as already pointed out, makes the unit more usable.

Resource Unit—Oceanography

Categories (file folders)	Examples of contents
Objectives	List from Course Guide—State Department of Public Instruction List from Teacher's Guide to basal textbook
Demonstrations	Xerox copies of demonstrations from *The Science Teacher, The American Biology Teacher,* etc. Descriptions of demonstrations on index cards
Labs	Lists of labs in basal and supplemental textbooks

Resource Unit (*continued*)

Categories (file folders)	Examples of contents
	Book of labs published by the state's Sea Grant University
Films	List of films available from County Media Center
	List of free films on oceanography
Filmstrips	List of oceanography filmstrips owned by Science Department of Public Instruction
	Filmstrips in County Media Center
Overhead transparencies	Collection of transparencies made in a teacher workshop on media
	Pages taken from journals which can be used as masters to make transparencies
Slides	Reference list of slides in personal collection
	Box of slides donated by former student
Games	List of games in County Media Center
	Ditto masters for crossword puzzles using oceanography terms
Worksheets and homework	Ditto masters for worksheets (commercially prepared)
	List of homework assignments—(Make a list of all the foods in your home that came wholly or in part from the sea; etc.)
Field work	Description of coastal processes that can be observed along the shoreline of many lakes or large ponds
	Water sampling activities that can be carried out in any body of water
Supplementary reading	List of books on oceanography in the school library
	List of articles on oceanography in recent issues of *National Geographic* and *Scientific American*
Bulletin Board displays	Map of Ocean Floor—*National Geographic*
	NASA satellite photos of earth, showing major oceans
Project ideas	Xerox copies of oceanography objects ideas from "The Amateur Scientist" in *Scientific American* and from other journals

Resource Unit (*continued*)

Categories (file folders)	Examples of contents
Individualized approaches	Collection of Instructional Modules and Learning Activity Packages—obtained at national meeting of science teachers and by writing school districts with oceanography courses
Evaluation	Copy of test questions accompanying basal textbook Collection of test items on 3 × 5 cards
Miscellaneous	Book—*Careers in Oceanography* List—Sea Grant Universities in the U.S. List—U.S. Government agencies that publish materials available to schools

COMPUTER-BASED RESOURCE UNITS

Educators have been experimenting with computer-based resource units since the mid-1960s. Although these units vary in format, they all contain ideas for teaching a given topic, such as soil conservation, chemical reactions, and the like. The resources in a given unit are intended primarily for teacher use and usually include objectives, activities, materials, and evaluation items.

In one format, a teacher selects the name of a unit from a master list and types the name into a computer terminal along with certain other information such as the age or grade level of the students. The computer responds by typing out a list of possible objectives or topics that could be taken up as part of the unit's work. The teacher then selects objectives and/or topics from the list and feeds these choices back into the computer. Next, the computer types out lists of materials and activities that can be used to achieve the objective or treat the topics selected. In some cases, the activities and materials are coded so that the teacher can select the ones most appropriate for average (or low-achieving students). Computer-based resource units are usually constructed so that the teacher is also furnished a list of test questions that can be used in evaluating student achievement.

Computer-based resource units, like other forms of resource units prepared by someone other than the teacher, have many advantages. The teacher saves time by using such units and benefits from the combined efforts of all those who were involved in assembling the unit. As in the case of teacher-constructed resource units, the teacher is free to choose among the many alternatives available and to add his or her own ideas along with those of students. Unlike computer-assisted instruction and computer-managed instruction, which are described in Chapter 8, using the computer to generate resource units enhances rather than detracts from the work of the classroom teacher and the students in planning the unit's work.

The use of computer-based resource units also has some notable limitations or disadvantages. First, the teacher has to have access to a terminal that is connected to a computer that contains the resource units. With the high cost of renting terminals, leasing telephone lines, and paying for computer time, many schools make little or no use of the computer in instruction. With microprocessors and other hardware made possible with the new electronics technology, schools in the future probably will be making less use of centralized computers of the type needed to store resource units. However, for schools with access to computers, the use of computer-based resource units can be a viable way of helping teachers with the time-demanding task of planning.

As in the case of any type of resource unit, it is important that provisions be made to keep computer-based resource units up to date. And as is too often the case in the development of education materials and ideas, funds are available to develop the units but not to revise and extend them.

TEACHING UNITS

The teaching unit, like the resource unit, contains many valuable ideas and resources for teaching a given topic. However, unlike the resource unit which is basically an organized collection of materials, the teaching unit is more like a collection of daily lesson plans. As such, teaching units suggest the order in which various topics are taken up as well as suggesting teaching strategies and materials.

The teaching units can be produced in various formats, but the most popular type is that illustrated in Figure 3.4. The number and headings for the vertical columns vary. Some teaching units are organized around objectives, others around a content outline, and still others, like the one in Figure 3.4, use a combination of objectives and a content outline. Most have columns in which strategies, materials, and references are specified. Suggested test questions and other evaluation items are sometimes included in a separate column.

An examination of teaching units produced by state educational agencies, curriculum workshops in local systems, and other groups reveals that most of these units emphasize the use of laboratory work, field work, demonstrations, and various kinds of media. This is intentionally done for two reasons. First, these kinds of strategies and activities are at the heart of a good science program, and their use is to be encouraged. Second, the units are usually prepared by experienced teachers as a means of informing less experienced teachers of the various possibilities that exist for teaching the unit.

Although teaching units often resemble lesson plans in format, they usually are not specific enough to replace lesson plans. Each teacher's

OBJECTIVES	CONTENT OUTLINE	STRATEGIES	MATERIALS	REFERENCES	NOTES (you are encouraged to make notes here and in other empty spaces as you teach the unit)
Given the appropriate materials, the student will be able to build a spectroscope and describe how it works.	VI Spectroscopes are used to separate light into its component colors	Demonstrate how a prism can be used to form a spectrum	Prism, light source or use direct sunlight		
	A. Spectroscopes can be made using prisms or diffraction gratings	Have students build a shoebox spectroscope (or demonstrate one that already has been assembled)	Shoe boxes, replica diffraction gratings (obtain from Edmund Scientific), aluminum foil (to form edges of slits), tape (masking or Scotch), scissors and/or knives for cutting holes in shoe boxes, water-based flat black paint and brushes (if inside of shoe box is to be painted)	Textbooks: *Physical Science: A Search for Understanding*, pp. 466-467 *Exploring Physical Science*, p. 443 *Interaction of Earth and Time*, pp. 358A-358B Also: Hynek, J. Allen and Norman D. Anderson. *Challenge of the Universe*. New York: Scholastic Magazine, Inc., 1964, pp. 135-136.	Have students keep their spectroscopes at school until you have finished Section VI.
Using the spectroscope constructed in the above activity, the student will be able to draw colored pictures of the spectra of three different light sources.	B. The spectra of light from various sources (stars, light bulbs, etc.) each have characteristic lines	Have students use their shoe box spectroscopes to view the light from various sources; have students make colored drawings of the spectra they observe.	Light Sources: -Incandescent light bulb -Fluorescent lights (different kinds of tubes produce different spectra) -Neon signs -Sunlight -Colored pencils or crayons		CAUTION: The spectroscope and other optical instruments (telescopes, field glasses, etc.) should not be pointed directly toward the sun. The spectra of the sun can be observed by pointing the spectroscope in the general direction of the sun, or if inside, toward a window.
Given the salts of sodium, copper, strontium, potassium, and calcium, the student can correctly identify three of the five using flame tests and reference books.	C. Each chemical element produces a characteristic spectra.	Have students do flame tests by placing chemicals on a nichrome wire and holding in the flame of a Bunsen burner or propane torch	Nichrome wires with handle Bunsen burners or propane torch Chemicals: chlorides of sodium, copper, potassium, strontium, and calcium (if the chlorides are not available, other salts of these five metals can be used.	*Physical Science: A Search for Understanding*, p. 207 *Exploring Physical Science*, p. 443 *Focus on Physical Science*, pp. 93-94	This activity can also be done as a demonstration. Place a teaspoon of the chemical on a piece of wire gauze and hold it over the flame of a Bunsen burner.
Using a shoe box spectroscope and flame tests, the student can match the spectra produced by sodium, calcium, and strontium with the colored pictures of a bright line spectra of these three elements.	D. The spectra produced during a flame test are bright line spectra	Have students draw a colored picture of the spectra of sodium, calcium, and strontium produced when a flame colored with each of these elements is viewed through a spectroscope.	Shoe box spectroscopes Bunsen burners or propane torches Nichrome wires with handles Chlorides of sodium, calcium and strontium Colored pencils or crayons	Textbooks containing pictures of bright line spectra: *Exploring Physical Science*, p. 444	
Student can explain what the spectra of a star reveals about its composition, temperature, and movement	E. The spectrum of the light from a star is used to determine the star's composition, temperature, and movement (Doppler Shift)	Use film or filmstrip	Films: *Instruments of Astronomy* (12 min., color) Filmstrips: *The Astronomer at Work* (39 frames, color) *Methods and Tools of the Astronomers* (42 frames, color)	Available in County Media Center County Media Center; also in some school media centers Check local school media centers	
		Demonstrate Doppler Shift (or have student(s) do as project	Modified Wave Tank	*Earth Science: A Search For Understanding*, pp. 641-642.	

FIGURE 3.4   Example of a page from a teaching unit.

situation is different, and the students in each class also differ. A teaching unit is useful in giving general direction. However, most teachers find it necessary and desirable to make more detailed weekly and daily plans as they teach the unit.

PROGRAM AND COURSE SYLLABI

A program or course syllabi contains, as a minimum, an outline of the content to be studied in a course or series of courses (usually called a program, such as a K-12 science program or a science education program at the collegiate level). Often, syllabi also contain many of the things found in resource and teaching units—lists or descriptions of laboratory investigations and demonstrations, lists of films and other audiovisual aids, lists of sources of free materials, etc.

Most syllabi are prepared by state educational agencies or groups of teachers working at the local level. For example, several science syllabi have been published by the New York State Education Department, some of which are for their "Regents Science Courses." These courses are for students who plan to go to college and take the statewide entrance examinations of the Board of Regents of the State of New York. Not all syllabi, however, are prepared by state and local educational agencies. The College Entrance Examination Board publishes syllabi for the Advanced Placement Program in biology, chemistry, and physics. Students taking these courses and passing the Advanced Placement Examination prepared by the Educational Testing Service can receive college credit at most major institutions of higher education. These and other examples of syllabi are frequently published in journals or special publications of professional organizations for science teachers.

Although syllabi prepared for use in a particular state, school system, or individual school may be of greatest use to teachers in that specific situation, most syllabi contain ideas and suggestions that can be utilized by all science teachers. A collection of syllabi can be a valuable part of a science teacher's professional library and another useful resource in planning for any phase of science teaching.

TEACHER-STUDENT PLANNING

When discussing planning, it is easy to forget students and to direct most of the attention to objectives, strategies, materials, and evaluation procedures helpful to the teacher. To neglect considering the "clients," however, is a serious mistake. As the recipients of the instruction being planned, students have ideas and interests that can contribute to more effective instruction. Besides, to deny students experience in various aspects of planning is to deny them the opportunity to achieve an important goal of education—to be self-directing individuals with the ability to analyze situations and to *plan* a course of action in light of this analysis.

There are many ways to involve students in planning. In some situa-

WHAT STUDENTS SAY

Planning

- I like my biology teacher because she is so organized and always seems to know what needs to be done.
- I love it when our science teacher lets us help plan our work for the week.
- Good teachers are those who plan ahead and use a lot of different things in class.
- One teacher I had could never remember the day of the week. He never knew where we were first period.
- I like surprises. A movie, a debate, or a walk outside can really liven up a day.
- Teachers who seem to know what's supposed to happen each day usually give tests that are more fair than do disorganized teachers.
- I feel much more comfortable in a class that's organized. Man, was I ever frustrated with science last year.

The students and the teacher in this picture are planning a laboratory investigation growing out of yesterday's discussion of invertebrates.

tions, students can take a major part in deciding what is to be taught in a course. For example, in a general science or elective science course, the students can suggest units they would like to study or they can choose from a list of units suggested by the teacher. Once the units to be included in a course are established, the students can have a voice in deciding what is to be included in a given unit (see Figure 3.5). Or they may be asked to suggest activities they would prefer doing as part of the unit's work.

Students also should share in the planning of the activities that make up a unit of work. Students can assemble the equipment and supplies needed for a laboratory investigation or a field trip. They can plan the displays and room decorations for an open house. Or they can plan a series of investigations to answer questions students pose in class. Do identical twins have different fingerprints? Does driving at slower speeds on the highway increase gasoline mileage? Does ESP really work? Do plants grow best if they are planted during a certain phase of the moon?

The teacher must *plan* to involve students if teacher-student planning is to work effectively. Will students be given a set of specific directions for doing an investigation, or will they be expected to design their own plan for the investigation? While introducing a unit, will student questions be solicited and their interests considered? Will students have any voice in how the unit will be taught or how their work is evaluated?

The involvement of students in planning can help change instruction from a passive to an active process for the students. But of equal importance, having students share in planning gives them practice in one of life's demanding tasks. And the better the students can plan, the better their chance of leading a fuller and more satisfactory life.

TEXTBOOKS

Research studies of science teaching practices in the United States, such as those conducted by the National Science Foundation, indicate the textbook gives the most direction to secondary school science teaching. In planning science courses, it is important to recognize both the potential contribution of textbooks and the limitations of their use.

The use of textbooks, as well as material published in modular and other forms, is one way of obtaining the organization needed for effective teaching. As such, textbooks can be especially helpful to the inexperienced teacher who often has difficulty "seeing the forest because of the trees." In other words, the teacher who has some grasp of the various things that can be included in a course, but doesn't see how the pieces all fit together, can use the textbook as a guide for organizing the course. The textbook can also help give students a sense of direction and, of course, contains valuable explanations, examples, problems, and suggested investigations, references, etc.

At best, however, science textbooks can serve only as a point of departure in planning and teaching a course. Planning does not stop with

Teacher:	Today we want to spend some time planning our next unit on astronomy. Let's start with the solar system. I'm going to put two columns on the chalkboard. The first one would be things you have observed in the sky and aren't sure you can explain. Let me give an example—the sun is higher in the sky at noon in the summer than in the winter (writes example on chalkboard).

Ⓐ

Ⓑ

Ⓒ

The second column I'm going to call "Questions I would like answered." An example would be "What is a black hole?" (also writes this on the chalkboard).

Once we have some ideas on the chalkboard, we can organize them into groups. So let's have your questions and ideas.

Ⓓ .... Pause (15–30 seconds) (No students volunteered information) I guess I asked a couple of $64,000 questions. I tell you what, let's stand with the earth's nearest neighbor, the moon. If you watch the moon for several nights in a row, what

Ⓔ do you notice?

Student 1: It changes shape.

Teacher: John says, it changes shape. Anyone know what word we use to
Ⓕ describe these shapes?

Student 12: Phases.

Teacher: The moon changes shape or goes through various phases. (Writes on chalkboard).

Student 4: What I don't understand is why we can't see the backside of the moon from the earth.

Teacher: That's ...

Student 11: Everybody knows the answer to that question!

Teacher: Whoa! I'm not sure everybody does know. Besides, all we want to do now is make our list. Then we will decide what we already know and how we are going to go about explaining what we have on our lists. (Writes question on chalkboard)

Student 4: I am not sure I understand eclipses.
Ⓖ

Ⓐ Teacher-student planning usually requires the teacher to set up the situation. Asking students to suggest astronomical objects and phenomena they have observed and questions they would like answered should produce better results than if the teacher says "Today we are going to start the astronomy unit. What would you like to study?"

Ⓑ Using an overhead projector or writing phenomena, observations, and questions on the chalkboard allows the entire group

FIGURE 3.5 Transcript of a portion of a teacher-student planning session.

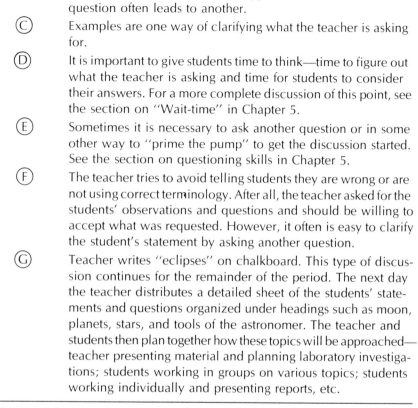

(C)   Examples are one way of clarifying what the teacher is asking for.

(D)   It is important to give students time to think—time to figure out what the teacher is asking and time for students to consider their answers. For a more complete discussion of this point, see the section on "Wait-time" in Chapter 5.

(E)   Sometimes it is necessary to ask another question or in some other way to "prime the pump" to get the discussion started. See the section on questioning skills in Chapter 5.

(F)   The teacher tries to avoid telling students they are wrong or are not using correct terminology. After all, the teacher asked for the students' observations and questions and should be willing to accept what was requested. However, it often is easy to clarify the student's statement by asking another question.

(G)   Teacher writes "eclipses" on chalkboard. This type of discussion continues for the remainder of the period. The next day the teacher distributes a detailed sheet of the students' statements and questions organized under headings such as moon, planets, stars, and tools of the astronomer. The teacher and students then plan together how these topics will be approached—teacher presenting material and planning laboratory investigations; students working in groups on various topics; students working individually and presenting reports, etc.

FIGURE 3.5 (continued)

the selection of a textbook. Even if it is decided to use the contents of a textbook as the general pattern for teaching a course, many decisions remain to be made. Will all parts of the book receive the same emphasis? Will it be necessary to leave out some units or chapters? If so, which ones? Will the order in which the chapters or units are taken up be changed from the way they appear in the book?

More importantly, how will the course be planned to reflect any uniqueness of students, teachers, and the community? Textbooks are prepared for national or even international use; there is no way any one book can adequately provide what is needed by all the students and all the teachers that use it. The five pages on the beach community may be insufficient for students along the ocean and of less interest to students in Kansas and Nebraska. In like manner, students and teachers with an interest in photography, wildflowers, or flying have knowledge and experiences that should be shared. The time required to do this would go beyond that suggested by the textbook's organization.

Resource units, teaching units, and syllabi are valuable planning aids even when a textbook is heavily depended on in a course. The following section should clearly illustrate how weekly and daily plans are needed even in situations where the textbook is the major determinant of the course content and method of presentation.

WEEKLY AND DAILY PLANNING

Policies dealing with weekly and daily lesson planning vary widely from school to school. Some schools require that a written lesson plan for each day be turned in weekly, and these are regularly checked by the science department chairperson, the principal, or some other supervisory official. In other situations, the responsibility for planning is left almost entirely to the teacher. Regardless of the school's policies, most teachers find it helpful to make plans for each week's work and more detailed plans for each lesson.

Many school systems provide each teacher with a plan book which contains a series of blank weekly calendars plus space to record other planning information. Figure 3.6 shows one page from such a plan book.

The plan book has the advantage of providing the busy teacher a centralized and portable place to record the hundreds of items that must be remembered or acted upon each year. When did I arrange for the visiting speaker of fission? What are the dates for the science achievement test? When are the next ninth week's grades due? When would be the best time to schedule a field trip to Lake Deep Hole?

Along with a grade book, the plan book is one of the teacher's most indisposable tools.

LESSON PLANS. Yes—lesson plans, like resource and teaching units, and like yearly and weekly plans, can take many forms and be quite general or very specific. The inexperienced teacher in a subject may find it helpful to prepare several pages of detailed plans for each lesson. On the other hand, the experienced teacher may be able to teach the same lesson with the notes made in one corner of the chalkboard or on the back of a used envelope. In addition to the teacher's experience, other factors affect the amount and kind of planning required. For instance, showing a film may not require as much planning as taking a field trip. Teaching a group of able students how to use a pH meter may require less planning than helping a class of less able students master the concepts of significant numbers or the difference between precision and accuracy in measurement.

A sample lesson plan is shown in Figure 3.7. The sample lesson contains most of the things typically included in a lesson plan, and the comments illustrate additional aspects of daily planning. Teachers usually have their own preferences for lesson plans, and beginning teachers will want to experiment with the kind of plans that work best for them.

WEEK OF _December 6_

PERIOD	MONDAY	TUESDAY	WEDNESDAY	THURSDAY	FRIDAY
1 Biology 10	Show film on Gregor Mendell. Give students questions to answer as homework assignment.	Conduct discussion session on major ideas central to Mendell's theories from film.	Divide class into small groups. Give them simple monohybrid crosses to derive expected phenotypic and genotypic ratios.	Give students module containing activities on probability, multiple alleles and sex-linked inheritance.	Assembly
2 Biology 10	Same as Period 1	Same as Period 1	Same as Period 1	Same as Period 1	Give quiz covering genetics problems dealt with in class during week. Introduce human genetics topic for following week.
3 Advanced Biology	Let students record results from frog embryo experiments. Review procedures for writing up scientific investigations.	Show filmstrip on human fertilization processes. Assign outside readings on prenatal influences of alcohol, drugs, & tobacco on embryo and fetus.	Dr. Baker from county health dept. will speak on recent research on influence of prenatal nutrition on fetal development.	Allow students to react to Dr. Baker's talk. Have students prepare equipment for next week's lab activity on reproductive behavior of insects.	Begin students' reports on outside readings on influences of nutrition, alcohol, drugs, and tobacco on prenatal development.
4 Advanced Biology	Same as Period 3	Same as Period 3	Same as Period 3	Same as Period 3	Same as Period 3
5 Preparation Period					
6 Biology 10	Same as Period 1	Same as Period 1	Same as Period 1	Same as Period 1	Give quiz covering genetics problems dealt with in class during week. Last half hour: Pep Rally

THINGS TO DO:	APPOINTMENTS AND MEETINGS:	NOTES:
Have lab assistant set up movie projector Friday before leaving school. Check to see if ther are evough modules for three classes of Biology 10. Have advanced classes write Dr. Baker a thank-you letter.	Meet with students after school Thurs. who had difficulty with genetics module. Plan science club meeting with officers on Friday. Meet with PTA committee to plan field trip for advanced biology students	Be sure to give Mrs. Jenkins the film on Gregor Mendel. Order film on "Tragedy of the Commons" for next month. Order bacteria for lab activity in two weeks.

FIGURE 3.6   A weekly plan of a high school biology teacher.

(A) Teacher ___RDB___ Subject ___General Science___

Periods ___1, 2 and 4___ Date ___Wednesday, September 24___

Major Objectives: At the end of the lesson, the student should be able to:

(B) --Give at least two advantages of using the metric system of measurement.
--Compare a meter to other units of length, such as mile, yard, foot, and inch.
--Measure the length and width of a room to the nearest meter.

(C) If time permits: --Measure the length of at least five objects in centimeters and millimeters.

	TIME	ACTIVITY	MATERIALS	NOTES
(D)	9:05-9:15	Introduce film "The Metric System" by placing questions on chalkboard and having students copy them into notebooks. Emphasize students should be able to answer these questions after seeing film.	Film Film Projector Screen	Reserve film projector for periods 1, 2 and 4. Check Tuesday to see if film arrived.
(E)	9:15-9:27	Show film		
(F)	9:27-9:35	Discuss questions on chalkboard		
(G)	9:35-9:55	Have students measure room to nearest meter--have students work in pairs (largest class is 32)	16 sticks of wood one meter long Ditto record sheets to record data	Do not let students mark on sticks--they will use strips of paper tomorrow to develop a measuring device calibrated in centimeters and millimeters.
(H)	9:55-10:00	Clean up - Assignment:(have on chalkboard at the beginning of the period) Find at least five objects in your home that are labeled in some way with metric units. Record the names of these objects and units in student record books -- Due tomorrow.		
(I)				

FIGURE 3.7 Sample lesson plan.

Experienced teachers agree, however, that the important thing to remember is—PLAN!

Once the objectives and teaching strategies for a lesson are determined, the remainder of the necessary planning mainly involves identifying ways to use the various strategies effectively. In the case of the sample lesson plan in Figure 3.7, primary attention is given to introducing and following up the film and conducting the laboratory investigation. Because planning so closely influences the success of each teaching strategy, the discussion on teaching strategies in the following modules contains many suggestions for planning. For example, good planning plays a big

(A) Some teachers like to write lesson plans in detail; these plans are a valuable resource the next time a similar lesson is taught and can be used by a substitute if the teacher is absent.

(B) Although experienced teachers may not find it necessary to write out the objectives for each lesson in detail, it is important to have clearly in mind the major things to be accomplished by the lesson.

(C) Most teachers find it desirable to plan more than they may accomplish on a particular day. This is one way of providing an orderly transition to the material in the lesson that follows. Also, it provides a course of action when unexpected things occur-- the film does not arrive on time, the projector breaks down, etc.

(D) Not only does the introduction give focus to the lesson, but can be used to get the students quickly on tasks and thus reduce class management problems. In the case of films it is important for students to know what they are supposed to learn from viewing the film. This means the film should be previewed before showing it to the class.

(E) In the case of long films, it sometimes is desirable to break the film into segments by stopping the projector and having discussion over the segment that has just been viewed. Since the film on the metric system being used is only 12 minutes long, the plan is to show it without interpretation.

(F) Films, laboratory work, and many other activities carried out in the science classroom should be followed with a class discussion or other means of summarizing and reviewing what has been learned.

(G) Having all the equipment ready to go can greatly reduce the time required. Confusion that sometimes accompanies laboratory work and similar activities also is reduced when students know what they are supposed to do. Lab assistants, when available, can be used to prepare equipment.

(H) Time should be allowed for clean-up and the return of all equipment and supplies to the proper places.

(I) Many lessons involve the giving of an assignment. Assignments yelled as an afterthought as the students leave the room seldom are effective. Time should be budgeted so that the assignment can be properly explained (what the student is to do, the form that assignment should be in, due date, etc.).

part in conducting successful demonstrations and field trips. Evaluation activities, such as test construction and grading, also require planning, and ideas on this kind of planning are presented in Chapter 6. Important points that summarize lesson planning are presented in the form of a checklist in Figure 3.8.

Planning for Alternative Approaches to Instruction

Most secondary school science teaching involves one teacher working with a group of twenty to thirty-five students at a time for a period of fifty to sixty minutes each day. There are, however, various alternatives to the group approach and this method of scheduling classes. Although the

☐ 1. Are the objectives consistent with the major goals of the course?

☐ 2. Can the objectives be communicated clearly to students?

☐ 3. Can student achievement of the objectives be evaluated?

☐ 4. Are the instructional strategies to be used the most effective means for helping students accomplish these specific objectives?

☐ 5. Do the instructional strategies take into account individual differences of students?

☐ 6. Is there variety and change of pace in this lesson?

☐ 7. Have provisions been made for necessary equipment and materials?

☐ 8. Does an opportunity exist whereby student progress can be checked by the end of the lesson?

☐ 9. Does this lesson build on earlier work and provide for a transition to future work?

☐ 10. Have provisions been made to allow feedback from students about the lesson?

FIGURE 3.8   Checklist for evaluating lesson plans.

planning guidelines and techniques discussed thus far can be applied to all forms of instruction, most alternative approaches usually require additional planning.

TEAM TEACHING

There are many different patterns of team teaching, but they all involve two or more teachers working as a team to instruct a given group of students. In some cases, the instruction is organized so that students receive some instruction in large groups (often one hundred students or more), some instruction in smaller discussion groups (twelve to twenty students), and perhaps some in very small groups (two to five), or even on an individual basis. Such an approach requires very careful planning in order to coordinate the roles of the various teachers and to assure that each student is receiving appropriate instruction.

A must for successful team teaching is time to plan. A teacher working individually can plan while taking a shower, traveling to school, or proctoring an examination. Team planning, however, requires time for members of the team to meet regularly at the same time and place. Time is required not only to determine who is going to do what next, but also to jointly review what has been accomplished since the team met last. Lack of time available for planning is probably the major reason why team teaching is not used more frequently in secondary schools.

MODULAR SCHEDULING

Most schools schedule classes so that subjects such as science and mathematics meet each day for fifty to sixty minutes. In some schools, subjects such as chemistry and physics have a double period for laboratory work once or twice a week. A few schools use a modular scheduling plan in which each module of time lasts for fifteen to twenty minutes.

Modular scheduling is often used with team teaching and various plans for individualizing instruction. Modular scheduling can also be used in situations where individual teachers are responsible for the instruction of twenty to thirty-five students at a given time. A sample weekly modular schedule for a science teacher is shown in Figure 3.9.

The schedule shown in Figure 3.9 is based on a two-week cycle. For example, General Science I meets for three long periods (four mods, or one hour and twenty minutes) and two short periods (two mods, or forty minutes). The following week, General Science I will meet for two long periods (four mods) and three short periods (two mods). The schedule the third week will be the same as the one shown in Figure 3.9. The last four minutes of each period, except the last one, are used by students to move to the next class.

An important advantage of modular scheduling for the science teacher is that the longer periods can be used for laboratory work, field investigations, and extended class discussions. For example, life science and earth science classes in Figure 3.9 have one period each week that lasts five mods, or one hundred minutes. The shorter periods are well suited for giving tests, showing films, giving assignments, and for reviewing the process of students doing various kinds of individual work.

The use of a modular schedule places extra demands on planning. In situations where class periods are of equal length, work not completed one day can be carried over to the next. The same is true when the schedule is disrupted by assemblies, standardized tests, and the dozens of other activities that must be squeezed into the school day. Not so with modular scheduling. Each activity, such as a lab or film, must be carefully matched to the time available each day. Unless individualized instruction is being used, disruption of the school sometimes means major reorganization of the teacher's weekly plan.

INDIVIDUALIZED INSTRUCTION

As in the case of team teaching, modular scheduling, and other educational innovations, there are many forms of individualized instruction. Most individualized instruction, however, involves students working independently part of the time, and working at their own pace, which requires that they take more responsibility for their own learning.

Teacher   <u>Dean Reed</u>   Week   <u>April 5-9</u>

Module	Time	Monday	Tuesday	Wednesday	Thursday	Friday
1	8:30-8:50	General	GS 1	GS-1	GS-1	GS-1
2	8:50-9:10	Science				
3	9:10-9:30	Class 1				
4	9:30-9:50		GS-2		GS-2	
5	9:50-10:10	General Science		GS-2		GS-2
6	10:10-10:30	Class 2				
7	10:30-10:50	Earth	ES-3		ES-3	
8	10:50-11:10	Science		ES-3		ES-3
9	11:10-11:30	Class 3	ES-4			
10	11:30-11:50				ES-4	
11	11:50-12:10	Earth Science				ES-4
12	12:10-12:30	Class 4		ES-4		
13	12:30-12:50	Lunch	Lunch	Lunch	Lunch	Lunch
14	12:50-1:10					
15	1:10-1:30		Preparation			
16	1:30-1:50	Preparation		Preparation	Preparation	Preparation
17	1:50-2:10					
18	2:10-2:30		LS-5			
19	2:30-2:50	Life Science		LS-5	LS-5	LS-5
20	2:50-3:20	Class 5				

FIGURE 3.9   Sample weekly modular schedule for a junior high school science teacher.

In planning for individualized instruction, there are two important points to keep in mind. First, the teacher's role changes from directing a group's work and giving directions orally to that of assisting students as they work through a unit of work. This means that materials, such as books, worksheets, audiotapes, and videotapes must carry a big share of the load in individualized instruction. Thus, planning for individualized instruction means identifying or developing these materials ahead of time and organizing them so that students can use them effectively. Ideas on planning this phase of individualized instruction are presented in Chapter 8.

Second, individualized instruction requires more, not less, planning than other forms of instruction, and this planning has to be done further in advance. If a person designs and builds his or her own home, minor changes are easily made as construction progresses. Not so if one person designs the house and another person does the actual construction. In like manner, teachers can easily make minor changes in a lesson plan when they are teaching a group of students. Changes are not as easily made when instruction depends on tapes, answer sheets, and other supplies, and when students need all these things at different times.

The fact that individualized instruction requires more planning should not be a deterrent to using this approach to teaching. Rather, teachers planning to use individualized instruction should be cognizant of the planning demands required by this form of instruction.

In Perspective

A prospective science teacher was overheard to comment, "With all the time and effort required for planning, I don't see how teachers ever find time to teach."

Planning does take time. But consider what happens when a teacher does not do at least some planning;

Carl Butler wheels into the last spot at the far end of the faculty parking lot. Late again. On the way to class he slows down enough to grab his room keys in the office and a doughnut in the lounge next door. Surely an appropriate breakfast for a biology teacher who loves to extoll the virtues of good nutrition.

Fortunately, the custodian left his room unlocked, and his first period students have already taken their seats. Mary Jane, his student assistant, has already taken roll. Give Carl Butler one gold star for planning—at least he had the foresight to give Mary Jane responsibility for taking attendance.

"Let's see, where were we Friday?" Carl queries the class.

"You said we were going to have a film today!" responds a chorus of students.

"Did I? Well, I forgot to pick it up and besides we don't have a projector reserved."

"Well, I guess what we had better do is move on through the plant kingdom," Carl reflects aloud as he thumbs through the textbook and tries to find where he left off last week. "Let's see, did we finish the algae on Friday?" Without waiting for an answer to see if the students feel the algae have been "finished off," he goes on, "Why don't you look at the stuff on fungi. Let's see, that starts on page.... 147 and runs over to page.... 154."

"While you are at it, why don't you do the questions at the end of the chapter on fungi. Let's see, that would be number.... 7,... 8,... 9,... 10 and 11 on page 161.

"Any questions? No? Then let's get to work—You have the rest of the period."

An exaggeration? Perhaps. A poor lesson caused by lack of planning? There is little question about the quality of the lesson, and from what we have been told, it would appear that better planning would have resulted in a much more meaningful experience for the students. Besides, how important do you think this lesson will appear to the students after they watch Mr. Butler in action?

Getting organized is an important part of planning and can help make for more efficient use of time. Make a written record of what you plan to do in a unit or for the next month, week, or day. Once your plans are written down, you will not have to use energy remembering all the things you intend to do, nor will time be spent redoing things that have been forgotten. Written plans also allow you to easily make notes as ideas occur to you before and during a lesson. And, of course, using resource units or a file system is a good way to organize the many "goodies" available for teaching a lesson or unit.

Planning is a job that is never completely finished. In planning for teaching, like planning for a social event, all you can do is give it your best effort with the time available. Hopefully, a science teacher can find enough time for planning so that there will be few disasters like the lesson described above.

Perhaps even more important than all of this is the attitude that is conveyed to students. When a teacher is organized, knows what is to happen, and knows how to handle contingencies, students not only are allowed more time to learn but they are also taught, indirectly, to respect what happens each day in their science class.

Review Questions

1. Describe several ways, including both theoretical and more practical approaches, that can be used to identify objectives for science instruction.

2. List several factors that should be taken into consideration in selecting objectives for a course, unit, or lesson.

3. Compare and contrast the views of Bruner, Gagne, and Ausubel on organizing objectives, content, and experiences.

4. What factors should be considered in deciding whether or not to use a particular strategy or type of instructional material?

5. Describe what you would expect to find in a resource unit and a teaching unit and explain how these types of units differ.

6. What are several advantages of having a yearly calendar for each course? A program or course syllabi?

7. Describe several ways that teacher-student planning can be used in teaching science. What are some advantages of using this type of planning?

8. What items are usually included in weekly and in daily lesson plans?

9. How does planning for alternative approaches to instruction, such as

team teaching, modular scheduling, and individualized instruction, differ from planning for more traditional approaches?

For Application and Analysis

1. Read the article by Lee S. Shulman, "Psychological Controversies in Teaching" in the September, 1968 issue of *The Science Teacher* (Vol. 35, pp. 34–38, 89–90) in which he discusses, among other topics, discovery learning (Bruner), guided learning (Gagne), and readiness (Piaget). Write lesson plans for teaching a particular topic that reflect each of these psychological theories. How are these lesson plans similar and how do they differ?
2. Analyze the statement "The teacher's job is not to cover the subject, but to uncover it."
3. Use the students' comments on page 94 (What Students Say: Planning) and other comments you can obtain from teachers and students to prepare a list of principles for effective planning.
4. Explain the advice given a student teacher by a cooperating teacher, "The most important thing to remember is to always have a Plan B!"
5. Some people are detailed planners, while others take the position "Let come what may." How do you feel toward the importance of planning in education? Defend your position.

References

Ausubel, David P., Joseph D. Novak, and Helen Hanesian. *Educational Psychology, A Cognitive View.* **Second Edition.** New York: Holt, Rinehart, and Winston, 1978.

An updated edition of Ausubel's work cited earlier in this chapter, this book presents a cognitive view of educational psychology along with a discussion of learning by discovery, problem-solving, creativity, and other types that should be of special interest to science teachers.

Gagne, Robert M. *Conditions of Learning.* **Second Edition.** New York: Holt, Rinehart and Winston, Inc., 1970.

The description of eight classes of performance change, or learning, and the corresponding sets of conditions for learning that are associated with them makes this a valuable resource in planning for science teaching.

Novak, Joseph D. *A Theory of Education.* Ithaca, N.Y.: Cornell University Press, 1977.

The author is a science educator, and so his treatment of learning theory and the work of David Ausubel has many implications for planning science instruction.

Tyler, Ralph W. *Basic Principles of Curriculum and Instruction*. Chicago: University of Chicago Press, 1949.

In addition to the model for curriculum development described in this module, Tyler provides useful advice on selecting and organizing the experiences used to achieve the objectives identified using the Tyler Model.

Wadsworth, Barry J. *Piaget for the Classroom Teacher*. New York: Longman, 1978.

This is an excellent treatment of theoretical foundations and related teaching principles and practices, with one chapter devoted to the development and learning of mathematics and science concepts.

CHAPTER 4

Science Teaching and the Laboratory

THE EFFECT OF GAMMA RAYS ON MAN-IN-THE-MOON-MARIGOLDS
(A Play)

Near the end of the play Tillie is making her presentation at a high school science fair:

TILLIE (*deathly afraid but referring to her cards*): The Past: The seeds were exposed to various degrees of . . . of gamma rays from radiation sources in Oak Ridge. (*Pause.*) Mr. Goodman helped me pay for the seeds. (*Pause.*) Their growth was plotted against . . . time.

She loses her voice for a moment and then the first gong sounds.
The Present: The seeds which received little radiation have grown to plants which are normal in appearance. The seeds which received moderate radiation give rise to mutations such as double blooms, giant stems and variegated leaves. The seeds closest to the gamma source were killed or yielded dwarf plants.

The second gong rings.
The Future: After radiation is better understood a day will come when the power from exploding atoms will change the whole world we know.

With inspiration.
Some of the mutations will be good ones—wonderful things beyond our dreams—and I believe, I believe this with all my heart, THE DAY WILL COME WHEN MANKIND WILL THANK GOD FOR THE STRANGE AND BEAUTIFUL ENERGY FROM THE ATOM.

Later, in the last lines of the play, Tillie is back home:

TILLIE'S VOICE: *The Conclusion:* My experiment has shown some of the strange effects radiation can produce . . . and how dangerous it can be if not handled correctly. Mr. Goodman said I should tell in this conclusion what my future plans are and how this experiment has helped me make them. For one thing, the Effect of Gamma Rays on Man-in-the-Moon Marigolds has made me curious about the sun and the stars, for the universe itself must be like a world of great atoms— and I want to know more about it. But most important, I suppose, my experiment has made me feel important—every atom in me, in everybody, has come from the sun—from places beyond our dreams. The atoms of our hands, the atoms of our hearts . . .

All sound out. Tillie speaks the rest live, hopeful, glowing.
TILLIE: Atom. Atom. What a beautiful word.
Curtain.

Webster's dictionary defines the laboratory both as a place equipped for experimental study and as a period of time set aside for laboratory work. Whether one uses the word to mean a *place* or a *period* of time, the term *laboratory* is as much a part of science as the white coat is a part of the image of the scientist. The word "lab" or "laboratory" in the minds of most people is synonymous with scientific investigation.

Laboratories vary, ranging from well-equipped rooms with benches, shelves, test tubes, and microscopes, to poorly equipped rooms in basements or garages. Laboratories also range from tents or grass huts in Africa to a backyard of a nearby park. The laboratory is where a scientist works, and this can be anywhere a person chooses to investigate natural phenomena.

If the laboratory is where scientists do their work, then it follows that much of science can best be learned in this setting. But this is not the only reason for considering the laboratory to be "the heart" of a good science program. The laboratory allows students to have experiences that are consistent with the goal of scientific literacy, that make sense in terms of how we believe people best learn science, and that are in harmony with the unique characteristics of secondary school students. To highlight the importance of the laboratory in science teaching, this chapter is devoted to ways of using the laboratory—the trademark of effective science teaching.

Major Functions of the Laboratory

Over one hundred functions of laboratory work have been described in the literature on science teaching. Most of these functions, however, can

---

WHAT STUDENTS SAY

Labs

When I think of science I think of lab work. I love things like that.

At the beginning of the year I swore I would never touch a frog. I really surprised myself—it was actually neat dissecting the little critter.

I wish we had more labs. I get so tired listening to my teacher talk about science. I want to do it firsthand.

I take lab time seriously. Some kids kinda treat it like play-time.

Those white coats really turn me on. There is something exciting about working in a laboratory.

We did a lot of labs in eighth grade. I guess that is when I really got interested in science.

What do I remember most about labs? The smells!

If it hadn't been for my good grades in the lab, I would never have passed the course.

What we did in lab never seemed to have anything to do with what we studied in class.

be grouped under five categories. These five major functions represent important goals in science education and demonstrate how teaching science in the laboratory is congruent with the enterprises of science and technology.

LEARNING ABOUT THE NATURE OF SCIENCE AND TECHNOLOGY

Science is a way of doing things, which involves observing natural phenomena, quantifying what has been observed, and trying to bring meaning to these observations. In some cases, variables can be controlled and manipulated so that cause-and-effect relationships can be identified. But science, while orderly and precise, is not based on certainty. Rather, events in science must be interpreted in terms of probability that things usually happen a particular way. For this reason, scientific findings are frequently open to multiple interpretations.

The enterprise of science in the purest sense is a quest for truth. The desire to know how or why something happens is a major compelling force behind scientific investigation. As science produces new knowledge, others attempt to apply these findings to human and social problems. The way in which scientific knowledge is applied is what we call technology. While the fundamental nature of science and technology differ, the two enterprises are nurtured by each other and in the minds of most people are inseparable.

By allowing students to experience a full range of activities in the laboratory, they can come closer to understanding science and technology and how the two enterprises interrelate. By providing opportunities to behave like scientists, students also stand a better chance of learning that answers are seldom as neat, clean, and clear-cut as they appear in textbooks. Part of science involves the art of handling frustration, mistakes, and, sometimes, even failure. Much of this can only be learned in the laboratory.

LEARNING PROBLEM-SOLVING SKILLS

In some of the elementary school science programs, lessons are built around helping students develop skills that relate to basic processes of science. For example, *Science—A Process Approach* (SAPA), a program developed by the American Association for the Advancement of Science, has units entitled "Observation," "Classification," "Using Numbers," "Communicating," and "Predicting." Instead of the lesson being built around topics such as "Rocks," "Butterflies," or "Plants," students are taught how to become more skillful observers, how to arrange objects into different groups, how to construct graphs that display scientific relationships, and how to predict future events from past recordings. Of course, students using the SAPA materials also learn about rocks, butterflies, and plants; however, unlike many programs, the emphasis is on learning how to better use the processes of science.

Science has been described as a process that makes knowledge. The laboratory is a place where scientists work, generate data, and analyze these data. From the laboratory come new observations, new interpretations, and a search for the meaning of things. It is the ability to solve problems and produce new ideas that characterizes scientific methodology. Allowing students opportunities to develop basic thinking skills has long been recognized as a major goal of science education. A laboratory setting is an excellent place for students to learn how to observe, discriminate, arrange, classify, measure, experiment, evaluate, and engage in the other processes of science.

LEARNING MANIPULATIVE SKILLS

In addition to mastering the mental skills associated with the processes of science, students should be able to perform certain "bench skills," such as measuring with a pipette, focusing a microscope, bending glass tubing, dissecting a flower, or lighting a Bunsen burner. These skills require

Learning how to use scientific equipment is an important part of laboratory work.

students to coordinate their knowledge with rather complex muscular control, and the laboratory is a place where students can learn how to master these basic manipulative skills. These and other skills are often taken for granted. However, students do not learn how to use scientific equipment properly unless they are given opportunities to handle materials. The laboratory is the major way and place that these skills are taught.

LEARNING MAJOR
CONCEPTS AND
PRINCIPLES

Another important goal of science teaching is that of helping students organize facts and other small pieces of information into meaningful relationships. The laboratory affords an excellent opportunity for students to gain exposure to factual information and scientific phenomena in a direct, firsthand manner. As a result of these concrete experiences, students are better able to grasp relationships such as concepts and scientific principles.

Research in learning psychology supports the idea that students are able to think better at abstract levels if they first experience phenomena in more concrete terms. Laboratory activities also provide an excellent means for students to discover for themselves the "big ideas" in science. These major ideas, such as the conservation of mass, and energy, represent the cornerstones of knowledge upon which science rests. In addition, learning these ideas in the laboratory is an effective way to teach students how theories in science are derived over time.

DEVELOPING
INTERESTS,
ATTITUDES AND
VALUES

The results of most studies on teaching practices suggest that student interest in science is increased when opportunities for hands-on experiences are provided. Secondary school students like to get involved with "the real thing," and investigations initiated in the school laboratory can often lead to follow-up activities at home or elsewhere. Many of the phenomena investigated in the laboratory may also lead to or increase interest in science-related careers, hobbies and other leisure-time activities.

Haney[1] has proposed that there are eight aspects of "scientific attitude." These attitudes are (1) curiosity, (2) open-mindedness, (3) objectivity, (4) intellectual honesty, (5) rationality, (6) willingness to suspend judgment, (7) humility, and (8) reverence for life. These attitudes or values foster the human enterprise of science and can be nurtured when students are placed in a stimulating and challenging laboratory environment.

---

[1] R. E. Haney, "The Development of Scientific Attitudes," *The Science Teacher*, 31:(1964): 33–35.

RESEARCH REPORT

A Ranking of the Roles of the Laboratory

Janice Lee,[2] in a study at North Carolina State University, asked faculty, teaching assistants, and students in an introductory college biology course to rank the basic roles of the laboratory. She categorized the various laboratory functions as skills, processes, knowledge, nature of science, and attitudes.

When faculty were asked to rank the five functions for nonscience majors, the results, in order of importance, were: (1) nature of science, (2) attitudes, (3) knowledge, (4) processes, and (5) skills. When asked to rank the five roles of the laboratory in order of importance for science majors, the following results were obtained: (1) processes, (2) skills, (3) knowledge, (4) nature of science, and (5) attitudes.

When the students were asked to rate the same five categories, both science majors and nonscience majors ranked them as follows: (1) skills, (2) processes, (3) nature of science, (4) attitudes, and (5) knowledge.

It is interesting to compare the faculty ranking of laboratory roles for science and nonscience majors. For students taking biology as part of their general education, but not their major, the faculty rankings imply that the laboratory may serve as a strategy for introducing students to "how science works" and to fundamental attitudes and values associated with science. The faculty, on the other hand, thought that science processes and skills were most important for those majoring in science.

Although Lee's study focused on an introductory college course, the results have implications for secondary school science laboratories. For example, the results of this study suggest that the role of the laboratory should differ depending on the needs and goals of students. Since the majority of secondary school students do not go to college and major in science, the most important objective of laboratory instruction at this level would appear to be that of introducing students to the nature of science and important attitudes and values associated with scientific methodology.

[2] Janice Taylor Lee, "The Role of the Laboratory in Introductory College Biology," Unpublished doctoral dissertation, North Carolina State University, Raleigh, N.C., 1978.

Types of Laboratory Activities

Many types of laboratory activities are associated with secondary school science, a summary of which is presented in Figure 4.1, along with examples and the teacher's role in each. It is important to recognize the contributions that can be made by each type and to remember that any particular laboratory, regardless of type, can contribute to several outcomes. For example, a laboratory designed to teach students how to measure relative humidity may also teach them how to read a thermometer, that evaporation is a cooling process, and the difference between relative and absolute humidity.

Type of Lab	Major Objective	Example	Role of Teacher
Vertification	Allow students to experience in a concrete fashion abstract knowledge.	After students are told how oxygen can be produced, they are allowed to do it in a chemistry lab.	Teacher provides opportunities for students to witness events that have previously been discussed in class or described in reading assignments.
Exploratory	Encourages students to become aware of and interested in new materials and phenomena.	Students are given mealworms and asked to describe the way they behave.	Teacher encourages students to probe and investigate new materials and phenomena in an "open-ended" fashion.
Inductive	Allow students to organize facts into meaningful generalizations and principles.	Students investigate the effect of the mass of the bob and the length of the string on the period of a pendulum.	Teacher asks questions rather than giving answers. Students are guided toward discovering a relationship or important concept on their own.
Deductive	Allow students to explain events in terms of major concepts or principles.	Students set up crosses with fruit flies and predict genotypic and phenotypic ratios.	Teachers encourage students to apply previously learned principles in explaining, predicting, or describing an event.
Skill Development	Mastery of skills needed to perform laboratory activities.	Using a balance, making a wet mount, and finding the hardness of minerals.	Teacher provides opportunities for practice and appropriate feedback or assistance until students have mastered prescribed skills.
Process Development	The ability to use the problem-solving processes of science.	Students predict what will happen when a marshmellow is placed in a vacuum and then be able to test their predictions.	Teacher pays particular attention to how students go about solving problems and formulating answers. Direct assistance is given to students having difficulty with objectives of lab.

FIGURE 4.1 Types of laboratory activities.

VERIFICATION
LABS

When a biology teacher describes cells, explains their basic structure and function, and suggests that all living matter is composed of these building blocks, students should also be given opportunities to see these things for themselves. By using microscopes, slides, razor blades, and several kinds of living materials, students can experience directly the ideas presented by their teacher. The objectives of the lesson are reinforced by allowing students to verify firsthand what has been explained.

Using the laboratory to verify major concepts and principles has been a common objective of laboratory activities since the use of laboratory work was first introduced in secondary school science classrooms. Many lab activities in high school chemistry and physics follow this format. It is the immediate reinforcement through a concrete experience that makes this type of laboratory activity so appealing to most teachers and students. However, in addition to verification labs, there are several other types, and each has its advantages and limitations.

EXPLORATORY
LABS

The major purpose of many laboratory activities is to expose students to new ideas, materials, and opportunities. These activities are designed to

Models are often useful in learning abstract ideas in science.

foster interest, provide students with new experiences, and to explore phenomena that are to be studied later in depth. During these types of laboratory experiences, students become aware of scientific relationships and are encouraged to probe and expand upon their initial observations. Providing students with a flashlight battery, a bulb, and pieces of wire allows them to explore ways of getting the light to come on. Students then may pursue other ways to complete an electrical circuit and discuss things in their classroom or home that operate on the same principle. In this setting, the teacher stimulates exploration and encourages open-ended responses. The teacher may not necessarily be concerned at this point with which students get "the right answers," but rather with how they go about exploring the materials that have been provided.

INDUCTIVE LABS

Inductive learning occurs when students go from the specific to the general. When laboratory activities are designed to furnish students with basic facts upon which to "discover" important concepts, inductive learning can follow. For example, students are given bar magnets with the poles marked and pieces of string with which to suspend them. The objective of the lab is to enable students to discover that "like poles repel and unlike poles attract."

The purpose of this kind of laboratory activity is to encourage students to gather facts and learn how to organize these facts into meaningful ideas. This is one of the ways in which science operates; inductive labs, therefore, allow students opportunities to behave like scientists.

DEDUCTIVE LABS

Deductive learning involves going from the general to the specific. Often, a major concept or principle will be discussed in class, and the teacher wants the students to be able to describe or predict events on the basis of the newly learned knowledge. For example, after having studied the behavior of fluids, students are given a block of wood or other object and are then asked to find ways of predicting if it will float and, if so, how far it will stick out of the water.

Students can think deductively when they are able to explain single events in terms of overriding concepts and principles. Lab activities designed to reinforce major concepts by allowing students opportunities to explain subsequent events also allow them to experience the deductive side of science.

SKILL
DEVELOPMENT
LABS

Learning to use a microscope, titrate an acid, or calibrate an oscilloscope are basic skills that often require long periods of time for development. Therefore, considerable time must be devoted to laboratory work designed to help students acquire these basic skills. Once these are attained, students can move to more complex lab activities which integrate these skills into other scientific processes.

PROCESS
DEVELOPMENT
LABS

Science involves processes such as observing, classifying, using numbers, measuring, communicating, and controlling variables. Frequently, the major purpose of a lab activity is to develop competence in one or more of these areas. For example, students may be asked to record enzyme reaction times and construct a graph showing how temperature influences enzyme activity. Or students may be asked to measure objects of varying size and thus gain practice in this important scientific process. In many cases, the most important objective of a laboratory investigation is learning how to use the underlying scientific processes.

**Conducting
Laboratory
Activities**

Important aspects of laboratory work include identifying the ideas or problems to be investigated, orienting the students to what is to be accomplished, arranging students into working groups, making logistical arrangements for carrying out the work, notifying the students of their responsibilities for caring for the equipment and for cleaning up, and directing follow-up activities such as discussion sessions and the writing of laboratory reports.

IDEAS FOR
LABORATORY
ACTIVITIES

Where does a science teacher get ideas for laboratory investigations? Many textbooks contain laboratory work as an integral part of each chapter and suggestions for "further investigation" at the end of the chapters. In addition, many textbooks have an accompanying laboratory manual. In some cases, the school system will purchase these lab manuals for students. (Examples of lab activities from textbooks and lab manuals are displayed in Figures 4.2–4.5.)

However, many science teachers must develop laboratory investigations by drawing from a variety of sources, and there are several advantages to doing so. One of the best places to get ideas for investigation is from student questions growing out of class discussions. A student will often ask a question that can serve as a springboard for an investigation by the entire class. Does hot or cold water freeze first when placed in an ice cube tray in the refrigerator? Why, on a cold morning, do the windows of some cars have more frost on them than others? Why does ice on a sidewalk melt when salt is placed on it? Does it make any difference which way bean seeds are positioned when they are being planted? Do students who participate in athletics have larger lung capacities, in general, than those who do not engage in sports? If so, how can the difference in lung capacity be explained?

When students are involved in the planning phase of laboratory work, interest is boosted and the students experience "behaving like a scientist." Students should learn that many of their questions can be investigated in the laboratory. Laboratory work is not only relevant to learning science, but the methods of science used in the laboratory are useful in solving many problems encountered elsewhere.

In addition to ideas in textbooks and student questions, there are many other sources of ideas for laboratory work. Supplementary textbooks and source books for science teachers are two such sources. A list of these source books can be found in Appendix A.

Ideas from elementary school science programs such as the *Elementary Science Study* (ESS) and the *Science Curriculum Improvement Study* (SCIS) can be used with students in middle and junior high schools. The ESS program, for example, contains fifty-six separate units, many of which are recommended for students in grades seven through nine.

Other rich sources of ideas for laboratory investigations are professional journals published for classroom teachers. *The Science Teacher, The American Physics Teacher, The Journal of Geological Education, The Journal of Chemical Education,* and *The American Biology Teacher* are examples of such journals published by science teacher organizations. These journals serve

Making a map of your school building

MATERIALS:

A large sheet of paper, a pencil, a ruler

PROCEDURE:

Go outside and stand about 5 meters away from your school building. Could you draw a map from this position? How accurate would it be? If you had never seen the back of the building, could you guess its shape and size?

Now prepare to draw a more accurate map of the outline of the building by walking around it, counting the number of paces it takes. The first thing you will have to do before you begin to draw is to decide on a scale for your map. Perhaps you will want to represent one step with a line one centimeter long. Or perhaps one step should be represented by a line only one-half of a centimeter long. What are the advantages and disadvantages of each of these scales?

When your map is completed, compare it with the maps made by your friends. Are all of them exactly alike? If not, can you explain why? How could you make your maps more accurate?

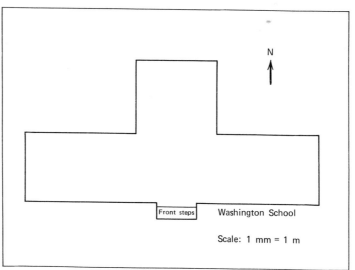

FIGURE 4.2 Example of a laboratory investigation that appears in a textbook in earth science. (*Source:* Reprinted by permission of Harper & Row Publishers, Inc., New York. Brown, Walter R., and Norman D. Anderson, *Earth Science: A Search for Understanding,* pp. 12–13. Copyright © 1977, 1973 by J. B. Lippincott Company.)

as ''idea banks'' for practicing science teachers. A listing of these resources is contained in Appendices B and C. Most states also have science teacher organizations with newsletters or journals, many of which contain ideas for lab work in each issue.

A-23 Relative masses of atoms

In this experiment you will convert a sample of pure copper (II) oxide, CuO, to metallic copper, Cu, by allowing it to react with the gas used to fuel your Bunsen burner. If the burner gas is assumed to be methane, CH_4, the reaction may be expressed this way:

$$4CuO(s) + CH_4(g) \rightarrow 4Cu(s) + CO_2(g) + 2H_2O(g)$$

Since all products except the copper escape from the system as gases, the amount of copper produced can be easily determined.

Determine the mass of a clean, dry 18 × 150 mm test tube to the nearest 0.01 g. Roughly weigh about 2 g of copper (II) oxide on a piece of paper. Assemble the equipment needed to conduct this experiment as shown in the illustration.

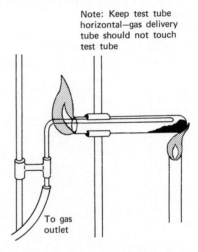

Note: Keep test tube horizontal—gas delivery tube should not touch test tube

To gas outlet

Fold a piece of paper into a tight cylinder and place it in the previously weighed test tube. Transfer the CuO sample to the bottom of the test tube through the paper cylinder. Carefully remove the paper cylinder, leaving the CuO confined to the bottom of the test tube. Determine the mass of the test tube containing the CuO sample to the nearest 0.01 g. Record the mass in a data table.

Complete the apparatus setup. Adjust a *slow* flow of burner gas through the glass tube (do not blow the CuO around!) and with a match promptly ignite

FIGURE 4.3   Example of a laboratory investigation in chemistry that appears as an integral part of the student text. (*Source:* Reprinted by permission of Harper & Row Publishers, Inc., New York. Atkinson, Gordon and Henry Heikkinen, *Reactions and Reason: An Introductory Chemistry Module,* pp. 40–41. Copyright © 1978, 1973 by Chemistry Associates of Maryland, Inc.)

the gas at the mouth of the test tube. Adjust the gas flow to obtain a 4-cm-high flame at the tube mouth.

Caution: *Keep clothes and hair away from the test tube mouth.*

Now light and adjust the flame of a Bunsen burner to obtain the hottest possible flame. Heat the CuO by slowing moving the burner flame under the end of the test tube. Continue to heat the copper (II) oxide until it is fully converted to metallic copper. (How can you determine this?) The reaction usually takes about 5 minutes. Carefully heat the wall of the test tube to "chase out" any condensed moisture, which is another product of the reaction.

Remove the Bunsen burner, but allow the gas to continue to flow through the glass tube and to burn at the tube mouth. Wait 5 minutes, or until the test tube is cool to the touch. When the tube has cooled, turn off the gas flowing to the tube. There should no longer be a flame at the tube mouth. Extinguish it if necessary.

Carefully remove the cooled test tube from your equipment assembly and determine the mass of the tube with the metallic copper inside to the nearest 0.01 g.

Enter the results in your notebook:

a. mass of empty tube	_____ g
b. mass of test tube + CuO	_____ g
c. mass of test tube + Cu	_____ g
d. original mass of CuO (b - a)	_____ g
e. final mass of Cu (c - a)	_____ g
f. mass of O in original CuO sample (d - e)	_____ g

Shake the solid copper plug from the test tube and rub it firmly on a hard surface or hammer it. Can you observe the characteristic metallic luster of the copper? Is it malleable?

Calculate the mass ratio, Cu/O, from your data, expressing your answer as a decimal fraction:

$$\frac{\text{mass of copper (e)}}{\text{mass of oxygen (f)}} = \frac{m_{cu}}{m_o} = \underline{\quad\quad}$$

Compare your Cu/O mass ratio result with that of other class members. This mass ratio will be important in your study of the relative masses of atoms that follows.

FIGURE 4.3 (*continued*)

47
MEASUREMENT
of resistance; voltmeter
ammeter method

PURPOSE: (1) To measure the resistance of conductors by the voltmeter-ammeter method. (2) To determine the effect of length, diameter, and material on the resistance of a conductor.

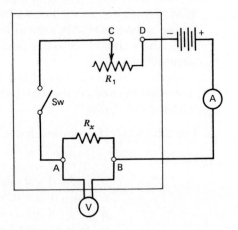

APPARATUS: Battery, 6 v (four No. 6 dry cells in series will serve); d-c ammeter, 0-1/10 a; d-c voltmeter, 0-7.5 v; tubular rheostat; annunciator wire, 18 ga for connections; 3 nickel-silver resistance spools, 30 ga-200 cm, 28 ga-200 cm, 30 ga-160 cm (Constantan or German-silver spools may be used); 1 copper resistance spool, 30 ga-2000 cm; brass connectors, double momentary contact switch, SPST. See Appendix A for instructions in the use of meters.

SUGGESTIONS: A convenient board for permanent use may be made as follows. Select a board from 10 to 12 inches wide and 15 inches long. Near one end, at A and B, Fig. 47-1, fasten two universal binding posts about 3 inches apart. At C and D fasten two universal binding posts. Attach a momentary contact switch to the board at sw and connect its terminal at A and C by means of 14 ga insulated copper wire.

FIGURE 4.4   Example of a laboratory investigation from a physics laboratory manual. (*Source:* Reprinted with permission of Holt, Rinehart & Winston, Inc., Publishers, from *Exercises and Experiments in Physics,* by John E. Williams et al., Holt, Rinehart & Winston. Copyright © 1972.)

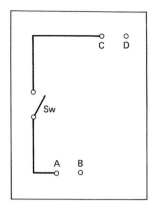

INTRODUCTION: Various substances offer different amounts of resistance to the passage of an electric current. In general metals are good conductors of electricity, but even among the metals we find a wide range of conductivity. Silver and copper, for example, are much better conductors than iron, lead, nickel-silver (an alloy of copper and nickel), or nichrome (an alloy of nickel, iron, chromium, and carbon), which is used in electric heaters.

Physicists have discovered that there are four factors which determine the resistance of a conductor to the passage of electricity. These factors are (1) the temperature of the conductor; (2) the length of the conductor; (3) the cross-sectional area of the conductor; and (4) the material of which the conductor is made.

In this experiment we shall observe the effect the length, the diameter, and the material have on the resistance of a conductor. Care must be exercised to keep the resistances at room temperature to avoid the introduction of an error as a result of the increase in temperature of the resistance.

PROCEDURE: Before you connect a wire to a binding post or to a piece of apparatus, you must remove the insulation from about one-half inch of the end of the wire, and scrape the exposed metal with a knife or rub it with sandpaper until it is bright and clean. Tarnish on a metal offers considerable resistance. Connect the apparatus as shown in Fig. 47.2. The voltmeter V is connected in *parallel* with the spool of wire R_x whose resistance is to be measured. The ammeter A is connected in *series* with the spool of wire, the battery, and the rheostat R_1, which can be varied and serves merely to limit the circuit current.

With the rheostat resistance R_1 all in the circuit and the 200-cm spool of 30 ga nickel-silver wire connected across the terminals AB as R_x, gradually reduce the resistance R_1 until the ammeter reads 0.3–0.5 a. Read both the voltmeter and the ammeter, estimating to the nearest tenth of the

FIGURE 4.4 (*continued*)

smallest scale division. Then open the switch immediately. Can you give two reasons for adjusting R_1 for the small current?

Substitute for the coil just used each of the other coils in turn, adjust the resistance R to a suitable value, and read the voltmeter and ammeter to the precision each instrument allows.

CALCULATIONS: The voltmeter gives the potential difference across the resistance spool, while the ammeter gives the current in the resistance spool. By Ohm's Law,

$$R_x = \frac{V_x}{I}$$

calculate the resistance for each spool to the precision your measurements allow. The diameters and crosssectional areas of wires are given in Table 21 of Appendix B. Determine the resistivity of the metal composing each spool, compare with the accepted constants (Table 20, Appendix B), and determine your error.

Trial	Metal	Gauge number	Length (cm)	Cross-sectional area (cm²)	V_x (v)	I (a)	R_x (Ω)
1							
2							
3							
4							

Trial	Resistivity (experimental) (Ω cm)	Resistivity (accepted value) (Ω cm)	Absolute error (Ω cm)	Relative error (%)
1				
2				
3				
4				

FIGURE 4.4 (continued)

2
HYPOTHESES AND THE DESIGN OF EXPERIMENTS

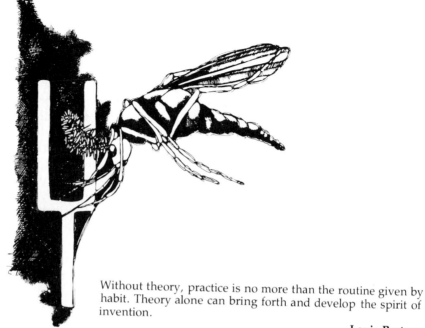

Without theory, practice is no more than the routine given by habit. Theory alone can bring forth and develop the spirit of invention.

Louis Pasteur

Louis Pasteur was a superb experimentalist; yet, as he points out in the quotation above, he realized the importance of theory. If we were to reword his quotation, we might say, "Without ideas to guide us, research can become very routine." Both Bernard and Pasteur have indicated the importance of ideas in science. Hypotheses, which are products of the human mind, are among the most creative parts of science.

Science is an interaction of experiments (facts, observations) and ideas (explanations, hypotheses, theories). The nature of the interaction varies. Researchers are artists. Some start with many facts. Some start with many ideas. But nearly all start with a problem they would like to solve, such as "What causes a muscle to contract?" In trying to solve a problem, they formulate hypotheses. A hypothesis is a tentative solution to a problem.

A hypothesis has also been described as a logical link between *if* and *then*. Consider the hypothesis that nerves are necessary for the contraction of muscles. In this case, we are proposing that *if* nerves are necessary for the contraction of muscles, *then* cutting the nerves leading to a muscle should result in the muscle failing to contract. This working hypothesis leads us to design an experiment in which we sever the nerves and ob-

FIGURE 4.5 Example of a laboratory investigation from an advanced biology textbook. (*Source:* Reprinted by permission of the authors, from *Biological Science: Interaction of Experiments and Ideas,* Third Edition, Biological Sciences Curriculum Study, 1970, pp. 14–21.)

serve the effect on the muscle; we collect data. If these data confirm that cutting the nerves results in a loss of muscle contraction, we may say that our hypothesis has been supported. However, if the muscle continues to contract, the data do not support our hypothesis.

The sequence of events in the above example started with a problem. We devised a hypothesis as a possible solution to the problem. We restated our hypothesis to include something we could test, and from the working hypothesis, we designed an experiment. The data obtained from the experiment either supported or did not support the working hypothesis.

When an experiment is performed to test a hypothesis, data may be gained that are not pertinent to evaluating the hypothesis. These new data, however, may lead to new questions, new problems, and new experiments. This is what Conant means by "fruitful" (page 7).

A. N. Whitehead, an outstanding British philosopher, remarked that "science is almost wholly the outgrowth of pleasurable intellectual curiosity." This curiosity has provided the fruitful sequence of problems and questions that serve as riddles for scientists to answer. A good problem or question asked of nature is almost as creative as the hypothesis needed to solve the problem, and some scientists have been more famous for the problems they posed than for the answers they gave. A piece of information prompts a question; a hypothesis is formed to answer it; and an experiment is designed to test the hypothesis.

As you work with the investigations in this book, practice stating the hypotheses in the "if... then" form to guide you in designing experiments and in evaluating the data they may yield.

2-1 Investigation: Relationship Between Food and Energy

Common baker's yeast has been selected as the organism with which to begin the laboratory studies in this course, because it is readily available and easy to work with. A study of the growth and metabolism of yeast offers experience in many aspects of biological research. The yeast you are to investigate derives its name from an early observation that it is a sugar-consuming fungus; hence the name *Saccharomyces* (*saccharum* = sugar, and *myces* = fungus).

Studies of brewer's or baker's yeast, both of which are varieties of the species *S. cerevisiae*, have provided much of our present knowledge of carbohydrate metabolism. Charles Cagniard-Latour and Louis Pasteur attempted to explain how yeasts were able to convert sugar to ethyl alcohol (ethanol) and carbon dioxide. When maintained under anaerobic conditions (without oxygen). *S. cerevisiae* forms ethanol and carbon dioxide from sugar. This process is an ethanolic (alcoholic) fermentation.

FIGURE 4.5 (*continued*)

The following equation summarizes what happens in this kind of fermentation:

$$C_{12}H_{22}O_{11} + H_2O \xrightarrow{\text{yeast}} 4CH_3CH_2\,OH + 4\,CO_2 + \text{energy}$$

$$\text{SUCROSE} \qquad\qquad\qquad \text{ETHANOL}$$

Since yeasts change sugar (food) to ethanol and CO_2 and release energy, there must be a relationship between the food available and the amount of energy produced. What is this relationship? Instead of measuring the energy produced, which might be beyond our facilities or skills at the moment, we could measure the CO_2 produced. Our problem now is, What is the relationship of food concentration to CO_2 production by yeast?

Figure 2-1 is one hypothesis of what this relationship might be. Read through the entire procedure, and then formulate two or three other

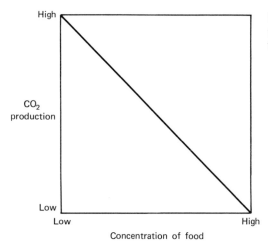

FIGURE 2.1 One hypothesis of the relationship of food concentration to CO_2 production in yeast.

hypotheses that also might explain this relationship. Multiple working hypotheses are a common situation in science. Each team should select the one they feel is most valid and test it.

Since molasses contains a high proportion of sugar and we know yeast can use it as food, we will use it as a source of sugar.

Note: A well-organized and *safe* laboratory operation is possible only when certain procedures are carefully followed by the investigator.

1. Keep all glassware and other laboratory equipment clean and in the proper place. The use of chemicals and microorganisms introduces potential hazards; cleanliness should always be stressed.

FIGURE 4.5 (*continued*)

Materials

(per class)
package of dry yeast in 1 liter distilled water
500 ml commercial molasses distilled water

(per team)
graduated cylinder, 100-ml
graduated cylinder, 10-ml
2 Erlenmeyer flasks, 125-ml or 250-ml (with stoppers)
test tube rack (for large test tubes)
10 test tubes, 22 × 175 mm
10 test tubes, 13 × 100 mm (culture tubes without lip are recommended)
2 rubber stoppers (for large test tubes)
millimeter ruler
marking pen

---

2. Handle all laboratory equipment such as microscopes and balances according to instructions.

3. Prepare for each investigation in a professional way. Label all containers and arrange your equipment in an orderly manner.

4. Discard living materials and other wastes in the place specified in your laboratory.

PROCEDURE

DAY 1

1. Number the large test tubes from 1 to 10.

2. Prepare a yeast suspension by adding 30 ml of the stock yeast suspension to 70 ml distilled water in a 125-ml flask. Stopper this for future use.

3. Prepare, by serial dilution in the 10 large test tubes, a series of molasses concentrations from very high in tube 10, to very low in tube 1. This is done as follows:

Tube 10: Measure 25 ml of pure molasses in the 100-ml graduated cylinder and pour it into tube 10.

Tube 9: Measure 25 ml of pure molasses in the graduated cylinder and add 25 ml distilled water. To insure a uniform mixture, pour the molasses-water mixture back and forth between the graduated cylinder and a clean 125-ml flask. From the flask, pour 25 ml of the mixture into the graduated cylinder, carefully pour this 25 ml into tube 9.

FIGURE 4.5 (continued)

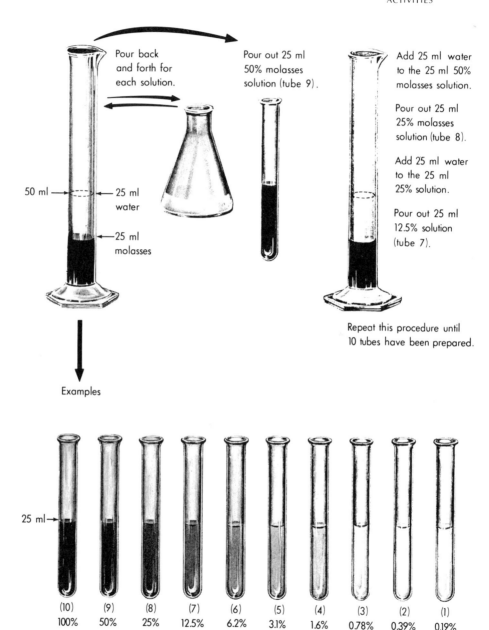

Pour back
and forth for
each solution.

Pour out 25 ml
50% molasses
solution (tube 9).

Add 25 ml water
to the 25 ml 50%
molasses solution.

Pour out 25 ml
25% molasses
solution (tube 8).

Add 25 ml water
to the 25 ml
25% solution.

Pour out 25 ml
12.5% solution
(tube 7).

50 ml → ← 25 ml
water

25 ml
molasses

Repeat this procedure until
10 tubes have been prepared.

Examples

25 ml →

(10)   (9)   (8)   (7)   (6)   (5)   (4)   (3)   (2)   (1)
100%   50%   25%   12.5%   6.2%   3.1%   1.6%   0.78%   0.39%   0.19%
molasses
solution

FIGURE 2.2   Serial dilution technique.
FIGURE 4.5 (continued)

Tube 8:   Add 25 ml distilled water to the graduated cylinder and add the molasses-water mixture you have left in the flask. Again, pour the mixture back and forth between the graduated cylinder and the flask. When the mixture in the flask is uniform, measure 25 ml in the graduated cylinder; carefully pour this into tube 8. Save the remaining half in the flask for tube 7.

Repeat this operation until a final dilution of molasses in water is obtained for tube 1. Discard the remaining 25 ml in the flask. Each of the 10 tubes should contain 25 ml of solution. The molasses concentration in the 10 tubes will be:

Tube 10:	100%	Tube 5:	3.1%
Tube 9:	50%	Tube 4:	1.6%
Tube 8:	25%	Tube 3:	0.78%
Tube 7:	12.5%	Tube 2:	0.39%
Tube 6:	6.2%	Tube 1:	0.19%

Note: We have serially cut the concentration of each solution in half until the final concentration is reached. Each successive solution contains one-half the concentration of molasses that is in the preceding solution. (Future experiments will require the same basic technique, although the dilution factor may vary. The details of serial dilution will not be described in future experiments.)

4. Thoroughly shake the flask containing the 100 ml of yeast suspension (the suspension you prepared in step 2) and add 5 ml of yeast suspension to each tube. Stopper each tube of the yeast-molasses mixture as you shake it thoroughly to insure a uniform mixture. Remove the stopper, rinse thoroughly in distilled water, and dry it before using it for the next tube.

5. Invert one of the small test tubes into each of the 10 large tubes containing the yeast-molasses mixture. All of the small tubes must be filled with the suspension. To do this, stopper a large tube and hold it on its side. When the small tube is filled with the suspension, slowly move the large tube back to its upright position. If there are any air bubbles in the small tube, repeat the procedure until no air is present. Remove the stopper. This is illustrated in Figure 2-3 on the following page.

6. When all the large test tubes have been prepared, place them on a convenient area where they will not be disturbed for 24 hours.

DAY II

1. Observe what has taken place in the 24 hours since the investigation was started.

FIGURE 4.5 (*continued*)

FIGURE 2.3   Preparing fermentation tubes.

2. Measure the quantity of gas collected in the top (actually the bottom) of each small test tube by measuring the height of the gas column with a millimeter ruler.

3. Plot the different concentrations of molasses (by test tube number from 1 to 10) on the horizontal axis of linear graph paper, and the quantity of carbon dioxide produced in 24 hours on the vertical axis.

4. Write the findings from each team on the chalkboard. Determine the average for the class. Plot these average readings on the same graph that shows your team's readings.

Questions and Discussion

1. Does the class-average curve approximate the one for your team?

2. Compare the graph prepared from your experimental results with the graphs you hypothesized prior to the experiment. Be prepared to explain any differences or to substantiate any similarities.

3. Based only on the results from this investigation, what relationship seems to exist between the concentration of available food and the production of CO_2 by yeast cells?

FIGURE 4.5 (continued)

Most science teacher organizations also conduct conferences and meetings, and the programs usually contain sessions devoted to doing various kinds of laboratory work. This allows the individual science teacher to benefit from the ideas of colleagues at the state or national level, rather than being limited to the sharing of ideas with fellow science teachers up and down the hall.

PREPARING STUDENTS FOR LABORATORY ACTIVITIES

In the world of science, the designing of investigations and experiments is an important part of the work. Secondary school students should also be given the opportunity to have experience in the planning phase of science. Questions should be raised, related literature reviewed, alternative designs for the investigation debated, and needed equipment and materials identified. In many cases, homework assignments can include planning for lab work. The more thought students give to a laboratory investigation in which they are going to be engaged, the more meaningful the experience generally will be.

Most scientific investigations require supplies and equipment. Students should be encouraged to share the responsibility of preparing the things that will be needed to conduct the investigation. If extensive preparation is necessary, sometimes a small group of students can be appointed to do this part of the work. For example, a group of students can collect the plants needed for a photosynthesis investigation or prepare the solutions required for a chemistry lab on rates of reactions.

Some laboratory investigations involve procedures and materials that must be dealt with in a safe manner. If this is the case, procedures should be reviewed before doing the lab. There are many ways to emphasize safety in the laboratory. Several good films on safety are available from state departments of education and other sources. A demonstration on "how to" and "how not to" will usually impress upon students the importance of following safety procedures. Still another technique is to have students read a set of safety rules or precautions and sign that they have read and understand the material. It may also be appropriate to include some of these safety items on the week's quiz. A more detailed description of safety rules and precautions is included later in this chapter.

ARRANGING STUDENTS INTO WORK GROUPS

The optimum way of grouping students depends upon factors such as the objectives of the investigation, the amount of equipment available, the number of sinks and gas outlets in the room, the amount of time needed to complete the investigation, the amount of available working space in the room, and the amount of teacher supervision required. Ideally, if enough equipment and materials are available, there are advantages to letting students work individually or in pairs. Students should do as much work as possible on their own. However, shy or less involved students, when placed in large groups, will sometimes hold back and let more active students do most of the work; small groups or individual work can help eliminate this problem. Another advantage of individual small group work is that it allows students to do a lab or to work through a unit at their own pace. On the other hand, working in larger groups provides opportunities for the sharing of ideas and for learning from each other.

The amount of time allotted for a laboratory activity is an important variable for a teacher to consider. While a few schools schedule double periods for lab work, most schools do not. Laboratory work, therefore, must usually be conducted during periods of time ranging from forty-five to fifty-five minutes. Laboratory investigations that take more time than this must be conducted over a period of two to three days. Since time is often a limiting factor, it may be desirable for the students to be grouped, briefed, and the planning completed on the day before the actual investigation.

During most lab sessions, students will finish the work in varying lengths of time. For those students who finish early, it is suggested that optional activities be available for them to pursue. For slower students, it may be necessary to allot additional time. Some students, particularly those who have not had much experience doing laboratory work, will complete their work prematurely and should be encouraged to go back and complete the work in a more thorough fashion. An important thing for students to learn during laboratory work is that not everyone will or should arrive at the same answer or require the same length of time to do so.

LOGISTICS OF LABORATORY WORK

Relatively simple logistics are required to direct the laboratory work of small groups where there is limited use of equipment and supplies. In these cases, the needed materials can be placed in a designated area of the lab. This allows the teacher to circulate among the students, making sure that proper procedures are being used and that appropriate progress is being made.

Additional systems of effective management may be needed in cases where extensive equipment and materials are required. This is also true in situations where students work individually or in pairs, or where the lab work is self-paced. An effective management system should include a file for locating and returning equipment to its proper storage position and a file of the directions that explain how to use various equipment and perform specific techniques (see Figure 4.6). For example, a file can tell the students where to find a balance needed in an investigation on specific gravity. A set of directions shows the students how to position the balance on a ring stand so that the weight of a submerged object can be found.

In laboratory work involving expensive equipment, such as oil immersion microscopes, pH meters, and oscilloscopes, often there is not enough equipment to allow all the students in a class to do the same laboratory work at the same time. As a way of getting around this problem, some science teachers set up stations around the room. Individual students or small groups rotate from station to station. For example, at station one, they might view bacteria through an oil-immersion microscope, at station two, they are asked to identify algae using a taxonomic key, and so on. It is usually desirable to have more stations than there are groups of students; otherwise, traffic jams will develop at the stations requiring the most time.

In some schools, advanced students are assigned to teachers as "lab

LOCATOR AND INVENTORY CARD

Item of Equipment _Reflecting Telescope_ Location

204	B	3
Room	Cabinet	Shelf or Drawer

Brand or Source _Starscope_ Model Number _403 EM_

Date of Purchase _3/2/79_ Cost _$360.00_ Other _See separate card for extra eyepieces_

Serial Number(s) _019326_

Date	Number on Hand	Date	Number on Hand	Date	Number on Hand
4/1/79	1				
2/14/80	1				
1/29/81	1				

FIGURE 4.6 This type of card is useful in setting up a file for locating and inventorying equipment and supplies in the science department. Note how the location is noted by using room numbers, letters to label the various storage cabinets, and numerals to label the drawers and shelves within each storage unit.

assistants." They can take major responsibility for assembling the equipment and supplies needed in an investigation. They can also see that the equipment is kept clean and stays in proper working order, and that locator files and inventories are up to date. Not only do teachers and their students benefit from the help of student assistance, but also the assistants gain in their own knowledge of science and laboratory work.

An integral part of all laboratory work is the responsibility for cleaning up equipment, picking up any leftover materials, and returning everything to its proper storage area. Students should be taught from the beginning that "lab" is not over until all of these things are done. If each student is taught to be responsible for cleaning up and storing all materials used, the student will be taught a valuable lesson in responsibility and the teacher will be spared many additional hours of needless effort.

FOLLOWUP OF
LABORATORY
WORK

Just as scientists devote considerable effort to planning for their laboratory work, so must they also devote a great deal of effort in analyzing their work once it is completed. This is also the case in the school laboratory. After skills are developed, concepts are discovered, and data are collected, it is important that appropriate activities be designed to synthesize what has been learned. Some laboratory work can best be summarized by having students write lab reports. In lab reports, students may be required to identify the purpose of the investigation, generate hypotheses when appropriate, review related literature, list equipment and materials that were used, present results in a clear fashion, and summarize the most important aspects of the study. In other situations, class discussion may be the most effective way to follow up the actual work in the lab. In this case, the teacher asks key questions that help students focus on major ideas from the investigation. Asking questions is also an excellent way for the teacher to evaluate what the students learned during the laboratory work.

In situations where students have worked in larger groups, it is appropriate for group reports to be given to the class. The reports can be handled in much the same way as papers are presented at meetings of scientific societies. Each group report can be discussed and questions asked by both students and the teacher. This technique, as well as written lab reports and teacher-led discussions, encourages students to pay attention to what they do in the lab and to share important ideas with other members of the class.

Many of the major objectives of laboratory work can be accomplished through the use of appropriate follow-up activities. Students learn to construct graphs, figures, and tables, to communicate major findings to other students, and to search for answers to important questions. And most importantly, additional unanswered questions will emerge. From this students can learn that science is an on-going enterprise where an investigation frequently leads to more questions being raised than answered.

**Facilities and
Equipment
Needed for Doing
Laboratory Work**

Although the innovative science teacher can find ways to do laboratory investigations in a poorly equipped room, facilities and equipment are often the limiting factors on how much lab work gets done. Thus, the availability of adequate facilities and equipment is highly desirable, and every effort should be made to obtain at least the essential items.

FACILITIES FOR
LABORATORY
WORK

Unfortunately, most science teachers do not have the opportunity to design their own "dream" laboratory; instead, they must make the best use of the facilities available. However, when the time comes for remodeling or building new facilities, the following are some of the things that should receive top consideration. Facilities with these features will encourage the use of laboratory work and be safer places to work. Figure 4.7 shows the layout of a modern secondary school science suite.

FLAT TABLE SURFACES.   Individual student desks with flat, level tops or larger tables are necesssry before many laboratory activities can be properly conducted. Student desks with slanted tops are inappropriate for most lab activities. The table tops should be resistant to heat, flames, and strong chemicals. Tables that can be moved and arranged for small-group activities generally work best. There should be enough space for all students to have ample room for their work since crowding can result in safety problems.

SOURCES OF WATER.   A large number of laboratory activities require sinks and running water. Ideally, there should be one sink with water for at least every five or six students. Rooms equipped for doing general science and physics investigations usually require fewer such facilities. However, it is usually best to equip all science labs with adequate water outlets and drains so that they can serve multipurpose uses. Sinks and

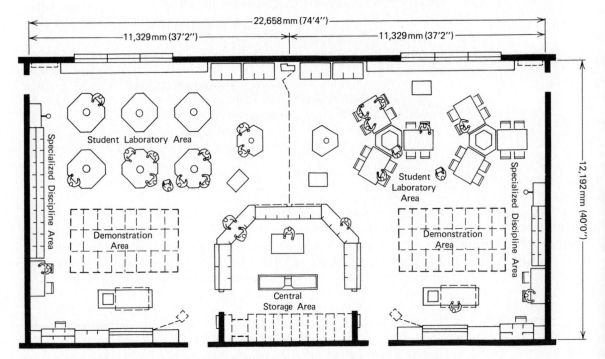

FIGURE 4.7   A modern science suite.

Courtesy of Sheldon Laboratory Systems, a division of General Equipment Manufacturers, Crystal Springs, MS 39059.

drains should be resistant to strong chemicals, and, when possible, both hot and cold water should be available.

ELECTRICAL OUTLETS.   Most science courses include investigations that require sources of electricity. In biology, for example, many student microscopes require artificial light sources, and thus conveniently located electrical outlets are needed. In chemistry, an outlet for hot plates, centrifuges, and other electrical appliances may be needed for every four or five students. Electrical outlets are commonly found around the periphery of most science laboratories. In some classrooms, outlets are also placed in the floor, thus allowing for a source of electricity at tables throughout the room.

GAS OUTLETS OR SOURCES OF HEAT.   Bunsen burners are commonly used in many laboratory activities, and this is particularly true in chemistry and biology. When equipping classroom laboratory areas for chemistry and biology students, ample outlets for gas should be available. It is sometimes advisable to use alternative sources of heat such as electrical hot plates or self-contained units that operate on alcohol, propane, or similar fuels. Electrical heating appliances have the advantage of being safer and allowing better control of the amount of heat being produced.

STORAGE AREAS.   When planning science facilities, a sizable area should be provided for storage. Cabinets around the periphery of the room should be available for storing frequently used equipment such as balances, glassware, models, and microscopes. Sturdy shelves should be available for dispensing chemicals and other expendable items. When possible, science facilities should include separate rooms in which chemicals and more expensive pieces of equipment can be safely stored. Regardless of how the facilities are arranged, some area should be provided for storage under lock and key of potentially dangerous substances. While there are many types of furniture and arrangements for storing science materials, ample space should be allocated so that as more materials are collected they can be properly stored.

VENTILATION AND SAFETY FEATURES.   Special attention must be given to classrooms in which laboratory activities involve the production of harmful or unpleasant fumes and odors. Laboratories should include evacuation chambers or hoods that remove these fumes and odors. If facilities do not have proper ventilation, it is sometimes possible and even desirable to conduct certain investigations outdoors.

Many states and local governments require that all laboratories contain certain safety devices or provisions. Included in these may be the

Using proper safety procedures should become
a habit in doing laboratory work.

kind and placement of fire extinguishers, fire blankets, eye baths, safety showers, and room exits. If a science teacher is assigned to facilities that are believed to be unsafe, it is recommended that he or she report this in writing to the principal or other appropriate school official. A packet of materials produced by the National Science Teachers Association, *Guidelines for Self-Assessment of Secondary School Programs*, is useful in surveying the adequateness of science facilities. (See **References** at the end of this chapter.)

OTHER DESIRABLE FACILITIES.   In addition to the features already described, there are many other desirable features and components for science facilities. These include:

1. Provisions for growing plants and caring for animals. Greenhouses, plant growth chambers, or appropriately positioned artificial lights are desirable along with aquaria, terraria, and properly ventilated cages for small animals.

2. A special room or area where students can do individual project work.

3. A dark room in which photography and other activities requiring complete darkness can be performed.

4. A designated outside area where investigations of astronomical, meteorological, ecological, and similar phenomena can be conducted.

5. Although not possible or practical in every case, facilities such as natural areas, nature trails, school gardens, planetaria, and observatories can be significant assets to a science program.

EQUIPMENT AND
SUPPLIES FOR
LABORATORY
WORK

Many school systems distinguish between "equipment" and "supplies" by defining equipment as items that last a specified minimum number of years or cost more than a certain amount. Supplies are items, such as microscope slides, glass tubing, and cotton swabs, that are quickly consumed and that are usually less expensive than equipment items. Time can be saved in ordering and inventorying materials if the local school system's definition of equipment and supplies is used.

IDENTIFYING EQUIPMENT AND SUPPLY NEEDS. Several sources can be used to identify equipment and supply needs. Professional organizations, state agencies, and local school systems often publish lists of equipment and supplies recommended for teaching various science courses. The teacher's guides that accompany most science textbooks and laboratory manuals often contain lists of suggested equipment and supplies. The *Purchasing Guide for Programs in Science, Mathematics and Modern Foreign Languages*[3] contains basic, standard, and advanced lists of equipment for courses in biology, chemistry, physics, and general science. Although these lists are somewhat outdated, they still are useful in assembling a list or in cross-checking other lists for possible omissions. If equipment and supplies are being ordered for the science program in an existing facility, the items already available must be subtracted from a master list of needed items.

Several factors must be taken into consideration when deciding what equipment and supplies will be needed. What laboratory investigations are anticipated? How many laboratory stations are there in the room? How will the students be grouped? What equipment and supplies may be needed to investigate problems and questions raised by students? How much money is available for purchasing equipment and supplies, and how can maximum utilization of these funds be achieved?

Although this discussion of equipment and supply needs has focused on laboratory work, the needs for using other teaching strategies also should be considered. What models, projectors, and other special equipment are needed for doing demonstrations? Are games and other simulation devices to be included as part of the science department's equipment

[3] Council of Chief State School Officers *Purchase Guide for Programs in Science, Mathematics, and Modern Foreign Language,* New York: Ginn and Company, 1965.

and supply order? Should films, filmstrips, videotapes, and other audiovisual aids also be included?

ORDERING EQUIPMENT AND SUPPLIES. There are many scientific supply companies from which materials can be purchased. Some of these companies specialize in specific kinds of materials, such as chemicals, glassware, and living organisms. Other companies sell a wide range of items—almost anything a science teacher should need. A list of some of these companies and their addresses is contained in Appendix E.

In some school systems, teachers may order items directly from individual supply companies. In most school systems, however, the policy is to send requests to a central purchasing agent. The purchasing agent may be required to obtain bids; this is particularly true when ordering more expensive things such as microscopes, balances, water baths, incubators, and centrifuges. For expendable items such as chemicals, glassware, stoppers, and rubber tubing, a school system or the state educational agency may have arrangements for purchasing supplies from companies that have previously supplied low bids or offered special discounts.

A typical order form from a scientific supply company is shown in Figure 4.8. By using a catalog, the order number and price can be obtained, along with a description of each item being purchased. Since prices are subject to change, it is important to use the most recent catalog when preparing a purchase order. As can be seen in Figure 4.7, the terms of purchase may vary. Most supply companies will furnish institutions that are regular customers with a permanent order number. In this case, supplies may be ordered and paid for after they are received and checked. Under this arrangement, it is important to make sure the supplies are mailed to the proper address and that the bill is invoiced to the appropriate person and department within the school system. Most companies will also allow teachers to place personal orders and pay by check or mail order, usually in advance. In this case, transactions occur between the teacher and supply company without going through the business office within the school system. Teachers should determine a particular school's policies on personal orders and petty cash funds before placing any order.

When ordering live materials, it is important to specify the time they are to arrive. Most supply companies are able to respond to orders for living materials the same day they receive the request. If the materials are not needed immediately, a future arrival date should be specified. The company can then initiate the shipment the appropriate number of days ahead of this date so that the materials will arrive at the proper time. Airmail and special delivery, while more expensive, can be used when crucial materials are needed in a hurry.

TRIARCH INCORPORATED
P.O. Box 98
Ripon, WI 54971

PURCHASE ORDER

Ship To *Pine Street Junior High Science Department*	This order is: ☒ Institutional ☐ Personal
Address *AHn: Mrs. Bridger*	
300 Pine Street	SHIPPING INFORMATION
City/State/Zip Code *Davenport, Ohio 43999*	☒ Ship at once ☐ Ship to arrive_____ ☒ Send *2* additional catalogs
Invoice To *Mr. Richard Marcellin, Purchasing Agent*	
Address *Davenport School District*	TERMS Institutions: Net: 30 Days Individuals: Cash with order
1700 Central Avenue	
City/State/Zip Code *Davenport, Ohio 43999*	

Date *7/14/81*	Customer's Order No. *732-002*	Authorized Signature	Title

QUANTITY	CATALOG NUMBER	DESCRIPTION OF ITEM	UNIT PRICE	TOTAL
THANK YOU FOR YOUR ORDER				

FIGURE 4.8   A typical purchase order form.

Ordering supplies, especially live materials, requires considerable time and planning. Most teachers find it helpful to select as many laboratory activities as possible well in advance of doing them and mark on a calendar or master planner what materials are needed and when. Although the ordering of equipment and supplies adds to the total effort required to use the laboratory effectively, most teachers feel that the extra effort is worth it.

Safety in the Laboratory

The National Safety Council estimates that about 32,000 school-related accidents occur each year, 5,000 of which occur in science classrooms. While school principals and other administrators are responsible for the overall safety program in a school, the science teacher is responsible for the safety of his or her classroom. Thus, it is important that the science teacher takes appropriate safety precautions during laboratory work and knows what to do if an accident does occur. Not only is it highly desirable to avoid accidents, but the teaching of safety and the use of appropriate laboratory procedures are also important objectives of teaching science.

Emphasizing safety is also important in avoiding possible legal problems. For example, the Occupational Safety and Health Act (OSHA) of 1970 includes educational institutions in those covered by its strict safety standards, and the federal government has recently been focusing more attention on safety in elementary and secondary schools. In addition, teacher liability in the case of accidents may depend on whether or not appropriate safety precautions were taken.

ESTABLISHING GENERAL SAFETY PRACTICES

Before school starts each year, a list of safety precautions should be prepared, and this list should either be read to students or distributed in the form of a handout before the first lab is conducted. Some teachers have found it useful to pass out such a list periodically, ask students to read it carefully, and then ask them to sign it indicating that they have done so.

1. Students should know the locations and how to use all of the safety equipment in the classroom and/or laboratory (fire extinguishers, fire blanket, eye baths, safety showers, first aid kits, etc.).
2. Safety goggles or glasses should be worn when engaging in activities that could be hazardous to the eyes.
3. Long hair and loose clothing should be confined when working in the laboratory.
4. Aprons should be worn during lab activities.
5. Eating and drinking are prohibited in the laboratory.
6. Any accidents should be promptly reported to the instructor.
7. Students are not allowed to conduct unauthorized experiments in the lab, nor is anyone allowed to work alone in the lab.
8. Horseplay and practical jokes of any kind are not allowed in the lab.
9. All table surfaces should be thoroughly cleaned after each lab period, and all gas, water, and electrical outlets should be turned off.

10. All equipment used should be cleaned and properly stored after each lab activity.

One of the most important things regarding safety is student attitude. Students should not be made to fear handling chemicals or using certain equipment; rather, they should learn to enjoy laboratory work and appreciate the importance of appropriate safety procedures. One way to foster such positive attitudes is for the teacher to set a good example. When a lab procedure is being demonstrated or an investigation is being planned, the teacher should take the same safety precautions that are expected of students.

SPECIFIC SAFETY PRACTICES

After general safety practices have been established and students realize the importance of safety in the laboratory, attention can be given to more specific safety hazards and practices. The following illustrate some of the most common hazards in the science laboratory and the precautions that can be taken to prevent accidents and injuries.

HEAT AND FIRE SAFETY. Burns caused by handling hot materials and injuries resulting from fire are among the most common problems in the laboratory. Such accidents can be avoided by following the correct procedures and by using proper safety equipment. However, should an accident of this type occur, having first aid materials and knowing the correct procedures for using them can prevent serious injury.

Most burns can be avoided by using the correct tongs or asbestos gloves, and the proper heating procedures. Proper use of the Bunsen burner should be demonstrated to all students. Electric hot plates or a water bath should be used when heating flammable materials. Alcohol lamps are a common and inexpensive heat source but tend to be more dangerous than other sources of heat.

Should a fire break out in the lab, there are several effective ways to extinguish it. General-purpose fire extinguishers containing special dry chemicals are effective against A-, B-, and C-type fires. Class A fires (combustion of wood, textiles, and other ordinary carbon-containing materials) can also be extinguished with water or a fire blanket. Class B fires involve gasoline, alcohol, oil, grease, or other liquids that gassify when heated. These are best extinguished by a general-purpose extinguisher. Class C fires involve electrical equipment and can be extinguished by using a carbon dioxide or general-purpose fire extinguisher. Class D fires involve the burning of combustible metals such as potassium, sodium, and magnesium. Dry sand scooped on such a fire or the powder from a special extinguisher will contain a Class D fire.

One of the best ways to prevent fires is by not having highly combustible materials in the lab. In cases where flammable materials are needed to conduct an investigation, they should be properly labeled and handled. If possible, highly flammable materials should be stored in a fire-resistant cabinet when not being used. Storage areas should be well ventilated and properly secured when not in use. It is considered unsafe to store flammable materials below the ground level, and the storage area should be free of all heat sources. The mixing or transferring of chemicals and smoking should be prohibited in storage areas. By maintaining a clean and orderly storage area, many fires and other accidents can be prevented.

GLASSWARE SAFETY.   Many of the accidents in the science classroom involve cuts or other injuries from glassware such as beakers, flasks, glass tubing, or glass rods. In addition to burns from handling hot glassware, many students receive cuts from broken glass. Glassware used in the lab should be Pyrex or made of a similar type of heat-resistant glass. Special containers should be provided for broken glass. A broom and dustpan should be available for the cleanup of glassware when it is broken. All glassware should be kept clean, properly stored, and never used for drinking or eating.

Another source of injury in the science lab is the use of glass tubing. This tubing is usually purchased in long sections. Students should be properly instructed in how to cut and firepolish glass tubing and rods. If students are required to bend glass tubing or to insert glass tubing in rubber stoppers or corks, they also will need proper instruction on how to safely perform these potentially hazardous tasks.

ADDITIONAL SAFETY TIPS FOR THE EARTH AND PHYSICAL SCIENCES. Here are a few additional safety precautions that apply mainly to the teaching of earth science, physical science, chemistry, and physics:

- Appropriate protective devices for the eyes and body should be worn when hammering, clipping, or grinding rocks, minerals, or metals.
- Direct viewing of the sun should be avoided; the safest way to view sunspots or an eclipse of the sun is to project the sun's image on a screen.
- Minerals and other chemicals used in the lab should not be tasted as a means of identification.
- If volatile liquids such as alcohol, carbon sulfide, and benzene are heated, this should be done away from an open flame and under a fume hood.
- Breathing gases in high or pure concentrations can be very dangerous and should be avoided.
- When acid is diluted with water, slowly add the *acid to the water* and stir while doing so.

- When heating a liquid in a test tube over an open flame, the tube should be heated slowly and the open end should not be pointed toward anyone.
- All electrical equipment should be properly grounded.
- Students should be cautioned not to "experiment" with the 117-volt AC electrical current in home or school circuits.
- Mercury (from broken thermometers and other sources) is toxic and should not be handled; in the case of mercury spills, smaller particles should be pooled together and vacuumed (if possible, with a specially designed aspirator).
- When measuring chemicals with a pipette, a suction bulb should be used; mouth-pipetting should never be used.
- The U.S. Energy and Development Administration (formerly AEC) has approved certain radioisotopes for classroom use. If used, all such materials should be labeled "RADIOACTIVE" with the level, date, and kind and quantity also noted. These materials should be stored in a locked cabinet clearly marked "RADIOACTIVE MATERIAL."
- Cathode ray tubes used for classroom demonstrations can produce potentially hazardous X-rays. If used, the instructor, with appropriate protective covering, should hold the tube, and no student should be closer than eight feet from the tube while it is operating.
- Other sources of potential dangerous energy, such as ultraviolet rays, infrared rays, microwaves, and laser beams, should be used only after direction for their proper use and appropriate safety precautions have been given.

ADDITIONAL SAFETY TIPS FOR THE BIOLOGICAL AND LIFE SCIENCES. As with the physical and earth sciences, several potential hazards are associated with lab activities in life science and biology classes. A few such hazards and related safety tips are included here:

- Scalpels and other such cutting devices should have only one cutting edge; double-edged blades are extremely dangerous.
- Specimens should be properly secured before dissection begins; materials that are being cut, sliced, or dissected should *not* be held in the hand.
- Only nonpathogenic bacteria should be used in the classroom. All bacterial cultures should be sterilized before washing petri dishes. Most cultures can be killed by heating at 15 pounds of pressure per square inch for 20 minutes or by placing them in a concentrated solution of disinfectant overnight. An alternative is to use disposable plastic petri dishes.

- Pressure cookers or autoclaves should be used with caution. Pressure should not be allowed to exceed 15 pounds per square inch and should be gradually reduced to a normal air pressure before removing the cover or opening the door.
- Rubber gloves and an apron should be worn when washing bacteriological and chemical ware.
- Lamps or indirect sunlight should be used with microscopes; reflected direct sunlight can damage the eye.
- If ether is used as an anesthesia or killing agent, students should be warned of its toxicity and high flammability.
- Only sterile, disposable lancets should be used to obtain blood samples. If blood is being typed, students should be cautioned that the results do not constitute an official finding, such as one determined by a physician or certified medical technician.
- Blood samples should not be taken from students with a known abnormal blood clotting time or other blood disorder.
- When plant specimens are collected for identification, care should be taken to avoid poisonous plants such as poison ivy, poison oak, sumac, and other kinds of plants that produce allergic reactions.
- Plant materials should not be tasted or eaten. Students should be cautioned that many common plants possess berries, twigs, bark, roots, or leaves that are toxic and can be fatal if taken internally.
- All animals obtained for classroom use should be acquired in accordance with federal, state, and local laws. In most states, for example, a permit from the State Game and Fish Commission is needed before wild animals can be kept in captivity. If wild animals are obtained, it is generally desirable to return them to their natural habitat as soon as possible.
- There are strict laws governing the care and treatment of animals, and particularly the vertebrates; inhumane treatment or abuse of animals is prohibited.
- Animals that may be disease carriers, such as snakes, snapping turtles, wild rabbits, bats, or insects, should not be brought into the classroom or lab.
- All live mammals brought to the classroom should be inoculated for rabies unless purchased from a reliable scientific supply company.
- All animals should be kept in clean cages and be fed and watered regularly, including weekends and vacations. Animals should not be teased or handled unnecessarily. Students should wash their hands after handling or caring for animals.

The following guidelines for the use of animals were published by the Humane Society of the United States:

It is the policy of The Humane Society of the United States that any study of animals shall foster a humane regard for the animal kingdom and a respect for life. The Society believes all live animal experiments (other than those for the purpose of behavioral observations and ecological studies that involve no direct manipulations) should be prohibited in elementary and secondary schools. Learning experiences that entail animal suffering cannot be justified or add positively to a child's character development.

The Society recognizes, however, that although this goal may not be reached for some time, it is a humane imperative to minimize and eliminate where possible all animal suffering and has, therefore, developed the following guiding principles with this goal in mind.

GUIDING PRINCIPLES FOR USE* OF ANIMALS IN ELEMENTARY AND SECONDARY EDUCATION

In biological procedures involving living organisms, species such as plants, bacteria, fungi, protozoa, worms, snails, or insects should be used wherever possible. (Phyletically "lower" life forms should be sought as alternatives to "higher" warm blooded forms). Their wide variety and ready availability in large number, the simplicity of their maintenance and subsequent disposal makes them especially suitable for student work. In mammalian studies, non-hazardous human experiments are often educationally preferable to the use of species such as gerbils, guinea pigs or mice.

Choice of Subject:

Procedures to be performed on any warm-blooded animal that might cause any extreme physiological or psychological reactions; i.e. pain, suffering, anxiety, discomfort or any interference with its normal health should be avoided. (Warm-blooded animals include man, other mammals such as gerbils, guinea pigs, mice, rabbits, hamsters and rats. It also includes birds, such as hens, quail, and pigeons. This means that a student shall do unto other warm-blooded animals only what he can do to himself without pain or hazard to health). Birds' eggs subjected to experimental manipulations should not be allowed to hatch; such embryos should be destroyed two days prior to the normal hatching time. If normal egg embryos are to be hatched, satisfactory arrangements must be made for the humane disposal of chicks. No lesson or experiment shall be performed on a vertebrate animal that involves: Microorganisms which can cause disease in man or animal; ionising radiation; cancer producing agents; extremes of temperatures; electric or other shock; excessive noise; noxious fumes; exercise to exhaustion; overcrowding or other distressing stimuli. No alien substance (drug or chemical) should be exposed

Procedures:

* 'Use' implies preferentially the non-manipulative study of life forms; i.e., observation, which is no less educational and scientifically valid than direct manipulations and other treatments which should be discouraged.

to, given in the food or water, or injected into the animal, and no surgery shall be performed on any living vertebrate animal (mammal, bird, reptile, or amphibian).

Diets deficient in essential foods are prohibited. Food shall not be withdrawn for periods longer than 12 hours. Clean drinking water shall be available at all times (and shall not be replaced by alcohol or drugs).

Projects involving vertebrate animals will normally be restricted to measuring and studying *normal* physiological functions such as *normal* growth, activity cycles, metabolism, blood circulation, learning processes, *normal* behavior, ecology, reproduction, communication or isolated organ/ tissue techniques. None of these studies requires infliction of pain.

Supervision:

Observations must be directly supervised by a competent science teacher who shall approve the student's protocol before the study is initiated. Students must have the necessary comprehension and abilities for the work contemplated. The supervisor shall oversee all experimental procedures, shall be responsible for their non-hazard nature and shall personally inspect experimental animals during the course of the study to ensure that their health and comfort are fully sustained.

Care:

Vertebrate studies (except natural field or zoo or farm studies) shall be conducted only in locations where proper supervision and adequate animal care facilities are available; either in a school or an institution of research or higher education. No vertebrate animal studies shall be conducted at a home (other than observations of *normal* behavior of pet animals such as dogs or cats).

In vertebrate studies the housing, feeding and maintenance of all subjects should accord with established standards of laboratory animal care, established under the Animal Welfare Act of 1970. Palatable food shall be provided in sufficient quantity to maintain normal growth.

The comfort of the animal observed shall receive first consideration. The animal shall be housed in appropriate spacious, comfortable sanitary quarters. Adequate provision shall be made for its care at all times, including weekend and vacation periods. The animal shall be handled gently and humanely at all times.

In rare instances when killing of a vertebrate animal is deemed necessary, it shall be performed in an approved humane (rapid and painless) manner by an adult experienced in these techniques.

Respect for life shall be accorded to all animals, creatures and organisms that are kept for education purposes, and such respect shall take precedence over any inhumane experiment which might be otherwise rationalized and justified as a valid learning experience.

Note: Educators and students may obtain a free listing of recommended study projects and/or project book for pre-university levels by writing to one of the following sources:

Canadian Council on Animal Care
151 Slater Street
Ottawa, KIP 5H3, Ontario, Canada

The Humane Society of the United States
2100 "L" Street, N.W.
Washington, D.C. 20037

Reprinted by permission of The Humane Society of the United States, 1980.

In Perspective

The laboratory is to the science teacher what the studio is to the artist and the shop is to the industrial arts teacher. It is a powerful tool that when implemented properly, can move students closer to all of the major goals of scientific literacy.

But using the lab to teach science requires lots of extra work. Supplies must be purchased, activities must be selected or designed, students must be properly prepared, and everything must be cleaned up when the last investigation is over. Even more demanding is the long list of safety precautions a teacher must consider before and during each activity. It is this consideration that most concerns science educators these days.

No one can argue that safety in the laboratory is not important. Knowing how to establish safe conditions under which students are to work and knowing what to do in case an accident occurs are important competencies expected of all professional science teachers. It may be tempting, however, after reading lists of safety precautions and potential hazards, to avoid using the laboratory. In fact, many science educators have been concerned about the increased emphasis on safety resulting in less laboratory work being done.

Such a decline in the laboratory would be both unfortunate and unnecessary. Practicing safety is like practicing preventive health care or preventative maintenance on a car. It is something that is expected of responsible people, and it pays off. Accidents seldom occur in classrooms where safety is placed in proper perspective and students learn to display positive attitudes toward their work and the welfare of others. Learning to prevent diseases, mechanical failures, or accidents in the laboratory does not detract, but rather enhances, the opportunities for all involved.

Laboratory safety procedures, once established, become second nature and do not have to be considered "extra work." Emphasis on safety can result in more work in the laboratory instead of less.

Review Questions

1. According to the discussion in this chapter, what are the five major functions of the laboratory in teaching science in middle and secondary

schools? Give examples of laboratory investigations to illustrate each of these functions.

2. Briefly describe the various types of laboratory investigations, the major objectives of each, and the role of the teacher in each. Give at least two examples of laboratory investigations that illustrate each type.

3. What are some useful sources of ideas for laboratory work?

4. Summarize the things a science teacher should do to prepare the students for work in the laboratory, to handle the logistics, and to follow up the students' lab work.

5. Make a list of the major facilities that are desirable for teaching a particular science, such as middle school earth science or junior high school physical science.

6. What is the role of the science teacher in obtaining and caring for equipment and supplies for laboratory work?

7. Summarize the general safety rules that should be followed in doing any laboratory work in middle or secondary school science. What are several additional precautions that should be taken in teaching particular science courses, such as life science or chemistry?

8. Briefly describe some of the major points to be observed in using living organisms in laboratory investigations and other phases of science teaching.

**For Application
and Analysis**

1. Use the student comments in What Students Say on page 110 in answering the following:
   (a) What, if anything, does each of the comments indicate about how the students view the general purpose of the laboratory in a science course?
   (b) What, if anything, do the comments imply about the kinds of science courses the students took?
   (c) As a science teacher, would you consider each of the comments a compliment or insult if made about your course?
   (d) Why are the things referred to in the comments the things these students most remember?

2. Two biology teachers are asked to prepare a request for the equipment and supplies needed to teach five tenth grade biology classes of twenty-four students each in a new high school. The biology rooms already contain all the required safety equipment (fire extinguishers, aprons, goggles, first aid kits, etc.), and these safety items need not be included in the request. Each biology teacher is allowed to request up to $9,000 the first year; although the requests should be as specific as possible, it is permissible to lump together small items, such as various

pieces of glassware or chemicals. (Audiovisual materials and books are purchased from another fund and are not to be included in this order.) The requests prepared by the two teachers were:

Teacher A

Quantity	Item	Unit Price	Total Price
1	Human Torso (male and female)	$800.00	$ 800
12	Microscopes (10×, 43×, 100× oil immersion)	450.00	5400
1	Microscope (4×, 10×, 43×, 100× oil immersion), dual viewing body	650.00	650
12	Prepared Microscope Slide Set (35 slides)	70.00	840
60	Jars, each containing 10 preserved animals	4.00	240
1	Table Microtome and Accessories	230.00	230
1	Pressure Sterilizer	70.00	70
30	Dissecting Kit, BSCS	13.00	390
20	Dissecting Trays	5.00	100
	Glassware (beakers, flasks, test tubes, etc.)		180
	Chemicals and miscellaneous supplies		100
	TOTAL		$9,000

Teacher B

Quantity	Item	Unit Price	Total Price
12	Microscopes (10×, 43×), monocular	$200.00	$ 2400
1	Microscope (4×, 10×, 43×, 100× oil immersion), dual viewing body	450.00	450
1	35mm Camera with microscope attachment	400.00	400
1	Microscope, stereozoom, illuminating base, 10×-25×, 10× and 20× eyepieces	600.00	600
1	B & L Tri-Simplex Microprojector	340.00	340
1	Kymograph Kit	400.00	400
1	Aneriod Sphygmomanometer and Stethoscope	40.00	40
1	Unit Pack of Preserved Specimens (10 each of 10 animals)	45.00	45
1	Vertebrate Survey Set (doubly injected with latex)	40.00	40
2	Prepared Microscope Slide Sets (35 slides)	70.00	70
2	Basic Blood Typing Kit (for 50 students)	15.00	15
2	Human Genetics Kit (for 50 students)	7.00	14
4	Animal Cages with automatic water dispensers and exercise wheel	50.00	200

Teacher B (*continued*)

Quantity	Item	Unit Price	Total Price
2	Aquarium (29 gallon) plus pump, filter, and other accessories	95.00	95
2	Terrarium, 18″ × 10″ × 15″	35.00	70
4	Triple Beam Balance and Weight Set	54.00	216
12	Elementary Dissecting Kits	5.00	60
12	Dissecting Pans	1.00	12
1	Limnological Test Outfit	100.00	100
1	Major Soil Element Lab Outfit	70.00	70
1	Sling Psychrometer	28.00	28
1	Rain Gauge, Large	32.00	32
12	Bunsen Burners	4.00	48
12	Ring Stands, 3 rings each	9.00	108
12	Beaker Tongs	1.00	12
12	Utility Tongs	1.00	12
12	Thermometers, −20°C to 110°C	4.00	48
6	Hot Plates, electric	44.00	264
1	Hot Plate - Stirrer	135.00	135
1	Oven/Incubator, electric	135.00	135
12	Field Magnifer	3.00	36
1	Field Glasses, 7 × 50	80.00	80
2	Metabolism Experiment Kit	25.00	50
2	Plant Growth Stand (3 shelves and 3 adjustable lights)	350.00	700
2	Accessory Kit for Plant Growth Stand (seeds, soil testing kit, etc.)	70.00	140
2	Timer for Plant Growth Stand	25.00	50
1	Hydrophonics Outfit	120.00	120
1	Plant Press	20.00	20
1	Human Torso (adolescent)	130.00	130
1	Plastic Skeleton Model	35.00	35
	Living Material (to be ordered as needed)		300
	Chemicals and miscellaneous supplies		400
	Glassware (beakers, test tubes, etc.)		300
	TOTAL		$9,000

(a) On the basis of the two orders above, how do you think the views of Teachers A and B differ on the following aspects of laboratory work:

• The use of preserved and living materials in biology?

- Verification versus experimentation in the laboratory?
- Indoors versus out-of-doors investigations?
- Doing laboratory work in groups of two students each versus other arrangements?
- Encouragement of students with high science interest and/or high ability students to do independent work?
- Providing a basic laboratory program versus trying some new ideas and investigations?

(b) What other differences between Teacher A and Teacher B are suggested by the two orders?

3. What guidelines can you suggest for use in assembling an order of equipment and supplies for a new science classroom? For example, if safety equipment is not provided, what priority should it receive? Would the location of the school (urban-rural, southern-northern, coastal-inland) make a difference? the school's philosophy on individualizing instruction? on participating in science fairs and other competitive activities?

4. Although the laboratory is held to be the science teacher's most powerful single teaching tool, research reports indicate that many teachers make only limited use of the laboratory. Using the form below, list the major reasons why you feel this is so and suggest as many ways as possible for increasing both the quantity and quality of laboratory work.

Reasons Why Lab Work Is Not More Fully Utilized	Suggestions for Increasing Both The Quantity and Quality of Lab Work
Example: Takes too much teacher time for preparation.	Examples: Have student aids or the students themselves prepare solutions, collect specimens, set up equipment, and perform other preparation activities. If funds are available, buy kits that contain all the necessary materials.

5. Winston Churchill is quoted as saying, "We shape our buildings; thereafter they shape us." Explain the implications of this statement for science facilities.

6. During the last few years, teacher liability has been discussed in faculty lounges, staff meetings, and professional journals. By now most teachers are aware of the factors that contribute to gross negligence and thus to liability for accidents that occur in the classroom or the field. In each of the cases listed below, a science teacher was being

sued for liability. As a member of the jury, would you judge these teachers guilty or not? Assume that the relevant facts have been given. Answers are given below.

(a) A biology teacher requested a student to bring a glass beaker from the back of the room to his demonstration table. The student slipped and fell and received serious wounds from the broken beaker.

(b) A student in a chemistry laboratory injured himself while inserting a piece of glass tubing into a rubber stopper. The teacher had previously demonstrated and properly instructed all the students concerning the method and danger involved. The student attempted to force the glass tubing into the stopper and was injured when the tubing snapped and went through the palm of his hand.

(c) During a physics lab a teacher stepped out of the classroom for a few minutes to obtain a reference book from the library. In his absence, a serious accident occurred.

(d) On a field trip a science teacher led his students across a precarious looking footbridge. The bridge collapsed causing serious injury to several students.

(e) A teacher asked two students to clean a chemical stockroom, warning them of an unlabeled jar of acid on a high shelf. A scuffle caused the acid to fall and the students were seriously burned.

(f) A student was sent to the drugstore in his own car to purchase some hydrogen peroxide. While returning, he hit another car when he ran a red light. He had no insurance and the accident victim sued the teacher.

(g) A student was asked to water the plants in the greenhouse lab adjoining the botany classroom. The student carried a glass bottle full of water, tried to climb a chair, and was seriously injured when the chair collapsed. The chair was in good repair.

(h) Three students in a chemistry class were making up a lab exercise on the preparation and properties of oxygen. The teacher told them to gather the materials necessary for the experiment and to follow the safety directions in the writeup. Contrary to the directions in the writeup, the students mixed potassium chlorate with red phosphorus and ferric oxide and heated them with a Bunsen burner. An explosion resulted and several students were injured.

The Texas Science Teacher, October, 1975. Author unknown.

Answers: The jury voted guilty in (c), (d), (f), and (h). Did you?

References   Anderson, O. Roger. *The Experience of Science: A New Perspective for Laboratory Teaching.* New York: Teachers College Press, Columbia University, 1976.

This work discusses the role of the laboratory in modern science programs and gives examples of different types of laboratory activities.

Behringer, Marjorie P. *Techniques and Materials in Biology*. New York: McGraw-Hill Book Company, 1973.

This valuable resource is for those planning or conducting almost any laboratory investigation in the biological sciences.

Brown, Billye W. and Walter R. Brown. *Science Teaching and the Law*. Washington, D.C.: National Science Teachers Association, 1969.

This book presents a good overview of school law and its implications for various phases of science teaching—laboratory safety, accounting for equipment and supplies, avoiding trouble with pressure groups, etc.

Exline, Joseph D. *Individualized Techniques for Teaching Earth Science*. West Nyack, N.Y.: Parker Publishing Company, Inc., 1975.

This work contains open-end laboratory work, activities, and ideas that will be helpful in individualizing an earth science program.

Guidelines for Self-Assessment of Secondary School Science Programs. Revised Edition. Washington D.C.: National Science Teachers Association, 1978.

This packet is useful in the self-evaluation of a science program; it contains modules on curriculum, science teachers, student—teacher interactions, and *science facilities and teaching conditions*.

Joseph, Alexander, and others. *Teaching High School Science: A Source Book for the Physical Sciences*. New York: Harcourt, Brace, Jovanovich, Inc., 1961.

This reference is valuable for those conducting laboratory investigations in the physical sciences.

Novak, Joseph D. *Facilities for Secondary School Science Teaching: Evolving Patterns in Facilities and Programs*. Washington, D.C.: National Science Teachers Association, 1972.

This work discusses science teaching in terms of evolving patterns and makes many valuable suggestions for designing facilities to accommodate these modern practices.

Safety in the Secondary Science Classroom. Washington, D.C.: National Science Teachers Association, 1978.

This manual provides science teachers with general safety recommendations plus specific suggestions for biology, chemistry, and physics.

THE FIRST DAY OF HIGH SCHOOL

CHAPTER

Strategies for Science Teaching

Louis still had time to brush up rapidly for the high school examinations. He had chosen the English High rather than the Latin High. He was accustomed to thinking and acting for himself, seldom asking advice. His thoughts in mass were directed ever toward his chosen career; and he believed that the study of Latin would be a waste of time for him; the time element was present always as a concomitant of his ambitions. He wished always to advance in the shortest time compatible with sure results. He had no objection to Latin as such, but believed its study suitable only to those who might have use for it in after-life. He had a keen gift for separating out what he deemed essential for himself.

On September third, his birthday, he received a letter from Utica, filled with delicate sentiments, encouraging phrases, and concluding with an assurance that the writer would be with him in spirit through his high school days.

The English and Latin High Schools, in those days, were housed in a single building, rather old and dingy, on the south side of Bedford Street; a partition wall separating them, a single roof covering them. The street front was of granite, the side walls of brick. There were brick-paved yards for the recess half-hour with overflow to the street and a nearby bakery. It was a barn-like, repellant structure fronting on a lane as narrow as the prevailing New England mind of its day.

Louis passed the examinations and his name was entered in the year book 1870–71.

He was among those—about forty in all—assigned to a room on the second floor, presided over by a "master" named Moses Woolson. This room was dingy rather than gloomy. The individual desks were in rows facing north, the light came from windows in the west and south walls. The master's platform and desk were at the west wall; on the opposite wall was a long blackboard. The entrance door was at the north, and in the southwest corner were two large glass-paneled cabinets, one containing a collection of minerals, the other carefully prepared specimens of wood from all parts of the world.

The new class was assembled and seated by a monitor, while the master sat at his desk picking his right ear. Louis felt as one entering upon a new adventure, the outcome of which he could not forecast, but surmised would be momentous.

Seated at last, Louis glanced at the master, whose appearance and make-up suggested, in a measure, a farmer of the hardy, spare, weather-beaten, penurious, successful type—apparently a man of forty or under. When silence had settled over the mob, the master rose and began an harangue to his raw recruits; indeed he plunged into it without a word of welcome. He was a man above medium height, very scant beard, shocky hair, his movements were panther-like, his features, in action, were set as with authority and pugnacity, like those of a first mate taking on a fresh crew.

He was tense, and did not swagger—a man of passion. He said, in substance: "Boys, you don't know me, but you soon will. The discipline here will be rigid. You have come here to learn and I'll see that you do. I will not only do my share but I will make you do yours. You are here under my care; no other man shall interfere with you. I rule here—I am master here—as you will soon discover. You are here as wards in my charge; I accept that charge as sacred; I accept the responsibility involved as a high, exacting duty I owe to myself and equally to you. I will give to you all that I have; you shall give to me all that you have. But mark you: The first rule of discipline shall be SILENCE. Not a desk-top shall be raised, not a book touched, no shuffling of feet, no whispering, no sloppy movements, no rustling. I do not use the rod, I believe it the instrument of barbarous minds and weak wills, but I will shake the daylight out of any boy who transgresses, after one warning. The second rule shall be STRICT ATTENTION: You are here to *learn,* to *think,* to *concentrate* on the matter in hand, to hold your minds steady. The third rule shall cover ALERTNESS. You shall be awake all the time—body and brain; you shall cultivate promptness, speed, nimbleness, dexterity of mind. The fourth rule: You shall learn to LISTEN; to *listen* in *silence* with the *whole* mind, not part of it; to listen with your *whole heart,* not part of it, for sound listening is a basis for sound thinking; sympathetic listening is a basis for sympathetic, worth-while thinking; accurate listening is a basis of accurate thinking. Finally you are to learn to OBSERVE, to REFLECT, to DISCRIMINATE. But this subject is of such high importance, so much above your present understanding, that I will not comment upon it now; it is not to be approached without due preparation. I shall not start you with a jerk, but tighten the lines bit by bit until I have you firmly in hand at the most spirited pace you can go." As he said this last saying, a dangerous smile went back and forth over his grim set face. As to the rest, he outlined the curriculum and his plan of procedure for the coming school year. He stressed matters of hygiene; and stated that a raised hand would always have attention. Lessons were then marked off in the various books—all were to be "home lessons"—and the class was dismissed for the day.

Louis was amazed, thunder-struck, dumb-founded, over-joyed! He had caught and weighed every word as it fell from the lips of the master; to each thrilling word he had vibrated in open-eyed, amazed response. He knew now that through the years his thoughts, his emotions, his dreams, his feelings, his romances, his visions, had been formless and chaotic; now in this man's utterances, they were voiced in explosive condensation, in a flash they became defined, living, real. A pathway had been shown him, a wholly novel plan revealed that he grasped as a banner in his hand, as homeward bound he cried within: *At last a Man!*

Louis Sullivan ranks as one of America's greatest architects and is noted for his perceptive writings on architectural theory. He popularized the phrase "form follows function," which is the battle cry of modern architecture. In his book *The Autobiography of an Idea,* Sullivan tells of his first day at Boston English High School in the fall of 1870. Apparently, Moses Woolson had a great influence on Sullivan, just as other teachers then and now greatly affect the lives of the students they teach.

Roles of Today's Teachers

Teachers like Moses Woolson were primarily disseminators of information. They lectured to students, told them exactly what they were expected to learn, maintained strict discipline, and evaluated each student carefully through question and answer sessions conducted in class. Teachers today have a much wider range of roles than in Woolson's time. In addition to disseminating information from the front of the classroom, teachers spend much of their time diagnosing the learning difficulties of students, selecting appropriate learning materials, supervising student activities, stimulating classroom interaction, counseling students individually, using educational media, and administering standardized and teacher-made evaluation instruments.

Modern-day teachers have a different role than they did in earlier days.

Teachers use many strategies, or teaching methods, in addition to lectures and recitations, a technique whereby students are examined orally, one at a time, in class. Teachers show films, arrange for guest speakers, encourage discussions, ask open-ended questions, construct instructional modules, moderate debates, conduct field trips, and encourage students to use educational games. With many of these strategies the teacher plays the role of a "stimulator," "facilitator," "resource person," "organizer," "moderator," "evaluator," "referee," or "supervisor." In the broadest sense, today's teacher is a "manager of learning."

Learning can be defined as any response to stimuli that leads to a residual change in behavior. Put another way, students learn when they interact with something in their environment that results in a new behavior. A young child sees $1 + 1 = 2$ on an educational television program and later is asked, "What's $1 + 1$?" Learning is said to have occurred if the correct answer is given. When a physical science student is able to identify various elements using a flame test, learning also has occurred. When students discover that all insects have six legs and three main body regions, the students have learned how to distinguish between insects and other kinds of animals.

Teaching involves helping students learn. It follows from our earlier definition of learning that teachers are primarily involved with changing student behavior. To some, this may sound restrictive or appear as though the teacher is manipulating or forcing students to do something against their will. But when one realizes that the ability to *add numbers, identify elements,* or *classify animals* is actually *behavior*, it is easy to accept this definition of teaching. This definition also illustrates the many and varied roles associated with teaching.

Within the context described, *teaching* is an act designed to produce *learning.* To foster learning teachers decide, usually ahead of time, how they will "teach" a given objective—for example, a concept, a skill, or an attitude. This predetermined method or manner used by the teacher to promote learning among students is defined as a *strategy* or an *instructional strategy.* A *strategy,* a carefully prepared plan or method, well describes the teacher's role in instruction. For example, a teacher asks, "What is the best way to help students learn to identify the most common trees in the vicinity of the school?" The teacher can use several strategies to help students achieve this objective. Students can be taken outside and be shown examples of maple, oak, and pine trees. Or 35mm color slides can be shown in class which illustrate the most important characteristics of common trees. Or the teacher may elect to bring specimens of leaves to class and allow students to use a key to classify trees. The *instructional strategy* used on a given day may depend on many factors, including the amount of time available, the age of the students, the availability of specimens, the availability of audiovisual materials, or the weather.

Classifying Instructional Strategies

Instructional strategies can be classified in several ways. Strategies in which the teacher has direct control are referred to as "teacher-centered" or "teacher-directed;" examples are lectures, demonstrations, and teacher-led discussions. Strategies that allow students to play a more active or self-guided role are referred to as "student-centered"—for example, laboratory activities, panel discussions, and independent projects.

Another way instructional strategies can be classified is according to the way the material is presented. For example, a teacher may provide experiences in which students organize several facts into a major concept or principle. This is an example of an *inductive approach* which involves the learners moving from "the specific" to "the general" and can be classified as *indirect teaching*. The teacher may elect, however, first to introduce a major concept and then to demonstrate how a set of known facts fit this generalization. Since students are guided from "the general" to "the specific," this is a *deductive approach* and can be classified as *direct teaching*.

Strategies can be classified using both of these systems. This classification system is shown in Figure 5.1 along with examples of strategies in each of its four categories. It should be noted that some

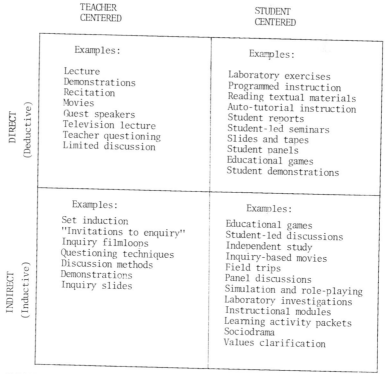

	TEACHER CENTERED	STUDENT CENTERED
DIRECT (Deductive)	Examples: Lecture Demonstrations Recitation Movies Guest speakers Television lecture Teacher questioning Limited discussion	Examples: Laboratory exercises Programmed instruction Reading textual materials Auto-tutorial instruction Student reports Student-led seminars Slides and tapes Student panels Educational games Student demonstrations
INDIRECT (Inductive)	Examples: Set induction "Invitations to enquiry" Inquiry filmloops Questioning techniques Discussion methods Demonstrations Inquiry slides	Examples: Educational games Student-led discussions Independent study Inquiry-based movies Field trips Panel discussions Simulation and role-playing Laboratory investigations Instructional modules Learning activity packets Sociodrama Values clarification

FIGURE 5.1 A system for classifying instructional strategies on the basis of teacher versus student centeredness and the direct versus indirect approach.

widely used teaching strategies do not fit precisely into one category. For instance, the degree of directness or nondirectness may vary as well as the extent to which the class is controlled by the teacher or the students. The research report on page below and on page 163 shows a way teaching can be quantified as well as categorized.

It is important to recognize that the use of various instructional strategies can be viewed in a systematic and rational manner. By the same token, these classification systems illustrate how researchers in science education study teaching strategies and are not necessarily construed as *the way* to view teaching. While teaching can be studied from a "scientific" view, it is also recognized that many things a teacher does are more akin to "art." In other words, the successful bringing together of the many important practices associated with teaching requires more than a knowledge of these skills. The effective teacher tempers this knowledge with an ability to do the right thing at the right time. Like the famous violin maker, Stradivarius, the master teacher is the one who puts everything together in the "right" combination. Using the same analogy, teachers, like Stradivarius, cannot be replaced by computers or production line teaching. There are far too many variables to consider at any given time; only the artist can produce a balanced final product of superb quality.

RESEARCH REPORT

Classifying Instructional Strategies

Russell Yeany, Jr., of the University of Georgia has reported on the use of the Teaching Strategies Observation Differential (TSOD).[1,2] This instrument, developed by Ronald Anderson and others at the University of Colorado, measures the degree of directness or indirectness of various teaching strategies. One end of the ten-point scale is direct verbal methods of teaching. The exposition of facts by lecturing is rated as one. As one moves to higher numbers on the scale, the degree of teacher control and directness decreases while student-centeredness and indirectness increases. At ten on the scale, students plan and conduct their own investigations, which is instructional strategy with maximum control by students. The scale uses a behavioral hierarchy as shown:

Direct Verbal
- 1. Exposition of facts (lecture)
- 2. Giving directions or opinions
- 3. Asking limiting questions

Direct Nonverbal
- 4. Demonstrations
- 5. Student exercises ("cook book")

---

[1] Russell Yeany, Jr., "A Case from the Research for Training Science Teachers in the Use of Inductive/Indirect Teaching Strategies," *Science Education*, 59,4(1975): 521–520.
[2] Russell Yeany, Jr., "The Effects of Model Viewing with Systematic Strategy Analysis on the Science Teaching Styles of Preservice Teachers," *Journal of Research in Science Teaching*, 14,3(1977): 209–222.

Indirect Verbal
- 6. Asking open-ended questions
- 7. Teacher response to student questions
- 8. Teacher guidance and probing

Indirect Nonverbal
- 9. Teacher-planned open-ended investigations
- 10. Student-planned investigations

Yeany has constructed the following conceptual model to show the relationships that exist among students, teacher, and science when a direct, expository teaching method is used:

The use of direct instructional strategies leads to science being communicated largely through the teacher to the student. When teachers employ indirect strategies, the model looks more like the one below:

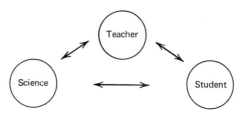

This model illustrates the change in role of the teacher when indirect strategies are used to teach science. The teacher's role, as Yeany suggests, is largely that of a facilitator and supplier of materials.

By summarizing several research studies, Yeany concluded that indirect instructional strategies appeared to produce superior results in achievement and attitude. He recommended that science teachers attempt to analyze their teaching strategies and, if needed, adjust them to include more indirect strategies.

Questioning Techniques

Nothing we do portrays the spirit of science more vividly than the act of questioning. The curious mind and the art of asking the right questions represent the heart and core of scientific inquiry. Thus, teachers involved in helping students understand the nature and processes of science use questioning as a primary teaching tool. In fact, some educators suggest that helping students learn how to ask good questions is as important as finding appropriate answers.

THE USE OF QUESTIONING AS AN INSTRUCTION STRATEGY

Not only is questioning an important part of science, but it is also an integral part of most methods and strategies for teaching science. Without questions, class discussion would not be possible, nor could student attention be directed during a demonstration or laboratory investigation by asking "What is happening?" Questions are the stock and trade of the science teacher.

The act of questioning also serves many other important functions. Initially, questions allow the teacher to gather information about student backgrounds, interests, and levels of understanding. A carefully worded question allows the teacher to detect if students have failed to grasp a major concept or principle. Questions are also used to summarize and to review the material that has been learned by a class.

Perhaps even more dramatic is the way questions are used to stimulate and motivate. "Do you think there is life on other planets?" "What will happen if I mix substance X with substance Y?" Questions like these are great for getting student attention at the beginning of a class or when the class is changing from one activity to another. Carefully worded questions not only serve to stimulate thinking but also help students see the relevancy of a topic.

Sometimes questions can be posed for which there is no readily available answer. Such questions not only motivate students to search for answers, but also serve to illustrate the open-ended nature of science. While questions can stimulate the thinking of an entire class, some questions should be directed to specific students. This allows the teacher to draw nonparticipating students into the discussion.

OPEN AND CLOSED QUESTIONS

Questions can be classified as being open or closed. A closed question, as the name implies, has a specific, or correct, answer. "How many times a year does the moon revolve around the earth?" and "What infectious agent causes influenza?" are examples of closed questions. With closed questions students are usually required to recall data or factual information. Closed questions, however, can also be used to stimulate convergent thinking at a higher level of cognition. For example, "Which blood vessels should be hooked up to a heart-lung machine during open-heart surgery?" This question requires students to analyze several factors before giving an answer. Closed questions can be used effectively to review, summarize, and evaluate student achievement.

While closed questions require students to think convergently, or to arrive at predetermined "acceptable" answers, open questions do the opposite. Here students are required to think divergently. With open questions, a variety of appropriate answers may exist, and these questions allow students to construct creative answers based on their own background and frames of reference. Opinions, attitudes, and values also enter into a student's response to open questions. In other words, students have more freedom to speculate and evaluate when they are asked open questions. "What major problems would be faced by astronauts if they had to remain in a spaceship for two or three years?" "What are important variables that must be considered in studying animal behavior in a laboratory?""Do you think our country should promote the use of nuclear energy for the generation of electricity?" Open questions like these stimulate thinking and encourage students to explore a wide variety of answers.

DIRECTING QUESTIONING SESSIONS

Asking the right kind of questions is an important part of establishing an environment of inquiry and investigation in a science classroom. Equally important is the way teachers respond to students' questions and answers. The manner in which student replies are handled does much to set the stage for the future behavior of students. For example, students are reluctant to answer questions if they think their responses will be treated lightly or ridiculed. While all student responses may not be appropriate or correct, most answers represent the learner's best effort and should be acknowledged both sincerely and seriously. By showing respect for each answer, a teacher quickly communicates that what the student said is important. If the student's response is incorrect or inappropriate, the teacher may wish to pause and wait for other responses. As other students contribute to the idea, the "right" or "best" answer will usually emerge. By acknowledging the more appropriate responses, the teacher reinforces the best ideas without "putting down" the less appropriate student responses.

TYPES OF RESPONSES TO STUDENT QUESTIONS

How a teacher responds to student questions depends on the objectives of the lessons, the amount and type of prior instruction, the amount of time available, the background of the student, and many other factors. Some of the alternatives are discussed below.

1. Give the Student a Direct Answer

This is often the best answer when the student needs a piece of specific information in order to proceed with an investigation or develop an idea. "Where are the rubber stoppers?" "What can I do to get more light through my microscope?" "Let's see, is chlorine or bromine the more active?" Sometimes, however, giving a student a direct answer discourages further thinking and destroys the opportunity for the student to "figure something out for myself." Thus, a direct response may *not* be the best answer when a student asks, "What is the best way to train my dog to sit up?" The natural thing for most of us to do is answer questions directly. Often, however, it is important to help students discover ideas for themselves. By doing so, students will learn a lot in the process.

2. Respond by Asking the Student a Question

"Mr Bell, can you tell me again the difference between an atom and a molecule?" This question suggests that the student is having difficulty conceptualizing the structure of matter. By asking the student a question, the teacher can often help the student discover his or her difficulty. For example, "Do atoms combine to form molecules or do molecules combine to form atoms?" Asking a question in this manner prompts the student to look at the material in a new way and may be all that is required for the student to grasp the idea.

3. Make Specific Suggestions About How or Where the Students Can Find Their Own Answers

Students often seek information that is readily available in a textbook or a reference source. In such cases, a good reply is, "That topic is discussed in chapter nine of your textbook." Or a student can be told, "Have you tried the library, I believe they have a good book on lasers." By using replies like these, the teacher shifts some of the responsibility for learning to the student. This approach may also result in a much richer source of information for the student than the teacher can supply verbally.

4. Allow Other Students to Answer the Question

Responses can be solicited from other members of the class when a student raises a question. Often, this happens quite naturally as other students show an eagerness to answer the initial question or share their ideas. If not, the teacher can reply to the question by saying, "Is there anyone who can answer Tim's questions?" The teacher may wish to pause after the first student response and ask, "Are there other ideas on this topic?" Or ask, "Do all of you agree with the answer that Jennifer gave?" Encouraging other students to expand on an initial answer is an excellent technique for increasing the involvement of a class in a discussion.

5. Indicate that You Do Not Know the Answer

There is something inherently refreshing about questions that have no answers and about people who admit they do not know the answer to a question. This, again, authentically portrays the nature of science. Sometimes students ask questions to which teachers are unable to quickly recall an answer. In this case, "I'll try to find the answer" may be the best response. Or, better yet, in many cases, "Let's see if we can find the answer together." Some teachers feel embarrassed when they occasionally do not have the answers to seemingly simple questions. But they shouldn't because, with the knowledge explosion in science, no one can be expected to have all the answers even in one small area of science. Students appreciate teachers who honestly reply that they do not have an answer to a particular question, and such honesty is helpful in establishing positive teacher-student relationships.

Many of the questions raised by students have no answers. Here the teacher has an excellent opportunity to illustrate the on-going investigative nature of science by replying, "We don't have the answer to that question yet," or by observing, "Scientists have been trying to answer that question for a long time."

MAINTAINING CLASS CONTROL DURING QUESTIONING SESSIONS

Some teachers find that maintaining class control is one of the most difficult aspects of questioning. Frequently, a few students will try to dominate, while others shy away from responding. There are several things that can be done to establish a desirable environment and to increase control in the classroom during questioning sessions.

1. Questioning, like other teaching techniques and methods, requires good planning. The major concepts and ideas to be discussed by the students should be mapped out ahead of time. Whenever possible, carefully worded key questions should be formulated. Master teachers have years of experience and dozens of their old favorites on which to rely; however, inexperienced teachers should not depend on "divine inspiration" to "reveal" the exactly right question at the precise moment it is needed in the lesson. While spontaneity and divergent thinking should be encouraged, the main objectives of the lesson should not be lost. Planning is the best way to make sure this does not happen.

2. Attention should be directed to the substance of the questions and answers rather than to the individual responding. "What are the forces acting on an orbiting satellite?" is better than "John, I can't believe that you didn't think of gravity." Students, no matter how inappropriately they respond, should never be "put down" or ridiculed.

3. Students should be encouraged to develop good listening skills. If the teacher avoids repeating the question and the answers, many students will learn to listen more carefully. The teacher should also insist that the person talking, whether teacher or student, have the attention and respect of the entire class.

4. When asking a question, it is generally best to state the question, pause for an ample period of time, and then call on an individual student. By saying, "Mary, can you explain . . . ?", other students may interpret this as an opportunity to think about something else.

5. Shy students should be encouraged to participate more and vocal students encouraged to listen more. A teacher can accomplish this by calling on several students to expand on an original answer. Just as the use of pausing can improve questioning sessions, in some instances, brisk pacing will result in more students getting involved and having a more stimulating session. Master teachers sense the mood of the class and learn to pace their questions accordingly.

IMPROVING
QUESTIONING
BEHAVIOR IN THE
CLASSROOM

The research findings of Mary Budd Rowe and others suggest that there are several ways teachers can improve their questioning skills and, thus, increase student learning in science. When a teacher pauses after asking a question, students are given more time to think. This not only allows more students to get involved but also leads to "better" responses. By pausing more, a teacher is also able to observe and listen more carefully to what students say. When students think a teacher is *really* listening, they are more likely to give higher level answers. A mixture of lower order and higher order questions is recommended. Other studies have shown that higher level questions produce higher level thinking.

By withholding praise some of the time, teachers can help students think more carefully about their answers. If done properly, reductions in *external reinforcement* (teacher reward) can lead to students placing more value on *internal reinforcement* (self-satisfaction and self-esteem). In this way, students are encouraged to mature. More emphasis is placed on helping students develop appropriate thinking skills, while less emphasis is directed toward "what will be the teacher's reaction to my answer."

As has been stated before, good questioning skills are the trademark of an effective science teacher. The use of carefully planned, open-end, higher level questions to stimulate learning, reinforced by increased wait-time and careful listening by the teacher, creates a classroom climate that fosters a spirit of inquiry. According to research findings, this improves both the quantity and quality of student behavior in the science classroom.

RESEARCH REPORT

Questioning Behavior

Major research findings concerning the questioning behavior of teachers and students have been reported by Mary Budd Rowe[3] at the University of Florida. Dr. Rowe, a science educator, analyzed more than a thousand tapes of teacher-student conversations over a six-year period and found many interesting relationships that have direct application in the science classroom.

Dr. Rowe investigated the influence of a variable she calls "wait-time" on the development of language and logic in children. Wait-time refers to the amount of time a teacher pauses after asking a question. Rowe found the average wait-time of teachers to be on the order of one second. After a teacher asks a question, students must begin a response within an average time of one second. If they do not, the teacher repeats, rephrases, or asks a different question or calls on another student. A second wait-time is involved. When a student makes a response, the teacher normally reacts or asks another question with an average time of 0.9 seconds.

---

[3] Mary Budd Rowe, "Wait-time and Rewards as Instructional Variables, Their Influence on Language, Logic, and Fate Control: Part One—Wait-Time," *Journal of Research in Science Teaching*, 11,2(1974): 81–94.

When teachers were trained to extend their average wait-time to 3–5 seconds, Rowe discovered that the following results occurred with students:

1. The length of responses from students increased.
2. The number of unsolicited but appropriate responses increased.
3. The number of students failing to respond decreased.
4. The confidence of students appeared to increase.
5. An increase of student to student comparisons of data resulted.
6. Students became more speculative in their thinking and made more inferences.
7. The number of questions asked by students increased.
8. The number of investigations proposed by students increased.
9. Contributions from lower achieving students increased.
10. The variety of responses by students increased.

Rowe also found that, when the wait-time of teachers was extended, the following changes in teacher behavior resulted:

1. Teacher exhibited greater flexibility in accepting responses from students.
2. The rate of questioning dropped from seven to ten questions per minute to an average of two to three per minute.
3. Teachers asked fewer informational questions and more leading and probing questions.
4. Teacher expectations of performance from lower achieving students appeared to increase.

Lectures and Class Discussions

Consider the following brief introduction to a lecture. Note that student comments appear in italics.

Let's ask some questions about biology, about the science of life. What do you want to know about life?

"What is life?"

Life has many, many aspects. We could, presumably, fight it out on a broad front and engage the subject all along the line, but "two hands for a beginner" is pretty good advice. Let's try for a narrow front, something more manageable; let's separate, for convenience, structure from function and take these two parts up one at a time.

All right, what then is the structure of life? Does life have a structure? If it has a structure, what is that structure? What is that structure without which there would be no life? Is there any such structure? Is it knowable? It is, and you can answer these questions. If you can ask good questions you have your own self-starters.

What are you going to do with our question, with your question and mine? How does one learn what an elephant is? How does one learn whether life has a structure, and if it does, what it is? How do you go about finding out what an elephant is? You know the story of the blind men and the elephant:

[Here is read the poem "The Blind Men and the Elephant" by John Godfrey Saxe. Six blind men, approaching the elephant from different directions, felt only parts of the animal. One, feeling its side, described it as a wall; one its tusk, "like a spear"; one its trunk, "like a snake"; one its knee, "like a tree"; one its ear, "very like a fan"; one its tail, "very like a rope."]

How are we going to find out whether life has a structure and if it has, what the structure is? What is it we have to do?

"We have to have all the facts."

All? We have to have all the facts, all the facts there are on the morphology, the anatomy, the histology, and the cytology, that is to say the structure, of better than two million species; all the facts that deal with the structure of living things?

"Oh, no. Not in a three-hour course."

Before we throw in the sponge, let's see if by identifying the relevant facts we cannot do in three weeks what we might not be able to do in three years were we just to assimilate facts as they were given to us. If this can be done, it will, you say, be a modern miracle.[4]

How would this lecture, if continued, be accepted by students in an advanced biology class? Does this lecture possess the potential for stimulating students to think? While reactions to these questions will vary, it is clear that the lecturer was not simply telling a story that students could read in a book or hear on a tape. He was not merely presenting facts or "covering material." Nor was he using big words to impress his students. Rather, he introduced the topic in an interesting manner and communicated directly with the students. Probably most students were especially attentive as this teacher moved about the room, smiling and looking students directly in the eye. Instead of taking notes, most were undoubtedly thinking about some of the lecturer's penetrating questions. Biology was being presented to these students with a freshness, a

[4] Reprinted by permission of Heldref Publications, 4000 Albemarle St., NW, Washington, D.C. 20016. From *Improving College and University Teaching*. Hatch, Winslow R., "The Lecture," Vol. 6, No. 1, p. 22, 1958.

curiosity, and an enthusiasm that make people "come alive." The subject was not being covered—it was being uncovered.

Many of us have experienced speeches or lectures that have captured out imagination, aroused our interest, or prompted us to action. The drama of such a setting is penetrating, and students seldom forget such experiences or such teachers. While many lectures do not compare favorably with the one in the example, it does illustrate the potential quality of this teaching method when it is used properly. When teachers ask questions, stimulate thinking, encourage discourse, and introduce new topics with the zeal of a curious scientist, a science class can come alive. When teachers probe the minds of students, when they communicate at the appropriate level, and when they help students to become actively involved in learning, an environment is created that stimulates thinking and leads to learning. This can happen when lecturing is designed to promote interaction between *science* and *students*. In this way, facts are not merely transmitted from the teacher's notebook to the notebooks of students.

In most secondary school science classes, the lecture is combined with a variety of other strategies such as demonstrations, questioning, discussion, and review sessions. Inexperienced teachers often find that lecture combined with discussion is the easiest strategy for which to plan. It offers the most efficient means for including all the topics in the curriculum guide they are required to teach. And perhaps most significantly, they feel the lecture-discussion gives them the most control over discipline problems.

The following are suggestions for improving the effectiveness of this instructional strategy:

- Plan short, well-organized lectures that lead to class discussion, or other learning activities. Combining lectures with other methods of instruction helps overcome the short attention span of younger students.

- Use lectures as a means of stimulating interest in a new topic. Ask thought-producing questions that will encourage students to examine major ideas in science.

- Most people are capable of thinking faster than they can speak. This is one reason why listening to someone talk can be boring. Lecture-discussions should be briskly paced, while at the same time allowing students ample time to think about the important concepts being presented.

- Introduce novel techniques such as short demonstrations, brief role-playing episodes, and the use of props or media such as overhead projectors, charts, and pictures. One professor in California periodically dresses up like a famous scientist when he lectures about important individuals. A science teacher in Nebraska brings unusual objects, such as four-leaf clovers or odd-shaped fossils to his class in hopes that his students will ask questions.

- Move around the room, maintain eye contact with students, and exhibit interest by smiling and other means. Teachers should not be afraid to share with students some of their feelings and enthusiasm, and should feel free to reveal some aspects of their personality.
- When lecturing, stop frequently to see if the "students are with you." Carefully directed questions will help you decide. Another technique is to stop briefly after a period of notetaking by students and allow them to compare what they have written with other students seated nearby. During this time, they may be able to clear up difficult points by asking their classmates or the teacher pertinent questions.
- The best lectures are those designed to lead to discussion and activity. Lectures should be used to transmit ideas, stimulate curiosity and prompt students to ask questions. Textbooks, films, records, tapes, filmstrips, magazines, and journals are more efficient ways of transmitting factual information than are lectures.

Although lecturing is a widely used method of instruction in most secondary schools, science teachers seldom adhere rigidly to the formal lecture so prevalent in college classrooms. Lectures are usually combined with demonstrations and other strategies discussed in the remainder of this chapter.

Demonstrations

Many things are difficult to communicate to others without showing them. Teaching someone how to swim, dance, or play bridge usually calls for a demonstration. Since science deals with observable and measurable phenomena, many topics in the science classroom can be effectively presented to students with demonstrations. Furthermore, research findings suggest not only that learning is enhanced by visual displays, but also that students prefer teachers who make use of objects and events as is done during a demonstration.

WAYS DEMONSTRATIONS CAN BE USED

A wide range of objectives can be achieved using demonstrations. Some of the ways that demonstrations can be used to do this, along with examples of each, are:

1. To show methods or techniques

Focus a microscope.
Use universal indicator paper to find the pH of a solution.
Correct an ammeter in a circuit.

2. To display objects or specimens

Rocks and minerals.
Leaves.
Parts of a television set.

3. To demonstrate phenomena

Optical illusions.
Formation of a cloud in a large flask.
Effect of exercise on rate of breathing and heart-
beat.

4. To verify facts and principles

Freezing point of water is 0°C.
Water expands when it freezes.
The boiling point of water in an opened con-
tainer is affected by air pressure.

5. To show applications

Use of a hygrometer to test the liquid in the
battery or cooling system of a car.
Operation of a light meter on a camera.
Effects of fertilizers on plant growth.

6. To solve problems

Does a piece of steel expand more or less than a
piece of copper when they are each heated
the same amount?
How will the direction of growth be affected when grass seedlings are placed for
twenty-four hours on a rotating surface?
How can sugar be separated from white sand?

7. To identify problems for further investigation

Should hot or cold water be used when making
ice cubes in a refrigerator?
Is the way people clap their hands (right thumb
over left thumb or vice versa) related to right
and left handedness?
Should seeds be positioned in any certain direction when they are planted?

CHARACTERISTICS OF A GOOD DEMONSTRATION

Good demonstrations have several characteristics in common. The following criteria, based on these characteristics, can be used in designing and
carrying out effective demonstrations.

1. The Objectives to be Achieved by the Demonstration Should Be Clearly Identified

Although it is not always necessary, or even desirable, to communicate
these objects to students at the beginning of the demonstration, the
teacher should know in advance what is to be gained by using it. Advantage should also be taken of unexpected results and student questions.

2. The Demonstration Should Be Easily Seen by Everyone in the Room

The apparatus can be placed on a tall table, and lights adjusted so
that visibility is increased. Some equipment is made extra large for demonstration purposes. Many demonstrations, such as the one using iron
filings to show the magnetic field around a magnet, can be performed on

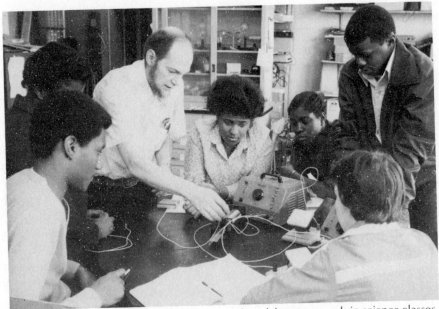

Demonstrations are an excellent way to introduce laboratory work in science classes.

an overhead projector and the results cast on a large screen. The Tested Overhead Projection Series (TOPS) of chemistry demonstrations are done in specially designed containers on the stage of a vertical overhead projector. By using this equipment, a demonstration can be effectively presented in a large room to a hundred or more students at one time.

3. The Equipment Should Be as Simple as Possible

Complicated equipment can easily obscure what is being shown. The pitch of sound, for example, may be demonstrated more effectively in many situations with a set of tuning forks than with a complicated electronic signal generator. The use of common household devices, such as egg beaters and tin cans, adds interest and shows the relevance of science to common events.

4. The Demonstration Should Work

Although demonstrations that do not work often can be used as springboards for interesting discussions and investigations, most of the demonstrations performed by the science teacher should work as planned. Otherwise, students will get the impression that Ohm's Law, photosynthesis, and acid-base reactions are products of science that occur in some capricious manner.

The best way to insure that the demonstration works properly is to try it out before presenting it in class. By doing so, the science teacher can make sure the needed equipment and supplies are available and everything is in working order. A rehearsal also allows the teacher to check for potential hazards and to take appropriate safety precautions. If an accident does occur, an important factor in establishing negligence and liability may be whether or not the demonstration was tried before it was used with students.

5. Adequate Time Should Be Allowed so the Benefits of the Demonstration Can Be Fully Utilized

Did the students see the things or events they were supposed to observe? Do they understand what they saw? Do they comprehend the ideas that were illustrated by the demonstration? If the demonstration failed to work exactly as planned, can they suggest hypotheses to explain what went wrong? Can they design experiments to test these hypotheses?

The actual amount of time devoted to discussion and questioning will depend on the complexity of the demonstration and the nature of the results obtained. Many "quickies," such as floating an uncooked egg in a beaker of water or letting sunlight strike a prism, can be used to get student attention and to pose questions for later consideration. The overuse of involved demonstrations that require a class period or more have the same disadvantage as other teaching strategies that fail to recognize the short attention span of many secondary school students.

6. A Variety of Approaches Should Be Used in Presenting Demonstrations

The teacher talking and doing is only one of many ways a demonstration can be performed. The silent demonstration, for example, can provide an interesting change of pace. Students are told to observe as much as possible while the teacher, without comments, pumps the air from bell jars containing a balloon with an open mouth, a partially inflated balloon, and a fresh marshmallow. The silence, besides being enjoyable to a tired science teacher at the end of the day, adds interest and increases the dramatic effect of the marshmallow swelling to the size of a softball. At the completion of the demonstration, students can be asked to discuss orally or describe in writing what they saw and why they think it happened.

Students like to perform demonstrations themselves, and this approach has the advantage of getting them more involved. Not only do the students benefit from planning, collecting materials, trying out the demonstration, and then presenting it, but this approach also can save valuable time for the teacher.

ADVANTAGES AND LIMITATIONS

Demonstrations possess many advantages as a teaching strategy. Chief among these is that demonstrations, like laboratory work, allow students to observe real objects and events. Demonstrations, in contrast to laboratory work, are usually more economical of both teacher and student time. Demonstrations, like the one shown in Figure 5.2, also require less equipment and supplies. In some cases, the equipment or materials used in the display of a concept or principle involve safety hazards; thus,

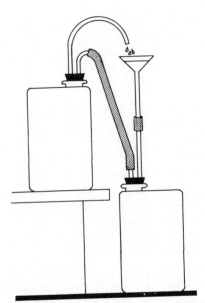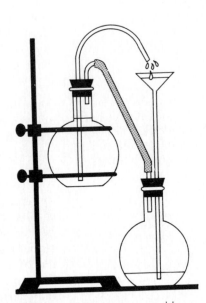

FIGURE 5.2 Demonstrations can be used to stimulate students, pose problems, evaluate understanding of scientific principles, and in many other ways. For example, when a small amount of water is poured into the funnel in the apparatus on the left, water flows out of the top most tube and continues to do so for some time. Is the water flowing uphill? The glass apparatus on the right, which is assembled the same way as the one on the left, should be helpful in figuring out what is happening.

demonstrations can be used to show things that might be too dangerous for students to investigate individually.

Class control is usually easier to maintain during a demonstration than during laboratory work or other activities where students are working more independently. This is especially true during the first few weeks of a course when classroom routines have not yet been fully established.

As in the case of other teaching strategies, the demonstration also has its limitations. In addition to those already mentioned, such as the time required for preparation and execution, demonstrations have several drawbacks when compared with laboratory investigations. Students are forced mainly to observe, and participation is limited to mental activities. Just as watching a group of acrobats walk on their hands does not mean you can do it, many objectives, both at the lower and higher levels of cognition, can best be achieved by students having "hands-on" experiences. Seeing someone else do it or explain it is not enough.

Demonstrations, when improperly used or "overdone," can give students the impression that science is "slick," that there are magical qualities involved, and that science is best described by a "gee-whiz." Science often involves spending large amounts of time in planning, sometimes doing messy and tedious work, and having failures as well as successes. It is important that students in secondary schools somehow see this side of science as well as its long list of accomplishments.

Inquiry Techniques

The art of good teaching is assisting discovery. This, of course, suggests that teachers should help students learn for themselves. During recent years many educators have advocated "discovery learning" and the "inductive approach." Several inquiry teaching techniques and programs have been developed to teach science using this approach.

THE SOCRATIC METHOD

I use the Socratic method here. I ask a question—you answer it. I ask another question—you answer it. Now you may think you have sufficiently answered the question but you are suffering a delusion. You will never completely answer it. (Law professor's remarks paraphrased from the movie *Paper Chase*.)[5]

The roots of many modern-day inquiry techniques are found in Plato in descriptions of his teacher Socrates. The Socratic method involves using a long line of questions and testing them with alternative, conflicting possibilities. Socrates taught both youth and adults using this method but was careful not to expect too much from younger learners. On the other hand, he drew experiences from older, wiser learners upon which these adults could build more knowledge.

The following account depicts Socrates raising a mathematical issue with a boy:

Tell me, boy, is not this a square of four feet which I have drawn?

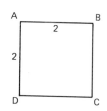

Boy: *Yes.*

Socrates: *And now I add another square equal to the former one?*

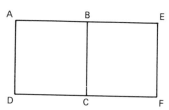

Boy: *Yes.*

Socrates: *And a third, which is equal to either of them?*

---

[5] Glenn McGlathery, "Analyzing the Questioning Behaviors of Science Teachers," in *What Research Says to the Science Teacher*, Vol. I (Mary Budd Rowe, ed.), NSTA, 1978.

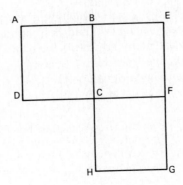

Boy: Yes.

Socrates: *Suppose that we fill up the vacant corner?*

Boy: *Very good.*

Socrates: *Here, then, there are four equal spaces?*

Boy: Yes.

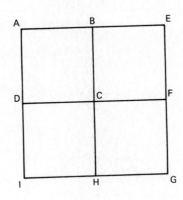

Socrates: *And how many times larger is this space [AEGI] than this other [ABCD]?*

Boy: *Four times.*

Socrates: *But we wanted one only twice as large, as you will remember.*

Boy: *True.*

Socrates: *Now, does not this line, reaching from corner to corner, bisect each of these spaces [DB, BF, FH, HD]?*

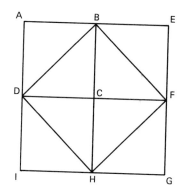

Boy: Yes.

Socrates: *And are there not here four equal lines which contain this space? [DB = BF = FH = HD; they contain space DBFH.]*

Boy: *There are.*

Socrates: *Look and see how much this space is.*

Boy: *I do not understand.*

Socrates: *Has not each interior [line] cut off half of the four spaces?*

Boy: *Yes.*

Socrates: *And how many such spaces are there in this section [DBFH]?*

Boy: *Four.*

Socrates: *And how many in this [ABCD]?*

Boy: *Two.*

Socrates: *And four is how many times two?*

Boy: *Twice [that is, DBFH is twice as big as ABCD].*

Socrates: *So that this space [DBFH] is of how many feet?*

Boy: *Of eight feet.*

Socrates: *And from what line do you get this figure?*

Boy: *From this [DB].*

Socrates: *That is, from the line which extends from corner to corner of the figure of four feet?*

Boy: *Yes.*

Source: *From* The Dialogues of Plato: The Meno, *translated by Benjamin Jowett (4th ed., 1953), Vol. 1, pp. 93–98. Reprinted by permission of Oxford University Press.)*

While this is not a typical Socratic dialogue, it does demonstrate in a simple way how one can be taught a generalization or concept. It also demonstrates Socrates' care in considering the boy's prior knowledge and what he was capable of learning. In more typical dialogues, Socrates often dealt with moral issues instead of mathematics, and with adults he often chose to motivate them by using increasingly perplexing questions. An additional point of interest is that Socrates used others as a source of information and authority instead of himself. In trying to make a point, he provided opportunitites for others to summarize what they knew or had learned, hence allowing them to formulate their own conclusions.

THE SET INDUCTION TECHNIQUE

As was mentioned in Chapter 3, learning theorist David Ausubel has suggested that students learn science based on what they already know. New material presented to students, he claims, is subsummed by formerly held concepts. Robert Schuck has proposed a teaching method called set induction which incorporates the ideas of Ausubel. Using set induction, the teacher reviews with students an "old" concept that it is likely they already understand. Then the teacher proceeds to help the student discover a "new" concept, similar to but usually more sophisticated than the first. Schuck[6] used as an example a familiar concept, "how milk is produced," to illustrate how students can be helped to discover more efficiently a new concept, "photosynthesis." In this situation, the idea that milk comes from cows, which take in grass and water and produce milk and manure, helps the student establish a "set." The set, or predisposition to think in similar terms, allows students to discover more readily the idea that plants take in carbon dioxide, water, and minerals and produce sugar and oxygen. The two processes are parallel in some ways, and, therefore, by first understanding how cows make milk, one can more easily learn how food is made in green plants. Once the students "discover" the basic concept of photosynthesis, the teacher can go in other directions, adding more specific information as it is appropriate. The main advantage of this method is that the teacher, by refamiliarizing the students with something they are capable of understanding, helps them discover *for themselves* a new, important concept. Most learning theorists agree that once students understand a major concept they are able to organize ensuing facts into more meaningful relationships.

Figure 5.3 illustrates how the organization of a book can be used to help students understand the importance of cells as fundamental units of life. By reviewing this organization and demonstrating that missing words in a sentence lead to nonsense fragments, the teacher can help students understand that the basic unit of structure in life is the cell. Like words in a sentence, essential parts of the cell must be present in order for the cell to function properly. When key cell parts are removed, the cell will die.

---

[6] Robert F. Schuck, "Set Induction as an Instructional Strategy for Science Educators," *The Science Teacher*, 37,5(1970): 63–65.

Some books contain all of the essential information on a given subject.	Each human being is a unique combination of inherited and acquired characteristics.
↓	↓
In order to convey ideas more clearly the book is arranged by chapters, each presenting information on a specific topic.	In order to survive each human must have systems for nutritional procurement, gas exchange, transport and regulation.
↓	↓
Chapters are organized into paragraphs, each one containing a main idea or major concept.	Within each system are specialized organs and tissues capable of functioning together as a unit.
↓	↓
The basic unit of the paragraph is the sentence. If certain words are removed from a sentence the thought becomes nonsensical. (Example: Many birds migrate south in the winter. Remove the word "migrate" and the sentence does not have a complete thought.)	All living matter is composed of small building blocks called cells. If certain parts of the cell are removed this basic unit can no longer function. (Example: Removal of the nucleus from most cells leads to disfunction and eventual death of that cell.)

FIGURE 5.3 An example of the set induction technique in helping students discover the role of cells in the human body.

INVITATIONS TO ENQUIRY

Invitations to Enquiry was developed by Joseph Schwab during the early 1960s at the University of Chicago. His *Invitations* pose situations where students are asked to identify problems, design experiments, or, in more advanced ones, identify relationships in existing data. These *Invitations* can be "made up" by the teacher or drawn from those Schwab has carefully prepared.

The *Invitations* are designed to show students how knowledge is obtained by the interpretation of data. Through this means, students learn that the search for data proceeds on the basis of assumptions and concepts that change as knowledge increases. Teachers do not *tell* this to students but rather allow them to experience the inquiry process through questioning, group discussion, and debate. The following invitation developed by Schwab, though a simple one, shows how a teacher can initiate discussions that can lead to other, more difficult questions. Comments to teachers are contained in brackets and demonstrate how this problem relates to scientific thinking.

TO THE STUDENT: You may already know that animals and plants are made of one or more very small living units called cells. You may also know that most kinds of cells contain a still smaller part called the nucleus. A biologist wanted to know whether the nucleus of cells is necessary for life, or whether cells could live without a nucleus. He found a way to break cells into two pieces so that one piece contained the nucleus and the other piece did not. He performed this experiment on a number of different kinds of cells.

Suppose the results of this experiment were that all the cell pieces without the nuclei died. All the cell pieces that had nuclei soon reformed into smaller but normal-looking cells, grew then to their former size, and in all other ways continued to behave exactly as do cells that have not been broken. What interpretation would you make of this experiment and its results?

[The evidence, as stated, will probably impel most of the students to conclude that the nucleus is necessary for the continued normal life of the cell. Even in this highly idealized Invitation, however, in which all the data are artificially perfect, there are, of course, doubts that could be raised and almost endless qualifications that could be added to the interpretations to make it "safer." We may suspect, for example, that the nucleus is necessary only for the repair of injury—hence the death of the non-nucleated fragments. Or, ignoring that, we may doubt whether what was found to hold for the kinds of cells tested necessarily holds for all cells. Or we could take pains to point out that the conclusions should be restricted to cells that normally have nuclei, and so on.

[Doubts such as these lurk behind almost all the general statements our textbooks ordinarily assert to be scientific "truths." Nevertheless, doubt can be cast on almost any statement that goes beyond the immediate and particular (such as, "That *one* automobile in front of *this* house is black in *this* light to *my* eye.") Hence it is not the business of science to be infinitely cautious as a condition for being "right." Overcaution is just as much a handicap to the growth of dependable knowledge as reckless overgeneralization. Scientific knowledge increases and becomes more dependable only as we do draw conclusions, interpret our data, and go on to further problems that these interpretations in turn suggest—to further experiments designed to solve these new problems, to new data, and to new interpretations of the whole body of data. The life blood of science is not indefinite caution and indecisiveness, but ongoing enquiry, enquiry that refines earlier conclusions, makes them more precise, and extends their scope. Perhaps that is why scientific work is called research.

[The present Invitation and those following it develop along similar lines. Later Invitations will successively exemplify one and then another of the common sources of error in interpreting experimental data, and different ways of refining and expanding scientific knowledge. Hence, for the moment, it is desirable that the students be permitted to have confidence in the unqualified conclusion to which the idealized data of this Invitation will probably lead them—that the nucleus *is* necessary to the continued life of a cell. Indeed, if some students have a habit of overcaution instilled into them, it might be desirable to point out some of the ideas we have stated.][7]

The following example is an Invitation dealing with the process of measuring. It allows students to discuss the concept of error and to discover the many natural ways error is introduced during scientific investigation. Here, too, Schwab includes comments (found in brackets) that are helpful to teachers.

SUBJECT: MEASUREMENT IN GENERAL TOPIC: SYSTEMATIC AND RANDOM ERROR **INVITATION**

[This Invitation introduces the concept of experimental error. It can be omitted if your regular laboratory projects cover the following points:

1. Experimental error is inevitable; it can be reduced but not eliminated.

2. Since error is inevitable, data are practically always equivocal. That is, the defensible interpretation is almost always "cleaner" than the data, for what we are reluctant to include in our interpretation we can often ascribe to experimental error.

3. One investigator's "experimental error" may be food for the next investigator's research. That is, the variation in the data may not have been due entirely to experimental error. The variation may indicate a factor overlooked in the design of the experiment.]

TO THE STUDENT: (a) During the course of a week, four students made five measurements each of a metal bar that was kept in the laboratory. They were led to believe that they were measuring a different bar each time. The record of their measurements (in millimeters) is shown in Table 5.

TABLE 5.1

Measurement	Student 1	Student 2	Student 3	Student 4
1	500.0	500.0	499.8	500.1
2	499.9	500.0	499.9	500.1
3	500.0	500.0	500.1	500.2
4	500.1	500.0	500.2	500.3
5	500.2	500.0	500.2	500.3

[7] Reprinted by permission of John Wiley & Sons, Inc. Mayer, William V., editor, *Biology Teacher's Handbook*, Third Edition, Biological Sciences Curriculum Study. Copyright © 1978, John Wiley & Sons, Inc.

Notice the difference between the measurements reported by Student 2 and those reported by Students 1, 3, and 4. How would you describe the difference? What do you think explains it?

[The difference between the report of Student 2 and the others lies in the uniformity of Student 2's measurements. Some of your students—those least experienced in the laboratory—may explain this as due to the greater accuracy of Student 2. The more sophisticated of your students may suggest the contrary—that Student 2 let a first measurement influence the reading of later measurements, or even that the student was cheating in an extremely silly way. You can then appeal to their own experience to indicate that the first interpretation is the *less* likely of the two—that uniformity is *not* characteristic of actual measurements and is always suspect. This point should end by introducing the term "experimental error," meaning unavoidable inaccuracy and inconsistency of measurement.]

TO THE STUDENT: (b) Now compare the measurements reported by student 4 with the other reports. What overall difference is there? How would you explain this difference? Hint: Think of the measurement you should obtain if you read the right end of the measuring stick while standing at its left end, with the stick on top of the measured bar. Then think of what the measurements might seem if you stood in line with the right end of the measuring stick.

[Student 4's measurements are uniformly higher than most. The hint is intended to lead the student to see that conditions of measurement may vary from one investigator to another and thus lead to different data. You may wish to have these variations actually experienced. If so, obtain a measuring stick and have one student stand well to the left, another well to the right, while each estimates some measurement.
[If you feel your class is ready for it, you can drive the idea of experimental error home by clarifying the difference between *random* error and *systematic* error. Student 4 represents a case of systematic error. The entire group of measurements, irrespective of the students making each measurement, would come close to exemplifying random error. The most important reason for making the distinction between random error and systematic error is that our common ways of making use of numerous measurements (by calculating their arithmetic mean, their mode, or their median, for example) are ways of correcting random error. We have no readily available way of detecting or correcting systematic error except by watching our habits. Hence systematic error is potentially a source of danger, whereas a reasonable amount of random error is not.]

TO THE STUDENT: (c) Suppose a later experiment required an estimate of the length of the bar to be used in *many* arithmetic calculations. In that case, what estimate would you choose as being "good" enough and also convenient?

If the future experiment required the best estimate from these data of the length of the bar, what number would you choose to use, and how would you go about calculating it?

[The two questions are put together so that the students will have a chance to contrast the idea of a "convenient" measure with the idea of a "best" measure. The most convenient measure would, of course, be 500.0. One "best" estimate, making no further allowances for differences between early and later measurements and measurements done by different students, would be a simple arithmetic mean, an average. This is computed, of course, by adding all the measures and dividing by the number of measurements.]

TO THE STUDENT: (d) What could we do to make this "best" estimate even more reliable?

[The answer, of course, is to secure more measurements.]

TO THE STUDENT: (e) There are two ways to secure additional measurements. One would be to have the same students do the job. Another would be to call on additional students to contribute. What kind of error, systematic or random, would be reduced more by the second method than by the first?

[Method 2 would reduce the overall systematic error more than would Method 1, if you are lucky or wise in your selection of students.
[Thus far, we have treated the problem of measurement only from the viewpoint of error introduced by the investigator. In the remaining portion of this Invitation, we deal with error introduced by unnoticed changes in the thing being measured. This is, of course, one of the kinds of problems to be met in controlling an experiment.]

TO THE STUDENT: (f) Now inspect each column of measurements from the top down. What trend is noticeable? What—besides a new sort of systematic error—might explain this trend? *Hint:* Remember that the measurements were made during the course of a week. Remember, too, that the bar being measured was made of metal, and that metals are subject to changes due to environmental factors.

[There is a clearly noticeable trend (ignoring Student 2) toward larger measurements on the later days. The second hint is intended to turn the student's attention to the possibility that the bar actually became longer as the days grew warmer. You will probably need to guide the students into seeing and understanding this possibility.
[In actuality, no readily available metal has a coefficient of expansion as great as is indicated by our fictitious measurements.]

TO THE STUDENT: (g) Suppose that the trend just discussed had been overlooked or treated as experimental error. Further, suppose that the measurements were used to support a certain theory according to which the rod ought to be nearer 500.1 mm long than to 500.0. Unless this experiment were repeated by others at different times and places, what might happen to the field of study that defended this theory?

[It might well have adopted the theory in question. Then, only when later inconsistencies appeared would the theory have been called into question. Only then might the experiment have been repeated by someone and the error discovered.

[This exemplifies the point made in the introduction to this Invitation— that what one investigator ascribes to experimental error may become the basis, through research, of other and more useful investigations.]

TO THE STUDENT: (h) In view of your answers to (e) and (g), explain what is meant by saying that science is a social enterprise.

[The idea here is that for some problems many heads are better than one—that science depends on debates and differences, on alternative approaches to problems.

[By now, your students are, hopefully, on the way to regarding data as only approximations of what is, and to seeing that what is is ever elusive, although we may refine our attempts to define it more accurately.][8]

Important things teachers should do when using *Invitations to Enquiry* include:

- Select or construct an Invitation that is relevant to the current topic being studied. The Invitation, however, should allow students to examine problems in a divergent manner. Therefore, students should be allowed to explore facets of the problem that may lead to other topics and take them in various directions.
- Start with simple Invitations; after students become familiar with what is expected of them, more sophisticated Invitations can be used.
- Prepare by carefully studying the Invitation selected. Note whether it will require graphs on the chalkboard, overhead transparencies, or duplicated materials for the students.
- The aim of an Invitation is to allow *students* to use *their* skills in generating information and solving problems. Teachers should, therefore, practice restraint in giving students answers. Rather, the teacher's role

---

[8] Reprinted by permission of John Wiley & Sons, Inc. Mayer, William V., editor, *Biology Teacher's Handbook,* Third Edition, Biological Sciences Curriculum Study, Copyright © John Wiley & Sons, Inc., 1978.

is to ask good questions and see to it that the discussion proceeds in a productive direction.

- In planning Invitations, a teacher should formulate a list of potential questions that may be appropriate to ask at opportune times during the activity. If an already developed Invitation is used, the accompanying notes for teachers should be studied. Questions, possible student reactions, and other ideas worth discussing should be listed in outline form and used by the teacher in allocating appropriate amounts of class time for each Invitation.

- While a teacher should be flexible and should allow students freedom to explore as many rational viewpoints as possible, there should be a general idea of what students should accomplish by the end of the activity.

In many cases, an Invitation can serve as a means of stimulating further laboratory work, small-group activities, or independent study, including homework assignments. In other cases, Invitations can serve as a vehicle for summarizing a unit of study and encouraging students to draw conclusions from available data. In either event, the teacher should plan in advance how an Invitation will fit into the weekly or unit instructional plan and how it will be used to help students accomplish the educational objectives of a particular science program.

Several of the Invitations that have been developed by Schwab are shown in Figure 5.4. The primary skills being addressed in each Invitation are listed in the right hand column. While these have been primarily developed for biology classes, others can be developed by biology teachers as well as by teachers in other areas of science. As stressed earlier, an Invitation can consist of a simple situation or set of questions, or it can include a well-developed set of research data requiring more sophisticated analyses.

INQUIRY FILMLOOPS AND FILMS

Inquiry materials also have been developed on film which can be presented to the students using either 8mm or 16mm projectors. The material for 8mm projectors is usually packaged in a cartridge, which makes loading and unloading as easy as placing a cassette in a tape recorder. These cartridges are often called filmloops, since the film is in the form of a loop and thus does not need to be rewound. Although the older filmloops were silent, most of the newer ones have sound.

INQUIRY FILMLOOPS

The Biological Science Curriculum Study (BSCS) developed a series of filmloops, as have other film producers, that actively involve students in the process of inquiry while they learn about specific aspects of science. The teacher shows segments of a film, stops the projector at designated points, and asks students questions about what they have just seen. As

INVITATIONS TO ENQUIRY, GROUP ONE

SIMPLE ENQUIRY: *THE ROLE AND NATURE OF GENERAL
KNOWLEDGE, DATA, EXPERIMENT, CONTROL,
HYPOTHESIS, AND PROBLEM IN SCIENTIFIC
INVESTIGATION*

INVITATION	SUBJECT	TOPIC
1	The cell nucleus	Interpretation of simple data
2	The cell nucleus	Interpretation of variable data
3	Seed germination	Misinterpretation of data
4	Plant physiology	Interpretation of complex data
INTERIM SUMMARY ONE: KNOWLEDGE AND DATA		
5	Measurement in general	Systematic and random error
6	Plant nutrition	Planning of experiment
7	Plant nutrition	Control of experiment
8	Predator-prey; natural populations	"Second-best" data
9	Population growth	The problem of sampling
10	Environment and disease	The idea of hypothesis
11	Light and plant growth	Construction of hypotheses
12	Vitamin deficiency	"If . . . , then . . ."analysis
13	Natural selection	Practice in hypothesis
INTERIM SUMMARY TWO: THE ROLE OF HYPOTHESIS		
14	Auxins and plant movement	Hypothesis; interpretation of abnormality
15	Neurohormones of the heart	Origin of scientific problems
16	Discovery of penicillin	Accident in enquiry
16A	Discovery of anaphylaxis	Accident in enquiry

FIGURE 5.4   A list of invitations to enquiry. (*Source:* Reprinted by permission
of John Wiley & Sons, Inc. Mayer, William V., editor, *Biology Teacher's
Handbook,* Third Edition, Biological Sciences Curriculum Study. Copyright
© John Wiley & Sons, Inc., 1978.)

additional segments of the film are shown and the dialogue continues, the
teacher helps students organize the factual information in the film. As
with *Invitations to Enquiry,* students are encouraged to seek answers on
their own.

One of the BSCS single-topic inquiry entitled "Social Behavior in
Chickens," is an excellent example of this type of film. Students are
shown several scenes showing chickens interacting. The first scene shows
five chickens of differing wing colors feeding at the same tray. The film is

stopped, and students are asked to tell what they saw. The teacher encourages as many observations as possible, but at this point does not add to those mentioned. Some of the observations are:

- "One chicken pecked another one."
- "The chicken that was pecked moved away from the tray."
- "When the chicken was pecked the others stopped briefly and shifted their positions."

Students will often volunteer statements that either are erroneous or go beyond objective observation. Statements like "The roosters started to fight" or "The red chicken got mad at the blue chicken" lack correctness and objectivity. The chickens in this scene are hens, not roosters. Their inclination to "fight" or "get mad" are inferences that go beyond the information at hand. In such cases, the teacher should encourage students to clarify their own statements and to disagree with the statements by other students that they find unacceptable. The teacher remains in the background as much as possible while students are discovering major ideas in the film. At the end, the teacher can clarify or summarize.

During ensuing scenes from this film, the five female chickens are placed in cages, two at a time, and are allowed to interact. After each encounter, the projector is stopped and students are asked to record their observations. Some of the observed behaviors include:

Pecking

Erect posture, tail feathers, and head held high

Crouching, head held low

Wing-flapping

Scratching

Freezing (remaining motionless)

Fighting

Puffing of neck feathers and wings

Mounting (assuming the male position, as during copulation)

After each of the ten possible pairings of chickens has been viewed students are asked to determine the dominant and submissive chicken in each of the combinations. Students are then asked to design ways to report his information. Figure 5.5 illustrates how a "dominant-submissive" chart can be made. After further dialogue, students may discover that a matrix is more useful. Figure 5.6 shows how a 5 × 5 matrix can be constructed that allows the viewer to count quickly the number of times each bird was dominant.

By viewing and discussing the film, students are able to discover that a social hierarchy or "pecking order" exists among these birds. In discussing this hierarchy, factors such as size, health, age, hormone levels, sex, past experience, and genetics can be examined in light of how they may affect an individual's position in a social group. Another area that can be examined is the extent to which this arrangement offers advantages and disadvantages to individual members and the society as a whole. During this discussion students will often speculate about human societies and extrapolate the findings of this experiment to human behavior.

It is also possible to discuss with students the experimental design used in this investigation. "Do you think there are limitations in the experiment?" "Do you think that the color painted on the wings influenced the behavior of the chickens?" "Was the order in which the chickens were paired an influencing factor?" These are examples of additional questions that can be explored using this film.

Decide, if you can, the dominant and submissive chicken in each of the pairings that you saw. (For help, review your notes and the observations recorded on pages 32 code A through 36 code B.) Make a chart showing the dominant and submissive chicken in each encounter.

There are several ways in which a "dominant-submissive" chart may be made. Perhaps the simplest is the one shown below.

Encounter	Dominant	Submissive
Red × Purple	Red	Purple
Yellow × Blue	Yellow	Blue
Purple × Blue	Purple	Blue
Yellow × Purple	Yellow	Purple
Red × White	Red	White
Yellow × White	Yellow	White
Blue × White	White	Blue
Red × Blue	Red	Blue
Purple × White	White	Purple
Yellow × Red	Red	Yellow

FIGURE 5.5 An example of a chart that can be used to record dominance and submissiveness. (*Source:* Reprinted by permission of the authors from "Social Behavior in Chickens: A Self-Instructional Guide to Independent Inquiry," Biological Sciences Curriculum Study, 1972, p. 28.)

This chart, although simple to construct, may not be as useful in retrieving data as are some other kinds of charts. Perhaps you organized your data in a more concise way. For example:

The letter in the square indicates the dominant bird.

	Y	R	P	B	W		
Y		R	Y	Y	Y	4	Red
R			R	R	R	3	Yellow
P				P	W	2	White
B					W	1	Purple
W						0	Blue

Or Red chicken dominant over *yellow, white, purple,* and *blue.*
   Yellow chicken dominant over *white, purple,* and *blue.*
   White chicken dominant over *purple and blue.*
   Purple chicken dominant over *blue.*
   (Blue never dominant.*)*

FIGURE 5.6 An example of a matrix showing which chicken was dominant in each encounter between the chickens. (*Source:* Reprinted by permission of the authors from "Social Behavior in Chickens: A Self-Instructional Guide to Independent Inquiry," Biological Sciences Curriculum Study, 1972, p. 28.)

A later edition of "Social Behavior in Chickens" has been designed to serve as a self-instructional guide to inquiry. Using this format, students can independently view the film and answer questions on their own. A guidebook provides students with directions and discussions of what they have viewed in each section of the film. The following was taken from the self-instruction guide for "Social Behavior in Chickens":

The study of social behavior in chickens has produced much information concerning the phenomenon of dominance. It has shed light on questions asked by psychologists, sociologists, and biologists and has proved helpful in solving practical problems of poultry husbandry.

Peck order among chickens was first described by T. Schjelderup-Ebbe, a Norwegian psychologist, who found that one hen usually dominated the others in a flock. It would peck any other hen without being pecked in return. The hen just below it in the social order pecked all but the top hen. The social positions of the remainder of the flock were arranged in descending order, with a hen at the bottom that was pecked by all the others but would not peck any of them. Cocks have their own peck order, separate from that of hens. As a result, there are usually two hierarchies in a breeding flock—one for each sex.

If hens are raised in isolation and are placed in a pen, each takes on one opponent at a time, engaging in encounters with all the others until a peck order has been established for the entire flock. Some encounters may be very short because some chickens may lack aggressiveness, fighting skill, or strength. After the peck order has been determined, encounters decline in frequency as members of the group establish relationships to the others. Eventually a subtle raising or lowering of the head may be enough to signify dominance or submission. The group then becomes comparatively peaceful; as a result, fewer individuals are hurt in fighting, and energy is conserved within the flock.

In groups of young chickens, peck orders may be established among females when they are only ten weeks old. Males may establish a peck order even earlier.

Once the social order has been established in a flock, a strange bird must fight each member to establish its status. Only an aggressive outsider can gain a respectable social position under these circumstances.

There are advantages for the dominant chicken in a peck order, including privileged feeding, roost position, and choice of nest boxes. High ranking hens feed regularly during the day and crowd together on the roosts, gaining warmth at night. Lower ranking birds must feed either in the morning or in the evening, while the dominant members of the group are roosting. At night the low ranking birds remain on the outer edges of the roosting group.

Among other things, peck order can be correlated with sexual behavior. In groups of young chickens, the lower ranking members take longer to reach sexual maturity than those higher in the social order. Males at the top of the peck order win out over their inferiors when competing for mates. Dominant males are the most successful in obtaining mates, while those lowest in the group are the least successful. The dominant males also father the most offspring, while the low ranking cocks may fail to fertilize any eggs at all. Likewise, rank in the peck order of a group of hens affects their sexual activity. The hens at the top of the group are comparatively unreceptive to males and less likely to be successful in mating than lower ranking group members (presumably because they do not often assume the submissive crouching posture necessary for mating).

Sex hormones seem to control the aggressiveness of chickens. If hens are given injections of the male sex hormone, they fight their way up the social order and eventually assume more dominant positions. Female sex hormone injections cause individuals to become more submissive.

The film *Social Behavior in Chickens* provides an opportunity to observe and gather data on behavior within a flock of chickens, leading to recognition that a social hierarchy exists in the group. You should realize that because social hierarchy accounts for organization within a group, the relationships involved are much more significant than a simple "peck order" chart might indicate.[9]

INQUIRY FILMS.   While it is possible to stop any films for discussion, some films are made especially to be used this way. One such film, *Cosmic Zoom*,[10] begins with a boy in a boat. As the camera moves closer and closer, it depicts a fly on his hand, then detailed structures of the fly, and finally smaller and smaller units of life. The sound accompanying the movie contains music but no words. As the levels of organization become smaller, cells, cell organelles, molecules, and finally sketches of atoms are shown. At this point, the viewer has journeyed from a boy in a boat to atoms comprised of nuclei and electrons. The film then changes directions and moves from atoms to molecules and from molecules to cells. It gradually ends up back where everything began—with the boy in the boat. Then the viewer is taken on a different journey, one through space. As things become larger, the lake is seen, the world is viewed, our sun and other planets are depicted, and, finally, other solar systems are intimated along with visions of the entire galaxy. The film ends with a gradual reduction back to the boy paddling the boat.

This film is an example of how a strong stimulus can be used to initiate thinking in science. After showing the film, the teacher may choose to say nothing and wait for student reactions, or the teacher can ask an open question. "What do you think was the main point of the movie?" "How did you feel as you watched the movie?" Questions such as these can be followed by more specific questions. "What did the film show after the scene of the earth floating in space?" Using such a method allows students to discover for themselves the meaning of science and how different topics interrelate.

Another popular film designed for inquiry teaching is *The Tragedy of the Commons*.[11] This film is based on ideas presented by Garrett Hardin in an article by the same name that was published in *Science*. The film opens with a scene of an uncrowded pasture in eighteenth-century England where a system of common land, "the commons," was used by herdsmen. Gradually, each herdsman adds to his herd, and by the end of

---

[9] Reprinted by permission of the authors from "Social Behavior in Chickens: A Self-Instructional Guide to Independent Inquiry," Biological Sciences Curriculum Study, 1972, pp. 38–39.

[10] *Cosmic Zoom*, 8 minutes, Film Board of Canada, National Film Board of Canada, 1251 Avenue of the Americas, New York, N.Y. 10020, 1969.

[11] *The Tragedy of the Commons*, 1974, Education Programs Improvement Corporation, Boulder, Colorado, (distributed by BFA Educational Media, 2211 Michigan Avenue, P.O. Box 1795, Santa Monica, California 90406).

the first segment the commons is filled with cattle and the grass has been destroyed. At this point, a large question mark appears on the screen, and the teacher is directed to stop the film and turn on the room lights. Students are broken into small groups and given about five minutes to discuss their impressions of the film thus far. One spokesperson from each group is then given an opportunity to summarize briefly the major ideas of his or her group. An instructional guide accompanying the film suggests questions the teacher may wish to ask after the students have made their reports. As with the other inquiry techniques, the teacher is cautioned to avoid giving too much information. Most points the teacher wants to make initially will usually be covered by the student discussion.

This film contains four parts, each one dealing with issues associated with concepts presented in the first segment. The film is highly stimulating and guides students toward thinking about how fundamental concepts in ecology affect human conditions and values in modern-day societies. The last segment raises four powerful points:

1. Natural controls such as starvation and disease do exist for human populations.
2. Technological controls do exist for human populations.
3. The U.N. Declaration says families should control themselves by voluntary means.
4. It may be necessary to legislate family size.

As one can see, each of these points can serve as a springboard for further discussion and class activity.

While two examples have been singled out to describe how films can be used to foster inquiry, it should be mentioned that others similar to these do exist. In addition, most traditional films can be used in this manner. At appropriate points the film can be stopped, and both broad and specific questions asked. Using a film in this manner enhances the effectiveness of this medium and is yet another technique for teaching students via the inquiry method.

INQUIRY SLIDES

In addition to inquiry films and filmloops, sets of 35mm slides have been developed that emphasize an inquiry approach. Many of the inquiry slide programs commercially available include sound. One of the most widely used programs is a series of sound-slide sets developed by the Biological Sciences Curriculum Study and produced by Mankind, Incorporated. In this program, the slides are keyed to a narrative sound track recorded on both cassette tapes and LP records. The slides are packaged in Kodak Carousel trays which make them easy to store and to keep in the proper sequence. The slides can be presented by the teacher or automatically advanced by a synchronization device on the projector which is designed to detect an inaudible signal.

The role of the teacher using inquiry slides is the same as with films and filmloops. The slides are presented, and at predetermined points time is taken for questioning and student discussion. As many ideas as possible should be included in the discussion, and alternative solutions encouraged. The teacher should receive all responses graciously and without personal bias.

One of the BSCS inquiry slide programs is entitled *The New Genetics: Rights and Responsibilities.* [12] The excerpt below describes how the program is introduced and how the interest of students is encouraged.

(Slides 2-11) Part I emphasizes the individual—the hopes, the fears, the shame, the guilt, and the helplessness that often affect the family of a severely deformed or retarded child. It opens with a brief account of the effects of Tay-Sachs disease in one family. Tay-Sachs disease is perhaps the simplest, most straightforward of genetic diseases; it is inherited as a double recessive, and it is always fatal in the first few years of life. What makes Tay-Sachs disease especially tragic is that during the first six months the affected baby develops normally. It is only after this initial development period that the symptoms begin to appear. The child goes downhill very slowly, dying in stages over a period of two to three years. The family setting was chosen to focus the viewer's attention on the human drama rather than on the objective clinical aspects of the disease. (These are touched upon in Part II.)

The following excerpt illustrates how the tone of the program shifts to a more objective format between slides 16 and 40. This section reviews the general principles of Mendelian genetics and fundamental vocabulary terms that are used throughout the remainder of the program.

A brief history of ideas about inheritance, from ancient times until the mid-19th century, is introduced. The viewer is shown many of the ways that these ideas were applied and envisioned, from selective breeding of domestic animals and agricultural crops to Plato's dream of selectively breeding human beings for specific social stations. This informal understanding of inheritance served for many centuries, though its actual mechanism was not understood. Then came the work of Gregor Mendel. The Austrian monk's extensive, detailed observations of the inheritance of traits in pea plants, coupled with his

---

[12] *The New Genetics: Rights and Responsibilities,* 1974, Biological Sciences Curriculum Study, P.O. Box 930, Boulder, Colorado 80302.

acute deductions and interpretations, provided a tool for accurate predictions of the occurrence of specific traits. This section presents a few of Mendel's observations and interpretations, using only one trait for simplicity of discussion.

Mendel's work was not widely known, or perhaps its significance was not realized, until the 20th century. It was then found that his ideas could be generalized to other organisms, including man. Although not all human characteristics are inherited in a Mendelian fashion, many genetic diseases, especially metabolic disorders, are the result of one gene, or one pair of genes, and are inherited in accordance with Mendelian ratios.[13]

The transcript below, taken from the program guide of *The New Genetics: Rights and Responsibilities*,[14] demonstrates questions that can be asked to stimulate discussion. In the right hand column are important points or techniques the teacher may find helpful while leading discussion on the first forty-one slides.

Questions to stimulate discussions:	*Strategies and points for emphasis:*

PART ONE

STOP 1 –(OPTIONAL)–SLIDE 27

WATCH FOR THE WHITE SQUARE ON THE SLIDE IF YOU CHOOSE TO USE THIS OPTIONAL FIRST STOP. A SENSITIVE AND SOPHISTICATED AUDIENCE OR CLASS MAY NEED NO MORE STIMULUS THAN THE FIRST QUESTION BELOW (1.1) TO ELICIT DISCUSSION OF THE MAJOR IDEAS PRESENTED. ADDITIONAL QUESTIONS MAY BE USED IF NEEDED TO HELP CLARIFY IDEAS THAT ARE MISSED.

1.1. What were Mendel's observations? Suggest explanations for these observations.

Mendel observed that when he crossed true breeding end-flowered plants with side-flowered plants, the first generation offspring were always side-flowered. When these first-

[13] Reprinted by permission of the authors from Program Guide 1002, *The New Genetics: Rights and Responsibilities*, Biological Sciences Curriculum Study, 1974, p. 9.

[14] Reprinted by permission of the authors from Program Guide 1002, *The New Genetics: Rights and Responsibilities*, Biological Sciences Curriculum Study, 1975, pp. 17–20.

*Questions to stimulate
discussions:*

*Strategies and points for
emphasis:*

generation offspring were crossed among themselves, the second-generation offspring were of both types in a ratio of three side-flowered plants to one end-flowered plant. One explanation is that each plant has two "somethings" which determine the expression of flower position. Each parent contributes one of these "somethings" to its offspring. These "somethings" seem to come in two forms: one form is expressed whether one or two "somethings" of that form are present, the other form is expressed only when both "somethings" are of that form.
STUDENTS MAY WELL CALL THE "SOMETHINGS" GENES. THIS QUESTION SERVES AS AN OPPORTUNITY TO REVIEW THEIR KNOWLEDGE OF MENDELIAN GENETICS.

1.2 How is Tay-Sachs disease, discussed in the first few slides, inherited?

Tay-Sachs disease is inherited as a double recessive, that is, the presence of two genes for this trait is necessary for its expression. One gene is inherited from each parent. But the parents, having only one gene each for Tay-Sachs disease, are not affected.

STOP 2—(MAJOR DISCUSSION BREAK)—SLIDE 41

IF THIS IS THE FIRST, RATHER THAN THE SECOND STOP USED, THE IDEAS REVIEWED ABOVE SHOULD BE INCLUDED IN THIS DISCUSSION TO PROVIDE A REVIEW OF THE CONCEPTS OF MENDELIAN GENETICS.

2.1 Review the ideas presented about genetics.

At this point a review of the concepts and terminology introduced is essential for fullest understanding of the

*Questions to stimulate
discussions:*

*Strategies and points for
emphasis:*

rest of the program. The following factual information is most important:

—Genes occur in pairs.

—Each parent contributes one gene of each pair to each of his or her offspring.

—A gene may be dominant or recessive.

—A dominant gene is expressed in two instances: when both genes of the pair are dominant and when only one gene of the pair is dominant.

—A recessive gene is expressed *only* when both genes of the pair are recessive.

—Reproductive cells contain one gene of each pair—all other cells contain two genes of each pair.

AFTER SMALL-GROUP DISCUSSION AND GROUP INTERACTION, YOU MIGHT ASK THE CLASS TO LIST ON THE CHALKBOARD THE RULES OF INHERITANCE. THIS LIST CAN BE USED FOR REFERENCE THROUGHOUT THE REST OF THE PROGRAM. IF STUDENTS DO NOT INCLUDE ALL THE POINTS LISTED ABOVE, ASK QUESTIONS TO ELICIT THOSE RESPONSES. WHEN MISINFORMATION IS GIVEN, GIVE MEMBERS OF THE CLASS AN OPPORTUNITY TO CORRECT IT BY ASKING SUCH QUESTIONS AS: "DOES EVERYONE AGREE WITH THAT?" OR "ARE THERE ANY OTHER EXPLANATIONS FOR THAT?"

*Questions to stimulate
discussions:*

*Strategies and points for
emphasis:*

Other general points which are likely
to come out include the following:

—Some diseases can be inherited.
  Some inherited diseases are fatal;
  others are not. Research is going
  on to detect and eliminate genetic
  disease.

—Ideas about certain characteristics
  being inherited are very old and
  have been used by farmers and
  animal breeders for centuries.
  Human inheritance, too, has long
  been discussed.

2.2 List all the diseases that you
think are inherited.
(If response to this question is extremely limited, ask the audience to list all the *traits* that they
think are inherited in people.)

The extensiveness of group lists will
depend in large part on the experience of the viewer. Over 1600 inherited diseases and defects have been
detected. The inherited diseases and
defects listed below are ones which
have received coverage in mass
media or are common textbook
examples. High school students are
likely to report at least some of the
following:

—cleft lip and/or palate
—color-blindness
—cystic fibrosis
—diabetes
—dwarfism
—extra fingers and/or toes (polydactyly)
—giantism
—hemophilia
—mongolism (Down's syndrome)
—muscular dystrophy
—sickle-cell anemia

Adult audiences are likely to have

*Questions to stimulate
discussions:*

*Strategies and points for
emphasis:*

some familiarity with the following
inherited diseases:

—clubfoot

—Cooley's anemia

—deaf-mutism

—extra sex chromosomes (Klinefel-
ter's syndrome and others)

—galactosemia

—glaucoma

—Huntington's disease (Huntington's
chorea)

—missing sex chromosomes
(Turner's syndrome)

—open spine (spina bifida)

—pernicious anemia–

—PKU (phenylketonuria)

—small or pin head (microcephaly)

—Tay-Sachs disease

—water on the brain (hydrocephaly)

Part I of this program includes eighty slides (one carousel) and deals
with several additional issues related to inheritance of human diseases
and genetic counseling. Part II of this program includes an additional
eighty slides and develops further the topics presented in Part I.

A part of one program has been presented as an example of how
inquiry slides can be effectively used in the science classroom. In addition
to the many excellent commercially developed programs, teachers can
design their own. Slides taken on a field trip or vacation can be arranged
and shown to students, and questions can then be asked that will promote inquiry and discussion. As seen with the example presented here,
carefully selected pictures can serve as an excellent means for building on
the natural interests of students and thus promoting stimulating interaction in a science class.

FOLLOWUP
ACTIVITIES

There are many ways of effectively following up *Invitation to Enquiry* and
other methods and materials used to foster inquiry. Listed below are
several suggestions from which teachers may select:

1. Students can be assigned related topics to pursue outside of class.
These can be in the form of homework, independent projects, laboratory
investigations, reports, or group projects.

2. Speakers can be invited to class to expand on issues raised during inquiry sessions. For example, a genetic counselor, a member of the Zero Population Growth or Planned Parenthood groups, a nuclear engineer or physicist, or a specialist on animal behavior can be used as well-informed specialists after students have been exposed in some detail to a given topic. Local politicians and city administrators are another source of speakers for some topics.

3. Surveys can be conducted and citizens asked to respond concerning how they feel about pertinent issues that have been discussed in a science class.

4. Books, journals, and other documents can be provided so that interested students can proceed further with questions raised in class.

The important thing to remember is that inquiry is a continuous activity in science. In like manner, the science teacher should continually be looking for ways to foster this kind of behavior in students.

Student comments (below) illustrate that field trips are a powerful educational tool. Field trips capitalize on the principle that many things are learned best from direct experience. A water treatment plant, an oak-hickory forest, or a sandy beach is a superior place to learn about the phenomena that occur there. In addition to the opportunity to observe things firsthand, students usually develop strong feelings about their observations as a result of field trips. Probably no other teaching method can change student attitudes as dramatically as a field trip. In fact, it is likely that students will remember *all* the field trips they ever take and something of what they learned on each.

The last student comment illustrates what is too often the case—

WHAT STUDENTS SAY

Field Trips

- Our science club visited a radio telescope when I was a junior. We all were impressed by elaborate equipment. However, the thing I remember most was their short-wave receiver sitting on a Sunkist orange crate. I guess scientists always have to improvise, regardless of how much money they have for research.

- The first time I saw farm animals was when our first grade teacher took us to a petting zoo in a shopping center a few blocks from the school. A baby goat licking my hand is something I'll never forget.

- Lucky me, I went to a small school. Each year the seniors went on a trip and our class chose Washington, D.C. As it turned out, so did 10,000 other schools. What a crowd, but we had fun. I met a boy from Memphis who lived only a few blocks from Elvis Presley's house. There were so many things, I don't know what I liked best. I guess the Smithsonian and the Focault pendulum stick in my mind most clearly.

- Field trips in science? I can't remember ever taking one—not even going outside to do something on the playground....

RESEARCH REPORT

Value of Field Trips

Anthony V. Sorrentino and Paul E. Bell[15] compared the values attributed to field trips with the results obtained in seven empirical studies of the field trip as a teaching strategy. Their analysis indicated that field trips provide bigger gains in knowledge of the environment than other teaching methods. Limited evidence also was identified that showed field trips (1) produce an interest, motivation, stimulation, or appreciation of some phase of science; (2) improve observational and perception skills; (3) assist in developing an interest in a vocation; and (4) improve the retention of knowledge.

The investigators concluded that, although the evidence for the superiority of field trips over other strategies is limited, there is little evidence that would negate its effectiveness in teaching science. As in the case of most strategies, substantial research is needed to determine the ways and conditions under which the field trip is most effective.

---

[15] Anthony V. Sorrentino and Paul E. Bell, "A Comparison of Attributed Values with Empirically Determined Values of Secondary School Science Field Trips," *Science Education* 54 (July-September, 1970): 233–236.

many students never have the experience and excitement of a science field trip. There are many reasons why field trips are not used more, but the principal ones are the time and effort required for planning and carrying out a field trip.

Few teaching methods require more planning than taking a field trip. Initial planning begins with selecting the site or sites of the visit. Field trips can be taken on the school grounds, a field adjacent to the school, sites within the city, or places located some distance from the school. The location often mediates other important factors such as transportation and the amount of time needed for the trip. For field trips to sites on or near the school grounds, a regular class period may be sufficient. If the site requires much travel time, then students will have to be excused from other classes if the trip is taken during a school day. To avoid interfering with other classes, it is sometimes possible to take field trips on Saturday, after school, during vacation days, or on teacher planning days.

If the trip requires a greater distance for travel, an entire day or two may be necessary. In such cases, special permission may be required from school administrators other than the school principal. When students are going to miss other classes, it is necessary that the matter be discussed with the other teachers well ahead of time and that students be prepared to complete assignments in advance.

The schedule for a one-day field trip to a beach about 150 kilometers from the school is presented on pages 203–204. The schedule and comments illustrate the importance of good planning. It is strongly recommended that teachers without experience in planning and conducting

(A)   Field Trip - Science Club
                              Saturday, April 7
                   Field Trip Leader - Ms. Tyner (telephone: 791-1118)

(B)   7:00 AM   Depart from east door of O'Keef School in school vans driven
                  by Ms. Tyner and Mrs. Wilcox (791-1249)
(C)   9:00-9:20   Rest stop - McDonald's in Oceanview (food, restrooms); (815-923-6142)
(D)   9:40-11:40 Investigation of geological process and features on an open beach.
(E)   12:00-1:00 Sack lunches at picnic tables near bath house at Ft. Hall State
                  Park (815-923-7151); cold drinks and sacks available at concession
                  stand.

      1:00-2:00   Complete beach investigations and pack equipment in van.
(F)   2:00-3:30   Walking tour of marine ecosystems, lead by Sadie Burrow, park
                  naturalist.
      3:30-3:45   Break - Ft. Hall Bath house (815-923-7151)
(G)   4:00-5:00   Delaney Aquarium and Nautical Museum (free admission); (815-923-4911)
(H)   5:15-6:30   Dinner, Captain Tony's (815-923-9223)
      6:30   Depart for home
      8:00   Rest stop at Homer's Service Station in Centerville
(I)   9:00   Arrive at east door of O'Keef (the office will be unlocked so students
                  can use telephones to call for transportation).

(J) Students should bring suntan lotion, sunglasses, insect repellant, raingear,
     cameras, binoculars, pencils and notebooks, plastic bags and bottles for
     collecting, money for sacks and dinner, and a sack lunch. School will provide
     in each van, a first aid kit, flashlight, iced water and paper cups and equip-
     ment needed for beach investigations.

(K)   Safety Committee
              Dalmolin, Carle, Chairman (791-4213) (T)
              Brickman, Barry   (428-9040) (M)
              Ford, Leon   (428-8362) (T)

                             Follow-Up Committee
              Ross, Marilyn, Chairman   (793-1421) (T)
              Bridges, Jane   (791-9042) (T)
              Dalton, Victor   (791-2767) (M)
              James, Janet   (791-5848) (M)
              Northart, Ron   (793-9918) (M)

                             Planning Committee
              Gray, Rebecca, Chairman   (791-8297) (T)
              Hegi, Ernest   (793-0489) (M)
              Morrison, Jon   (791-5911) (T)

           Team Leaders for Open Beach Investigations

              Middlebrooks, Warren, Chairman (793-0900) (M)
              Schiei, Tom   (791-7252) (T)
              Anthony, Joyce   (791-4520) (T)
              Desai, Hermant   (793-4595) (M)

(continued)

Equipment Committee

Plake, Christina, Chairman	(793-7507)	(T)
Funderburk, Perry	(482-2195)	(M)
Zepeda, Willie	(791-9328)	(M)

EXPLANATION

(A) Each student is given two copies of the agenda--one to leave at home so the parents know how to contact the group and one to take on the trip so each student could keep posted on the various activities. Copies also are left with appropriate school officials.

(B) Time and place of departure are clearly noted along with method of transportation. The (T) and (M) following students' names indicate in which van they are to ride.

(C) Rest stops and breaks are planned at least once every two or three hours. Telephone numbers of most stops are supplied so the field trip group can be contacted in case of emergencies.

(D) A major part of the field trip is devoted to investigative activities which the students have carefully planned prior to taking the trip. The time before and immediately after lunch is for observations and data collecting. This part of the field trip was scheduled while the students were still fresh. The data will be analyzed upon returning home by the science club members.

(E) Lunch is scheduled at a site having a pleasant environment, a choice of drinks, and adequate restroom facilities. Sack lunches reduce costs, speed up eating, and add to the fun by encouraging students to trade food items. In case of rain, picnic tables will be suitable since they are in a shelter.

(F) The use of a resident naturalist provides a "change of pace" and is a quick way to get an overview of the ecosystems in the area.

(G) As in the case of the walking tour by the naturalist, this stop was scheduled in advance by a telephone call. A museum employee will be on hand to welcome the group and give a five minute slide presentation on what to see.

(H) The planning committee and the other students selected this eating place because of its varied menu, inexpensive prices, and because they can eat there wearing the same clothes they wore on the beach.

(I) Time and place of arrival are clearly noted. The building will be opened so equipment can be unloaded and students can call for rides.

(J) Safety equipment and other items to be furnished by the students or provided by the school are clearly designated.

(K) Each student is a member of a committee or a team leader for the open beach investigations. Home telephone numbers are given so students can contact each other and so the field trip leader will have telephone numbers in case of an emergency.

field trips start out on a small scale. Taking a class outside to measure the sun's altitude on September 21 or to a pet store down the street will provide the teacher with valuable experience for conducting more ambitious trips later. Besides, field trips do not have to be to distant places in order to be effective.

One of the joys of teaching is coming upon an unexpected situation and capitalizing upon that rare "teachable moment."

GUIDELINES FOR USING FIELD TRIPS

Using field trips effectively demands careful planning, skillful execution, and appropriate followup and evaluation. For most field trips, it will be necessary to answer the following questions before embarking on the field trip.

1. What is the purpose of the field trip?

2. Could the objective proposed for the field trip be accomplished more easily and in less time with some other instructional strategy?

3. What sites and resources are available to use during the field trip?

4. How much will the field trip cost, how will transportation be provided, and what other logistical problems must be solved?

5. What arrangement must be made with school officials, parents, adult

supervisors taking the trip, and resource people to be used at the sites visited?

6. What legal requirements, such as insurance coverage and parent permission forms, must be met?

7. Has every precaution been taken to insure a safe field trip and has the location of the nearest hospital, physician and rescue squad been determined?

8. Has an agenda been prepared and have routines been established so that the time spent on the field trip can be maximumly utilized?

9. If the field trip is being taken for the first time, has the field trip leader made a "dry run"?

10. Do students know what they are to bring on the trip, what they are to accomplish, and how they are to act?

11. How will the field trip be evaluated?

12. Will the field trip be followed up by drawing from the students' experiences in various class activities that follow and by sharing with those not taking the trip through reports, displays, and assembly programs?

Using Resource People

In most communities, there are many people who are willing to share their expertise with science students. This can be a stimulating change of pace for a science class. It can also give students a better grasp of what scientists, technicians, and other people engaged in science-related activities actually do. Other groups that can be used are local environmentalists, public utilities officials, public health personnel, local industrialists, and representatives of public or private agencies whose work relates to the many interactions between science and society.

BRINGING RESOURCE PEOPLE TO THE CLASSROOM

Certain things should be done when arranging for guest speakers and other resource personnel. Identifying appropriate guest speakers requires careful planning. How will the use of a guest speaker augment the course objectives? What will the speaker specifically be asked to do? Why has the person being invited been chosen? Most speakers prefer to know specifically what it is they should do while visiting the class. Not all people in the community make good guest speakers. Some specialists are far too technical for secondary school students, while others "talk down" to young people. Any past performances of a potential guest should be checked out. The teacher also should try to ascertain if the person is likely to be most successful in a middle, junior, or senior high school setting.

Once a guest speaker has been identified, the person should be asked well in advance of the date he or she is needed. Even people who are very busy find it difficult to turn down thoughtful invitations received several weeks or months in advance. In most cases, the earlier a speaker can be invited the better. In general, a guest speaker should be invited several weeks before the time of the appearance. This is particularly important in cases where the teacher does not know the speaker or where the person has never been invited before. In some cases, the speaker may have to spend considerable time preparing for the visit.

The topic on which the visiting speaker is being asked to speak should be outlined as specifically as possible. The speaker should be given an overview of what the student will have been exposed to before he or she arrives. The speaker should also be given a short list of objectives that can serve as a guide to how the speaker's presentation can supplement or complement the goals that have been established for the students. Most speakers prefer this kind of guidance as opposed to, "Speak on anything you like."

Speakers also want to know what time they should arrive, how long they should speak, how much time they should leave for student questions, and whether or not they will be expected to give their presentation to more than one class. In most cases, the speaker should be encouraged to leave ample time for student questions. A common error of many speakers is to talk too long, leaving little or no time for interaction with the students who are usually anxious to ask questions. Teachers should emphasize this to speakers ahead of time and suggest that twenty to thirty minutes be reserved for questions. In addition, it is usually good to agree ahead of time that students may ask questions whenever misunderstanding occurs or clarification is needed.

Finally, in preparing for the speakers it is necessary to make a decision as to the number of classes to which they will be expected to talk. It is usually inappropriate to ask a speaker to stay all day. Most of the time, one or two classes per day is preferable. In cases where the teacher desires to provide three or four classes with the same opportunity, multiple speakers should be considered, or the same speaker should be invited back on a successive day. Some science teachers make audio- or videotapes of visiting speakers. If several speakers are used during the year, they arrange the schedule so that each class has at least one "live" speaker.

Directions concerning where to park and how to find the office should be sent to the speaker ahead of time. Arrangements should be made on the day of arrival for someone to meet the speaker at the main office of the school. If the teacher is available to meet the guest, it is usually an appropriate gesture to introduce him or her to the principal. If the teacher cannot be at the office, a student should be available to greet the speaker and to serve as an escort. If the speaker has had to travel considerable distance, opportunities for a break and for refreshments should be offered.

What should a teacher do if the speaker fails to talk on the topic previously agreed upon, or if it becomes apparent that the level of the talk is inappropriate for the students? With proper planning such problems seldom arise; however, should a teacher experience either situation it should be remembered that a teacher's first responsibility is to the students. In such situations then, it is appropriate for the teacher to interrupt politely and to say something like, "I think perhaps some of the students have questions that will help clear up the points you are making," or "We have not talked about _____ yet this year. Would you mind discussing_____ in order to give us a little more background?" Speakers, especially those who are not accustomed to speaking to secondary school students, will usually appreciate this assistance, and the students will profit from this intervention.

It is always a good practice to write all speakers a thank you note a few days after their visit. The preparation and time from those individuals represent a major contribution to the schools, and a letter acknowledging this is certainly fitting. In some cases, it is appropriate to let students help in this process either by letting all class members sign the letter or, as teachers of younger students sometimes do, by allowing all students to compose letters which can then be delivered to the speaker along with a note from the teacher.

Most schools do not have money to pay speakers an honorarium. This fact should, of course, be mentioned when a speaker is initially invited. Sometimes travel expenses can be provided for speakers who do not receive remuneration from their companies or institutions. However, this matter should be worked out carefully through the appropriate school officials before reimbursement is promised. While most speakers do not expect pay for their contributions to schools, it is a point that should be mentioned or clarified beforehand. In any event, should the speaker be able to stay for lunch, it is a nice gesture to arrange for the payment of the person's meal. These and other amenities are usually considered ample compensation by speakers, and this kind of treatment will frequently elicit comments such as, "I'll be happy to come back next year" or "I know someone else who might be interested in talking to your class."

GOING TO THE
RESOURCE PEOPLE
IN THE
COMMUNITY

Although resource people perhaps are most often used as visiting speakers, it is also possible to utilize their expertise by going to them. The field trip is one way of doing so. Other ways of taking advantage of the expertise and experience of people in the community include:

(a) Having individuals or small groups of students interview appropriate resource people on topics such as local environmental problems, the operation of nearby scientific and technological laboratories and industries, and the opportunities for employment in science-related jobs and careers.

(b) Apprenticing advanced students with scientists and others in science-related work.

(c) Using scientists and others as advisors on scientific investigations being conducted by students.

Educational Games

Games in the science classroom are becoming as commonplace as Monopoly and Scrabble in the living room of our homes. Interest in this method of teaching has increased during the last few years, and there are many new and interesting games on the market.

The term *game* implies "fun" and "competition," and usually provides an opportunity for individuals or groups to end up with some type of tangible reward—to "collect points" or "win." For some students, games stimulate interest and increase motivation. Games represent a way of getting some students involved who might not otherwise participate. Some games make subject matter relevant by using real-life situations.

Some games use simulation or role-playing techniques. These can be used both to develop intellectual skills and to examine student attitudes toward a current issue or problem in the community. While playing these games, students have an opportunity to act out different roles in a creative way. This allows them to experience the broad, interdisciplinary nature of many issues and problems relevant to society.

SELECTING GAMES FOR THE CLASSROOM

There are many things for a teacher to weigh before using an educational game as an instructional strategy. In selecting or devising games for classroom use, the following should be considered:

1. What Objectives Can Be Achieved by Using the Game?

The objectives embodied by the game should be congruent with the educational objectives of the science curriculum. In other words, the content, processes, and outcomes of the game should be consistent with the knowledge, skills, and attitudes that a teacher is helping students attain.

2. How Many People Can Participate?

Some games are designed for an entire class to play at one time, while others must be played in smaller groups or by individuals. Since games are used to maximize student participation, care should be taken to insure that all students be actively involved.

3. Is Prerequisite Information Needed before the Students Can Play the Game?

Some games require that participants possess specific knowledge before they are able to play the game effectively. Other games provide opportunities for students to start where they are and learn as they play. Hence, some games can be used to review what the students have already learned, while other games can serve to introduce new material and motivate students.

4. Does the Outcome of the Game Depend on Skill or Chance?

Some games require that students possess skills for planning and implementing sophisticated strategies in order to win. Other games are based more on chance. For less able students, a game may be less fun if it requires too much skill; for more mature and able students a game involving too much chance may be boring and unchallenging.

5. Are the Rules Easy to Explain and Enforce?

It is important that there be a minimum of complicated rules when dealing with large numbers of students. Some games that otherwise would be excellent teaching strategies are not appropriate for classrooms because of lengthy lists of cumbersome rules that are difficult to follow.

6. What Is the Format of the Game?

The most distinguishable characteristic of any game is its format. The format may call for one person to work a puzzle, four people to play cards, or the entire class to engage in a simulation or quiz show. Many games can be purchased, or if the general format is understood, students and teachers can devise their own games.

Educational games come in a wide variety of formats. The following section discusses some of the most common game formats and gives examples of each.

SIMULATIONS

Simulations allow students to play roles that revolve around real-life situations. In the popular game **Redwood Controversy**,[16] a United States Senate hearing is conducted, and students play the parts of senators and people called upon to testify. The drama focuses on the question of "Should parts of the Redwood Forest be bought by the Government and preserved as National Forestop" or "Should the lumbermen and citizens of Redwood Gulch be allowed to continue their life-long practice of harvesting these giant trees?" Students playing senators attempt to influence each other to vote for or against certain proposals. This game well illustrates the complex, multidisciplinary nature of this issue.

The format of a game like **Redwood Controversy** can easily be adapted to a local issue. By designing a game around a local problem, students can role-play people in their own community and experience an even greater feeling of relevance.

BINGO MATRIX

Nearly everyone has played Bingo, and the format is easy to adapt for classroom use. It allows equal participation of all students and is particu-

---

[16] The Redwood Controversy, Educational Research Council of America, 1971 (distributed by Houghton Mifflin Company), 110 Tremont Street, Boston, Massachusetts 02107.

larly appropriate when used for reviewing material at the end of a topic or unit. Questions can be constructed so that students knowing the answers can work toward a "Bingo." One example of this format is shown in Figure 5.7.

PATHWAY
FORMAT

The structure of a game of this type follows that of **Monopoly**. As students answer questions or make proper decisions, they are allowed to move toward a desired goal. A commercial game called **Pollution** and another called **Space Hop** are examples of this format. In **Space-Hop**, knowing the answers to questions about the stars and planets allows the space traveler to proceed more quickly to other planets and ultimately win more points.

CARD FORMAT

Many educational games are based on popular card games. In some instances, collecting a series of cards that represent a complete class of objects or a completed system allows the student to discard and win the game. The kinds of card games that can be bought or "made up" by students or teachers are almost endless. Most card games are played with groups of four to six students. Figure 5.8 shows an example of a card game that can be constructed by a teacher and students.

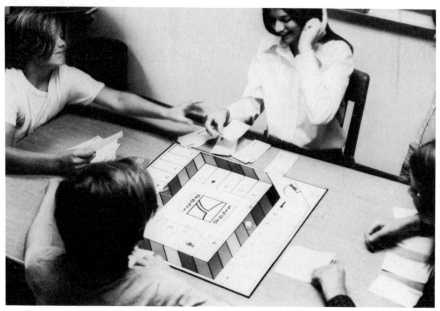

Students in the BSCS Human Sciences Program play a commercial game about pollution, as a part of the program's extensive field tests.

BIOLOGY

B	I	N	G	O
1	6	11	16	21
2	7	12	17	22
3	8	13	18	23
4	9	14	19	24
5	10	15	20	25

Directions:

In this game the teacher, along with students, can compose 25 questions over material students have studied. The questions can be placed on small cards, shuffled, and then a student or the teacher will call these out to the class. If a student can answer the question he is allowed to place a chip over the number of that question. When a person gets a "Bingo," he or she is required to answer the questions. To reduce the chance of ties, more numbers and questions can be used so that each card is not the same.

FIGURE 5.7 Example of educational game: Biology Bingo.

Directions: The object of this game is to get as many "books" of cards as possible. Students, usually four per game, are dealt cards containing chemical reactants, chemical reactions, and chemical products. Played the same as the popular card game Rummy, when a person gets four cards representing a complete chemical reaction he lays down the set of cards and receives one point for the book. The student with the most books at the end of the game wins.

Some of the cards that could be constructed by the teacher or students and that represent a book are:

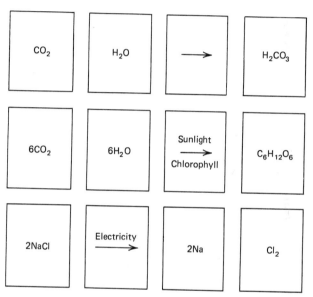

FIGURE 5.8   Example of educational game: Chemical Reaction Rummy.

QUIZ SHOW
FORMAT

Television quiz shows allow a person or groups of people to win prizes by answering questions. Most of these contests can be easily adapted for classroom use. A noticeable advantage of this format is that students can form teams and large groups can participate. Games of this type foster a "team spirit" and friendly competition, which motivate some students who otherwise might not want to "get involved." Quiz-type games are particularly good for learning factual material and helping students review large amounts of subject material. Games of this type are easy to construct and inexpensive to use.

INDIVIDUAL
GAMES

Crossword puzzles, word scrambles, riddles, and many other similar games can be used to heighten interest and increase participation. Most students are challenged by the thought of "figuring something out" and will frequently spend inordinate amounts of time trying to master a game that requires individual logic or reasoning. Individual games can often be used as a bonus question on a test or serve as an interesting homework assignment. An example of a crossword puzzle is displayed in Figure 5.9.

REVIEW GAMES

Many experienced teachers have found that various kinds of "review games" help encourage students to prepare for weekly quizzes or unit tests. Such games can be adapted to follow a baseball, basketball, or football format, where answers to different questions count as "base hits," "homeruns," "baskets," "first downs," or "touch-downs," and points are awarded for "correct answers." Figure 5.10 presents an example of a review game used by a junior high school science teacher in Franklin, Massachusetts.

Strategies Useful with Small Groups

There are several ways a teacher can work effectively with students in small instructional groups. Generally, this approach allows students to play a more active role in the learning process and places more of the responsibility for learning on students. Through small-group interaction, students learn to exchange ideas with each other and often become more interested in the material than when the teacher is the center of attention. Using small-group strategies also allows the teacher to shift roles. Instead of being preoccupied with disseminating information, the teacher can take time to observe students, encourage those who need extra help, and be in a better position to evaluate student progress.

Many of the strategies discussed in the remainder of this chapter can be used in combination with large-group activities. For example, students can be broken into small groups and later reassembled so that the entire class can share results. Perhaps as important as group size is the characteristic of student involvement and participation which typifies small-group strategies. Additional small-group strategies are discussed in Chapter 7, which deals with the teaching of attitudes and values.

BRAINSTORMING

Brainstorming is a creative problem-solving technique that has been used successfully in government, business and industry, and, to some extent, education. It is a way of getting the greatest number of ideas in the shortest length of time. Unlike most methods used in science teaching, brainstorming emphasizes the spilling out of ideas as quickly as possible and defers until later judgments on their worth. The following are the steps usually followed in a brainstorming session:

1. *The class is divided into groups of five to seven members.* Keeping the size small encourages each member of the group to participate.

Crossword puzzle provided will help you review some of the terms from the lesson.

ACROSS

3. the process by which a cell uses energy to move materials through the cell membrane (two words).

5. a process in which the molecules of a substance spread out.

7. this forms when a large particle is engulfed.

9. the molecule that is transported in the active transport model.

11. used to show how active transport takes place.

12. materials plants absorb from soil water by active transport.

13. an organism that engulfs its food.

14. example used to explain passive and active transport.

DOWN

1. another term for diffusion (two words).

2. the molecule that transports materials in the active transport model.

4. a cell surrounds and a large particle.

6. materials may enter a cell by being enclosed in small pockets or_____in the cell membrane.

8. selective boundary of a cell (two words).

10. a cell requires this for active transport

1. Passive transport
2. Carrier
3. Active transport
4. Engulfs
5. Diffusion
6. Folds
7. Vacuole
8. Cell membrane
9. Passenger
10. Energy
11. Model
12. Minerals
13. Ameba
14. Bicycle

FIGURE 5.9   Example of a crossword puzzle. (*Source:* Reprinted by permission of Holt, Rinehart & Winston, *Life Science*, 1978.)

Directions:

To make the game, cut 44 pieces of scrap plywood or paneling 8" × 11". Next, on pieces of paper the same size as the wood, write 44 review questions (for example, 30 cm = _____m). Mount each question on a panel, then place it inside a large plastic freezer bag (to keep it clean). Fasten the bag to the board with thumb tacks.

After moving desks and chairs out of the way, arrange the "question bags" face down, in the pattern shown in the figure. Then divide the class into two teams, and have each elect a member to start at position 10. The first student from Team One picks up the question and reads the question *number*, then his *answer*. The teacher announces whether or not the answer is correct.

If the student gives a correct answer, he or she moves ahead to row 9 and tries a question on that level. If an incorrect answer is given, it becomes the other team's turn. When it becomes Team One's turn again, the student next in line picks up with the question that his team member missed. If three people from the same team miss the same question, the fourth person may advance to the next row.

The game is over when a team member correctly answers the question in row one.

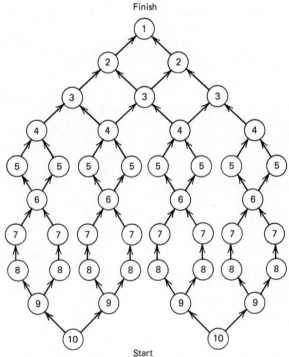

FIGURE 5.10 Example of a review game. (*Source:* Reprinted by permission of *The Science Teacher*. Circe, Jeffrey, "Review Game," Vol. 45, No. 1, p. 35, 1978.)

2. *The teacher appoints a leader for each group or each group selects its own leader.* It is also a good idea to have a recorder in each group make a list of the ideas that are generated.

3. *The rules for brainstorming are explained.* The idea is to get as many ideas as quickly as possible. Critical judgment is ruled out; that comes later. "Free-wheeling" is encouraged—the wilder the idea the better. "Hitchhiking" is encouraged—a student can suggest an idea that builds on a previous suggestion or can suggest how two or more ideas can be combined.

4. *The problem is stated.* The problems that work best are simple, specific, and have many possible answers. Some examples are:

- How can the school reduce its consumption of electricity?
- What would happen if the earth stopped turning on its axis?
- How can money be raised for an upcoming field trip by the science club?
- How can the laboratory be made a safer place in which to work?
- How can the temperature of the sap inside of a tree be measured?

5. *The leader keeps the pace brisk and the discussion on track.* The leader can call for volunteers to get started. If more than one person has ideas, it usually works best for the participants to take turns making their suggestions. If suggestions get too far removed from the problem, the leader should restate the problem. Since negative comments are not allowed in brainstorming, the leader and other members of the group must refrain from statements such as "that idea doesn't have anything to do with the problem" or "that's a dumb idea."

6. *The ideas generated can be evaluated.* Once as many ideas as possible have been identified, they can be evaluated by the usual means used. For example, the ideas can be tested by use of a series of questions. Is the idea feasible? Is it realistic? Is it an improvement over what has been done? The exact nature of the question, of course, will depend on the idea being tested.

Another approach is for the various groups to pool their ideas. This can be done either before or after the ideas have been evaluated.

BUZZ SESSIONS

This method is similar to brainstorming but differs in that groups of four to six students are asked to come to a conclusion about a question or problem. In other words, rather than thinking divergently, students must think convergently. In small groups of four to six, students are asked, "Why has Darwinism been so controversial?" or "How has putting a man on the moon changed the thinking of society?" During buzz sessions, the teacher circulates among the students and helps any group that seems to be having difficulty. Buzz sessions can vary in time from five to thirty minutes, usually depending on how productive the discussion continues to be. As with brainstorming, it is usually beneficial to allow members in each group, if time permits, to share their main ideas with the entire class. Buzz sessions can also be used to initiate other group activities such as laboratory investigations, group projects, or individual reports.

CASE STUDIES

Another small-group strategy is to give students a "problem situation" for them to resolve. This practice is widely used in the training of doctors where they are given a patient's medical history and symptoms and must come up with a diagnosis and a plan for treatment. Case studies differ from brainstorming sessions and buzz sessions in that students are given some of the details of a situation or "case" rather than just being given a question or problem.

Case studies can be designed by science teachers to include a variety of topics. A case study below is given as an example.

Dr. Martha Howard, after four years of investigation, has found that high levels of a common artificial sweetner causes cancer in the bladder of white rats. She has petitioned the Food and Drug Administration to ban the use of this chemical in all products consumed by humans. Manufacturers of the artificial sweetener claim there are no recorded cases in the United States where their product has been shown to cause cancer in humans. Dr. Pierre Bardot, a physician in Paris, claims that humans and rats are too different to allow predictions to be made about what will or what will not induce cancer. You are a member of a special investigative committee that must make the decision on whether or not to take this product off the market. What is your recommendation? What are the major factors that should be considered when making decisions of this type? Other case studies might be developed and include topics such as:

- Use of vitamin C in treating colds
- Appropriation of money for investigations concerning sightings of UFOs
- The use of alternative sources of energy
- Safety regulations for nuclear power plants
- The nutritional value of "fast-food"
- The banning of cigarette smoking in public areas
- Dealing with the disposal of toxic chemicals

Case studies can also be used to study historical developments in science. Although written for college use, the *Harvard Case Studies*[17] pro-

---

[17] James B. Conant, (Ed.), *Harvard Case Studies in Experimental Science.* Volumes 1 and 2, Cambridge, Mass.: Harvard University Press, 1957.

vide illustrations of topics that might be studied using this approach. These materials can be adapted for secondary schools, or other materials specifically prepared for this age group can be used. Historical topics studied using case studies, or case histories as they sometimes are called, might include:

The Overthrow of the Phlogiston Theory
The Atomic-Molecular Theory
Plants and the Atmosphere
Pasteur's Study of Fermentation
Boyle's Experiments in Pneumatics

PANEL DISCUSSIONS

The panel discussion is a common format used for exchanging information at professional and scientific meetings. It can also be used with relative ease and to good advantage in the science classroom. In most instances, a panel discussion involves three to five "experts," along with a moderator who introduces the topic and the members of the panel. Three to five minutes (this time can be longer with a smaller panel) are allocated to each panelist to introduce the topic and state his or her position. The moderator then usually opens up the discussion to the audience, allowing individuals to make comments or ask questions of selected members of the panel. Another approach is for the moderator to allow questions immediately after the subject and panel have been introduced. Still another technique is for one, two, or three "reactors" or "discussants" to comment first on the prepared remarks by the panelist before allowing questions from the audience.

When using panel discussions in secondary school classrooms, it is helpful to select students who are to serve as panelists well ahead of time. This way they will have time to prepare adequately. These students become "experts" so that on the day of the panel discussion they will be knowledgeable in a specific area and be able to handle questions from other members of the class. Assigning a student to serve as moderator usually works better than the teacher assuming this role. The moderator must see to it that both the panelists and members of the class have opportunities to express their views and ask pertinent questions. At the end of the period, the moderator or teacher should summarize the major ideas discussed and make concluding remarks. Information from the panel discussion should be related to past and future topics to which the students have or will be exposed.

MODIFIED DEBATES

The modified debate is one of the most stimulating methods of dealing with issues or controversial topics. The term *modified debate* implies more flexibility than is the case with formal debate. Modified debates involve two teams of students with usually three or four individuals per team. The two teams of students are assigned a topic, and the teams agree ahead of time to represent opposite views. For instance, one team will agree to represent the pro side of building more nuclear power plants and the other team the con side. In addition to obvious social issues that conjure up polarized views, new scientific theories that deal with topics such as quarks, chemical evolution, and sociobiology can be chosen as topics. By introducing new theories that are currently being debated by scientists, students can experience science as it actually happens.

On the day of the debate, one member from each team is allowed approximately five minutes to make a formal presentation. After the two opposing positions have been offered, another student from each team is allowed approximately five minutes for rebuttal. The third member from each team is then allowed to direct a question to any member of the other team. While the procedure can vary, it is usually a good practice to allow other students in the class to ask questions. This involvement gives all students the freedom to participate, which is an advantage over the format of a formal debate. Toward the end of the class period, the fourth member of each team is given approximately three minutes for a closing argument and summary. In the remaining time, students from the class can comment on the positions of the two teams and draw conclusions as to the strengths and weaknesses of the opposing views.

The moderator, who can be a student or the teacher, plays an important role in debates. The moderator should strictly enforce the time limits previously agreed upon. The moderator should also make sure that the pro-con sequence is maintained in a balanced way. The teacher should help the students focus on ideas rather than on personalities. It should be pointed out to class members that those on the debate team may be representing positions that are not necessarily consistent with their personal opinions. An advantage of this instructional strategy, therefore, is that students can be taught to probe, question, and vigorously discuss opposing views while learning to respect alternative opinions. Moreover, students can learn to put their ideas on the line for critical review without worrying so much about their own ego and personal gain. As students learn to use this method effectively, they can be assigned to argue views that they do not personally hold. This method of teaching further encourages tolerance and objectivity and is a lesson most students remember.

STUDENT
REPORTS

Oral and written reports are one way of exposing students to a large number of topics not treated by the other strategies used in a class. These should be assigned one or more weeks ahead of time, depending on the length and depth of the report. Some or all of the students can be asked to present their reports to the class. If all students give reports, it is usually necessary to establish and enforce time limits. One way to reduce the amount of class time consumed is to divide students into two, three, or four groups, with one student reporting at a time in each group. Grouping can be done by interests, by random assignment, or by asking students to devise a method.

If written reports are used, the students should be given a set of guidelines. The number of references required, approximate length, basic organization, and acceptable format(s) of the report are helpful guidelines for students. Similar guidelines are helpful to students giving oral reports. In addition to giving their reports orally, the teacher may want the students to turn in a written copy of their reports prepared according to the given guidelines.

STUDENT-LED
SEMINARS

The seminar is a popular format for advanced science courses in college. The term *seminar* generally implies student or faculty presentations and discussions of current research results. This format can be used successfully in secondary schools and particularly in advanced classes. Students can report their findings from laboratory investigations or independent study projects. The seminar can be led by one or several students.

The spirit of a seminar, a medium frequently used by practicing scientists, is to allow open examination and evaluation of research results or current theory. A seminar usually consists of a formal presentation followed by questions and discussion. Presentations can be enhanced by using transparencies, slides, charts, or other graphic aids. Handouts for each seminar participant are also helpful. Through the use of this instructional strategy, students can be taught to display and interpret data, formulate conclusions, and communicate results to others. Discussion sessions that accompany seminars are also an excellent way for students to learn how to probe and question scientific results. By encouraging open dialogue and rigorous debate, science teachers allow students to experience at firsthand many important facets of science. Instead of telling students how scientists behave, why not let students behave like scientists?

Improving Reading Skills in Science

The reading ability of American students has received considerable attention during the past few years, and test scores indicate that many students in secondary schools read several years below their grade level. The continual push by many parents and other citizens to emphasize the teaching of the basic subjects has influenced teachers at all grade levels to pay more attention to how well their students read. When faced with the problem, it is tempting for the science teacher to reply, "I'm a science teacher, not a reading teacher. Let the reading, language arts, or English teacher solve the problem." Upon closer examination, however, it is constructive to note that many of the so-called reading skills are closely associated with the important processes of science.

Students, parents, and teachers should recognize that reading, writing, and arithmetic are not the only basic subjects in the school curriculum. Science is also a *basic*, and not only because we live in a scientific and technological society. By helping students learn science, the processes associated with communication and calculation can be improved. Not only does better reading produce better learning in science, but the reverse is equally true. A better understanding of science helps students become better readers.

IDENTIFYING
POOR READERS IN
THE CLASSROOM

Science teachers can evaluate the reading levels of their students in several ways. The easiest method is to give students something to read in class and then ask questions about what they have just read. A more comprehensive way to evaluate student reading levels is to use an informal group reading inventory. The inventory contains a sample question for each reading skill. After students are given reading material in science, they might, for example, be tested on their ability to use a glossary or a table of contents, or to summarize the main idea of an assigned passage. After student answer sheets are tabulated, a table (similar to the one in Figure 5.11) can be constructed with students' names recorded in the left column and skills listed across the top. Columns corresponding to incorrect answers for each student in the class can be checked. With this kind of record for each class, it is easy to determine at a glance areas of general weakness.

Another way to identify students who may be having difficulty with assigned reading material is to use the Cloze technique described in Chapter 6. To use the Cloze technique, the teacher copies a passage from current science reading material and blanks out every fifth or sixth word, until a total of fifty words have been omitted. Students are then given the sheet and asked to fill in the blanks with the words they believe have been omitted. The sheets are then scored with two points being given for each correct answer. If a student's score is less than 41, it is assumed that the student will have difficulty with the material. Scores from 41 to 60 suggest that the student will be able to read the material but that teacher assistance may be needed. If a student scores over 60, the individual should be able to read the material without assistance.

If a teacher finds that the reading level of a given class is unusually high or low, textbooks and other reading materials can be selected with this information in mind. The Fry Formula is commonly used to evaluate the average reading level of instructional materials. A graph showing how

Name	Using the Text			Vocabulary Skills			Study Skills			Comprehension Skills						
	Index	Glossary	Table of Contents	Contextual Clues	Technical Vocabulary	Structural Clues	Use of References	Use of Diagrams	Use of Dictionary	Main Idea	Pattern of Writing	Noting Details	Organization	Problem Solving	Drawing of Conclusions	Applications
	1	2	3	4	5	6	7	8	9	10	11	12	13	14	15	16
John	×			×	×			×								
Susan								×								
Phyllis	×	×	×	×			×		×						×	×
Robert	×	×		×			×						×			
etc.																

FIGURE 5.11 Sample of an informal group reading inventory, where "x" signifies problem areas.

this formula works is presented as Figure 9.4 in Chapter 9. The technique consists of selecting three 100-word passages at random and counting both the *number of syllables* and the *average number of sentences* per 100 words. The values, once plotted on a readability graph yield an estimate of the reading level of the material. Since factors in addition to number of syllables and sentences influence readability, the Fry Formula suggests only an approximate grade level of the materials.

HELPING STUDENTS TO BECOME BETTER READERS

Once a teacher has determined that a class contains slow readers, what can be done to help these students? One approach is to obtain the help of a guidance counselor or reading specialist. Such consultants, frequently employed by school systems and state departments of education, are trained to administer, score, and interpret standardized reading tests. They can also offer the classroom teacher helpful tips on how to work with minor problems and are often available to work closely with students who have severe reading problems.

Science teachers can help students improve their reading skills by creating interest in vocabulary development. Teachers, for instance, who introduce new words with enthusiasm will often find their students becoming excited about word etymologies and other interesting associations. Crossword puzzles, acrostics (see Figure 5.12), and word search games are enjoyable ways of developing and reinforcing a science vocabu-

```
B  N  I  F  R  O  G  E  N  N  E  G  O  R  D  Y  H  S  E
T  I  N  O  D  E  N  Z  I  N  O  B  R  A  C  U  L  O  F
L  S  O  G  N  I  T  R  I  O  F  G  M  U  I  C  L  A  C
A  P  R  Z  R  T  B  R  H  P  H  O  S  P  H  O  R  U  S
B  T  I  O  X  Y  U  Y  U  L  M  U  I  D  O  S  X  B  P  R
O  C  N  L  R  S  U  T  I  D  O  A  O  N  C  I  Z  Y  B  P  R
C  H  Y  U  L  T  I  D  O  R  G  C  A  R  N  B  G  O  G  E
D  X  R  F  N  S  B  O  R  G  A  N  G  A  S  E  S  E  R  U  P
H  F  A  J  S  U  M  M  A  N  G  A  S  E  N  A  G  N  A  M  P
K  L  C  A  I  L  O  X  Y  E  S  E  N  A  G  N  F  L  A  U  O
T  O  T  P  D  F  I  O  N  S  B  T  O  N  F  L  A  C  R  C
P  U  R  R  O  U  I  D  E  I  O  D  I  N  E  O  C  R  C
M  C  N  Z  I  R  O  M  Y  U  C  D  S  O  I  U  M  P  T
    U  N  E  D  B  Y  L  O  M  P  H  S  O  R  P  U  S  N
```

Directions: Find and circle the following elements in the puzzle above. Words may be listed frontwards, backwards, from top to bottom, from bottom to top, or diagonally.

Hydrogen	Potassium	Zinc
Oxygen	Sulfur	Manganese
Carbon	Sodium	Copper
Nitrogen	Chlorine	Fluorine
Calcium	Magnesium	Iodine
Phosphorous	Iron	Molybdenum
		Cobalt

FIGURE 5.12   An example of an acrostic.

lary. New words should be repeated, written on the chalkboard, and used as frequently as possible during class discussions. This helps students become more comfortable with new words in their vocabularies.

Beyond vocabulary development comes a host of other reading skills that relate to comprehension and meaning. A helpful study guide developed by Harold Herber[18] illustrates one method teachers can use to help students improve reading comprehension. Herber's procedure consists of assigning specific readings and, by means of the study guide, leading students through increasingly difficult levels of comprehension. The levels are as follows:

Level I: "What the Author Says"
Level II: "What the Author Means"
Level III: "Application of the Material to a New Situation"

[18] Harold Herber, *Teaching Reading in the Content Area*, Englewood Cliffs, N.J.: Prentice-Hall, 1970.

After all the students have completed a required reading, they are heterogeneously grouped and given worksheets consisting of questions on the first level of comprehension. Members of each group, working together, complete the worksheet, referring back to the original reading as necessary. Then, they move on to complete worksheets on the next two levels. These worksheets are usually not graded and serve as "study notes" for the unit.

Skills such as observing, identifying, and describing are examples of science processes that correspond closely to basic reading skills. Figure 5.13 shows several important science processes, along with a list of corresponding reading skills and suggested science activities that can be used to increase reading ability. As this figure demonstrates, the teaching of reading and science need not be competing activities; rather, they should be taught so that each reinforces the other.

Forming a Theory Of Instruction

While teachers may use a wide variety of instructional strategies, Jerome Bruner[19] has urged educators to organize their approaches around a sound theory of instruction. There are several theories of instruction that attempt to explain the important sequences of events that occur when teachers teach and students learn. Bruner claims his theory is consistent with other learning and developmental theories.

The first segment of Bruner's *Toward a Theory of Instruction* deals with developing a *predisposition* among students toward learning. This means that teachers must "set the stage," "prime the pump," or, in other words, provide stimulation so that students will be motivated to learn when the science lesson begins. Stimulating questions, interesting demonstrations, stories that relate past experiences to new topics, or a summary of yesterday's lesson are techniques that can raise the anticipation level of students.

Many educators say that students do better when they are told ahead of time what it is they are expected to learn. Some teachers find that sharing the objectives of a lesson with the students at the beginning of the lesson helps students develop a proper frame of mind for learning. Regardless of the techniques used, it is important to realize that effective instruction begins by considering where students are and how they can best be prepared to take the next step.

The second consideration basic to an instructional theory is how the knowledge, skills, or attitudes to be learned are *structured*. Here the teacher must organize what is to be learned into a framework that will be ultimately meaningful to the learner. Content can be structured so that it

[19] Jerome S. Bruner, *Toward a Theory of Instruction*, Cambridge, Mass.: The Belknap Press of Harvard University Press, 1967, pp. 39–72.

Science processes	Corresponding reading skills	Examples of activities for teaching reading skills in science
OBSERVING	Discriminating shapes	Break new words down when listing them on chalkboard.
	Discriminating sounds	Have students pronounce new words aloud.
	Discriminating syllables and accents	Mispronounce a few words and give bonus points to those who correct you.
IDENTIFYING	Recognizing letters Recognizing words Recognizing common prefixes Recognizing common suffixes Recognizing common base words	Take a prefix, suffix, or base word common in science, define it, and list as many words as possible in which it is used. Play a game where as many of these words as possible can be recited.
		Hydro (water) Micro (small) hydrogen microorganism hydrosphere microscope hydrozoa microspore hydrochloric micron hydrocarbon microsurgery hydrophilic microphotograph hydrophone microgram hydroplane micrometer
DESCRIBING	Isolating important characteristics	Construct dichotomous keys for leaves, rocks, shells, etc.
	Enumerating characteristics	Play vocabulary games such as "Password," crossword puzzles, matching exercises.
	Using appropriate terminology	Ask students to state purpose of an experiment.
	Using synonyms	Identify an object from three or four characteristics.
		Devise a game called "Name That Plant," (or "Animal," "Element," etc.).

FIGURE 5.13   Science processes, corresponding reading skills, and examples of activities for teaching reading skills in science.

Science processes	Corresponding reading skills	Examples of activities for teaching reading skills in science
CLASSIFYING	Comparing characteristics Contrasting characteristics Ordering, sequencing Arranging ideas Considering multiple factors	List steps in the life-cycle of an insect or a plant. Construct dichotomous keys. Construct a chart which compares and contrasts characteristics. Order chemical reactions on cards

DESIGNING INVESTIGATIONS	Asking questions
	Looking for potential relationships
	Following organized procedures
	
	Developing outlines
		Assign students to:
		  Use a "library corner"
		  Design an experiment from an outline
		  Write lab reports in an original manner
		Outline facts and concepts on a chalkboard.

COLLECTING DATA	Taking notes Surveying reference materials Using several parts of a book Recording data in an orderly fashion Developing precision and accuracy	Use library and classroom resources to prepare bibliography. Refer frequently to table of contents, glossary, chapter headings, etc. Use laboratory activities which incorporate quantitative skills. Allow students time to compare and discuss notes with classmates.
INTERPRETING DATA	Recognizing cause-and-effect relationships Organizing facts Summarizing new information Varying rate of reading Inductive and deductive thinking	Discuss factors that could affect the health of an organism. Teach students to "scan" and/or "skim" textbook. Organize notes in outline form. Arrange new facts and concepts in a flowchart. Have students "pre-read" (read only selected parts ahead of time) a chapter in textbook.

FIGURE 5.13 (*continued*)

Science processes	Corresponding reading skills	Examples of activities for teaching reading skills in science
FORMULATING CONCLUSIONS	Generalizing Analyzing critically Evaluating information Recognizing main ideas and concepts Establishing relationships Applying information to other situations	Ask "What If" questions. List applications of scientific laws and principles. Use a "case study" technique to stimulate critical thinking. Have students spot erroneous conclusions.
COMMUNICATING RESULTS	Using graphic aids Logically arranging information Sequencing ideas Knowledge of technical vocabulary Illuminating significant factors Describing with clarity	List events chronologically leading to a scientific discovery. Graphically illustrate the results of a laboratory investigation. List scientific discoveries on a time line. Ask for conclusions from a graph or figure depicting results of an experiment.

FIGURE 5.13 (continued)

can be learned deductively or inductively. With deductive learning, the teacher attempts to "paint the big picture" and then helps students see how the smaller pieces fit together. Alternatively, inductive learning implies that students will be exposed to smaller pieces of information and then be given the opportunity to see how these bits form the whole. Through inductive thinking, students learn to synthesize information into concepts and higher order principles.

The third part of an instructional theory involves the sequencing and pacing of learning experiences. Does the teacher present concrete material first? Or does the instructor start with a problem or something that is unfamiliar to the students? How much time is allotted for exploration and discovery? What does the teacher do to optimize the chances that each student will be able to sort out what is being learned and eventually internalize the meaning? Knowing when to provide information, when to ask questions, when to pause, or when to change directions in a discussion are related to sequencing and pacing and are important aspects of the process of instruction.

Finally, effective instruction depends on appropriate reinforcement. Rewards to students can be both internal and external. The teacher must assess the students' maturity and blend these two reward systems so that the most effective kind of reinforcement is delivered. Younger and less mature students usually require more frequent reinforcement. Older and more mature students often function best when the teacher gives fewer "pats on the back" and allows them to develop their own internal systems of reinforcement. Regardless of the approach used, reward and punishment have significant effects on the ultimate outcomes produced by any instructional strategy. Most theories of instruction hold that students tend to increase those behaviors for which they receive rewards and decrease those behaviors for which no rewards are given.

In Perspective

As you look back to the story of Louis Sullivan at the beginning of the chapter and then think about the strategies that have been described, one important idea emerges—the role of the teacher has changed over the past century. In addition to being formal authorities and disseminators of information, science teachers today perform many other tasks. They serve as purchasing agents, organizers, and implementers. They plan, interact, facilitate, and evaluate. In fact, there are few jobs that require as many skills as that of teaching.

As this chapter illustrates, there is an arsenal of useful strategies that can help science teachers accomplish their objectives. The most appropriate strategy for a given moment depends on such things as the objectives of the lesson, the maturity of the students, the available time, the available materials, the background and personality of the teacher, and the nature of the students within a given class. And no one strategy is best. They all possess advantages and disadvantages. No "new innovation" is a panacea or an answer to all the problems of a teacher.

After reading about so many different strategies, it is only natural to feel somewhat overwhelmed and possibly confused. "Will I ever be able to pull all of this off? Why wasn't I taught this way? Where will I get all the materials and equipment to do all of this?" These and similar questions come to the minds of most inexperienced teachers.

It is important to remember that the science teacher is not expected to be perfect. Nor is the science teacher expected to put on a polished "show" that can compete with prime time television. Rather, the science teacher should be willing to operate in the spirit of science and to experiment with the use of various strategies. Through this approach the science teacher can develop the professional skills associated with different strategies, and students can benefit from studying science in an environment characterized by experimentation.

Review Questions

1. Describe how the role of the American teacher has changed from that of Louis Sullivan's teacher at the Boston English High School. How would the methods used by Moses Woolson be received by parents and students today?

2. Define the following terms based on what you have read in this chapter about strategies for science teaching: teaching, learning, instructional strategy, teacher-centered strategies, and student-centered strategies.

3. Contrast indirect teaching (inductive approach) with direct teaching (deductive approach) by giving a specific example of how each could be used to teach a particular topic.

4. Why is questioning so important in science teaching? What is meant by "wait-time," and why is it important for teachers to understand this concept?

5. When the lecture method is used, what are some ways to improve the effectiveness of this instructional strategy?

6. Describe the "set induction technique." Design a short lesson where this technique is used (use an example other than the ones given in this chapter) and identify the major concepts you are trying to help students learn.

7. Briefly describe the term *Invitation to Enquiry* and discuss some of the other instructional strategies that have evolved from this teaching technique.

8. Name at least six game formats that can be used in science classes and give an example of each.

9. List several ways that the demonstration can be used in teaching science and several characteristics that good demonstrations have in common.

10. What are some things that can be done to increase the effectiveness of field trips?

11. Describe as many ways as possible that resource people can be used in teaching science.

12. Give two examples of how each of the following might be used in a science class: brainstorming; buzz sessions; case studies; panel discussions; modified debates; student-led seminars; and improving reading in the content area.

Application and Analysis

1. Below is a chart in which can be listed instructional strategies described in this chapter. Across from each strategy list major advantages and disadvantages associated with its use.

Strategy	Major Advantages	Major Disadvantages

2. The chart below describes six roles that teachers play.[20] One column contains major goals associated with each role, and another column contains specific teacher skills associated with each role, and another column contains specific teacher skills associated with those goals. Fill in the instructional strategies in the last column that you think would help a science teacher play each of these roles. Which role(s) do you see yourself emphasizing? Rank the roles in importance to you and compare your results with those of others completing this exercise.

The Teacher's Roles	Major Goals	Characteristic Skills	Appropriate Instructional Strategies That Can Be Used
Expert	to transmit information, the concepts and perspectives of the field	listening, scholarly preparation, class organization and presentation of material; answering questions	
Formal Authority	to set goals and procedures for reaching goals	defining structure, and standards of excellence; evaluating performance	
Socializing Agent	to clarify goals and career paths beyond the course; to prepare students for these	clarifying rewards and demands of the major, the field, and academic	

(continued)

[20] Reprinted by permission of Dr. McKeachie and John Wiley & Sons, Inc. From *Teaching Tips*, by Wilbur J. McKeachie, D. C. Heath and Company, 1978. This chart was derived from material in *The College Classroom: Conflict, Change, and Learning*, by Richard M. Mann, et al. Copyright © 1970 by John Wiley & Sons, Inc.

The Teacher's Roles	Major Goals	Characteristic Skills	Appropriate Instructional Strategies That Can Be Used
Facilitator	to promote creativity and growth in student's own terms; to help overcome obstacles to learning	bringing students out, sharpening their awareness of their interests and skills; to use insight & problem solving to help students reach goals, avoid blocks	
Ego Ideal	to convey the excitement and value of intellectual inquiry in a given field of study	demonstrating the ultimate worthwhileness of, or personal commitment to, one's material/educational goals	
Person	to convey the full range of human needs and skills relevant to and sustained by one's intellectual activity; to be validated as a human being; to validate the student	being self-revealing in ways which clarify one's totality beyond the task at hand; being trustworthy and warm enough to encourage students to be open as well	

3. Plan and teach a short science class to your peers while being videotaped. Review the tape by responding to the following questions or statements:
   (a) What were your instructional objectives?
   (b) What teaching strategies did you use?
   (c) How did you evaluate your "students?"
   (d) Describe how you felt when you viewed yourself on the videotape.
   (e) What were some things you noticed about yourself that surprised you?

4. With permission, tape record a science class in a local secondary school. List your primary observations while you are there. Later, analyze the audiotape by listing some of the following:
   (a) How much time was spent with the teacher talking?
   (b) Did the teacher ask questions? If so, what kinds of questions did he or she ask?
   (c) What were the major responses elicited from the students?
   (d) How many different instructional strategies were employed by the teacher?

5. Using what you consider to be five of the most important instructional objectives in your teaching field, list under each objective at least five appropriate instructional strategies. Select the strategy you think is best in each case and tell why you did so.

References

DeVito, Alfred, and Gerald H. Krockover. *Creative Sciencing: A Practical Approach.* Boston: Little, Brown & Company, 1976.

Designed for teachers of younger students, this book contains many practical ideas for science activities along with discussions on "Why Teach Science?" and "Changing Your Objectives".

DeVito, Alfred, and Gerald H. Krockover. *Creative Sciencing: Ideas and Activities for Teachers and Children.* Boston: Little, Brown & Company, 1976.

This is a companion book to *Creative Sciencing: A Practical Approach.* While written with a focus on elementary school science activities, the book contains many excellent ideas appropriate for middle school science programs.

Farmer, Walter A., and Margaret A. Farrell. *Systematic Instruction in Science for the Middle and High School Years.* Reading, Mass.: Addison-Wesley Publishing Company, 1980.

The general approach used in this book is that of the competency-based teacher education (CBTE) model, wherein important skills needed by teachers are prescribed and the means for developing these skills are outlined.

Funk, H. James, James R. Okey, Ronald L. Fiel, Harold H. Jaus, and Constance Stewart Sprague. *Learning Science Process Skills.* Dubuque, Iowa: Kendall/Hunt Publishing Company, 1979.

This book is filled with activities designed to help students develop both basic and integrated process skills in science. Observation, classification, and experimenting are examples of the sixteen different skills covered in this book.

Mayer, William V. (Ed.). *Biology Teachers' Handbook.* New York: John Wiley and Sons, Inc., 1978.

This book is an accumulation of many topics, ideas, and suggested techniques appropriate for biology teachers, especially those who are using Biological Science Curriculum Study materials.

Smith, Carl B., Smith, Sharol L., and Larry Mikulecky. *Teaching Reading in Secondary School Content Subjects: A Bookthinking Process.* New York: Holt, Rinehart and Winston, 1978.

This is an excellent book for classroom teachers who wish to learn more about the fundamentals of reading and how to help secondary school students become more proficient readers in subject matter areas.

ANGELS ON A PIN

CHAPTER

What Have
Students
Learned?
The Whys
and Hows
of Evaluation

Some time ago, I received a call from a colleague who asked if I would be the referee on the grading of an examination question. He was about to give a student a zero for his answers to a physics question, while the student claimed he should receive a perfect score and would if the system were not set up against the student. The instructor and the student agreed to submit this to an impartial arbiter, and I was selected.

I went to my colleague's office and read the examination question: "Show how it is possible to determine the height of a tall building with the aid of a barometer."

The student had answered: "Take the barometer to the top of the building, attach a long rope to it, lower the barometer to the street, and then bring it up, measuring the length of the rope. The length of the rope is the height of the building."

I pointed out that the student really had a strong case for full credit, since he had answered the question completely and correctly. On the other hand, if full credit were given, it would well contribute to a high grade for the student in his physics course. A high grade is supposed to certify competence in physics, but the answer did not confirm this. I suggested that the student have another try at answering the question. I was not surprised that my colleague agreed, but I was surprised that the student did.

I gave the student six minutes to answer the question, with the warning that his answer should show some knowledge of physics. At the end of five minutes, he had not written anything. I asked if he wished to give up, but he said no. He had many answers to this problem; he was just thinking of the best one. I excused myself for interrupting him, and asked him to please go on. In the next minute, he dashed off his answer which read:

"Take the barometer to the top of the building and lean over the edge of the roof. Drop the barometer, timing its fall with a stopwatch. Then, using the formula $S = \frac{1}{2}at^2$, calculate the height of the building."

At this point, I asked my colleague if *he* would give up. He conceded, and I gave the student almost full credit.

In leaving my colleague's office, I recalled that the student had said he had other answers to the problem, so I asked him what they were. "Oh, yes," said the student. "There are many ways of getting the height of a tall building with the aid of a barometer. For example, you could take the barometer out on a sunny day and measure the height of the barometer, the length of its shadow and the length of the shadow of the building, and by the use of a simple proportion, determine the height of the building."

"Fine," I said. "And the others?"

"Yes," said the student. "There is a very basic measurement method that you will like. In this method, you take the barometer and begin to walk up the stairs. As you climb the stairs, you mark off the length of the barometer along the wall. You then count the number of marks, and this will give you the height of the building in barometer units. A very direct method.

"Of course, if you want a more sophisticated method, you can tie the barometer to the end of a string, swing it as a pendulum, and determine the value of 'g' at the street level and at the top of the building. From the difference between the two values of 'g,' the height of the building can, in principle, be calculated."

Finally he concluded, there are many other ways of solving the problem. "Probably the best," he said "is to take the barometer to the basement and knock on the superintendent's door. When the superintendent answers, you speak to him as follows: 'Mr. Superintendent, here I have a fine barometer. If you will tell me the height of this building, I will give you this barometer.'"

People often shudder at the mere mention of the word "evaluation." To many, evaluation is synonymous with "tests" and "grades," both of which are viewed with a great deal of unpleasantness. However, evaluation should be seen in a much broader and more positive way. Both students and their teachers can benefit from a wide range of evaluation activities, and evaluation need not be limited to what can be learned by giving tests.

What is Evaluation?

Evaluation is a process whereby information is gathered, analyses made. The root word of evaluation is "value," and the process of valuing is that of placing worth on something. This placing of worth, of course, always involves the making of judgments. We judge or decide that something is "good" or "bad," "satisfactory" or "unsatisfactory," or only "average" in quality on the basis of the information we have and the values we use in making our decisions.

Most of us evaluate a variety of things every day. We buy a particular automobile because of its price, gasoline mileage, or appearance. We decide to go camping because of a favorable weather forecast and because camping costs less than staying in a motel. Evaluation also plays an important role in every phase of the science teachers's work as shown by the following examples.

Student-Related Evaluation	Can the students correctly balance an oxidation-reduction equation? Is the class ready to move on to the use of topographic maps? Does Jake have what it takes to be successful in high school chemistry?
Teacher-Related Evaluation	How should I present the mole concept? What is the best way to evaluate my students' ability to critically examine scientific ideas? What do my students like most and least about my teaching?
Program-Related Evaluation	Which textbooks should be selected? What mathematics courses should be required as prerequisites for high school physics? Would it be better to construct a greenhouse or use artificial light to grow plants for life science classes? How good is the science department at Washington Middle High School?

Evaluation involves students, teachers, and programs, and the above questions illustrate how these three are interrelated. This chapter deals with reasons for evaluating these three aspects of science teaching and means for doing so. The evaluation of teacher effectiveness is examined in Chapter 12, which deals with the professional activities of science teachers. Many of the references listed at the end of this chapter provide valuable information on evaluating science teachers and science programs.

Major Functions of Evaluation

Evaluation serves three major functions in the evaluation of student achievement in science: (1) providing information for the teacher; (2) providing information for the student; and (3) providing a basis of grading or reporting progress. It is helpful for the teacher to know how much students know at the beginning of a course, an instructional unit, or a lesson. This is the diagnostic function of evaluation. One of the easiest ways to perform this function is by asking the students questions. "What is the meaning of the term photosynthesis?" "Did you study chemical bonding last year?"

DIAGNOSTIC EVALUATION

Some teachers find it useful to give a pretest in order to ascertain the level at which their students are functioning. Students who already possess considerable knowledge on a topic can do enrichment activities such as individual projects or supplemental reading. They can also act as aides, assisting the teacher with those students who are having difficulties with the material or who have missed some of the work. Or if circumstances permit, students who score sufficiently well on the pretest can go on to the next unit of work.

Many sources of tests can be used to diagnose a student's level of understanding. Many standardized tests in science, such as the Nelson Biology Test or one of the Cooperative Tests in Science, can be used at the beginning of a course. The tests that accompany textbooks can be used as pretests at the beginning of units or chapters. Tests that have been previously developed for the course are also useful. Some teachers prefer to develop their own pretests and to emphasize certain knowledge and skills. For example, chemistry and physics teachers often want to know if entering students possess particular mathematics skills.

Reading is an area where it is usually important to diagnose the level of student achievement early in the year. Science teachers need to know which students will have difficulty in reading the textbook and other written material. The Cloze technique, which is one way of determining the reading level of students, is described in Figure 6.1.

FORMATIVE EVALUATION

A second function of evaluation is to provide students *feedback* on their performance. All of us like to know how well we are doing, and experiencing success is a strong motivation to continue our efforts to learn. Even evidence that we have not accomplished a task may cause us to try harder. Of course, continuous failure usually has negative effects and may lead to students giving up or even dropping out of school. Because education has such strong effects on student actions, teachers must be especially cognizant of how their evaluation activities affect students.

Realistic feedback can serve to reinforce students on things they are doing well and show them where improvements are needed. In this way, evaluation serves to shape student behavior in a desired direction. Students learning to balance chemical equations need to know what they are doing right and what they are doing wrong. Often, students do not perform the way the teacher wants them to simply because they are not aware of *where* they are making their mistakes.

Evaluation that is designed to give students immediate feedback, or

Purpose: Reading materials can be tested for individual student comprehension using this technique.

Directions: Select a passage from the material to be evaluated and copy it. Blank out every fifth or sixth word, until a total of 50 words have been omitted. Students are then given the sheet and asked to fill in the blanks with the words they believe have been omitted.

Example: An excerpt from the following passage shows how to construct this. The blocked words are the ones to be blanked out.

An electrically balanced, or neutral, atom always has as many electrons outside the nucleus as there are protons inside the nucleus. The number of neutrons, however, may vary. This does not change the electrical nature of the atom. For example, the less common varieties of hydrogen atoms have one or two neutrons, but they still have only one proton and one electron. Because they have one proton and one electron, they have the characteristics of hydrogen.

Scoring: Give two points for each of the 50 blanked-out words the student correctly replaces. The following scores tell how well the student should be able to handle this material:

40 or below - material may be very difficult for student
41-60   - material may be used with teacher guidance
61 or above - students should be able to use material independently

FIGURE 6.1   Using the Cloze technique.

to serve a developmental function, is one kind of *formative evaluation*. With formative evaluation, the objective is to do what the word implies—to help form or shape the student's learning. It should be a continuous process that takes place throughout the instruction.

SUMMATIVE
EVALUATION

A third function of evaluation is to provide a means of *reporting* student progress. Summative evaluation is a summing up and takes place at the end of the instruction. Most secondary school teachers are required to assign grades to all students every six or nine weeks. Report cards, an example of summative evaluation, give students and their parents an overall indication of how well the student has performed in each of his subjects.

Grades are important and especially to the students who receive them. These "final" performances of students go with them as labels or designations which have "good" and "bad" connotations. These judg-

**RESEARCH
REPORT**

National
Assessment of
Achievement in
Science

The National Assessment of Educational Progress (NAEP), a Denver-based group established by the Commission of the States and funded by the National Institute of Education (NIE), each year measures the educational attainment in one or more school subjects of students aged nine, thirteen, and seventeen, and adults aged twenty-six to thirty-five. The tests are given to a sample of people in such a way that the results for each group can be generalized to the entire national population. Some of the test items are given to more than one age group and are used more than one time so comparisons can be made between groups and between testing periods.

The three administrations of the science test (1969–1970, 1972–1973, 1976–1977) have shown a general decline in achievement of the questions that have been on the test three times. The proportion of correct answers dropped 2 percent for nine-year-olds, 3.6 percent for thirteen-year-olds, and 4.7 percent for seventeen-year-olds. The weakest performances by all three groups tested in 1976–1977 were in the physical sciences.

An example of a question that was asked thirteen-year-olds in all three science assessments was:
"Some air is pumped out of a car and the car collapses. Which of the following explains why this happened?"

A. Air molecules inside the car collapsed.

B. Pumping out the air molecules weakened the car.

C. The air molecules inside the car condensed to form water.

*D. The air pressure inside the car became less than the pressure outside the car.

E. Pumping the air out of the car increased the number of air molecules around the car.

F. I don't know.

The average proportion of correct answers (D) declined from 72.2 percent in 1970 to 63.9 percent in 1973 to 63.0 percent in 1977.

NAEP stresses assessment, which implies measurement, and leaves the evaluation of the results, or the placing of worth, to other groups. The National Science Teachers Association issued a statement upon the release of the 1976–1977 report which in part said, "The science curriculum of today, which emphasizes broad concepts and investigative skills, is quite different from the fact-oriented exercises which constitute a major portion of the tests."

Other factors suggested as being related to declining scores include decreasing enrollments in high school chemistry and physics, the proliferation of electives that many high school students may substitute for science courses, and the alleged lack of time for science instruction in the lower grades.

ments may determine whether a student passes from one grade to another, graduates, is accepted by a certain college, or gets into medical school. Since grades are so important, it is imperative that they be based on reliable information about the student and be assigned using appropriate procedures and in a fair manner.

Setting Standards and Analyzing Grades

Of the three methods commonly used in setting standards for educational achievement and in assigning grades, the first method involves judging the student's achievement in terms of his or her ability. Using this method, students with high ability must achieve more than average students in order to receive the same grade.

Some schools have ability groups in science, or students are assigned to various classes on the basis of test scores, previous grades, or other data. In such situations, the able students are usually expected to achieve more to get an "A" than the "sweathogs" in a lower section. As a result, one student may earn an "A" by learning only half as much of the material as another student in a higher section.

Students are encouraged to work at their own pace in programs such as the junior high science program developed by the Intermediate Science Curriculum Study (ISCS). Students with high interest and ability in science generally progress faster and further than students with less ability and interest. However, students in some schools are graded only on the work that is completed. In this situation, each student receives a grade based on his or her capabilities to proceed through the program. In other words, a slow student could end up with as much reward, as far as grades are concerned, as a talented science student.

Some teachers use what is called *contract grading*. With this method, objectives are established for each individual depending on the student's needs and abilities. Students are then evaluated on how much progress they make or on how hard they try, rather than being compared to students in their class or against some standard. This might be compared to the concept of scoring handicaps in sports such as golf and bowling.

NORM-REFERENCED EVALUATION

A second method of setting standards and assigning grades is based on how students rank with others in their group. This method is known as "grading on the curve," and the grade the student gets is heavily dependent upon how well the peer group does. If a student gets only 75 percent of the questions correct on a test, but this is the highest grade in the class, the individual gets an "A." Likewise, if 75 percent is the lowest grade in the class, the student might be assigned an "F."

This method of setting standards and assigning grades is an example of *norm-referenced evaluation*. Standardized tests such as the Scholastic

Aptitude Test (SAT), the Graduate Record Examination (GRE), and conventional IQ tests are examples of norm-referenced tests. Scores on an IQ test and other norm-referenced tests will tell how an individual compares with others in a given population. For example, a twelve-year-old getting 100 on an IQ test has scored as well as the average twelve-year-old in the population for which the test is designed. Or a ninth grade student making an average score on a standardized science test would be said to be on the 50th percentile, which means scoring better than 50 percent of those taking the test.

Norm-referenced evaluation, or grading on the curve, has both advantages and limitations in a classroom situation. Comparing a student's performance on a test or other activity with others in the class is often the best way to give meaning to a score. For example, if a test has never been given before, the teacher can use overall class performance to judge the difficulty of the test and the worth of each student's mark. On the other hand, the nature of the students or the course may make it inappropriate to grade on the curve. Most teachers would not want to assign the same number of "Ds" and "Fs" as "As" and "Bs" to a group of high ability students in chemistry and physics. Moreover, unhealthy competition may be fostered when students realize that their grade is dependent upon how others perform. Norm-referenced evaluation tends to maximize differences in students' abilities and has limited meaning when applied to other than random populations of students with natural ranges of abilities.

CRITERION-
REFERENCED
EVALUATION

A third way to establish standards and assign grades is by setting predetermined levels of performance and grading students according to the level they attain. For example, mastering 90 percent or more of a given set of instructional objectives might be considered an "A." Mastery of 80 to 90 percent of the objectives would be a "B," and so on. In this method of evaluation, the grades of students are not a function of how well they compare with other members of their group, but are based on how many of the objectives they are able to accomplish. These grades also do not reflect differences in ability among the students.

This method is called *criterion-referenced evaluation,* since criteria, or levels of performance, are established before achievement is assessed. Although the terminology is fairly recent, the idea of criterion-referenced evaluation is not. There are many situations both within and outside of schools where certain standards must be met. Many states require students to make at least a certain minimum score on a competency examination in order to receive a high school diploma. People who wish to drive a car must make 70 percent or some other minimum score on the driver's license test.

As in the case of other methods of evaluation, criterion-referenced evaluation has its advantages and disadvantages. There are many situations where students must reach certain levels of performance before moving on to new material. This is especially true in mathematics and the quantitative phases of science. In these cases, the material is more sequential, and the student cannot perform a task, such as balancing an equation, without first being able to perform other tasks, such as writing chemical formulas. In many situations, it is difficult to set criterion levels, and those that are established reflect little more than the value judgments of a teacher.

Which of these methods should science teachers use in evaluating their students' work? Many factors will affect the answer to this question. Some schools have published policies on grading practices which must be followed. Students in a junior high science course for special education probably will be evaluated differently than those in advanced science course for seniors. In most cases, a combination or modification of all three methods is used, with the emphasis depending upon the situation and the philosophy of evaluation embraced by the teacher and the school.

Regardless of which methods are used, students like to know ahead of time how they are being evaluated and how grades will be assigned. School officials, parents, and others expect a teacher to be able to explain how a student's grade is determined. Thus, each teacher should have well thought-out plans for evaluating students and assigning grades.

RECORD OF STUDENT ACHIEVEMENT

A page from a teacher's grade book (see page 244) illustrates one method of recording student scores and indicates the progress made during the first half of a six-week grading period. An explanation is given below.

(A) Listing students alphabetically by last name speeds up the recording of grades and their transfer to other school records.

(B) There are several advantages of recording numerical scores: final grades are easier to determine, and the weighing of various tasks is facilitated. Note that the test is given four times as much weight as the quiz and the lab reports. Some scores are reported as multiples of five, as in the case of the oral reports on careers, or in multiplies of two, as in the case of lab reports. This is done because of the difficulty of grading some work to the nearest point.

(C) Class participation was graded subjectively and assigned one of three grades. These grades can be converted to numerical scores and included in the total grade, or they can be considered when assigning letter grades to numerical scores. The latter approach was used in the example shown.

(D) "Ab" recorded in pencil indicates the student was absent, and it can be replaced by the appropriate score once the grade is made up.

(E) Midterm numerical scores can be converted to letter grades using one or more of the methods described on pages 241–243. In the case of the example, the scores were arranged in numerical order and lines drawn, which resulted in the grades being assigned as follows:

95–105	A	65–75	D
85–94	B	74 and below	F
75–84	C		

(F) According to the grading scale, a score of 93 is a "B"; however, high marks in class participation served as justification for assigning Pat an "A."

1st Period 7th Grade Science	Safety Quiz	Home work — metric System	Oral Reports — Covers	Test — Chapter 1	Lab Report — microscope	Lab Report — Cell Division	Class Participation First 3 Weeks	midterm Grades Total	midterm Grade	
Names (A)										
Possible Points (B)	10	15	20	40	10	10	V+ V++ (C)	105	(E)	
Abbott, James	8	10	15	29	6	8	V	76	C	
Abernethy, Pat	9	13	20	33	8	10	V++	93	A	(F)
Baker, Donald	10	15	20	35	6	6	V	92	B	
Banner, Rodney	10	15	15	40	10	10	V++	100	A	
Buchanan, Mary	7	15	10	32	Ab	Ab (D)	V	Inc		
Daughtry, Pat	5	4	10	20	6	6	V	51	F	
Edmund, Cecil	8	12	15	36	10	10	V+	91	B	
	10	13	20	35	8	6	V	92	B	
				21	10	8	V	80	C	

Collecting Data for Evaluation

Students, like radio stations, are always transmitting. What science teachers must do is to tune their ears to hear the many things they are saying. Of course, teachers must temper or ignore the "static"—the frequent complaints about the difficulty of homework or the unreasonableness of having to learn the symbols of twenty elements. And, as is always the case in evaluation, teachers must interpret student responses and make judgments about their meaning.

In other words, there are many ways to evaluate students in addition to giving tests. The following list summarizes some of these ways and gives examples of each.

Action	*Opportunities to Observe*
1. What do students say?	Class discussion Oral reports, panel discussions Informal conversations during laboratory work, field trips, and during extracurricular activities
2. What do students produce?	Results in laboratory and on research projecs Construction of equipment and displays
3. What do students write?	Written homework Reports of laboratory work and research projects Reports on field trips, interviews, and outside reading Quizzes and tests
4. What do students do?	Choose or ignore science-related articles, books, television programs, and other forms of education and entertainment Choice of hobbies and careers Changes in habits, such as eating a more balanced diet or getting regular exercise

These data can be used for many purposes besides assigning grades. Part of them deal with student attitudes and interests, and are felt by some to be inappropriate evidence for use in determining grades. However, these data are helpful in situations such as judging a teacher's effectiveness and determining which changes need to be made in a science curriculum.

In collecting and analyzing data like these, it is important to remember that we can collect only a sample of a student's behavior. We can observe only a small percentage of what each individual student does or says in the laboratory. On the final examination, we can only ask questions about a portion of what the student has been expected to learn.

Important Attributes of Achievement Tests

Even though there are numerous ways students can be evaluated, tests are the principal method used by most science teachers. Since tests play such an important role, several test attributes should be given careful consideration when constructing or selecting a science achievement test.

VALIDITY

A *valid* test is one that measures what it is supposed to measure and is determined primarily by the course content and the instructional objectives. If a test is valid, the questions will not appear strange or incomprehensible to others who are competent in the subject matter being tested.

The validity of a test is dependent upon the test being *balanced*. The nature and number of items and the time required to answer them should reflect the amount of time spent teaching a given topic or objectives. If 25 percent of the time during a unit was spent on photosynthesis, then the topic should receive approximately the same emphasis on the unit test. The same is true of high- and low-level objectives; if the instruction emphasized recall and recognition, then the test should not be mainly application questions.

Figure 6.2 illustrates one way to analyze the distribution of items on a general science test on astronomy. Note how the levels of objectives are shown on the horizontal axis, while the major topics covered by the test are shown on the vertical axis. The numbers correspond to the number of each item on the test; in this case, the test was composed of fifty items. Figure 6.2 shows that the items are evenly distributed on the basis of content but that more items deal with knowledge than with the higher order objectives of analysis, synthesis, and evaluation.

Validity is one of the most important attributes of any test. A test that

Content	Classification of test items according to Bloom's taxonomy				Total number of test items
	Knowledge	Comprehension	Application	Analysis, synthesis, and evaluation	
I. Tools of Astronomy					
A. Telescopes	1,3	4	2		4
B. Spectroscopes	5		6,7	8	4
C. Space Vehicles	9	10,11		12	4
II. Solar System					
A. Sun		13,14	15	16	4
B. Motion of Planets	17	18	19,20		4
C. Characteristics of Planets	21,22,23	24			4
D. Moon	25		26,27	28	4
E. Meteors and Comets	29,30				2
F. Origin of Solar System	31,32	33	34		4
III. Beyond the Solar System					
A. Locating Stars in the Sky	35,36,37	38,39			5
B. Classification of Stars	40,41	42,43		44	5
C. Galaxies and Other Features	45,46	47			3
D. Origin of the Universe	48,49	50			3
Total Number of Test Items	22	14	9	5	50

FIGURE 6.2   Two-axis chart for a General Science Examination.

does not measure what it is intended to measure is of little value in evaluating student achievement.

RELIABILITY

A test should be *reliable,* or it should measure a person's knowledge and understanding of a subject in a consistent manner. If a test is reliable, it should yield the same results in two or more measurements. A test is said to have a low reliability if a student scores 95 and then scores 50 on the same or a similar test the same day.

The reliability of an achievement test can be raised by increasing the number of questions or scorable units it contains. Reliability is also affected by the quality of the questions. For example, "tricky" questions or questions that encourage guessing decrease reliability.

OBJECTIVITY

A test should be as *objective* as possible since objectivity increases reliability. A test is objective if it receives the same grade or score when it is read by the same reader on two different occasions. High objectivity is also indicated by high agreement among experts as to what the answers are on a test.

Students are always concerned about the fairness of a test and rightly so. Tests that are valid and possess high objectivity are the ones that students rate as being the fairest. Means of increasing the objectivity of test items and scoring procedures are discussed later in this chapter when various kinds of questions are considered.

ECONOMY

Tests should be economical of the student's time in taking them and of the teacher's time in grading the papers. The economy or efficiency of the test is the amount of achievement that can be measured in a given period of time. If a test elicits a high number of responses, hence, requiring the student to demonstrate much of what he has learned, we say that the test is efficient. Closed-type questions, such as multiple choice or true–false, are usually more efficient than discussion or essay questions.

REASONABLENESS

The questions on a test should represent reasonable tasks for students to perform, and students should have reasonable amounts of time to do them. The well-prepared student should be able to finish the test and have a feeling of accomplishment.

Just how hard should a test be? Many teacher-made tests are criterion-referenced and thus measure the student's mastery of a set of specific objectives. In other words, their purpose is to differentiate between those who have achieved mastery and those who have not. In constructing these tests, the difficulty of the items is adjusted so that those who possess the desired competencies will make more than some predetermined minimum score. For example, students who can success-fully work inclined-plane problems will score 90 percent or more on the test.

The purpose of norm-referenced tests is to spread out students so that those with differing levels of achievement can be compared. In order to do this, the test must contain questions of varying levels of difficulty. In other words, the test must contain some items that most of the students will get correct and some items that only a few students will get correct.

The *level of difficulty* of a test item can be found using the formula:

$$\frac{\text{Number of students getting item correct}}{\text{Number of students taking the test}} \times 100 = \text{level of difficulty in percent}$$

For example, if seventeen out of twenty-seven students get an item correct, its level of difficulty is $17/27 \times 100$, or 63 percent. Whether or not this item is too easy or difficult depends on its intended use and the other items on the test.

Some teachers find it useful to calculate the level of difficulty for each item on the tests they give. An easy way of doing so is by having students volunteer to raise their hands if they got the item correct. The hand-held calculator or a slide ruler is an aid in calculating the level of difficulty in percent.

DISCRIMINATION   The ability of a test to *discriminate,* or to distinguish among students with differing levels of achievement, is an especially important attribute of norm-referenced tests. The ability of a test to discriminate is related in part to the level of difficulty of the items. In order to be a discriminating item, it should not be answered correctly by all the students, nor should it be missed by all the students.

Tests experts find the *index of discrimination* for each item by compar-ing the number of students in the top 27 percent of the class getting the item correct with the number in the bottom 27 percent getting the same item correct. An *approximate* index of discrimination can be found by using all the responses and the following formula:

$$\frac{\begin{array}{c}\text{number in top half of class} \\ \text{getting the item correct}\end{array} - \begin{array}{c}\text{number in the bottom half} \\ \text{of the class getting the} \\ \text{item correct}\end{array}}{\text{total number of students in class divided by two}} = \text{index of discrimination}$$

For example, twelve of the fourteen students in a class of twenty-eight that made the top scores on a test got an item correct. Only two of the fourteen making the lowest score got the item correct. The index of discrimination is:

$$\frac{12\text{-}2}{14} = 0.71$$

The index of discrimination for an item can range from $+1.0$ (all the top students and none of the bottom students got the item correct) to -1.0 (none of the top students and all the bottom students got the item correct). Many factors affect what is an acceptable index of discrimination for an index; however, it should always be positive and generally should be $+0.5$ or higher when the above formula is used.

RELEVANCE

The items on a test should be *relevant*, which means that they are appropriate for a given group of students. In this sense, relevance is closely related to validity. At least some of the items also should be *life-like*, or they should require students to perform tasks that often are associated with common, everyday experiences. "What are some things that should be checked if a table lamp doesn't work" is more life-like than "list the different parts of the water cycle." Competency tests, which some states require for graduation and promotion, often emphasize life-like items.

How to Write Different Kinds of Test Questions

We have discussed important attributes of a good test and some general things to consider when selecting items to make up a test. Let us now look at some specific types of test items that are appropriate for measuring achievement in science and consider a few guidelines for constructing these items. Most test items can be categorized as being either **open** or **closed**. Each possesses noticeable advantages and disadvantages.

CLOSED TEST ITEMS

Closed test items are those that call for definite, specific answers. Multiple choice, matching, true–false, and fill-in-the-blanks are examples of closed test items. These items are sometimes referred to as "objective" questions. This stems from the high objectivity of these items, which in turn results from the high agreement among experts concerning the appropriate answers. As a result of high objectivity, closed questions usually possess greater reliability because there is a higher degree of consistency among student scores from one test time to another. One of the major advantages of closed questions is their high degree of efficiency. More student time can be spent on reading and thinking since a minimum of writing is required. As a result, more responses per unit of time can be elicited from students. Another noticeable advantage is that they can be scored much faster. The grader, by using a key, can grade a page of multiple choice or matching items in a matter of a few seconds.

The ease of grading closed questions is offset by the fact that considerable time is required to construct items of this type. Good multiple choice and matching questions are difficult to construct and require a great deal of time and skill on the part of the teacher. However, when major examinations are given to large numbers of students, closed questions are generally advantageous. Experienced teachers usually keep good test items of this type in a file and use them over again. Another of the major disadvantages of closed questions is that they often are written to measure only lower level learning—recognition or recall of factual information. With additional skill and experience, a teacher can learn to construct closed test items to measure higher level thinking skills.

Essay, short answer, and other kinds of open questions are discussed later in this chapter.

MULTIPLE CHOICE TEST ITEMS. Multiple choice items are among the most frequently used closed type of test question. This format contains a **stem** and four or five **options** from which the best answer is selected. The incorrect options are called **distractors**. A stem may be a complete statement, a question, or an incomplete statement lacking only a word or phrase. The following multiple choice question contains a poor example of a stem:

_____ 1. An ion

    A. Is any charged particle
    B. Is formed when any substance dissolves in water
   *C. Is formed when atoms gain or lose electrons
    D. Is present only in solutions which can be electrolyzed
    E. Results only when atoms gain electrons

In the above example, the student is not sure what the question is asking until all the options are read. A better way to write this item is demonstrated by the following question:

_____ 2. Which of the following statements best describes the condition under which ions are produced?

    A. When any substance receives an electrical charge
    B. When any substance dissolves in water
   *C. When atoms gain or lose electrons
    D. Only when solutions are electrolyzed
    E. Only when atoms gain electrons

In the second example, a student has a better idea of what to look for among the options. In a good multiple choice question, all the options should agree as closely as possible with the focus of the stem. It is generally considered advantageous to keep options as short as possible and to avoid repeating the same phrases in each option. The above question could be rewritten another way to eliminate further duplication in the options:

_____ 3. Which of the following conditions always produces an ion from an atom?

    A. Electrical current
    B. Dissolving a substance in water
  *C. A loss or gain in electrons
    D. Heating a substance
    E. A gain in neutrons

As you can see, one of the most difficult tasks in constructing multiple choice items is associated with writing good options. A few suggestions are:

- All answers should sound plausible to the student who has little or no knowledge of the idea being tested.
- All answers should relate to the topic contained in the stem.
- Common misconceptions make good options.
- True statements, but in the wrong context, make appropriate options.
- Options are best if they are nearly equal in length and style.
- The correct answer should be positioned randomly, and readily distinguishable patterns of responses should be avoided.
- Tenses should be consistent between the stem and options.
- Avoid words like "all," "never," "always" which may serve as clues to students that the response is not plausible.
- Options like "none of the above" or "all of the above" should be used sparingly and, if used, sometimes be the only acceptable answer.

Multiple choice items are particularly suitable for examining higher level thinking skills. As stated before, it is tempting to use closed questioning techniques only for the recognition of factual information. The following multiple choice questions demonstrate how higher level learning thinking can be elicited from students.

_____ 4. Which of the following levels of organization represents the simplest unit at which living processes can be maintained?

    A. compounds
    B. organelles
  *C. cells
    D. tissues
    E. organs

In the above question, students must comprehend the idea that cells constitute the basic unit of life in order to answer this correctly.

_____ 5. Which of the following substances does not belong in this general grouping?
    A. coal
    B. diamond
    C. graphite
    D. charcoal
    *E. silica

In the above questions, students are required to think in terms of how substances are classified. The first four substances are carbon-containing compounds while silica is not.

_____ 6. Assuming red is completely dominant over white in roses and follows simple monohybrid patterns of inheritance, what ratios would you expect to find in the offspring if you crossed heterozygous parents?
    A. all red
    B. all white
    C. ½ red and ½ white
    *D. ¾ red and ¼ white
    E. ¼ red and ¾ white

To answer the above question correctly a student would not only have to understand the basic concepts of Mendelian genetics but also be able to work a problem where a monohybrid cross is involved. Here, students are called upon to apply what they know to a new situation.

As one can see from these examples, multiple choice questions can be constructed to test higher levels of understanding. Research data can be presented and students asked to interpret results. With test equations like these, students are called upon to analyze, synthesize, and evaluate ideas at the highest levels of Bloom's taxonomy. Questions used to evaluate the various levels of cognition are presented in Figure 6.3 (pages 254–255).

MATCHING QUESTIONS. Another type of closed question similar to multiple choice is the matching question. With this type of question, several items dealing with common topics are placed in a grouping, and students are asked to discriminate among several similar options. Matching questions possess high efficiency; that is, a large number of student responses can be elicited in a relatively short amount of time. Below is an example of a poor matching format. See how many faults you can find before reading the paragraph following this example (on page 256).

Knowledge
(ability to recognize
terminology and recall
facts)

_____ The person who first promoted the germ theory and dispelled spontaneous generation was:

    A. Harvey   B. Galileo   *C. Pasteur   D. Aristotle   E. Darwin

_____ The term *Homo sapiens* represents the genus and species name of which organism?

    A. Horse   B. Gorilla   C. Dog   D. Cat   *E. Human

Comprehension
(ability to understand
and explain ideas)

_____ Consider the following graph.
Results from this graph indicate that:

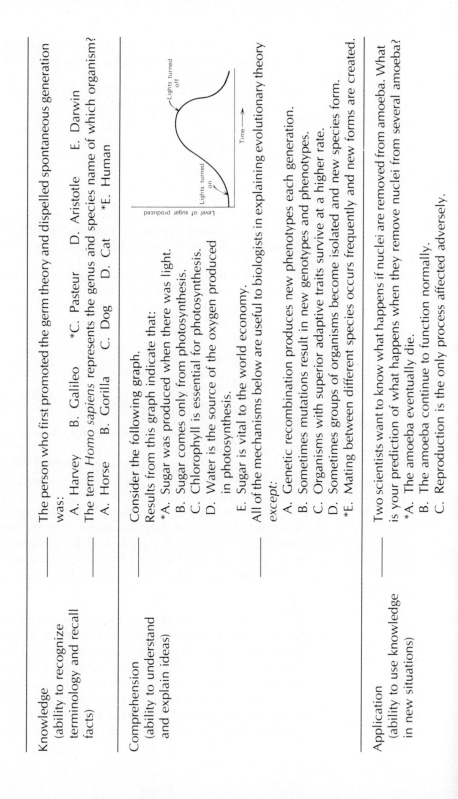

   *A. Sugar was produced when there was light.
    B. Sugar comes only from photosynthesis.
    C. Chlorophyll is essential for photosynthesis.
    D. Water is the source of the oxygen produced in photosynthesis.
    E. Sugar is vital to the world economy.

_____ All of the mechanisms below are useful to biologists in explaining evolutionary theory except:

    A. Genetic recombination produces new phenotypes each generation.
    B. Sometimes mutations result in new genotypes and phenotypes.
    C. Organisms with superior adaptive traits survive at a higher rate.
    D. Sometimes groups of organisms become isolated and new species form.
   *E. Mating between different species occurs frequently and new forms are created.

Application
(ability to use knowledge
in new situations)

_____ Two scientists want to know what happens if nuclei are removed from amoeba. What is your prediction of what happens when they remove nuclei from several amoeba?

   *A. The amoeba eventually die.
    B. The amoeba continue to function normally.
    C. Reproduction is the only process affected adversely.

D. The amoeba go through temporary shock, then recover.
E. Since amoeba don't have nuclei this experiment cannot be done.

_____ A botanist has found a new kind of buttercup and thinks it is a new species. Which of the following characteristics is the best one to use in distinguishing it from previously established species?

A. Leaf size
B. Root branching pattern
C. Odor
D. Soil type preference
*E. Floral structure

Analysis, Synthesis, and Evaluation
(ability to summarize, formulate, and interpret concepts)

_____ If a taxonomy of living organisms was developed based on the kinds of DNA possessed by each organism, which of the following techniques would be the most accurate method for quantifying this information?

A. Studies on the organism's native environment.
B. Embryological investigations of cleavage patterns.
C. Description of external morphology.
*D. Serological study of proteins.
E. Description of internal morphology.

_____ Biologists classify chemical substances based on their contribution to life. Which of the following functions best describes chlorophyll?

A. Movement
*B. Energy transformation
C. Reproduction
D. Excretion
E. Nutritional procurement

FIGURE 6.3   Examples of multiple choice items written at various levels of Bloom's taxonomy.

I. Matching

1. An enzyme found in some animals capable of digesting wood.
2. A branch of biology that deals with the study of birds.
3. The "currency system" of life's energy system.
4. Small, spherical granules in cells where protein synthesis is known to occur.
5. Two men responsible for formulating the chemical structure of genes.

A. ribosomes
B. Hooke
C. ornithology
D. ATP
E. cellulase
F. respiration
G. Watson and Crick

The above matching question lacks directions. It is not clear what the student should do in responding to this set of items. Item 1 calls for an enzyme, and most students know that the names of enzymes usually end in the letters "ase." The second column contains not only one option that is a match for this statement, but also only one word with an "ase" ending. For item 2, there is only one term in the column at the bottom representing a branch of biology. Item 3 calls for an energy-laden compound, and ATP is the only answer that fits this category. Statement 4 calls for a plural answer, and ribosomes is the only plural word in the list of options. Item 5, like the other items, calls for an answer that could be none other than "G." In constructing items, all options should be plausible answers; yet, "Hooke," a person's name, and respiration, a chemical process, do not represent possible answers for any of the items.

The following example shows how a matching question can be constructed to remedy many of the shortcomings of the previous example.

II. In Column I are statements defining basic units of matter. You are to match each item in Column I with the appropriate word in Column II by placing the letter in the blank provided at the left of each statement. Answers in Column II may be used once, more than once, or not at all.

Column I

(A) 1. The smallest particle of an element that can exist and still maintain its identity

(F) 2. A small, charged particle found in the nucleus of atoms

Column II

A. atom
B. electron
C. ion
D. molecule

Column I   *Column II*

(B) 3. A negatively-charged particle   E. neutron

(D) 4. The smallest particle of a compound that   F. proton
      can exist and still maintain its identity

(B) 5. The particle found in atoms that possesses
      the least amount of mass

(C) 6. A particle such as H^+, NA^{++} or O^{--}

With the above example, clear directions are provided. Each term in Column II is a plausible answer since they all represent particles that make up matter. Each statement in Column I calls for a single answer, and each term in Column II is singular. With this format, students are required to discriminate among items within a similar category.

In constructing matching items, care should be taken so that:

• Items cover the same general topic or category.

• All options are plausible answers.

• The basis on which items are to be matched is defined in the directions.

• Options are written in the same tense.

• At least six items are included in each column and no more than twelve to fifteen per column.

• When several options are present, the words are arranged in alphabetical order.

• Some items may be used more than once or not at all.

COMPLETION-TYPE QUESTIONS.   The completion or "fill-in-the blank" question represents another kind of closed question. Unlike the multiple choice and matching format, they are relatively easy to construct. While items of this type require less time for construction, there are many pitfalls that should be avoided. The following item is a classical example of how student perceptions may fail to match the meaning intended by the teacher writing the item:

1. Three states in which matter exists are _____, _____, and _____. The intended answer is gas, liquid, and solid. What would you do if a student responded with *Arkansas, California,* and *Texas*? While this example may seem a bit exaggerated, it actually happened and illustrates how completion-type questions may have more than one possible answer.

Completion questions require students to recall information, while multiple choice, matching, true–false, and other closed-type questions call for *recognition*. In cases where *recall* is desired over *recognition*, the completion question has a distinct advantage. In problem-solving situations, particularly in chemistry and physics, it may be appropriate to ask for the actual answer the student calculates. In this case, the completion format is superior to having students select from a series of options.

Guidelines to follow when writing completion-type items are:

- Blanks should be of uniform length with sufficient space for the answer; blanks of varying length serve as unnecessary clues to students.
- Directly copied statements from the textbook or standard definitions should be avoided since they encourage students to memorize the answer. Also, when statements are taken out of context they can take on different meaning.
- Articles such as "a" or "an" in front of the blank should either be avoided or both options provided, such as "... a(an) _____.
- Blanks should be avoided at the beginning of statements; blanks appearing later in the sentence or at the end help students determine what the item is asking for.
- Only key words should be left blank, and one or two blanks per sentence works best.
- Blanks should be for a word or two, not for long phrases.
- Items should be written in such a way that each blank calls for a specific response. Credit should be given when students respond with closely related synonyms.
- Clear directions should be given; students may write directly in the blanks or the blanks numbered and student responses placed in separate blanks to the side of each item.

TRUE-FALSE ITEMS. True–false statements represent a fourth kind of closed test question. They are easy to construct and easy to grade. As in the case of multiple choice, they are particularly suitable for determining how well students can analyze or evaluate important concepts. True–false statements may be written to help students make judgments, evaluate variables, and enter into other decision-making processes. In addition, true–false questions allow for testing students' knowledge of the characteristics of science. Statements like "Science deals with absolute truth" or "Scientific investigation usually produces facts which are unchangeable" allow teachers opportunities to determine whether students understand the basic tenets on which science rests.

Unfortunately, true–false items too often are used to evaluate only factual level knowledge. In some cases, students look only to see if key words are right or wrong. This may lead to a guessing game instead of students thinking about the overall meaning of each statement. Students may also become overly concerned about being tricked into wrong responses. For this reason, true–false test items generally possess low reliability. Another thing that many experienced teachers have noticed is that higher achieving students often "read more into the question" and, hence, may do comparatively less well with true–false items.

There are modifications of the true–false format that some teachers find useful:

Directions: Read the following statements carefully; one key word in each statement is italicized. If the statement is true, write "true" in the blank to the left of each number. If the statement is false, *change* the italicized word so that the statement becomes true. Write this word in the blank to the left of each number.

<u>energy</u>   1. The first Law of Thermodynamics states that *matter* can be changed from one form to another.

<u>Cold-blooded</u> 2. *Warm-blooded* animals are those whose body temperatures vary with the temperature of the environment.

Another modification of true–false is to present research results or a series of related data that students are then asked to respond to pairs of associated statements concerning the topic:

Write "A" in the blank if both statements are true.
Write "B" in the blank if both statements are false.
Write "C" in the blank if statement 1 is true but statement 2 is false.
Write "D" in the blank if statement 1 is false but statement 2 is true.

<u>3. (A)</u>

1. Technology is an attempt to apply scientific knowledge to human problems.
2. It is often said that "necessity is the mother of technology."

<u>4. (B)</u>

1. Science is based on fact, hence scientific results should not be questioned.
2. Only people who are geniuses should consider entering the field of science.

The following suggestions should help avoid some of the common weaknesses associated with true–false questions.

• Each statement should be clearly correct or incorrect.
• Avoid making items tricky.
• Avoid double negatives such as "not unlike" or "membranes are not unaffected by concentrations of . . ."
• Avoid the use of words generally associated with false statements such as "all," "always," and "never"; likewise, avoid words that hedge and give clues that the statement is probably true, such as "sometimes," "generally speaking," and "possibly."
• When possible, statements should encourage higher level thinking.
• Lifting statements or definitions verbatim from textbooks should be avoided since taking statements out of context often changes meaning.

• If a statement represents an individual scientist's hypothesis or theory, that person should be cited, such as "Darwin's Theory of Evolution" or "Professor Jones' hypothesis concerning..."

OPEN ITEMS

Thus far, we have discussed questions that call for closed responses, or what are often referred to as "objective" questions. Another general category of test items calls for more open responses. Essay, discussion questions, or oral test questions require students to formulate their own answer. These questions usually result in a wider range of student responses. Often, the intent of the question is to elicit divergent thought from students. For example, "Design a spaceship capable of carrying four astronauts on a four-year trip to another planet." This question obviously calls for the organization and synthesis of information different from what the response to most closed questions would elicit. With this question, students would be required to apply many concepts of science and communicate their ideas in writing.

One of the advantages of open questions is that students can be more creative in demonstrating what they have learned. This type of question also allows a teacher to find out where the students' misconceptions lie. For this reason, essay or short answer test questions are useful as "weekly quizzes," in "daily evaluations," or as pretests to determine the level at which students are functioning.

One way of evaluating science understanding is to ask students to explain a natural event with which they are familiar.

Discussion questions usually take less time to construct than most closed items. However, since discussion and other open questions often yield lengthy student responses, more time is required for grading and the responses are most difficult to score. The more open a question is, the wider the range the responses will be; the more varied the responses, the more difficult it is to grade each question fairly and consistently. As a result, the reliability of essay questions is usually much lower than that for short answer and objective items. In an attempt to raise the reliability and objectivity of discussion questions, it is often advisable to write questions that are more specific. Examine the following pairs of questions and select the one from each pair you think would elicit responses you could evaluate most objectively.

1A. What is photosynthesis?
1B. Discuss at least three ways photosynthesis differs from respiration.
2A. Discuss what is meant by the term *quantum mechanics.*
2B. Outline at least two important concepts on which our current understanding of quantum mechanics rests.
3A. What is meant by the term "food chain?"
3B. Arrange a garter snake, salamander, hawk, and a small green plant so they form a food chain and label the role of each organism in this food chain.

The first member of each pair is very broadly stated and open-ended. Questions with little or no direction usually result in such a variation of answers that a uniform grading standard is difficult to attain. In each case, the second question of the above pairs gives the student more information or direction. Thus, the person grading a particular question has built-in standards to go by and can be more objective in evaluating each answer.

It is important to know ahead of time what a student should be able to do after a given unit of instruction. Important cognitive behaviors asked for in test questions should coincide with those present in the instructional objectives. Figure 1.4 in Chapter 1 presents examples of key words that can be used in open-type questions designed to measure achievement at various cognitive levels.

Another use of open questions is the oral examination. While oral exams are sometimes given in small college classes, they are not commonly used in secondary schools because of the large number of students each teacher must evaluate. Nevertheless, when circumstances permit, examining students by asking oral, open-ended questions can be an excellent method of evaluating achievement.

Essay and short-answer discussion questions offer many advantages in the overall evaluation of student performance. In summary, here are a few suggestions to consider when using open questions.

• Relate discussion questions to the major objectives for the unit; ask for behaviors in the test question that correspond to what was emphasized in class.

- Construct discussion questions that measure not only factual recall, but also an understanding of concepts and principles, and other important outcomes; factual material is usually tested more efficiently by using closed questions.

- When constructing open test questions, consider carefully the time factor and allow students ample time to complete the test.

- Establish criteria for grading the question at the time of construction; the more specific the question, the greater the objectivity and reliability.

- When scoring discussion questions, grade one question at a time on all the papers before moving to the next question; rearrange the papers randomly after reading the answers to each question so the answers on a given paper are not always read first or last.

- If possible, grade papers anonymously. It is tempting to grade individual responses in light of the student's ability level or past performance. A fairer job of grading is possible if you do not know whose paper is being read.

- When answering essay questions, students should be encouraged to organize their ideas and prepare well-written responses. In some cases, it may be appropriate to award points for basic communication skills employed in answering the questions.

ADDITIONAL TESTING TECHNIQUES

In addition to the commonly used methods that have been discussed, there are many other techniques that can be used in evaluating student achievement.

OPEN BOOK TESTS.   This technique deemphasizes memorization while emphasizing the ability to find correct answers or to solve problems using material in the book. Open book tests are "life-like" in that this is the kind of "test" people usually face once they leave school. Students should know ahead of time if an examination is going to be open book or closed book because it will affect how they prepare for the test.

LABORATORY PRACTICAL EXAMINATIONS AND SKILL TESTS.   Evaluation procedures that allow students to demonstrate what they know or what they can do serve as excellent methods for testing. Having students focus microscopes, find unknown compounds, identify properties of substances, and recognize parts of plants or animals are all good ways to evaluate the "hands-on" abilities as well as the mental skills of science students. Particularly in psychomotor evaluation, exercises can be designed to test students' abilities. Bending glass tubing, using a pipette, measuring materials accurately, and building apparatus in a physics laboratory are examples of skills that can be evaluated by observing student performance.

TAKE HOME EXAMINATIONS. Students can learn a great deal from taking tests outside the classroom, and occasionally it is desirable to give them take home exams. While the teacher has less control and cannot be sure that all students will do the examinations as directed, their use is justified as a means of helping students develop a sense of responsibility. Tests of this type are often used during a course as a learning experience and thus are more formative than summative in nature.

PEER TESTING. In order to help students identify their difficulties and mistakes, it is sometimes helpful to let students evaluate each other. Working in pairs or small groups, students can administer written or oral tests to each other, grade them, and offer immediate feedback on areas of strength and weakness.

PUZZLES AND GAMES. Crossword puzzles, riddles, and other individual or group games can be used as evaluative measures. They can also be used for review and preparation for end-of-term examinations. The "quiz-show" format is also a good technique for reviewing material. Puzzles and games are most often used in formative evaluation or as an instructional strategy.

Constructing a Classroom Test

Portions of this teacher-made test illustrate several things that should be done in assemblying a test.

(1 of 2 pages)   Ⓐ

Ⓑ Name _____   Ⓒ Date _____

Ⓓ Class or period _____   Ⓔ Total Score _____

Test #3 (40 minutes)

Ⓕ Environmental Science

Ⓖ Part I. Circle T if the statement is true and F if it is false (1 point each).

T F   1. Cold-blooded animals are found living only in cold climates.

T F   2. Lichens are composed of algae and fungi living together in a symbiotic relationship.

(2 of 2 pages)   (A)

(B) Name _____

(H) Part II. Answer each of the following questions with one or more complete
sentences in the space provided (5 points each).

1. Explain what a community and an ecosystem have in common and how they
differ.

(I)

Explanation

(A) This method of numbering pages illustrates one method of insuring each
student gets all the pages of the test.

(B) The student's name on each page of the test is desirable since some of
the pages may get separated during grading.

(C) The date the test is taken is useful information, especially in the
case of make-up tests.

(D) This information is especially useful when the teacher has two or more
sections of the same course.

(E) Student's total score and grade can be reported here; the position close
to the student's name speeds the recording of the score in a grade book.

(F) Most teachers like to title or number a test and indicate the amount of
time the students will have to complete the test.

(G) The test should be organized so that all questions of one type are
grouped together, appropriate instructions are provided, and the weights
for each item are indicated.

(H) Most teachers prefer to place some of the easier items first in each
section; others feel it is better to arrange the items in the approximate
order the material is studied in class.

(I) In short answer and essay questions, it often is desirable to allow space
for the answers immediately following the question; this facilitates
grading and space limitations discourage "long winded" responses.

**Using
Standardized
Science
Achievement
Tests**

In selecting a standardized science achievement test, it is important to have clearly in mind what is to be accomplished by using the test. A particular test may be excellent for predicting success in a course but totally inappropriate for assessing what students know at the end of the course. Selection of an achievement test should also take into account test attributes such as validity, reliability, and reasonableness, which were described earlier in this chapter. Several excellent reference books that list and discuss standardized achievement tests are described in Chapter 9.

Science teachers must be able to interpret the scores made on the tests they select or those given as part of schoolwide and statewide testing programs. The raw score, for example, 17, that a student makes on one of these tests has little meaning. However, 17 correct out of 20 questions, or 85 percent on a criterion-referenced test, represents satisfactory performance when the minimum acceptable score is some percentage below 85.

On a norm-referenced test, the meaning of a score of 17 is determined by comparing it with the scores of others taking the test. The results can be reported to students and parents using one of the following terms:

> *Age-equivalent*—the age (for example, 14.3 years) for which a given score (17) is the average score on the test. In other words, a student who scored 17 did as well as the average score made by a group of students 14.3 years old. If the student is younger than 14.3 years, his or her score of 17 would be considered above average. Students with scores of 17 who are older than 14.3 years could be considered below average in achievement.

"Test time" for many students is a time of anxiety and frustration.

Grade-equivalent—the grade level (for example, 9.2) for which a given score (17) is the average score on the test. As you can see, grade equivalent scores are very similar to age-equivalent scores.

Percentile rank—the percent of scores in a group equal to or lower than the score corresponding to a given rank. For example, 17 might represent a rank of 62 percentile, which means the student scoring 17 did as well as or better than 62 percent of those taking the test. Since a student's score is included in the total and he or she cannot be better than or worse than himself or herself, the range of percentile ranks is 1 to 99. The 50th percentile is average, and students scoring below or above the 50th percentile are considered, respectively, below or above average in achievement.

Most standardized tests have a test manual that describes the various features of the test and explains how to interpret the results. Science teachers and others using these tests should use the manuals to become thoroughly familiar with the tests and aware of their limitations as well as their potential usefulness. After all, one of the major purposes of science teaching is to encourage people to collect appropriate data and to use these data in the solving of problems. Should science teachers not act in the ways of science in using standardized tests and the other means of evaluating every phase of the science program?

Evaluating Behavior in the Affective Domain

The affective domain, as you will recall, deals with interests, attitudes, and values. There are many techniques for evaluating how students feel toward science, their learning environment, and the many topics in the science curriculum. Some educators believe that the way students *feel* toward these and other topics is as important as cognitive development in science. The willingness of students to apply their knowledge in science, the way they react to issues in the future, and indeed, the extent to which science becomes an important part of their lives is influenced largely by the attitudes and values with which they leave our secondary school science classrooms.

THE LIKERT SCALE

The Likert Scale is one of the most commonly used methods for measuring attitudes and values. This method requires students to respond to statements designed to probe feelings, using a scale such as "strongly agree," "agree," "undecided," "disagree," or "strongly disagree." For example, the statement "I really get upset when I see people dumping trash on the highway" elicits feelings toward one aspect of pollution. A "strongly agree" response to this statement indicates strong feelings or concern and is scored five points. An "agree" response would receive four points and so forth down to one point for the "strongly disagree." This scoring system is easy to use since all responses have positive values.

Likert Scale items are also written to elicit disagreement. For example, "I see nothing wrong with those who dump their trash on the highway" is scored in an opposite manner to scoring positive items. Five points are given to the "strongly disagree" responses to negative items on down to one point for "strongly agree." Figure 6.4 is an example of a Likert-type scale that could be used to measure attitudes toward pollution.

Directions: We would like to find out how you feel about certain environmental topics and ask that you be totally honest in your responses. This is not a test and you need not sign your name on this form. Respond to each item by using the key below and circling one response for each item.

I Strongly Agree	I Agree	I Am Undecided	I Disagree	I Strongly Disagree	
					1. Much of the talk about pollution is propaganda that should be ignored.
					2. The Federal Government should pass strict laws that punish those who pollute the environment.
					3. I think using insecticides can be very dangerous.
					*4. The more people our country has the better off we will all be.
					*5. The so-called energy crisis is a story "made-up" just to scare people.
					*6. Plants and animals were put on Earth for humans to dominate and use as they please.
					7. I have ill feelings toward people who throw trash out their car windows.
					*8. I think the pollution problem is only temporary and will soon blow over.
					9. Schools should teach about the dangers of overpopulation.
					*10. The world has so much land that isn't being used that its silly to panic over the thought of running out of space.

----

*These items would be scored in reverse, 5 for strongly disagree, 1 for strongly agree.

FIGURE 6.4   An example of a Likert-type scale for measuring attitudes toward environmental issues.

THE SEMANTIC DIFFERENTIAL

The semantic differential is another technique for measuring student attitudes. Developed by Osgood, Suci, and Tannenbaum, this scale measures one's feelings toward a variety of concepts such as "school," "science," and "myself as a science student," by asking students to place an "X" in the blank between pairs of opposing adjectives. The following example would indicate a very positive feeling toward "science" and would receive a score of 7:

Science

Good __X__ ____ ____ ____ ____ ____ ____ Bad

Likewise, the following response would indicate a very negative attitude toward "school" and would receive a score of 1:

School

Good _____ _____ _____ _____ _____ _____ _X_ Bad

Figure 6.5 is an example of a semantic differential scale that can be used to measure attitudes toward different objects or concepts. Scores of 1 to 7 are assigned to each response and are summed to give a total score for each student toward a particular concept.

Directions: The following pairs of words will help you tell us how you feel toward certain things. Place an "X" between each pair in the blank that best describes where your feelings lie. For example, if you have very good feelings or very much like dogs, your response would look like this:

Dogs

Good   X   _____ _____ _____ _____ _____ _____ Bad

(Concept Such as "science," "school," etc.)

Good*	_____ _____ _____ _____ _____ _____ _____	Bad
Sad	_____ _____ _____ _____ _____ _____ _____	Happy*
Helpful*	_____ _____ _____ _____ _____ _____ _____	Hurtful
Dirty	_____ _____ _____ _____ _____ _____ _____	Clean*
Pretty*	_____ _____ _____ _____ _____ _____ _____	Ugly
Strong*	_____ _____ _____ _____ _____ _____ _____	Weak
Still	_____ _____ _____ _____ _____ _____ _____	Moving*
Bright*	_____ _____ _____ _____ _____ _____ _____	Dull
Irrelevant	_____ _____ _____ _____ _____ _____ _____	Relevant*
Rough	_____ _____ _____ _____ _____ _____ _____	Smooth*
Successful*	_____ _____ _____ _____ _____ _____ _____	Unsuccessful
Useless	_____ _____ _____ _____ _____ _____ _____	Useful*

Adjectives marked with an " * " represent positive feelings and should receive a maximum score of 7 points. Student scores for this instrument could range from 12 (extremely negative feelings) to 84 (extremely positive feelings).

FIGURE 6.5   Example of a semantic differential scale.

SUBJECT
PREFERENCE
SCALES

A subject preference scale can be used to compare attitudes of students toward "science," "biology," or other science courses with their attitudes toward other school subjects. With this scale, students are asked to circle their favorite subject in each pair. Figure 6.6 is an example of how this scale is constructed. To determine preference toward science, the scorer adds up the number of times science is circled and compares this with the total number of times other subjects are circled. In addition, preference for science courses over nonscience courses can be found by comparing the number of times science courses are circled with the number of times nonscience courses are circled. This scale can be used to detect changes that occur between the beginning and end of the school year.

In using all of these scales, it is important to have students remain anonymous and to treat the results as indications of group attitudes rather than individual attitudes. With the preference scale in particular, comparisons should be avoided that might reflect negatively on other teachers or subject areas.

Directions: Below are pairs of subjects with which you are familiar As you glance at each pair, circle the subject you like best. Do not sign your name on this paper.

Mathematics ___ ___ ___ ___	Science
Social Studies ___ ___ ___ ___	English
Physical Education ___ ___ ___ ___	Mathematics
Foreign Language ___ ___ ___ ___	Science
English ___ ___ ___ ___	Mathematics
Physical Education ___ ___ ___ ___	Foreign Lanauge
Science ___ ___ ___ ___	Social Studies
Foreign Language ___ ___ ___ ___	Mathematics
English ___ ___ ___ ___	Science
Social Studies ___ ___ ___ ___	Physical Education
Foreign Language ___ ___ ___ ___	Social Studies
Science ___ ___ ___ ___	Physical Education
Mathematics ___ ___ ___ ___	Social Studies
Physical Education ___ ___ ___ ___	English
English ___ ___ ___ ___	Foreign Language

FIGURE 6.6 Example of a subject preference scale.

OBSERVATION
SCALES

In addition to knowing how students feel toward things as a group, it is helpful to have evaluation measures for individuals of the attitudes, values, and interests of individual students. One way of doing this is to utilize a student observation form which is used to record student behavior in the laboratory. Important objectives relating to attitudes and values communicated to students at the beginning of the year are evaluated systematically by observing students while they are working independently in a laboratory setting. Figure 6.7 is an example of how a science teacher can evaluate students in each class by observing attitude-related behavior during laboratory work. Different scales, including numerical scores for grading, can be established.

	Comes to lab prepared and familiar with activities	Reads directions before asking for assistance from others or instructor	Cooperates with other students in group activities	Appears serious in the lab and carefully puts time to use	Can be depended on to properly care for equipment and clean up work area	Spends extra time in the lab with followup activities
1. Adams, Sue						
2. Basset, John						
3. Collier, Phillip						
4. Dorsey, Joan						
5.						
6.						

Possible Key:

5 = With consistency (excellent)
4 = Almost always (good)
3 = Part of the time (fair)
2 = Only on occasions (poor)
1 = Seldom, if ever (unsatisfactory)

FIGURE 6.7   Example of a student observation form.

UNOBTRUSIVE
MEASURES

Methods for spotting both positive and negative indicators of interests, attitudes, and values are discussed in an interesting book entitled *Unobtrusive Measures*.[1] Unobtrusive measures are observations of behavior that

---

[1] E. J. Webb, D. T. Campbell, R. D. Schwartz, and L. Sechrest, *Unobtrusive Measures: Non-reactive Research in the Sciences*, Chicago: Rand McNally and Company, 1966.

teachers and others can make without being noticed or without obstructing the student's activities. For example, interest in metric education can be assessed by noting the number of students who freely select metric rulers that have been placed on a table for them to take. The most popular exhibits in museums can be determined by noting the amount of wear on the carpet or floor. Teachers can determine the topics in which students are most interested by checking library withdrawals. These library observations may also signal which students are the most interested in pursuing scientific investigations beyond required assignments.

Another interesting clue to interests and attitudes is to observe the diameter of a circle during student discussions. As student feelings become more positive, the diameter of the circle will become smaller. Unobtrusive measures, like other evaluation data, can be misinterpreted. These data should be analyzed carefully and combined with other sources of information before attempting to make the actual interpretations.

If promoting positive attitudes toward science is an important goal of science education, it should be evaluated. The feelings with which students leave their science courses is an important educational outcome. By evaluating students in the affective domain, teachers can gain valuable information for improving student achievement and rethinking the objectives and strategies they use.

In Perspective

Evaluation is more than giving tests and assigning grades. Rather, evaluation should involve all the means of gathering and analyzing data about student achievement. The results of this analysis should not only tell us how the student is doing but also serve as indicators of our own effectiveness as teachers. In other words, it is difficult to make a case for success as a teacher when the student has failed.

Effective science teachers make use of a wide variety of evaluation techniques and instruments. In doing so, it is important that they be aware of which approach they are using—norm-referenced evaluation or criterion-referenced evaluation. For example, a major purpose of norm-referenced tests is to spread out and compare students with different levels of achievement. Thus, it is appropriate to calculate the level of difficulty and the index of discrimination of individual test items. On the other hand, the purpose of criterion-referenced tests is to determine if a student has mastered the material or objective at some predetermined level. In this case, the results on a test have to be interpreted in a different manner. Teachers should continually ask themselves, "What am I trying to accomplish as an evaluator? How will I accomplish it? Are norm-referenced tests appropriate? Or should I use criterion-referenced tests to evaluate my students?"

As in the case of strategies for science teaching and other aspects of the profession, it is easy to be overwhelmed by this discussion of evaluation. This is not all bad. Professionals charged with the responsibility of evaluating other human beings and making decisions that could affect them for the rest of their lives should take this part of their work seriously and make every effort to develop expertise in all phases of evaluation.

Review Questions

1. Explain how the "why of evaluation" is more than "grading" and the "how of evaluation" is more than "testing."

2. Describe how evaluation functions in diagnosis, in providing students feedback, and in reporting student progress.

3. Give several examples of how *formative evaluation* and *summative evaluation* might be used in a secondary school science course.

4. Briefly discuss three bases for assigning grades. Which is an example of criterion-referenced evaluation? Norm-referenced evaluation?

5. Define each of the following test attributes in your own words and describe one or two things that can be done in constructing a test to insure the presence of the particular attribute:
(a) Validity
(b) Reliability
(c) Objectivity
(d) Economy
(e) Reasonableness
(f) Discrimination
(g) Relevance

6. How do *closed* and *open* test questions differ? What are some types of questions that are examples of each?

7. List as many things as possible that can be done to improve the following types of items:
(a) Multiple choice
(b) Matching
(c) Completion
(d) True–false

8. Briefly discuss several things that can be done to improve the use of open questions.

9. In addition to paper-and-pencil tests taken in class, what are several other kinds of tests that can be used to evaluate student achievement in science?

10. Explain how age-equivalent scores, grade-equivalent scores, and percentile ranks are used in reporting results on a standardized test.

11. How are each of the following used to evaluate in the affective domain?

(a) Likert Scale
(b) Semantic differential
(c) Subjective preference scale
(d) Observational scale
(e) Unobtrusive measures

For Application and Analysis

1. List as many reasons as possible that support and refute the following statement: "Defining an 'A' as being equivalent to 93–100 and a 'B' as being 85–92, and so on is the biggest intellectual fraud perpetrated upon students and parents in the history of education."

2. Assign each of the five students in a ninth grade science class a *letter* grade (A, B, C, D, and F) for the first three weeks of work in a grading period and justify your decisions. The five students have the following characteristics:

	John	Mary	Jim	Susan	Tom
IQ	97	131	110	101	80
Age	13	13	14	13	16
Achievement Test in Math (Grade Equivalent)	9.3	9.2	11.5	9.7	7.6
Achievement Test in Science (Grade Equivalent)	9.6	9.8	11.6	9.5	7.2
Days Absent during past 3 weeks (15 days)	0	1	2	6	4

Listed below are the scores that were recorded for the five students during a three-week period.

Quiz #1*	5	6	9	5	2
Quiz #2**	6	7	8	4	ab
Tests #1***	50	55	75	60	20
Homework****	30	40	60	70	40

*   10 points possible; range 2–9; *median* for class of 25 students was 6
**   10 points possible; range 2–10; *median* for class of 25 students was 7
*** 80 points possible; range 78–20; *median* for class of 25 students was 55
**** 70 points possible on homework

3. How many poor testing practices can you find in the following test and what could you do to correct each?

Name _____

1. What is the smallest unit of living matter?

2. _____ was the father of modern biology.

3. Five kinds of joints found in the human body are
_____, _____, _____, and _____.

4. _____ is the study of animals.

5. _____ is the study of plants.

6. All living things came from other living things (true or false).

7. A meter is longer than a yard (true or false).

8. The unit of metric volume measure is (a) a centimeter
(b) a liter (c) a cubic centimeter or "cc" (d) a mile (e) all of these.

9. A microscope (a) makes small things look larger (b) can be used
to observe only transparent objects (c) can use either light or
electrons (d) costs less than $20.00.

Match

10. Process of all division   A. Mitosis

11. A blood vessel   B. DNA

12. Deoxylibonucleic acid   C. Artery

13. Unit used to measure   D. Capillary
    energy content of food

References   Bloom, Benjamin S. *Handbook on Formative and Summative Evaluation of Student Learning.* New York: McGraw-Hill Book Company, 1971.

A goldmine of information on different ways evaluation can be used and evaluation techniques for different levels of educational objectives; Chapter 18 contains dozens of examples of test items in science.

Evaluative Criteria for the Evaluation of Secondary Schools. Fourth Edition. Washington, D.C.: National Study of Secondary School Evaluation, 1969.

This manual is used in the evaluation of secondary schools for accreditation by the various regional accrediting groups in the United States; Section 4–15 deals with science programs, facilities, and staff.

Hedges, William D. *Testing and Evaluation for the Sciences in the Secondary School.* Belmont, Calif.: Wadsworth Publishing Company, Inc., 1966.

This book contains an excellent discussion on how to effectively construct science tests, with hundreds of examples of science questions to illustrate the important ideas of testing.

Mayer, William V. (Ed.). *Biology Teacher's Handbook.* Third Edition. New York: John Wiley and Sons, 1978.

The material on pages 198–256 will be very useful to those evaluating inquiry-related objectives in the biological sciences.

Nedelsky, Leo. *Science Teaching and Testing.* New York: Harcourt, Brace, and World, Inc., 1965.

This is an excellent treatment of almost every phase of testing with dozens of sample questions to show how achievement of different categories of instructional objectives can be measured.

CHAPTER 7

The Development of Interest, Attitudes, and Values

TWO VIEWS OF THE SCIENTIST
Still True Today?

Positive Side of the Image of the Scientist

He is a very intelligent man—a genius *or* almost a genius. He has long years of expensive training—in high school, college, *or* technical school, *or perhaps even beyond—during which* he studied very hard. He is interested in his work and takes it seriously. He is careful, patient, devoted, courageous, open minded. He knows his subject. He records his experiments carefully, does not jump to conclusions, and stands up for his ideas even when attacked. He works for long hours in the laboratory, sometimes day and night, going without food and sleep. He is prepared to work for years without getting results and face the possibility of failure without discouragement; he will try again. He wants to know the answer. One day he may straighten up and shout: "I've found it! I've found it!"

He is a dedicated man who works not for money or fame or self-glory, but—like Madam Curie, Einstein, Oppenheimer, Salk—for the benefit of mankind and the welfare of his country. Through his work people will be healthier and live longer, they will have new and better products to make life easier and pleasanter at home, and our country will be protected from enemies abroad. He will soon make possible travel to outer space.

The scientist is a truly wonderful man. Where would we be without him? The future rests on his shoulders.

Negative Side of the Image of the Scientist

The scientist is a brain. He spends his days indoors, sitting in a laboratory, pouring things from one test tube into another. His work is uninteresting, dull, monotonous, tedious, time consuming, and, though he works for years, he may see no results or may fail, and he is likely to receive neither adequate recompense nor recognition. He may live in a coldwater flat; his laboratory may be dingy.

If he works by himself, he is alone and has heavy expenses. If he works for a big company, he has to do as he is told, and his discoveries must be turned over to the company and may not be used; he is just a cog in a machine. If he works for the government, he has to keep dangerous secrets; he is endangered by what he does and by constant surveillance and by continual investigations. If he loses touch with people, he may lose the public's confidence—as did Oppenheimer. If he works for money or self-glory he may take credit

Reprinted by permission of *Science.* Mead, Margaret, and Rhoda Metraux, "The Image of the Scientist Among High School Students," Vol. 126, pp. 384–390, August 30, 1957.

for the work of others—as some tried to do to Salk. He may even sell secrets to the enemy.

His work may be dangerous. Chemicals may explode. He may be hurt by radiation, or may die. If he does medical research, he may bring home disease, or may use himself as a guinea pig, *or* may even accidentally kill someone.

A scientist should not marry. No one wants to be such a scientist *or* to marry him.

An important goal of science teaching is to develop in students positive attitudes toward science. Not only do students with positive feelings toward science achieve more, but they are also more likely to incorporate science into their daily lives when they appreciate its importance. For this reason, science teachers should strive to make their subject interesting and their classrooms an environment where positive feelings and values are fostered.

Science and the Affective Domain

The term *affective* stems from the Latin word *affectus,* having to do with **feelings**. Krathwohl, Bloom, and Masia have constructed a hierarchy of educational objectives for the affective domain. This scheme is based on the gradual process of internalization that occurs as a person becomes *aware* of a phenomenon, is willing to *respond,* and eventually forms *values* that become part of a life outlook.

The willingness to *respond* to something is closely associated with the concept of *interest.* The predisposition to respond positively or negatively toward an object or phenomenon is commonly defined as *attitude.* Feelings toward specific referents such as "bacteria," "insects," "scientists," "science teachers," or "school" are generally described as one's "attitude toward" something. *Values* involve less specific referents. The degree to which one feels that "honesty," "democracy," or "open-mindness" is important depicts the values of that person. Values often fuse, forming high-level *value-systems* that combine with cognitive understanding to influence one's personal philosophy, ethical standards, and political views.

Science and scientists are often described as being "objective," "factual," or "amoral." In truth, those who practice science as well as those who consume it are surrounded by inescapable affective attributes that characterize this human endeavor. When a person exhibits curiosity, is willing to work cooperatively with others, or critically questions a current idea, the person is demonstrating an interest, an attitude, or a value. Science is a way of doing things, and as a result, it invariably encompasses a plethora of human feelings and values. An inventory by Crocker and Nay of common affective attributes of scientists is presented in Table 7.1 as an example of how interests, attitudes, and values are closely associated with science.

Perceptions young people develop toward scientists are influenced by what they watch on television or view in movies.

Several areas in the affective domain can be nurtured through the use of appropriate instructional strategies. For example, there are activities that can be used during the first few weeks of school to "break the ice" and boost interest in the opinions of others and the value of group decision-making. Other strategies can be used to foster self-esteem and expand the consciousness of students toward the world around them as well as of themselves. In this chapter, we shall examine a few strategies that science teachers can use to increase interest and produce attitudes and values that are consistent with the enterprise of science. Many of these strategies, moreover, will help students become more effective learners in other subject areas.

Stimulating Interest in Science

An experienced teacher recently remarked that she spends more time preparing for the first week of school than for any other week of the year. She stated, "If I can get students off to a good start during the first week I know I'm going to have a productive year." The impressions students get of their science course, science teacher, or the scientific enterprise can be significantly influenced by the feelings they develop during the early part of the year. Extra planning and the use of teaching strategies to develop interest among students can be an excellent investment of the teacher's time. The following are examples of ways that can be used to get the school year off to a good start.

ICE BREAKERS FOR THE FIRST CLASS MEETING

In situations where most of the students do not know each other, it is helpful to introduce students and encourage them to get acquainted. The simplest method and the one requiring the least time is to ask each student to stand up and tell his or her name to the class. To make it more interesting, students can also be asked to describe something funny that

TABLE 7.1 Inventory of Common Affective Attributes of Scientists

1. Interests
(The motivation for a person to become a scientist and continue to be one.)

Understanding natural phenomena
  Curiosity
  Fascination
  Excitement
  Enthusiasm

Contributing to knowledge and human welfare
  Altruism
  Ambition
  Pride
  Satisfaction

2. Operational Adjustments
(Primary behaviors which underlie competence and success in science, and performance at recognized standards.)

Dedication or commitment
  Perseverance (persistence)
  Patience
  Self-discipline
  Selflessness
  Responsibility
  Dependability

Experimental requirements
  Systematism (methodicalness)
  Thoroughness
  Precision
  Sensitivity
  Alertness for the unexpected

Initiative and resourcefulness
  Pragmatism (common-sense)
  Courage (daring, venturesomeness)
  Self-direction (independence)
  Self-reliance
  Confidence
  Flexibility
  Aggressiveness

Relations with peers
  Cooperation
  Compromise
  Modesty (humility)
  Tolerance

3. Attitudes or Intellectual Adjustments
(Intellectual behaviors which are foundational to the scientist's contribution to or acceptance of new scientific knowledge.)

Scientific integrity
  Objectivity
  Open-mindedness
  Honesty
  Suspended judgment (restraint)
  Respect for evidence (reliance on fact)

Willingness to change opinions
Idea sharing

Critical requirements
  Critical mindedness
  Skepticism
  Questioning attitude
  Disciplined thinking
  Anti-authoritarianism
  Self-criticism

4. Appreciations
(Relative to the foundations, interactions, and dynamics of science.)

The history of science
  The evolution of scientific knowledge
  Contributions made by individual scientists
  The exponential growth of science

Science and society
  The social basis of the development of modern science
  The contribution made by science to social progress and melioration
  The relationship between science and technology
  The interaction of the "two cultures"

The nature of science
  The process of scientific inquiry
  The tentative and revisionary character of scientific knowledge
  The strengths and limitations of science
  The value of one's own contribution and the debt owing other scientists
  The communality of scientific ideas
  The esthetics and parsimony in scientific theory
  The power of individual and cooperative effort
  The power of logical reasoning (rationality)
  The causal, relativistic, and probabilistic nature of phenomena

5. Values and/or Beliefs
(In the realm of philosophy, ethics, politics, etc.)

Philosophy
  The universe is "real"
  The universe is comprehensible (knowable) through observation and rational thought
  The universe is not capricious

Ethical
  Science is amoral but scientists have the responsibility to interpret the consequences of their work
  Humanism is the highest ideal

Social
  Science must serve the needs of society
  Science flourishes best in a free and democratic society

SOURCE: *Reprinted by permission of John Wiley & Sons, Inc. Crocker, Robert K., and M. A. Nay,* "Science Teaching and the Affective Attributes of Scientists," *Science Education, Vol. 54, pp. 59-60. Copyright © John Wiley & Sons, Inc. 1970.*

has happened to them, their hobby, or their favorite television show. Another technique that works well is to have students pair off and, for two or three minutes, to share information about each other. Then each student is asked to stand up and introduce his or her partner. Another technique is to have each student stand behind the person with whom they have just become acquainted and introduce themselves as though they were that person. For example, Sue might stand behind Nancy and say "Hello, my name is Nancy and I live on Hillside Road. I work after school at the A & P Store and have three pet gerbils in my room at home." Using this technique, students learn to put themselves in each other's shoes and to discover how it feels to "be someone else."

Another technique that can accompany introductions is to see which student, after everyone has been introduced, can remember the most names. If the classroom has flexible seating arrangements, it is beneficial to place chairs in a circle, semicircle, or U-shape.

One way to add interest to this activity is to ask each person to say his/her name and then state something they like that begins with the same letter of the alphabet as his/her name. For example, the first student will say "My name is *Charlene* and I like *chocolate*." The next student continues, "My name is *Winston* and I like *water-skiing*." The second student then repeats what the first student said, "Her name is Charlene and she likes chocolate." The third student says, "My name is Henretta and I like horses." The third student then repeats what the second student said, as well as the first. After several students have done this, it may be best to start over with a smaller group, particularly if individuals begin having difficulty remembering everything or if too much time is being consumed. At the end of this or similar activities, students can be asked to write down all the names they can remember. The student with the most names can be recognized as "the winner."

Through such activities the teacher communicates that every person is important and that it is worthwhile to get to know people with whom you work and play. This technique also emphasizes to students that it is important to listen carefully to what is said and to be courteous when others are speaking.

OTHER GETTING-
ACQUAINTED
ACTIVITIES

Another technique for getting students acquainted and for "breaking the ice" on the first day or so of class is to announce: "Within five minutes, find someone in the class that has the same (1) shoe size, (2) same month of birth, (3) same number of brothers and sisters, (4) same height, and (5) same favorite subject in school." This list can be shortened, lengthened, or modified to include other topics. During this activity, students move hurriedly around the room, making contact with a large number of people, getting acquainted in an informal fashion, and recording the names of students with whom they have something in common. The first student to complete the list is the winner and can be called upon to share his or her findings. While discussing each of the topics, the teacher can call on other students to tell what they discovered during the activity.

One technique that has been used successfully by teachers of younger students is that of asking students to make a collage to share with the class. A collage is an artistic composition of fragments of printed material, pictures, and other materials pasted on a sheet of paper or poster board. Suitable topics for students include (1) a picture of how I feel when I'm happy, (2) a list of things I most enjoy doing, (3) things I like most about people, (4) a topic in science I'd most like to study this year, and (5) a picture of something I don't like to do. When finished, the collage should communicate to others interesting and important information about the person. If room permits, the collages can be placed around the room and similarities and differences discussed by the class. As with the other "ice breaking" approaches, this technique not only allows students to get acquainted, but also lets students express their feelings, tell what is important to them, and, perhaps most importantly, communicates that each individual is an important member of the class and has something valuable to contribute.

ENCOURAGING STUDENT INVOLVEMENT

Another way to stimulate interest is to allow students an opportunity early in the school year to list topics they would like to study. It is also appropriate to ask students to suggest teaching methods, materials, and other resources they know of that can make the year's science class more interesting and stimulating. When students realize they have some say in what they will study in science, their interest will increase. Besides getting good ideas, teachers who allow students to help plan class activities usually find that as a result students assume more of the responsibility for learning.

In addition to student planning, it has been found that students are more likely to be highly motivated in science if they know ahead of time

---

WHAT STUDENTS SAY

Science, In One Word

The following descriptions were listed most frequently by a large group of secondary school students when they were asked to relate how they saw science in one word:

Research	Learn
Discover	Explore
Think	Intriguing
Confusing	Smart
Experiment	Observe
Crazy	Boring
Picky	Curiosity

RESEARCH REPORT

How Student Feelings Relate to Achievement

In *Human Characteristics and School Learning*, Benjamin Bloom[1] summarizes research findings from the United States and several foreign countries that demonstrate how attitudes correlate positively with achievement. Looking at student interest, for example, Bloom concluded that interest in science appears to account for 20 to 25 percent of the influence on achievement in science. Bloom also noticed that this relationship increased as students advance in grade level. In other words, student interest in science at the twelfth-grade level was more predictive of academic success than it was in elementary school grades.

Even more striking, however, are research findings on the relationships between academic self-concept and achievement. The way a student feels toward himself or herself *as a student* correlates higher with achievement in science than does interest. This relationship again, appears to increase with advancement to the higher grade levels. Bloom suggests that students who are consistently in the bottom 25 to 35 percent of their science class each year develop poor academic self-concepts and ultimately become convinced they cannot succeed in science.

In related research, Rowe[2] has found that students can be classified into two groups based on their degree of fate control. Fate control is defined as the belief that events are under one's own control. Rowe calls students who are high in fate control "bowlers" and those low in fate control "craps shooters." "Bowlers" believe that through work and skill they have some measure of control over the future. "Craps shooters" are oriented to the present and attribute their future to chance and the influence of powerful "others."

Fate control is closely tied to the variable called locus-of-control. This variable relates to the degree to which individuals believe that reinforcement is contingent upon their own behavior. In the Coleman Report,[3] locus-of-control proved to be the single best predictor of achievement for nonwhite students and the second best for whites. In other words, students who believe that what happens to them is directly related to their own actions, as opposed to luck, whim, or chance, achieve more in school.

In summary, what the research says to the science teacher is that students' feelings toward science and self correlate positively with how much they learn.

---

[1]B. S. Bloom, *Human Characteristics and School Learning*, New York: McGraw-Hill Book Company, 1976.

[2]M. B. Rowe, "Relation of Wait–Time and Rewards to the Development of Language, Logic, and Fate Control: Part II—Rewards," *Journal of Research in Science Teaching*, 11, 4, (1974):291–308.

[3]J. S. Coleman, *Equality of Educational Documents*, Superintendent of Documents, Catalog No. F, 55–238: 38001, Washington, D.C.: Government Printing Office, 1966.

how they will be evaluated. When criteria and procedures for grading are made public, students realize it is possible through hard work to be successful in science. For this reason, many educators today recommend criterion-referenced evaluation (see Chapter 6). Using this method of evaluation, students are graded according to how well they perform on a given set of objectives rather than how they rank with others in their class. When this method is used to evaluate students, 50 percent of the students do not have to be in the bottom half of the class.

Research shows that success in school breeds more success. When students are allowed to help select science objectives, when they know what they must do in order to make a certain grade, and when they feel that their teacher is behind them, expecting them to do well from the start, motivation and interest in science are heightened. According to many studies, including those mentioned in the Research Report on page 283, when students have positive attitudes toward science, and when they have positive views of themselves as science students, their achievement in science will be higher.

Fostering the Development of Self-Concept and Values

The following is an excerpt from *The Greatest: Muhammad Ali.*[4]

What was wrong? How could I explain I could never ask Mr. Sutcliffe to help me get a hamburger? I folded the letter and put it back in my pocket.

"What's wrong with you?" Ronnie kept saying.

How could I explain: my millionaires were the real rulers of Louisville. But I did not want to be considered "their" boy even in the eyes of those who hated me. I had earned my Gold Medal without their permission. It should mean something without their permission. I wanted that medallion to mean I owned myself. And to call, seemed to me, to be exchanging one Owner for the Other. And suppose they did come to my rescue? Then I could come and go in the "white only" places, but other blacks couldn't. Then what would I be?

I moved closer to the door, keeping my eyes on The Owner. I felt a peculiar, miserable pain in my head and stomach. The pain that comes from punches you take without hitting back.

... I held the medallion just far enough out so that it wouldn't tangle in the bridge structure, and threw it into the black water of the Ohio. I watched it drag the red, white and blue ribbon down to the bottom behind it. . . .

How could I put the answer together? I wasn't sure of all the reasons. The Olympic medal has been the most precious thing that had ever come to me. I worshiped it. It was proof of performance, status, a symbol of belonging, of being a part of a team, a country, a world. It was my way of redeeming myself with my teachers and schoolmates at Central High, of letting them know that although I had not won scholastic victories, there was something inside of me capable of victory.

---

[4]Reprinted by permission of Random House, Inc. Ali, Muhammed with Richard Durham, *The Greatest—My Own Story.* Copyright © 1975 by Random House, Inc.

"The Olympic Medal...was my way of redeeming myself with my teachers and schoolmates at Central High.... Although I had not
won scholastic victories, there was something
inside of me capable of victory."

Self-concept involves all the attitudes, beliefs, and values one has toward oneself. The autobiographies of many famous people, including Muhammad Ali's, reveal that the way these individuals felt toward themselves as students lingered years after leaving school. Lists of behaviors, one for a hypothetical student with a strong self-concept and one for a hypothetical student with a weak self-concept, are presented in Table 7.2. While attempting to foster positive attitudes and values toward science, the teacher should be aware that belief in one's self is perhaps the most lasting and significant of all affective outcomes in school.

Another important goal of science education is to produce citizens who are capable of making value judgments. For example, many times each day each person in our society has to make many decisions— everything from deciding what to wear to how one will vote in the next election. These decisions are made (or avoided) not only on the basis of information and logic, but also on the system of values the person possesses. As part of the development of a value system, a person should examine his own feelings, what is important to him, as well as how a given issue affects society as a whole. Several instructional strategies can be used to help students clarify their own values, which allow them to act out roles of people in various decision-making positions. Such strategies encourage students to develop strong self-concepts.

VALUES CLARIFICATION TECHNIQUES

"Values clarification" has become a popular term in recent years. This teaching technique allows students to probe, to ask questions, and to express themselves openly concerning the way they feel about events and

TABLE 7.2   A Comparison of Students with Strong and Weak Self-concepts

Possessor	Non-Possessor
Worth:	*Worth:*
Positive self-reference (self-accepting)	Seeks reassurance/denies own importance
Comfortable with people (poised)	Nervous around people
Is friendly (has friends)	Few friends/quarrelsome with peers
Can admit imperfections (take criticism)	Boasts
Independent	Dependent on authority or others
Flexible	Rigid
Not defensive/open	Easily defensive/denies actions
Trusting	Suspicious/wary
Warm (loving)	Cold
Spontaneous	Calculating/mean
Can relax (not tense)	Often tense/rarely relaxed
Happy	Unhappy
Can be quiet	Attention getting
Coping:	*Coping:*
Takes responsibility/good leader	Poor leader/irresponsible
Sees school work as challenging	Dislikes work
Curious/participates	Dislikes novelty/reluctant to participate
Problem-solving approach	Flounders
Likes school	Dislikes school
Competent in school work	Does poor work
Sociometrically chosen for tasks	Not chosen for tasks
Expressing:	*Expressing:*
Talks easily in class/outspoken	Does not volunteer to participate
Shares feelings (even negative)	Hides feelings/poker-face/fake smile
Takes positions on issues	Not clear what he believes
Open about feelings/self revealing	Denies feelings
Direct/blunt	Super tactful/unclear meaning
Constructive confrontations	Destructive/blows up/blasts
Less superficial talk	Chatters
Autonomy/Can Make Choices:	*Autonomy:*
Can disagree openly	Never disagrees or really agrees
Decisive	Wish-washy
Can take reasonable risks	Plays it safe
Thinks through issues and decisions	Impulsive/flip-flops
Resistance to authority/reality-oriented/tests for self	Authority oriented
Internal locus of evaluation	Dependent/checks out others

SOURCE: *Adapted from Beatty, Walcott, H., "Affective Measurement and the Self Concept," in* Evaluation in the Affective Domain, *Gephart, Ingle, and Marshall, editors. CEDR Monograph, 1976. Reprinted by permission of Phi Delta Kappa.*

people in their environment. When used properly, this technique can be a useful tool for helping students explore the many facets of science that impinge on personal beliefs and values. This technique can also be used by teachers to encourage students to express their feelings as the students develop their own sense of perspective and worth.

Values clarification sessions can be designed by individual teachers to fit the needs of a particular class of students. For example, a teacher might wish to hand out a short list of questions and ask students to think about how they would respond if they were being interviewed by a news reporter. Some sample questions are:

1. What is something you feel you can do well?
2. What is something that is very aggravating to you?
3. What is the worst habit you have?
4. What is the happiest time this year in your science class?
5. If you could make one New Year's resolution what would it be?

Using these questions, students can be broken into groups of four or five and be given an opportunity to share their answers with the group. It should be clearly established that no one has to answer any question about which he/she may feel uncomfortable. Students should also be told that some feelings are public and some are private, and that they should not feel compelled to express anything they consider to be private. In addition, everyone should understand that there are no right or wrong answers; each student is entitled to his or her opinion, and all members of the class should respect this right to an opinion.

A list of questions used with this technique can be shortened or lengthened. If six to eight minutes of time are spent on each question, the activity will generally take thirty to forty minutes. The time and format of this activity can be modified by teachers, depending on the age of the students, the number of questions, and the purpose of the activity. If there is time left at the end of the activity, the teacher can ask the class followup questions such as "How did you like the activity?", "Were you surprised by the way others in your group answered?", or "Did this activity help you focus more clearly on what is important to you?" There also may be some students who will want to share responses with the entire class.

Another values clarification technique is to use "I wonder statements." This technique has been described in *Values Clarification: A Handbook of Practical Strategies for Teachers and Students.* [5] This simple but powerful activity is particularly appropriate in science classes. The teacher in beginning this activity writes several incomplete statements on the chalkboard such as:

I wonder if . . .   I wonder about . . .   I wonder whether . . .
I wonder how come . . .   I wonder why . . .   I wonder when . . .

Students are then asked to write a completion to each sentence based on something that comes to their mind. After the students have finished, the

[5]Sidney B. Simon, Leland W. Howe, and Howard Kirschenbaum, *Values Clarification: A Handbook of Practical Strategies for Teachers and Students,* New York: Harcourt Publishing Co., Inc., 1972.

teacher calls on individuals to share one of their "I wonder" statements with the class. Students should be allowed to "pass," or to decline to share their statements, if they desire. The teacher should participate, too, possibly starting off each new statement with an example or two. Since the purpose of this activity is to stimulate creativity and spontaneous expression, the answers do not necessarily need to be discussed or elaborated on. Several modifications of this technique can be used, including the replacement of the written reactions with the immediate oral reactions of students.

Other values clarification techniques that can be used by a teacher involve presenting a problem situation. Students can be told something like, "Assume your family of four has built in the basement of your home a fallout shelter designed to protect you from radioactive fallout produced by a nuclear explosion. Assume that there is a nuclear explosion and that Civil Defense authorities warn that it is unsafe to leave your shelter for two weeks. You calculate that your water and food supply will last four people for two weeks only. Now assume that the family of six next door has failed to construct a fallout shelter as they were warned and that they come knocking on your door asking if they can stay with you for two weeks. Your family realizes that your own safety is in jeopardy if you let others in. What do you say to your neighbors?"

With this activity, the best discussion occurs if the class is broken into smaller groups of approximately five to seven individuals. After students have had ample time to reach a consensus, one member from each group can share his/her answer with the entire class. The purpose of this activity is to encourage students to establish criteria on which difficult decisions are made and to work toward group consensus by allowing individuals to express and debate their ideas and values. While agreement over difficult issues is ideal, students should be encouraged to express their opinions freely and to avoid being pressured into something that their value system will not allow. This activity is an interesting one and usually produces several unanticipated responses and positions.

One final example of a values clarification activity involves asking students to make a list of modern conveniences around their home that they use frequently and that make life easier for them. After they have listed most of the current products of technology that they use daily, ask the students to take away the item that was invented most recently. Allow several members of the class to share how life would be different without this most recently discovered item (i.e., color television). Then ask them to discuss how things would be different without the second most recently discovered item, the third, and so forth. Tied to this activity might well be a homework or library assignment in which students are expected to find out when each of these major projects of technology, such as electricity, antibiotics, automobiles, and microwave ovens was developed or made available for public use. How would our values be different if we did not have these items? How do you think people were different fifty years ago with regards to their interests, leisure activities, communication patterns, and values?

An additional way this activity can be used is to ask each student to mark the three items on the list he/she could do without most easily. Then ask each to make the three items he/she would have the most difficulty giving up. Through this values clarification activity, individuals are able to examine those things in their lives that are most important to them. Likewise, this activity provides an excellent opportunity for students to examine important relationships that exist among science, technology, and societal values.

ROLE-PLAYING

Providing opportunities for students to "act out" different roles within a contrived setting is a sure-fire way of getting students involved and to promote the development of valuing and their self-concept. This technique, known as role-playing, allows students to "get the feel" of what it would be like to be another person, another organism, or even an inanimate object. Role-playing is particularly suitable for learning about areas of science that are socially significant or controversial. In fact, the teacher who uses this method can deal with sensitive topics such as drugs, evolution, nuclear energy, genetic engineering, and smoking. By approaching issues and hard-to-resolve questions in science through role-playing, the teacher encourages students to express themselves openly and honestly. The teacher's role is more powerful if he or she helps students focus on relevant criteria without signalling an individual position or preference.

There are numerous role-playing formats, and we can easily adapt them to fit the topic being currently studied and the maturity level of the class. One of the simplest formats involves allowing students to act out how they think they would feel as another person, animal, plant, or object. For example, students can portray famous scientists from the past and tell how they felt when they made their biggest discovery. With younger students, asking them to "act out" what they think it would feel like to be a tree, fish, eagle, cloud, or one of many other objects is an effective way to initiate role-playing.

Another format for role-playing is the use of an "interview." Here, one student plays the role of a reporter and another student plays the person being interviewed. With this format, students can play an infinite number of roles, such as that of a scientist, engineer, senator, mayor, ecologist, owner of business, physician, or nurse. One derivation of this format is to ask students to role-play as though they were Rip Van Winkle just waking up from a long nap of ten to twenty or more years. The teacher can say, "Mr. Van Winkle, what changes have you noticed since you have awakened? Which changes do you like best and which do you like least?"

Another role-playing technique begins with the teacher reading a story to the students. The short story should contain several characters that are involved in a dilemma. After the story is read, students can volunteer or be assigned to play each character. A typical format might be something like the following example. "Sam Jones has just lost his job, and his wife is in need of expensive medication. Sam asks the pharmacist to sell the medicine to him at a price he can afford or to let him pay later when he gets a new job. The pharmacist will not agree to those terms. Two days later Sarah, Sam's wife, becomes extremely ill and desperately needs the medicine. In his frustration Sam steals the medicine from the pharmacist, but he is caught by the police. He is tried in court, and a jury and judge must decide his fate." In this situation, students can play such parts as Sam, Sarah, the pharmacist, Sam's physician, the judge, and the jurors.

Role-playing activities can also focus on current problems that are being experienced in a local community. What to do about a proposed dam site, the building of a new chemical plant, selecting a location for the next city dump, or whether or not the city should build a new multimillion dollar zoo are examples of problems faced by many communities. By using this format, students can be assigned to actual roles played by members of the community such as members of the city council, the mayor, local environmentalists, local business people, and other concerned citizens. When local problems are role-played, students usually become so involved that it is difficult to imagine that the situation is not the real thing.

An interesting technique used in conjunction with role-playing is called role-reversal. Using this technique, the teacher assigns students to opposite roles after they have finished an initial role-playing activity. After students have finished playing a role opposite to their former role, they are asked to compare the different feelings they experienced while playing the two roles. Needless to say, this technique allows students to discover that there are at least two viable sides to most issues and that it is possible to have more than one rational perspective.

When role-playing is first used in a class, a few students may balk at the idea or resist involvement. These students should not be made to feel uncomfortable but rather should be allowed to express themselves and choose between participation and nonparticipation. Teachers should also underscore that these are merely roles that are being "play-acted" and that all views, no matter how unconventional, have a right to be expressed. If a role-playing session reaches a "dead end" or gets off the subject, it is usually best to move to a new topic. The teacher, however, might wish to stop at that point and discuss what has been said or ask the class "What do you think we should focus on next?"

Another technique for keeping role-playing activities on target is to designate ahead of time a couple of students as referees and charge them with the responsibility of keeping the session moving in a positive direction. Over a period of time, the teacher should eventually encourage all students to volunteer for roles and see to it that the more aggressive students learn to relinquish some of their involvement to other students. The teacher's responsibility during role-playing is to provide equal opportunities for all students to become involved and to be free to express their views openly. Without taking sides, the teacher should protect the views of all students and minimize "putdowns," withdrawals, or domination by a few students. The best way for teachers to help students accomplish these goals is to set good examples themselves.

Robert Hawley in his book *Values Exploration Through Role Playing*[6] suggests how role-playing can be evaluated. Students who serve as observers can be handed a role-playing observer sheet ahead of time, or the items simply can be written on the chalkboard. During the discussion following the role-playing, the student observers can discuss things they noticed during the session. This can be done as an entire class or in smaller groups without the teacher being present. The following observer sheet is from Hawley's book:

Role-Playing Observer Sheet[7]

1. Characterize the opening exchange (cheerful, genial, guarded, threatening, questioning, bored, etc.).

2. How well did the participants listen to each other? Try to give a specific example of good or poor listening.

3. Characterize the participants' nonverbal behavior toward each other.

4. Did you hear any hidden messages? If so, jot down one or two.

5. Were there any turning points in the discussion? If so, where?

6. Characterize the behavior of the participants toward each other.

SOCIODRAMA

Sociodrama is a teaching strategy similar to role-playing. It expands, however, on some of the dramatic aspects of decision-making and has been used to show differences that exist between reality and one's ideals. For example, a cast of students can be selected to play key figures associated with the Manhattan Project. In this project, top scientists and

---

[6]R. C. Hawley, *Value Exploration Through Role Playing: Practical Strategies for Use in the Classroom*, New York: Hart Publishing Company, Inc., 1975.

[7]Reprinted by permission of Hart Publishing Company. Hawley, R. C., "Role Playing Observer Sheet," in *Value Exploration Through Role Playing: Practical Strategies for Use in the Classroom*, 1975.

government leaders had to grapple with the decision of whether or not to develop the atomic bomb during World War II. Many scientists, including Albert Einstein, were pacifists and knew that the bomb would be capable of killing thousands of people. On the other hand, they knew that should the enemy develop the bomb before the United States, our country would suffer great losses and perhaps lose the war. The agony of this dilemma was profound.

The conflict between one's political position and one's conscience can be explored using sociodrama. One way to use this strategy is to have some students play major roles, such as those of President Roosevelt, Albert Einstein, Professor Oppenheimer, and others who were deeply involved in making the decision about the atomic bomb. Students usually need time to become familiar with these roles. Another set of students can play the "consciences" of each of these individuals. For instance, if the person playing Oppenheimer says, "We must go ahead and develop the atomic bomb in order to save the lives of millions of Americans," the person playing his conscience can stand up next to "Oppenheimer" and say, "But are you willing to take the responsibility for the millions of lives around the world that may be lost as a result of this lethal weapon being developed?"

A third set of students can be observers and take notes on what they saw taking place during the sociodrama. These individuals can then discuss with the class what they though happened and mention any interesting changes they felt took place during the activity.

As one can see, sociodrama can be a powerful teaching method for developing self-concept. Students are encouraged to listen carefully to other points of view, while at the same time paying close attention to their own feelings and their "consciences." As students play-act these roles, the dramatic effect of group interaction and the complexity of decision-making become apparent.

Increasing Sensitivity and Group Orientation

In sociological terms, the classroom is a small group of individuals working toward common goals and outcomes. The extent to which the group is successful is in large measure a function of how sensitive the members are to each other and how well the individuals work together for the common good of all. Science is also a social enterprise. Most of the big ideas in science are a result of the thinking of many individuals over time and the willingness of these individuals to discuss, share, and debate their ideas.

PROMOTING GROUP DECISION-MAKING

During the 1950s, businesses, industry, and governmental agencies began to use the Training Group (referred to as T-group) method in order to train managers and executives to cope with change and group decision-making. The T-group is relevant to the field of education and specifically to classroom situations. A handbook developed by NASA contains a number of T-group activities. One of these is "Decision by Consensus." General and specific instructions follow, along with complete directions for using the activity.

DECISION BY CONSENSUS[8]

INSTRUCTIONS: This is an exercise in group decision making. Your group is to employ the method of GROUP CONSENSUS in reaching its decision. This means that the prediction for each of the 15 survival items *must* be agreed upon by each group member before it becomes a part of the group decision. Consensus is difficult to reach. Therefore, not every ranking will meet with everyone's *complete* approval. Try, as a group, to make each ranking one with which all group members can at least partially agree. Here are some guides to use in reaching consensus:

1. Avoid arguing for your own individual judgments. Approach the task on the basis of logic.

2. Avoid changing your mind only in order to reach agreement and avoid conflict. Support only solutions with which you are able to agree somewhat, at least.

3. Avoid "conflict-reducing" techniques such as majority vote, averaging, or trading in reaching decisions.

4. View differences of opinion as helpful rather than as a hindrance in decision making.

On the "Group Summary Sheet" (page 295) place the individual rankings made earlier by each group member. Take as much time as you need in reaching your group decision.

The Problem

You are a member of a space crew originally scheduled to rendezvous with a mother ship on the lighted surface of the moon. Due to mechanical difficulties, however, your ship was forced to land at a spot some 200 miles from the rendezvous point. During reentry and landing, much of the equipment aboard was damaged and, since survival depends on reaching the mother ship, the most critical items available must be chosen for the 200-mile trip. Below are listed the 15 items left intact and undamaged after landing. Your task is to rank-order them in terms of their importance for your crew in allowing them to reach the rendezvous point. Place the number 1 by the most important item, the number 2 by the second most important, and so on through number 15, the least important.

---

[8]*Human Relations Laboratory Training Student Notebook*, ED 018834, Washington, D.C.: U.S. Office of Education, 1961.

Boxes of matches	_____
Food concentrate	_____
50 ft. of nylon rope	_____
Parachute silk	_____
Portable heating unit	_____
Two .45 caliber pistols	_____
One case dehydrated Pet Milk	_____
Two 100 lb. tanks of oxygen	_____
Stellar map (of moon's constellation)	_____
Life raft	_____
Magnetic compass	_____
Signal flares	_____
First-aid kit containing injection needles	_____
Solar-powered FM receiver-transmitter	_____
5 gallons of water	_____

Scoring Instructions for Decision by Consensus

The prediction is that the group product will be more accurate than the average for the individuals. The lower the score, the more accurate. A score of "0" is a perfect score.

Each individual can score his own sheet. As you read aloud to the group the correct rank for each item, they simply take the difference between their rank and the correct rank on that item and write it down. Do this for each item and add up these differences. DISREGARD "+" and "−."

To get the average for all individuals, divide the sum of the individual scores by the number of individuals in the group. Compute the group score in the same way you computed each of the individual scores. If our hypothesis is correct, the group score will be lower than the average for all individuals.

Possible Questions for the Group

1. Did the group really go by consensus? Or did we gloss over conflicts?

2. Did the group stay on the intellectual or task aspects or did we stop to examine our process to see how we could work more effectively?

3. How satisfied were we with the way the group worked? How efficient were we?

4. How satisfied are you (as members) with the group?

5. How much influence did you feel you had as an individual on the group decision?

6. Did the group listen to you? Ignore you?

7. Did you stay involved in the exercise or did you give up?

8. In what ways could you change or improve your interaction with others?

Group Summary Sheet

	Individual Predictions											Group Prediction
	1	2	3	4	5	6	7	8	9	10	11	
Box of matches												
Food con-centrate												
50 ft. of nylon rope												
Parachute silk												
Portable heating unit												
Two .45 cal. pistols												
One case dehy-drated milk												
Two tanks oxygen												
Stellar map												
Life raft												
Magnetic compass												
Signal flares												
First-aid kit w/needles												
Solar-powered radio												
5 gallons of water												

KEY

Little or no use on moon	15	Box of matches
Supply daily food required	4	Food concentrate
Useful in tying injured together, help in climbing	6	50 ft. nylon rope
Shelter against sun's rays	8	Parachute silk
Useful only if party landed on dark side	13	Portable heating unit
Self-propulsion devices could be made from them	11	Two .45 caliber pistols
Food, mixed with water for drinking	12	Dehydrated Pet Milk
Fills respiration requirement	1	Two tanks of oxygen
A principal means of finding directions	3	Stellar map
CO_2 bottles for self-propulsion across chasms, etc.	9	Life raft
Probably no magnetic poles; useless	14	Magnetic compass
Distress call when line of sight possible	10	Signal flares
Oral pills or injection medicine valuable	7	First-aid kit with injection needles
Distress-signal transmitter, possible communication with mother ship	5	Solar-powered FM receiver-transmitter
Replenishes loss from sweating, etc.	2	Five gallons of water

After this activity the students assess how the group functions and how each individual facilitates group problem solving. This can be done through the use and understanding of group functions. These functions have been grouped into two overall areas: helping functions and hindering functions. Hindering functions include four activities:[9,10]

1. Seeking recognition: Calling attention to oneself through unusual behavior such as telling stories, boasting, and loud talking.

2. Digressing: Getting away from the topic or the group task.

3. Out of field: Withdrawing from the discussion.

4. Blocking: Interfering with the group task by arguing excessively or by continually bringing up a "dead" issue.

---

[9]K. P. Benne, and P. Sheats, "Functional Roles of Group Members," *Journal of Social Issues,* 4, 2, (1948).

[10]From *Humanizing the Classroom: Models of Teaching in Affective Education* by John P. Miller. Copyright © 1976 by Praeger Publishers, Inc. Reprinted by permission of Holt, Rinehart, & Winston.

The helping functions are divided into two subgroups. Some functions are related to the group task and others are concerned with maintaining and developing the proper emotional climate.

Task functions are:

1. Initiating: Proposing and defining the task for the group.

2. Seeking information or opinions: Asking questions about relevant information; or asking for expression of feelings or personal value.

3. Giving information or opinion: Offering relevant information; stating opinion or expressing personal value.

4. Summarizing: Bringing ideas together so that the group can refocus on the problem; offering a conclusion that the group can accept or reject.

5. Clarifying: Clearing up misunderstanding; defining terminology; rephrasing a statement to facilitate understanding.

6. Consensus testing: Checking with the group to see whether they are reaching a decision.

Maintenance functions include:

1. Encouraging: Supporting other group members; indicating through nonverbal gestures acceptance of another's thoughts.

2. Harmonizing: Trying to reconcile disagreements; reducing the anxiety level.

3. Compromising: Willing to yield status or admit error so that the group can function.

4. Gate keeping: Keeping channels of communication open; asking others to participate; suggesting procedures that allow others to participate.

5. Standard-setting: Exploring whether group members are satisfied with procedures.

Often these functions can be used in an inner- and outer-circle situation. Some students sit in the inside circle and discuss a problem, while other students sit on the outside and record how the individuals in the inner circle helped or hindered group functioning. Students in the outer circle can use a chart to indicate how students on the inner circle are performing the various functions. The data collected by the outer circle then can be used in giving feedback to the students in the inner circle.

TABLE 4

TASK FUNCTIONS	A	B	C	D	E	F	G	H	I	J	K	L	M	N
1. Initiating														
2. Seeking information														

3. Giving information																
4. Summarizing																
5. Clarifying																
6. Consensus testing																
MAINTENANCE FUNCTIONS																
1. Encouraging																
2. Harmonizing																
3. Compromising																
4. Gate keeping																
5. Standard-setting																
HINDERING FUNCTIONS																
1. Seeking recognition																
2. Digressing																
3. Out of field																
4. Blocking																

SOLVING
PROBLEMS
THROUGH
GROUP
INTERACTION

The U.S. Forestry Service has developed an activity called "Six Bits" that demonstrates some of the processes in which people engage while solving problems in group situations. This activity also helps individuals become more sensitive to some of the important things that should be present when groups of people work productively together.

In order to initiate the activity, the teacher or group leader asks the class or audience to arrange themselves in groups of six and, if possible, in circles. Six pieces of paper are then distributed to each group, with each person in a group receiving a different bit of information. The "six bits" of information are shown in Figure 7.1. The activity leader announces to all groups, each of which has received identical information, "There is a

1	2
Although you may tell your group what is on this slip, you may not pass it around for others to read.	Although you may tell your group what is on this slip, you may not pass it around for others to read.
Information:	Information:
The Dinosaurs had Tom for a teacher during the third period. Dick and Belinda did not get along well and so they did not work together. During the first period the Team Leader taught the group that Harry liked best.	All teachers taught at the same time and exchanged troups at the end of each period. Each teacher liked a different group best. During the second period each teacher taught the group he liked best. Each teacher taught every group during one of the first four periods of the day.

3	4
Although you may tell your group what is on this slip, you may not pass it around for others to read.	Although you may tell your group what is on this slip, you may not pass it around for others to read.
Information:	Information:
The Freznel Elementary School Intermediate Unit has two teacher's aides, four teachers, and four instructional groups of students. Each instructional group had chosen its own name. Sybil was the Team Leader for the Intermediate Unit.	Your group members have all the information needed to find the answer to the following question. Only one answer is correct. You can prove it. IN WHAT SEQUENCE DID THE APES HAVE THE VARIOUS TEACHERS DURING THE FIRST FOUR PERIODS? Some of the information your group has is irrelevant and will not help solve the problem.

5	6
Although you may tell your group what is on this slip, you may not pass it around for others to read.	Although you may tell your group what is on this slip, you may not pass it around for others to read.
Information:	Information:
Belinda and Ralph disagreed about how it would be best to handle the Bombers who had always had trouble settling down to work. Dick preferred to work with the Champs over all other groups. Although the Team Leader had been at Freznell School for five years, this was a shorter period of time for the other team members.	The Team Leader taught the Dinosaurs the second period. Harry worked with the Bombers in the third period. Sybil had been at Freznel School a shorter period of time than any of the other teachers at the Intermediate Unit.

FIGURE 7.1   The "Six Bits" Activity. These "six bits" of information are cut into six smaller slips of paper and passed out to each group of six participants. Each person receives one "bit" or slip of paper.

problem to solve. You may tell anyone in your group what is on your piece of paper, but you may not show it to others."

As the problem-solving session progresses, the leader writes the word TRUST on the chalkboard after five to eight minutes have lapsed. After eight to twelve minutes have passed, the words VISUAL DISPLAY are written on the board. Finally, after twelve to fifteen minutes, the word MATRIX is written on the board.

The activity leader should continue to move around the room, listening to what is taking place in each group and giving out as little information as possible concerning potential answers to the problem. Occasionally, a group will get "stuck" and will need a little help, but this does not happen often. It is usually best to let participants discover as much as possible on their own. Gradually, most groups will come up with answers to the question (which is on one of the pieces of paper): "In what sequence did the Apes have the various teachers during the first four periods?" It usually takes twenty to forty minutes to answer the question. Although a few groups may not have the answer, the activity should be halted in a reasonable length of time and a discussion held for the entire class.

During the discussion, the following questions should be asked: "What kept you from solving the problem to begin with?" "What helped you to solve the problem later?" "What did you learn about problem-solving from doing this activity?"

The developers of this activity felt that it contains elements of involvement that groups go through when working together on common problems. For example, there must first be **trust**. The participants must trust that the teacher or leader gave them a solvable problem. They, in turn, must also trust each other. Careful listening must follow. During the early stages of this activity, the participants can be seen listening in merely a ritualistic manner, but after they become more serious about solving the problem, individuals listen more intently to what others are saying.

Another tool used to solve this problem is the use of **visual displays**. With so many bits of information to remember, it is virtually impossible for a group to solve this problem without writing down some of the information. In fact, the most logical way to solve this problem is to construct a **matrix** in which relevant information concerning the four teachers and four periods can be recorded. This is a common tool used to record scientific information, and it is appropriate for solving problems such as the one given here.

An important aspect of this activity is the fact that every person has something valuable to contribute. When any participant withholds information, the problem cannot be solved. One idea that can be reinforced by the group leader is that "none of us is as smart as all of us." To underscore this statement, it also should be written on the chalkboard. The most important outcome of this activity is not the answer the group arrives at, but the techniques and skills learned about group problem-solving. When this activity is used with students and other groups, the importance of working together in a cooperative mode is demonstrated. The importance of human communication, which plays a crucial part in scientific methodology, is also emphasized.

Expanding Consciousness

Interesting research by several investigators over the past few years has shown that the two hemispheres of the brain are responsible for different modes of consciousness. For instance, the left side of the brain, which controls the right side of the body, is largely responsible for analytical thinking. The left brain operates in a linear fashion and processes information sequentially; language, mathematics, and some processes of science depend heavily on this mode of consciousness. The right hemisphere, which controls the left side of the body, operates in a more spatial or global mode. Artistic and creative behaviors are associated more closely with right brain activities. Intuition and the tendency to view things holistically are also characteristics of right hemispheric consciousness.

Learning in science requires that both right and left hemispheric learning take place. While some scientific thought draws heavily upon analytical, linear thinking, other aspects of science require spatial and holistic modes of interpretation. Activities that expand the consciousness level of students to include both hemispheres of the brain are needed if education is to include all "sides" of science.

CONFLUENT EDUCATION

During the past decade, many educators called for an integration of the affective, cognitive, and psychomotor domains of learning. This "flowing together" of many dimensions is called "confluent education." In *Human Teaching for Human Learning: An Introduction to Confluent Education*,[11] Brown introduces many topics and methods associated today with confluent education.

Lazarus[12] has proposed the acronym BASIC ID to represent seven components of human functioning: behavior, affect, sensation, imagery, cognition, interpersonal relations, and drugs. Others, including Gerler and Keats,[13] have recommended that the BASIC ID be used as a model for reorganizing and expanding school curricula.

---

[11]G. I. Brown, *Human Teaching for Human Learning: An Introduction to Confluent Education*, New York: Viking Press, 1971.
[12]A. A. Lazarus, "Multimodal Behavior Therapy: Treating the Basic ID," *Journal of Nervous and Mental Disease*, 156 (1973):404–411.
[13]E. R. Gerler, and D. B. Keats, "Multimodal Education: Treating the Basic ID of the Elementary Classroom," *Humanist Educator*, 15 (1977):148–154.

A promising technique called *Inner Change* has been designed to expand the consciousness level of students and to incorporate some of the important aspects of confluent education. Specifically, Inner Change helps students accomplish four things: (1) increased skill in listening, (2) increased willingness to open up and express oneself, (3) improvement of self-concept, and (4) reduction in the notion that one is unique. The last objective focuses on the idea that adolescent students are prone to possess a "delusion of uniqueness." Simply stated, many young people hold the idea that the fears, problems, and frustrations they experience are unique and, therefore, uncommon to other people. The fact is that most of their fears as well as their joys are common ones and are shared by most other persons.

Inner Change is a flexible approach that can be used in a variety of settings. The activity involves asking five or six students to sit voluntarily in a small circle facing each other. Several other students are asked to sit in a larger circle which surrounds the smaller inner circle. The teacher then asks students in the small circle a question designed to stimulate creative thought and the expression of value judgments. For example, students might be asked to name the animal (other than human) they would most like to be and tell why they chose that particular animal. Students in the outer circle are asked to observe very carefully the behavior and reactions of the respondents and to be prepared to discuss these observations later.

The teacher may also wish to sit in the inner circle and respond. Answers to this question may include such responses as "I'd like to be a bear because bears are so powerful and seem so confident"; "I'd love to be an eagle and be able to view things from the air"; "I've always thought I'd

Providing students an opportunity to discuss ideas and feelings in smaller groups is an excellent way to promote positive attitudes in the science class.

like to be a Saint Bernard. They are so big and yet so gentle and trustworthy."

After each person has had ample opportunity to respond, students in the outer circle are asked to make comments. Interesting reactions like these may follow: "I noticed that John leaned forward when he spoke"; "Mary used her hands a lot when she described how she thought it would feel to be a dolphin"; or "It seemed to me that everyone wanted to be an animal that was a lot like his own personality."

After this format has been established, the teacher may wish to use it periodically to help students' attitudes and beliefs that relate to science topics discussed in class. Eventually, all students in the class who want to should have an opportunity to sit in both the inner and outer circles. Discussions can go in many directions as the teacher encourages students to express themselves openly and freely. It has been found that this technique not only teaches students to open up and express their positive and negative feelings, but it also teaches them to listen more carefully. A few research studies have confirmed that over time students do develop a greater self-identity and more positive self-concept. In many classrooms where Inner Change has been used, discipline problems have been reduced and cooperation and communication have increased.

SYNECTICS

In *The Metaphorical Way of Learning and Knowing*,[14] William J. J. Gordon introduces activities and materials for classroom use that are designed to encourage the development of creativity and imagination. Through the use of a technique called synectics, emotional elements of the creative process are combined with intellectual processes. The key to synectics training is the use of metaphors. With metaphors, students are able to make **the familiar strange** and to **make the strange familiar**. An example of **making the familiar strange** can be seen in the following example of William Harvey's discovery of circulation:

> In the sixteenth century, people thought that blood flowed from the heart to the body, surging in and out like the tides of the sea. Harvey was FAMILIAR with this view and believed it till he closely observed a fish's heart that was still beating after the fish had been opened up. He expected a tidal flow of blood, but he was reminded of a pump. The idea of the heart acting like a pump was most STRANGE to him and he had to break his ebb-and-flow connection to make room for his new pump connection. HE MADE THE FAMILIAR STRANGE.

The use of synectics is based on the assumption that creativity and imagination can be developed in a group setting. Through group interac-

---

[14] W. J. J. Gordon, *The Metaphorical Way of Learning and Knowing*, Cambridge, Mass.: Porpoise Books, 1966.

tion, an individual's emotional and intellectual capacities are often stimulated to a higher degree than through individual experience. Using samples similar to the one above, science teachers can encourage students to discuss various concepts and principles in science and to make analogies with things familiar to them but normally considered outside the realm of science.

Gordon suggests that there are three types of analogies. First, through *direct analogy* a simple comparison of two objects can be made. An example is the analogy of the heart and a water pump. Another example is "a crayfish moves backwards like a sneaky shoplifter." The following lists potential direct analogies which Gordon suggests can be used to stimulate class discussion:

Compare the wheel of a car to the following moving objects:

1. The cutter on a can opener
2 The rotor of a helicopter
3. The orbit of Mars
4. A spinning seed pod
5. A hoop snake

Since analogies are not necessarily meant to represent substantive knowledge, some are more strained than others. The first analogy above is a closer parallel than the others since both objects are circular, metallic, and manufactured by humans for a specific purpose. The last analogy is quite strained since snakes do not actually form hoops that roll down hills (as has been perpetuated by myth).

A second type of analogy suggested by Gordon is the *personal analogy*. The following example demonstrates how a student might react to the question "Describe how you might feel if you were a large fiddler crab."

> O.K. I'm a fiddler crab. I've got armor all around me—my tough shell. You'd think I could take it easy, but I can't. And that big claw of mine! Big deal! It looks like a great weapon, but it's a nuisance. I wave it around to scare everyone, but I can hardly carry it. Why can't I be big and fast and normal like other crabs? No kidding! That claw doesn't even scare anyone![15]

Compressed conflict, the third form of analogy, involves trying to explain two words that do not seem to go together. An example in science is the term *safe attack* which Pasteur used before he discovered antitoxins. This form of analogy is probably the most sophisticated of the three since the "compressed" words usually provide initial surprise. Compressed

---

[15]W. J. J. Gordon, *The Metaphorical Way of Learning and Knowing,* Cambridge, Mass.: Porpoise Books, 1966, p. 25.

conflict, however, is an excellent method for helping students understand and express many important principles in science.

Teachers and students can add interest to many topics in science by using synectics at appropriate times. Divergent, creative thinking should always be encouraged. Students should also be encouraged to express how they feel about objects and phenomena that are central to the science curriculum. The use of synectics not only helps students understand important concepts in science but also allows them to develop other skills through creative expression.

Moral Development

Lawrence Kohlberg, a Harvard psychologist, has described various stages of development at which people reason about moral issues.[16] He asserts that these stages of development are universal, even though individuals from various cultures may move from one stage to another at different rates. Briefly outlined, Kohlberg's six basic stages are as follows:

Stage I. Punishment and Obedience Orientation. Here an individual behaves on the basis of physical consequences. Young children, for example, will often do something if they think there is an immediate reward awaiting them. They will also behave, or not behave, in a certain manner if they realize that punishment is probable. So, rather than considering the good or bad consequences of an action, an individual at this stage of development interprets things in terms of the physical power of those who establish the rules.

Stage II. Instrumental Relativist Orientation. In this stage, individuals base "right" and "wrong" actions on the satisfaction of their needs and occasionally the needs of others. Instead of being guided by higher principles, an individual is most likely to take the position "I'll scratch your back if you'll scratch mine."

Stage III. Interpersonal Orientation. At this stage, individuals behave primarily on the basis of family or group expectations. Behavior is often rigid and stereotyped and is guided by what is considered to be "natural" and "acceptable." Individuals in this stage consider acceptance by parents, teachers, and peers to be extremely important.

Stage IV. Authority Orientation. People in this stage are conscious of "doing one's duty" and following the rules and regulations of society. Showing proper respect for authority and maintaining a socially acceptable status are among the most important incentives for behavior at this stage of development.

[16]Lawrence Kohlberg. *Collected Papers on Moral Development and Moral Education.* Cambridge, Mass.: Harvard Graduate School of Education, Spring 1973.

Stage V. Social-Contract Legalistic Orientation. By this stage, individuals behave largely on the basis of principles that they have examined and have found to hold validity and utility. Instead of the "law and order" orientation of Stage IV, the orientation here is based on a combination of personal values with those things that are constitutionally and democratically agreed upon.

Stage VI. Universal Ethical-Principle Orientation. Individuals who function at this stage are able to make decisions based on broadly defined ethical principles that are universal in nature. These principles are more abstract (i.e., The Golden Rule) than concrete moral rules like the Ten Commandments. People at this stage are more concerned with the quality of human rights and respect for human dignity than with the enforcement of specific rules or the immediate personal gains possible by behaving in a stereotyped, expedient manner.

The aim of moral education in Kohlberg's view is not to accelerate development through the various stages outlined but, rather, to avoid retardation within a given stage. Kohlberg's research suggests that if children or adolescents stay at a lower level of development too long, they may become entrapped by that stage and be unable to grow intellectually to a higher level.

Several techniques discussed in this chapter are appropriate for encouraging moral growth and development. The basic aim, of course, is to help students gain insight into what is fair and just for the individual and the group in given situations. The best situations for accomplishing this are associated with those problems that have no "right" answer. Role-playing, sociodrama, values clarification, or group decision-making activities afford opportunities for students to examine issues, consider salient aspects of each issue, and express their views based on their own ethical judgments. The role of the teacher during such activities is a crucial one. By encouraging students to examine multiple views, by allowing them freedom to express ideas, and by showing respect for the rights of all people to express views, the teacher can facilitate moral growth and development in the science classroom.

Kohlberg's work demonstrates vividly how affective and cognitive development are interrelated. His stages of development parallel those of Piaget's which describe the intellectual stages of development through which all people pass. Oftentimes, students have difficulty understanding important concepts in science because they are unable to think at more abstract levels. Likewise, some secondary school students are unable to behave appropriately because they are unable to view the consequences of their behavior in terms of how it affects them in the long run or how it affects others. The development of constructive attitudes and values is a major goal of science education. Helping students become logical and ethical in their science-related work should be a major objective for all professional science teachers.

In Perspective

For many people in this country, the term *affective domain* conjures up feelings of mistrust and strong opposition. For schools to teach their youngsters "attitudes" or "values," they insist, is for our educational system to overstep its bounds. For others, such instruction is "soft" and means that the teacher must be neglecting important "basics."

As we have discussed in this chapter, neither science nor any other human activity is value-free. The moment a person accepts honesty or rejects dogmatism, values are implied. The enterprise of science is filled with individual and cultural preferences, all of which emanate, again, from basic human values. To think that science or any other subject in the curriculum can be taught with no reference to human feelings and values is based on misunderstanding and ignorance.

When teachers do elect to incorporate the affective domain into the science curriculum, they should realize that they must accept additional responsibility. Students should be free to explore, agree, disagree, and honestly express themselves without fear of pressure from their peers and their teachers. The science classroom should be an ever-expanding forum for questioning, for debate, and for critical analysis.

For those who believe strongly in "basics," science also has much to offer. While it is appropriate to spend time in class fostering positive attitudes and exploring human values, it is also the responsibility of science teachers to expose students to the fundamental cognitive aspects of science. By combining attitudes, skills, *and* knowledge, students can learn science in a way that is consistent with the fundamental nature of this subject.

Review Questions

1. Define the term *affective* as commonly used by educators.

2. Make a list of affective behaviors and demonstrate how these might be important outcomes in science education.

3. Outline several techniques that can be used on the first day of class to promote positive attitudes toward science.

4. Research has shown that students with positive self-concepts behave differently in school from those with negative self-concepts. List at least five ways you might be able to distinguish between such students.

5. Discuss what is meant by "values clarification" and mention three positive outcomes that can arise from such activities.

6. Define "role-playing" and outline three examples where this teaching technique can be used in a science class.

7. Discuss three important educational outcomes from the activity "Six Bits" discussed in this chapter.

8. Describe briefly Kohlberg's levels of moral development and demonstrate how they relate to important objectives in science education.

**For Application
and Analysis**

1. In the Keynote address at the North Carolina Science Teachers Association Annual Meeting in 1979, Harry Wong, a well-known California science teacher, described some of the techniques he uses to begin the school year:

- He meets each student at the door as they enter.
- He gives each student a card with special instructions on where they are to sit.
- He asks each student to fill out a small file card which asks for positive things about himself or herself.
- He provides each student in his room with a mailbox.
- He asks all students to pronounce their names.
- He calls each parent during the first week and says something positive about their work, then quickly hangs up.
- He gives each student a "map" (lesson plan) for each two- to three-day lesson.
- He gives a short quiz every two to three days.
- He emphasizes major concepts in his class.
- He teaches students how to read selectively by using short paragraphs prepared on overhead transparencies.
- He keeps books in his classroom that range from easy to difficult reading levels.

Think about each of the techniques Mr. Wong uses and list the potential advantages a science teacher might gain from using such approaches.
Why do you think Mr. Wong works so hard to implement these practices?
Can you think of other practices that could serve similar functions?

2. Study carefully the responses of students under What Students Say on page 282 of this chapter. Write a brief essay on how you think these students feel toward science based upon their one-word descriptions.

3. Attend a city council meeting, a legislative session, or a meeting of some type where a science-related issue is being discussed or debated. Write a brief report addressing the following questions:
   (a) What specific knowledge of science was necessary in order to understand the issue?
   (b) What attitudes and/or values did you hear expressed or see operating that influenced any decisions that were made.
   (c) What processes occurred which helped the group reach a decision?
   (d) What processes occurred which hindered the group in reaching a decision?
   (e) Was there any misunderstanding of scientific principles that were

present that interfered with the group's ability to deal with the issue?

4. Select one of the following topics and plan a lesson or unit that would be appropriate for a science class in middle or junior high school: sex education, drugs, UFOs, nuclear energy, evolution, space travel, or environmental education.

References

Brown, George. *Human Teaching for Human Learning: An Introduction to Confluent Education.* New York: Viking Press, 1971.

This is an account of the Ford Foundation-Esalen Institute Project which produced extensive examples of affective techniques and their classroom applications. This book is considered an introduction to the emerging field of confluent education.

Castillo, Gloria A. *Left-Handed Teaching: Lessons in Affective Education.* New York: Praeger Publishers Inc., 1974.

This 223-page paperback book is considered one of the most complete sourcebooks on confluent education. It contains many excellent activities and references.

Hawley, Robert C. *Value Exploration Through Role Playing: Practical Strategies for Use in the Classroom.* New York: Hart Publishing Company, Inc., 1975.

This is a large collection of role-playing activities, many of which can be used in the science classroom.

Miller, John P. *Humanizing the Classroom: Models of Teaching in Affective Education.* New York: Praeger Publishers, Inc., 1976.

This excellent book contains a wide range of both theories and examples of activities applicable to the science classroom. Many valuable suggestions for conducting various activities are included.

Raths, Louis, Merril Harmin, and Sidney B. Simmon. *Values and Teaching: Working with Values in the Classroom.* Second edition. Columbus, Ohio: Charles E. Merrill Publishing Company, 1978.

This up-to-date edition of the standard reference on values clarification contains many practical suggestions for teaching values in secondary school classrooms.

Rogers, Carl. *Freedom to Learn.* Columbus, Ohio: Charles E. Merrill Publishing Company, 1969.

This is a classic which suggests the direction of education for years to come. Rogers explains in detail how classrooms can be organized to free students to learn.

Simon, Sidney B., Leland W. Howe, and Howard Kirschenbaum. *Values Clarification: A Handbook of Practical Strategies for Teachers and Students.* New York: Hart Publishing Company, Inc., 1972.

This treasury of activities for teachers in all fields is a valuable contribution to the field of affective education.

ANIMAL SCHOOL

CHAPTER

8

Individualizing
Science
Instruction

Once upon a time the animals decided they must do something to meet the problems of the "New World," so they organized a school. They adopted an activity curriculum consisting of running, climbing, swimming, and flying and to make it easier to administer, all animals took all subjects.

The duck was excellent in swimming, better in fact, than his instructor, and made passing grades in flying, but he was poor in running. He had to stay after school and also drop swimming to practice running. This was kept up until his web feet were badly worn and he was only average in swimming.

The squirrel was excellent in climbing, until he developed frustration in the flying class, where his teacher made him start from the ground up instead of from treetop down. He also developed charlie-horse from overexertion and then got a "C" in climbing and a "D" in running.

At the end of the year, an abnormal eel, who could swim exceedingly well, and also run, climb and fly a little, had the highest average and was valedictorian.

The prairie dogs stayed out of school and fought the tax levy because the administration would not add digging and burrowing to the curriculum. They apprenticed their children to a badger and later joined the groundhogs and gophers to start a successful private school.

Source: From "The Animal School" by George Reavis. In: *Catcher in the Wrong: Iconoclasts in Education*, edited by Billy L. Turney, F. E. Peacock Publishers, Inc., copyright © 1968. Reprinted by permission of Phi Delta Kappa Educational Foundation.

Mary Ann is bright, fifteen years old, an avid volleyball player, and plans to attend a local nursing school upon completion of high school. Sue is fifteen, makes below-average grades, hates science and mathematics, and is interested mostly in clothes and boys. Bill, barely seventeen, in trouble with the law, works forty hours per week at night and on weekends, and loves animals. Warren is an average student—average grades on his report card, average height and weight, average age for his grade in school, just about average in every respect.

Providing for Individual Differences

What happens when Mary Ann, Sue, Bill, and Warren, along with twenty-six other students, are placed together in a tenth grade biology class? True, these thirty students have many commonalities, but there are also tremendous differences among them. For example, ability to read may vary from the fourth grade level or lower to that expected of college students. Interests range from careers in health sciences to not the foggiest notion of what they will be doing next week. How can a science teacher provide effective instruction for a class of thirty students who have a wide range of abilities and needs?

At one time in our history, most schools were small, and teachers could work with students on an individual basis. As the size of schools grew, it became necessary to group students, and this was most often done on the basis of age. Six-year-olds were placed in first grade, seven-year-olds in second grade, and so on. Although some students who failed to master the work were retained in a particular grade for a year, most students were promoted each year. And as much as the distance between fast and slow runners increases, the longer they run, the differences in achievement between able and slower students increases as they try to move through a school at the same pace.

In an attempt to decrease the amount of variation in a class, many schools group students according to their ability, a practice called *homogeneous grouping.* As the name implies, students are assigned to groups so that members of a class are as much alike as possible. This practice is in contrast to *heterogeneous grouping,* which involves placing students with a wide range of abilities, interests, and career plans in the same class.

The disadvantages of heterogeneous grouping are obvious with classes of thirty or more students of wide-ranging abilities and interests. It is virtually impossible for a teacher to adequately provide for individual differences using conventional approaches such as lecturing, class discussions, demonstrations, and various kinds of media. There are also major disadvantages to homogeneous grouping. First, we lack the instruments and techniques to accurately and precisely measure student ability and achievement. Research studies show that students in homogeneously grouped classes often exhibit as wide a range of individual differences as the total population from which they were selected. Second, there are many reasons why it is both desirable and necessary for science classes to be made up of students representing various backgrounds and abilities. For example, the legal requirements and educational desirability of including students with various kinds of handicaps in regular science classes are discussed in Chapter 10.

Although the pros and cons of ability grouping continue to be argued, most educators feel the solution to the problem of providing for individual difference lies in the individualization of instruction.

Types of Individualized Instruction

An examination of various plans, materials, and techniques for individualizing instruction reveals two important characteristics. First, most plans allow for students to take varying lengths of time to complete a task or learn certain material. Students are usually allowed to determine their own rate of progress; hence, these programs are called *self-paced*.

The idea of allowing students varying amounts of time is complementary to the idea of mastery learning advocated by Block and others.[1] The basic assumption of mastery learning is that most students can master a body of material if they are given enough time. This is in contrast to the more traditional practice of giving all students the same amount of time (one week to learn to do Punnett squares or vector problems) and then moving on to the next topic, with student comprehension of the previous topic ranging from near zero to 100 percent. In other words, with mastery learning, *time* becomes the major variable, and with traditional learning, *achievement* is the primary variable. Operationally, mastery can be defined as completing a prespecified percentage, say 90 percent, of the evaluation items presented at the end of a lesson or unit. Many of the programs and materials for individualizing science instruction described in this chapter are based on a mastery learning approach.

To some, individualized instruction suggests students seated at carrels or in cubicles, reacting with a computer, working through a set of programmed materials, or watching a program on educational television. Individualized instruction should be more than automated instruction and the use of educational technology. Ideally, individualized instruction should allow students to have choices in **what** is to be learned and **how** it is to be learned as well as the rate at which they will work. Thus, a second characteristic of individualized instruction involves the roles of teachers and students in the selection of objectives and the strategies or activities by which these objectives can be achieved.

[1]James H. Block (Ed.), *Mastery Learning: Theory and Practice.* With selected papers by Peter W. Airascah, Benjamin Bloom, and John Carroll, New York: Holt, Rinehart & Winston, 1971.

RESEARCH REPORT

Comparison of Individualized and Conventional Modes of Instruction

In a review of the literature dealing with comparisons of individualized and conventional modes of instruction in science, Marchese[2] concludes:

1. Individualized instruction provides an environment for greater student participation and acceptance of responsibility.

2. Individualized instruction provides an increased ability for the student to evaluate his or her own progress.

3. Individualized instruction attains just as much, and sometimes more, learning of subject matter.

4. Individualized instruction seems to produce a more positive attitude towards the students themselves, the school, and the subject.

Marchese also adds a note of caution. The research reviewed deals with various kinds of individualized instruction, such as modular, programmed learning, audiotutorial, and multimedia. Because there may be common inadequacies in these instructional materials, erroneous conclusions concerning the relative effectiveness of different teaching methods may result. Nevertheless, Marchese feels that the evidence supports the view that individualized instruction can be a refreshing and invigorating world of realistic learning for many science students.

[2]Richard S. Marchese, "A Literature Search and Review of the Comparison of Individualized and Conventional Modes of Instruction in Science," *School Science and Mathematics,* 77, 8 (December, 1977):669–703.

A schema for analyzing individualized instruction is presented in Figure 8.1. The roles of teachers and students in deciding what is to be learned (objectives) and how it is to be learned (strategies) are represented on the horizontal and vertical axes. A few examples of individualized programs will illustrate how this schema can be used and will show that decisions on objectives and strategies are often made jointly by teachers and students.

Secondary school science programs have been developed that allow students to work individually or in small groups. One of the first such programs was initiated at Nova School in Broward County, Florida. The Nova 7–12 science program was composed of a series of Learning Activity Packages (LAPS). Each LAP consisted of a printed study guide and various kinds of supportive materials. Teachers assisted as students worked at their own pace to perform investigations, complete reading assignments, and carry out the other activities specified in LAPS. Students completing the fifty-five LAPS making up the secondary science program before they graduated from high school were allowed to do independent investigations. Since the teacher made most of the decisions on objectives

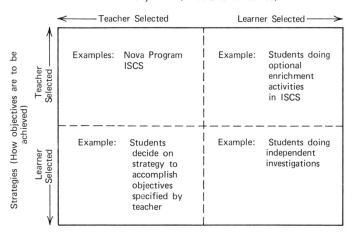

Objectives (What is to be learned)

FIGURE 8.1   A schema for analyzing the degree of teacher control
and student control in the selection of objectives and strategies.

and strategies, the Nova program would be placed in the upper left corner
of the schema in Figure 8.1. However, students who completed the fifty-
five LAPS and engaged in independent investigations would for the most
part select their own objectives and strategies. For example, a student
who wants to know more about a career in engineering might arrange for
an internship in a local electronics industry. This part of the program
would be in the lower right corner of the schema (Figure 8.1).

The Intermediate Science Curriculum Study (ISCS) developed an
individualized, self-paced, activity-centered, sequential set of instructional materials for the intermediate grades. Headquartered at Florida
State University and supported by the National Science Foundation, ISCS
was designed using a multitrack approach. Each student is expected to
complete the activities making up a core of material, which is represented
by the broad horizontal arrow in Figure 8.2. Branching out from this core
are excursions, which can be classified as remedial or enrichment (also see
Figure 8.2). Self-evaluation tests allow students to work at their own pace
and direct them to remedial activities when test scores indicate additional
instruction on a particular topic is needed. An example of these tests is
given in Figure 8.3 and an example of optimal material is shown in
Figure 8.4.

The core part of the ISCS is similar to the Nova program; the objectives and strategies are selected by the teacher and those designing the
program. However, students doing the optional enrichment activities
have a voice in the selection of objectives by deciding which ones, if any,
to do. (See the upper right corner of the schema in Figure 8.1.)

In addition to the three alternatives already discussed, it is possible
for the teacher to select the objectives and let the students decide how

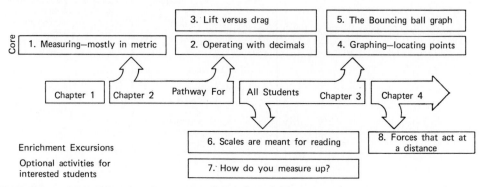

FIGURE 8.2   Core and optional activities of Level 1 of the Intermediate Science Curriculum Study.

they will achieve these objectives. For example, students can choose from several possibilities: doing laboratory investigations and activities, viewing films or videotapes, reading, doing a library report, interacting with a computer, and so on. For those believing there is a common core of material that should be learned by all students, this approach to individualizing instruction has great appeal.

Some educators prefer the term *personalized instruction,* which implies that the instruction is carried out on a more personal basis and allows for interaction among students and between students and the teacher. One

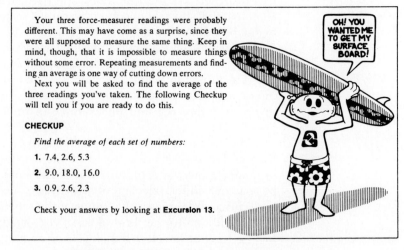

FIGURE 8.3   An ISCS self-test or check-up exercise.

EXCURSION 13: Answers to Check-up
1. *5.1*   2. *14.3*   3. *1.9*
(If you missed any of these, do this excursion now.)

Averaging

Smokey Bear seems to be smarter than the average bear. What does that mean? What is an "average bear"? Does it mean that Smokey is smarter than all bears? What is an average?

If you've used averages, you probably know what funny things averages are. Then you don't have to do this excursion. But if you're not sure what averages are, this excursion should help you.

Suppose someone asked you, "How long is your arm?" You could ask, "Which arm?" Did you know that most people have one arm that is longer than the other? Let's find your "average arm length." The only piece of equipment you will need is a meterstick.

FIGURE 8.4   The answers to the check-up on averaging shown in Figure 8.3 and the beginning of an excursion to improve the student's ability to average numbers.

Some students learn more efficiently when they are allowed to work at their own pace, in their own unique way.

such personalized system of instruction (PSI) is the Keller Plan,[3] which was originally developed to teach psychology at the college level. The system allows the student to: (1) move at his or her own pace through successive units of a course of study, (2) be tested as often as necessary to assure mastery of each unit of work, with no penalty for failure, and (3) be graded on each test by a well-prepared and well-guided student proctor.

A comparison of the Keller Plan with other approaches to individualized instruction reveals that self-pacing is the major characteristic they all have in common. The development of new instructional approaches and advances made in educational technology has made it possible for students to work at their own pace and, to some extent, to have a voice in what is to be learned and how it is to be learned. Several of these approaches have stood the test of time; others are more recent developments. Since most individualized science programs are a mix of the old and new, it is important that professionals considering the implementation of individualized programs be familiar with these various approaches.

Teaching Machines and Programmed Instruction

In the 1920s, Sidney L. Pressly of Ohio State University invented a small machine to score multiple choice examinations automatically. The machine presented one question at a time, with the student responding by pressing a key. If the question was answered correctly, the machine allowed the student to go on to the next question. If not, the student had to keep pressing keys until the correct answer was selected. A record of each student's score was made, and the students were provided immediate feedback of their results, which in itself was rewarding.

Although Pressly and his graduate students performed many experiments with this and similar devices, their use in teaching was not fully utilized. The idea of teaching machines was reintroduced in the 1950s by B. F. Skinner of Harvard University. Skinner was particularly interested in the teaching machines because subjects using them were given immediate reinforcement. Since that time, various kinds of teaching machines have been developed, ranging from cardboard devices costing a few dollars to complicated packages of electronics and optics costing thousands of dollars.

Most of the programmed material presented to the student by teaching machines can also be presented by programmed texts and other forms of printed material (workbooks, flash cards, etc.). The following example illustrates how one kind of programmed material is presented. To use it, cover the answer column (on the right hand side of the page) with a piece

---

[3]Fred S. Keller and J. Gilmour Sherman, *The Keller Plan Handbook*, Menlo Park, Calif.: W. A. Benjamin, Inc. 1974.

1. In a programmed text, the educational material is broken up
    into small portions called <u>frames</u>. If you read these carefully
    you will be able to fill in any gaps in the <u>frames</u>. You are
    now reading the first fr____ of a specimen program.   (fr)ame

2. Each frame involves some question, or several questions, or
    blanks to fill in. The whole collection of frames makes up the
    program or _____med text.   program(med)

3. If all students of a programmed text have to go through all
    the _____, we call this a <u>linear program</u>. The other
    kind of program is called a <u>branching program</u>. When some   (frames,
    students read different parts of a program from others, we   questions)
    call this a _____ program.   branching

              linear/branching

4. The contents of a programmed text, which we call the
    _____, could be put onto a film or paper strip. A   program
    device for presenting this, one frame at a time, is called
    a <u>teaching machine</u>. This teaching machine is then, technical-
    ly speaking, using the same _____ as a programmed   program,
                                                                    material
    text.

5. Is this true or false: "A teaching machine in which all the
    students go through all the frames is using a <u>linear</u> pro-
    gram, by contrast with a <u>branching</u> program."[4]   true

*Reprinted by permission of the Indiana University Press. Scriren, Michael, "The Case for and Use
of Programmed Texts," in* Programmed Instruction, Bold New Venture, *edited by Allen D.
Calvin, pp. 4–5, 1969.*

of paper and move it down after you have attempted to complete each
frame.

All programmed materials, regardless of how they are presented,
have four characteristics in common:

1. They present information and questions, to which the student must
select or construct a response.

2. They provide immediate feedback to the student by indicating whether or not the response is appropriate.

3. The sequence in which the items are presented is controlled by the program.

4. They allow the student to work individually and at his or her own pace.

Numerous programmed materials were developed for presenting material in secondary school science. Figure 8.5 presents a page from a programmed unit in chemistry. Many science teachers find this useful material for reviewing what already has been presented in class or as a way for students to make up work.

Although many schools experimented with the use of teaching machines, few are in use today. The chief disadvantages are their expense, the unavailability of personnel in secondary schools to maintain them in working order, and their lack of portability. In contrast, a pro-

---

1. In a methane molecule (CH$_4$), _____ carbon atom is   1
                           (number)
   connected to _____ hydrogen atoms.   4
               (number)

2. Later on we will see why these connections between
   atoms occur. Meanwhile, we want to learn what
   connections take place. For example, we just saw that
   in CH$_4$, 1 C atom is connected to 4 _____ atoms.   H
                                      (symbol)

3. We may represent the CH$_4$ molecule by the diagram
        H
   H-C-H. The lines in the diagram show that 1 connection
        H
   is made between the _____ atom and each of the
                                                                  carbon,
   _____ atoms.   hydrogen

4. We may represent an ethane molecule (C$_2$H$_6$) by the
       H H
   diagram: H-C-C-H
       H H
   The lines in the diagram show that each carbon atom

   is connected to _____ C atom and _____ H atoms.   1, 3

FIGURE 8.5   A sample page from a programmed chemistry unit. To use this material, cover the answer column (on the right) with a piece of paper and move it down after you have attempted to complete each frame.

grammed book is relatively inexpensive and can be used by the students whenever and wherever they have the time to do so.

Programmed instruction of all types also has several inherent disadvantages. Most programmed instruction places the emphasis on reading as the primary means of learning, whereas laboratory investigation and other activities are seen as the cornerstones of a good science program. In addition, the availability of computers opens up the possibilities of a wider range of instructional activities than is possible with typical programmed materials. Nevertheless, programmed instruction had an impact on science teaching as shown by a comparison of the characteristics of programmed material listed above with those of other means of individualizing instruction.

The Audiotutorial Approach

The audiotutorial approach, now often called the autotutorial approach,[4] was used at Purdue University by Samuel N. Postlethwait and his colleagues as a means of teaching an introductory college botany course. Rather than the typical college lectures and laboratory sessions, the activities of the courses were scheduled as a part of Independent Student Sessions, General Assembly Sessions, Small Assembly Sessions, and under the heading of "Other Activities."

THE INDEPENDENT STUDY SESSION

Students self-schedule independent study sessions in a learning center consisting of booths for individual work and tables for bulky materials. Each booth is equipped with a tape recorder, an 8mm movie projector, and other equipment, such as microscopes and slides, that are needed for the week's work.

Upon entering the learning center, the students pick up a list of behavioral objectives for the week's work and assign themselves a booth. By means of a tape recorder, the voice of the senior professor tutors (hence the term *audiotutorial*) the students through a variety of learning activities. These activities may include reading a short passage in the textbook, viewing a film, observing specimens through a microscope, doing experiments, answering questions on a work sheet or in a laboratory manual, and even taking a field trip. Portable tape recorders provide the directions for field trips. One or more instructors are available in the learning center to assist students who need help with any of the activities.

Students like being able to decide when during the week they will do

---

[4]The early programs relied heavily on the use of audiotape recorders for giving directions, explaining biological phenomena, and generally guiding the student; hence the term *audiotutorial*. More recently, such programs have utilized new media such as videotape players and computers, and the term *autotutorial* has been introduced to indicate that the program is more multisensory.

a particular activity and how much time they wish to spend in the learning center. An important advantage of the independent study sessions is that students are placed in a more active role than they are, for example, with lectures. Moreover, a wide variety of methods and materials can be used to teach a given unit of work.

THE GENERAL ASSEMBLY SESSION

The general assembly session is held near the end of the week and is used for activities that can best be done in large groups. Guest lectures, long films, review sessions, and major examinations are examples of activities conducted in general assembly sessions. General assembly sessions also allow the student and senior professor who conducts them to become better acquainted.

THE SMALL ASSEMBLY SESSIONS

The small assembly sessions meet approximately an hour at the end of each week and involve approximately eight students and an instructor. These sessions have been used in various ways. One use has involved their being called Integrated Quiz Sessions and being used as a time for oral and written tests on the week's work. Some instructors using the audiotutorial approach prefer the students to take the weekly tests whenever they think they are ready and as part of their work in the independent study session. In this case, small assembly sessions may be used for discussion on science-related topics, for the presentation of oral reports by the students, and for planning student research projects.

OTHER ACTIVITIES

Some desirable activities, such as student research projects, cannot be accomplished within the sessions already described. At Purdue, all students are required to do one research project, and students wishing to earn an "A" in the course must do a second project.

ADVANTAGES AND LIMITATIONS OF THE AUDIOTUTORIAL APPROACH

The audiotutorial approach used at Purdue is described in greater detail in books by Postlethwait and others (see References at the end of this chapter). This approach has been modified for use in other subjects and in secondary schools. As is true for many other forms of individualized instruction, some important advantages and limitations of the audiotutorial approach are:

1. Students can work at their own pace. In secondary schools with fixed time periods for class, this can also present problems. Some students may need more time than is available during the school day to complete a unit of work. In like manner, provisions must be made for students who finish early.

2. Students assume more active roles and take more responsibility for their own learning. Although this is a very desirable outcome, many secondary school students, unlike college students, need more direction and guidance than is permitted by the teacher-student ratio. In addition, the lack of staff time makes it difficult to schedule small assembly sections in most secondary schools.

3. A multiplicity of approaches and educational technology can be used. The audiotutorial approach reflects the desirability of presenting material in a variety of ways. Certain material lends itself to a particular type of presentation, and most students also have individual preferences for the way they like to learn. However, lack of the facilities and equipment needed to carry out an audiotutorial approach can be a serious problem.

Computers in Education

Computers have had tremendous effects on education just as they have greatly influenced every other aspect of our lives. At first, computers were used mainly to perform administrative and research and development tasks. Some of these tasks are listed in Figure 8.6. Computers have also found their way into the classroom, and all predictions point to their playing a bigger role in instruction in the future. These uses of computers in science classrooms can be grouped under two headings (see Figure 8.6).

COMPUTER-MANAGED INSTRUCTION

Computers can be a valuable tool in managing instruction. For example, in cases where instruction is individualized, computers greatly reduce the problem of keeping track of each student's progress. In like manner, a

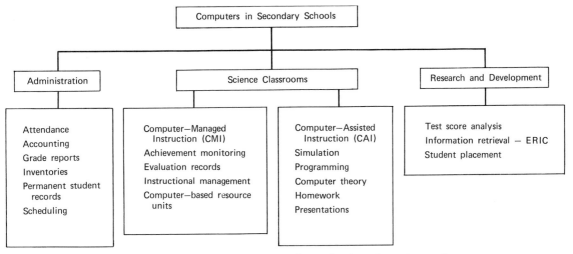

FIGURE 8.6 Uses of computers in secondary schools and in science classrooms.

computer program can be designed to indicate when remedial work is needed, when a student is ready to move on to new material, and to prepare regular evaluation reports of various kinds. Computer-based resource units are described in Chapter 3. These and similar uses make up what is called computer-managed instruction (CMI). The teacher and perhaps teacher aides use a computer to schedule, monitor, and otherwise manage the many activities of the classroom. Although CMI has been used primarily in reading and mathematics, it can also be used in individualized science instruction.

COMPUTER-
ASSISTED
INSTRUCTION

The use of computers to provide instruction directly to pupils is most often called computer-assisted instruction (CAI). As this term suggests, the computer is used to supplement the efforts of teachers. Figure 8.6 shows some of the functions comprising CAI.

TYPES OF
COMPUTER
HARDWARE,
SOFTWARE, AND
SYSTEMS

Many of the advantages of using the computer in CAI are closely related to the type of computer *hardware* and *software* available. These two terms are used to denote the computer, teletypewriters, cathode-ray display units, etc. (hardware), and the *programs* (software), which tell the computer what to do.

Computers are used in homes as well as classrooms and have become an important learning tool for today's student.

Schools often use centralized computers that are classified as *interactive-time sharing* and *batch*. In an interactive-time sharing system, many schools and students share a computer and are able to interact with it simultaneously by means of a terminal, such as a teletypewriter and/or a cathode-ray tube unit. Each terminal is connected to the computer by means of cables or by means of a telephone. The material in Figure 8.7 beginning on page 326 is an example of a program used in an interactive-time sharing system. An important advantage of this type of system is that the students get immediate feedback to the information entered into the system. In addition, students do not have to know a computer language, such as FORTRAN (FORmula TRANslator) or BASIC (Beginner's All-purpose Symbolic Instruction Code) in order to interact with the computer. Of course, those who wish to write their own computer programs must have a knowledge of computer language.

Recent advances in electronics and computer technology have led to the development of relatively inexpensive *microcomputers*, or *microprocessors* as they are often called. Most are composed of a unit similar to an electric typewriter and a display unit that looks like a standard television receiver, some of which produce colored images. They can store programs and data on disks or cassette tapes like those used in tape recorders. These units are capable of performing a majority of the computer tasks involved in CAI in secondary school science. Because of their low costs and adaptability, people are buying them for home use; thus, some students already have access to a computer for homework and other educational activities. Microcomputers in the home potentially have the same revolutionary effects that television and hand-held calculators have had.

USES OF CAI

Several uses of computer-assisted instruction are shown in Figure 8.6. Perhaps the simplest use is that of presenting drill exercises and opportunities to practice various skills. For students with little or no experience with computers, this has value in its novelty of approach as well as providing, in the case of interactive systems, immediate feedback. The following are examples of drills and practice exercises that can be done with CAI:

- Give the symbols for the chemical elements as the computer displays the names.
- Convert English units of measurement to metric units.
- Calculate the calories in a meal when given a calorie chart.
- Find the amount of product in a given chemical reaction.
- Solve various problems in mechanics and other areas of physics.

The computer can also be programmed to make presentations of material new to the student or to serve as a tutor. One such system, PLATO

(Programmed Logic for Automatic Teaching Operations), has been under development at the University of Illinois since 1960. Based on a program selected or developed by a teacher, the computer presents the material on a screen, and checks the student's performance and the effectiveness of a particular program. Programs have been developed in many areas, including astronomy and physics, and have been field tested with thousands of students across the United States.

Since computers play such a big part in our lives, today's students must develop computer literacy. Computer theory and programming skills can be taught in various secondary school courses—mathematics, business education, vocational education, and specific courses in computer science, to name a few. These ideas are also included in some science courses such as physics and physical science. If such topics are included in science, it is very desirable for students to have hands-on experience with computers.

Perhaps the most interesting use of CAI in science is that of providing simulations. An example is the material developed by the Huntington II Simulation Project headquartered at the State University of New York at Stony Brook. Figure 8.7 presents a beginning student's response to a simulation on water pollution. Notice how the student doing this simulation is engaged in important processes of science—for example, predicting results, manipulating variables, interpreting data presented in tables and graphs, and drawing conclusions.

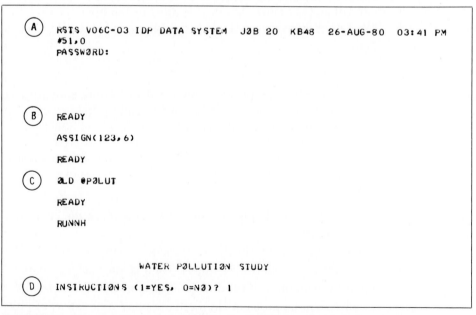

FIGURE 8.7   The responses of a student to a Huntington II simulation on water pollution made on an interactive time-sharing system.

IN THIS STUDY YOU CAN SPECIFY THE FOLLOWING CHARACTERISTICS:

(E)
A. THE KIND OF BODY OF WATER:
   1. LARGE POND
   2. LARGE LAKE
   3. SLOW-MOVING RIVER
   4. FAST-MOVING RIVER

B. THE WATER TEMPERATURE IN DEGREES FAHRENHEIT:

C. THE KIND OF WASTE DUMPED INTO THE WATER:
   1. INDUSTRIAL
   2. SEWAGE

D. THE RATE OF DUMPING OF WASTE, IN PARTS PER MILLION (PPM)/DAY.

E. THE TYPE OF TREATMENT OF THE WASTE:
   0. NONE
   1. PRIMARY (SEDIMENTATION OR PASSAGE THROUGH FINE
              SCREENS TO REMOVE GROSS SOLIDS)
   2. SECONDARY (SAND FILTERS OR THE ACTIVATED SLUDGE
                METHOD TO REMOVE DISSOLVED AND COLLOIDAL
                ORGANIC MATTER)

****

(F)
BODY OF WATER? 3
WATER TEMPERATURE? 60
KIND OF WASTE? 2
DUMPING RATE? 9
TYPE OF TREATMENT? 0

(G) DO YOU WANT: A GRAPH(1), A TABLE(2), OR BOTH(3)? 3

AFTER DAY 2 THE GAME FISH BEGIN TO DIE, BECAUSE
THE OXYGEN CONTENT OF THE WATER DROPPED BELOW 5 PPM.

TIME DAYS	OXY. CONTENT PPM	WASTE CONTENT PPM
0	8.56	2.67
1	6.88	9.16
2	4.85	12.14
3	3.67	13.51
4	3.08	14.14
5	2.8	14.42
6	2.67	14.56
7	2.61	14.62
8	2.58	14.64
9	2.57	14.66
10	2.56	14.66
11	2.56	14.66
12	2.56	14.67
13	2.56	14.67
14	2.56	14.67
15	2.56	14.67
16	2.56	14.67
17	2.56	14.67
18	2.56	14.67
19	2.56	14.67
20	2.56	14.67

(H)

FIGURE 8.7 (Continued)

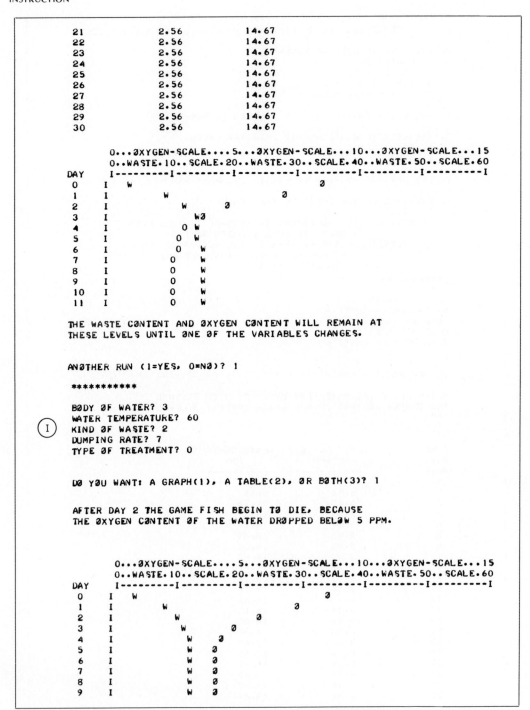

```
            21            2.56            14.67
            22            2.56            14.67
            23            2.56            14.67
            24            2.56            14.67
            25            2.56            14.67
            26            2.56            14.67
            27            2.56            14.67
            28            2.56            14.67
            29            2.56            14.67
            30            2.56            14.67


            0...ØXYGEN-SCALE....5...ØXYGEN-SCALE...10...ØXYGEN-SCALE...15
            0..WASTE.10..SCALE.20..WASTE.30..SCALE.40..WASTE.50..SCALE.60
      DAY   I---------I---------I---------I---------I---------I---------I
       0    I  W                                   Ø
       1    I        W                       Ø
       2    I          W         Ø
       3    I            WØ
       4    I        O  W
       5    I       O   W
       6    I       O    W
       7    I      O     W
       8    I      O     W
       9    I      O     W
      10    I      O     W
      11    I      O     W

      THE WASTE CØNTENT AND ØXYGEN CØNTENT WILL REMAIN AT
      THESE LEVELS UNTIL ØNE ØF THE VARIABLES CHANGES.


      ANØTHER RUN (1=YES, 0=NØ)?  1

      **********

      BØDY ØF WATER?  3
      WATER TEMPERATURE?  60
      KIND ØF WASTE?  2
      DUMPING RATE?  7
      TYPE ØF TREATMENT?  0


      DØ YØU WANT: A GRAPH(1), A TABLE(2), ØR BØTH(3)?  1

      AFTER DAY 2 THE GAME FISH BEGIN TØ DIE, BECAUSE
      THE ØXYGEN CØNTENT ØF THE WATER DRØPPED BELØW 5 PPM.



            0...ØXYGEN-SCALE....5...ØXYGEN-SCALE...10...ØXYGEN-SCALE...15
            0..WASTE.10..SCALE.20..WASTE.30..SCALE.40..WASTE.50..SCALE.60
      DAY   I---------I---------I---------I---------I---------I---------I
       0    I  W                                   Ø
       1    I     W                          Ø
       2    I       W              Ø
       3    I         W         Ø
       4    I            W    Ø
       5    I            W   Ø
       6    I            W   Ø
       7    I            W   Ø
       8    I            W   Ø
       9    I            W   Ø
```

FIGURE 8.7 (Continued)

```
         THE WASTE CONTENT AND OXYGEN CONTENT WILL REMAIN AT
         THESE LEVELS UNTIL ONE OF THE VARIABLES CHANGES.


         ANOTHER RUN (1=YES, 0=NO)? 1


         ***********

         BODY OF WATER? 3
   (J)   WATER TEMPERATURE? 60
         KIND OF WASTE? 2
         DUMPING RATE? 7
         TYPE OF TREATMENT? 1


         DO YOU WANT: A GRAPH(1), A TABLE(2), OR BOTH(3)? 1


              0...OXYGEN-SCALE....5...OXYGEN-SCALE...10...OXYGEN-SCALE...15
              0..WASTE.10..SCALE.20..WASTE.30..SCALE.40..WASTE.50..SCALE.60
         DAY  I---------I---------I---------I---------I---------I---------I
          0   I    W                                   O
          1   I       W                             O
          2   I        W                        O
          3   I        W                      O
          4   I        W                    O
          5   I        W                 O
          6   I        W                 O
          7   I        W                 O
          8   I        W                 O
          9   I        W                 O

         THE WASTE CONTENT AND OXYGEN CONTENT WILL REMAIN AT
         THESE LEVELS UNTIL ONE OF THE VARIABLES CHANGES.


         ANOTHER RUN (1=YES, 0=NO)? 1


         ***********

         BODY OF WATER? 3
         WATER TEMPERATURE? 50
         KIND OF WASTE? 2
   (K)   DUMPING RATE? 7
         TYPE OF TREATMENT? 1


         DO YOU WANT: A GRAPH(1), A TABLE(2), OR BOTH(3)? 1
```

FIGURE 8.7 (Continued)

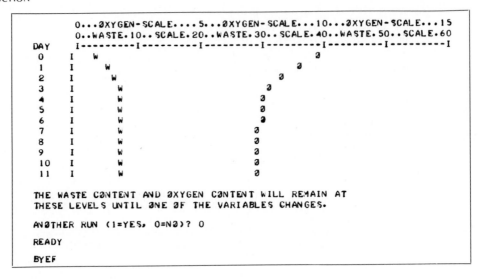

```
         0...OXYGEN-SCALE....5...OXYGEN-SCALE...10...OXYGEN-SCALE...15
         0..WASTE.10..SCALE.20..WASTE.30..SCALE.40..WASTE.50..SCALE.60
   DAY   I---------I---------I---------I---------I---------I---------I
    0    I   W                                    O
    1    I     W                               O
    2    I      W                          O
    3    I       W                       O
    4    I       W                    O
    5    I       W                    O
    6    I       W                    O
    7    I       W                  O
    8    I       W                  O
    9    I       W                  O
   10    I       W                  O
   11    I       W                  O

THE WASTE CONTENT AND OXYGEN CONTENT WILL REMAIN AT
THESE LEVELS UNTIL ONE OF THE VARIABLES CHANGES.

ANOTHER RUN (1=YES, 0=NO)? 0

READY

BYEF
```

(A) This program was run on an interactive-time sharing computer connected to a tele-typewriter by means of telephone. Notice that the printout gives the data and time the program is started.

(B) Each student, class, or school is assigned a user number. This number is used to bill the school for the time the computer is in use.

(C) The title of the Huntington II Simulation Program on Pollution is entered by the student; the computer already contains this program in its memory.

(D) This tells the student to answer "yes" by typing "1" and "no" by using "0".

(E) The student is given certain background information and is requested to make choices about the values of the variables that will be used.

(F) The Teacher's Guide suggests water temperature in the range of 32° to 70° Fahrenheit is a reasonable choice and that the rate of dumping should be kept between 0 and 14 parts per million per day.

(G) On the first run, the student requests both a table and a graph.

(H) Both the table and the graph show what happens to the oxygen content and the concentration of the wastes in the river over a period of time; this represents a dying situation.

(I) In this run, all variables are kept the same as the first run, except for the amount of waste dumped; result—the fish still die.

(J) The student continues to change one variable at a time so the effect of doing so can be observed; in this run, the wastes are given a primary treatment (sedimentation of passage through fine screens to remove gross solids). Oxygen content of the water stays above 5 PPM and thus fish continue to live.

(K) Student experiments with the effect of temperature on the river's ability to support life.

(L) Indicates the date and time the student signed off.

FIGURE 8.7 (Continued)

WHAT STUDENTS SAY

Using Computers to Learn Science

- I think it would be fun to try.
- Great idea, but some changes would have to be made—we can't even use hand-held calculators in my advanced math class.
- No—I'm not very good at math and I'm sure that it would be mass confusion.
- Fun for awhile, but then the novelty would wear off—this is what happened at home when we got our minicomputer last Christmas.
- After my schedule got screwed up by the computer and I had PE three times a day, I'm not sure.
- Sure would beat listening to the teacher talk or doing worksheets.
- Would depend on the course—chemistry and physics, "yes," but probably not in biology.
- I know someone who is a computer nut. What is it with these people?
- I've heard you can play games on computers.

Other Hunting II Simulations in science include:

Ecology, Bison
Milliken's Oil Drop Experiment
Weight Control; Food Intake versus Standard Diet
Genetics: Monohybrid Cross
Genetics: Hardy-Weinberg Principle, Rates
World Growth Model: Population and Food Supply
Enzymes: Competitive Inhibition, Lock and Key Model
Disease: Malaria Epidemic
Enzymes: pH Specificity
Effect of Cleanliness and Poison on Rats
Population
Rutherford Alpha-Particle Study
Young's Double-Slit Experiment, Light
Insect Control: Sterile Males or Pesticides

Each of these includes a resource handbook and teacher's guide that gives the information needed to use the simulations effectively.

Instructional Modules

Instructional modules, which are sometimes called Learning Activity Packages (LAPS), allow students to complete a small segment of work on their own or with minimal help from the teacher. At a minimum, an instructional module consists of objectives, activities, and evaluation items. It may be short enough so most students can complete it in an hour, or it may require several days or even weeks. Some mini-courses lasting from a few weeks to a semester are presented entirely by means of instructional modules.

An advantage of instructional modules is that students can become involved in learning activities that are tailored to their particular needs or interests. Another advantage is that students can proceed at their own pace, working until they have successfully completed a unit of study. For example, a student who has missed several days of class can catch up on instruction missed on genetics; or an accelerated student in chemistry can do a special investigation in the biochemistry of lipids. A student who has difficulty understanding the metric system can spend extra time mastering basic measuring skills. Since modules contain objectives written in terms of expected student performance, it is possible to assess these outcomes at the end of the module and redirect students to additional activities if they have not been successful in completing the objectives. Some modules also contain a pretest, which can be used to determine if the students already possess the knowledge, skills, and other objectives treated by the module.

THE PARTS OF AN INSTRUCTIONAL MODULE

Although instructional modules can be purchased in modular form, it is also possible for teachers to construct their own modules. Often, these commercially available modules have components in addition to those found in the materials developed by teachers. The following components are needed in a module, regardless of whether it is developed commercially or by a teacher.

TITLE.   A title that sounds interesting or "relevant" to secondary school students is usually preferred over more traditional titles. For instance, "Major Causes of Heart Attacks" is more interesting than "Coronary Thrombosis." "Searching for the Mysterious Bug" is more appealing to most junior high school students than "Causative Agents of Four Major Diseases." Titles do not have to be "catchy" or "cute," but a module is usually a more appealing learning package when additional thought is given to finding a label with an interesting ring.

INTRODUCTION.   A short, snappy introduction, usually no more than two or three short paragraphs, helps prepare students for the module. Teachers constructing modules should "talk" directly to students, and in a manner that increases interest in the topic to be studied. "Have you ever been in a big thunder storm and wondered where all the noise came from?" is a better opening sentence than "There are several important factors that influence the intensity of a thunder storm."

A good introduction should whet student appetites and encourage them to read further. The introduction should also explain in general terms what the module is going to cover and what the student will be doing in the module. By the end of the introduction, the student should be interested in reading further and should have a "feel" for what he or she is to accomplish in the module. The following section is an example of a good title and introduction for a middle or junior high school science class.

TITLE

INTRODUCTION

> ## And Let There Be Light!
>
> Ever tried to hook up an electric train or automobile race track and fail to get it to work? Perhaps someone helping you said, "There must be an open circuit keeping it from running." What is a circuit?
>
> Or perhaps you decide to wire up a battery-operated radio so you can plug it into a household receptacle. "Stop! What do you want to do—burn down the house? That radio is designed for DC, not AC electricity!" your friend advises you. What is DC electricity? How does it differ from AC electricity?
>
> In this module, you will use flashlight bulbs, dry cells, wires, and your textbooks to answer these and other questions about circuits and direct current electricity. And as the title suggests, most of the activities involve connecting a flashlight bulb to a dry cell so that it lights!

OBJECTIVES. One trademark of a good module is that clear, concise objectives are presented in terms of things each student will be expected to do by the end of the module. Below are two objectives. Which of the following gives students the best idea of what they are expected to do?

A. You will understand the ways an electrical current flows.

B. You will be able to demonstrate a circuit by arranging a dry cell, a bulb, and a piece of wire in such a way that the bulb will light.

The second objective not only communicates more specifically to students what they are to learn, but it also illustrates what they are to do in order to successfully achieve the objective. Objectives that are clear and to the point work best in modules.

Modules can be designed to last from one period, or less, to several periods. Generally, modules with three to five objectives are suitable for one instructional period and work better with secondary school students than longer modules. The following objectives would be suitable for the portion of a module designed for one instructional period for middle school or junior high school science students.

Objectives: After you have finished this module you should be able to:

1. Arrange a dry cell, a bulb, and a piece of wire in such a way that the bulb will light and make a drawing that shows the arrangement necessary to light the bulb.
2. With two dry cells, a bulb, and a wire, sketch at least three different pictures of arrangements that would cause the bulb to light.
3. After reading page 94 in your textbook, and using your dry cells, bulb, and wire as examples, define the terms "electricity," "dry cells," "electrical circuit," and "direct current."
4. List at least three items in your home or your classroom that use direct current electricity.

ACTIVITIES.   Modules differ from programmed instructional materials; instead of being mainly reading passages followed by questions, modules are designed to guide students through a series of hands-on activities. The activities should correspond to the objectives that have been established. For example, if the student is expected to be able to separate the pigments found in a green plant using paper chromotagraphy, then it follows that one or more of the activities would involve the use of this process. This point illustrates a major limitation of instructional modules. In many cases, it is difficult to identify an activity to teach a specific outcome. For example, what activity do you have students do to have them discover that electricity is a flow of electrons when they cannot see or handle the electrons? That the landscape of the earth changes very slowly? That gravity in the moon is only one-sixth that on the earth?

A list of *what* materials will be needed and *where* these can be found should accompany the activities section. Since a module is a self-contained unit, the students' progress can also be facilitated by having carefully written directions contained within the package. This reduces the need for the student and teacher to spend time discussing simple procedures.

Directions are usually easier for students to follow when activities are broken into sections. For example, "Activity One" can deal with the first two objectives in the module, while "Activity Two" can correspond to the third objective. As stated before, activities are usually more interesting when they involve at least some hands-on, manipulative experience. It is also appropriate within a module to refer students to their textbooks or other reference books. This works best when the reading assignments are kept short and they relate closely to the activities.

The following is an example of activities corresponding to the sample objectives cited earlier.

ACTIVITY ONE (Objective One)

Obtain from the table in the front of the room one of each of the following: a *dry cell* (also called a flashlight battery or a D battery), a *flashlight bulb*, and a small piece of *wire*. At your work area and on your own, arrange the dry cell, bulb, and wire until you are successful in getting the bulb to light. Once you are able to do this, make a drawing in the space below which shows the arrangement you found that causes the bulb to light. You should take all the time you need to "discover" how to light the bulb. If, after a lengthy period of time, you are unsuccessful, you should ask your teacher for help.

Make drawing here:

Once you have finished your drawing, you are ready to proceed to Activity Two.

ACTIVITY TWO (Objective Two)

Obtain *one* additional dry cell from the table in the front of the room. At your work area and on your own arrange the bulb, wire, and *both* dry cells so that the light bulb will light. Make a sketch of this arrangement here:

Drawing of two dry cells, a wire, and a lighted bulb:

After you have made the bulb light with two dry cells; experiment with other ways you can get the bulb to light. Take your time and do not worry about what others are doing. The important thing is for you to learn as much as you can about how electricity travels through a circuit. Make at least two additional drawings of different arrangements you found that will light the bulb. In which arrangements, if any, does the bulb light more brightly with two dry cells than the one? Circle the drawings in which the bulb lights more brightly.

Make additional drawings here

ACTIVITY THREE (Objective Three)

Turn to page 94 in your textbook and carefully read the section entitled *Electrical Circuits*. Make notes that will help you understand this topic in the box below.

Makes notes here:

After you have carefully read page 94, define the following terms in your own words in the box below:

Define terms here:

Electricity-

Dry cell-

Electrical Circuit-

Direct Current-

ACTIVITY FOUR (Objective Four)

Now that you understand how direct current works, let's find some things that use direct current electricity. To begin, list below as many things as you can in your school or home that use some kind of electricity:

List things here that use electricity:

You read on page 94 in your textbook that some electrical devices use direct current (DC) and some utilize alternating current (AC). Go back to your list of items listed above and circle those which operate on direct current. Hint: Most electrical devices operating on DC electricity run on dry cells or batteries.

Now that you have finished all your activities it is time to test yourself. Turn to the next page and read carefully the instructions.

EVALUATION. The last major section of a module usually involves ways for students to find out how well they have mastered the objectives. The questions should be constructed so that students can check their own answers. To accomplish this, an answer may be posted somewhere in the room or may even be placed inconspicuously at the end of the module. Sometimes answers are placed upside down at the bottom of the page so that students cannot easily view them.

In order to allow students to check their own answers, it is usually necessary to ask closed rather than open questions. Multiple choice, matching, completion, and true–false items are examples of closed items (see Chapter 6 for more information on types of test items). Essay or discussion items usually must be graded by the teacher and, therefore, are less appropriate for use in a module.

One of the strengths of the modular method of instruction is that students can proceed with learning activities on their own, which means that they can assess their own progress and stop working on the module once they have accomplished the objectives. When students fail to answer one or more of the questions correctly at the end of the module, provisions should be made for giving them additional help. Such help can include directing them back to the objectivities and activities they have not yet mastered, having them do similar activities, or having them discuss with the teacher what they should do in order to successfully achieve the objective(s) they have not mastered.

When constructing test questions for a module, the items should reflect the objectives at the beginning of the module. The following questions are examples of how a teacher can evaluate the sample objectives and activities displayed earlier.

SELF-ADMINISTERED TEST

You have completed all the activities and now it is time to see how much you have learned. The following questions have been designed to measure your mastery of the objectives given at the beginning of the module. Good luck!

Directions for Question 1 (Objective 1)

Below are four drawings. Each contains a dry cell, a bulb and a piece of wire. Select the drawing that represents an arrangement where the bulb light will come on and place the letter only in the blank to the left.

_____ 1.

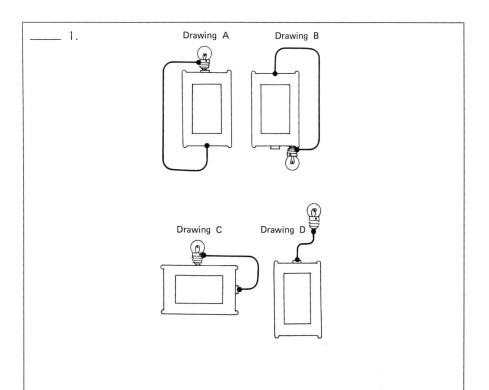

Directions for Question 2 (Objective 2)

Below are four drawings each of which contains *two* dry cell batteries, a bulb, and a piece of wire. Select the drawing that represents an arrangement where the bulb will light by placing the letter only in the blank to the left.

_____ 2.

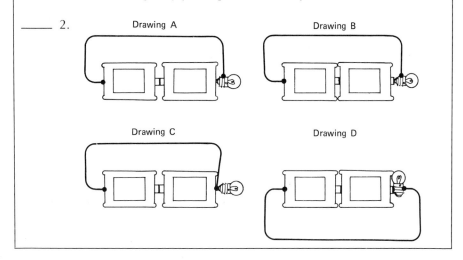

Directions for Questions 3 -6 (Objective 3)

The following multiple choice questions will measure your understanding of the terms "electricity," "dry cell," "electrical circuit" and "direct current." Select the *best* answer for each question by placing the letter only in the blank to the left of the question.

_____ 3. Which of the following statements best *defines* the word "electricity"?

A. The spark you feel when you walk across a carpeted room and touch a metal object.

B. The form of energy that causes molecules to move faster and farther apart.

C. A flow of electrons.

D. The juice supplied by an electrical power company.

_____ 4. All the following statements below accurately describe a "dry cell" *except*:

A. The source of electricity used in a flashlight.
B. Produces AC (alternating current) electricity.
C. Produces low-voltage (about 1.5 volts) electricity.
D. Produces electricity by chemical action.

_____ 5. Which of the following statements best *describes* the term "electrical circuit"?

A. A closed loop or pathway followed by an electrical current.
B. The small wire in a bulb that lights when electricity flows through it.
C. The wire used to connect a flashlight bulb to a dry cell.
D. The rod in the center of a dry cell.

_____ 6. Which of the following statements best *defines* the term "direct current"?

A. A current that flows back and forth through a circuit (often 60 times per second).
B. A current that flows in one direction through a circuit.
C. The current that flows through an electrical device when it is plugged into a household receptacle.
D. The electricity produced by the friction between two objects.

Direction for Question 7 (Objective 4)

Select the best answer(s) for the following question by placing the letter(s) only in the blank to the left of the question. In this question there may be more than one answer; therefore, it may be necessary to place more than one letter in the blank.

_____ 7. Listed below are several items commonly found at school or at home. Which of these items operate with direct current?
   A. Battery-operated radio   B. Table lamp
   C. Washing machine   D. Hand-held calculator
   E. Flashlight   F. Electric heater

Directions for Checking your Answers

After completing this test, you may check your answers by turning to the next page. The answers are upside down at the bottom of the page. If you got any questions wrong, go back to the objectives at the beginning of the module that corresponds with the test question you missed. Then move to the activity that was designed to help you achieve that objective. Review what you did during that activity and try to find out why you missed the question. If necessary, do the activity again. Repeat this procedure for each question you got incorrect. If you still are unable to answer the test questions you missed, ask for assistance from your teacher.

OBTAINING STUDENT FEEDBACK ON MODULES

Developing instructional modules is hard work and a time-consuming process. Despite all the teacher's efforts to get the "bugs" out, there are always ways of improving an instructional module. One of the best ways to improve a module is to ask students for suggestions at the time they are doing the module. This can be done by attaching an evaluation form to the end of the module. After the module has been used by several students, the teacher may wish to revise it based on their comments. For example, if half the students indicate that the directions for Activity 2 are confusing, some changes are in order. Student feedback of this kind can be most helpful in eliminating the "bugs" or "rough spots" in a module and, thereby, improving the quality of the product.

A sample evaluation form is shown on page 342.

NOTE: If modules have not been used before, it may be helpful for the teacher to ask students to discuss their preference for this method of learning compared with other teaching methods.

Independent Work

Giving students individual assignments and having them work individually or in small groups is perhaps the strategy most commonly used by science teachers to provide for individual differences. This approach is particularly useful with the more able students. They can do the regular work in a science class in less time than the other class members and thus have class time available for individual projects and investigations. In

TO: Students who have completed this module
FROM: Your teacher
RE: Evaluation of the module

Please respond in an honest fashion to the following questions. This will help us assess the effectiveness of this module and it will help to improve future editions.

1. What did you like most about the module?

2. What did you like least about the module?

3. Are there parts of the module that were confusing or incomplete? If so, please list them.

4. What other things could be done to improve the module?

5. In general, I would rate this module:

_____Excellent.   Other students should be able to use this module without difficulty.

_____Good.   With minor changes, this module should be used again.

_____Fair.   With major changes, this module should be used again.

_____Poor.   This module should NOT be used in the future. (Please give your reasons).

_____

_____

addition, these students usually have the skills and work habits that allow them to work effectively with minimum supervision.

The following list illustrates the variety of ways some students might do independent work in a high school biology class:

- Take care of the greenhouse, aquarium, or animal care facility
- Help establish and/or maintain an outdoor nature center or trail
- Assist the teacher in preparing for laboratory work and demonstrations
- Get practical experience by serving as a "Candy Striper" or nurse's aide in a hospital, as an assistant to a doctor, dentist, veterinarian, greenhouse operator, etc.
- Perform individual laboratory work on a problem of the student's

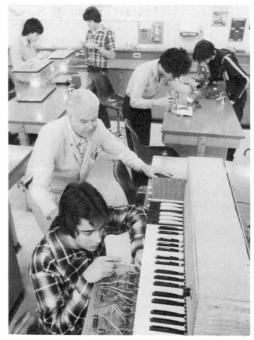

Successful project work is enhanced by adequate facilities and guidance from the teacher.

choosing and taken from sources such as the BSCS Laboratory Blocks or
the BSCS Invitations to inquiry
• Do investigations that can be entered in competitive events, such as
science fairs and the programs carried on by the Junior Academy of
Science.

These and other ideas are also discussed in the section dealing with
gifted and talented students in Chapter 10. In considering these various
options, it is important to realize the importance of providing for the
individual differences of students.

In Perspective

The need to individualize instruction has long been recognized, and
some progress has been made toward accomplishing this goal in the
science classroom. Many things have contributed to the progress that has
been made, including the recognition of the importance of the student
taking more responsibility for his or her own learning. Advances in educational technology and the preparation of instructional materials in an
individualized format have also supported teachers' efforts to make better
provision for individual differences.

Large classes, inadequate equipment and supply budgets, and heavy teaching schedules are but a few of the factors that make the individualization of instruction difficult in many schools. In addition, individual teachers often experience great difficulty when they try to teach in a way different from others in a building or school system. The success of individualized science programs depends heavily on administrative commitment, the availability of time for planning, and the availability of needed resources. Although there are isolated cases of science teachers individualizing instruction without this support, these programs depend on teachers compensating by working harder, and thus the programs are often short-lived.

Many science teachers use various forms of individualized instruction to supplement more teacher-directed strategies. Students needing a review of the metric system use a programmed booklet to do so. A unit on photosynthesis is presently using an audiotutorial approach. Students in chemistry may complete a LAP on "Chemistry and the Energy Crisis," and computer-assisted instruction may be used to present a series of simulations on environmental problems. Some students may elect to do independent investigations in place of the regular laboratory work or as extra credit work. Rather than reject individualized instruction as a "dream" possible only in a "Utopia," these teachers use individualized approaches whenever it is possible.

Review Questions

1. Explain the difference between heterogeneous grouping and homogeneous grouping and give the advantages and disadvantages of each practice as a means of providing for individual differences.

2. Describe the various types of individualized instruction in terms of teacher and student roles in selecting objectives and strategies.

3. What are the major characteristics of programmed material? How does a linear program differ from a branched program?

4. Describe the major components of an audiotutorial program such as the programs used by Postlethwait at Purdue University. How does an audiotutorial program differ from an autotutorial program?

5. List several ways that computers can be used in schools. Which of these are examples of computer-managed instruction? Computer-assisted instruction?

6. What are several advantages and possible limitations of using computers to engage students in simulations?

7. Describe each of the major components of an instructional module or LAP.

8. Make a list of ways students can do independent work in a middle or secondary school science class and give at least two examples for each

way. You may wish to draw all your examples from a particular course, such as seventh grade general science or high school chemistry.

**For Application
and Analysis**

1. React to the following in terms of their implication for individualizing instruction in middle and secondary school science:
    (a) Do students in an individualized program have the choice of working in groups as well as working individually?
    (b) A major problem with individualized instruction is that it requires more teacher time and effort. Over the long haul the approaches used by a majority of teachers are those that require the least effort—that is the chief reason why lecturing is so popular.
    (c) With the widespread appearance of radios in classrooms and homes, education in the 1920s looked for ways to use radio in teaching. Some even went as far as predicting that radio would replace the teacher. Then it was 16mm films, followed by television, teaching machines, and computers. However, it now appears that the role of computers will be different than that of the earlier types of education technology. Computers are here to stay and will revolutionize science teaching in this country.
    (d) Most approaches to individualizing instruction place much of the load on a student's ability to read, especially the ability to read directions. Yet, reading ability is one of the major ways that students differ in achievement, and reading directions is one of the most difficult reading skills. In light of this fact, is individualizing instruction a realistic alternative?
2. Analyze the student responses in What Students Say on page 331. From these statements and others you obtain by talking with students, make a list of advantages of using computers in the science classroom. Also make a list of potential shortcomings and suggestions for avoiding these limitations.
3. If you have not had the opportunity to interact with a computer, make arrangements to do so. Use a tape recorder to make a record of your thoughts and feelings as you work through a program. How do you think your experience would be similar to and different from that of science students using a computer for the first time?
4. Based on the description of instructional modules in this chapter, develop an instructional module to teach a topic that typically can be mastered in one or two class periods. The module you develop might deal with one of the following functions:

Function	Example
Remedial	How to graph data
	How to multiply fractions

Function	*Example*
Enrichment	Finding star locations using declination and right ascension
	Classifying fossil shark teeth
Skill	Using a pH meter
	Finding science references in the library
Investigations	Describing the microclimate of the classroom
	Predicting the intrusion of direct sunlight into a classroom at various times of the day and days of the year

References

Bybee, Rodger W. *Personalizing Science Teaching.* Washington, D.C.: National Science Teachers Association, 1974.

This small monograph emphasizes the importance of the science teacher's interaction with students.

Howes, Virgil M. (Ed.). *Individualizing Instruction in Science and Mathematics.* New York: The Macmillan Company, 1970.

This is an excellent selection of readings from professional journals on programs, practices, and the uses of technology in individualizing instruction.

Postlethwait, Samuel N., Joseph D. Novak, and Hal Murray. *The Audio-Tutorial Approach to Learning Through Independent Study and Integrated Experience.* Third Edition. Minneapolis: Burgess Publishing Company, 1972.

The authors describe the audiotutorial approach in botany at Purdue University and give many helpful suggestions for initiating and operating such a program.

Triezenberg, Henry J. (Ed.). *Individualized Science—Like It Is.* Washington, D.C.: National Science Teachers Association, 1972.

This book explains the individualized programs in science, describes five well-established programs, and offers suggestions for individualizing a single course or an entire program.

CHAPTER

Programs and Resources for Science Teaching

THE SABER-TOOTH CURRICULUM

Three fundamentals marked the first educational curriculum:

1. Catching fish with the bare hands.
2. Clubbing tiny horses to death.
3. Frightening saber-toothed tigers with torches.

By studying those three subjects in their "schools" the stone-age people got along fairly well until there came a changed condition caused by the movement of ice from the north, the forerunner of the ice age.

The stream became muddied and fish could not be seen to catch with the bare hands, so someone invented the net, made of vines. The tiny horses fled and the antelopes replaced them. The stone-agers invented antelope snares. The saber-toothed tigers died of pneumonia, but the big ice bear replaced them, and the stone-age men dug pits to trap them. So net-making, twisting antelope snares and digging bear pits became the three essentials of life.

But the schools continued to teach fish-catching with the hands, horse-clubbing, and tiger-scaring because they had taught them for years. Some "liberal" wanted to teach net-making, snare-making, and pit-digging but he was met with opposition. Some even wanted to do away entirely with the old subjects, but they aroused a storm and were called radicals.

The old subjects must be retained for their "cultural value," the school people contended. The proposed new subjects had no place in the curriculum.

The conservatives said: "Training to catch non-existent fish with bare hands is the best way to achieve muscular coordination and agility; training in clubbing horses that do not exist is an education in stealth and ingenuity; practicing to frighten tigers that do not exist develops courage. Some things are fundamental and sacred in education and must not be changed."

Reprinted by permission of John Wiley & Sons, Inc. From an address by Harold Benjamin in Douglass, Harl and Calvin Grieder, *American Public Education*, 1948. This quotation parallels Dr. Benjamin's book, *The Saber-Tooth Curriculum*, published by McGraw-Hill Book Co., 1939. Permission also granted by McGraw-Hill.

The status of science education at the beginning of the second half of this century was, in many people's minds, similar to that described in *The Saber-Toothed Curriculum*. Critics claimed that much of the content of science textbooks was outdated and that factual information was being emphasized at the expense of concepts and the big ideas of science. In like manner, science programs were relying too heavily on reading and discussion; the laboratory and other teaching strategies emphasizing firsthand experience were not being sufficiently utilized. The reasons mentioned most frequently for this "sad state of affairs" were inadequately prepared science teachers and the unavailability of up-to-date and appropriately designed textbooks and other instructional materials.

Since 1950, many efforts have been made to improve science teaching in our schools. One of the most important forces in this effort has been the federal funds made available for science education and primarily through the National Science Foundation (NSF). A majority of these NSF funds for science education have been used to support summer and academic-year activities for the upgrading of science teachers and for various course improvement projects.

The NSF Course Improvement Projects

The Physical Science Study Committee (PSSC), organized in 1956 at the Massachusetts Institute of Technology, was the first of many national course improvement projects. The creation of PSSC was motivated primarily by a dissatisfaction among physicists with the state of high school physics. The PSSC felt that physics textbooks reflected an outlook unrepresentative of modern science and that they lacked unity. The textbooks presented a massive amount of material to be learned and were overly concerned with the applications of science to technological problems. In addition, the laboratory was being used to verify the concepts presented in the textbook and not as an opportunity for scientific investigation.

As the above paragraph illustrates, PSSC and the other NSF course improvement projects that followed began with an indictment of what was wrong with a particular science course. The response of PSSC was the proposal to develop a new high school physics course. The following criteria were used in designing the course:

1. The course should stress the major principles of physics, with less emphasis on application.

2. The course should develop student insight into the manner in which these principles were developed and occasionally superseded by others.

3. The course should be a unified story in which the interrelatedness of all physics would be illustrated.

4. Physics should be presented as a human activity set within society and carried on as a part of the historical development of mankind.

"Hands-on" activities in the science classroom
and laboratory help students develop important
skills that are an integral part of the scientific
enterprise.

5. The laboratory should be an important part of the course and a place
where students can discover some of the major ideas of physics.

To produce the materials for the new course, PSSC organized a team
of university physicists and secondary school physics teachers. This team
developed a student textbook, teacher's guide, and set of laboratory activities using simplified apparatus. These materials were field-tested in pilot
schools across the country, revised, retested, and finally published commercially after several years of use. Also developed by PSSC were a film
series, standardized achievement tests, and a series of paperback books
on various special topics. NSF financed summer institutes to help physics
teachers learn how to use the PSSC materials.

A summary of the purposes and activities of selected projects in
secondary school science supported by the National Science Foundation
is presented in Figure 9.1. As an examination of the table will reveal, each
project developed an assortment of instructional materials, although the
means for doing so varied slightly from project to project. For example, as

Project name and date of initiation	Purpose of project	Examples of material produced
Biological Sciences Curriculum Project (BSCS) 1959	The improvement of biological education through the development of curriculum materials dealing with the study of biology.	Three versions of a first course for 10th grade—molecular (blue version), organismic (yellow), and ecological (green); BSCS advanced biology course (12th grade); special materials for low-ability students; laboratory blocks; biology teacher's handbook; single topic inquiry films; inquiry slide series; series of biological investigations for secondary school students. Recent activities include the *Human Science Program* (*HSP*) for grades 6–8; *Me and My Environment* (*MAME*) for educable mentally handicapped (EMH) students; also *Me in the Future and Me Now* for EMH students.
Chemical Bond Approach Project (CBA) 1959	The design of a high school chemistry course that emphasized bonding and chemistry as a process of investigation.	Textbook; student laboratory guide; teacher's guide; self-instructional programs on selected chemistry topics.
Chemical Education Materials Study (CHEM Study) 1960	The development of a high school chemistry course based upon experimentation and observation that leads to the synthesis of unifying principles, which in turn are used to interrelate diverse phenomena.	Chemistry textbook; laboratory manual; teacher's guide; programmed instruction pamphlets; 8mm filmloops; teacher training films.
Engineering Concepts Curriculum Project (ECCP) 1965	The development of course materials in science, mathematics, and social science that emphasize the use of a systems approach to solving social, personal, political, and environmental problems.	Text (*The Man Made World*); laboratory manual; teacher's manual; discussion "games"; and tests.
Earth Science Curriculum Project (ESCP) 1963	To provide an interdisciplinary treatment of earth science with an investigative approach.	Textbook (*Investigating the Earth*); laboratory manual; comprehensive teacher's guide; reference series pamphlets; subject matter

Project	Objectives	Materials
		films; equipment for laboratory investigations; teacher training film and teacher preparation packet. Also conducted the Environment Studies Project (ES) which developed instructional materials for environmental education.
Harvard Project Physics (HPP) 1964	To present physics in a broad, humanistic context; to design into the course the maximum flexibility with regard to content, emphasis, and teaching strategies; to increase, in numbers and in diversity of ability and interests, the population of students taking high school physics.	Textbook; teacher's guide; student handbooks; laboratory and demonstration apparatus; overhead transparencies; filmloops and filmstrips; test booklets.
Intermediate Science Curriculum Project (ISCS) 1966	To develop a comprehensive, self-paced, science program for grades 7–9 with supplemental materials for accommodating both better than average and below average students.	Three textbooks with core and excursion materials; teacher's editions of texts; student response books which include self-tests; equipment package.
Introductory Physical Science (IPS) 1963	To develop basic attitudes and skills with regard to science and to show students how scientific knowledge is acquired, as well as providing for a beginning knowledge of physical science.	Textbook; teacher's guide; laboratory equipment and apparatus; achievement tests; laboratory tests; films.
Physical Science Study Committee (PSSC) 1956	To present physics as a unified but continuing process by which the nature of the physical world is understood; to use laboratory experimentation to encourage the spirit of inquiry.	Textbook; laboratory guide; teacher's resource book and guide; laboratory apparatus; PSSC films; tests; over 40 paperback books on science topics related to physics.

FIGURE 9.1   Summary of selected course improvement projects in secondary school science supported by the National Science Foundation.

experience was gained in the development of instructional materials, psychologists, philosophers, science writers, and others were added to the writing teams. To encourage diversity of thought and to provide for options, two projects (the Chemical Bond Approach Project and the Chemical Education Materials Study Project) were funded in chemistry, and the Biological Sciences Curriculum Study developed three (blue, yellow, and green versions) programs for the introductory secondary school biology course.

Just as science education prior to development of the NSF programs had its critics, so did the so-called Alphabet Curriculum Projects. Some claimed the material was too difficult for the average student, and others objected to much of the traditional content being omitted. Schools claimed they lacked funds to initiate the laboratory program which was an integral part of most of the NSF projects. Schools also claimed they could not find teachers who had been properly prepared to teach the new programs. This inclusion of material on evolution, sex education, and other controversial topics made the material unacceptable in some parts of the country.

This criticism cumulated in a congressional investigation and a series of research studies by the National Science Foundation in the late 1970s (see Research Report—the Status of Science Education in the United States). Although the NSF studies revealed many serious problems with science teaching, these studies were not designed to demonstrate cause-and-effect relationships between the NSF programs and science teaching practices in elementary and secondary schools. The 7–12 NSF science programs used by more than 5 percent of the school districts in the United States are shown in Figure 9.2.

In addition to the impact of the NSF programs in the school districts using them, the materials produced by NSF projects greatly influenced materials produced by state and local educational agencies and by commercial publishers. For example, most science materials published during the 1970s placed greater emphasis than had been previously true on the use of the laboratory, on the processes of science, and on the interaction of science and society.

Other Efforts to Improve Science Programs

Course Improvement Projects and other activities of the National Science Foundation have been only one part of the massive effort since 1950 to improve science teaching. Projects carried out by federal agencies other than NSF, by professional societies, by state departments of education, by local school districts, and by various other groups also have had a major impact on today's science programs. Space does not allow for a comprehensive treatment of these many projects; however, a few examples seem in order as a means of illustrating the magnitude and diversity of these efforts.

Curriculum materials	Percent of districts using materials
1. Introductory Physical Science (IPS)	25
2. Biological Science: An Ecological Approach (BSCS Green)	19
3. Biological Science: An Inquiry into Life (BSCS Yellow)	16
4. Chemical Education Materials Study (CHEM Study)	15
5. Probing the Natural World—Intermediate Science Curriculum Study (ISCS)	12
6. Project Physics Course (Harvard)	12
7. Physical Science Study Committee Physics (PSSC)	11
8. Investigating the Earth—Earth Science Curriculum Project (ESCP)	10
9. Biological Science: Molecules to Man (BSCS Blue)	8
10. Individualized Science Instructional System (ISIS)	7
11. Biological Science: Patterns and Processes	6

FIGURE 9.2   NSF Curriculum Materials in 7-12 Science used by more than 5 percent of the U.S. school districts. (*Source:* Iris R. Weiss, *Highlights Report: 1977 National Survey of Science, Mathematics, and Social Studies Education.* Research Triangle Park, N.C.: Center for Educational Research and Evaluation of the Research Triangle Institute, 1978.)

GOVERNMENT AGENCIES

Most government agencies have an educational component as part of their mission. For example, the Soil Conservation Service of the United States Department of Agriculture produces booklets and other teaching aids suitable for use in secondary school science. Activities of the Department of Energy include traveling exhibits, programs on nuclear, solar, and other energy sources, workshops for teachers, and the production of various kinds of teaching aids.

PROFESSIONAL SOCIETIES

A few of the many activities of the National Science Teachers Association (NSTA) should illustrate the role of professional societies in science teaching. To give a sense of direction to science education, NSTA has produced several statements dealing with the general goals of science teaching. These include *Theory into Action* and *School Science for the Seventies*. NSTA has also assisted with the more practical aspects of teaching by producing a series of How-to-Do-It Pamphlets (*How to Handle Radioisotopes Safely, How to Investigate the Environment in the City: Air and Water*, etc.) and a

RESEARCH REPORT

The Status of Science Education in the United States

In response to congressional criticism of its science education programs, the National Science Foundation in 1976 funded three research studies to determine the status of science, mathematics, and social studies education in the United States. The three studies were: (1) a survey of school administrators, supervisors, and teachers conducted by the Center of Educational Research and Evaluation of the Research Triangle Institute (North Carolina); (2) a literature review by the ERIC Center for Science, Mathematics and Environmental Education at Ohio State University; and (3) in-depth case studies of a variety of school systems by educational researchers at the University of Illinois-Urbana.[1] Several professional organizations, including the National Science Teachers Association, were selected by NSF to evaluate the results of these studies. The following quotes from the NSTA report indicate that, although progress has been made during the twenty years (1955–1975) of major NSF support for science education and although the science programs in some schools include many of the characteristics advocated by the NSF Course Improvement Projects, many practices in science teaching have remained relatively unchanged since the 1950s.

—Classroom observers reported that at all grade levels the predominant method of teaching was recitation (discussion), with the teacher in control, supplementing the lesson with new information (lecturing). The key to the information and the basis for reading assignments was the textbook.

—The next most frequently observed activity was the demonstration, conducted in two out of five classes once a week or more. The number of classes using hands-on experiences once a week or more increases from one-in-three in elementary to three-in-four in senior high schools.

—Student reports and projects are used once a month or more in half of the classes. Other teaching techniques such as field trips, guest speakers, simulations, contracts, programmed instruction, and similar programs are used once or more in less than 10 percent of the classes and are never used in 50 percent of the science classes surveyed—with the exception of field trips, which are never used in 31 percent of the classes.

—The secondary school science curriculum is ordinarily organized with a textbook at its core. More than half the science teachers sampled in the survey reported that they used a single text, with approximately one-third indicating that more than one text was required for their course.

—Survey data suggest that the domination of the curriculum by the textbook tends to discourage use of inquiry techniques which require students to do more than look up information in the text and then recite or record it. In addition to reading and recitation, teachers report that

---

[1] *The Status of Pre-College Science, Mathematics and Social Studies Educational Practices in U.S. Schools: An Overview and Summary of Three Studies.* Washington, D. C.: U.S. Government Printing Office, 1978 (Stock Number 038–000–00 383–6).

workbook exercises provide much of whatever activity exists in typical classrooms.[2]

Findings like those cited above can be easily misinterpreted and overgeneralized. For example, the findings show there are a wide range of practices found in elementary and secondary school classrooms and some programs can be classified as being exemplary. It should also be pointed out that many forces in addition to efforts by NSF were affecting science education during the twenty-year period studied. Most groups, including the NSTA panel, that have studied the results of the three studies have recommended that additional research is needed and that the status of science teaching should be continuously examined.

---

[2]James V. DeRose, J. David Lockard, and Lester G. Paldy, "The Teacher Is the Key: A Report of Three NSF Studies," *The Science Teacher,* 46, 4 (April, 1979):31-37.

series of activity packets on energy, and by publishing a continuous supply of new ideas in the organization's three journals (see Appendix B).

STATE DEPARTMENTS OF EDUCATION

Most states have one or more state science supervisors, or science consultants as they often are called. These professionals, working in cooperation with local systems, provide many services as part of a statewide effort to assist teachers. The following list illustrates the nature of these services:

- Serve as consultants to school districts working on curriculum development, facility design, accreditation, etc.
- Prepare or arrange for the preparation by others of instructional materials on metric education, environment education, career education, etc.
- Cooperate with colleges and universities, other state agencies, and various private groups in the organization of activities such as short courses on laser technology, teacher workshops on state parks, and the production of instructional materials by electric companies and the coal industry.

Many of the publications and other materials produced by the science education division of a state educational agency can be obtained by individual science teachers. Consulting services and other assistance are normally requested by the superintendent or science supervisor of a local school system. In other words, a science teacher should check on the policies of his or her school system before contacting the state educational agency.

LOCAL EFFORTS
TO IMPROVE
SCIENCE
PROGRAMS

Thousands of local school systems and science departments have been engaged in efforts to improve science instruction during the last quarter century. An examination of professional journals dealing with science teaching (Appendix B) and of the convention programs of professional organizations for science teachers reveals the diversity of these efforts. The following description of two such projects should further illustrate the potential impact of these activities.

The Marine Science Project in Carteret County, North Carolina, began with a conversation in 1965 between the local superintendent of schools and a scientist at the Duke Marine Laboratory, which is located in that particular coastal county. Many changes were occurring on the coast. What could be done to get people to examine the region's attitude toward a sea that embraces it physically, culturally, and economically? What part should the public schools play? What should be included in the science program about the sea?

The school system prepared a proposal and was awarded funds for planning from Title III (now Title IV–C) of the Elementary and Secondary Education Act of 1965 (ESEA). The following year funds were received to initiate several activities:

- A full course in marine ecology was offered at the senior level, with the emphasis on field work and the students doing research projects under the guidance of working scientists at the marine laboratories in the area.
- A course in coastal affairs, which emphasized the application of ecological knowledge to the problems of managing coastal resources, was offered as a high school elective.
- Several booklets were developed to assist teachers in the teaching of marine topics in the elementary and secondary school curriculum; titles included *The Field Approach to Coastal Ecology*, *The Sea and Modern Man*, and *Dune Detective*.
- The school purchased a bus, and a field specialist was employed to facilitate field work, thus allowing teachers with little or no preparation in field work to learn along with their students.

The work in Carteret County, along with similar projects in Delaware, Florida, California, and other states, has given impetus to the present high interest in marine education. In addition, dozens of teachers and thousands of students benefited from having participated in these experimental programs.

The Career Oriented Pre-Technical Physics (COPP) curriculum was developed by the Dallas, Texas, Independent School District with funds received from the United States Office of Education. The curriculum attempted to meet the threefold challenge of preparing secondary school students for careers in a technology-oriented society, tailoring the choices in the technical physics curriculum to better meet individual needs or interests, and reversing decreasing physics enrollments.

The COPP curriculum includes twenty-nine modules plus a teacher's guide. Modules include *The Automobile Ignition System, Electronics as a Hobby, The Physics of Sports, So You Gotta Wear Glasses,* and *Stereo Sound and Acoustics.* Each module, or mini-course, has a stated rationale, a list of terminal objectives, a list of enabling objectives, activities, resource packages, and self-tests with answers. The length of time required for completion varies from one and a half to six weeks, with an average completion time of about three weeks. The modules can be used with self-paced and individually prescribed instruction or with more traditional approaches.

The COPP curriculum was first field-tested in four Dallas high schools during 1973–1974. Since then it has been field-tested in other schools in Texas and in other states. A recent article in *The Physics Teacher* described it in greater detail and reports on its use in San Diego, California.[3]

Resources for Science Teaching

A wealth of resources are available for science teaching, including textbooks and other kinds of printed material, media, and a variety of community resources.

TEXTBOOKS AND ANCILLARY MATERIALS

Many research studies, including the NSF studies summarized in the Research Report on pages 354–355, have demonstrated the impact of textbooks on secondary school science in the United States. Although many science educators believe there is too much reliance on textbooks, their popularity with teachers and students is difficult to dispute. In many school systems, the textbook is the most important determinant of the science program.

There are approximately one to two dozen textbooks available for each major science course. Some of these are the products of NSF course improvement projects (see Figure 9.1) or other activities funded by government agencies and private groups; others have been produced in a variety of ways by commercial publishers. Ancillary materials, which are available for use with most textbooks, include laboratory guides and record books, teacher's guides or annotated editions, mastery tests, and various kinds of laboratory kits and media packages.

About half of the states in the United States, most of which are in the South and West, have some type of system for the state adoption of textbooks. In these states, a state textbook committee selects from three or four to several textbooks for each subject. These state adoptions usually last from four to six years. A local school system in these states selects one or more textbooks from the state-adopted list. In states that do not have

---

[3]Willa Ramsay and Walt Elliot, "Career Oriented Pre-Technical Physics Curriculum in San Diego." *The Physics Teacher,* 17, 6, (September 1979):374–377.

state adoptions, local school systems are free to choose any textbook they wish to use.

The selection of textbooks, because of their impact on the science program in most school systems, is a very important undertaking. Most school systems use a committee to select the books, and their choice usually must be confirmed by the local board of education. Committee members may include science teachers, supervisors, administrators, school board members, and, sometimes, parents and/or students. It is customary for all science teachers to have the opportunity to examine the materials being considered and to indicate their preference to a committee member. Most textbook committees find it desirable to have a plan for systematically evaluating textbooks and making their decisions. One such plan is described in the literature by two science educators from Pennsylvania.[4]

A sample of the kind of form used to evaluate textbooks is shown in Figure 9.3. In evaluating textbooks and other educational materials, it is important to remember that they are all products of compromise. A wheelbarrow would be required to move a textbook that contained all the features and materials desired by all the teachers and students using it. A science textbook editor has commented, "Deciding what to include is an easy decision compared to deciding what to omit."

Compromises are also required of teachers and others who select textbooks. Are the laboratory activities included as an integral part of the program more important than additional photographs and line drawings? Is price more important than the total length of the book? In making these compromises, it is important to recognize that there also may be imperatives. For example, a textbook with an eleventh grade reading level should not be chosen for use with a class of average seventh graders, even though the book has many desirable characteristics. (The Fry Formula shown in Figure 9.4 can be used to determine reading level.) Similarly, a book might be rejected because it does not adequately reflect the content outline of a course, or perhaps because it represents an unbalanced treatment of issues, or because it omits controversial topics such as evolution, sex education, or experimentation on human subjects.

OTHER KINDS OF PRINTED MATERIALS

In addition to textbooks and ancillary materials, many other kinds of printed materials are valuable resources for science teaching. The following list illustrates the nature and variety of this material:

- Supplemental books, both in hardback and paperback
- Science articles in news magazines and newspapers

---

[4]James V. DeRose and Jon R. Whittle, "Selecting Textbooks: A Plan That Worked," *The Science Teacher*, 43, 6 (September, 1976):38–40.

- Science magazines, such as *Scientific American, Science Digest,* and *Science 80*
- Science magazines specifically for secondary school students, such as *Current Science* and *Senior Science*
- Brochures, pamphlets, and booklets published by commercial publishers, government agencies, private foundations, business and industry, and other groups.
- Charts and posters from commercial and noncommercial sources.

MEDIA

Nonprint media include films, filmstrips, overhead transparencies, slides, audio recordings, models, kits, games, bulletin boards, displays, television, and computers. These media are powerful tools for teaching science and can be used effectively and efficiently to present many science concepts. Perhaps no other school subject has such a rich resource of media as does science.

FILMS. Films for school use are available in both 8mm and 16mm and in both a reel-to-reel and closed-loop format. Films have been made on a wide range of topics and have several important advantages over many other types of media. They can be used to show distant places impossible to visit on a field trip, scientific phenomena that occur irregularly, and experiments and demonstrations that cannot be performed in a school laboratory. Close-up sequences often are superior to what the student can see in a demonstration or through a microscope or telescope. Time-lapse and special effects photography makes possible observations too fast or too slow to be otherwise seen, and animation can be used to present difficult concepts.

While many films are descriptive in nature, others emphasize techniques, inquiry, and issues. In many schools, 8mm filmloops are the preferred format when demonstrating laboratory techniques or using individualized instruction. Many of the inquiry films are available in two versions: a version for class used by the teacher and a version that can be used by small groups or individual students. Films produced by BSCS that encourage an inquiry approach to selected issues include *Energy to Burn, Tragedy of the Commons,* and a series of three films entitled *Projections for the Future.*

FILMSTRIPS. Filmstrips are popular with science teachers. They are relatively inexpensive as is the required projection equipment, thus allowing individual schools or departments to own filmstrips rather than depend on an often unreliable rental system. While older filmstrips usually have a caption on each frame, many of the new ones have sound which is

NAME OF TEXTBOOK: _Junior High School Science, Book 2_

NAME OF PUBLISHER: _Zebra Publishing Company_

NAME OF EVALUATOR: _Ruth Kelly_

DATE: _June 16, 1980_

DIRECTIONS: It is suggested that you decide on the importance of each characteristic by circling the appropriate number in Column 2 before evaluating each book. Also, feel free to add characteristics in Column 1 that you think should be considered in the evaluation process. In evaluating a book, circle the appropriate number in Column 3 for each characteristic and record your comments in the column on the right. The rating for each characteristic is found by multiplying the circled number in Column 2 times the circled number in Column 3. The overall rating of a book is found by totalling the ratings in Column 3. See the Cautionary Note at the end of this form before using the overall rating to choose a book.

CHARACTERISTICS (Column 1)	Importance of Characteristics (Column 2)				Presence of Characteristics (Column 3)				RATING (Columns 2 x 3)	COMMENTS
	No importance; not desired or needed	Some importance	Very important	An imperative	Absent; totally lacking	Only partially provided	Average in terms of most books	Superior treatment		
CONTENT										
Appropriate objectives and content	0	1	2	**3**	0	1	**2**	3	6	
Up-to-date content and accurate information	0	1	2	**3**	0	1	2	**3**	9	
Reflects the nature of science (tentative, relationship to other subjects, etc.)	0	1	**2**	3	0	**1**	2	3	2	
Probable interest to students	0	1	**2**	3	0	1	**2**	3	4	
OTHERS:										
Behavioral objectives in either student or teacher edition	0	1	2	**3**	0	1	**2**	3	6	
Contents can be understood by most students	0	1	**2**	3	0	1	**2**	3	6	
Career Education emphasis	0	1	**2**	3	0	1	**2**	3	4	

OTHERS: (continued)

Item	0	1	2	3	0	1	2	3	Score	Comments
Historical development of science	0	1	②	3	0	①	2	3	2	Check of index shows only the names of five famous scientists.

ORGANIZATION:

Item	0	1	2	3	0	1	2	3	Score	Comments
Appropriate choice and sequence of units and chapters	0	1	②	3	0	1	②	3	4	Would prefer a book that has chapters broken down into 5-10 sections - makes giving assignment easier.
Material within chapter organized for easy use	0	1	②	3	0	①	2	3	2	
Book allows for flexibility (chapters can be taken up out of order or chapter(s) omitted)	0	1	②	3	0	1	2	③	6	

OTHER:

Item	0	1	2	3	0	1	2	3	Score	Comments
Good placement of seasonal chapters (living things in the fall and spring)	0	1	②	3	0	1	2	③	6	Good placement but not enough mention of plants and animals found in large city.
Materials on metric education, safety, and laboratory procedures included in textbook	0	1	2	③	0	1	②	3	6	Mass and weight are used interchangeably; no mention of neutrons.

FIGURE 9.3 Sample textbook evaluation form.

362

CHARACTERISTICS (Column 1)	Importance of Characteristics (Column 2)				Presence of Characteristics (Column 3)				RATING (Columns 2 x 3)	COMMENTS
	No importance; not desired or needed	Some importance	Very important	An imperative	Absent; totally lacking	Only partially provided	Average in terms of most books	Superior treatment		
PRESENTATION:										
Appropriate reading level	0	1	2	(3)	0	1	2	(3)	9	Range of 6.5 to 7.5 with an average of 7.0 on the five passages checked using the Fry formula.
Concepts appropriate for grade level	0	1	2	(3)	0	1	(2)	3	6	
Technical terms properly introduced and defined	0	1	(2)	3	0	1	(2)	3	4	
Photos and line drawing attractive, properly captioned and included for their instructional value.	0	1	(2)	3	0	1	2	(3)	6	
Text and illustrations not racially or culturally biased	0	1	2	(3)	0	1	(2)	3	6	
Text and illustrations not sexually biased	0	1	2	(3)	0	1	(2)	3	6	
Useful end of chapter features:										
Summary	0	1	(2)	3	0	1	(2)	3	4	
Vocabulary List	0	1	(2)	3	0	1	(2)	3	4	Vocabulary list placed at beginning of chapter.
Review Questions	0	1	2	(3)	0	1	(2)	3	6	
Suggested Readings for students	0	1	(2)	3	0	1	(2)	3	4	
Suggested research reports and/or additional laboratory activities	0	1	(2)	3	0	1	(2)	3	4	

PRESENTATION: (continued)

End of book features

	Scale 1					Scale 2				Total
Glossary	0	1	2	③		0	1	2	③	9
Accurate and complete index	0	1	2	③		0	1	2	③	9

OTHER:

Middle of road approach (neither authoritarian nor a strictly inquiry approach)

	Scale 1					Scale 2				Total
	0	1	2	③		0	1	2	③	9
	0	1	2	3		0	1	2	3	
	0	1	2	3		0	1	2	3	
	0	1	2	3		0	1	2	3	

LABORATORY PROGRAM

Investigations and activities:

	Scale 1					Scale 2				Total
Within range of students, mental and physical development	0	1	2	③		0	1	②	3	6
Contribute to an understanding of the concept being developed	0	1	2	③		0	1	②	3	6
In addition to knowledge, emphasize processes of science and other components of scientific literacy	0	1	2	③		0	1	2	③	9

Checked entries for mass, cell, solar system, force and inertia.

FIGURE 9.3 (Continued)

CHARACTERISTICS (Column 1)	Importance of Characteristics (Column 2)				Presence of Characteristics (Column 3)				RATING (Columns 2 x 3)	COMMENTS
	No importance; not desired or needed	Some importance	Very important	An imperative	Absent; totally lacking	Only partially provided	Average in terms of most books	Superior treatment		
LABORATORY PROGRAM: (continued)										
Emphasize safety and the humane use of living materials	0	1	2	(3)	0	1	(2)	3	6	
Are reasonable in terms of facilities and equipment available in the school in which the book will be used	0	1	(2)	3	0	1	(2)	3	4	
OTHER:										
Investigative and activities included as integral part of textbook rather than as separate lab. manual.	0	1	(2)	3	0	1	(2)	3	4	
Possible to do labs in one 50-minute period.	0	1	(2)	3	0	1	(2)	3	4	
Possible to skip labs and to do "old favorites" from other books and sources.	0	(1)	2	3	0	1	(2)	3	2	
		1	2	3	0	1	2	3		
PHYSICAL AND MECHANICAL FEATURES:										
General attractiveness	0	1	(2)	3	0	1	(2)	3	4	
Appropriate overall size	0	(1)	2	3	0	1	(2)	3	2	
Print size	0	1	(2)	3	0	1	(2)	3	4	
Design of most pages is open rather than crowded	0	(1)	2	3	0	1	(2)	3	4	
Durability (especially cover and binding)	0	1	(2)	3	0	1	(2)	3	4	

OTHER:
_____
_____
_____
_____

TEACHER AIDS:

	0	1	2	3	0	1	2	3		Points
Teacher's Guide and/or annotated edition	0	1	2	③	0	1	②	3		6
Mastery tests and answer book	⓪	1	2	3	0	1	②	3		0
Master list of equipment and supplies	0	①	2	3	0	1	②	3		2
List of suggested media materials	0	①	2	3	0	1	②	3		2

OTHER:

	0	1	2	3	0	1	2	3		Points
List of supplemental library books	0	①	2	3	0	1	②	3		2
Games, puzzles, review exercises	0	1	②	3	⓪	1	2	3		0
Laboratory/record book	0	①	2	3	⓪	1	2	3		0
Work book	0	①	2	3	⓪	1	2	3		0

OVERALL RATING (TOTAL OF RATINGS IN COLUMN 3)	220*

Handwritten note: Although I don't need, I feel many teachers will want these and they should be considered when our committee gets together.

FIGURE 9.3 (Continued)

* CAUTIONARY NOTE: Since each person evaluating books can add characteristics, the total number of characteristics and thus the total number of possible points may vary from person to person. If a committee is using this form, the overall ratings should be used as follows: Each person rates all the books being considered and uses his or her overall ratings to rank order the books. Points are then awarded based on the book's rankings; for example, 10 points to the book that rated highest in a group of 10 books, 9 points to the second highest book, and so on. These points obtained from each committee member's rankings are then totalled and used to decide which book or books to select. In using this system, it is important that each committee member rate each book.

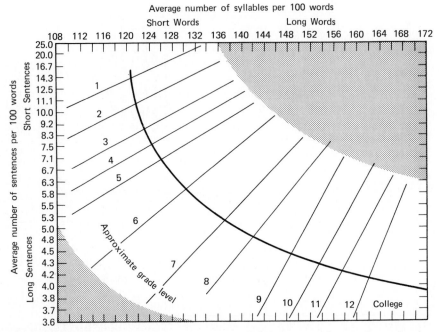

FIGURE 9.4 *The Fry Graph for estimating readability.* to use the graph, randomly select three 100-word passages from a book. Count the total number of sentences and the total number of syllables in each passage and find the average of each. Plot the average number of sentences and syllables on the graph. The point at which the two meet represents the approximate grade level of the material. The upper right-hand and lower left-hand corners (shaded areas) are areas in which readability findings are considered unreliable.

provided by audio cassettes or records. These sound recordings generally contain signals that can be used to advance the frames automatically. Because of the modest cost and the simplicity of the projectors, filmstrips are an important part of most individualized science programs.

OVERHEAD TRANSPARENCIES. Today, transparencies projected by an overhead projector are used to show many of the things that previously had to be written or drawn on a chalkboard. This can result in a saving of time for the teacher and the presentation of more easily read material for the student. Overhead transparencies are easily made using machines available in most schools and are also commercially available at a modest cost. Because transparencies and projectors are relatively inexpensive, many schools have an overhead projector in each science classroom. Since the teacher faces the class when using the overhead projector and it can be used in a partially darkened room, discussion is encouraged and class control problems are reduced.

Many science teachers take advantage of having an overhead projector in the classroom by using it to perform demonstrations. Iron filings sprinkled on a piece of clear plastic covering a bar magnet produce a dramatic illustration of a magnetic field. Tree leaves placed on the projector result in silhouettes that emphasize size and shape. Water in a glass cake pan can substitute for a wave tank, and the entire class can easily see the results produced by placing an electric brush in the water. Petri dishes partially filled with water colored with various vegetable dyes, when placed on top of each other on an overhead projector, provide an excellent means of studying the science of colors.

35mm SLIDES.   Many science teachers use 35mm slides to supplement class presentations and to add interest to what might otherwise be a rather boring subject. Slides of a volcano eruption, of one of the remaining whooping cranes, or of a motorcycle jumping a row of trucks elicits a response far different from that obtained by lecture or discussion. In addition to slides available commercially, slides taken by the teacher, students' parents, and others in the community can be used.

Recently, a special kind of slide, the Daylight Blackboard Projection slide, has become available for use in science classrooms. These daylight slides have two major advantages. First, discussion is encouraged and class control problems are reduced because these slides can be used in a lighted classroom. Second, teacher and students can easily modify what is being projected because a chalkboard rather than a screen is used. For classrooms that have no screens and that cannot be properly darkened, the daylight slide is a must.

Instructional materials have been developed using daylight slides to present controversial material through an inquiry approach. Two such resources for biology teachers are the BSCS *Inquiry Slides for Daylight Blackboard Projection* and *Life Science: Man and Nature.*

As in the case of filmstrips, many slide sets are now available with a sound track on cassettes or records.

AUDIO RECORDINGS.   Recordings of important speeches, panel discussions by scientists, interviews, sounds of nature such as bird calls, and various musical phenomena are available in cassettes or as records. These recordings can be very useful; however, most students lose interest quickly if they are asked to listen to a recording without also receiving other simulation. For example, in the audiotutored approach described in Chapter 8, the students receive directions and listen to short presentations on a tape recorder. However, they also read, look at specimens through a microscope, perform experiments, and engage in other activities, all of which minimize the monotony that can result from just listening.

In addition to their use as listening devices, tape recorders can be used as a tool by students actively investigating a problem. When the sound made by the sirens of a passing ambulance are played back on a receiver connected to an oscilloscope, is it possible to observe the Doppler effect? If so, can the speed of the passing ambulance be estimated? Is it possible to hear rapidly growing corn on a warm, still night? How does the human heartbeat differ from individual to individual?

MODELS, KITS, AND GAMES.   The human torso and models of the ear, leaf, and stem are examples of models used in the biological sciences. Models of the cross-section of the earth and of volcanoes and geysers can help make earth science more meaningful. Models have the advantage of being three-dimensional and students can feel as well as see. This is especially important in working with visually handicapped students, as is described in Chapter 10.

Some kits, such as the Invisible Man and the Invisible Woman, can be used to construct models. Other kits are available for constructing radios, telescopes, and plastic-embedded specimens. Still another type of kit is used in doing laboratory and field work; examples are water pollution kits, blood typing kits, and radioactive tracer kits.

Games have been designed to do everything from reviewing factual information, such as the chemical symbols or metric units, to permitting students to engage in high-level problem-solving skills. The use of games is described in Chapter 5.

BULLETIN BOARDS AND OTHER DISPLAYS.   It has been said that "You shouldn't have to ask what is being taught to know when you are in a science classroom." Bulletin boards and displays of students' work, specimens, and models are an effective way to give the science classroom its own personality. In addition, these media can serve important instructional functions. A bulletin board on the solar system can help students learn the planet names and their positions, and to more fully appreciate their relative distance from the sun. A display of fossils collected by the science club on their most recent field trip is a sure way to boost attendance at the next club meeting. Most of the time bulletin boards and other displays assembled by students are the real winners!

TELEVISION.   The earliest use of television in secondary school science involved entire courses in physics, earth science, and other subjects being broadcast on educational channels. Some of these were designed for students as supplements to their regular classroom activities; others, such as Continental Classroom broadcasts in the early morning in many parts of the country, were designed to upgrade the teacher's knowledge.

Although broadcast television is still used in many schools, easy-to-

science

Plants of the Desert

This combination bulletin board and display can make the science room more attractive as well as help increase curiosity and interest.

use and relatively inexpensive videotape equipment has resulted in increased use of this format. Programs can be purchased in cassettes, copied from broadcast television, or made in a school studio or classroom. Care should be taken not to violate federal copyright laws in taping television programs, films, and other kinds of media.

As in the case of other media, it is desirable for students to have the opportunity to participate actively in the production of videotapes. A program they make on water pollution in their own community will mean more than a similar program made by someone else about a community in another part of the country. Such student-made programs can be saved and used with other classes in following years.

COMPUTERS. The stage is set for computers to begin to significantly affect and perhaps to revolutionize certain aspects of science teaching. With the availability of self-centered units at an ever-decreasing price, computers may soon become as commonplace in the classroom as overhead projectors and pocket calculators. Since computers have such great potential for individualizing instruction, their use in science teaching is described in Chapter 8.

SELECTING MEDIA.   The task of selecting media is similar in many ways to that of selecting textbooks. The following questions are illustrative of those that should be asked in deciding which media to use and if a specific film, filmstrip, or other item is appropriate.

WHICH TYPE OF MEDIA TO USE?

- If it must be purchased or rented, are funds available?
- How expensive is it compared to other media (for example, the prices of a film compared to that of a filmstrip)?
- Is required hardware, such as projector or television, readily available?
- Does it require a darkened room and, if so, is this possible?
- Does its use encourage the active involvement of students?
- Does its use contribute to good class management procedures?
- Will it be used with an entire class, small groups, or by individual students?
- Is it reliable, or do breakdowns frequently result in long delays in its being used?

WHAT SPECIFIC FILM, FILMSTRIPS, OR OTHER MEDIA ITEM SHOULD BE USED?

- Will its use contribute to the objectives of the lesson or unit?
- In terms of reading level, concept level, and other factors, is it appropriate for use with the students for whom it is being considered?
- Does it present the material effectively and with an efficient use of time?
- Is the material unbiased, technically accurate, and up to date?
- Does it encourage students to make further inquiries and to engage in problem-solving?
- Is it attractive, the sound of good quality, and otherwise well-produced material?

In selecting media items, it is important to know what is available. In addition to guides prepared by local school systems and catalogs published by suppliers, there are several excellent reference guides to various kinds of media. These are described in a later section of this chapter.

COMMUNITY RESOURCES FOR SCIENCE TEACHING

A community resource is a person, place, or thing available from outside of the school, thus in the community, that can be used in teaching sciences. The two most common uses of community resources are having experts come to the school as visiting speakers and taking field trips to sites away from the school. These two important resources are discussed in Chapter 5 along with suggestions for their effective use. However, there are many additional ways to utilize these resources.

PEOPLE.   In addition to bringing resource people to the school, teachers and students can profit by going to them. Interviews can be conducted on audio- or videotape of professionals or amateurs in fields ranging from astronomy to zoology. Many of these resource people are willing to assist students working on science projects, investigation, and reports. They also represent valuable sources of information on how to do things like bird banding and tree graphing or where to find things such as photographic accessories or electronic components.

PLACES.   Public libraries, museums, aquariums, planetariums, nature centers, and state and national parks are examples of places that are a storehouse of resources for science teaching. Nor should laboratories in hospitals, research centers, and colleges and universities be overlooked. Not only are these places that can be visited on field trips, but also they represent sources of information and assistance. A telephone call to the local hospital may be the easiest way to answer a question on genetic counseling raised by a biology student. In like manner, a student doing a

A naturalist from a park or museum can help bring science into the classroom.

WHAT STUDENTS SAY

Media

- I like to see movies, except our teacher always gives us questions to answer. Then he turns all the lights off and I can't see to write.
- Slides our teacher took last summer in the Rocky Mountains was the best thing we have done all year in earth science. I'd give anything to really see those mountains in the winter time—sure would be different than January in Miami.
- Television in school is boring. My mother says I already watch too much TV at home.
- Bulletin boards put up by kids in a class are best.
- Our teacher uses the overhead projector a lot. The only trouble is that she sometimes goes too fast and we don't have time to copy all the information in our notebooks.
- Films and filmstrips? In our school they are all a disaster! We have one of the most modern junior high schools in the county—except there is no way to get the room dark nor is there a good place to put the screen. Also, we have open classrooms and the teacher next door is always complaining that the projector is too loud.
- I could watch science films about wildlife and explorers all day.
- The thing I remember most about physical science is that we got to use a computer. I guess that is how I got hooked and decided to major in computer science in college.

science investigation on the effects of energy from high voltage-transmission lines may find helpful literature in the scientific journals of a college library.

THINGS.   In addition to free or inexpensive printed material available from sources outside the school, many groups also produce and loan films, filmstrips, slides, and other kinds of media to schools. In many communities, local businesses and industries lend or give surplus equipment to schools. The local florist shop can be the source of wilted flowers for a laboratory on the reproductive parts of the flower. The meat market is the source of bones used in the study of anatomy. Gifts of oscilloscopes, computers, and electron microscopes are not unheard of. The chances of obtaining such items can be enhanced by letting people know your needs. One teacher posts a list of wanted items on the bulletin board in the science classroom. Another asks the school newspaper and the PTA newsletter each year to run a "Help Wanted" notice. This science teacher typically gets a roomful of items ranging from aluminum pie tins, which make great disposable containers, to old radios and television sets, which can be salvaged for parts.

LOCATING AND USING COMMUNITY RESOURCES. Some school systems have developed guidebooks for locating potential resources in their community. A page from such a guidebook is shown in Figure 9.5. Ex-

RESOURCE PERSON   Code: *Junior High & High School Science*
Form RG-3
Central County Schools   Expertise: *SCUBA Diving and underwater Photography*

Name: *Roy Carver*

Residential Address: *1937 3rd Street*   Telephone: *731-4962*

Big Tree, Minnesota

Business Address: *Same as above*   Telephone: *same as above*

Occupation, Hobbies: *Former U.S. Navy diver; continues diving in local lakes and takes ocassional trips to the Bahamas and other islands in the Caribbean; expert underwater photographer.*

Availability: *Is willing to give 5 to 10 presentations per year to science classes; prefers no more than 50 to 60 people per group and no more than 2 presentations per day.*

Type of service offered: *Will present an illustrated lecture on SCUBA diving (45-50 minutes) in which safety and the scientific aspects are emphasized; will address questions following lecture; also will work with groups getting started in underwater photography.*

Procedures for contacting: *Prefers to be called at home between 7-9 p.m. on week nights; since he works parttime, he must be contacted at least two weeks before date of appearance so he can arrange his schedule.*

Other: *Furnishes own projector and extension cords; school must furnish screen (at least 4' x 6') and a room which can be completely darkened is desirable.*

FIGURE 9.5   Sample page from a guidebook to community resources.

perienced teachers and the local public library are also good sources of information. References described later in this chapter are useful in locating certain kinds of community resources.

In using community resources, care should be taken that they meet the same standards imposed on other resources. For example, in the case of printed materials, are they technically accurate, up to date, and presented at the appropriate reading level? Are the materials unbiased and free from advertising and sales promotion? And, most importantly, how effectively will their use contribute to the science program?

Identifying Resources

There are many excellent publications and services that can be used to identify resources for science teaching. These are available at most public or university libraries and at media centers operated by state education agencies and local school systems.

PERIODICAL LITERATURE AND RESEARCH REPORTS

Science teachers have the twin responsibilities of keeping up to date on developments in professional education and in science. The following are valuable aids in locating appropriate references on the teaching of science and other topics in professional education:

1. Publications of the Educational Resources Information Center (ERIC) include *Resources in Education (RIE)* and *Current Index to Journals in Education (CIJE)*. *RIE* provides abstracts of curriculum materials, conference addresses and reports, bibliographies, and other professional materials (see Figure 9.6). Approximately 14,000 items are abstracted each year, and copies are available in microfiche or hard copy from the ERIC Document Reproduction Service in Arlington, Virginia. The *CIJE* includes indexes and annotations for more than 750 education and education-related journals (see lower part of Figure 9.6). Many universities and school systems have facilities for doing computer searches of the *RIE* and *CIJE* files.

A group of clearinghouses located across the country prepare abstracts and annotations for inclusion in *RIE* and *CIJE*. The ERIC Information Analysis Center for Science, Mathematics and Environmental Education (ERIC/SMEAC) is located at Ohio State University. In addition to processing documents and articles, ERIC/SMEAC has an extensive publications program, which includes bibliographies, research reviews, abstracts of papers presented at professional meetings, and sourcebooks of activities for teaching subjects such as environmental education and energy education.[5]

---

[5]For additional information or to request a list of current publications, contact ERIC/SMEAC, The Ohio State University, 1200 Chambers Road, Columbus, Ohio, 43212.

Document resume from resources in education (RIE)

ERIC Document——ED 144 787   SE 022 923——Clearinghouse
accession or   Suggested Activities for Environ-   accession number
identification   mental Education in the Secondary
number   Schools.
                      Texas Education Agency, Austin. Div.——Organization
Title   of Curriculum Development.   where document
                      Pub Date 77   originated
Publication Date   Note—47p.; For related document,
                        see SE 022 922; Not available in
                        hard copy due to colored print
                        throughout entire document
EDRS price—   EDRS Price MF-$0.83 Plus Postage.
cost from   HC Not Available from EDRS.
ERIC Document   Descriptors—*Classroom Materials,   Descriptors—
Reproduction   Curriculum Enrichment, *Curricu-   terms which
Service   lum Guides, *Environmental Edu-   characterize
                        cation, *Instructional Materials,   the content
                        Learning Activities, Resource Ma-
                        terials, Science Education, *Secon-
                        dary Education
                      Identifiers—Texas Education Agency.
                        This publication is designed as a   Identifiers
                        model to assist middle school and   (Identifying terms
                        high school teachers in developing   not found in
                        environmental education activities in Thesaurus of
                        all subject areas. Both public school ERIC Descriptors)
                        and college educators developed this
                        guide to help make young people
                        aware of the value of the environ-
                        ment and of the responsibility they
                        have for conserving it. Discussions
Abstract   of the curriculum model for the guide
                        and the program format and criteria
                        are included for the teacher. The cur-
                        riculum model demonstrates the inter-
                        relationships of personal concerns,
                        environmental concerns, and educa-
                        tional process. A multidisciplinary
                        approach is an important component
                        in every suggested activity topic.
                        Some of the areas covered are en-
                        vironmental ethics, government and
                        law, land use, pollution, population,
                        energy, and economics. Each topic
                        includes a short overview and a listing
                        of generalizations and suggested pupil
                        activities. The educational experiences

FIGURE 9.6   Sample résumés from *Resources in Education* and the *Current Index to Journals in Education.*

and activities are designed to individualize student learning, emphasize
community involvement, and encourage exploratory and investigative
learning. A companion guide is also
available for elementary grades.
(Author/MA)

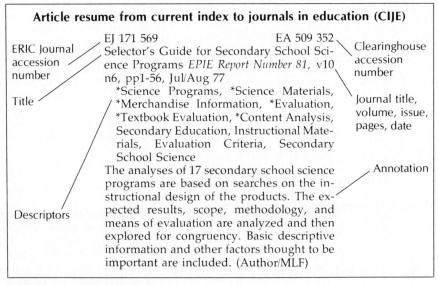

Article resume from current index to journals in education (CIJE)

FIGURE 9.6   (*Continued*)

2. *Education Index.* New York: H. W. Wilson Company, 1932 to date. A
detailed subject index and guide to professional literature in the field of
education, issued ten times yearly and cumulated frequently. A list of
periodicals indexed is included at the front of each volume.

3. *Dissertation Abstracts: A Collection of Abstracts of Doctoral Dissertations
and Monographs Which Are Available in Complete Form on Microfilm.* Ann
Arbor, Michigan: University Microfilms, 1938 to date. The abstracts of
dissertations in education, science, and other fields are published in two
sections: A—Humanities and Social Science, B—Sciences and Engineering. A computerized searching service, DATRIX (Direct Access to Reference Information), is available for searching the entire file of *Dissertation
Abstracts.*

In addition to the sources just described, other references provide
information about science and science teaching. The following are useful
in locating articles on science and more general topics.

1. *Reader's Guide to Periodical Literature.* New York: H. W. Wilson Company, 1900—. Cumulated.

2. *New York Times Index.* New York: New York Times, 1913—. Semimonthly with annual cumulation. A subject matter index to articles appearing in the *New York Times.*

BOOKS AND OTHER PRINTED MATERIALS

In addition to book reviews published in professional journals, booklists cited in textbooks, and bibliographies prepared by various groups, the following are useful in locating appropriate books and other printed material.

1. *Books in Print.* New York: R. R. Bowker Company, 1948—. Annual. Consists of two 2-volume indexes. The first by author and editor, and the second by title and series. Gives bibliographic information, including price.

2. *Subject Guide to Books in Print.* New York: R. R. Bowker Company, 1957—. Annual.
A subject listing of books from *Books in Print.*

3. *El-Hi Textbooks in Print.* New York: R. R. Bowker Company, 1970—. Annual. A listing of elementary, junior high, and senior high school textbooks; also includes reference books, maps, teaching aids, and programmed materials in book form.

4. Deason, Hilary J. (Comp.). *The AAAS Science Book List: A Selected and Annotated List of Science and Mathematics Books for Secondary School Students, College Undergraduates and Nonspecialists* (Third Edition). Washington, D.C.: American Association for the Advancement of Science, 1970.
Includes 2,441 titles of trade books, textbooks, and reference books in the pure and applied sciences, arranged by subject.

5. *Ulriches International Periodicals Directory: A Classified Guide to Current Periodicals, Foreign and Domestic* (Seventeenth Edition). New York: R. R. Bowker Company, 1977.

6. *Educators Guide to Free Science Materials.* Randolph, Wis.: Educators Progress Service, 1960—. Annual.
This publication contains descriptions of materials, names and addresses of sponsoring organizations.

MEDIA

There is a rich resource of media available for science teaching, including films, filmstrips, overhead transparencies, audio-and videotapes, games, and other nonprinted materials. In addition to reviews of new media in professional journals, the following sources are useful in identifying media equipment and materials.

1. The National Information Center for Educational Media (NICEM) at the University of Southern California operates a computer data bank that includes over a half million media listings, with approximately 50,000 items being added each year. Various listings of media are published on a regular basis, which are especially useful to science teachers:

Index to Ecology (Multimedia)
Index to Educational Audio Tapes
Index to Educational Overhead Transparencies
Index to Educational Slides
Index to Educational Video Tapes
Index to 8-mm Motion Picture Cartridges
Index to 16-mm Educational Films
Index to 35-mm Filmstrips

2. *Educators Guide to Free Films*. Randolph, Wis.: Educators Progress Service, Inc., 1941—. Annual.

This comprehensive guide contains a listing of over 4,000 films, most of which are 16mm. Check current edition for new listings.

Educators Guide to Free Filmstrips. Randolph, Wis.: Educators Progress Service, Inc., 1949—. Annual.

This guide contains a list of approximately 500 filmstrips, some of which can be borrowed and some of which are donated to schools.

Educators Guide to Free Audio and Video Tapes. Randolph, Wis.: Educators Progress Service, Inc., 1955—. Annual.

This guide contains a list of approximately 1,000 items, including both audio- and videotapes.

3. Seltz-Petrach, Ann and Kathryn Wolff (Eds.). *AAAS Science Film Catalog*. Washington, D.C.: American Association for the Advancement of Science, 1975.

This catalog contains the title, grade level, running time, price, and a brief annotation for some 5,600 films.

4. Hounshell, Paul B., and Ira R. Trollinger. *Games for the Science Classroom, An Annotated Bibliography*. Washington, D.C.: National Science Teachers Association, 1977.

This guide contains all the information needed for choosing or making over one hundred games in science, along with a brief summary of their rules.

STANDARDIZED
TESTS AND OTHER
EVALUATION
INSTRUMENTS

The following references are useful in identifying and selecting standardized tests and other evaluation instruments:

Buros, Oscar K. (Ed.). *Science Tests and Reviews: A Monograph Consisting of the Science Sections of the Seven Mental Measurements Yearbooks*. Highland Park, N.J.: Gryphon Press, 1975.

This thorough compilation of standardized science tests highlights reviews of each test.

Buros, Oscar K. *The Seventh Mental Measurement Yearbook.* Highland Park, N.J.: Gryphon Press, 1972.

This book contains descriptions and critical reviews of standardized tests and other instruments used in all phases of education; earlier volumes should be consulted for information on tests that have been in use for several years.

Buros, Oscar K. *Tests in Print II.* Highland Park, N.J.: Gryphon Press, 1974.

This index to tests, test reviews, and the literature on tests includes a section on science tests.

Wall, Janet, and Lee Summerlin. *Standardized Tests: A Descriptive Listing.* Washington, D.C.: National Science Teachers Association, 1973.

This short book contains important information about standardized tests available in all areas of science.

In Perspective

It is interesting to ask experienced science teachers what they remember about their first national convention of a science teachers organization. Chances are they can recall the time, place, weather conditions, the names of the major speakers, and the menu for the annual banquet. But most of all, they recall their excitement at seeing the exhibit hall packed full of thousands of "goodies" for science teaching. Even those who have attended national conventions for years admit to feeling like a small child in a candy store or supermarket. With so much material available, how do I even decide what to use?

For many there is an easy way of solving the problem; there are never enough funds to purchase all the equipment, all of the books, and all of the films. Nor would there be time to use all of them if they were available. In actual practice, science teachers have to make choices about what science programs they will use and what resources they will purchase.

In making these choices, many factors must be taken into consideration. How much money is available each year for science? What limitations are imposed by the science facilities of the school? What are your personal preferences? In general, do you prefer films or filmstrips, slides or overhead transparencies, laboratory work or demonstrations?

But most importantly, the students must not be forgotten. Just as the supermarket shopper can easily be carried away by fancy displays and forget the nutritional requirements of the people for whom the food is being purchased, so can a teacher's judgment be adversely affected by the attractiveness of many of today's tools for science teaching. Teachers should be careful this doesn't happen. A bulletin board display assembled by several science students may be superior to one purchased and put up by the teacher. A demonstration of the effects of air pressure using a pair of "plumber's helpers" may be remembered longer than one using a pair of Magdebury hemispheres obtained from a commercial supplier.

Teaching is not entertaining. The availability of such a rich resource of science materials can tempt the teacher into viewing a course as a series of extravagances. To do so is to forget the students and their need to be actively involved in the learning process. The best secret is to use a particular resource when it represents the best way to teach a concept or idea. Of course, variety is also important. Even high interest media such as films and videotapes lose their effectiveness if they are used several days in succession.

In summary, effective science teachers use a wide variety of resources in their work, but the resources are a means to an end and not an end in themselves.

Review Questions

1. Describe the problems that existed in science education in the United States in the mid-1950s and the efforts of the National Science Foundation since then to improve science teaching in middle and secondary schools.

2. Give at least two examples of efforts to improve science teaching that have been carried out by each of the following:
(a) Agencies of the federal government
(b) Professional societies
(c) State educational agencies
(d) Local school districts

3. List at least ten characteristics that should be taken into account when selecting textbooks and other instructional materials.

4. Briefly discuss how each of the following can be used in middle and secondary school science and the relative advantages and disadvantages of each:
(a) Printed materials other than textbooks
(b) Films
(c) Filmstrips
(d) Overhead transparencies
(e) 35mm slides
(f) Audio recordings
(g) Models and kits
(h) Games
(i) Bulletin boards and other displays
(k) Television

5. What items are classified as community resources? Give at least two

examples of how each type of community resource can be used in teaching science.

6. What services are provided by the Educational Resources Information Center (ERIC)?

7. Name two or more documents that can be used to identify the following resources:

(a) Articles about science teaching in professional journals
(b) Articles about science in newspapers of general journals
(c) Books about science
(d) Media for science teaching
(e) Standardized tests in science

For Application and Analysis

1. Use the form shown in Figure 9.3 to evaluate at least three current textbooks used in a particular science course. In what ways does the form reflect what you feel are the desirable features of a textbook? What other characteristics do you believe should be considered? How does the overall rating you obtained agree with your general impression of the three books? In other words, would you choose the book that received the highest overall rating using the form?

2. Compare a science program developed as an NSF Course Improvement Project (for example, one of those listed in Figure 9.3) with a science program available from a commercial publisher at that time. In what ways are they different? If the NSF program has been revised, in what ways has it been changed?

3. Develop a form for evaluating a film, filmstrip, or some other kind of media. You may wish to use a format similar to the one used in Figure 9.3. Use the form you have developed to rate at least three examples of the type of media for which it is intended. If possible, also have several other people use the form you have developed and make any revision warranted by their reactions.

4. Choose a topic that can be taught in one day, such as kinds of telescopes, laser technology, fuel cells, or alternation of generations. Examine several science programs to see how the topic you have chosen is developed. Also, using references such as those described in the last major section of this chapter, assemble a list of resources (film titles, magazine articles, library books, and the names of possible speakers) that could be used in teaching the topic.

References

Lockard, J. David, Charlene Pritzker, and Susan Snyder (Eds.). *Twenty Years of Science and Mathematics Curriculum Development* (the Tenth Annual Report of the International Clearinghouse). College Park, Md.: University of Maryland Science Teaching Center, 1977.

This reference describes curriculum projects in elementary and secondary school science and mathematics in the United States and in numerous foreign countries.

Nelkin, Dorothy. *Science Textbook Controversies and the Policies of Equal Time.* Cambridge, Mass.: The MIT Press, 1977.

This report of the battles over evolution and creationism, MACOS, and other controversial topics in science education makes for interesting reading.

Woodbury, Marda. *A Guide to Sources of Education Information.* Washington, D.C.: Information Resources Press, 1976.

This is a useful guide to directories and other reference books for obtaining information on education products, curricula resources, instructional materials, etc.

ACHIEVEMENT IN SCIENCE

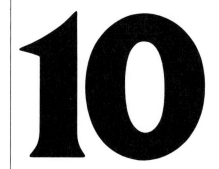

CHAPTER 10

Science for Exceptional Students

"A veterinarian? Of course you can be a veterinarian," the doctor said, giving my parents a knowing wink. It was January in 1947. One month earlier a bout of meningitis had left me completely deaf. Now I was wondering what effect deafness would have on my career choices. At age 14 I hadn't exactly decided what I wanted to do. Like most girls in those days I supposed I'd work for awhile then maybe get married. Science and math were my best subjects and my parents had never discouraged my interest. My father was a biochemist and I had visited his laboratory and played with his rats. Then I had received a doctor kit at an appropriate age and my sister and I had converted a quarter of the basement into a hospital ward with rows of beds to care for our dolls and stuffed animals, all of which had suddenly become sick. A veterinarian would not have to talk to her patients, I reasoned. It would be a perfect career for a deaf person! It never occurred to me then that deafness might mean I couldn't finish high school and college and then earn my own living.

Years later, after I had done just that and had earned a doctorate, as it turned out not in veterinary medicine but in biochemistry instead, I learned that others had not been so certain. The social workers at Columbia University's Vanderbilt Clinic had told my parents that deafness would make it impossible for me to continue in a regular classroom. But, when my parents tried to enroll me in a school for the deaf, they found that my years of normal hearing had placed me far ahead of my deaf age peers who had to spend extra time learning to speak and to use language. My parents therefore decided that I should return to my regular ninth grade classes and they arranged for me to have instruction in lipreading once a week on Saturday morning.

My classmates, who lent me their notes and relayed assignments, and teachers, who wrote extra comments on my papers and on the blackboard, were especially helpful at this time. The major hurdle was learning to study. People who hear take for granted the tremendous amount of information they get effortlessly by overhearing conversations around them. Suddenly deprived of this input, I had to learn to acquire the information by looking it up in a book. Often it felt as though I was reading half the library just to be sure that I did not miss the one point the teacher thought to be important.

In 1950 I entered Oberlin College. I chose Oberlin not only because it was a medium sized college with a reputation for academic excellence but also because it was 500 miles away from home. The latter was important to me because I wanted a chance to develop independence. No special arrangements were made for me,

Reprinted by permission of the National Science Teachers Association. Hoffman, Helenmarie H., and Ricker, Kenneth S., editors, Sourcebook: Science Education and the Physically Handicapped. *Washington, D.C.: National Science Teachers Association, 1979, pp. 42–43.*

and I made no attempt to lipread the lectures. Usually I asked a classmate if I could copy her notes as she took them down, and I relied heavily on the textbooks. Later on, in graduate school, I found that I could lipread some of the lectures if the teacher's speech was clear, but notes of my classmates were still very helpful because it is impossible to write anything down while lipreading.

I did exercise some selection in the courses I took. To satisfy the fine arts requirement, I took studio drawing instead of music appreciation. To fulfill the language requirement, I took German, which was taught by reading, instead of French, which was taught conversationally. Science courses, because they required hands-on laboratory work were always more fun than the more abstract and unillustrated history or philosophy lectures.

I received a bachelor's degree in zoology and enrolled at Wayne State University in a master's degree program in medical technology. After graduation I worked as a research medical technologist for eleven years, during which time I authored and published several papers in immunochemistry and protein chemistry. I encountered few problems that could be related to deafness. I could tell by touch whether a centrifuge was operating properly. I was usually able to communicate with my coworkers by lipreading, although we occasionally resorted to pencil and paper. There was always someone else around who could answer the telephone. I eventually reached a position where I supervised the work of several technicians.

I encountered considerable opposition to the idea of a return to school. My friends and family exerted subtle pressures. There were dire predictions that I would not be able to find a job because I would be over-educated. I was warned that higher standards of excellence would be required of me, and there would be questions about my abilities to carry out the professional duties of a chemist. Nevertheless, I went ahead and eventually obtained a PhD in biochemistry with a distributed minor in chemistry and, after four years of postdoctoral training at Mayo Clinic in 1975 I joined the faculty at Albert Einstein College of Medicine to organize a monoamine assay laboratory for the Departments of Psychiatry and Neurology. I have special expertise in the analysis of neurotransmitter amines which are chemicals thought to play an important role in brain function. I am involved in several research projects designed to give insight into the nature of changes in neurotransmitter amine metabolism associated with various neurological and mental disorders as well as with normal fluctuations of mood and behavior. It is fascinating work and I have never regretted my decision to go for a doctorate.

Today's science classrooms often contain students with many kinds of handicaps and learning disabilities, as well as so-called normal students and students classified as gifted and talented. The term *exceptional student* is used to describe students at both ends of the continuum, ranging from students who can barely cope in a school environment to those

TABLE 10.1   Percent of U.S. Children with Varying Handicapping
Conditions, 1976 [a]

Speech Impaired	3.50
Learning Disabled	3.00
Mentally Handicapped	3.00
Behavioral Disorders	2.00
Orthopedic/Health Impaired	0.50
Hearing Impaired	0.60
Visually Impaired	0.10
Multiply Handicapped	0.60
Total	12.0

[a] Based on U.S. Government Statistics, 1977.

SOURCE: Bureau of Education for the Handicapped, 1977.

with superior intelligence and talent. According to Hallahan and
Kauffmann, "exceptional children are those who require special education and related resources if they are to realize their full human potential."[1]

Various agencies of the federal government have regulations dealing
with the classification of exceptional individuals and their education. In
addition, many states have laws governing the handicapped and the
gifted and talented. The most commonly used categories and the percentage of the population contained in each is shown in Table 10.1. Each of
these categories, along with suggestions for teaching science to the individuals with each of these types of exceptionality, is described in greater
detail in this chapter.

Alternatives for Teaching Science to Handicapped Students

The presence of handicapped students in regular classes is a recent event
in most schools. Public Law 94–142, the Education for All Handicapped
Children Act, was signed into law by President Gerald Ford on November
29, 1975. This law requires all schools to place each student, regardless of
the nature of any handicaps or learning disabilities, in the "least restrictive environment."

THE CASCADE SYSTEM

Shortly before P.L. 94–142 became law, the Council for Exceptional Children adopted the "cascade" system as one model for delivering educational services to exceptional students. This system, first introduced
by Maynard Reynolds in 1962, is based on a series of alternative settings that move from the least restrictive to most restrictive educational

---

[1]Daniel P. Hallahan and James M. Kauffmann, *Exceptional Children: An Introduction to Special
Education,* Englewood Cliffs, N.J.: Prentice-Hall, Inc., 1978.

RESEARCH REPORT

Science Education and the Handicapped Student

In April, 1978 a special conference entitled Science Education for the Handicapped was sponsored by the National Science Teachers Association (NSTA) in Washington, D.C. Helenmarie Hoffman, a staff member at NSTA, edited the following position which was endorsed by those attending the conference:

Handicapped children have a right and a need to learn basic science content and skills. Research indicates that handicapped children are interested in and capable of learning science. This research in addition to court rulings has established the "principle of normalization". Handicapped students have similar needs to other students, and they develop concepts in a similar manner. Therefore, it is necessary that equal education opportunities are offered to these students.

Science courses should be an integral part of the education of all handicapped students from kindergarten through high school. The teacher who teaches science to the physically handicapped must possess a strong comprehensive science background. Outstanding science teachers utilizing multisensory instructional techniques and laboratory-centered programs are able to effectively teach physically handicapped students in regular classes. Physically handicapped students should receive comprehensive exposure to the various fields of science. Aspects of the science curriculum should include process, content, and career education with emphasis placed on early childhood and elementary programs as well as middle/junior high school and secondary science. The instructional strategies, techniques, and procedures found most effective with the physically handicapped in science are also most effective with the non-handicapped. A great need exists to disseminate science educational information about materials, techniques, conferences, workshops, etc. to regular and special education teachers.

Although many of the conference recommendations are costly, failure to meet these obligations will most probably cost more, through the loss of physically handicapped individuals' particular contributions to science and/or society. The societal loss will be professional, human, and economic. The anticipation of this loss provides the necessary rationale for following through on these recommendations.[2]

The above position statement reflects the attitude and position of many science educators today. The conference from which this position statement emerged was financed by a grant from the National Science Foundation and suggests the direction that science education for the handicapped is likely to follow.

[2]Helenmarie Hoffman (Ed.), "A Working Conference on Science Education for Handicapped Students: Proceedings," Washington, D.C.: National Science Teachers Association, April, 1978.

environment. The trend today is to place students in an environment where they can be successful and face the least number of restrictions. This "mainstreaming" concept provides opportunities for mildly handicapped

Handicapped students have the same interests, emotions, and social needs as do other students their age.

individuals to spend most or all of their time in regular classes. More severely handicapped students are placed in more restrictive environments. As students develop additional skills and learn to overcome various disabilities, they are moved to educational environments that are less restrictive. Conversely, when it is determined that additional support systems are needed, a student can be moved to a more restrictive environment.

The cascade system is shown in Figure 10.1 with ten alternatives illustrated in a hierarchical fashion. A brief description of each alternative should help clarify how this system works.

REGULAR CLASSROOM.   The regular classroom is the least restrictive of all educational environments. In this setting, the regular teacher with minor adjustments instructs the handicapped along with other students.

REGULAR CLASSROOM WITH CONSULTANTS.   In this setting, an educational specialist works with teachers and exceptional students in the regular classroom. This approach requires extensive planning and cooperation between the regular teacher and the specialist. This approach is most often used in elementary schools.

REGULAR CLASSROOM WITH ITINERANT TEACHERS.   Some handicapped students can function well in regular classrooms but require instruction from specially trained teachers on a regular basis. In such instances, the special education teachers "travel" from one classroom to another.

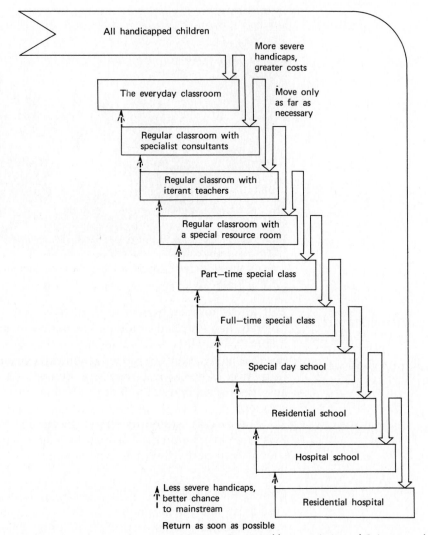

FIGURE 10.1   The cascade system. (*Source:* Reprinted by permission of *Science and Children.* Molloy, Larry, "Law and the Handicapped," Vol. 13, No. 6, pp. 7-10, March 1976. Copyright © 1976 by the National Science Teachers Association, 1742 Connecticut Ave., NW, Washington, D.C. 20009.)

REGULAR CLASSROOM WITH A SPECIAL RESOURCE ROOM.   Some classrooms are adjacent to special areas where, for example, students with seeing or hearing impairments can receive additional assistance. Supplies, media, and other special curriculum materials allow many handicapped students to function part of the time in class and part of the time in resource rooms.

PART-TIME SPECIAL CLASS.   In some instances, a handicapped student can function well in, for example, social studies and music, but needs extra help in mathematics and reading. In such cases, handicapped students attend regular classes part of the time and classes taught by special educators part of the time.

FULL-TIME SPECIAL CLASS.   It may be necessary for students with more serious disadvantages to attend special classes all of the time. Classes for blind, deaf, or mentally handicapped students are housed in many regular schools across the country today. Lunchroom, library, and other facilities are shared, and regular students have the opportunity to observe and get to know students with handicaps.

SPECIAL DAY OR RESIDENTIAL SCHOOLS.   Some special schools for exceptional students operate during the day only, with students returning to their homes each evening. Other special schools serve also as a place of residence. State-supported schools for deaf or blind students are examples of residential schools that have been common in the past.

HOSPITAL SCHOOLS AND RESIDENTIAL HOSPITALS.   Some students with severe physical handicaps need extensive medical care or other hospital services while going to school. For these students it is usually necessary that their learning environment be established in a hospital. In some cases, students attend during the day and return home at night. With more severe cases students stay at a hospital full time.

HOMEBOUND.   Students who are too fragile to move must stay at home where special teachers instruct them. Since these students seldom leave home, this is the most restrictive of all educational environments.

IMPLICATIONS
FOR PLANNING

P.L. 94–142 requires all school personnel to establish an Individualized Education Program (IEP) for each handicapped student who is placed in a regular classroom (mainstreamed). The IEP contains objectives, learning activities, and modes of evaluation that are to be followed by the teacher and student. This mandatory plan must be agreed upon not only by appropriate school personnel, but also by the parents.

Since P.L. 94–142 provides teachers with assistance, IEPs are not the sole responsibility of the classroom instructor. Rather, it is the joint responsibility of specialists, administrators, and teachers to propose a plan that is satisfactory to the student and his or her parents. Once this is agreed upon, all parties involved are obligated to follow and complete the plan to the best of their ability. Procedures used to establish IEPs vary some from school system to school system. A sample copy of an IEP is shown in Figure 10.2, and represents the important features of such a plan as followed by most school systems.

Hearing-Impaired Students

Most of us have watched a portion of a television program without the sound turned up. Under such circumstances, it does not take long to realize how much we rely on sound for communication. Individuals with partial or full loss of hearing live in a world of reduced stimulation and communication. Science can be a particularly valuable subject for such students. Teaching science to hearing-impaired students is a challenge that has only recently begun to receive special attention.

The term *hearing impaired* or *hearing handicapped* refers to (1) the deaf and (2) the hard of hearing. Deaf individuals are those whose hearing loss is so severe that it precludes the normal development of language. Most individuals who are hard of hearing are able to develop some spoken language. And many have near normal speech.

As with all handicaps, the degree of impairment can range from mild to severe. Since youngsters who are congenitally deaf do not develop

---

WHAT STUDENTS SAY

Mainstreaming

- At first I thought it was gross to have a blind student taking chemistry. After we got acquainted, I really changed my mind. Boy was I wrong about what blind people can do.

- If you mean putting a special ed students in regular classes, it was a disaster. We must have had a half dozen in ninth grade physical science and the teacher didn't get much done all year but try to control them.

- I don't think our school has mainstreaming. At least I don't know anything about it.

- I had never thought about how difficult it was for deaf persons to learn new words until James was assigned to our physics class. While he is not totally deaf, he is not able to learn in the same way the rest of us are. It really makes you stop and think.

- I used to feel sorry for anyone in a wheelchair. Now that we have a couple in class I marvel at what they can do instead of pitying them.

- I've heard my parents complain about mainstreaming. I think most of my friends quickly accept handicapped students.

- I think students with learning problems should go to a special school.

- This kid in my earth science class has convulsions once in awhile. I'm not as scared as I used to be when she has a seizure.

Date _____ Student's Name _____ Birthdate _____ School _____

Grade _____ Parents' Name _____ Address _____ Phone _____

CLASS SCHEDULE		
Period	Subject	Teacher
1		
2		
3		
4		
	Lunch	
5		
6		
7		

CHECKLIST

Date	Action
_____	Referral by _____
_____	Parents contacted
_____	Initial Evaluation
_____	Parents Scheduled
_____	Committee Meeting
_____	IEP Developed
_____	IEP approved

GENERAL HEALTH

General Physical _____

Vision _____

Speech _____

Hearing _____

Emotional _____

Other _____

_____

COMMITTEE MEMBERS

_____

_____

_____

_____

_____

_____

RANGE OF SERVICES TO BE USED: _____

_____

_____

_____

_____

_____

TEST INFORMATION

Date   Test   Interpretation of
                      Results

GENERAL OBJECTIVES	METHOD OF EVALUATION	DATE ACHIEVED
1. _____	_____	_____
2.		
3.		
4.		
5.		
6.		
7.		

FIGURE 10.2   A sample page from an IEP form used with exceptional students.

normal language patterns, they are not placed in regular classes. A few hard-of-hearing individuals, however, are being mainstreamed today, and science teachers are learning how to better accommodate these students in their classes. An estimated 0.5 percent of the school population in this country can be classified as hard of hearing and .075 percent as deaf.

CHARACTERISTICS OF THE HEARING IMPAIRED

Individuals who do not possess normal hearing may be different from others in language development, intellectual development, educational development, and emotional development.

LANGUAGE DEVELOPMENT.   The most noticeable characteristic of hearing-impaired students is that they lag in language development. Be-

RESEARCH REPORT

Educators'
Attitudes Toward
Mainstreaming
and
Individualized
Education
Programs

Dorothy Semmel[3] has conducted research to find ways to predict what variables most influence the attitudes of educators toward mainstreaming and the use of IEPs. As might be expected, she found that classroom teachers and principals had less positive attitudes toward mainstreaming than did special education teachers. She did find, however, that knowledge of IEP regulations by regular teachers and principals heavily influenced their attitude toward mainstreaming.

The fact that IEPs are mandatory may influence how teachers feel toward mainstreaming. Many teachers also apparently feel that handicapped students have a moral right to the best possible education. The most important factor in predicting how teachers and principals react to mainstreaming, however, is knowledge of Public Law 94–142 and its provisions for Individualized Education Programs. In summary, Semmel's research suggests that the more educators know about IEP regulations the more positive their attitudes will be toward mainstreaming.

[3]Dorothy S. Semmel, "Variables Influencing Educators' Attitudes Toward Individualized Education Programs for Handicapped Children," Paper presented at the American Educational Research Association Annual Meeting, San Francisco, April, 1979.

cause of decreased stimulation and interaction with others, their vocabularies are limited and they fall behind in reading skills. In fact, the *average* reading level of a hearing-impaired high school graduate is between second and fourth grade level. Hands-on science activities are an excellent means of introducing hearing-impaired students to facts, concepts, and principles in a concrete and meaningful way.

INTELLECTUAL DEVELOPMENT. Because of the lag in language development and reading skills, the intellectual development of deaf students usually falls behind that of normal students. This may be due at least in part to the mode of testing. Studies have shown, however, that the intellectual development of partially hearing students is not necessarily inferior to that of normal hearing students. While partially hearing students do fall behind in verbal skills, they apparently compensate in other ways and are able to demonstrate logical thinking skills in much the same way as normal hearing students. Such findings support the theory of Inhelder and Piaget[4] that formal language is not necessary for the development of logical thinking. By using appropriate instructional strategies, science teachers can contribute significantly to the intellectual development of hearing-impaired students.

[4]B. Inhelder and J. Piaget, *The Early Growth of Logic in the Child,* New York: Harper and Row, 1964.

EDUCATIONAL ACHIEVEMENT. The average deaf student is at least three to four years behind other students in educational achievement, with reading problems being the most severe. Partially hearing students are generally from one-half to two years behind. With early detection of hearing difficulties and with increased efforts to meet the needs of these students, it is generally agreed that this lag, so common in the past, can be greatly reduced in the future.

EMOTIONAL DEVELOPMENT. Because of lags in language development and educational achievement, hearing-impaired students often mature more slowly and are more dependent on others for assistance. During childhood, individuals who have partial hearing often do not perceive themselves as being different from other students. During the stressful period of adolescence, however, the hearing-impaired student is vulnerable to psychological and social strain that may lead to a decline in self-esteem and personal confidence.

The role of the teacher, of course, is crucial in helping the hearing-impaired student adjust emotionally in the regular classroom. The teacher not only needs to help students with hearing handicaps believe that they can be academically successful, but the teacher must also be alert to how such students relate to their peers. By communicating to the student that science can be learned in much the same fashion as by students with normal hearing, the teacher demonstrates to other members of the class that a hard-of-hearing student is a regular member of the class and should be treated as such. By assuring hearing-impaired students that they can be successful in science, the teacher removes one of the major "restrictions" that has been so prevalent in the past.

HEARING AIDS AND TRAINING DEVICES

Many hearing-impaired students can be helped significantly by the use of hearing aids. When properly diagnosed and treated, the hearing of some students can be restored to almost normal, although no hearing aid can ever compensate completely for a hearing loss. By making sure these students are seated near the teacher, most activities in the science class need no further modification. Auditory trainers worn about the neck are also a big help to many students who suffer appreciable loss of normal hearing (see photograph on page 394).

Lip reading can be facilitated by facing and speaking carefully to the individual. The teacher can also urge other students to develop such helpful means of communicating. Many teachers have been successful in working with hearing-impaired students through the use of signing, finger spelling, and other signals easily understood by students. The use of diagrams, charts, and pictures is also very helpful to students with hearing difficulties. In some classrooms, media centers have been established where hearing-impaired students have access to materials that fur-

This meeting of a counselor, teacher, principal, parent, and student was held to approve the student's IEP.

ther reinforce the lesson being taught. By being considerate and patient, and by learning to listen attentively to hearing-impaired students, communication can be improved significantly.

Many science programs have been successful with hearing-impaired students. Materials developed by the Science Curriculum Improvement Study, Science—A Process Approach, the Elementary Science Study, and the Biological Sciences Curriculum Study, ME NOW have been found to be extremely useful. More recently, projects funded by the National Science Foundation have adapted traditional programs and materials for use with hearing-impaired students.

The key to teaching science to deaf and partially hearing students is the use of hands-on materials and equipment. When these students are able to experience science *firsthand* in a tangible and "real" manner, the development of appropriate concepts, skills, and attitudes can be facilitated. Instead of perpetuating the idea that "science is too hard for hearing-impaired students," as has often been the case in the past, science can be presented as a subject where students "learn by doing." It is this opportunity for direct experience that makes science a particularly relevant subject for deaf and partially hearing students.

SUMMARY OF METHODS FOR HELPING HARD-OF-HEARING STUDENTS IN SCIENCE

In summary, the following are suggestions for teaching science to students with hearing impairments:

- Visuals should be used freely. In addition to illustrations on the chalkboard, important ideas in science can also be communicated to hearing handicapped students using overhead transparencies, slides, charts, and films. Some films are available with captions especially designed for hearing-impaired students.

- Ask hearing handicapped students where it is best for them to sit. It is usually desirable for them to be close to the teacher or interpreter.

- Have note-takers available when they are needed. Hearing handicapped students often have difficulty watching the teacher or interpreter and trying to take notes at the same time.
- Provide outlines for hearing-impaired students; this allows them to get back on track if they are momentarily distracted.
- Cooperate with special education teachers. Most school systems and state departments of education employ specialists who are trained to assist teachers with hearing handicapped students.
- Reduce the reading level of materials and vocabulary used when necessary. When communicating with hearing-impaired students, it is helpful to use short sentences.
- When necessary, use individualized tests for hearing-impaired students.
- During certain lessons or activities, pair hearing handicapped students with hearing partners.

Visually Impaired Students

Visually impaired students range from those who are totally blind to those who can read regular print under special conditions. Students defined as legally blind are those who have acuity of 20/200 or less in the better eye with corrective glasses, or who have a peripheral field so contracted that they cannot see beyond an angle of 20 degrees. Partially seeing individuals are legally defined as those seeing between 20/200 and 20/70 in the better eye with corrective glasses.

For the teacher, however, the most relevant distinction between blind and partially seeing students has to do with how they function in the classroom. Approximately 80 percent of all visually impaired individuals have some vision, and approximately three-fourths of the people who are legally blind can read print. While seriously impaired students usually must depend on braille and other tactiles, a majority of partially seeing students need only large print or regular print under special conditions. There are many exceptions to this distinction, however, and factors such as age of onset of visual impairment, chronological age, maturity level, intellectual ability, and achievement background often mediate the extent to which special help is needed.

INTELLECTUAL CHARACTERISTICS

Visually impaired students are restricted in their ability to receive some kinds of stimuli from the environment and must rely more heavily on the senses of touch, smelling, taste, and hearing. For the congenitally blind student, many things such as mountains, buildings, and stars are too large and too far away to experience. Conversely, bacteria, protozoa, and other microscopic objects are too small for them to touch or feel. Other objects, organisms, or phenomena may move too fast, be too fragile, or be too dangerous for them to experience through touch. Visually impaired students, however, learn to experience objects and phenomena in other ways and to use their senses to a higher degree than seeing students.

The space perception of totally blind students is different from that of seeing students. Research shows that visually impaired students "see" things differently with their fingers than other students do with their eyes. It is important that teachers of visually impaired students realize this difference. A teacher, for example, should not assume that a blind student who handles a model of a heart or a plant specimen will conceptualize that object in the same manner as do the other students.

Visually impaired students are not generally considered to be significantly different from seeing students in intelligence and ability to achieve in school. The major difference appears to be in the area of vocabulary and the ability to conceptualize objects and events. The use of "normal" vocabulary by visually impaired students can be misleading to teachers; for example, knowing a word should not be interpreted to mean an understanding of a concept. Moreover, limited contact with the environment usually hinders the blind student's opportunity to conceptualize and understand many of the phenomena to which seeing students have ready access.

Kenneth Ricker, a science educator at the University of Georgia, has found that blind students necessarily approach all new learning tasks inductively. Only by collecting all bits of evidence or information possible—size, shape, texture, odor, sound, number, for example—can a blind student begin to form a concept of the whole object, process, or idea. Blind students, he concludes, cannot learn deductively except at the verbal level where they have had previous inductive experience with the topic being learned. Special materials are thus needed to simulate objects, events, or ideas being studied.

The following reasons help explain why in the past many visually impaired students have fallen behind in academic achievement: (1) slow diagnosis of impairment, (2) slow implementation of services, (3) loss of time in school due to treatment, (4) slower acquisition of information and slower reading rates, and (5) lack of concrete inductive experiences in the classroom.

EMOTIONAL
DEVELOPMENT

In the past, visually impaired individuals have been viewed by many as helpless and of less value to society than seeing persons. These and other stereotyped attitudes of society have resulted in the self-devaluation of many visually impaired individuals. For visually handicapped students who accept this devaluation, adjustment problems can ensue. Further, attitudes toward blind students are often different from those toward partially seeing individuals. Partially seeing students, for example, are able to function on a par with other students in the classroom but are restricted in some athletic activities. Such restrictions can influence the social development of these students, resulting in lowered expectations and social rejection by their peers. The major cause of maladjustment among visually impaired youngsters, however, is negative societal reaction.

Attitudes toward visually impaired students must be changed. Through mainstreaming at earlier ages and through developing an increased awareness of the intellectual and emotional needs of blind and partially seeing students, educators can help improve the self-acceptance and independence of these individuals and, hence, help them to become better-adjusted individuals.

METHODS FOR ASSISTING VISUALLY IMPAIRED SCIENCE STUDENTS

The amount of assistance needed by a visually handicapped student depends on the extent of the impairment. It is important that all students be provided mobility. It is also important that visually handicapped students be encouraged to interact with their peers. For some partially seeing students, a seat on the front row may be the only major change that is needed. With these students the teacher, of course, should make sure that charts, transparencies, and all writing on the chalkboard are visible. Clean chalkboards and carefully prepared visual displays are helpful. Demonstrations that can be easily viewed can also assist partially seeing students. In most cases, it is helpful to ask handicapped students what the teacher can do to help them.

With some students, specially printed materials are necessary. Some of these materials are available commercially, and others can be made with the use of large characters that fit on certain typewriters. When printed materials are clean and possess good contrast, some students can read regular print with the aid of special magnifying lenses.

For partially seeing students with very limited acuity and for blind students, the use of braille is common. Many museums and outdoor learning centers have displays that are accompanied by braille and audio presentations. Since most blind students are not mainstreamed, braille is normally not used in regular classrooms.

Audio presentations are available today that allow blind students to "read" books, articles, and other published materials. When large amounts of information must be covered, a technique called compressed speech can be used. With compressed speech, a special device is used to discard very small segments of the speech from an audiotape of the lesson. Thus, when played back, the time of presentation is shortened without hampering the individual's ability to understand the material. In some cases, compressed speech can be used to reduce the listening time by as much as 50 percent.

The American Printing House for the Blind (American Printing House for the Blind, P.O. Box 6085, Louisville, KY 40206) has recently

Three-dimensional models, or tactiles, are particularly useful in teaching science to visually impaired students.

developed a series of "tactiles" that allow blind students to experience more directly things such as the stages of mitosis or the parts of a cell. These tactiles are made of plastic and possess raised portions that represent chromosomes, cell membranes, and other cell structures. Examples of such tactiles used for learning the stages of meiosis are shown above. Instructions for using such tactiles can be put on audiotape or printed in braille.

USING MODELS FOR TEACHING SCIENCE TO BLIND STUDENTS

The work of Piaget and others indicates that concepts cannot always be communicated to seeing students by language alone. Many important concepts in science are best learned through direct sensory experience. The use of manipulative and hands-on experiences is a particularly effective way to help visually impaired students learn science.

The use of models is particularly useful with blind and partially seeing students. When models are adapted for use with visually impaired students, colored areas should be changed to surfaces having various textures. When models that require assembling are used, small magnets that allow easier fitting should replace nails or other types of fasteners.

USING REAL MATERIALS TO STUDY STRUCTURE AND FUNCTION

Since tactiles and models lack true size, texture, definition, and warmth, actual plant and animal materials can supply an even greater degree of reality to the learning process. For increased authenticity, fresh specimens are superior to those that have been preserved in formaldehyde or other preservative.

The following activity is an example of an activity that has been used successfully with blind students (see Figure 10.3). The heart of a pig or sheep is used because it is large enough to "show" the details that might be missed in smaller specimens. Working in groups of two, the teacher gives directions orally and asks related questions as the students progress through the exercise. Taped (or printed) guides allow students to work in a self-paced manner. In some cases, a sighted student can be paired with a nonsighted student. With this particular exercise, raised diagrams and models are used to supplement the sheep or pig heart.

Laboratory Procedure

The heart of a sheep or a pig is given to each student group. In all specimens, two cuts have been made through the walls of the ventricles—one through the left and the other through the right.

In addition, each student group is given the following materials:

- Four probes of two different textures: two wooden and two glass; or, for the sighted, two of one color and two of another.
- Braille rulers; or, for the sighted, regular rulers or micrometers.
- A balance for the blind; or, for the sighted, a regular balance.
- A small laboratory guide in braille alphabet or in conventional characters containing the entire unit's activities, instructions, and questions.

FIGURE 10.3   Teaching the mammalian heart to the visually handicapped. (*Source:* Reprinted by permission of the National Science Teachers Association. Hoffman, Helenmarie H., and Ricker, Kenneth S., editors. *Sourcebook: Science Education for the Physically Handicapped.* Washington, D.C.: National Science Teachers Association, 1979, pp. 213–216.)

- Board and modeling clay; or wax-filled dissection pan or aluminum foil to draw on.

Students are told only that the mammalian heart is a four-chambered organ, with right and left atria and ventricles, and that a cut has been made through the wall of each ventricle. They are told that the left ventricle wall is thicker than the right ventricle wall. We also tell the students the name of the animal being studied and its approximate body weight (kilograms) and size (meters). They are then asked to follow written directions:

Gently pass your fingers over the entire outer surface of the heart, then answer the following questions: (a) What type of tissue is this organ built of, hard or soft? (b) Are all parts of the heart of a uniform degree of hardness? (c) If your answer is no, which parts are softer, the upper or the lower? (d) Knowing that the heart functions as a pump, what type of tissue would you suppose the heart is predominantly built of? (e) Since the lower parts are harder, predict whether their muscle content differs from that of the upper parts. (f) Can you feel any external feature which suggests a separation of the heart into right and left? Does this depression separate the ventricles equally? (g) Can you feel any raised lines (tube-like) on the heart wall or in the area of the depression? What do you think these might be? Because these blood vessels supply blood to the heart itself, they are named coronary vessels.

Weigh the heart; measure its length; measure it at its greatest width. Compare these to the animal's approximate weight.

Put your fingers into the left ventricle. Measure the thickness of the left ventricle wall. Do the same for the right ventricle wall: (a) Which wall is thicker? (b) Based on your knowledge of how the heart functions, try to explain your results. (c) Is there more muscle tissue in the left ventricle wall than in the right one?

Push the wooden stick into the left ventricle and the glass stick into the right ventricle. Push both sticks straight up. If you get caught in something, push the tissue aside so you can pass through. Now you have passed into the upper parts of the heart, called atria: (a) Feel the external size of the two atria. Are they different? (b) Can you feel your sticks by pressing on the atrial walls? By pressing on the ventricle walls?

Make a small cut in the wall of each atrium, then measure the wall thickness: (a) Is there any difference in the thickness of the two atrial walls? (b) Since atrial walls are less thick than ventricle walls, are they less muscular? What can you predict about the function of the atria? (c) How might the blood therefore pass from the atria to the ventricles?

Search with your fingers for the structures which interfered with your pushing the sticks through from the ventricles into the atria: (a) Describe the structural materials these are built of. (b) How many are there in each ventricle? (c) Do you find any similarity between their structure and that of a

FIGURE 10.3 (Continued)

parachute? (d) From this structural similarity, and the fact that they prevented your sticks from readily passing from ventricles to atria, how would you explain their function? (e) What do we call a structure which can open or shut to allow fluid to flow in a given direction?

Push through the other sticks which you have (again, the wooden to the left, and the glass to the right). Try to find another passage out of the ventricles. (a) Did you encounter any obstacle? (b) What did your stick enter? Blood vessels which carry blood away from the heart are called? Those which carry blood to the heart are called? (c) Do you think the blood vessels connected to the ventricles are arteries or veins? (d) On what fact do you base your conclusion?

Measure the wall thickness of the arteries and also their cross-sectional diameters on both sides of the heart: (a) Compare these arteries. Which is bigger and more muscular? Do you know its name? (b) Explain the above fact, basing your explanation on what you already know about how the heart functions.

Now find the veins entering the heart: (a) Push the first two sticks you used for finding the atrioventricular node further up, and look for other entrances into the atria. Did you find any? (b) What are they opening into? These vessels are the veins entering the atria. (c) Measure the wall thickness, the diameter of the veins entering the left and those entering the right atria, and compare your measurements. Are there any differences? What are they? (d) Can you explain your findings? The main vein entering the right atrium is the superior vena cava, and those entering the left atrium are called the pulmonary veins.

Compare all of your data for measurements of veins with those for measurements of arteries in the left and right sides of the heart: (a) Which type of vessels (arteries or veins) are bigger in tube diameter, have thicker walls, and are more muscular? What might be the differences in function?

Now, summarize your data on the double blood cycle by making a schematic drawing showing the double blood cycle. Check it against the drawing provided.

Arteries are muscular; they contract to help push the blood forward: (a) What problem might arise to interfere with a one-directional arterial blood flow? (b) How might this problem be solved? (c) Now it is clear why you encountered no hindrance to pushing your stick through in the direction from ventricles to arteries. (d) How can you prove the existence of valves? Push a stick through in the opposite direction, from arteries into ventricles. Did you encounter anything? (d) Describe the valves you encountered. Are they similar in structure to those between ventricles and atria?

Try to find an opening between the left and right parts of the heart. Did you find one? (a) The left side of the heart receives its blood supply from the _____ where it has been oxygenated. This blood therefore is high in _____

FIGURE 10.3 (Continued)

gas. This oxygenated blood passes into the _____ _____ and is pumped to the organs and tissues of the _____. (b) The right side of the heart receives blood from the organs and tissues of the body. Thus, this blood is oxygen-deficient and high in carbon dioxide gas. This blood passes through the _____ _____ which pumps it to the _____ where it picks up fresh _____ and gives up carbon dioxide. This oxygenated blood then returns to the _____ _____. It is obvious that blood arriving at the cells and tissues of the body brings _____ and removes _____ _____ gas. Also, blood arriving at the lungs brings carbon dioxide to be exchanged for fresh oxygen. (c) In your opinion what would happen if there were a passageway between the left and right sides of the heart? What type of gas would the cells of the body get? (d) Since the oxygen provided to cells is used for energy production, receiving less oxygen would result in? This would produce a lower metabolic rate (body activity), and a lower body temperature.

Summary

We have learned that the mammalian heart structure provides the possibility for the existence of two entirely separate circulatory systems. One system is responsible for gas exchange with the environment (via the lungs); the other for gas exchange with the tissues. The efficiency of energy production that results from these separate systems makes possible homeothermy: warm-bloodedness and a constant body temperature.

The different components of the heart structure are each fully adapted for their specific functions and enable a one-directional blood flow: From veins through the atria and ventricles to the arteries—with valves to guard that flow.

FIGURE 10.3 (Continued)

While blind students seldom are mainstreamed, students with various other visual impairments are placed in regular classrooms. Most of these visually impaired students can do well in a regular classroom, and this is especially the case when the teacher is aware of the student's problem. Several strategies can be used to help these students learn science, and hands-on experiences are particularly effective.

Speech and Language Disorders

Speech and language disorders are the most common handicap of students in today's schools. Since many of those with such disorders outgrow their handicaps, speech and language problems are more prevalent in the earlier grades.

One of the major problems faced by secondary school teachers is the use of nonstandard English. This problem is associated more commonly with students from economically disadvantaged environments and those from minority groups. Some educators feel that failure to speak standard English interferes with normal cognitive development. Other educators minimize this factor and suggest that students should be taught to use the language best suited for their own survival. Although there is disagreement among educators, the majority of school systems advocate the use of standard English and teachers in all subject areas are faced with the problem of helping students overcome nonstandard speech patterns.

Most individuals with disorders are extremely sensitive about how they sound to others. When they detect that their speech patterns are unacceptable by others, they often resist further communication and help. The watchword when working with students who have speech or language disorders, therefore, is that of being careful not to draw unnecessary attention to the problem.

TYPES OF ORAL LANGUAGE DISORDERS

Most language disorders can be classified as those related to central nervous system malfunctions or those associated with environmental factors.

APHASIA. The term *aphasia* is used to designate a wide range of language disturbances associated with injury to the central nervous system. In some cases, the injury occurs before individuals learn to speak, and in other cases after. Aphasia is often difficult to diagnose since students with such conditions may appear mentally retarded, hard of hearing, or emotionally disturbed. Upon close examination, however, many students with aphasia are intellectually alert, but lack the ability to express their thoughts orally. Aphasia varies greatly in extent, and the educational arrangement must be tailored for each individual depending on the mode by which he or she learns best. This frequently leads to the aphasic student being taught, at least part of the time, in special classes.

ARTICULATION PROBLEMS. Failure to pronounce words properly involves a variety of articulation problems. One common disorder is caused by an inability to include all necessary letters in a word. When a child says "ouse" instead of "house," the individual may be accused of "baby-talk," but in essence it is the omission of the "h" that creates the mispronunciation. In other cases, letters such as "t" for "k" and "b" for "v" are substituted uncontrollably. The "th" for "s" substitution is commonly referred to as a "lisp." A third kind of articulation problem is called a distortion. This is often caused by allowing too much air to escape from the sides of the teeth, thus resulting in a muffled sound such as "buthday" instead of "birthday." Fortunately, children outgrow most articulation problems. Most others can be eliminated with special exercises designed to help the youngster concentrate on using the tongue properly. Individuals experiencing these types of problems should be referred to a speech pathologist or therapist for diagnosis and treatment. The teacher can be most effective when working closely with a speech specialist.

VOICE DISORDERS. Damage or irritation to the larynx can lead to abnormal voice qualities. Voice disorders can involve pitch (degree of highness or lowness), loudness (strength), and other deviations of voice quality. With most voice disorders, it is important to have the student examined by a physician so that the extent of damage can be ascertained and proper treatment can be prescribed.

STUTTERING. Stuttering is one of the most common, yet complex, of all speech disorders. Stuttering usually passes through stages of varying severity over time. The symptoms consist of sound repetitions, hesitations, or prolongations that are frequently associated with certain words. The causes of stuttering are not well understood, but both physical and emotional factors are thought to be involved. A child, for example, may exhibit a slight stutter which in turn is complicated by the reaction of the parents. One of the most serious problems associated with stuttering is that others often fail to accept this deviation as "normal." When the person who stutters feels that others cannot accept the deviation, the situation often worsens. The best way to help a student who stutters is to be accepting and reassuring. Fortunately, many children who stutter do so only temporarily.

LANGUAGE DISABILITIES ASSOCIATED WITH NONSTANDARD ENGLISH

Many students in today's schools have not had preschool experiences in which they have used standard English. As mentioned earlier, these culturally different language patterns are often used by young people from economically deprived backgrounds and by members of various ethnic groups. Many educators suggest that such language should be viewed as "different," not "deficient," or as nonstandard rather than substandard.

All classroom teachers must share the responsibility for teaching standard English. This should be done with patience and by setting good examples. The teacher should not denunciate or destructively criticize the use of nonstandard English but, rather, demonstrate to students that in today's complex world it is advantageous to be able to master standard English. Learning to use science terminology correctly is part of this process.

SUGGESTIONS FOR HELPING STUDENTS WITH SPEECH AND LANGUAGE DISORDERS

The classroom teacher's role in helping students with speech or language disorders is both crucial and central. Since most secondary school students with such disorders take regular classes, it is up to the regular teacher to identify problems, seek additional help when needed, and give these students the emotional support they need. In the case of serious problems, the teacher's most important role is that of working with specialists.

The following list suggests ways to help students who have speech and language difficulties.

1. Teachers should carefully observe all students at the beginning of the school year and watch for unusual speech patterns. Some school systems have procedures for identifying such students which leads to referral and diagnosis. Teacher referrals are one of the most effective and efficient means school systems have for helping students.

2. Students with speech or language disorders are usually sensitive about their problems. They quickly detect the reactions of others toward their actions. One of the most effective ways to deal with these students is to exhibit patience and acceptance. Once a stutterer, for example, realizes that his or her problem is not seen by someone else as a deterrent to their communication or their relationship, the "disorder" can be dealt with in a positive, nonthreatening fashion.

3. The use of nonstandard English should not be ridiculed. Rather, the teacher should help students understand their own "language" and build from there to standard usage. Nonstandard English should not be considered as "all wrong" and standard English as "the only way." The advantages of standard over nonstandard verbiage can be taught without indicting or criticizing what the student has learned at home or on the street. In some cases, standard English is taught as a second language, and students learn that in given environments or settings they must use this second language in order to be successful.

4. Students with articulation problems should first be taught to be good listeners. Before many students can reproduce correct sounds, it is necessary for them to recognize and distinguish between correct and incorrect versions of these sounds. Speech clinicians can provide techniques and materials for teachers who wish to help individual students.

5. Students with overly loud or soft voices should be taught to make judgments on their performance and be encouraged to make necessary corrections. When problems appear to be physical in origin, parents should be consulted and encouraged to check with a speech pathologist.

6. Teachers should look for "good days" of those who experience speech difficulties and encourage students to participate freely at times when they are experiencing success.

7. Teachers should avoid rushing students who have language difficulties. Often, a little extra time will be sufficient in prompting successful performance.

8. Teachers should help other students become tolerant and accepting of those who experience difficulty communicating orally. Immature students are often prone to make fun of others who are different. The classroom teacher is in a position to influence the attitudes of other students toward those with speech and language problems.

9. Success breeds success. Teachers should try to place students in situations where they can communicate successfully and, hence, build additional self-confidence.

10. On the other hand, students with language difficulties also need to learn to handle their failures. Certain disorders require long and hard work before they can be overcome. The teacher is in a position to help students realize that things are not always easy and that there is no disgrace when one is not successful.

Orthopedic and Other Health Impairments

Among the most common physical handicaps are those associated with the use of bones, muscles, or joints. Such handicaps may be due to disease or accident, or be congenital. Among the most common disorders in this category are those resulting from cerebral palsy, birth defects, skeletal deformities, muscular dystrophy, multiple sclerosis, arthritis, osteomyelitis, and other bone imperfections. Teachers should also be aware of other health problems students may have, including epilepsy, rheumatic fever, cystic fibrosis, diabetes, asthma, sickle-cell anemia, and hemophilia.

In the past, many students with serious diseases or impairments were educated at home or in special institutions. Today, more and more of these students are entering regular classrooms and are engaging in activities alongside students their own age. The health problems mentioned above vary greatly in magnitude. In some cases, students need specialized care and can attend regular classes only on a limited basis. In other cases, however, students are able in most school systems to receive all of their education in regular classes. With some of the disorders, teachers and school officials need only to be aware of students who are affected and to know what to do in cases of sudden illness or emergency.

BEING AWARE OF ORTHOPEDIC AND OTHER DISORDERS

With today's emphasis on mainstreaming handicapped students, it becomes important for all teachers to be able to recognize the most common orthopedic disorders. The following section deals briefly with the major characteristics of the most common disorders and discusses a few precautions and safeguards for working with people so affected.

A few modifications may be needed in most classrooms in order to accommodate the orthopedically handicapped. Physical as well as social barriers should be removed. Communication should occur with medical and other support personnel. Plans for dealing with irregular attendance need to be established. The teacher should also become familiar with common side-effects of medications taken by students with orthopedic disorders.

CEREBRAL PALSY. Cerebral palsy (CP) is one of the most common orthopedic and neurological disorders. This disease is caused by many factors, some of which are still not well understood. Factors include those that are prenatal, natal, and postnatal in origin. Cerebral palsy can be classified into four broad categories: spastic, athetoid, ataxia, and mixed. Damage in the central nervous system is characteristic of all three types. Convulsions and mental retardation may also be found with all types.

Spastic.　About 50 to 60 percent of all cerebral palsy cases are related to spasticity. This form is characterized by explosive, jerky, and other exaggerated responses in the muscular system as well as muscle tightness, abnormal reflexes, and limited movement. Although the lack of muscular coordination may be severe in some individuals, many are capable of learning at a normal rate. Utilizing notetakers, readers, and tapes of class discussions can be helpful to this student when studying science.

Athetoid.　This type of cerebral palsy is characterized by almost constant motion. Athetoid individuals may exhibit tremors, as with the other types of CP, and "stiffness" or "rigidity." Speech problems are common, and there is often a tendency to drool. Several forms of athetoid CP may exist in the same individual, with different forms predominating from one day to the next. About 20 to 25 percent of all cerebral palsy cases fit into this category.

Ataxia.　This form of cerebral palsy is caused by lesions in the cerebellum and is characterized by loss of balance. Individuals with ataxia also frequently lack spatial orientation and muscular coordination.

While sources differ as to the extent of mental retardation among palsied children, it is generally estimated that close to half of the individuals with this disorder suffer from some mental deficiency. Approximately three-fourths exhibit speech and/or hearing impairments.

Mixed.　A fourth category of CP exists where students demonstrate a combination of symptoms. Seizures, speech delays, mental retardation, visual limitations, perceptual-motor problems, drooling, and a general lack of muscular control are among the most common symptoms of this multihandicapping condition.

Physical therapy and speech therapy programs are usually central to the treatment of most students with cerebral palsy. Science programs that foster the development of manipulative and communication skills are, therefore, of particular importance to these students. But modifications are usually necessary depending on the type of symptoms displayed by each individual.

BIRTH DEFECTS.　The National Foundation for the March of Dimes[5] defines birth defects as "structural or metabolic disorders present at birth, whether genetically determined or the result of environmental interference during embryonic or fetal life. Birth injuries are not included." It

[5]*Facts and Figures*, The National Foundation for the March of Dimes, New York, 1969.

is estimated that 7 percent of all newborn children in the United States have defects that are evident at birth or that can be detected during the first year of life. More than a million deaths each year occur as a result of birth defects.

The most common birth defects among students in secondary schools are clubfoot (foot turns inward or outward), polydactyly (extra fingers or toes), cleft palate (improper formation of upper mouth and lips), congenital amputees (missing limbs), curvature of the spine, hip dislocation, and congenital heart defects.

Today, most of these defects can be partially improved or totally corrected by surgery. In severe cases, however, medical attention may only eliminate a portion of the disorder. Students with such defects are usually fully capable of learning in regular classrooms. For such students the school grounds, corridors, and classrooms need to be barrier-free. Recently, schools and colleges around the country have spent large sums of money to eliminate physical barriers that impeded movement of physically handicapped students.

The most important thing for classroom teachers to be aware of is that students with birth defects may be sensitive and insecure concerning their looks or physical features. It is important for the teacher also to be aware that some of the other students may be inexperienced in dealing with those who have certain defects. In both instances, sensitivity and careful observation can reveal any initial problems. Teachers are usually in a position to set examples that other students will follow. While it is important to be aware of physical defects that possibly can limit certain activities, with prior planning there is usually little, if anything, these students cannot be a part of. By treating such students *like everyone else,* feelings of "I'm different from others" or "I'm not capable of doing that" can be effectively eliminated. In other words, when students with physical defects are treated as normal individuals, they do not grow up thinking of themselves as different or as handicapped.

MUSCULAR DYSTROPHY.   The disease is characterized by progressive loss of muscular strength. The mortality rate of individuals with muscular dystrophy is quite high for children between three and thirteen years of age.

Students with muscular dystrophy often have not been given the care and attention they deserve. Treatment today can alleviate some of the symptoms, and the student with muscular dystrophy usually gains a great deal both intellectually and emotionally when he or she is allowed to remain in regular classes.

MULTIPLE SCLEROSIS.   Multiple sclerosis is a disease of the central nervous system. It is more prevalent among young adults than among children or adolescents. Multiple sclerosis, like muscular distrophy, is progressive, and as yet there is no cure. Individuals with multiple sclerosis experience muscular weakness and can also be affected by hearing loss, visual impairment, and speech difficulties. Most high school students with multiple sclerosis can follow the regular curriculum and, except for strenuous exercise, can do everything other students can. The teacher must be able to balance activity with rest for these students. Multiple sclerosis is characterized by periods of remission or noticeable improvement followed by periods of decline and weakness. Though the disease is progressive, many young adults with multiple sclerosis live for several years, sometimes well into their late thirties or forties.

ARTHRITIS.   While arthritis is a common disease of older people, it does affect younger individuals. It is an inflammation of the joints and is characterized by swollen fingers, knees, and elbows. Teachers of arthritic students should be aware that mild to severe pain can accompany this disease and that this can affect both directly and indirectly the cognitive as well as psychomotor performance of students. While arthritis does not seriously impair learning, it is important to be aware that intermittent pain and discomfort can influence a student's ability to concentrate and engage in certain activities some of the time. With proper medication and with the understanding of teachers, most students with arthritis can function normally in regular classes. It is important, however, to check with medical and therapeutic personnel concerning the limitations of an arthritic student.

OSTEOMYELITIS.   Osteomyelitis is an inflammation of the bone marrow and affects the long bones of the body. In the past, affected individuals usually required long periods of inactivity in order to recover. Today antibiotics and drugs are used to control this disease, and it is seldom an educational problem.

EPILEPSY AND SEIZURES.   There are many forms of epilepsy and other forms of seizures that result in periodic convulsive disorders that may occur in the classroom. It is extremely important for the teacher as well as students to react to such a disorder both rationally and responsibly. With grand mal seizures, convulsion can last for several minutes, and unsuspecting teachers and students can find themselves at a loss for what to do. Petit mal seizures are much shorter, usually involving brief lapses of consciousness for a few seconds.

When a teacher is apprised of an epilepsy case, its type, and whether medication is being used, the management of the seizure is relatively simple. To the naive observer seizures, particularly the grand mal, are very upsetting and often, individuals who try to help overreact. Most seizures can be prevented with medication.

A grand mal seizure is often preceded by a shrill cry or other sensation known as an aura. With many individuals the aura comes in advance, leaving time for the person to be taken to a place to lie down. The violent jerks of a grand mal seizure usually last for only one or two minutes. When a seizure occurs in class, the teacher should make sure the student is lying on the floor away from furniture or other objects that could be harmful and make sure something soft is under the head. The jerking movements should not be constrained. Science teachers need to pay particular attention to equipment and other objects that could harm a student experiencing a seizure.

The most important thing during and after seizures in the classroom is that the teacher remain as calm and reassuring as possible. The teacher should explain that seizures are basically harmless and that they are not contagious. After a seizure, the student will probably be very tired and should be allowed to rest. His peers should be reassured that the individual is all right. When the teacher exhibits an understanding of epilepsy and remains positive and supportive of those who have this illness, students usually pick up on this attitude and respond in a similar manner. With this kind of leadership, both the patient and observers can be taught to accept epilepsy as a physical disorder not unlike many other illnesses.

RHEUMATIC FEVER.   Rheumatic fever is caused by bacterial infection that results in damage to the heart. Today, rheumatic fever generally can be controlled by the use of antibiotics and by limiting physical activity. In cases where permanent heart damage has been sustained, it is important that a physician advise school faculty as to the level of physical activity in which the student should be allowed to engage.

CYSTIC FIBROSIS.   Cystic fibrosis rivals cancer as a cause of death among children. The mortality rate is high, and death is usually a result of pulmonary complications. Affected individuals periodically have to spend time in the hospital when respiratory or intestinal symptoms persist. Improved treatment has led to longer life spans for individuals with cystic fibrosis.

DIABETES.   While diabetes mellitus can be controlled through diet and the administration of insulin, this metabolic condition can result in temporary losses in alertness and vitality in school. Severe diabetes may lead to visual and tactile loss of which the teacher should be aware. For youngsters who have been recently diagnosed, the teacher may have to help with the initial regulation of the treatment. When a diabetic student becomes dizzy, suffers abdominal pain, or goes into insulin shock, the teacher should know what to do to restore the person to normal. This should be done by checking with medical personnel, the family, and the student ahead of time.

ASTHMA AND ALLERGIC CONDITIONS.   Asthma and other allergic conditions are very common among young people. As with many of the other health problems discussed, the teacher needs to be aware of those who have these conditions and to be apprised of the medication that is used when such reactions occur. Allergic conditions are of particular concern when students are working outside or are on field trips. A list of students with a history of asthma or other allergies (particularly to bee stings) should be made, along with appropriate medication to be given in the case of any reactions. In more serious cases, the teacher should contact parents and/or physicians concerning possible restrictions that need to be imposed.

BLOOD-RELATED DISEASES.   Sickle-cell anemia, hemophilia, leukemia, hepatitis, and infectious mononucleosis are diseases that may affect the general activity level of students while they are at school. As mentioned before, teachers need to be aware of such conditions among their students and to know if there are limitations regarding the amount of physical activity these individuals can endure. In most cases, proper medication and regular checkups by physicians allow students with such conditions to function normally at school.

As stated before, several things can be done to help students with orthopedic and other health impairments in the regular classroom. Some need help with taking notes. Some need special assistance with reading. Tape recordings of class discussions can be very helpful. Science is an excellent opportunity for developing psychomotor and manipulative skills through hands-on activities. In addition to removing physical barriers, the science teacher should work hard to remove social and emotional barriers. Science should be communicated in such a way that *all* students come to realize that it is a course in which they can attain some degree of success.

Learning Disabilities

One of the newest areas of focus to evolve within the field of special education is that of "learning disabilities" or "specific learning disabilities." Earlier, students with learning disabilities were classified as "brain injured" or as having "minimal brain dysfunction." Today, these disorders are viewed in more specific terms and include problems associated with certain motor skills, or visual, auditory, and speech perceptions. Most of these disorders affect the reading, spelling, writing, or mathematics abilities of students. Some learning disabilities are the result of a combination of physical and environmental problems and lead to problems involving memory, attention span, hyperactivity, and ability to organize and conceptualize information. In most cases, students with learning disabilities are of near average, average, or above average intelligence; yet, to an unfamiliar teacher they may appear as below average.

Most science teachers will not have to deal with many of the exceptionalities described and discussed in this chapter. Learning disabilities, however, are more common and are encountered by most classroom teachers. For this reason, it is important that teachers be able to recognize common learning disabilities and to know how to deal with them in the regular classroom.

RECOGNIZING AND DEALING WITH VARIOUS KINDS OF LEARNING DISABILITIES

Teachers of science need to be made aware of common learning problems that interfere with learning. Some of the most frequently occurring disorders are as follows.

MOTOR DISORDERS. The ability to perform various behaviors depends on a combination of gross and fine motor skills. Gross motor abilities include walking, running, climbing, lifting, and balancing. Fine skills include folding, tying, cutting, sketching, calibrating, and adjusting. In some instances, a combination of certain motor disorders can seriously alter one's ability to perform a variety of cognitive tasks, including reading. Usually, students with severe motor disorders are diagnosed at a young age and have received special training before they enter middle school or high school.

AUDITORY PERCEPTION. The proper discrimination of speech sounds is central in the learning process. One's ability to read, conceptualize, or process information from sounds depends heavily on this mode of communication. Special training in how to detect sound-blends and the proper articulation of sounds, words, or sentences is available and can be used to improve most problems associated with auditory perception. One of the common characteristics of students with auditory perception problems is that they read poorly. This is one way teachers have of identifying this kind of disorder.

ORAL LANGUAGE DISORDERS. In addition to major speech handicaps which are discussed elsewhere in this chapter, there does exist a series of milder or more subtle oral dysfunctions that interfere with normal learning. For example, some students have difficulty putting certain letters together so that one word instead of two or three comes out. "Biology" might come out like "b—logy" with a long pause between the two sounds. Oral disorders are easier to detect and are often dealt with and corrected while students are in elementary school.

READING DISORDERS. Some students possess specific reading disorders wherein letters or words are transposed or processed backwards. This condition has received widespread attention in recent years, and several methods have been successfully used to teach basic reading skills. Students with moderate to severe reading disorders need special help from reading specialists. Most school systems employ such specialists, and classroom teachers are able to call on them for assistance.

SPELLING DISORDERS.   It is not uncommon for students with reading problems to exhibit spelling problems as well. While not all poor spellers have difficulty reading, some of the basic motor skills needed for spelling are common ones used in reading, listening, and speaking. The treatment of spelling disorders depends on the extent to which it is associated with other psychomotor skills for a given individual. In many cases, techniques for improving spelling are tied closely to techniques used to improve basic reading and writing skills.

OCULAR-MOTOR DISORDERS.   A few students with normal visual acuity lack the ability to coordinate eye muscles properly or to process images and words into meaningful patterns or sentences. This is one reason why some students develop reading problems at an early age. Students with perceptual problems need to be diagnosed by a specialist and to receive at least some specialized help. Prescribed exercises designed to strengthen eye muscles or improve coordination have been used in many cases with success.

Some students with moderate to serious ocular-motor problems experience difficulty in handwriting. One perceptual disorder, although rare, is mirror writing. In mirror writing, students transpose letters in reverse; hence, they oftentimes appear exactly backwards. Tracing exercises can be used to help improve mild to moderate handwriting disorders. Students with more severe disorders often have to be taught to use the typewriter.

MATHEMATICS DISORDERS.   Many students with visual-spatial disorders have difficulty learning basic mathematical skills. Others have difficulty thinking in quantitative or abstract terms. These skills, of course, are also basic to science and are of particular concern to science teachers. Severe cases of mathematics dysfunction caused by brain damage are referred to as dyscalculia. Hands-on, manipulative materials have been used successfully in teaching quantitative skills and concepts to many students with mathematics disorders. It is important to pace this instruction carefully and to emphasize the *process* necessary in solving problems. Most science programs offer excellent opportunities for students to learn through direct experience skills and processes that relate to basic understanding in mathematics. With both reading and mathematics, science can be used as a ''medium'' or ''vehicle'' through which basic skills can be taught.

SPECIFIC
STRATEGIES FOR
HELPING
STUDENTS WITH
LEARNING
DISABILITIES

The following suggestions may be of particular value to science teachers when working with students with learning disabilities.

- Determine the way the student can learn best, then expose the individual to science in this fashion; for example, some learn best visually, some best through auditory means, and still others best through the use of manipulatives.
- Utilize peer tutoring where an advanced student can summarize the material for the handicapped student.
- Use alternative forms of evaluation if necessary, such as oral or motor tests.
- Tape record sections from the textbook and use these to reinforce students who have reading difficulties. As the student reads, he or she can listen to the tape.
- Highlight key concepts in the text *after* the end of lessons or activities.
- Use educational media to demonstrate key concepts and processes in science.
- Establish learning centers where students can interact with manipulative materials.

The development of basic learning skills is of particular importance when working with students who have learning disabilities. Science is a subject that allows this to take place in a natural way. For this and other reasons, science teachers are in an excellent position to help these students become successful in school. The development of language skills parallels closely the development of basic science skills.

Mental Handicaps

Approximately three out of every one hundred students in our schools are mentally retarded. While the degree of retardation varies greatly, most of these individuals have difficulty becoming adaptive members in society and need special attention. Mental retardation is usually associated with factors that affect the normal development of children. Chromosomal abnormalities such as Down's Syndrome (mongolism) and genetically caused metabolic disorders such as phenylketonuria are known causes of retardation. The classroom teacher seldom, if ever, works with these students. Brain injuries, serious childhood diseases, and selected socioeconomic factors are among other common causes of mental retardation.

CLASSIFICATION

As with all disorders, it is often difficult and misleading to place mentally handicapped individuals into categories. Although controversial, scores on IQ tests are still widely used to classify mentally retarded individuals.

Traditionally, individuals with IQ scores below 20 have been regarded as profoundly retarded. At best, these individuals are capable of learning a few ambulatory skills such as feeding and toileting, but rarely are they capable of learning to speak, and in practically all cases they are incapable of self-care and require permanent nursing care.

Individuals with IQ scores between 20 and 35 are classified as severely mentally retarded. Much of their education is directed toward custodial training and the development of self-help skills. While these individuals need permanent care as adults, some are capable of performing chores and other simple tasks.

Individuals with IQ scores ranging from 35 to 65 are classified as moderately retarded or trainable mentally handicapped (TMH). These youngsters are usually capable of school learning up to approximately the third grade level, and special schools or classes are necessary. As adults, some moderately retarded individuals are capable of employment in supervised unskilled occupations.

Mildly retarded or educable mentally handicapped (EMH) individuals are those with IQs ranging from 60 to 75. It is common practice in some school systems to consider individuals with IQs between 75 and 85 as borderline mentally handicapped. Mildly retarded individuals are capable of learning academic skills commonly taught in the middle grades, with borderline students being able to handle some high school level work. Most mildly retarded individuals are potentially capable of vocational, personal, and marital independence in adulthood. It is important that they lose their identification as mildly retarded during adulthood.

Classifying students on the basis of IQ scores has some serious drawbacks. Some students who have not been taught standard English reading skills, for example, will test low on standardized tests, yet function normally in a verbal setting. Foreign students, along with those from very low socioeconomic backgrounds, also sometimes test low and therefore stand a chance of being improperly labeled. When working with students who have been classified as mentally handicapped, it is always important to look for additional signs that represent their ability to learn. An alert teacher is often in a position to detect a specific physical handicap or learning disability that is the cause of a learning difficulty rather than mental retardation. It is also important to note that the mildly mentally handicapped (or EMH) students are usually the only group of mentally handicapped students found in regular classes.

SCIENCE AND THE MENTALLY HANDICAPPED

Recently, there has been considerable interest in using science as a vehicle for teaching basic skills to mentally retarded students. Science offers opportunities for concrete, hands-on experiences that lead to opportunities for abstract thinking, language development, and the acquisition of quantitative skills. With this in mind, science becomes a particularly appropriate subject for mentally handicapped students, both in special schools or classes, or in situations where mildly retarded students are partially or completely mainstreamed with regular classes.

The Biological Sciences Curriculum Study has developed three programs that have been successfully used with special students. ME NOW is a program in science and health for students between the ages of ten and thirteen. ME AND MY ENVIRONMENT is an environmental science program for the mildly mentally handicapped student between the ages of thirteen and sixteen. ME IN THE FUTURE is a course dealing with careers and decision-making processes relative to the future. ME NOW is a self-image building program that focuses upon four content areas: digestion and circulation; respiration and body wastes; movement, support, and sensory perception; and growth and development. The program contains teacher's guides (these guides enable teachers with little or no science background to use the program), daylight slides, posters and pictures, filmloops, worksheets, models, laboratory supplies, and evaluation materials. The following features of the program exemplify a special orientation that is particularly suitable for mildly mentally retarded students:

- Focus on "me" as the natural entry point and primary target of interest
- Nondependence on vocabulary and reading ability, although language skills emerge
- Development of activities in small, discrete, slower paced units that build upon or reinforce skills
- Attention and special help to individual needs and differences
- Communication of basic ideas in a simple, straightforward, uncluttered manner
- A balance between motivational activities and presentation of detailed information
- Focus on the mastery of *useful* or relevant concepts
- Development of a sense of success and personal accomplishment

Likewise, ME AND MY ENVIRONMENT uses curriculum guides, audiovisual materials, games, posters, booklets, and other laboratory equipment to teach problem-solving skills and basic concepts in science. In this program, fundamental environmental topics comprise the five basic units of the curriculum. The major objectives of this program are:

- Develop in each child a sense of identity as a person who has some degree of control over, and who can act on, his or her environment
- Develop in each child a success syndrome
- Develop in each child an interest that could become a hobby or avocation over a lifetime

- Develop in each child a sense of relationship and empathy with other things
- Develop in each child an understanding of conditions that will lead to a sense of responsibility for the environment and to actions that protect or improve it

The focus and major objectives of these two programs communicate the basic orientation that is needed with mentally handicapped students. At present, additional programs in science are being developed to meet the needs of this group of students who in the past have not had many opportunities to learn science. Additional research on how mentally handicapped students learn will no doubt help science teachers understand more clearly how all students can learn science more effectively and efficiently.

Behavioral Disorders

Another area of exceptionality is referred to as behavioral disorders. This group of students includes those who are emotionally disturbed or are socially maladjusted. Usually, this behavior is chronic and may require special diagnosis and treatment by experts. It is often difficult, however, to categorize many students with behavioral disorders. For example, if a student from a very poor family steals something, we might tend to consider that individual as socially maladjusted, concluding that this individual does not understand that members of our society must work in order to purchase goods and services. If a youngster from an affluent home, on the other hand, steals the same thing, we would tend to suggest that the individual is emotionally disturbed—that he or she performed such an act as a means of getting attention from the parents or peer group.

TYPES OF BEHAVIORAL DISORDERS

When teachers deal with chronic behavioral disorders among students, it is helpful in most cases to identify major characteristics associated with the problem. Quay[6] has developed a classification system that can be helpful to educators. The four dimensions of Quay's classification are listed below and include major characteristics of each category:

Conduct Disorder—This kind of behavior includes attention-seeking devices such as boisterousness, rudeness, and both physical and verbal aggression. Many students who display these kinds of behaviors are hyperactive and require physical restraint from time to time.

---

[6]H. C. Quay, "Dimensions of Problem Behavior and Educational Programming," in P. S. Graubard (Ed.), *Children Against Schools*, Chicago: Follett, 1972.

Anxious-Withdrawn—In contrast to conduct disorders, students displaying these kinds of behaviors are frequently "underactive." They often possess feelings of inferiority, lack self-confidence, and are commonly fearful or anxious concerning school and learning.

Inadequate-Immature—Students in this category often lack interest in school work. They are frequently lazy, sluggish, and have difficulty concentrating. They are prone to daydream, play with objects in class, or mark furniture.

Socialized Delinquent—Behavior in this dimension is characterized by truancy, failure to abide by middle-class ethics, and loyalty to group delinquent acts. While these students are capable of subscribing to acceptable codes of behavior, they prefer to follow the standards set by delinquent peer groups and gang organizations.

It is important for teachers to realize that students with behavioral disorders do not usually fit neatly into a single category. Rather, they frequently exhibit a combination of the behavior types discussed by Quay. Furthermore, there are other, more serious, disorders that are not covered by Quay's system. It is, nevertheless, helpful for teachers to understand these kinds of disorders and to develop a variety of techniques suitable for the various categories of behavior.

DEALING WITH BEHAVIORAL DISORDERS IN THE REGULAR CLASSROOM

All teachers must deal at one time or other with students who display certain types or combinations of behavioral disorders. In many cases, outside help is necessary. In severe cases, it is usually necessary to temporarily remove disruptive students from class, make arrangements for remediation or special assistance, and then gradually bring such students back to the regular classroom. The following procedures are appropriate in most cases and can serve to assist the classroom teacher in dealing with students who exhibit inappropriate or delinquent behavior.

IDENTIFYING BEHAVIORAL DISORDERS. Early in the school year, teachers should carefully observe the behavior of all students. Those thought to have behavioral disorders should be identified and watched more closely. The teacher should keep a record of unusual behaviors and note the frequency of these displays.

Some school systems regularly administer standardized tests in order to diagnose and predict the extent to which various individuals possess behavioral problems. Two such instruments that have been used for diagnosis and prediction are the Glueck Prediction Scale and the California Test of Personality. A drawback with these and other instruments is that they sometimes predict behaviors that do not in fact actually follow. In most cases, however, testing by trained counselors or school psychologists is a good way to identify problems and to plan for dealing with these problems. It is important to remember that the most valid measure from an educational standpoint is the observation and records of the teacher. These observations, when combined with external assessments from counselors, parents, peers, and supervisors, serve as an excellent base of information on which to make decisions.

UNDERSTANDING THE CAUSES OF BEHAVIORAL DISORDERS.   Aberrant behavior can be divided into two categories: biological and environmental. Some of the most severe types of behavioral disorders are a result of genetic factors. Schizophrenia, for example, has been found to occur in some families more frequently than in others. In cases where monozygotic twins have been studied, data show that when one twin has been diagnosed as having schizophrenia chances are quite high that the other twin has the same condition. Extreme cases of hyperactivity and central nervous system (CNS) dysfunctions are frequently linked to physiological disorders. In other cases, biologically mediated disorders may also stem from chronic physical diseases.

Environmental or psychological disturbances are caused by interactions between individuals and other significant people in their lives. Students who are extremely shy, overanxious, or disinterested often suffer from inadequate home environments. The home may lack intellectual stimulation, emotional security, adequate supervision, or proper health care.

Theorists such as Carl Rogers and Eric Berne believe that many behavioral disorders stem from the lack of healthy emotional development during childhood. This school of thought holds that when children fail to establish a personal identity they often carry with them later in life unconscious feelings of inadequacy, confusion, and low self-esteem. From this perspective, it is the incongruence between "self" and "experience" that accounts for the emotional disturbance of many young people in our schools. It is on this basis that Carl Rogers and others have called for the major aim of education to be that of promoting self-identity and self-actualization. Other psychologists such as B. F. Skinner believe that maladaptive behaviors, like other behaviors, are learned and that when they are manifested it is due to the fact that appropriate learning has not taken place.

HELPING STUDENTS WITH BEHAVIORAL DISORDERS IN THE REGULAR CLASSROOM.   Most special educators agree that students with serious or highly disruptive behavioral disorders should be moved out of the regular class for remediation and then gradually brought back. Students with moderate or mild disorders can often be dealt with more successfully when allowed to remain in the regular classroom. Dealing with such students requires additional patience and skill on the part of already busy classroom teachers. The rewards, however, are great, and many students can be taught with the help of skilled teachers to make necessary adjustments for daily living in our society.

Teachers can take several approaches to help students with behavioral disorders improve classroom performance. One approach involves implementing the recommended practices of Carl Rogers, an approach whereby the curriculum becomes student-centered and the teacher strives to help the student become a self-directed learner. With many students of this type, the most important aspect of teaching becomes that of demonstrating understanding and convincing them that they can be successful. With this approach, the teacher allows students some choice in selecting what they study. As students begin to experience success, the teacher can then guide individuals to other appropriate learning activities. For these students the anxiety-producing climate of lesson tasks, assigned readings, lectures, tests, and teacher criticism give way to an environment where students are allowed to engage in activities that are relevant to both their emotional and cognitive needs. The role of the teacher with such students, therefore, becomes one of promoting strong interpersonal relations and self-acceptance. Science is an especially excellent vehicle for this approach. Independent projects and hands-on activities are a means through which students can experience concrete learning and attain tangible rewards.

Other human relations models can be applied to students with behavioral disorders. In addition to the Carkhuff Model (which applies to many of the ideas of Rogers) discussed in Chapter 2, Transactional Analysis (TA) and Glasser's Reality Therapy (RT) are also appropriate. One of the goals of TA is to help individuals develop feelings of "I'm OK." Since many students with behavioral disorders are "I'm not OK" individuals, TA can be used to elevate self-esteem and build self-confidence. Similarly, RT can be used to help students become more responsible for their own actions. Often, behavioral disorders are associated with students who demonstrate low levels of maturity. By allowing students to set goals and follow through with plans they have developed, the teacher is able to facilitate growth in maturity. As stated, the models discussed in Chapter 2 have special implications for working with students who demonstrate many of the most common behavioral disorders.

Another approach used by classroom teachers to deal with students with behavioral disorders is known as behavior modification. Rather than focusing on diagnosing students, this method involves attempts to suppress or extinguish inappropriate behaviors that occur in the classroom by substituting and reinforcing more desirable behaviors. For example, when a student brings a toy to class to play with, a piece of science equipment can be substituted for the toy. As the student learns to use the new piece of equipment appropriately, he or she is rewarded by the teacher. Another example is that of getting students in their seats. Demonstrating to students that they can participate in an interesting educational game *when* they are seated and quiet serves as incentive and reinforcement for this kind of behavior. A key to behavior modification is that one kind of behavior actually be substituted for another. Asking students to sit passively in their seats is not an *active* behavior for which reinforcement can be given. When one type of active participation (i.e., playing a game) is substituted for another kind of behavior (i.e., running around the room), the teacher can modify and hence to some extent control the activities of students.

Token reinforcement contingent upon academic behavior has been used successfully to improve scholastic performance in several school systems. Special awards, extra privileges, or points added to a final grade are examples of extrinsic rewards that often encourage immature students to exhibit desirable behaviors. As students become successful and more mature, teachers can promote a shift to intrinsic reward systems. For example, by learning to be a good listener students discover that they become more popular with other students. Similarly, by learning to read well students discover that they can understand new material with greater ease. Eventually, this feeling of self-satisfaction can take the place of token, more superficial rewards.

In addition to working with students on an individual basis, many group activities can be used to help change inappropriate behavior. When students are allowed to establish goals jointly and are given opportunities to implement and evaluate their activities, a sense of self-control emerges that is conducive to academic growth. In this setting much of the reinforcement is governed by the peer group, a source of control that is often more potent than the teacher. Most educators who work with behavioral disorders agree that in the long run positive reinforcement is superior to punishment. Again, however, it is important to recognize that when the behavior of such a student becomes so disruptive that other members of the class cannot function normally, the student should be removed from the group temporarily until he or she can behave appropriately.

The amount of control, support, and consistency demonstrated by the teacher influences the kind of climate found in any classroom. A climate conducive to learning by students with behavioral disorders is usually the same kind of climate that facilitates efficient learning by all students.

Gifted and Talented Students in Science

Students with superior intellectual ability are frequently referred to as *gifted* or *talented*. Those who are unusually precocious and possess exceptionally high intelligence or creativity are considered in the gifted cate-

**RESEARCH
REPORT**

Important
Competencies
Needed by
Teachers of
Students with
Behavioral
Disorders

Bullock and Whelan[7] completed a study in which experts ranked the important competencies needed by teachers of students with behavior disorders. The twelve items below represent the final ranking of these items:

1. A knowledge or understanding of the advantages of providing experiences in which pupils can be successful.

2. A knowledge or understanding of the education and psychology of various types of exceptional children.

3. The ability to tolerate antisocial behavior, particularly when it is directed toward authority.

4. A knowledge or understanding of basic human physical and psychological needs.

5. A knowledge or understanding of techniques adaptable to classroom situations for relieving tensions and promoting good mental health.

6. A knowledge or understanding of the advantages of flexibility of school programs and schedules to permit individual adjustment and development.

7. The ability to establish "limits" for social control (neither overprotective nor overrestrictive).

8. The ability to develop self-imposed social control within the pupils.

9. The ability to establish and maintain good working relations with other professional workers, such as social workers and psychological personnel.

10. The ability to teach remedial reading.

11. The ability to avoid identical, stereotyped demands of maladjusted pupils.

12. A knowledge or understanding of curriculum and methods of teaching the "normal" pupil.

It is interesting to note that most of these competencies are skills that regular classroom teachers can use to improve the behavior of all students. These competencies, of course, are directed specifically toward dealing with students with behavioral disorders and demonstrate the importance of establishing sound human relations in the classroom.

[7]L. Bullock and R. Whelan, "Competencies Needed by Teachers of the Emotionally Disturbed and Socially Maladjusted: A Comparison," *Exceptional Children*, 31, (1971):7.

gory. According to the U.S. Office of Education, this group is comprised of approximately the top 3 percent of the population in this country. Using the same classification system, students who rank within the top 15 to 20 percent of the general school population and who are considered strong candidates for four-year colleges or universities are considered talented. Definitions of giftedness and talentedness vary, of course, as do methods for identifying these students.

RECOGNIZING
THE GIFTED AND
TALENTED

School systems and teachers who are committed to providing special programs or enrichment activities for gifted and talented students face the challenging task of identifying these individuals. Gifted or talented students are frequently those who:

- Are more mature than the average student
- Learn rapidly and easily
- Read rapidly and recall what they have read
- Go beyond class discussions and assignments in search of additional information
- Recognize quickly important concepts, principles, and relationships and can think readily at high levels of abstraction
- Ask stimulating, high-level questions
- Are creative and self-directed
- Possess outstanding leadership capabilities
- Volunteer to do extra-class projects and engage in extra-school activities
- Possess large working vocabularies and can express themselves well in written form
- Possess or display special talents in areas such as art and music

Most school systems have developed ways of selecting students for gifted and talented programs, and several criteria are used to identify these students.

TEACHER OBSERVATION AND RECOMMENDATION. While many tests and other standardized procedures are helpful in identifying gifted and talented students, one of the most valid means is through careful observation by teachers. Students who possess a combination of the behaviors previously mentioned can be identified by teachers who are on the lookout for gifted and talented individuals. Many school systems ask teachers for recommendations at the end of each school year of students who may qualify for special programs or enrichment activities

DEMONSTRATION OF PAST ACHIEVEMENT. Another method of identifying gifted and talented students is to look carefully at the past performance of students. Students who consistently perform high in science and/or mathematics are often those who need to be placed in special programs designed to challenge their high capacity for achievement or to enrich the basic curriculum they are following.

PERFORMANCE ON INTELLIGENCE TESTS. Many group or individual tests of general intelligence are available for use by school systems for determining which students potentially qualify as gifted and talented. In some schools, cutoff scores such as 130 for gifted and 115 to 120 for talented are used. Educators have found that selection procedures are more valid and fair when other criteria are used in addition to IQ scores.

PERFORMANCE ON CREATIVITY TESTS. There are several tests that measure divergent thinking and other factors associated with creativity. While research shows a positive correlation between creativity and IQ, psychologists agree that there are many aspects of creativity that are independent of IQ. Many gifted and talented programs place heavy emphasis on the identification and continued development of creativity.

NOMINATION BY PARENTS. As has already been mentioned, most school systems have attempted to broaden the base of students from which the gifted and talented are identified. Many such school systems allow parents to nominate and provide additional information about their children that may be useful in placing students in appropriate programs. This has the advantage of identifying the special talents and abilities of some students that would otherwise possibly go unnoticed. The drawback to this method, as one might suspect, is that the pool of applicants is often quite large since many parents in this country are convinced that their children are gifted.

When teachers or school systems attempt to recognize gifted and talented students, it is important not to overlook youngsters who are quiet or shy, who are physically handicapped, or who are members of economically depressed groups. Often, students from these groups lack verbal skills or do not have much encouragement from home. Yet, in instances where individual teachers or school systems have made a special effort to identify such students, many gifted and talented individuals have been found in such groups. Most school systems and state departments of education have specialists who can help identify these students.

PROGRAMS FOR
THE GIFTED AND
TALENTED

There are many approaches for dealing with gifted and talented students. Special schools such as the Bronx High School of Science[8] and the North Carolina High School of Science and Mathematics[9] exist for students with outstanding ability in science and related fields. Many universities have programs that allow local students to take courses while still in high school. The National Science Foundation sponsors summer courses in

[8]The Bronx High School of Science, 75 West 205th Street, New York, N.Y.
[9]The North Carolina School of Science and Mathematics, West Club Boulevard and Broad Street, Durham, N.C. 27705.

The Bronx High School of Science is one of the nation's best known schools for gifted and talented students.

which talented high school students study with scientists during the summer. Many states also sponsor special schools in the summer in which outstanding students spend several weeks on a college campus taking special enrichment courses in science, mathematics, art, and other subjects. In some cases, students begin college work early, which is the suggestion of Julian Stanley who directs the Johns Hopkins University's Study of Mathematically Precocious Youth.[10]

The College Entrance Examination Board (CEEB) and the Educational Testing Service (ETS) jointly sponsor the Advanced Placement Program.[11] This program covers thirteen subject areas, including biology, chemistry, and physics. Under Advanced Placement (AP) programs, students can take college-level science courses during the last two years of high school. At the end of each AP course, students take a standardized examination administered by ETS. With satisfactory scores, students are eligible to receive college credit for introductory courses in biology, chemistry, or physics. This is an excellent program for students who wish to stay at home and continue in high school but are ready to take college-level courses in some subject areas. The Advanced Placement Program has grown in popularity during recent years as many states and individual school systems have given increased attention to gifted and talented students.

MAINSTREAMING THE GIFTED AND TALENTED

In addition to the many special programs that exist for gifted and talented students, other things can be done in conjunction with the regular science class. Many of the techniques for individualizing instruction that are dis-

---

[10]Dr. Julian Stanley, Study of Mathematically Precocious Youth, The Johns Hopkins University, Baltimore, Md.
[11]Advanced Placement Program, College Entrance Examination Board, 888 Seventh Avenue, New York, N.Y. 10019.

cussed in Chapter 8 are appropriate. The following methods can be used with gifted and talented (G&T) students in regular classes:

- Science teachers should attempt to identify G&T students at the beginning of the school year. Several or all of the criteria previously discussed in this chapter can be used.
- G&T students should be encouraged to engage in enrichment activities that correspond to their areas of special interest and ability.
- Additional reading materials should be readily available for use by G&T

RESEARCH REPORT

Teachers for the Gifted

David Kuhn[12] of Duke University has reported several studies that underscore the importance of the teacher in working with gifted and talented students. Not only should science teachers working with these students have strong academic backgrounds and high intellectual ability, but they should also be flexible, enterprising, and open to young people who have divergent views and who approach learning in many ways.

Kuhn Cites Paul Brandwein[13] who has worked many years with gifted students:

Investigations of the career commitments of the gifted in science clearly indicate that a key figure was significant in their choice of a career in science. The prime period of influence of this key figure has been found to occur in the early years of the gifted child, in the junior and senior high-school years, mainly in the former.

Kuhn also cites the work of Magary and Freehill[14] with biographies of the gifted, in which they identified important characteristics of influential teachers:

These studies indicate that the gifted prefer to be taught by teachers who have qualities most like their own; for example, high intellect, flexibility, humane motives, a sense of humor, curiosity, personal magnetism, sensitivity to others, widely varying interests, receptivity to help from other people, enthusiasm for self-improvement, outstanding scholarship, and excellent organization, from which they . . . can depart at any time.

There is renewed interest in this country in trying to meet the needs of *all* students in our schools. This is also a renewed national commitment to academic excellence. By helping our gifted and talented students, many educators feel that we can move closer to realizing these important educational goals.

[12]David J. Kuhn, "Giving the Gifted Their Due," *The Science Teacher*, 46, 2 (1979):32–34.
[13]Paul Brandwein, "Teaching Gifted Children Science in Grades Seven Through Twelve," California State Department of Education, Sacramento, 1975. ERIC No. ED 112632.
[14]J. Magary and F. Freehill, "Critical Questions and Answers Relating to School and Society in the Education of the Gifted," *The Gifted Child Quarterly*, 16, 3 (1972):185–194.

students. College-level textbooks, journals, and books on specialized topics should be available in the school library or in the classroom.

- G&T students should be encouraged to engage in independent research projects and to do additional laboratory activities. These activities can be done while the teacher works with slower learners, poor readers, or students who need more direct supervision; or they can be done after school or at home.

- G&T students who wish to participate should be used as tutors for other students. In some school systems, mature high school students are allowed to visit elementary schools to assist teachers with science lessons. These programs have proved to be very successful.

- In many schools, G&T students are allowed to serve as laboratory or teaching assistants and, in some cases, recceve credit for doing so. Not only do the students learn to prepare chemical solutions, set up equipment, and assist in the general planning needed for such work, but they also learn to perfect certain laboratory skills that are important to those who wish to enter fields of science and technology.

- Science teachers should facilitate the use of resource people in the community. Arrangements should be made for G&T students to work with local scientists, engineers, mathematicians, and other nearby specialists.

- Parents of G&T students also provide a rich source of help. They are often happy to assist with science club activities, special tours, or field trips. Parent organizations such as the PTA, the PTO, or other civic groups are often willing to provice money for extra equipment, enrichment activities, science awards, or scholarships.

- G&T students should be encouraged to participate in such activities as the Future Scientists of America Club (sponsored by the National Science Teachers Association), the Junior Science and Humanities Symposium (Sponsored by the U.S. Army), the Junior Academy of Science (sponsored by state academies of science), the Junior Engineering Technical Society (JETS), the Westinghouse Talent Search, and local and state science fairs.

These and other approaches can be used to cultivate the science talent in our middle and secondary schools. It is from this pool of talent that many of our future scientists, engineers, physicians, and leaders will come. The science teacher has a key in nurturing this talent, and, although working with any student can be professionally rewarding, for many teachers working with the gifted and talented is what makes science teaching such an exciting profession.

In Perspective

Wait! Don't throw up your hands in despair! Being asked to provide for students with various kinds of exceptionalities is not just one more thing that classroom teachers are being asked to do. An analysis of the nature and scope of the problem and the complications for science teaching should help put the problem in proper perspective!

First, look back at Table 10.1 on page 385. The percentage of the population having the various types of exceptionality is relatively small. Also remember that severely handicapped students are seldom found in regular classes. The result is that regular classes more often than not contain only one or two mildly handicapped students at the most. In other words, regular classroom teachers should not expect to have a class made up mostly of handicapped students. This is the job of special education, which usually involves classes with fewer students and teachers with special training to handle these problems.

Second, P.L. 94–142 requires not only that handicapped students be placed in the least restrictive environment but also that schools to provide assistance to teachers who have handicapped students in their classes. This includes assistance in preparing an IEP for the student and providing support personnel, equipment, and supplies.

Third, efforts to provide for the educational needs of a special group often result in strategies and materials that are equally effective with regular students. Films, filmstrips, drawings, and other visuals used with hearing-impaired students also work well with regular students. Likewise, the models and tactiles designed for visually handicapped students can be used with regular students. In fact, science programs for the handicapped students that emphasize hands-on experience and multisensory learning also make sense with regular students. Thus, science teachers who regularly use laboratory work and a wide variety of media should find less modification needed for handicapped students than in cases where lecture and class discussion are the primary means of instruction.

Fourth, and most important, students with handicaps or students who are classified as gifted and talented, although different in some ways, also possess many commonalities. When we first met a person with an exceptionality, we may be tempted to concentrate on the person's blindness or superior talent in music. This is much the same experience many of us have in learning to know people from racial groups or ethnic backgrounds different from our own. Once we get acquainted, these factors usually become less and less obvious. Instead, their personalities, interests, and abilities are what we remember. Once a teacher has had the opportunity to work with students possessing various kinds of exceptionality, the job of providing for their unique needs should take on manageable dimensions. And many teachers have found this to be one of the most rewarding parts of their profession.

Review Questions   1. In the chapter opener, an account by Dr. Nansie Sharpless describes some of the joys and difficulties she encountered during her formal edu-

cation. What were the major problems she faced and how did she overcome them?

2. List the seven areas of handicappedness that are officially recognized
by the U.S. government.

3. Briefly describe P.L. 94–142 and outline the major implications it has
for public school teachers in science.

4. What is meant by the cascade system? How can this model be helpful
to schools in determining the best learning environment for handicapped
students?

5. What is an IEP? What are the major components of an IEP?

6. There are certain things science teachers should be aware of when
working with any handicapped student. List these considerations and
discuss how they can help improve the learning environment for both
teacher and students.

7. Define what is meant by "gifted" and "talented." Outline several
techniques that can be helpful when working with these students.

8. List five methods that have been successfully used to teach science to
blind or visually impaired students.

9. Name at least five resources that are available for science teachers and
that can be used to help better meet the needs of handicapped students.

10. Students with behavioral disorders commonly present problems for
science teachers. What are some promising techniques for dealing with
these students in science classes?

For Application and Analysis

1. Select a science topic, such as plate tectonics or animal diversity, from
a secondary school science course. Make a list of strategies and materials that could be used to teach the topic to students with the various
exceptionalities listed in Table 10.1 on page 385. Which of these might
also be effectively used with regular students?

2. Make an inventory of the physical barriers in a science classroom
and/or laboratory that might cause problems in trying to teach students
with various kinds of handicaps. Propose alternative ways for removing these barriers. For example, measure the amount of force required
to open the classroom door. Can this door be opened easily by a
student in a wheelchair or using a walker? If not, how can the door be
modified? In making your inventory, don't overlook potential safety
hazards to handicapped students.

3. If possible, interview a handicapped or gifted and talented secondary
science student. In conducting your interview, remember the person
has feelings and goals just as you do. Rather than concentrate on the
person's handicaps and ask questions such as, "What does it feel like
to be blind?", or "Are there times you miss playing basketball?," ask
about the person's interests, hobbies, school activities, and future
plans.

References

Brown, Dean R. "Teaching Science to Handicapped Students: Learning By Doing." *What Research Says to the Science Teacher* (M. B. Rowe, Ed.), Vol. II. Washington, D.C.: National Science Teachers Association, 1979.

This chapter is an excellent review of research dealing with how to teach handicapped students. The author demonstrates why science activities are effective with students who learn in ways that are sometimes different from students who have full use of all their senses.

Coble, Charles R., Paul B. Hounshell, and Anne H. Adams. *Mainstreaming Science and Mathematics: Special Ideas and Activities for the Whole Class.* Santa Monica, Calif.: Goodyear Publishing Company, Inc., 1977.

Although directed primarily toward the elementary school classroom, many of the ideas and activities will also work with mainstreamed students in middle and junior high school science classes.

Hoffman, Helenmarie H., and Kenneth S. Ricker. *Science Education and the Physically Handicapped.* Washington, D.C.: National Science Teachers Association, 1979.

This is perhaps the most complete collection of articles to date dealing with science for physically handicapped students. This publication deals with a wide range of topics and contains many activities that have been used by experienced teachers.

Jordan, June B. (Ed.). *Exceptional Students in Secondary Schools.* Reston, Va.: The Council for Exceptional Children, 1978.

This book covers all areas of exceptionality in depth and suggests practical methods for meeting the needs of both handicapped and gifted students.

Hadary, Doris E., and Susan Hadary Cohen. *Laboratory Science and Art for Blind, Deaf, and Emotionally Disturbed Children: A Mainstreaming Approach.* Baltimore, Md.: University Park Press, 1978.

This publication contains a collection of activities and teaching methods useful for handicapped students of all ages.

Turnbull, Ann P., Bonnie B. Strickland, and John C. Brantley. *Developing and Implementing Individualized Education Programs.* Columbus, Ohio: Charles E. Merrill Publishing Company, 1978.

This book contains an extensive collection of IEPs with many suggestions for developing individualized programs for exceptional students.

CHAPTER 11

Dealing with Controversial and Contemporary Topics

INHERIT THE WIND

ACT ONE

Scene One

In and around the Hillsboro Courthouse. The foreground is the actual courtroom, with jury box, judge's bench, a raised witness chair and a scattering of trial-scarred chairs and counsel tables. The back wall of the courtroom, from waist-level up, is non-existent. In full stage, at a raked elevation, is the courthouse square and the Main Street of Hillsboro, including a practical drug store and dry-goods store.

It is an hour after dawn on a July day that promises to be a scorcher.

RACHEL *enters. She is twenty-two, pretty, but not beautiful. She wears a cotton summer dress. She carries a small composition-paper suitcase. There is a tense, distraught air about her. She may have been crying. She looks about nervously, as if she doesn't want to be seen. She bumps into a chair, and jumps, as if somebody had touched her. The courtroom is strange ground to her. Unsure, she looks about. Then, with resolution, she crosses and touches the empty jury-box.*

RACHEL *(tentatively, calling).* Mr. Meeker . . . ?

(After a pause, MR. MEEKER, *the bailiff, enters. There is no collar on his shirt; his hair is tousled, and there is shaving soap on his face, which he is wiping off with a towel as he enters.)*

MEEKER *(a little irritably).* Who is it? *(Surprised)* Why, hello, Rachel. 'Scuse the way I look. *(He wipes the soap out of his ear. Then he notices her suitcase.)* Not goin' away, are you? Excitement's just startin'.

RACHEL *(earnestly).* Mr. Meeker, don't let my father know I came here.

MEEKER *(shrugs).* The Reverend don't tell me his business. Don't know why I should tell him mine.

RACHEL. I want to see Bert Cates. Is he all right?

MEEKER. Don't know why he shouldn't be. I always figured the safest place in the world is a jail.

RACHEL. Can I go down and see him?

MEEKER. Ain't a very proper place for a minister's daughter.

RACHEL. I only want to see him for a minute.

MEEKER. Sit down, Rachel. I'll bring him up. You can talk to him right here in the courtroom. (RACHEL *sits in one of the stiff wooden chairs.* MEEKER *starts out, then pauses.*) Long as I've been bailiff here, we've never had nothin' but drunks, vagrants, couple of chicken thieves. (*A little dreamily*) Our best catch was that fella from Minnesota that chopped up his wife; we had to extradite him. (*Shakes his head.*) Seems kinda queer havin' a school-teacher in our jail. (*Shrugs.*) Might improve the writin' on the walls.

(MEEKER *goes out. Nervously,* RACHEL *looks around at the cold, official furnishings of the courtroom.* MEEKER *returns to the courtroom, followed by* BERT CATES. CATES *is a pale, thin young man of twenty-four. He is quiet, shy, well-mannered, not particularly good-looking.* RACHEL *and* CATES *face each other expressionlessly, without speaking.* MEEKER *pauses in the doorway.*)

MEEKER. I'll leave you two alone to talk. Don't run off, Bert.

(MEEKER *goes out.* RACHEL *and* CATES *look at each other.*)

RACHEL. Hello, Bert.

CATES. Rache, I told you not to come here.

RACHEL. I couldn't help it. Nobody saw me. Mr. Meeker won't tell. (*Troubled.*) I keep thinking of you, locked up here—

CATES (*trying to cheer her up*). You know something funny? The food's better than the boarding house. And you'd better not tell anybody how cool it is down here, or we'll have a crime wave every summer.

RACHEL. I stopped by your place and picked up some of your things. A clean shirt, your best tie, some handkerchiefs.

CATES. Thanks.

RACHEL (*rushing to him*). Bert, why don't you tell 'em it was all a joke? Tell 'em you didn't mean to break a law, and you won't do it again!

CATES. I suppose everybody's all steamed up about Brady coming.

RACHEL. He's coming in on a special train out of Chattanooga. Pa's going to the station to meet him. Everybody is!

CATES. Strike up the band.

RACHEL. Bert, it's still not too late. Why can't you admit you're wrong? If the biggest man in the country—next to the President, maybe—if Matthew Harrison Brady comes here to tell the whole world how wrong you are—

CATES. You still think I did wrong?

RACHEL. Why did you do it?

CATES. You know why I did it. I had the book in my hand, Hunter's *Civic Biology*. I opened it up, and read my sophomore science class Chapter 17, Darwin's *Origin of Species*. (RACHEL *starts to protest.*) All it says is that man wasn't just stuck here like a geranium in a flower pot; that living comes from a *long* miracle, it didn't just happen in seven days.

RACHEL. There's a law against it.

CATES. I know that.

RACHEL. Everybody says what you did is bad.

CATES. It isn't as simple as that. Good or bad, black or white, night or day. Do you know, at the top of the world the twilight is six months long?

RACHEL. But we don't live at the top of the world. We live in Hillsboro, and when the sun goes down, it's dark. And why do you try to make it different? (RACHEL *gets the shirt, tie, and handkerchiefs from the suitcase.*) Here.

CATES. Thanks Rache.

RACHEL. Why can't you be on the right side of things?

CATES. Your father's side.

July of 1925 in Dayton, Tennessee, was a hot one. Not only was the weather scorching, but the trial at the Rhea County Courthouse generated a heat of its own. A young science teacher, John Scopes, was accused of violating a Tennessee law which prohibited the teaching of evolution. Defending Scopes was Clarence Darrow, one of the country's most famous criminal lawyers. Assisting the prosecution was William Jennings Bryan, noted orator and three times an unsuccessful candidate for President of the United States. Bryan won the case but died soon after while recovering from the exhausting trial. Scopes was fined $100. It was more than thirty years later that the law was repealed under which Scopes had been convicted.

The play *Inherit the Wind* is based in part on the "monkey trial" and has been presented in theaters across the country. The movie version has been shown several times on television. For many people, the Scopes trial of the 1920s is an amusing incident, but something that couldn't happen today. Wrong! In many parts of the country, the controversy surrounding the teaching of evolution is every bit as strong as it was a half century ago.

What should schools and teachers do? It is tempting to omit controversial subjects such as evolution, sex education, and drug abuse. There are two reasons why this cannot be done; one reason is a matter of principle, and the other one of practicality.

A course in life science or biology cannot be taught without dealing with topics such as evolution or human sexuality. To do so would be to distort the science of life and to violate a basic value of science—the importance of free and open inquiry. And even though some might convince themselves that these topics should be omitted because of their controversial nature, on a practical basis they cannot. Students ask questions, and these questions often draw teachers into the discussion of controversial topics. These unplanned discussions may represent a greater danger than a well-planned and more deliberate approach.

Four general areas of problems, issues, and controversies are described in this chapter. In addition to evolution, sex and population education, drugs, and environmental and energy education, there are dozens of other areas of controversy. However, the descriptions of these four should provide a general approach for dealing with this type of material and illustrate important reasons for doing so.

The creationism-evolution debate has been in
the news off and on for many years and is likely
to be a controversial issue for years to come.

Evolution

Ever since the publication of Darwin's *Origin of Species* over a century ago,
the topic of evolution has been debated, championed, and discredited.
Textbooks describing Darwin's ideas on evolution were not widely accepted until the 1950s. Even after the Scopes trial and after anti-evolution
laws were repealed, authors and publishers of the leading biology texts
continued to include little material on evolution.

EVOLUTION IN TEXTBOOKS

During the late 1950s, several federally funded curriculum projects
brought together leading scientists and educators in an effort to upgrade
the content and quality of secondary school science textbooks. One such
group, the Biological Sciences Curriculum Study (BSCS), produced three
new textbooks that included comprehensive treatments of evolution. As
was expected, the books came under fire from pressure groups in several
parts of the country. Increased support from the scientific community,
along with newly passed laws that limited religious influence in the
schools, served to protect these newly available textbooks. Dr. Addison

Lee of the University of Texas, who was chairman of the Board of Directors of BSCS in 1972, outlined the position BSCS took on the teaching of evolution (see Figure 11.1).

Dr. Addision E. Lee, Professor of Science Education and Biology, and Director of the Science Education Center, The University of Texas at Austin, serves as Chairman of the Board of Directors of the Biological Sciences Curriculum Study. His distinguished accomplishments as science educator and biologist enable him to write with authority in support of the BSCS position on the teaching of evolution. Dr. Lee's many publications as author or editor include *Laboratory Studies in Biology* and a monograph series entitled *Research and Curriculum Development in Science Education*.

The BSCS program began in 1959 amid considerable debate about the approach to be taken in the teaching of biology: Should it be molecular, organismal, developmental, ecological, or other? Should it include one textbook or several? How much and what kind of attention to laboratory work should be given? Amidst all these debates, however, it was an early consensus that certain themes should be included in all biology programs, no matter what approach is selected, and whatever attention may be given to various details. These themes were identified and have consistently pervaded the several approaches and different materials developed by the BSCS during the past twelve years. They are:

1. Change of living things through time: evolution
2. Diversity of type and unity of pattern in living things
3. The genetic continuity of life
4. The complementarity of organism and environment

FIGURE 11.1 "The BSCS Position on the Teaching of Biology" by Addison E. Lee. (*Source:* Reprinted by permission of the authors from BSCS Newsletter, pp. 5-6, November 1972, Biological Sciences Curriculum Study, Boulder, Colorado.)

5. The biological roots of behavior
6. The complementarity of structure and function
7. Regulation and homeostasis: preservation of life in the face of change
8. Science as inquiry
9. The history of biological conceptions

It should be noted that these unifying themes were identified and accepted by a large group of distinguished scientists, science teachers, and other educators. And although members of this group represented many interests, specialities, and points of view, there was and has continued to be general agreement concerning the importance, use, and nature of these themes.

It should also be noted that evolution is not only one of the major themes but is, in fact, central among the other themes; they are interrelated, and each is particularly related to evolution.

The position of the BSCS on the importance of evolution in teaching biology has been clearly stated in both the first (1963) and second (1970) editions of the *Biology Teachers' Handbook:*

> It is no longer possible to give a complete or even a coherent account of living things without the story of evolution.
>
> On the one hand, many of the most striking characteristics of living things are *products* of the evolutionary process. We can make good sense and order of the similarities and differences among living things only by reference to their evolution. The relations of living things to the particular environments in which they live, their distribution over the surface of the earth, the comings and goings of their parts during development, even the chemistry by which they obtain energy and exchange it among their parts—all such matters find illumination and explanation, in whole or in part, from the *history* of life on earth.
>
> On the other hand, another great group of characteristics of living things can be fully understood only as the *means* and *mechanisms* by which evolution takes place. There are first, and conspicuously, the events of meiosis and fertilization, universal in sexual reproduction. It is only in terms of the contribution of these processes to the enhancement and sorting out of a vast store of heritable variations that we make sense of them. The same point applies to the complex processes that go under the name of mutation. Similarly, we see everywhere the action and consequences of natural selection, of reproductive isolation of populations, of the effects of size and chance on intrabreeding groups.
>
> Evolution, then, forms the warp and woof of modern biology. . . .

Evolution is a scientific theory in the sense that it is based on scientific data accumulated over many years and organized into a unifying idea widely accepted by modern biologists. The BSCS is concerned with any scientific theory relevant to the biological sciences that can be dealt with in terms of scientific data accumulated and organized. It is not, on the other hand, concerned with religious doctrines that are based only on faith or beliefs, nor does it consider them relevant to the teaching of biological science.

FIGURE 11.1 (*Continued*)

The BSCS program was carried through an extensive tryout period during its early development; feedback and input from hundreds of scientists and science teachers was used in the initial edition that was made available to biology teachers in the United States. A revised second edition of the three major textbooks produced has been published, and a revised third edition is nearing completion. In spite of efforts of various groups to force changes in the content of the texts by exerting pressures on textbook selection committees and on local and state governments, throughout the last twelve years the BSCS position on using the unifying themes of biology remains unchanged.[2]

FIGURE 11.1   (Continued)

A new controversy arose during 1969, however, that marked the beginning of a new series of debates between evolutionists and creationists. On October 9, 1969, a document entitled *Science Framework for California Public Schools* was presented for adoption by the State Board of Education. The document had been carefully prepared by an advisory committee appointed by the California State Board that consisted of distinguished scientists and educators. The document, which outlined a K–12 science structure for the state, was presented for review and comment in a series of conferences held in different locations throughout California. At the Board of Education meeting, one board member raised the issue of creation and was quoted as saying, "I think we would be remiss if we did not include the theory of creation along with the evolutionary theory of life."[1] Another board member stated, "I believe in the creation theory, not evolution. You people should try to find out more of a scientific background of creation..."[2] A thirteen-page statement containing the views of a Mr. Vernon L. Grose was presented to the California State Board of Education during their November meeting. This statement recommended in essence that equal time be given to the biblical version of creation when teaching about evolution. As a result of this document, changes were made in the Science Framework and were adopted by the State Board at this meeting. California's decision to require that special creation be taught alongside evolution was eventually reversed; however, a series of similar bills were either introduced or passed in several other states. While in all cases such legislation was eventually struck down by United States courts, it does demonstrate the influence of pressure groups in deciding what should be taught in biology in our schools.

The U.S. Supreme Court has held that no state policy can be justified which rests on the religious views of some of its citizens. While it is

---

[1]*Sacramento Bee,* October 10, 1969.
[2]*Los Angeles Times,* October 10, 1969.

unconstitutional for a state to "blot out" the teaching of evolution (as was earlier the case in some states) or to require that creationism described in the book of Genesis be given equal time, some states have made available on their textbook adoption list a high school biology book entitled *Biology: A Search for Order in Complexity*.[3] This textbook, written by a committee sponsored by the Creation Research Society, champions the position of special creationism. The Creation Research Society is an organization comprised of members required to possess master's or doctoral degrees in some area of science. The major beliefs of the organization are expressed as follows:

1. The Bible is the written Word of God, and because it is inspired throughout, all its assertions are historically and scientifically true in all the original autographs. To the student of nature, this means that the account of origins in Genesis is a factual presentation of simple historical truths.

2. All basic types of living things, including man, were made by direct creative acts of God during the Creation Week described in Genesis. Whatever biological changes have occurred since Creation Week have accomplished only changes within the original created kinds.

3. The great flood described in Genesis, commonly referred to as the Noachian Flood, was a historic event worldwide in its extent and effect.

4. We are an organization of Christian men of science. . . .[4]

An extensive review of *Biology: A Search for Order in Compexity*[5] was published by Simpson and Anderson in 1975. The reviewers concluded that the textbook failed to treat properly the topic of modern evolutionary thought, and that while its authors claim to give equal time to both creationism and evolution, they presented biology reminiscent of a century or more ago.

Several major scientific societies and professional organizations in science education have published position papers on the teaching of evolution. Among the most notable of these organizations are the American Association for the Advancement of Science, National Academy of Sciences, American Chemical Society, National Association of Biology Teachers, and National Science Teachers Association. The following statement is a reprint of the position taken by the National Science Teachers Association.

[3]John N. Moore and Harold Schultz Slusher (Eds.), *Biology: A Search for Order in Complexity*, Second Edition, Grand Rapids, Mich.: Zondervan Publishing House, 1974.
[4]As quoted by John A. Moore in "Creationism in California," *Daedalus* 103, 3 (1974):176.
[5]Ronald D. Simpson and Wyatt W. Anderson, "Same Song, Second Verse—A Review of Biology: A Search for Order in Complexity, Revised Edition," *The Science Teacher*, 42, 5 (1975):40–42.

Throughout his recorded history, man has been vitally concerned in finding out all that he can about his universe. He has explored it in many ways, raised questions about it, designed methods by which he could increase and organize his knowledge, and developed systems to aid him in understanding and explaining his origin, and nature, and his place in the universe. Among these systems are philosophy, religion, folklore, the arts, and science.

Science is the system of knowing about the universe through data collected by observation and controlled experimentation. As data are collected, theories are advanced to explain and account for what has been observed. The true test of a theory in science is threefold: (1) its ability to explain what has been observed; (2) its ability to predict what has not yet been observed; and (3) its ability to be tested by further experimentation and to be modified as required by the acquisition of new data.

The National Science Teachers Association upholds the right and recognizes the obligation of each individual to become informed about man's many endeavors, to understand and explain what each endeavor has contributed to mankind, and to draw his own conclusions in each area.

The National Science Teachers Association also recognizes its great obligation to that area of education dealing with science. Science education cannot treat, as science, those things not in the domain of science. It cannot deal with, as science, concepts that have been developed in other than scientific ways. Moreover, the National Science Teachers Association vigorously opposes all actions that would legislate, mandate, or coerce the inclusion in the corpus of science, including textbooks, of any theories that do not meet the threefold criteria given above.

NSTA's position on "Inclusion of Nonscience Theories in Science Instruction"

The positions taken by the other organizations are similar to the position taken by NSTA. The key point in the positions of these organizations is that creationism does not qualify as science and as such should not be included as an "alternative scientific theory" in the science curriculum. This does not mean that science teachers should avoid discussion of various interpretations of origins. Indeed, science teachers should help students understand that science is not the only way for humans to perceive meaning. Human experience also occurs through art, philosophy, religion, and many other avenues. Perhaps science educators have been guilty in the past of teaching many topics, including evolution, as dogma. Science is based on probability, not certainty, and many of the beliefs of today will change as new knowledge is found. The topic of evolution serves as an excellent reminder to all teachers that even the most cherished ideas in science should not be presented to students as final, unchangeable knowledge.

It is important, however, for science teachers to recognize that most biologists view the concept of evolution as the single most important principle of biology. In large measure, modern evolutionary thought gives meaning to all other concepts in biology. To teach biology void of this notion is to take from the discipline its foundation. The teaching of evolution, however, does not mean a teacher must try to convince students that humans evolved from simpler forms of life. Rather, more fundamental concepts including adaptation, mutation, natural selection, niche, speciation, and the unity and diversity of organisms should be focused upon. Once students understand these and other basic concepts in biology, they are equipped to deal more intelligently with questions concerning origins and to resolve personal conflicts in values that may arise.

Teachers of science can use evolution as an example of how scientific findings sometimes conflict with human values. Just as Copernicus's suggestion that the earth was not the center of the universe caused people to interpret things differently, so has Darwinism produced shifts in the way we view our origin. While it is difficult to resolve conflicts between Darwinian evolution and literal interpretation of the Bible, most science teachers and students accept the idea that science and religion operate at different ends of the spectrum of human knowledge and that the two enterprises do not necessarily conflict.

A SUMMARY OF THE EVOLUTION-CREATIONISM CONTROVERSY

Proponents of creationism claim that the teaching of evolutionary theory as the sole scientific explanation of origins is indoctrinary. Indeed, teachers do risk being indoctrinary when they fail to include in their teaching all rational views of any topic in science. The key is the word "rational." When earth science teachers discuss the shape of our planet, they do not include the "Earth is flat" theory. Similarly, when biology teachers cover human reproduction they do not give equal time to the stork theory. The reason, of course, is that the "flat earth" and "stork" theories are not rational explanations.

The same holds true for the theory of special creation. Biblical-based creationism, especially when interpreted literally, is *not* a product of science. Theories that cannot be tested and, hence, potentially falsified, fall outside the realm of science. Since there is no way to empirically prove or falsify special creation, the theory does not qualify as science.

Science teachers should be sensitive to the fact that the topic of evolution may produce conflicts with the religious views of some students. Moreover, science teachers should always be quick to help students realize that many forms of knowledge fall outside the realm of science and that science indeed possesses many limitations. Discussions among students on such issues should be allowed, and they should have the opportunity to express divergent opinions. Open and free discourse should be a distinguishing characteristic of all science classes.

RESEARCH REPORT

Tennessee "Genesis Law" Overturned

The following is an account of how the involvement of a professional science teachers organization led to repeal of a state law that would have meant that science teachers would have been required to teach the biblical version of creation in amounts equal to Darwinian evolution.[6]

The National Association of Biology Teachers' long struggle to obtain a federal court judgment against the Tennessee "Genesis Law" ended successfully on April 10 when the United States Court of Appeals for the Sixth Circuit ruled the Tennessee law unconstitutionally established a preference for the teaching of the biblical account of creation over the theory of evolution. The Court called the case a new version of "the legislative effort to suppress the theory of evolution which produced the famous Scopes Monkey Trial of 1925."

The Appeals Court ruled that the result of the Tennessee legislation was "a clearly defined preferential position for the Biblical version of creation as opposed to any account of the development of man based on scientific research and reasoning. For a state to seek to enforce such a preference by law is to seek to accomplish the very establishment of religion which the First Amendment to the Constitution of the United States squarely forbids." The Court also stated that the law was unconstitutional in other respects, and that "the District Court clearly erred in abstaining from rendering a determination of the unconstitutionality of the statute on its face." Judges George Edwards and Pierce Lively voted in the majority; Judge Anthony Celebrezze dissented on procedural grounds saying he believed the federal District Court in Tennessee should have heard the case.

At its meeting on June 15–16, 1973 the NABT Board of Directors unanimously moved to assume the role of plaintiff against the State of Tennessee in litigation challenging the constitutionality of the new "Genesis Law." On October 11 NABT formally retained Frederic S. Le Clercq, attorney at law and associate professor of law at the University of Tennessee, and instructed him to initiate a lawsuit as early as possible. Three co-plaintiffs were named: Joseph Daniel, Jr., Arthur Jones, and Larry Ray Wilder. Daniel and Jones are professors of zoology at the University of Tennessee and Wilder is a teacher in the Knoxville public schools. The suit was filed on December 28, 1973 in the United States District Court for the Middle District of Tennessee, and appellant's motion to convene a three judge court was granted.

---

[6]Special supplement to NABT *News and Views*, 1974.

But it is fallacious to suggest that biblical creationism and Darwinism are equally attractive scientific theories. This practice not only represents a misunderstanding of science, but also forces students to choose between two nonparallel theories. One is a product of religious thought, and the other of scientific thought. To accept the position that special creationism does not qualify as science is not an attempt to indoctrinate students. Rather, it is a recognition of the fact that religion and science are different ways of viewing phenomena and that creationism does not qualify as science. To help students understand this is to help them experience the true nature of science—and to prepare them to cope with a world of multiple perspectives.

Sex Education

Except for perhaps the topic of evolution, no other subject engenders as much controversy as sex education. Yet, like evolution, it is a topic that underpins and unifies the entire field of biological science. Few topics are more pervasive than this one, and few are more relevant to the interests and needs of both students and society.

WHY INCLUDE SEX-RELATED TOPICS IN THE SCIENCE CURRICULUM?

Some people are against including sex-related topics in the science curriculum. Many say, "This is a subject that should be dealt with at home or by the church." They argue that, by exposing young students to sex education, we run the risk of increasing premarital sex, teenage pregnancies, and sexually transmitted diseases. Still others object to sex education for religious reasons. They view open discourse on sex as antiscriptural

---

WHAT STUDENTS SAY

Sex Education

- Sex is something we all have interest in, but somehow most teachers find a way to avoid it.
- The thing I remember most about biology was our unit on sex education. I thought our teacher did a good job answering all our questions.
- Most kids already know a lot about sex. I don't think teachers really have that much more to teach us.
- Boy did my biology teacher really get nervous when we got to sex education. I noticed he would sweat a lot.
- The part I thought was most helpful in biology was when the doctor came and showed us different birth control devices. Believe me, that's something kids my age need to know about.
- It seems to me that spending more time on how plants and animals reproduce would be a good idea.
- At first I was real nervous when we took up the unit of human reproduction, but later on it didn't bother me. You should have seen my parents squirm when I'd mention some of the things we'd discussed at school.
- Our minister says sex education should be covered at home. Gosh, my parents would die if I brought up the subject.
- Our life science teacher had the neatest way to deal with sex education. I couldn't believe she was so relaxed. Since then I've been able to talk more freely about such things with my family.

and feel that schools are overstepping their bounds in an area where they have no right to be.

The majority of our citizenry, however, believes that at least some attention should be paid to sex-related topics in the schools. Professional educators cite the fact that little is done at home or in the church to educate young people on this topic, and most feel strongly that it is a responsibility of the schools to deal with important aspects of sex education. The following reasons are given in support of sex-related topics being included in the science curriculum:

1. Reproduction is a Basic Function of Life	From the study of mitosis and meiosis at the cellular level to the study of the behavior of organisms in an ecosystem, the reproductive processes of animals, plants, and microorganisms are a central theme in biology. There are few topics in biology that are not related in some way to the reproductive nature of living things. The fact that the organisms of today have survived over such long periods of time suggests that the maintenance of successful strategies for reproduction is central to life. To study biology without emphasizing reproduction is to eliminate from the discipline one of the most important principles in the entire field of science.
2. The Major Physical Characteristics and Functions of All Living Organisms Are Tied Closely to the Way in which They Reproduce	The overall structure and function of all members of a species is largely a product of how they have successfully reproduced over time. Moreover, much of the behavior of all organisms, including humans, can be explained through the necessary mechanisms needed to insure reproduction. An excellent way to introduce sex-related topics in the biology curriculum is to introduce students to the reproductive function and behavior of more simple life forms. By understanding how organisms reproduce, students are able to learn about other important characteristics of individual species.
3. Many Social Problems of our Day Are Related to the Reproductive Capacities of Living Organisms	Biologists know that practically all species possess a tendency to produce more offspring than are needed to insure their survival. It is the interplay of this strong biotic potential with the carrying capacity of a given environment that influences the birthrate, deathrate, and well-being of any animal, plant, or microbial population. World problems such as food shortages, overcrowding, competition, war, and disease, all impinge on the capacity of all forms of life to reproduce and survive.
4. The Current Rise in Teenage Pregnancies in this Country is of National Concern	There is evidence that young people in our society are becoming sexually active at an increasingly early age. The number of teenage pregnancies is rising, and the percentage of unplanned babies in our country is estimated by the Planned Parenthood Association to be around 50 percent. In order to insure that parenthood is a responsibility that is planned for in advance, more information is needed by the populace in order to make responsible decisions.

5. The Incidence of Sexually Transmitted Diseases is Increasing

While most communicable diseases are decreasing in the United States, the incidence of gonorrhea and syphilis is increasing and these diseases are now outranked only by the common cold.[7] The incidence of another sexually transmitted disease, herpes virus, is also increasing. Diseases of this type are a serious national health problem, and most health educators feel that schools should teach young people about these diseases.

6. Research Indicates that While Persons in our Society are Exposed to Sex-Related Matters at an Earlier Age and at an Increased Rate, Young People Today are Ignorant of Many Facts Associated with Reproduction and Sex

Sex stimuli abound through advertising, television, movies, and magazines. Many teenagers feel confident that they know a lot about sex and human reproduction; however, research evidence does not support these claims. Many members of our society lack an understanding of basic biological facts of reproduction and of other aspects of sex education. For many individuals, tenth-grade biology is the first and last opportunity for exposure to accurate information concerning human reproduction. Many students marry upon leaving high school, have children, and rear families. The interests, attitudes, and values fostered in high school biology, therefore, become the foundation on which their adult lives are led. This part of the secondary school experience may well represent the most relevant topic in the science curriculum.

INCORPORATING SEX-RELATED TOPICS INTO THE SCIENCE CURRICULUM

Whether or not a teacher consciously elects to cover some aspect of "sex education," all teachers in one way or another "teach" sex education. The pregnant history teacher who shares how she feels toward the upcoming event with her class, the English teacher who reads aloud a poem about love, or the industrial arts teacher who explains his wife's Rh factor, all are dealing with knowledge or expressing attitudes that relate, at least indirectly, to sex education. Sex education not only includes knowledge of reproductive biology, but also many other subjects as well as a complex set of attitudes and values. In fact, many sex education specialists argue that it is not knowledge that is so important in sex education, but the attitudes and values one learns from parents, teachers, and peers.

In teaching sex education, it is important to establish a positive, emotional climate in the classroom. Teachers (and parents) often become "different" when sex-related topics are discussed. Instead, a teacher should establish rapport and openness ahead of time and encourage students to talk about things that are on their minds. Within this context, "sex" topics are dealt with no differently than other topics. One of the major reasons for anxiety toward sex among young people is that adults treat the topic differently. Children are particularly adept at picking up differences in

---

[7]William V. Mayer, "Sex Education," *Biology Teachers Handbook,* New York: John Wiley and Sons, 1978.

attitudes among their parents. The teacher who can establish the appropriate emotional environment in the classroom will usually be successful in dealing with sex-related topics.

Life science and biology teachers must decide which sex education topics to include in their courses. Some topics are so basic to the study of biology that including them in the science curriculum is seldom controversial. These topics include comparison of asexual and sexual reproduction, descriptions of the structure and function of female and male reproductive systems in plants and animals, and discussion of venereal diseases. The same holds true for many other topics, such as sex hormones, body changes at puberty, fertilization, mating behavior of lower animals, embryonic and fetal development, birth, amniocentesis, Rh incompatibility, menstruation, the human reproductive system, and genetical determination of sex. The junior high life science teacher and the high school biology teacher can almost always include these and comparable topics without controversy.

Some topics of high interest to students, however, are potentially controversial. Because of their controversial nature, they are usually not found in the most commonly used textbooks in schools. Some of these topics include: methods of contraception, abortion, premarital sex, *in-vitro* fertilization, artificial implantation, sperm banks, and sexual behavior of humans. Most science and health educators believe these subjects are important and should be dealt with somewhere in the curriculum of our schools. Whether or not they are included in a life science or biology course depends on the following: (1) policies of the state educational agency and of the individual school system, (2) attitudes of the community, (3) support of school administrators, (4) philosophy of the science teacher and his or her department, (5) experience and skill of the teacher, (6) availability of supplementary instructional materials, (7) attitudes and maturity level of the students, and (8) the presence or absence of a unified sex education program in the school system.

Coordinated, schoolwide sex education programs taught by specially trained teachers are not found in most school systems. Often, then, it becomes the responsibility of the science and health programs to expose students to some of the potentially controversial topics mentioned above. This requires careful planning and considerable skill on the part of the teacher. In a large number of cases, these topics will emerge naturally through questions asked by students. The skill of the teacher in handling these questions, therefore, is an important factor.

Drugs

We live in a drug-oriented society. Many people go to sleep with sleeping pills, wake up with coffee, relax with cigarettes, and take aspirin when they get a headache. Advertising bombards us with suggestions on what brands of beer to drink, which tranquilizers are best, and the kind of medication to ask for when one has an itch, ache, or drip.

Obviously, many drugs are helpful to human beings. Antibiotics save thousands of lives each year, and many serious diseases and disorders can be prevented, controlled, or cured by appropriate medication. The quality of life we now enjoy is due in large measure to the many scientific breakthroughs in chemistry and the various fields of medicine.

It is not the use of drugs that is the major problem today but, rather, the abuse of such substances. Teenagers are experimenting with drugs and alcohol at earlier ages than ever before. In many parts of the country, drugs that are potentially harmful to the human body are being sold illegally in recordbreaking quantities.

WHY DO PEOPLE ABUSE DRUGS?

A drug is defined as any substance that causes a change in the body. Characteristically, drugs can produce more than one response in a living organism. These responses depend upon such factors as level of dosage, age of the individual, tolerance level, past experience with the drug, general health of the individual, interaction with other drugs, and route of administration. Most drugs used by people may produce beneficial results; if used improperly, they also produce potentially harmful effects.

The reasons for taking drugs are almost as numerous as the number of available drugs. Many people take drugs for medical reasons, and when used wisely, these drugs can help alleviate pain and suffering. When taken indiscriminately, however, many drugs produce harmful side-effects and can lead to dependency, serious illness, and even death. Therefore, it is drug abuse, not drug use, that is the major problem in our society.

Why do so many young people today abuse their bodies with unwise use of drugs? One reason is that the United States is a drug-oriented society. Youngsters observe their parents using drugs, they see advertisements that glamorize smoking, drinking, and pill taking, and they quite naturally want to participate in these adult-like behaviors. For many youngsters, the desire to experiment with drugs is a passing fancy, and mature decisions eventually follow with regards to tobacco, alcohol, and other substances classified as drugs.

For some people, however, the discriminate use of drugs is not possible. Since there is a thin line between use and misuse, individuals who lack maturity, self-esteem, confidence, and accurate information about drugs are vulnerable to misuse or abuse of drugs. In many youth cultures, there is peer pressure to use various drugs at a young age. For some, drug usage is seen as a means of gaining attention and becoming popular with peers. For others, drugs serve as an escape from family problems, failure in school, and other miseries associated with unhealthy environments. Still others are maladjusted, unhappy, or depressed, and drugs serve as a

In many communities the use of alcohol is as serious a problem as the use of illegal drugs.

way to avoid facing these painful feelings. Whatever the reason for taking drugs, teachers need to know that, for many youngsters, drugs serve as an escape mechanism. For these young people, drug abuse may be an outgrowth of deeper and more serious problems. Not all individuals, however, take drugs because of emotional problems. Some begin for simple, seemingly irrelevant reasons such as finding themselves in a situation where drugs are being used or befriending a drug user.

In teaching about drugs in the science class, it is important for teachers to realize that drug abuse is not simply a question of right versus wrong. Rather, it is related to a complex set of circumstances that involve both the nature of people and the nature of the society in which they live.

MAJOR CATEGORIES OF DRUGS

Drugs can best be described in terms of how they affect living systems, and it is on this basis that drugs are usually classified. The following is a brief summary of the major categories of drugs.

STIMULANTS. Substances that directly stimulate the central nervous system are called stimulants. The most widely used stimulant in this country is coffee, which contains caffeine. Caffeine is also found in tea, several kinds of soft drinks, and in certain prescriptions sold to prevent drowsiness and falling asleep. Since caffeine in naturally occurring substances is socially acceptable and produces relatively mild effects, it is not considered a major drug problem. Recent research, however, suggests that excessive coffee drinking may be harmful to one's health. Many

WHAT STUDENTS SAY

About Drugs

- If people want to smoke marijuana, that should be up to them.
- I know a lot of elementary school kids who experiment with drugs.
- The unit in science on drugs was a big help. I didn't know as much about things as I thought.
- I know of a girl who freaked out on acid. That was enough to convince me.
- Teachers should be more open and let us discuss drugs honestly—and on our terms.
- When some adult starts preaching about drugs, I just tune them out, man.
- My uncle rants and raves about kids taking drugs, then pops a tranquilizer every night before hitting the sack.
- Why should I worry about marijuana when my parents get drunk every weekend.
- I like the way Mr. Harris handles the drug question in biology. He lets us do most of the talking. I respect him for that.
- When you find out how such small amounts of some chemicals affect the body, it makes you think twice about taking drugs.

kinds of diet pills, which contain high levels of caffeine, are also potentially harmful.

Amphetamines is a class of stimulants used by physicians to treat patients with certain types of health problems. These stimulants are sold as Benzedrine ("bennies"), Dexedrine ("oranges"), and Methedrine Desoxyn ("speed"). These "pep pills" or "uppers" can lead to physical and psychological dependence when taken indiscriminately and can be very dangerous when taken in combination with other drugs. Cocaine is an odorless, white powder that comes from the leaves of the coca bush. It is a stimulant that is also widely used today. Users generally sniff it, since it is too strong to be taken orally or by injection. Death from respiratory failure can result from overdose.

Stimulants have long been recognized as having therapeutic value for many kinds of physical and emotional illnesses. However, when taken regularly without a doctor's guidance, potential abuse and drug dependency are highly probable.

SEDATIVES. This group of drugs includes a large number of depressants and barbiturates that are commonly used to control epilepsy, insomnia, depression, and hypertension, and to alleviate pain. Chronic misuse and illegal traffic with these drugs, however, is common. Pentobarbital ("yellow jackets") and secobarbital ("red devils") are often taken orally as mood elevators by amphetamine, heroin, and morphine users. Dependent users of barbiturates usually suffer from withdrawal reactions when attempting to stop, and they may undergo periods of delirium, hallucination, and mental confusion for several days. While sedatives are of great value to physicians and psychiatrists, their indiscriminate or illegal use often leads to serious side-effects. Their use can also aggravate underlying neurotic or psychotic problems.

Though not considered a prescription or illegal drug, alcohol is classified as a depressant. Most forms of alcohol are sold and consumed legally for nonmedical purposes. Yet, alcohol upon entering the blood stream does cause rapid and noticeable changes in both the circulatory and central nervous systems. While estimates vary, perhaps as many as 10 percent of the adults in this country have a drinking problem. At least half of these individuals are thought to have problems serious enough that jobs and family life are seriously affected. Alcoholism among teenagers is higher today than ever before. Many educators speculate that many parents, while attempting to discourage the use of hard drugs and marijuana among adolescents, "look the other way" when their youngsters consume beer, wine, and other alcoholic beverages.

TRANQUILIZERS.   Unlike sedatives, tranquilizers theoretically produce calmness without bringing on drowsiness or sleep. The use of tranquilizers has increased during the past twenty years. Names such as Valium and Librium are common, and many physicians prescribe such drugs as medication for nervousness, anxiety, and mild depression. While tranquilizers were initially thought by many physicians to be nonhabit-forming, recent medical research suggests that regular usage over long periods of time can lead to dependence and possible withdrawal problems.

The use of tranquilizers is not yet a "street problem"; however, there is growing concern that many middle-aged and elderly persons depend too heavily on their use. Another problem is the degree to which they are taken in combination with other substances, including other kinds of prescribed medication. For this reason, many pharmacies today keep records on what medication is sold to each customer and warn the customer when potentially dangerous combinations are being purchased.

NARCOTICS.   Heroin, morphine, opium, and codeine are drugs that belong to the narcotic group. They are characterized by their pain-relieving and sleep-inducing qualities, and they are all addictive. Over long periods of usage, increased doses are needed in order to get the same effect; this leads to habituation and, later, extreme physical dependence. Prolonged use of narcotics can result in cell and tissue alterations. Withdrawal from drugs of this type is long-lasting, painful, and, in extreme cases, fatal.

When prescribed by physicians, some narcotics have important, life-saving qualities.

HALLUCINOGENS.   This group of drugs, the most common of which are LSD, mescaline, and marijuana, became well known during the late 1960s. Unlike most other drugs, hallucinogens have no established medical use at this time. Research on this group of drugs is being conducted, and many uses of the various hallucinogens have been suggested. These applications remain largely speculative at this time.

Hallucinogens produce distorted perceptions, feelings of euphoria, feelings of anxiety, hilarity, sadness, and "inner joy," and have many other effects. Many LSD users say that parts of their body seem to become detached, or "float away," and that their entire environment is rearranged. LSD also produces many physical changes, such as increased heart rate, elevated blood pressure, elevated temperature, loss of muscular coordination, and nausea. Reactions, of course, depend on dosage levels, presences of impurities, and differences among users. An LSD trip may last up to eight hours and may reoccur later. Some research has shown that LSD may lead to chromosome breakage and other serious genetic effects. While LSD is not believed to be addictive, it has been known to produce hallucinations long after usage.

Marijuana is currently the most widely used illegal drug. While marijuana is not considered a "hard drug" and does not produce effects as detrimental as LSD, it is classified as an hallucinogen. Marijuana comes from a plant grown in several parts of the world. The potency varies depending on a variety of conditions under which the plant is grown. Marijuana is a green, alfalfa-like substance that has a pungent, sweet odor when burned. It is usually smoked by rolling small amounts of the dried weed in paper and tucking in the ends. These "joints," as they are called, burn hotter than tobacco cigarettes and produce a much brighter tip.

There is still considerable debate over the long-term effects of using marijuana. A "trip," which lasts from three to five hours, may involve a variety of psychedelic reactions, some pleasant and some unpleasant. An unpleasant trip is known as a "bummer" or "downer." Since most trips are reputed to be rather harmless affairs with less effect than drinking a few ounces of alcohol, many people today believe that marijuana is harmless and should be legalized. Most drug experts presently believe that marijuana produces little lasting physiological harm when used occasionally. On the other hand, it is generally believed that regular use of marijuana produces significant psychological changes; the most noted of these are decreased motivation, indifference, lethargy, and self-neglect. While marijuana is not physiologically addicting, most drug experts suspect that chronic usage may reduce resistance to other, more harmful drugs. Currently, the use of marijuana as a toxicant is second only to the use of alcohol in our society. This topic is of extreme importance to teachers at all levels in today's school

TEACHING ABOUT DRUGS IN THE SCIENCE CLASSROOM

Drug abuse is one of the most serious problems in our society. Since drugs have such varying and profound effects on the human body and mind, the topic fits quite naturally into many science courses in the secondary schools, particularly general science, life science, biology, and chemistry. The following are important objectives that science teachers should consider when dealing with this topic.

EXPOSING STUDENTS TO ACCURATE INFORMATION. One of the most important objectives of drug education is to expose students to accurate, up-to-date, factual information about drugs. Since research on the effects of tobacco, alcohol, and marijuana is conflicting, this is not an easy task. Assistance from experts and the use of credible reading material are usually helpful. There are many good sources of information, including physicians, pharmacists, chemists, public health authorities, and local, state, and federal agencies. Many organizations produce accurate sources of information, including pamphlets, research documents, journal articles, books, films, and other instructional materials.

FOSTERING AN ENVIRONMENT OF DISCUSSION AND DEBATE. As with the treatment of all controversial topics, it is imperative that the science teacher foster an attitude in the classroom of open discussion and debate. Many aspects of drug education are subject to multiple perspectives. Research evidence and political views on marijuana, for example, are conflicting. Drug education cannot be successfully accomplished unless the teacher is willing to let the classroom become a forum for the examination of facts and interpretations.

EXAMINING EFFECTS OF DRUGS ON LIVING SYSTEMS. The science classroom is an excellent setting for students to study the effects of drugs on living organisms. All living processes are carefully regulated by enzymes and hormones. This is a basic concept of biology. One characteristic of this regulatory process is that small amounts of such chemicals can cause profound changes in living organisms. Biology courses are an excellent place to provide opportunities for students to experiment with this idea and to find out how various substances affect these processes in simple organisms. Laboratory activities, independent projects, and group or individual reports are particularly effective strategies for accomplishing this objective.

In doing laboratory activities involving living organisms, care should be taken to observe recommendations and laws governing the use of animals in experimentation. A copy of a statement on the humane treatment of animals appears in Chapter 4 on pages 147–149. Many science teachers use only bacteria in doing experiments on the effects of drugs. In doing so, care should be taken not to use pathogenic bacteria. Plants can also be used, and when animals are used, invertebrates should be considered. According to current humane treatment guidelines, the use of vertebrates for experimentation in science classes is not acceptable.

ALLOWING FOR HONEST ASSESSMENT OF DRUG PRACTICES.   The use of scare tactics and teacher moralizing has been shown to be an ineffective method for teaching about drugs. Secondary school students are usually more aware of drug practices by some of their peers than are their teachers. They appreciate the opportunity to discuss these and other practices in an environment where honesty and trust prevails. One important objective in drug education, therefore, is to allow students opportunities to share experiences and ideas relative to what is actually happening. In this setting, students can examine facts, discuss varying points of view, and arrive at conclusions based on rational discourse.

PROVIDING AN ENVIRONMENT FOR DECISION-MAKING.   One of the major outcomes of science teaching is to encourage personal decision-making about important, science-related matters in life. Decisions concerning the use of tobacco, alcohol, and other drugs must ultimately be made by each member of society. When teaching about drugs, the teacher should be aware that long-range decision-making rests on the shoulders of the students. For this reason, drug education should include opportunities for students to gain practice in decision-making. Role-playing, values clarification exercises, and group discussion techniques are particularly effective in teaching students about decision-making processes. One teacher has developed a game called Fact or Fiction. This quiz show format allows participants to decide whether various statements are based on scientific evidence or myth, and it rewards those who are the most skilled in discriminating between "fact" and "fiction." Students can take the lead in preparing statements on drugs that can be used in such a game.

BECOMING FAMILIAR WITH LOCAL, STATE, AND FEDERAL DRUG LAWS.
One important aspect of decision-making relative to drug usage is the law. Many drugs can be bought across the counter by individuals of any age. Some require doctors' prescriptions, and others require that the purchaser be of a certain age. Other drugs are illegal to sell or possess. When violations occur, those convicted can receive serious penalties, including up to life imprisonment. In some countries, penalties include capital

punishment. Many young people who experiment with drugs are not aware of such laws and may be victims of circumstance. While not tied directly to science content, the law is certainly an important aspect of drug education, and it should receive careful attention in some phase of the school program.

DEVELOPING ATTITUDES OF CONCERN AND SELF-WORTH.   One thing that should be communicated by teachers in *all* subject areas is an attitude dealing with the importance of human life. How each of us treats our own body is an important function of how we value our own lives and the lives of those around us. Many students who engage in drug usage lack self-confidence and self-esteem. By communicating to each student that his or her life is precious and that it is important to care about others, the teacher can help many develop a more positive and productive self-image. By combining attitudes and values with knowledge about drugs, teachers can be more effective in helping students achieve healthier mental and physical behavior.

DOS AND DON'TS WHEN TEACHING ABOUT DRUGS.   Here are a few suggestions to consider when incorporating drug education into the science curriculum:

- Do be well informed yourself about drugs. Teachers can use many resources to bring accurate and up-to-date information to the classroom.
- Don't use scarce tactics, but rather try to be honest with students about drugs. Establishing credibility with students is necessary if a teacher expects to influence attitudes and values.
- Don't stereotype "drugs" and "users." Drugs are not "good" or "bad," but, rather, they are used wisely or used foolishly. Most users of drugs are not addicts, criminals, or "way-out" people. For example, many teenage users are one-time or experimental users. Many alcoholics are very prominent, talented people who have made outstanding contributions to society.
- Do select movies and other drug materials that are unbiased, accurate, and up to date.
- Do select resource people carefully. Often police officers, ex-drug addicts, and other individuals close to the drug scene lack sufficient knowledge about many important aspects of drug education. Just because an individual has taken a lot of drugs does not make him or her an expert.
- Do allow students the freedom to express their views, regardless of what they are, and to debate these views with others. A teacher who is a good listener is able to facilitate student-directed discussions on drug

use and abuse more effectively than one who dominates discussion and tries to tell students what they should believe.

- Don't create an environment of suspicion and distrust. Like many parents, some teachers become moralistic and judgmental when views different from their own are expressed. The teacher's job is to help students to be able to make intelligent decisions about drugs, not to preach to them that drugs are wrong.

Energy and Environmental Education

Recently, the citizens of the United States and other developed countries have come to a fuller realization that many of their most cherished resources are rapidly being depleted. Limited gasoline supplies and rising costs for all forms of energy are familiar examples. Traffic jams, power blackouts, food shortages, worldwide pollution, and conflict between countries for valuable natural resources are realities of our time and of times to come. It would seem, as some have suggested, that human destiny is currently on a collision course and that unless many current trends are reversed, hunger, pestilence, war, and widespread human suffering are imminent.

Preparing young people to deal with current and future problems of society is a major goal of science education. How can energy and environmental education be incorporated into an already overcrowded science curriculum? How can these vital issues be addressed and young people prepared to deal intelligently with these topics?

ROLE OF SCHOOLS IN HELPING TO SOLVE PROBLEMS

John Dewey, the famous educator and philosopher, believed that education should be a way of life, not just a preparation for the future. Most educators and many citizens agree that, in addition to teaching students to read, write, and do arithmetic, schools should expose students to the problems faced by society. In fact, one commonly accepted goal of American education is to provide individuals within our society with the tools needed for survival. The survival of our society, and indeed others around the world, may depend on how successfully we can deal with the many science-related problems we presently face.

Exposing students to problems that face our nation is a major responsibility of both social studies and science teachers. With problems such as those of obtaining energy and protecting the environment comes the need for: (1) helping students become *aware* of important aspects of the problems, (2) helping students gain necessary information in order to more clearly *understand* the problems, and (3) allowing students to discover, discuss, and evaluate alternatives for *dealing* with the problems.

The important issues embodied by environmental and energy education should be treated throughout a science course by the use of appropriate teaching methods and materials. Students should learn how these issues relate to science, technology, and other aspects of our society.

WHAT ARE THE MAJOR GOALS OF ENVIRONMENTAL EDUCATION?

One of the primary goals of environmental education, particularly as a part of the science curriculum, is to teach students the major concepts of ecology. In fact, this should be a goal of most science courses. This topic does not need to be specifically labeled "environmental education" since it is so basic to all of science.

Ecology is the study of organisms and how they relate to each other and their environment. Ecology is a relatively new branch of science, but it has become a household word and has also become part of the vocabulary of elementary school children. In one popular elementary and middle school science program, the Science Curriculum Improvement Study (SCIS), *interaction* among organisms with their environment is an important, culminating theme. The concept of interaction is also taught in various physical science units in this program. An understanding of how natural resources and organisms interact, form systems, change, and interrelate with the environment is, in essence, the most fundamental of all topics in science.

Another important aim of environmental education is related to the beliefs, attitudes, and values of the citizenry. The manner in which any group of people interacts with its environment in the long run is a significant characteristic of that society. Many cultures live in subjugation to nature; that is, its members follow a "whatever will be will be" attitude and do little to change the basic forces of nature. Other people, such as those seen in many oriental cultures, attempt to live in harmony with nature, and individuals view themselves as merely a part of the harmonious whole. Many Western cultures, on the other hand, view nature and the environment as a means of improving human conditions. In these societies, science and technology have become tools to utilize more of nature's potential. Therefore, natural resources and the environment are viewed as something to "conquer" and "use" for the betterment of the human race.

The way young people in our society are taught to feel toward and interact with their environment has significant implications. Indeed, any society that does not learn to live within the constraints of its own limited resources ultimately faces the gravest consequences.

A major goal of environmental education in this country, therefore, should be to produce attitudes among our young people that will improve our chances for survival and human fulfillment in the future. The development of these attitudes and values should start early in the science curriculum of our schools and continue throughout formal education. As has been discussed in Chapter 7, teaching about attitudes and values is an important part of the science teacher's work. In the long run, the most important outcome of environmental education is how students as future citizens feel about and behave toward environmental issues.

A third goal of environmental education is to help students understand its multidisciplinary nature. Environmental relationships and problems are not mere "scientific" issues. These problems are also political, economic, cultural, and psychological in nature. This means that the study of natural resources, worldwide energy demands, population growth or decline, and the management of water and air, must be studied not only in terms of scientific principles but also on the basis of how they are influenced by the entire social system in which we live.

To accomplish this third goal, science teachers need to expose students to a variety of problem-solving activities that allow them to look at environmental education issues from many perspectives. What are the ramifications of strict air quality control? Does a government have the right to encourage, or possibly demand, birth control? Should hunting be allowed in certain regions of our country? These and other questions represent important multidimensional aspects of environmental education. They need to be studied in the science class in such a way that students learn to appreciate how each is tied to all other things within a system.

MAJOR CONCEPTS OF ENVIRONMENTAL EDUCATION

Eugene Vivian has listed several concepts which he calls "conceptual schemes" important in environmental education. These concepts are:

1. All parts of any environment, living or nonliving, are interdependent; their stability and existence are interconnected.

2. Environmental stresses placed on part of any community tend to produce additional stresses on other or all segments of that community.

3. Change is the most constant characteristic of the living or nonliving parts of any environment.

4. The continuous interaction between heredity and environment determines the characteristics of all life forms.

5. The relationships that develop among individuals, groups, and their environments determine the characteristics of those groups.

6. The history of any group of persons is a record of the interaction of individuals in that group, of that group with other groups, and the interaction of all of them with their environments.

7. The characteristics and behaviors of an individual are a result of the interaction of his/her heredity and all his/her environments—the biophysical, the social, and the cultural.

8. Governments are stabilized by tradition and law; governments are changed by modification of the people's perception of the governmental function.

9. The way an individual uses his/her environment is influenced by his/her perception of that environment.

10. The economy of a society is influenced by its perception of the relation of that society to its natural and human skills and resources.[8]

Vivian summarizes how these conceptual schemes relate to important concepts in ecology. Take, for instance, the central idea: All parts of an environment, living or nonliving, are interdependent; their stability and existence are interconnected. Disturbing the environment produces a situation much like the series of predicaments encountered by the old woman in the nursery tale when she wanted her pig to go over the stile. In her case, feeding the cat led to threatening the mouse to gnawing the rope to hanging the butcher to killing the ox to drinking the water to quenching the fire to burning the stick to hitting the dog to biting the pig to going over the stile.

This central idea is called a conceptual scheme because it relates or connects many other important concepts in ecology. The interdependence idea pulls together concepts such as the following:

1. When a series of larger animals feeds (and depends) on smaller animals or plants, that whole series is known as a food chain. For example, mice, which feed on seeds or grain, may be eaten by snakes, which, in turn, are caught by hawks or owls. This food chain is disturbed by people who deliberately try to exterminate snakes, hawks, and owls. The resulting change may produce a plague of mice. This leads to a second concept.

2. When one or more members of a food chain are eliminated, disastrous consequences may result for one or more members of the chain.

3. The more complex the food chains and other interrelationships in an environment, the more difficult it is to disrupt the web or interrelationships. Conversely, more simplified environments such as a farmer's field of corn are far more susceptible to disruption, by insect pests, for example, than a more complex community such as mixed vegetation, forests, or grasslands.

4. Any section of land on which people or animals are dependent for food has a definite limit or carrying capacity of population that it can support.

Each of these four concepts, in itself, illustrates the conceptual scheme of "interdependence."[9]

---

[8]V. Eugene Vivian, *Sourcebook for Environmental Education*, Saint Louis: C. V. Mosby Company, 1973.
[9]From Vivian, V. Eugene, *Sourcebook for Environmental Education*, pp. 17–18, 1973. Reprinted by permission of the C. V. Mosby Company, St. Louis.

THE MAJOR
GOALS OF
ENERGY
EDUCATION

Perhaps no other issue has hit the American public with more force than the so-called energy crisis. Lines at service stations and the price of gasoline have convinced most of us that the days of cheap energy are probably gone forever. In the future, the energy we use to heat and light our homes and propel our cars will be more expensive, and the energy from many of our traditional sources will be in short supply. Because this is such an important problem, energy education is now being included in science and social studies curricula at all grade levels.

The availability of energy in the future is a problem of worldwide significance. The standards of living and life-styles of all societies are highly dependent on the amount of energy that is available to individuals within the system. In the past, we have depended on fossil fuels as a major source of energy. Today, while demands for energy continue to increase, oil supplies appear to be shrinking and the use of other sources of energy is imminent. Turning to other sources of energy, of course, has created new problems. The potential safety hazards associated with the use of nuclear energy have become more apparent during the last few years and have emerged as a major political issue. Solar energy has been widely discussed, but its use depends on the development of a new technology and economic structure. Likewise, returning to coal as a major source of energy has also become a trend. This, of course, means that clean air standards that are now in force may have to be changed.

The ramifications of energy education are similar to those of environmental education. The major goals of energy education should include:

- Helping students understand the role of energy in the total scheme of life.
- Analysis of the major processes by which energy is converted from the sun, stored in many forms, and eventually consumed for human needs.
- Examination of alternative sources of energy and the feasibility, advantages, and disadvantages of each.
- Identification of how energy availability and usage affect societal activities such as agriculture, economics, and political organizations.
- Identification of how energy availability and usage affect human life-styles, attitudes, values, and interpersonal relationships.
- An understanding and appreciation of the importance of rational problem-solving and decision-making as they relate to worldwide human existence and universal moral responsibilities.
- An appreciation for the need to eliminate energy waste and to establish personal commitments and behaviors that are consistent with reasonable conservation practices.

These goals, as is the case with environmental education, encompass human behaviors such as *awareness, understanding, appreciation,* and *ac-*

tion. Many of the goals are already being achieved in science courses, since energy is such a central idea in all science curricula.

MAJOR CONCEPTS OF ENERGY EDUCATION

A conceptual scheme for energy education was developed as part of an energy conservation project at Florida State University. The main ideas are grouped into three functional categories:

1. The Universe of Energy
2. Living Systems and Energy
3. Social Systems and Energy

The Universe of Energy and Living Systems and Energy outline scientific ideas fundamental to basic energy concepts and energy flow models of which people are a part. Social Systems and Energy sets forth fundamental concepts in social systems, including governmental, economic, and moral systems, the understanding of which is vital in making decisions affecting the production, distribution, and consumption of energy resources.

This list of main ideas focuses on *energy conservation*—decisions by individuals, decisions by groups, and systemic decisions on matters affecting energy resources. These decisions range from when and where to turn on a light bulb, to personal life-style commitments, to vast matters of societal/global planning like design and industrial location. This is extensively rewritten from a schema produced by the John Muir Institute for Environmental Studies.

The Universe of Energy

1. Energy is the ability to do work.
2. Energy exists in many different forms, including light energy, electrical energy, chemical energy, mechanical energy, and heat energy.
3. Changes in the motion or position of matter only occur when energy is exerted.
4. Almost all of the energy available on earth comes from the sun.
5. The earth is an open system which constantly receives solar energy and which constantly gives off heat energy.
6. Life can exist on earth only because of the constant and steady arrival of solar energy and the equally steady loss of heat energy into outer space.
7. Machines and living organisms change energy from one form to another.
8. Energy can be changed, but it can never be created or destroyed.
9. Different forms of energy are able to do different amounts of work.
10. Kinetic energy refers to any form of energy that is actively doing work.

11. Potential energy refers to any form of energy that is inactive or stored. All matter contains potential energy.

12. Sources of energy for future use include organic matter, nuclear materials, and solar energy.

Living Systems and Energy

1. All living organisms require energy to maintain such characteristic functions as movement, responsiveness, growth, reproduction, and metabolism.

2. Green plants (producers) are the only form of life that can capture the energy available in solar radiation. They do it by means of a chemical reaction: photosynthesis.

3. Organisms, like humans, which cannot capture solar energy obtain energy from green plants either directly or indirectly. These non-green organisms are consumers.

4. Organisms that break down dead animals and plants into molecules and atoms are decomposers. Decomposers are usually bacteria and fungi.

5. Feeding relationships between producers, consumers, and decomposers form patterns called "food chains" or "foodwebs" that describe the paths by which energy is transferred from one organism to another.

6. The overall pattern formed by the movement of energy from producers to consumers is a complex foodweb called an energy pyramid.

7. As energy flows through a living system, it imposes order and organization on that system.

8. Under certain conditions, energy stored in the tissue of dead organisms may become a fossil fuel.

Social Systems and Energy

1. All people must consume energy to stay alive.

2. People transform and manipulate energy sources to satisfy their needs and wants.

3. People use energy to improve their environmental conditions, to power machines, and to maintain culture.

4. People are among the very few organisms that use large quantities of energy sources.

5. People have increased their consumption of energy resources throughout history.

6. Pepole living in technological cultures have greatly increased their consumption of energy resources in the last few hundred years.

7. Sources of energy have changed as new types have been found and as old sources have been depleted or found to be less desirable.

8. The major sources of energy have changed, from renewable ones such as plants and animals, to depletable ones such as coal, oil, and natural gas.

9. People use energy to create and sustain special ecosystems such as cities, recreation areas, and agricultural areas.

10. People have used energy resources to increase agricultural yields and thus increase the amount of food energy available to them.

11. People are beginning to look toward energy resources that are non-depletable.

12. All societies have wants greater than their resources are able to fulfill, creating the condition of scarcity. Economic systems, governmental systems, and moral systems are used to give direction in allocating scarce resources, including energy resources.

13. Energy consumers have interests, obligations, rights, and ideals which govern their personal and collective consumption of energy resources.

14. Energy producers have interests, obligations, rights, and ideals which govern their production and distribution of energy resources.

15. Social systems, including government, the economy, and societal networks, have interests, obligations, ideals, and rules affecting the production, distribution, and consumption of energy resources.

16. Individuals, groups, and the society-at-large face conflicts in self-interests, obligations, rights, and ideals as they make choices or rules affecting the production, distribution, and consumption of energy resources.

17. Energy conservation deals with increasing the efficiency of energy use and decreasing the amount of energy used.

18. Social systems that regulate energy supplies and use are important components in energy conservation.

19. People as energy consumers and decision makers are individually and collectively responsible for energy conservation.[10]

WAYS TO
INCLUDE ENERGY
AND
ENVIRONMENTAL
EDUCATION IN
THE SCIENCE
CURRICULUM

There are several ways to incorporate the common goals of environmental and energy education into science courses. The following suggestions represent some of the methods that can be used by science teachers.

SPECIAL UNITS.   One method commonly used by science teachers as assurance that important topics like energy and environmental education receive proper consideration is the creation of special instructional units. In a physics course, for example, a special unit on energy might be de-

---

[10]Reprinted by permission of the *Journal of Environmental Education*, 8(4):8–17, "Toward Goals for Multidisciplinary Energy Education," by Rodney F. Allen, David E. LaHart, George Dawson, and Marvin Dee Patterson. Heldref Publications, Washington, D.C., 20016, 1976.

signed for the end of the first semester. Such a unit would pull together what has been learned about energy and show how these energy concepts relate to some of the technological problems associated with limited energy supplies. A biology teacher might plan a separate unit on environmental education to follow the chapter on ecology in the textbook. In this unit, the teacher could help students better understand how many of the principles of ecology relate to common problems in our society such as air pollution and solid waste disposal. The use of special units represents a relatively easy and flexible way of adding emphasis to relevant topics of current concern.

INFUSION.   Rather than adding separate units to the curriculum, many teachers prefer to include various aspects of energy or environmental education throughout a science course. An earth science teacher might wish to spend time on water pollution during a unit on water, cover air pollution when dealing with atmospheres and weather, and include land management with a chapter on physical geography. Similarly, a physical science teacher may prefer to expand on current energy problems whenever this topic emerges. One advantage of the infusion method is that students study important aspects of energy or environmental education as an integral part of science and not as an "add-on."

MINI-COURSES.   A common practice in some schools over the past few years is the development of self-contained mini-courses. During the last six weeks of school, for example, a life science teacher might teach a mini-course on "alternative sources of energy," "worldwide food shortages," or "endangered species." Each "course" is independent of other topics treated during the year, and students are evaluated independently in each offering. In some cases, mini-courses are designed so that students can proceed through individualized learning activities at their own pace. With this format, students may have a choice of several mini-courses. This approach has worked well in many science courses and has the advantage of allowing students to change pace frequently and to select topics of high interest.

SPECIAL COURSES.   In some cases, semester or year-long courses on energy education or environmental education are offered as part of the science curriculum. During the senior year in high school, for example, students may be given a choice of taking physics, advanced biology, or environmental education. Courses such as environmental education or "interdisciplinary science" often are especially appealing to students who do not plan to enter science fields in college. Such courses are usually organized around topics of high interest to secondary school students and may attract students who would not otherwise elect to take additional science courses.

MATERIALS FOR TEACHING ENERGY AND ENVIRONMENTAL EDUCATION

There is an almost unlimited source of materials from which teachers can extract ideas for teaching energy and environmental education. The following examples represent a few such sources.

TEXTBOOKS. Most up-to-date textbooks include topics of current interest to science teachers and students. Material on environmental and energy education may be infused throughout the book or be found at the end of major units. If the textbook being used in the course does not contain up-to-date material on energy and environmental education, the teacher may wish to have the school purchase for use as reference books a few copies of textbooks that do contain such material.

SPECIAL PUBLICATIONS BY PROFESSIONAL ORGANIZATIONS. Organizations such as the National Science Teachers Association (NSTA) and the National Association of Biology Teachers (NABT) publish materials on environmental and energy topics. NSTA, for example, has published an entire series of curriculum guides on energy education. Samples of these materials may be obtained by writing to NSTA, 1742 Connecticut Avenue, Washington, D.C. 20009.

PROFESSIONAL JOURNALS. Journals such as *The Physics Teacher, Journal of Geological Education, Science and Children, American Biology Teacher,* and *Science 80* publish excellent articles that can be used by science teachers when developing units on energy and environmental education. A list of these and other journals with addresses are included in Appendix B.

NATIONAL ORGANIZATIONS. The Sierra Club, the National 4-H Club, and the Audubon Society are examples of national organizations that have prepared environmental education materials suitable for use in science classes. These materials can be adapted to fit any number of approaches a science teacher may wish to use.

FEDERAL AGENCIES. Agencies such as the National Parks Service, the Wildlife Federation, the Department of Energy, the U.S. Department of Agriculture, and the U.S. Geological Survey publish numerous pamphlets, booklets, and monographs that can be used as reference materials for energy or environmental education. These materials are either free or available for a small cost, and can serve as excellent sources of ideas.

STATE AND LOCAL AGENCIES.   Many local and state agencies promote
conservation, environmental education, and energy education. Many of
these agencies have speakers who are willing to visit science classes and
talk on topics that relate to environmental and energy issues. In many
cases, state, county, or city political leaders are also willing to speak to
classes on problems of local interest. Before contacting these officials, the
teacher should determine the local school system's policies and procedures for using such resources.

Additional Controversial Topics

Many other potentially controversial topics emerge from time to time in
science classes. Some of these are associated with areas outside the
mainstream of science, such as astrology, parapsychology, and various
forms of meditation. Other topics are associated with human aspects of
biology such as human behavior, genetic counseling, and biological engineering. Another topic of considerable interest is an emerging field
known as sociobiology. As the name implies, sociobiology represents a
fusion of the fields of sociology and biology. The behavior of humans and
societies is studied in terms of interactions between genetic and cultural
influences.

As can be seen, just about any topic that touches on the human
parameters of "behavior," "politics," or "religion," and that involves
attitudes, beliefs, and values is potentially controversial. In addition,
there has been an increase recently in the number of cults and pseudosci-
ence movements. The science teacher has the important task of helping
students discriminate between science and nonscience, and to help them
learn the boundaries of each. While today's mysticism lies outside the
realm of science and cannot be easily explained, it should not be automatically tossed out as totally irrelevant. Who knows, some of what is considered "mystical" today may be "scientific" tomorrow.

A Summary of Suggestions for Dealing with Controversial Topics

Regardless of the topic, there are several things science teachers should
consider before, during, and after dealing with controversial topics in the
classroom. Some important considerations are as follows:

• Teachers should know the local school system's policy on the teaching
  of controversial topics. Some such policies include provisions for students or parents to challenge or protest the coverage of a given topic.
• When it is planned to include topics of potential controversy in the
  curriculum, the teacher should consult with the department head and
  principal. Administrators contacted ahead of time often will have
  suggestions for presenting the material and, perhaps more importantly,

will be able to respond effectively if approached by an irate parent or student.

- Is the controversial topic under consideration one of educational value and significance? For example, a discussion on birth control may be deemed an important educational objective in a tenth grade biology course, while having students do reports on the topic of abortion might not be. A key question any science teacher must first ask is, "How important is it that my students learn this concept or skill at this time?"

- Are the age, ability, and maturity of the students commensurate with the level of instruction being planned? This is always an important factor when deciding whether or not to include any material.

- Provisions should always be made to insure that a fair and balanced treatment is given to any controversial topic. Science teachers have a professional and moral obligation to see that alternative rational views are considered. There are, for example, several rational and defensible views on the use of nuclear energy. The "stork theory," however, does not represent a rational view and would not be worthy of time equal to that given to the "live birth theory."

- Up-to-date, accurate information is essential. The use of credible sources from outside the classroom is therefore recommended. Books, pamphlets, journals, films, and outside speakers are excellent sources of information. Discussions, role-playing, and debates that allow all students the freedom to express opinions are desirable strategies to use when dealing with controversial topics.

- The nature of the community and the expertise of the teachers also are important variables to consider when planning for the inclusion of controversial material. The experienced teacher who attempts to go "all out" on "evolution" or "sex education" in a conservative community may have problems.

- Science teachers should be aware of official position statements concerning controversial topics that have been published by professional societies in science and science education (see Figure 11.2 as an example).

- Respect for divergent views should be encouraged at all times. Guidelines that foster careful listening, self-control, tolerance of divergent views, and mutual respect should be established ahead of time and carefully enforced. The teacher should serve as a model by being a good listener and by not "preaching" or "moralizing" to students. Focus should be on the issue and not the personality. Students should learn that their science classroom is a place where they can express their feelings both openly and honestly.

- In summary, the rights of students, parents, and teachers should be considered and respected when dealing with any controversial topics.

A teacher's freedom to teach involves both the right *and* the responsibility to use the highest intellectual standards in studying, investigating, presenting, interpreting, and discussing facts and ideas relevant to his or her field of professional competence. As professionals, teachers must be free to examine controversial issues openly in the classroom. The right to do so is based on the democratic commitment to open inquiry and on the importance to decision-making of the expression of opposing informed views and the free examination of ideas. The teacher is professionally obligated to maintain a spirit of free inquiry, openmindedness and impartiality in the classroom.

Many state legislatures, boards of education, and school administrators have shown disregard for the teacher's professional role in dealing with controversy in the classroom. Consequently, it is important that the National Science Teachers Association as a professional organization act forcefully to insure teachers a significant role in determining educational policy. If the freedom to teach is to be meaningful, teachers must participate in decisions regarding the organization, presentation, and evaluation of instruction and in determining the competency of other teachers and administrators. The same is true of the freedom to learn: commitment to it demands student involvement in curricular decisions, even in the evaluation of instruction.

Approved by the NSTA Board of Directors in 1976. This position is essentially the same statement previously adopted by the National Council for the Social Studies.

FIGURE 11.2   Excerpts from the National Science Teachers Association's Official Position on the Freedom to Teach and the Freedom to Learn.

It is the responsibility of science teachers to teach useful and important information. With this responsibility, however, comes the obligation to respect the rights and beliefs of students, parents, and other citizens.

In Perspective

Environmental education, energy education, sex education, population education, consumer education, drug education, career education, and education for leisure—what will the schools be asked to do next? And these requests for schools to assist in solving personal and societal problems are coming at a time when there is a knowledge explosion in science. How can time be found to do everything that is expected of science teachers?

It appears that time is not available to teach all the things demanded by our schools' various publics. Choices must therefore be made about what topics should be emphasized and what should receive less attention. In doing so, the following points should be considered:

1. It is often possible to treat issues such as evolution, sex education, and environmental education as an integral part of instruction primarily directed toward the teaching of important facts, concepts, and processes of science. Separate units of instruction may not be needed or even desirable; rather, an integrated approach may be better. A central idea of evolution is change—changes in rocks, landforms, living things, stars, and even the universe itself. A science program designed to promote scientific literacy teaches about these changes; the idea of evolution is but one of many ideas related to change. In like manner, reproduction is an important life process and should be considered in studying any form of life. The interdependence of living things and their nonliving environment is an important idea of ecology, which can be illustrated by dozens of cases taken from the records of environmental abuse.

2. As was described in Chapter 1, the development of scientific literacy involves more than teaching about the facts and methods of science. For example, students should be knowledgeable of the scientific enterprise, the values underlying science, and the relationship between science and society. The problems and issues facing our country and the rest of the world are "naturals" for teaching these goals. Are science and technology the chief culprits causing our environmental problems or the salvation for solving them? Will the energy crisis be solved by science and technology or by economic, political, and social changes? Should the exchange of scientific information between all countries be encouraged, or should it be limited to countries with certain types of governments or those countries with similar political beliefs? These are but three examples of the many problems we face and that have relevance and high interest to students. Failure to capitalize on this valuable resource is to teach a sterilized version of science isolated from its substrate.

3. Schools exist in large measure to equip students to solve the problems they face now or will face in the future. For many, it is now—teenage pregnancy, decisions about drugs, diets, and careers, and how to cope in a world of conflict and differing opinions. How can students best be equipped to solve these problems? Such a question has no easy answer. But certainly part of the answer is giving students a knowledge base they can use in solving problems. They need to know about different kinds of drugs, the major scientific principles involved in nuclear energy, and interaction of science with other aspects of our culture. But knowledge is not enough; students should also be given practice in solving problems—not just idealized problems, but problems they, their school, and their community face. In this context, science-related problems and issues such as those discussed in this chapter can give real "life" to any science course.

Review Questions

1. Briefly describe the evolution-creationism controversy as it exists today and describe why it is a particularly sensitive issue with which life and earth science teachers must deal.

2. What are the major beliefs of the Creation Research Society?

3. Briefly summarize the official position of the National Science Teachers Association on the teaching of creationism and evolution in science classes.

4. What are the major reasons for including sex education in the science curriculum?

5. Do you consider drugs a major problem in today's schools? Do you think the schools should include drug education in the curriculum? If so, how do you think this topic should be covered?

6. List and briefly describe the major categories of drugs.

7. Many people feel that schools in general and science in particular should not deal with attitudes and values. Yet, most environmental and energy issues include attitudinal and value judgments. How would you as a science teacher deal with this issue?

8. List six or seven things that science teachers should be aware of when dealing with controversial topics in the classroom.

For Application and Analysis

1. A small town politician was fond of saying, "The trick is to skin the skunk without making a stink." In what ways in this statement analogous to the effective teaching of controversial topics?

2. It has been suggested that the teacher should not interject his or her personal values into a discussion of a controversial topic. Do you agree with this recommendation? Is it possible for the teacher to be value-less? Is it desirable? If teachers are to be valueless, does this mean they should not insist on students treating data in a manner consistent with the methods of science? Is the way data is treated in science a value?

3. If several students are available, organize a debate on a topic that deals with some phase of the teaching of a controversial subject. For example, "Resolved: Teaching students about sex and drugs does more harm than good in that it gives students ideas and encourages them to try things they otherwise would not do."

4. Read the following account of a debate that was held at a National Science Teachers Association meeting in Atlanta and published in *The Science Teacher* and draw your own conclusions based on what you see as the major point of conflict.

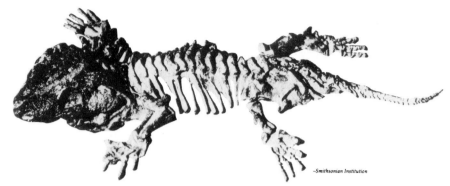

–Smithsonian Institution

EVOLUTIONIST–

At an NSTA area convention in Atlanta last fall, two creationists, Lane P. Lester and John N. Moore, met with evolutionists Ronald D. Simpson and Wyatt W. Anderson to debate whether or not accounts of special creation should be taught in biology courses alongside the biological theory of evolution. Here are their points of view.

EVOLU-TIONIST–CREATIONIST ROUND TABLE

Wyatt W. Anderson

The question before us is whether or not accounts of special creation should be taught in biology courses alongside the biological theory of evolution. I will base my remarks on a premise which seems self-evident to me as a practicing scientist, and which certainly must find accord among members of the National Science Teachers Association. It is simply that *science* should be taught in the science classroom.

Those like Drs. Moore and Lester who propose that special creation be taught in the science curriculum know they cannot disguise their essentially religious views as scientific. Rather, they attack the biological theory of evolution as unscientific on the basis of a misunderstanding of what constitutes science. Then they insist that since one "unscientific" theory is being taught, equal attention must be given a second—the Biblical account of creation. I find this a most curious position for "scientists." Their viewpoint may be illustrated with the following quotation from a creationist handbook:[1]

It should be clearly stressed that the creation-evolution issue is not an argument between religion and science. Since creation and evolution are both

---

[1] *Science and Creation: A Handbook for Teachers* by Morris, Boardman, and Koontz. Creation-Science Research Center, Ann Arbor, Mich. 1971. P. 7.

*theories of origins, incapable of scientific demonstration as nonrepeatable
events of the past, the choice between them is not a decision between scientific alternatives. The question of origins is ultimately a matter of faith, so that
both theories are equally "religious."*

Clearly it is not the cause of science that proponents of special creation serve;
they are seeking to introduce religious dogma in the guise of an acceptable
alternative theory for the origin and development of life.

No amount of confrontation with contrary facts seems to daunt the
creationists. Dr. Lester states, "Because of extensive empirical evidence of the
insufficiency of mutation to explain the living world, the creation model
includes a fourth source of variation, that created by a supernatural being."
The first part of his sentence is simply false; the empirical evidence is that
gene mutations do occur frequently enough to account for the evolutionary
process. In fact, recent studies indicate that only a fraction of mutations are
mobilized by natural selection for long-term evolutionary changes.

Dr. Moore asserts that after more than 70 years, there is a complete
dearth of evidence regarding any prediction of accumulation of small, continuous variational changes from generation to generation of living organisms.
This same criticism was raised a hundred years ago, in the decades immediately after Darwin proposed his theory of evolution by natural selection,
and it has been disposed of time and again (see, for instance, the books by
Grant and Simpson). Man, for example, has purposefully accumulated such
small, continuous variations over generations in producing the strikingly different breeds of dogs we know today. The fossil record has many instances of
transitional individuals which grade continuously between successive species
of a genus; good examples are found in the preserved shells of the pelecypods
and ammonoids. There are also examples of transitional individuals which
not only grade between successive species, but which cross from one higher
taxon to another; again, the pelecypods and ammonoids provide good cases,
although examples are found in a wide array of other groups. Creationists are
either ignorant of the facts or, worse, they choose to ignore them.

I am convinced that no discussion of facts with creationists will be profitable, because they view facts in a different way than do scientists. It is revealing that Dr. Lester speaks of two "models" for the history of life and that Dr.
Moore refers to the "megaevolution model." A model seems to be a belief to
which facts are fitted, and it is this approach which sets creationists apart from
biological scientists. Creationists are committed to fitting the facts to their
beliefs, and not to a free inquiry. It is easy to quibble over the small points of
this or that fossil, or over the precise date of one rock stratum or another—and
the creationists are masters at doing so. But the fundamental weakness of their
position lies in their commitment to an unscientific methodology, a commitment to a hypothesis and not to a continuing process of understanding the
world. I would like to explore the nature of science further, particularly with
regard to theories of evolution and of special creation.

The goal of science is the systematic organization of knowledge about the world in terms of principles subject to test. Science is thus a way of knowing about the world. It differs from ordinary, common-sense knowledge in several ways: First, science seeks to organize knowledge, revealing relationships which might not be immediately obvious. Second, science provides explanations of why observed events occur. Third, the explanations must be testable and subject to *possible rejection*. This last criterion is the most important characteristic of scientific methodology, for it means that science is self-testing and self-correcting. Hypotheses are tested and possibly rejected or modified. *Any hypothesis which admits no test, no possible change, can never qualify as science.*

It is sometimes claimed that scientific hypotheses must allow predictions which can be tested, and, in fact, one of the criticisms Dr. Moore and other creationists have leveled at evolution is that one cannot observe long-term processes in order to test predictions about, for example, the formation of species. Such a requirement is unduly restrictive, however, and is a carry-over from some areas of physical science where direct observation of an entire process—a chemical reaction, for example—is possible. There are certain fields of scientific knowledge where prediction is restricted by nature of the subject. Examples are events which occurred in the distant past, or events which occur over such long periods that observation in any one lifetime is not possible; these kinds of events are, of course, those of interest to the evolutionist. Other examples are objects too small for observation, such as atoms or subatomic particles—or processes too fast for observation; these subjects are part of chemistry and physics. The criterion of testability can, however, be satisfied for such hypotheses by requiring that they have precise consequences which *can* be tested. A set of hypotheses with broad explanatory power which successfully meets repeated tests becomes a scientific theory—an example is the current neo-Darwinian theory of evolution.

It is clear that special creation is not a scientific theory. It rests on faith and *cannot be falsified* by any possible test. It does not admit the possibility that a theory must be changed in the light of contrary evidence. Let me illustrate from a booklet written by Dr. Moore entitled "Should evolution be taught?" The closing sentence is, "In point of fact, the only unchanging explanation of 'origins' is that found in the Genesis account of creation." A scientific explanation can never be "unchanging," no matter how appealing such certitude may be. Attempts to "verify" creationist beliefs by showing that they fit selected data are meaningless, for the basic requirement of science, testability leading to possible rejection, is absent.

Just What Is "Science"?

Testing Evolution

The hypothesis that a gradual evolutionary process leading from simple to complex organisms has occurred, as opposed to a sudden creation of complex life forms, is subject to test in many ways. The two hypotheses do lead to quite different consequences which can be distinguished. For one thing, evolutionary theory requires that Earth be quite old, certainly older than the 6,000 or so years held by many creationists for so long. Radioactive dating techniques, among others, show that Earth is indeed not several thousand, but several billion, years old. For another, if evolutionary theory is true, we should expect to find progressive differences among fossils buried in successive rock strata of different ages, and fewer of what we call "higher" forms in older strata. We would not expect such differences under the creationist theory. Again, data support the evolutionary theory.

Hypotheses about the *processes* by which evolution occur, natural selection in particular, are far more difficult to test, as evolutionists have come to realize.

"Special creation . . . rests on faith and cannot be falsified."

Natural selection can be used to explain too many facts too easily, and, as we might expect, there are difficulties inherent in trying to understand the past in terms of the present. The methodological problems involved in evolutionary biology should not be underestimated; it is only by an awareness of these problems that evolutionary biologists can hope to properly frame hypotheses about the mechanics of evolution. But it is the use of a methodology aimed at understanding the world by a self-testing and self-correcting process that makes evolutionary biology a science. Let me give examples of the way evolutionary theory has been and is being tested—one from an older, and the other from the current, theory.

The first truly biological theory of evolution was proposed by Lamarck in 1809. Lamarck suggested that organisms changed in response to the environment, and that these alterations were passed on to their offspring. The mechanisms of his evolutionary model was "inheritance of acquired characteristics." We are all familiar with the fallacious example that giraffes which stretched their necks reaching for leaves would have offspring with longer necks. Lamarck's hypothesis of the inheritance of acquired characteristics was tested extensively—and rejected. For instance, the tails of mice were amputated for many generations with no effect on the tail length of offspring.

Over the past few years biochemistry has given us new techniques by which to test the accuracy of the theory of evolution. We have learned that genetic material—DNA—functions by determining the sequence of amino acids in proteins. Thus, protein differences between different kinds of organisms can be used to estimate the *genetic* differences between the organisms. And this data can then be compared with the distance separating the organisms in an evolutionary scheme built from *different* kinds of data—for example, the extent of mating barriers between groups of organisms at the lowest level, or the fossil record at a higher level. If evolutionary theory is correct, we should expect an accumulation of genetic differences as barriers to reproduction appear and morphological differences widen. And we expect organisms more closely related (that is, whose fossil record shows they diverged from common ancestors more recently in time) to show correspondingly fewer differences in the sequence of amino acids in a broad array of proteins. Both predictions are supported by the results of recent studies. Thus, evolutionary theory *is* being subjected to experimental test. No single test is likely to be critical by itself; it is repeated tests like this which have led to the acceptance of evolutionary theory as a cornerstone of modern biology.

In closing I should like to reiterate the major point of my remarks: Science is a way of learning about the world, with testability of hypotheses leading to rejection or modification its major characteristic. The biological theory of evolution is a scientific theory and as such belongs in the science classroom. Accounts of special creation are in no way scientific and do not belong in the teaching of science.

Bibliography

1. Ayala, F. J. "Biology as an Autonomous Science." *American Scientist* 56:207–221; 1968.
2. Grant, V. *The Origins of Adaptations.* Columbia University Press, New York, N.Y. 1963.
3. Moore, J. A. "On Giving Equal Time to the Teaching of Evolution and Creation." *Perspectives in Biology and Medicine* 18:405–417; 1975.
4. Newell, N. D. "Evolution Under Attack." *Natural History* 83:32–39; 1974.
5. Popper, K. R. *The Logic of Scientific Discovery,* Second English Edition. Harper Torchbooks, Harper and Row, New York, N.Y. 1968.
6. Simpson, G. G. *The Meaning of Evolution,* Revised Edition. Yale University Press, New Haven, Conn. 1967.

John N. Moore

Evolution is often defined as a change in gene frequency. Necessarily then, at least two degrees of change must be explicated: that between kinds of organisms, and that within kinds of organisms. Change between kinds may be labeled *megaevolution;* that within kinds, *microevolution.* Since the latter is just genetic variation within limits, it need not be considered here. But how scientific is megaevolution?

The nature of science is aptly conveyed in the following quotation from G. G. Simpson:

The important distinction between science and those other systematizations [e.g., the arts, philosophy, and theology] is that science is self-testing and self-

correcting. The testing and correcting are done by means of observations that can be repeated with essentially the same results by normal persons operating by the same methods and with the same approach.[1]

Corroboration of this view is found in the words of Francisco J. Ayala:

A hypothesis is empirical or scientific only if it can be tested by experience . . . A hypothesis or theory which cannot be, at least in principle, falsified by empirical observations and experiments does not belong to the realm of science.[2]

I assert that megaevolution does not meet these criteria. All the evidence grouped under morphology, embryology, anatomy, and blood and protein analyses are only itemizations of prevailing circumstances.

Any suggestion that basic similarities between kinds of organisms are evidence for megaevolution is based solely upon the *assumption* that the degree of relationship between organisms may be correlated with their degree of similarity. However, as many scientists point out, no family lineages of organisms are established by such evidence—contrary to claims of evolutionists.

Actually the only evidence of import is genetic and fossil. Yet all genetic tests of family lineage leave one with the clear impression of "fixity of kinds"—that is, inviolate genetic barriers exist between major groups of living things. Researchers always conclude their work with the same kind of organisms they began with. Further, fossils are, in general, identified without much difficulty as previously existing examples of currently present kinds of plants and animals. Also, the long list of "living fossils" fits the concept of "fixity of kinds."

There simply are no real tests of evolution, when this is meant to involve amoeba-to-man changes. The biochemical studies to which Dr. Anderson refers have nothing to do with genetic lineages of groups of organisms. An ability "to calculate the genetic differences between groups of organisms" does not result in establishment of any genetic familial lineages and hence is not a test of amoeba-to-man evolution.

When Dr. Anderson refers to "closely related" organisms he *assumes* that which he supposedly would use the theory of evolution to clarify. This is plainly fallacious reasoning—he is assuming that which is to be supported. And, of course, mutilation of animals by amputation of tails (as in mice) is surely no test of inheritance because no changes of genes result. There are no "repeated tests" as Dr. Anderson claims.

In sum, there is no experimental test that can either confirm or falsify megaevolution. And exactly the same objection can be applied to creationism.

---

[1]G. G. Simpson *et al.* editors, *Notes on the Nature of Science.* Harcourt, Brace and World, Inc., New York, N.Y. 1961-62. P. 9.
[2]Francisco J. Ayala, "Biological Evolution: Natural Selection or Random Walk?" *American Scientist* 62:700; November-December, 1974.

The two models can, however, be used to make comparative predictions as to: (a) the character of the array of living organisms, (b) the character of basic laws of nature, (c) the nature of the fossil record, (d) the nature of biologic change, and other points. For example, the creation model is a basis for predicting that the basic laws of nature are conservative and deteriorative, as confirmed by the two Laws of Thermodynamics. A proponent of evolution has to accommodate these laws by one or more secondary assumptions, which are still nontestable.

The major prediction from the megaevolution model is that (as Darwin presumed) small, continuous variational changes should be expected to accumulate from generation to generation to the point where completely new organisms eventually appear. No confirmation of such a prediction is obtained through any amount of analysis of genetic study. After more than 70 years, a complete dearth of evidence exists which might confirm this prediction. Thus, the major prediction from megaevolution is a failure.

A major prediction from the creationist model is that researchers should find gaps between distinct kinds of living and past animals and plants, and that different degrees of variability should occur within known kinds of animals and plants. Full confirmation of this prediction can be obtained from careful research and interpretation of data from comparative anatomy, embryology, serology, biochemistry, genetics, and fossil materials. Without doubt, all of the data of gene combination and recombination, hybridization, mutation, isolation, distribution, and selection may be interpreted meaningfully, and conclusively, in support of the creationist model.

Testing Predictions

> **"Any belief in spontaneous generation of life on Earth is a violation of the law of biogenesis, as well as the assumption of uniformity of natural events."**

Both evolutionist panelists have missed the point made repeatedly by leading creationist scientists—that aspects of the creationist model can be discussed without reference to the Bible or other religious literature or doctrines. The basic beliefs of the creationist model are accepted widely by orthodox Jews, Moslems, as well as by evangelical Protestants. (I regularly explain to my students that Hindus and Buddhists just do not have much to say about first origins.) Thus there is essentially no risk of omission, and there is no religious group trying to impose its singular beliefs. Creation scientists are not proposing the teaching of "religion." In no way would practices of worship or procedures be a part of public school study of the creation model.

Not Pushing "Beliefs"

Dr. Simpson is reminded that teaching *about* the beliefs of people is fully legal and consistent with U.S. Supreme Court rulings. I, for one, regularly teach about the beliefs of people on first origins at Michigan State University.

Incidentally, Dr. Simpson's article seems to assume that either Dr. Lester or I have proposed or supported legislation regarding this controversy. This is erroneous. We have both recorded our disagreement with any attempts at legislation in this matter.

There is concern that the creation model is based upon supernatural creation of basic kinds; but let it be clearly understood that megaevolutionists themselves repeatedly utilize concepts entailing events *beyond* the natural events observable by careful scientists. Megaevolutionists are dealing in the supranatural whenever they insist that life on Earth arose by spontaneous generation, or that new physical traits have ever come into existence through mutation. Neither spontaneous generation nor the appearance of new physical traits can be documented in any sense of the nature of science as presented by Simpson and Ayala. Furthermore, any belief in spontaneous generation of life on Earth is a violation of the law of biogenesis, as well as the assumption of uniformity of natural events. I should note, too, that megaevolutionists express their ideas in a depth of belief and commitment easily identified as "dogma."

Selected indoctrination of young people at various levels of education regarding origins of life and of humankind need not continue. Because the megaevolution model and the creation model are put forth as conceptual frameworks to explain "origins," science teachers are properly exercising their academic freedom and responsibility to present both models to their students. On the grounds of constitutional and civil rights of students and science teachers, alike, there are no significant reasons why science teachers in the United States or abroad cannot teach both models.

Lane P. Lester

Whenever concepts of origin are taught—whether of the universe, life, or man—the models of both evolution and creation should be presented. This position is morally imperative, first because each of the models has both a religious and a scientific nature; second, because students are denied academic freedom when allowed to study only one model; and third, because citizens overwhelmingly support presentation of both positions.

Much of the opposition to a balanced treatment of the two models arises from a misunderstanding of the similarities and differences between them. If such misunderstanding can be even partially eliminated, teachers will be more likely to make the teaching of origins an experience in scientific reasoning, rather than one of indoctrination.

Probably the most important difference between the two views lies in how each describes the origin of life. According to evolution, the first living system resulted from a gradual accretion and accumulation of molecules. The creationist model postulates a supernatural bringing into existence of many *baramins*. (Creationists have found it necessary to invent this word, from Hebrew derivatives, to express the concept of organisms which originated directly by divine creation, because genetic evidence shows that no single taxonomic group—species, genus, etc.—can serve the purpose.)

Tree or Forest?

Variation is one of the striking characteristics of life on Earth. It can, of course, result from environmental effects, but such variation is not inherited, and its significance does not extend beyond the individual organism. Among organisms reproducing sexually, variation can also arise from genetic recombination. But the only source of new genetic information since the origin of life is mutation. Indeed, the evolution model has only mutation to account for the variety of life throughout its history and for the diversity of life on Earth today. Because of extensive empirical evidence of the insufficiency of mutation to explain the living world, the creation model includes a fourth source of variation—that created by a supernatural being. Thus, at the time each baramin was created, there was included a certain amount of genetic heterogeneity, which has been sorted into various combinations throughout the history of life and which accounts for virtually all of the adaptive variation seen today. One baramin—or created kind of organism—has, for example, produced horses, zebras, donkeys, and similar species which can be shown to be genetically related. Another has given rise to cats, lions, tigers, and so on.

In evolutionary theory, all organisms are related back through time to the first primitive organisms; thus, the history of life may be viewed as one large tree. Creationists, on the other hand, see the history of life as a forest of small trees, where each tree represents a baramin. As discrete populations of a particular baramin colonized different environments, natural selection of the best combinations of created variation, plus genetic drift, caused the populations to become dissimilar.

Dr. Anderson's main point is that evolution is testable and creation is not. This is both an error and an oversimplification in that neither model is falsifiable, but both involve hypotheses that can be tested. Anderson's own example of Lamarckism illustrates this, for while Lamarck's hypothesis for the mechanism of evolution was rejected, the concept of evolution was not. Examples abound: Evolutionists predicted a continuum of fossils, but the fossil record is composed of distinct groups. Evolutionists predicted embryonic recapitulation, but this could not be demonstrated; they predict the occurrence of beneficial mutations, but examples of these can be counted on the fingers of one hand. Evolutionists predict that homologous structures will arise from the same areas of the embryo, yet the forelimbs of the newt arise from trunk segments 2-5, those of the lizard from segments 6-9, and those of the human, segments 13-18. In each case the model of evolution is changed to fit the latest findings.

This process of improving a model without rejecting it has also occurred in the creationist model. The early model, for example, stated that *all species* were separately created, which led to predictions that no new species would arise and that there would be no genetic interchange between species. Later evidence required modification of this model. The essential point is that while hypotheses must be capable of being proved false, it is *not* necessary that the models of which they are a part must also be falsifiable. Both the evolution and creation models have illustrated this principle repeatedly.

**"In evolutionary theory . . .
the history of life may be
viewed as one large tree.
Creationists, on the other
hand, see the history
of life as a forest of
small trees. . . ."**

In his negative reply to the qeustion "Should both evolution and creation be taught in the public schools?" Dr. Simpson relies on the artificial distinction between evolution as science and creation as religion. Having erected this straw man, Dr. Simpson then goes on to do an excellent job of showing why religion should not be taught in the science classroom. Unfortunately for his case, the study of origins cannot be so neatly categorized into scientific or religious.

A person who denies the existence of supernatural forces does, of course, eliminate himself from the discussion. His philosophy requires that he accept evolution, and his examination of the data can never be objective. Those who accept the existence of the supernatural may, however, examine the question of origins scientifically. They may consider alternative hypotheses, weighing the evidence for each. Some may conclude that an evolutionary explanation best fits the data. Others that creation is superior. The important question is whether students will have the opportunity, and the academic freedom, to consider alternatives. Will they be involved in the scientific enterprise of using data to support or reject competing hypotheses, or will they continue to be indoctrinated?

Bibliography

The following publications are available from Creation Life Publishers, Box 15666, San Diego, CA 92115.

1. Bliss, Richard. "Origins: Two Models."
2. Gish, Duane T. "Evolution—The Fossils Say No!"
3. Lammerts, Walter E., editor. "Why Not Creation?" Scientific Studies in

Special Creation." (Anthologies of articles from the "Creation Research Society Quarterly.")

4. Morris, Henry M. "Scientific Creationism."
5. Morris, Henry M. "The Twilight of Evolution."

Drs. Lester and Moore have shared their views on creationism and evolution. It is relevant for readers to know that they are members of the Creation Research Society, an organization which expresses its beliefs as follows:[1]

Ronald D. Simpson

1. The Bible is the written Word of God, and because it is inspired throughout, all its assertions are historically and scientifically true in all the original autographs. To the student of nature, this means that the account of origins in Genesis is a factual presentation of simple historical truths.

2. All basic types of living things, including man, were made by direct creative acts of God during the Creation Week described in Genesis. Whatever biological changes have occurred since Creation Week have accomplished only changes within the original created kinds.

3. The great flood described in Genesis, commonly referred to as the Noachian Flood, was a historic event worldwide in its extent and effect.

4. We are an organization of Christian men of science....

Drs. Lester and Moore represent the position that the above view should be taught alongside Darwinian evolution as an equally attractive scientific theory. Much of their support for creationism is based on what they consider to be weaknesses of the evolution model.

I did not agree to debate the merits of creationism vs. evolutionism. What I did agree to, and what I will do, is to discuss whether biblical creationism should be formally included in the science curriculum of our schools.

Dr. Anderson has demonstrated why the concept of special creation does not qualify as science, and it is primarily on this basis that we oppose its formal inclusion in science curricula. It is helpful, however, to look at how the courts of this country see the issue. During the past few years, every attempt to eliminate Darwinism from the classroom or to legislate mandatory teaching of biblical creationism has been ruled unconstitutional. For example, in *Epperson vs. Arkansas*, The U.S. Supreme Court invalidated the Arkansas anti-evolution statute on the grounds that the law existed solely on the basis of fundamentalist sectarian conviction.[2] The court concluded:

What's the Law?

Arkansas' law cannot be defended as an act of religious neutrality. Arkansas did not seek to exercise from the curricula of its schools and universities all discus-

---

[1] As quoted by John A. Moore in "Creationism in California," *Daedalus* 103(3): 176; 1974.
[2] Frederic S. LeClercq, "The Constitution and Creationism," *The American Biology Teacher* 36:140; March 1974.

sion of the origin of man. The law's effort was confined to an attempt to blot out a particular theory because of its supposed conflict with the Biblical account, literally read.

Today, under the guise of "equal time" or "fair play," a movement still exists to dilute the freedom of biology teachers.

The First Amendment to the U.S. Constitution protects the right of any competent person to speak on matters within his or her profession. This means that under the Constitution teachers have the necessary freedom to teach. To legislate curriculum of any kind whereby professional teachers are forced to teach material *foreign* to the parameters of their academic discipline is to violate the First Amendment. To deny biologists the right to treat evolution in an intellectually honest fashion is to deny them academic freedom and to disfigure the discipline.

Likewise, the Fourteenth Amendment insures all citizens protection from arbitrary restrictions against the pursuit of useful knowledge. This means that students have the necessary freedom to learn. To ban or curtail the teaching of any principle deemed significant by those in that field limits free exercise of learners and endangers their potential to perform in our society. This is why the courts of this country do not exempt public school children of no matter what background from studying biology and Darwinism. Considering recent actions of the courts in California and Tennessee relative to this issue, the question of "equal time" is now moot.

Dr. Moore concludes, "Selected indoctrination of young people at various levels of education regarding origins of life and of humankind need not continue." He further asserts that "On the grounds of constitutional and civil rights of students and science teachers alike, there are no significant reasons why science teachers in the United States or abroad cannot teach both models."

This recommendation is fallacious for several reasons. It not only violates the U.S. Constitution, but it represents a gross misunderstanding of both science and religion by advocating an intrusion of fundamentalist religious doctrine that is unacceptable both to the overwhelming majority of biological scientists and to most modern-day theologians.

This practice would in essence force students to choose between "science" and "religion"—because by presenting two conflicting theories in the science classroom, we imply that one is "right" and the other "wrong." In reality, evolution represents a scientific view and creationism a theological view. Science and religion operate at different positions along the spectrum of human knowledge and experience. Helping students to recognize this is to help them cope with a complex world wherein there exists a multiplicity of perspectives.

As I have noted, science teachers in this country are by law given the necessary freedom to teach those principles deemed central to the understanding of their discipline. And modern evolutionary theory is what most biologists and practicing scientists consider *the single most important principle* in the discipline today. It also, in large measure, *gives meaning to all other concepts in biology.*

As with all examples of freedom, there follows a need for responsibility. Just as it is our responsibility to teach evolutionary biology in an intellectually honest fashion, so it is our responsibility to help students discover the limitations of science. Perhaps we have been guilty of teaching many of our most cherished ideas as "scientific dogma." Perhaps we have not communicated clearly enough that while science has a way of interpreting events, so too do religion, philosophy, and art. Those who understand most clearly the discrete roles of science and religion in our culture are usually those who see the least conflict between the two enterprises. I think most science teachers have been careful to avoid this unnecessary conflict between science and religion.

Intellectual Honesty

The unfortunate part of the Creation Research Society's position is that they unyieldingly fail to separate their religious beliefs from their "scientific" endeavors. Because contemporary theory associated with evolution does not fit precisely their narrow, literal, and unchanging interpretation of Genesis, they label it false, indoctrinary, and anti-religious. This approach is the antithesis of scientific methodology.

In the past, biology teachers in some states have been unable to teach certain major principles in their discipline because of external pressures. By exercising the freedom we now have and doing so in a responsible fashion, we increase the probability that our students will live in a society that respects truth.

Some NSTA members feel that discussion of this topic has no place in our programs or journals. Others believe that as long as there are science teachers who want to discuss issues openly, NSTA is correct in providing forums such as this. One thing is certain—science teachers and students have faced and will face pressures to dilute their constitutional freedom to teach and to learn. Through the work of our professional organizations, we have been able to preserve much of this freedom—a freedom we must be sure is never again taken from us.[11]

Bibliography

1. Ayala, Francisco J. "Biology as an Autonomous Science." *American Scientist* 207–221; 1968.
2. Biological Sciences Curriculum Study. *BSCS Newsletter* No. 49 (*Science, Biology, and Evolution*); November 1972.

[11]Reprinted by permission of *The Science Teacher*. Anderson, Wyatt W., Lane P. Lester, John N. Moore, and Ronald D. Simpson, "Evolutionist-Creationist Roundtable," Vol. 43, No. 11, pp. 34–39, 1976.

3. "Creationists and Evolutionists: Confrontation in California." *Science* 178: 724–728; November 17, 1972.

4. Dobzhansky, Theodosius. "Nothing in Biology Makes Sense Except in the Light of Evolution." *The American Biology Teacher* 35(3): 125–129; March 1973.

5. LeClercq, Frederic S. "The Constitution and Creationism." *The American Biology Teacher* 36: 139–145; March 1974.

6. Moore, John A. "Creationism in California." *Daedalus* 103(3): 173–189; 1974.

7. Simpson, Ronald D. and Wyatt W. Anderson. "Same Song, Second Verse." *A Review of Biology: A Search for Order in Complexity*, Revised Edition. *The Science Teacher* 42(5): 40–42; May 1975.

References

Abraham, Michael R. (Ed.). *Science Education/Society: A Guide to Interaction and Influence.* Columbus, Ohio: ERIC Clearinghouse for Science, Mathematics, and Environmental Education, The Ohio State University, 1978.

This 1979 Yearbook of the Association for the Education of Teachers of Science contains articles by some two dozen science educators on various controversial topics, such as drugs, sex education, and creationism, and the implications of these topics for the teaching of science.

Fowler, John W. *Energy-Environment Source Book.* Washington, D.C.: National Science Teachers Association, 1975.

Almost every phase of the energy crisis is covered, and the discussions of various energy sources and problems will be very useful for teachers who wish to incorporate material on energy with their teaching.

Garigliano, Leonard J., and Beth Jo Knape (Comps.). *Environmental Education in the Elementary School.* Revised Edition. Washington, D.C.: National Science Teacher Association, 1977.

This collection of fifty-two articles that have appeared in *Science and Children* is also a valuable resource for middle and secondary school science teachers. A majority of the articles deal with classroom activities, outdoor activities, and games.

Lunetta, Vincent N., and Leon J. Zalewski. *Interactive Incidents from Classroom, School, and Community.* Washington, D.C.: National Science Teachers Association, 1974.

Over one hundred incidents, many of which involve the teaching of controversial subjects, are briefly described and are followed by one or more questions for use in initiating a discussion.

Vivian, V. Eugene. *Sourcebook for Environmental Education.* Saint Louis: C. V. Mosby Company, 1973.

In addition to an overall view of environmental education and suggestions for developing instructional materials, this sourcebook presents a series of interesting case studies on human communities in various parts of the country.

CHAPTER

12

On Becoming a Master Teacher of Science

TO TEACHERS OF SCIENCE: A CHARGE AND A CHALLENGE

I. KNOW YOUR STUFF.

Build sound knowledge of your subject.
Renew and extend it continually.
Reach beyond habitual and comfortable levels.

II. KEEP ALIVE.

Observe, experiment, and THINK: ask questions of Nature.
Read widely: keep asking questions of yourself.
Grow with your students and with the changing times.
Keep your spark of originality alive: cherish the spark of curiosity as you find it in your students.

III. BE INSPIRED—BE INSPIRING.

Give of yourself: teaching is a highly personal job.
Have a sense of mission: what you are doing has long-range importance.
Awaken in your students a desire to learn: you can only help them develop their own powers.
Make full use of your skills and personality: they are YOU.

Reprinted by permission of *The Science Teacher*. Sutton, Richard M., "A Charge and a Challenge," Vol. 24, No. 8, p. 379, 1957.

Professor Richard Sutton was one of thousands of master science teachers who have left their mark. An outstanding performer of physics demonstrations, a warm, gentle person, an inspirer of students, Sutton also helped others to realize the tremendous opportunities and responsibilities of the science teacher. It is in the hands of the science teacher and the teachers of other subjects that our nation trusts its most valuable resource—today's students and tomorrow's leaders.

As in the case of other professions, preparation for science teaching begins at an early age. Many science teachers credit an elementary or secondary school teacher with getting them started in science teaching. And most of us continue to use the laboratory investigations, demonstrations, and anecdotes we learned from these teachers. Participation in in-service programs, graduate programs, and professional organizations also add to our professional expertise. And as science teachers near retirement, they look back and see that becoming a master teacher of science is truly a life-long process.

Programs for the Preparation of Science Teachers

More than a thousand colleges and universities in the United States are authorized to prepare secondary school science teachers. Although there are many differences among these programs, all have several features in common. For instance, all the undergraduate programs require course work and include experiences to provide the prospective science teacher with competency in general education, in the sciences and related fields, and in professional education. Figure 12.1 shows the relative distribution of the courses in these three broad areas.

GENERAL EDUCATION

Science teachers should not only be professionally educated with extensive backgrounds in science, but they should also be familiar with the major ideas of the humanities, the social sciences, and the arts. They should understand how science relates to other disciplines, and they should be capable of informed, intelligent, and interested participation with students and colleagues in discussions that range over the spectrum of human thought and accomplishment. Our society needs and depends upon teachers who are among the best and most broadly educated of its citizens.

The amount and nature of course work required in general education vary from institution to institution, but on the average about 25 to 30 percent of all course work is in general education. It should be pointed out that many courses cannot be classified strictly as general education, professional education, or academic preparation. Courses in the history or philosophy of science are a case in point. These are very desirable courses for prospective science teachers and can contribute to the development of

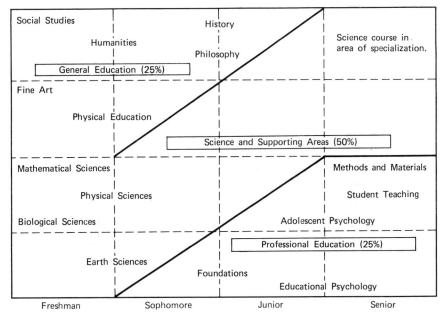

Social Studies | History | Science course in area of specialization.
Humanities
Philosophy
General Education (25%)
Fine Art |
Physical Education |
Science and Supporting Areas (50%)
Mathematical Sciences | Methods and Materials
Physical Sciences Student Teaching
Biological Sciences | Adolescent Psychology
Professional Education (25%)
Earth Sciences
Foundations
Educational Psychology

Freshman · Sophomore · Junior · Senior

FIGURE 12.1   This diagram of a teacher education program illustrates its hierarchial organization. General education and introductory science courses are usually taken first with advanced science and professional education placed later in the program.

RESEARCH REPORT

Characteristics of Outstanding Biology Teachers

The Outstanding Biology Teacher Award is given annually to a teacher in each state by the National Association of Biology Teachers. A panel of judges in each state selects the award winner. Dieter and Hounshell[1] studied the criteria used by 220 judges from forty-seven states to see which criteria were considered most important by the judges. From a list of 111 factors the judges were asked to rate, 21 were rated as the most important by the total group of judges. The top nine items are listed below:

• Interest and enthusiasm for biology
• Ability to encourage self-motivation in students
• Concern for student understanding of essential concepts
• Ability to inspire self-confidence in students
• Concern for student understanding of essential science processes
• Evidences of resourcefulness
• Adequacy of self-concept
• Concern for personal involvement of students in learning activities
• Evidences of ingenuity

[1]Donn L. Dieter and Paul B. Hounshell, "Biology Teacher Evaluation: Factors Significant in the Process," *Journal of Research in Science Teaching*, 12, 2(1975):139–146.

competencies in all three of the major divisions of a teacher education program.

PREPARATION IN THE SCIENCES

The major national committees of scientists and educators studying science teacher education in recent years all have recognized the need for both breadth and depth of preparation in science. Let's consider the need for breadth of preparation first.

The time is past when scientists can limit their pursuits to a single discipline. Likewise, science teachers need more than a passing acquaintance with the various fields of science. They should have such a command of the major areas of science that they can understand important advances as they occur on all of the major frontiers of sciences. In turn, they should be able to stimulate students and help them understand the web of disciplines comprising science. For the biology teacher, this means familiarity in chemistry, physics, mathematics, and the earth sciences as well as knowledge of botany, zoology, microbiology, genetics, ecology, and other areas in the biological sciences.

The first reason for depth of preparation emanates from the need of the teacher to be able to stimulate students intellectually. Much of this need is related to the teacher's competence in dealing with recent developments in science, directing student investigations, and serving as an advisor to those interested in scientific careers. In order to challenge students who will likely go on to college and major in science-related fields, rich, in-depth knowledge in specialized fields is needed.

A second reason for depth of preparation in science can be described as practical. Undergraduates preparing to teach science should also be prepared to do graduate work in one or more of the sciences if they are to improve their competence and keep abreast of recent developments. The ideas that today's college graduates are prepared, without a background for future graduate work, to teach in science until the middle of the twenty-first century is incomprehensible!

How are science teacher education programs structured to provide for both breadth and depth of preparation in science? Most contain a common foundation of courses that all prospective science teachers take. This common foundation, or core of courses, usually includes mathematics, chemistry, physics, and courses in the biological and earth sciences. This does not mean that every prospective science teacher takes the same courses. In institutions that have two or more introductory sequences, a student planning to specialize in physics might take the courses in physics, chemistry, and mathematics with the physical science majors and courses in the biological and earth sciences that are designed specifically for nonmajors.

In addition to the common foundations courses, each student usually takes courses in an area of specialization (sometimes called a major or a teaching field). This area of specialization may itself be fairly broad, such as earth science, biological science, and physical science, or in a more restricted area such as geology, physics, or botany. Most science educators feel it is important that the program provide for both breadth and depth of preparation. However, within that framework, there should be flexibility for institutions and individual students to design programs that best meet their needs. In other words, no one list of science courses is best for every prospective science teacher.

About 50 percent of the course work in most programs for the preparation of secondary school science teachers is devoted to science, mathematics, and other supporting subjects, such as statistics, computer science, and the history and/or philosophy of science. In spite of the fact that half of the four-year program is devoted to science, beginning science teachers often complain that they still do not know as much science as they feel they should. In addition, beginning teachers with strong science backgrounds may lack some of the specific knowledge and skills needed to effectively teach secondary school science.

As in the case of other professions, it is doubtful if any preparatory programs can ever include enough course work to satisfy everyone's needs. Moreover, there are many desirable competencies that probably are best learned through practical experience in other settings, and not in course work in the traditional sense. As a part of their professional development, prospective science teachers should take advantage of other opportunities, such as the following:

- Participate in science clubs and other out-of-class activities on the campus
- Attend science lectures, seminars, and meetings of scientific societies
- Take summer employment in research labs, summer camps, a hospital, or other places where science-related work is going on
- Attend a summer field camp, which is especially valuable for prospective biology and earth science teachers
- Serve as laboratory or teaching assistants in science courses
- Volunteer to judge a science fair or serve as an advisor to a high school student working on a research project
- Develop hobby interests, such as photography, scuba diving, amateur radio, and bird watching

PROFESSIONAL EDUCATION

As in the case of general education and preparation in the sciences, there are both commonalities and uniquenesses in the professional education phase of science teacher programs in the United States. Common courses include those dealing with the historical, philosophical, psychological, and sociological foundations of education. Some institutions teach general methods courses taken by all prospective teachers, while others offer science methods courses or more specialized courses such as biology methods courses. Student teaching or some type of internship program is an important part of every program for the preparation of secondary school teachers. Professional education courses usually make up 20 to 25 percent of a four-year undergraduate program.

In recent years, many universities have experimented with programs for the preparation of science teachers. This is appropriate, as a means not only of improving the program, but also of providing science educators with opportunities to apply principles of scientific methodology in their own day-to-day work. Prospective science teachers should not only encounter experimentation and research in their science courses, but they should also be participants in experimental professional programs and research studies in education.

Followup studies usually find that graduates of a program rank student teaching as the most valuable part of their professional preparation. They place high value on the opportunity to put into practice what they have learned, just as secondary school science students state that they learn science best through direct experience. Because of the advantages that accrue when prospective teachers have more contact with secondary school students, some institutions have developed field-based teacher education programs. These programs range from placing more emphasis on student teaching to teaching all professional courses in a secondary school. In the latter case, a team of faculty members (for example, a science educator, an educational psychologist, and a sociologist) may work with a group of eight to twelve prospective teachers in a clinical setting in a large secondary school.

There also is interest in spreading the professional education courses over the four years rather than concentrating them during the last year or two of the program. This allows students more time to develop the high-level professional skills required of teachers. Courses in the freshman and sophomore year also allow students to explore teaching as a possible career. In many cases, students find out that teaching is really what they want to do. In other cases, they find that teaching is not what they had expected, and so they still have time to transfer to some other collegiate program.

Figure 12.2 shows some of the activities performed by college sophomores who serve as teacher aides two half-days each week in middle or high school science departments. The teacher aide experience is part of an introductory course in science education at North Carolina State University. It represents one way of getting students involved earlier and making the program more field-based.

In addition to more emphasis on field-based programs, there have been efforts to develop competency-based teacher education (CBTE) programs. The rationale for these programs is similar to that for other competency-based programs, such as those mandated in some states and

Observing cooperating teacher's classes

Observing other science teachers' classes

Helping students during class with written work

Tutoring students who need remedial help

Working with able students on science projects and reports

Working with students in a science club or other school activities

Teaching a topic to a small group of students

Presenting a mini-lesson to an entire class

Accompanying students on field trips and other activities outside of school

Developing instructional modules

Identifying diagnostic instruments or techniques to assess student achievement

Assemblying equipment for laboratory investigations and demonstrations

Developing book lists and book orders in science for the library

Inventorying and/or cataloging science books and equipment

Locating and/or ordering filmstrips, films, and other audiovisual aids

Making models and other audiovisual aids

Assemblying bulletin boards

Checking homework and other written assignments

Grading tests and quizzes

Keeping records and recording student progress

FIGURE 12.2   Examples of activities performed by teacher aides in secondary school science classrooms

found in many elementary and secondary schools. In general, competency-based teacher education programs have three characteristics in common:

1. The desired outcomes or competencies to be possessed by those completing the program are made explicit and are shared with students before instruction occurs.

2. Techniques and instruments that assess these outcomes are developed and are used to determine if a student has acquired each of the competencies.

3. Instructional strategies, materials, and organizational plans are developed that allow students to progress through the program at their own pace.

Although many institutions claim to have competency-based teacher education, few have programs that incorporate all three of the characteristics described above. CBTE remains a controversial practice, and many educators feel it has strengths and limitations similar to those involved in practices such as using behavioral objectives, competency tests, and individualized instruction. But regardless of one's personal preferences and views on CBTE, it is important that all educators be receptive to new approaches and support experimentation in teacher education.

STUDENT
TEACHING

It is a common practice to require some clinical or on-the-job experience of all individuals entering a profession. Those preparing for careers in medicine and law engage in internships. Work experience often accompanies a program of study in fields such as engineering and architecture. Student teaching or some other type of internship is required in all accredited teacher education programs in the United States. It usually lasts from eight to fifteen weeks and may vary from a few hours each day to working full time in schools near the college or university campus. This is a crucial period of time for those majoring in science education. As stated earlier, it is an opportunity for prospective science teachers to apply their knowledge in science, to practice using the many instructional strategies learned in methods courses, and, perhaps most importantly, to find out how well they can work with younger students.

The first several days of student teaching involve getting acquainted with staff members, observing classes, learning the names of students, and locating the lunchroom, principal's office, and teachers' lounge. Typically, the student teacher has opportunities to teach on a limited basis during the second and third weeks. Most cooperating teachers and university supervisors agree that student teachers should begin to "get their feet wet" as early as possible but that a full teaching load should not be attempted until the student teacher is doing a good job with one or two classes. The amount of responsibility and the workload assigned should be based on several factors, one of which is the amount of prior field experience the student teacher has had. In field-based programs where education students are in the schools prior to student teaching, responsibilities can be accepted much sooner.

The primary objective of student teaching is to provide opportunities for prospective teachers to develop and demonstrate competencies that are considered necessary for entry into teaching. Obviously, it takes many years to develop fully the sophisticated skills we would like to see all teachers possess. Student teaching is a time, however, for aspiring teachers to assess their strengths and to continue efforts to improve weaknesses. In *Guiding a Student Teacher*, Thomas Brown outlines common teaching errors that occur among student teachers. These errors are displayed in Figure 12.3 and can be constructive to students preparing for student teaching. While this list may possess a negative orientation, it nevertheless contains many common pitfalls faced in student teaching. When used in a positive fashion, it can be quite useful in preparing for the many challenges of student teaching.

Prospective science teachers can benefit from working with younger children as well as students of secondary school age.

Lesson Aims:

1. Purposes of a lesson are not shared with pupils.
2. Subject matter is presented as if purpose was inherent in it.
3. Lesson aims are frequently too abstract to lead to understanding.
4. Lesson is begun where teacher thinks pupils should be rather than where they actually are.
5. The aim of the lesson, though clearly stated, may not be worth realizing.

Motivation:

1. Motivation is viewed as entertainment with no relevance to the lesson.
2. Interest of pupils may be taken for granted.
3. Too much time is spent on motivation with a topic that is inherently interesting to pupils.

FIGURE 12.3 Common teaching errors. (*Source:* Thomas J. Brown, *Guiding a Student Teacher,* Second Edition. New York: Harper & Row, Publishers, 1968, Appendix E.)

Audiovisual Aids:

1. Visual aids are assumed to require no study or are viewed as a convenient method of passing time; hence, teacher does not explain, discuss, or comment on them when used.
2. Charts, pictures, models, or demonstration material are not large enough or displayed well enough for all of the class to see.

Use of Chalkboard:

1. Material that would be clearer if placed on board is dictated or given orally.
2. Handwriting of teachers or pupils illegible, too faint, or too small for chalkboard material to be read by all pupils.
3. Chalkboards not cleared before beginning a new class.
4. Material inscribed on board with no logical order.

Pupil-Teacher Rapport:

1. Lack of graciousness or sympathy with pupil efforts.
2. Lack of faith in ability of a class is communicated.
3. Cooperative class attitude not developed: "Who will read that aloud for me?" "Tell me . . ." "I want you . . ."
4. Pupils not required to speak and be heard by others.
5. Group structure imperiled by singling out certain students for high praise or by making invidious comparisons: "Why can't you all do your work as neatly as Helen?"
6. Pupils not made aware of progress.
7. Pupils referred to as "children."

Lesson Development:

1. Pupils given information that might better be elicited from them.
2. An abstract concept may be illustrated with another equally abstract concept.
3. Pupil contributions not heeded or built upon.
4. Class activities not varied or, having found a good technique, teacher uses it until he destroys its effectiveness.
5. Lessons unrelated to present or future lives of pupils.
6. Lesson of the day plunged into without "setting the stage."
7. Relationships between concepts and facts not made clear.
8. Vague terms—social prestige, citizenship, etc.—go unchallenged.
9. Class time wasted and then pupils are pushed to finish: "Quick, quick. We haven't much time left."
10. Lesson developed with one or two pupils in the class.
11. A correct response by one pupil is assumed to be a measure of general understanding.

FIGURE 12.3 *(Continued)*

12. Statements such as "This is important to remember" are employed instead of the teacher presenting material so that it is important.
13. Teacher tends to be too helpful and to explain too much thoroughly, thus creating the idea in pupils' minds that their work is being done and will be done for them.
14. Class time of all pupils is taken to bring one pupil out of error.
15. Pupil answers evaluated by the teacher instead of sharing this responsibility with the class.
16. Tendency to moralize without submitting values for pupil analysis: "Always aim high." "Never lend money."

Questioning:

1. Questions may be asked and answers expected before providing pupils with any knowledge of the subject.
2. Questions asked without a specific frame of reference: "What happened in Chapter X?"
3. Pupils given no time to ponder an answer to questions asked.
4. Teacher answers own questions.
5. Questions not adapted to intelligence level of pupils.

Lesson Planning:

1. A discussion lesson is assumed to require no aim.
2. Transitions from one activity or aspect of lesson content to another not thought through.
3. Planning in detail neglected for inspiration.
4. Lesson plan may be imposed upon class.

Voice and Speech:

1. Unnatural terminology employed: "Leave my establishment of employment." "What then ensued?"
2. Monotone quality of speech creates the impression of a lack of enthusiasm.
3. Utterances habitually begun with "All right." "Now." "Well."

Classroom Management:

1. Too much time spent taking the roll and getting class under way.
2. Names of pupils not known by teacher.
3. Teacher either paces "like a tiger in a cage" or stays glued to one spot.
4. Teacher does not insist on immediate attention from the class at the bell and permits class to leave without formal dismissal.
5. Procedures for homework, pencil sharpening, roll, etc., not established or adhered to.

FIGURE 12.3 (*Continued*)

Student teaching represents a time when prospective teachers must learn to deal successfully with a wide spectrum of individuals. The relationship with the cooperating teacher is the most crucial. In most cases, student teachers are placed with proven master teachers, and personality factors are considered in making these placements. The student teacher must also learn to deal with other faculty members, the principal, assistant principals, and guidance counselors. Of course, another crucial group with whom the student teacher must learn to deal successfully is students. Research has shown that the major apprehension of beginning teachers is their concern over being accepted by their students. And finally, student teaching is a time to learn about dealing with parents. Student teachers should take advantage of opportunities to meet parents by attending parent conferences and PTA meetings. Learning to deal with different kinds of people is a professional skill that makes the difference between successful or unsuccessful teaching. The student teacher should feel free to ask for assistance from the cooperating teacher and university supervisor in establishing these many lines of communication. In most cases, the student teacher who is skillful in developing positive relationships with people at all levels within the education community will have a successful student teaching experience.

ALTERNATIVE PROGRAMS

Although many of the science teachers entering the profession each year have completed undergraduate programs in science education, others enter the profession via other avenues. One of the largest of the alternative programs is the Master of Arts in Teaching (MAT) degree. Although MAT programs vary from campus to campus, most have the following in common:

1. Students entering an MAT program have an undergraduate degree or background in the sciences.

2. The program consists of work in professional education and the sciences, usually about half in each area.

3. The program lasts twelve months or longer, with students usually entering at the beginning of a summer session.

4. Students do an internship, or student teaching, in a secondary school during at least part of the academic year.

5. Students completing the program receive a graduate degree (MAT) and graduate-level certification.

College science graduates may also prepare for secondary school teaching by enrolling in the professional courses required in an undergraduate science teacher education program. Although practices vary, students sometimes also have to complete undergraduate general education and subject matter requirements. For instance, a zoology major might have to take undergraduate botany courses and work in speech and history if he or she had not already done so.

In times of crucial teacher shortages, some state educational agencies issue temporary teaching certificates to college graduates who do not have the courses required for certification. Recipients of the certificates usually have two to three years to take the required courses by attending classes at nights, on Saturdays, and during the summer. Many science teachers who have entered the profession in this manner report that their first year of teaching was truly a "baptism under fire."

Entering the Profession

Teaching is usually classified as a profession, though not all educators agree on a definition of "profession." Regardless of the definition used, it is important to consider some of the major characteristics of a profession and what a person should do in order to be considered a professional teacher.

1. Professionals are essentially *service oriented*. A professional by most standards is one who desires to contribute to the betterment of humankind.

2. People in professions are characterized by a high degree of *commitment* to their chosen field. It is in the best interest of any professional group to attract and retain the highest caliber of membership possible. This includes the willingness to recruit and train the most qualified young people available.

3. Considerable *formal preparation* is necessary before one can enter a profession. Those preparing to enter medicine, law, or teaching must take general courses, specialized courses in closely allied disciplines, and engage in professional or clinical experiences before being eligible to practice their profession.

4. Professions possess *standards for entry*. There is almost always a formal licensing required; this process is usually external to the college or university and often involves passing national or state examinations before certification can be completed.

5. Professions usually have established *standards for maintaining status*. Those found incompetent can lose their license. In some cases, members who do not engage in required certificate renewal programs can also lose their credentials.

6. In addition to entry and maintenance standards, professions adhere to *codes of ethics*. Physicians are expected to provide the best possible health care for their patients, and lawyers are obligated to represent clients to the best of their ability. Teachers are expected to meet the needs of all students assigned to them and to operate within the policies of their school district and professional organizations. Most professions have pro-

cedures for removing members who engage in unethical or immoral practices.

7. Professions in their purest form in this country are *self-regulating*. In this regard, members have input into the establishment and regulation of standards. The professional is a recognized expert in his or her field and is afforded the necessary *freedom* and *respect* in which to perform this role. It is in this regard that most teachers question whether or not education qualifies as a profession. Teachers in this country have only limited input into many of the important decision-making functions that affect their status.

8. Perhaps the most distinguishing characteristic of professionalism is the *knowledge base* from which members draw. The mark of a true profession is that its members perform services based on a highly organized body of knowledge. The field of medicine is generally considered as one of the best examples of a true profession. This, in part, is due to the fact that physicians operate today from a highly refined base of research and theory and can demonstrate skills that members outside their group do not possess.

The last point deserves additional comment. Advances in the biological and physical sciences have been enormous during the past few decades. Research and theory in the behavioral and social sciences have been much slower in coming. However, as more is learned about human behavior, group dynamics, and human learning, the larger the arsenal of skills teachers will have. In the meantime, the more teachers know about planning, instruction, management, and evaluation, the more skilled they can be in practicing their trade. For the teacher who is capable of motivating all types of students, for the teacher who is able to teach something to every youngster in class and who, perhaps more than anyone else in society, literally influences the future of countless young people each year, one can hardly deny this person the distinction of being considered *a professional*.

CERTIFICATION

A teaching certificate is a license to practice and is required to teach in all public elementary and secondary schools. A half dozen or so states require a teaching certificate to teach in independent or private schools, and a few require such credentials for teaching in public post-secondary technical schools, junior colleges, and community colleges. Those interested in teaching in a particular state or type of institution should consult a certification guide such as one published annually by Woellner and Wood.[2]

---

[2]Elizabeth H. Woellner and M. Aurilla Wood, Requirements for Certification (Teachers, Counselors, Librarians, and Administrators for Elementary Schools, Secondary Schools and Junior Colleges), Chicago: University of Chicago Press (revised edition published annually).

WHAT STUDENTS SAY Science Teaching as a Career	• Although I like science, I've never thought about teaching. • Not for me! • Like the idea except for money. • Yes, but I would want to teach overseas or join the Peace Corps. • Has its ups and downs. • Yuk! • My Dad would have a fit, but my science teacher would be overjoyed. • Think it would have a lot of challenges. • A lot of people in my family are teachers. • I'm not sure I'd be patient enough. • If I could be as good as my chemistry teacher, I'd love it.

The issuance of teaching certificates in the United States is a responsibility of the states, and each of the fifty states has established a state agency for doing so. Although the requirements vary from state to state, holders of a valid certificate in one state often have little difficulty in obtaining a certificate in another state. Many of the states have reciprocity agreements. Graduates of teacher education programs accredited by the National Council for the Accreditation of Teacher Education (NCATE) will find this facilitates their getting a certificate in a state other than the one in which they graduated. A few states have unique requirements, such as requiring certain courses, such as "The History of Texas" or "American Government." These states will often issue a temporary certificate to applicants who do not have these courses and will allow one or two years to complete this requirement. A few states also require applicants to make a satisfactory score on an examination such as the National Teachers Examination. Certification requirements for teaching positions in the United States territories and various kinds of overseas schools vary. Applicants for positions in these schools should inquire about certification at the time of application.

OBTAINING A TEACHING POSITION

Obtaining a teaching position is a bit like going fishing. The more hooks you put in the water, the better your chance of getting the kind of position you really want. And like fishing, job hunting is more than a matter of luck. There are several things the applicant can do in addition to making numerous applications. The following should be considered by both inexperienced and experienced teachers when seeking teaching positions.

1. *Use the placement service at a college or university.* Most institutions of higher education maintain placement offices to assist their graduates in obtaining positions, both at the time of graduation and throughout their professional career. These services are usually free or are available for a

very modest fee. Some placement offices will also assist students who took courses at the institution but who did not complete a degree.

The placement office maintains a folder for each person desiring to use its service. This folder includes personal data, a record of courses taken and grades received, work experience, participation in out-of-class activities, and copies of letters of reference. By using a placement service, applicants are spared the expense and bother of sending transcripts and asking for letters of reference for each position for which they apply.

Placement services list positions that are open and schedule interviews for school officials coming to the campus during certain times of the year. Although practices vary, most will contact the applicant before sending his or her folder to a school with a teaching vacancy.

2. *Contact school officials in systems in which you might have an interest in teaching.* Most school systems have an administrator in their central office who has the primary responsibility for employing teachers. Inquiries about a possible teacher position can be made to this person by telephone or letter. It is customary to ask for an appointment if you wish to talk with this individual.

Figure 12.4 presents a sample letter than can be used for inquiring about a teaching position. The letter should be short, to the point, neatly typed, and give all the necessary information. A good thing to remember in job hunting is, "You don't get a second chance to make a first impression." Whether by letter or during an interview, always present yourself in a manner that maximizes your assets.

3. *Use personal contacts whenever possible.* Often, it is "who you know," *not* "what you know" that puts a person in contact with a prospective employer. Inexperienced teachers find it profitable to discuss their professional aspirations with their advisor and other college professors. Frequently, these faculty members know someone in the geographic area in which the student wishes to secure a position and are willing to give a personal reference or make a telephone call on the student's behalf. It is through these kinds of contacts that the person looking for a position is most likely to learn about vacancies in other parts of the country.

4. *Use the placement services of professional societies.* Some professional societies maintain a placement service similar to those provided by colleges and universities. There is usually a charge for the service, but in some cases it is paid for by the employer. Most societies also provide placement services as part of their state, regional, and national meetings. Most often, this consists of bulletin boards where those seeking teachers and teachers seeking employment can post notices. Personal contacts at professional meetings often prove to be very beneficial for teachers seeking employment.

5. *Consult newspaper and directories.* It is customary in some parts of the country for school districts to run ads in newspapers and professional journals. These ads are especially helpful to those desiring to relocate in a

February 16, 1980
(A) 103A Seaside Apartments
4900 Lighthouse Road
Cookville, Texas 75558

Dr. Jay Desmond
Personnel Officer
(B) Old Township Independent School District
1345 Henry Marshall Drive
Oiltown, Texas 78371

Dear Dr. Desmond:

(C) In May of this year I will be completing my undergraduate degree in science education at Cookville State College. I have specialized in chemistry and have taken extra courses in physics and mathematics. My student teaching was done in chemistry and physical science at Red Elm High School during the fall semester of 1979.

While a student here at Cookville State I have participated on the track team as a long-distance runner and have worked in the library approximately twenty hours per week. The past two summers have been spent as Waterfront Director at Camp Arthur.

(D) I would very much like to obtain a position beginning in the fall of this year as a teacher of chemistry. I also would consider teaching physics, mathematics, and physical science and would be interested in assisting with out-of-class science activities and the track team. If your school system may have such a vacancy in science, I would very much like to receive an application form.

(E) I can be reached at the above address or by phone (512-254-8907) until May 15; after that date, I will be at Camp Arthur (RFD 1, Box 74, Arthur, Texas, 75411; phone 512-362-9947.

Thank you for your consideration.

Sincerely,

Jane B. Rachelson

(A) Always include a complete inside address so that any response can reach you promptly.

(B) Letters sent to appropriate individuals often receive more positive response than those addressed to an impersonal "Dear Sir" or "Whom It May Concern"; most states publish annually an educational directory that gives the names, titles, and addresses of officials in each school district.

(C) Academic background, work experience, extra-curricular activities, type of position sought, and time of availability should be clearly and concisely stated.

(D) It is considered ethical to inquire about a possible vacancy in this manner; it is unethical to say you are available if the school district decides to replace an incumbent teacher or to mention the name of a teacher you would like to replace.

(E) It is of utmost importance that prospective employers be told how an applicant can be contacted by mail or phone. The lack of such information may be the major cause of qualified applicants not getting a position.

FIGURE 12.4 Sample letter of inquiry about a science teaching position.

different part of the country. There are several directories that are helpful to those interested in teaching positions outside of the United States.[3,4]

Several other steps are usually involved in obtaining a position in addition to locating potential positions using some or all of the approaches described above. Most school systems have an application form that they require all applicants to complete. Such forms should be taken seriously and completed as neatly and accurately as possible.

6. *Applicant Forms and Interviews.* Applicants also are usually required to have interviews with the personnel official and with principals and department chairpersons. The interview offers both school officials and teacher candidates an excellent opportunity to gather useful information and make important decisions. The interview, particularly if it is with the person who will make the decision on employment or the person to whom the teacher will be directly responsible, is the most important part of the entire job-finding process. It is only natural for candidates seeking their first position to be uneasy or nervous during an interview. Most interviewers recognize this and are skilled in helping those being interviewed to relax and enjoy the interview.

Among the most important things for the teacher candidate to remember during an interview are to be alert, enthusiastic, and honest, and to act as natural as possible. Another factor that interviewers look for is the kind of questions the candidate asks. The candidate should gather as much information as possible ahead of time and ask questions that reflect knowledge and interest in the school system. While asking good questions during an interview is highly desirable, too many questions may not give the interviewer ample time to learn about the candidate; therefore, they should be used in moderation and should be presented at the appropriate time.

Interviewers themselves have a list of favorite questions. Since they try to learn as much as possible about each candidate, it is best for the person being interviewed to give answers of moderate length. "Yes" or "no" answers are too terse, while verbose answers are too time-consuming. A few questions interviewers frequently ask inexperienced teachers include:

- "Why do you want to be a teacher?"
- "Why do you think you will be a successful teacher"
- "What is your philosophy of education?"
- "How do you plan to maintain discipline in the classroom?"
- "Are you willing to be involved in extracurricular activities? If so, which ones?"

[3]Department of Defense, Dependent Schools. *Overseas Employment Opportunities for Educators.* Alexandria, Virginia: DOD Schools, published annually.
[4]Harold E. Dilts, *Teacher's Guide to Teaching Positions in Foreign Countries—1979,* Seventh Edition, Ames, Iowa: Teaching Positions in Foreign Countries, 1979.

In addition to answering the interviewer's questions, the prospective teacher at an interview usually has an opportunity to ask about the school's science program.

- "Are you willing to teach a course outside your major?"
- "What additional skills or areas of interest do you have that you would be willing to share with our students?"
- "Why do you want to teach in this school system?"
- "What was your student teaching experience like?"

It is helpful for the prospective teacher to have a general idea of how he/she will respond to questions like these. Perhaps the most important rule to follow is that *one should be honest.* If you are not willing to coach, you should say so. If chemistry and physics are the only areas you feel comfortable teaching, this, too, should be stated. In the long run, interviewers appreciate honesty and are often dubious of candidates who promise to be "all things to all people."

There are other tips for interviewing, but most of these follow lines of good judgment and taste and need little elaboration. Obviously, one should be on time for the interview (arriving too early is not recommended either). Dress should be business-like—not too formal or too informal. Smoking and gum chewing are taboo during an interview. And, the first question asked should not be, "What does this job pay?" The candidate should concentrate on the interviewer and refrain from taking notes or looking around the room.

Looking for a job affords beginning teachers an opportunity to "sell their services to the highest bidder." After four or five years of hard work, an aspiring teacher does have something of value to offer, and the interview is an opportunity to demonstrate this.

Opportunities for Professional Growth

In addition to the satisfaction gained from working with students, the opportunity to grow intellectually, to learn about new ideas in science and pedagogy, to be free to try out new approaches in the classroom, to interact with exciting people through reading, travel, and participation in professional societies are the things that make science teaching an exciting profession. And these opportunities should not be wasted; rather, the master teacher of science is always looking for ways to improve his or her expertise and, in so doing, have a greater influence on the lives of students.

INSERVICE
PROGRAMS

State departments of public instruction, colleges and universities, governmental agencies, private groups, local school districts, and others provide in-service programs for science teachers. These faculty development programs take many forms. They may be offered late afternoons, evenings, Saturdays, on teacher workdays during the school year, or during the summer. They vary in length from a few hours to several days and may carry continuing education credit, certificate renewal credit, or, in some cases, credit that can be applied toward graduate degrees. Fees vary, with short programs often being free and extended programs carrying college credit being the most inexpensive. Some states and school districts require teachers to periodically earn a certain number of credits—for example, five hours of continuing education or college credit every five years. Some school districts pay for all the in-service work required of teachers.

Figure 12.5 shows examples of groups sponsoring inservice programs for science teachers and the kinds of programs offered. As can be seen from the example, inservice programs provide excellent opportunities for science teachers to expand and update both their academic and their professional preparation.

GRADUATE WORK

Before World War II, there were few graduate programs for science teachers in which they could continue both the preparation in the sciences and professional education begun in the undergraduate program. Fortunately, this is not true today, and most institutions offering graduate work have programs specially designed for science teachers. Many of these institutions offer classes in the late afternoon or evening, on Saturdays, and during the summer, so that science teachers can complete some or all of their graduate work while they are employed. Courses taught at branch campuses and extension centers make it easier for teachers located in remote areas to take these courses.

MASTER'S LEVEL PROGRAMS. Although graduate programs vary from campus to campus, most master's level programs in science education contain some or all of the following features:

1. Half or more of the program is in science, with the student in science education taking a broader range of courses than the graduate student specializing in a specific discipline. For example, a biology teacher might

Local School District	Implementation of a local curriculum for middle school science. Local school policies on teaching controversial subjects, such as sex education, use of tobacco, alcohol and controlled drugs, and environmental issues.
State Department of Public Instruction	Federal and state laws governing laboratory work in secondary school science classrooms. Meeting the needs of all students in a mainstreamed classroom.
Colleges and Universities	Energy Education Conference Teaching Advanced Placement Chemistry
Local Museum	Wildflower Biology Using Terrariums in the Classroom
Commercial Publishers and Equipment Suppliers	Implementing IAC Chemistry Using a Reflecting Telescope in Earth Science
Government Agencies	Water and Soil Conservation Practices The Science of Civil Defense
Commercial and Industrial Groups	Conserving Electrical Energy Industry's Contribution to a Better Life
Private Groups	A Meteorological Field Day (sponsored by local chapter of American Meteorological Society) Beautification of a School Grounds as a Science Project (sponsored by a local garden club)
Local Teacher Centers	A discussion session run by local teachers on how to improve average daily attendance. A debate on whether or not local teachers should develop a drug education program

FIGURE 12.5 Examples of inservice programs for science teachers.

take courses in botany, zoology, genetics, microbiology, biochemistry, ecology, and applied fields such as horticulture and animal science.

2. Some of the science courses are designed specially for science teachers. This type of course was emphasized in many of the Academic Year, Summer, and In-service Institutes supported by the National Science Foundation beginning in the mid-1950s. Examples would include courses with the titles of Recent Advances in Chemistry, Physics for High School Teachers, and Advanced Placement Biology.

3. Science courses emphasizing research participation and field experience are highly desirable parts of the science component of a science education graduate program. Unfortunately, not many science education students are able to include this kind of course in their graduate program.

4. About half of the total program is in professional education, with part of this being specifically in science education. Graduate science education

courses may deal with the historical, philosophical, sociological, and psychological foundations of science education, with curriculum development, and with various strategies and materials for science teaching. Graduate courses in professional education are often taken in several areas, including courses such as advanced educational psychology, tests and measurement, guidance and counseling, educational statistics, and foundations of education.

5. Although most master's programs at one time required the student to complete an independent investigation culminating in a thesis, many master's programs today consist entirely of course work. Students doing a thesis usually investigate a problem dealing with some phase of science teaching.

Figure 12.6 shows the graduate programs of two students with differing backgrounds and career goals who completed master's degrees at the same institution. In both cases, these students, as is usually the case at other institutions and in other states, were also eligible to receive a graduate-level teaching certificate.

SIXTH-YEAR PROGRAMS.   Graduate programs for an Educational Specialist Degree and/or Educational Specialist Certificate usually contain many of the same features found in master's programs in science education. These include course work of a higher level in the sciences, science education, and general professional education. Depending on the individual student's career aspirations, these programs may also include research requirements or an internship in supervision, teacher education, college-level science teaching, or some other area.

DOCTORAL PROGRAMS.   Programs leading to the Doctor of Philosophy (Ph.D.) and Doctor of Education (Ed.D.) degrees vary from institution to institution, and an individual's program usually reflects his or her background and career plans. Course work requirements most often include additional work in the sciences, science education, general professional education, and research tool courses such as statistics, experimental design, and test and measurements. The dissertation, in which a student reports the results of his or her research, is an important part of any doctoral program.

PROFESSIONAL
ORGANIZATIONS

In addition to the many national, state, and local professional organizations for all teachers, there are several professional organizations primarily for science teachers or specifically for teachers of biology, chemistry, physics, or earth science. The names, addresses, and journals published by each of these are listed in Appendix B.

Student 1		Student 2	
(Broad background in science and five years as a junior high science teacher; wishes to become department head and perhaps later to be a district science supervisor)		(Strong background in biological sciences and associated areas; plans to continue teaching general biology and advanced biology; has some interest in doctoral level work in science education)	
Master of Education in Science Education		Master of Science in Science Education	
Courses	Semester hours credit	Courses	Semester hours credit
Foundations of Science Education	3	Foundations of Science Education	3
Laboratory Practicum in General Science	2	Seminar in Science Education	2
Special Problems in Science Teaching	2	Tests and Measurements	2
Introduction to Guidance	2	Educational Statistics	3
Principles of Teaching Reading	2	Advanced Ecology	3
Exceptional Students	3	Human Genetics	3
Introduction to School Supervision	2	Recent Advances in Microbiology	3
Astrophysics	3	Biological Oceanography	3
Recent Advances in Geology	3	Cell Biology	3
Ecology	3	Research in Science Education (thesis)	5
Environmental Chemistry	3	TOTAL	30
Summer Field Camp in Geology	8		
TOTAL	36		

FIGURE 12.6 Sample master's programs in science education.

As in the case of other professional organizations, the primary purposes of organizations for science teachers are to further the development of the profession of science teaching and to assist members in becoming better science educators. Many services are provided to accomplish these purposes, including the following:

1. Journals, such as *The Science Teacher* and *The American Biology Teacher*, are published which contain articles about advances in science and teaching. Advertisements, book and film reviews, and other notices assist the reader in keeping up to date on tools available for science teaching.

2. Other publications, such as those published by NSTA entitled *What Research Says to the Science Teacher* and *Science Career Exploration for Women*, are produced which help the science teacher keep abreast of new ideas and provide materials for use with students.

3. Committees are appointed which study problems, such as the teaching of evolution and the use of live animals in experimental work, and issue position statements and reports.

4. National, regional, and state meetings, seminars, and workshops are held which afford thousands of science teachers the opportunity to exchange ideas with scientists and science educators from around the world. Figure 12.7 gives examples of these many opportunities which were a part of a recent national meeting for science teachers.

The relationship between professional organizations and science teachers is not a "one-way street." Meetings, publications, and other activities also provide opportunities for science teachers to share their ideas and experiences with other members of the profession. Preparing a speech or publication helps the individual organize his or her thoughts, provides for a sense of satisfaction, and often stimulates the person to greater achievements. Thus, both those appearing on a program and those in the audience benefit. This is the hallmark of a professional organization—a community of professionals working together to improve the teaching of science and their own expertise.

WORK, TRAVEL, AND LEISURE-TIME ACTIVITIES

Earlier in this chapter, the case was made that undergraduates preparing to teach science could enhance their preparation by engaging in extracurricular activities. In like manner, practicing science teachers have many opportunities for professional development that go beyond taking in-service and graduate courses and participating in professional organizations.

Many part-time and summer jobs contribute significantly by providing experience with new industrial materials, techniques, and applications. A teacher working in a hospital, as an environmental quality control technician, or an assistant to a veterinarian will gain experience that can be used to enrich a life science or biology course. Working as a counselor in a summer camp allows teachers to develop a better understanding of both nature and young people. Because of the potential contributions of work experiences, some schools and professional organizations assist science teachers in finding science-related positions.

Travel can be both recreational and educational. Trips to national parks, museums, and foreign countries can result in a rich resource for science teaching. A camera for taking slides is a must for such trips, and most science teachers also like to collect brochures and other available materials. Some science teachers find it desirable to plan their travel around a science theme, such as Astronomical Observations in the Western United States, Great Physicists' Laboratories in England, or Plants of the Everglades. Those interested in such travel may wish to check with professional organizations about the availability of science-oriented tours.

Types of convention activities	Examples
General Sessions (Total of three during the four days)	"Child Development"—Barbel Inhelder, Coworker of Jean Piaget, Geneva, Switzerland "Learning Chemistry with Chemical Lasers"—George C. Pimentel, National Science Foundation, Washington, D.C.
Concurrent Sessions (Approximately 220, each 1 to 1½ hours long)	"Curriculum Development for Handicapped Learners in Science" "Sociobiology—Its Theoretical Base" "The Education of Minorities in Science: Perspectives from Black Science Educators" "How and Why Should Endangered Species Be Studied in Science Classes"
Contributed Papers (Approximately 125, each 15 minutes long)	"Science and the Gifted Student: How Do We Challenge?" "A Program for Developing Creativity in Science" "An Interdisciplinary Approach to Energy Education for Science and Social Studies Teachers"
Seminars and Symposia (Approximately 50, each meeting 1½ hours for one to three days)	"Warm Blooded Dinosaurs? Why Did They Become Extinct?" "Black Holes" "Microelectronics in Science Education"
Commercial Workshops (Approximately 30, each meeting for 1½ hours)	"Bioelectricity" "Practical Approach to Teaching General Science" "Teaching Science to Problem Readers: Biology"
Film Showings (Total of 3 sessions)	"Meteor" (Special Showing) "A Festival of Distinguished Award Winning Films"
Breakfasts, Luncheons, and Banquets (Total of 6)	NSTA Annual Banquet (Speaker: Vance Packard, author of *The Hidden Persuaders* and *The People Shapers*) AETS/NSSA Luncheon (Speaker: J. Michael Lane, Director of Smallpox Eradication, National Center for Disease Control)
Tours (Total of 35, ranging from 2 hours to 1½ days in length)	North Side High Science Department and Planetarium (Atlanta) Lockheed Aircraft Company (Marietta) Skidway Marine Extension Center (Savannah)
Exhibits	Approximately 130 exhibits of books, audiovisual materials, science equipment and furniture, and materials available from private and governmental organizations Curriculum Materials Center (display of locally developed curriculum guides and materials)
Awards Presented	Robert H. Careton Award and NSTA Distinguished Service Citations Ohaus-NSTA Awards for Innovations in Elementary and Secondary School Science Teaching
Committee Meetings (Approximately 30)	NSTA Board of Directors Science for the Handicapped Association
Social Events	Coffee Hour sponsored by universities and other groups Receptions sponsored by commercial group Mixers each night sponsored by NSTA

FIGURE 12.7 Examples from the Program of the 27th Annual Convention of the National Science Teachers Association (Atlanta, Georgia, March 23-26, 1979).

In addition to travel, science can be an integral part of many other types of leisure activities. Reading affords the opportunity to become more familiar both with the work of the pioneers in science and with recent advances. Hobbies such as collecting rocks, gems, or shells, nature photography, and model-building all have a scientific dimension. The science teacher can also see examples of science while cooking, boating, and working in the garden. In fact, science permeates almost every phase of the master science teacher's life, and his or her teaching is enriched as a result.

ASKING STUDENTS FOR FEEDBACK

An important way a teacher can grow professionally is through a systematic gathering of information on how he or she is perceived by students. In an extensive search for what makes teachers credible, Lapan[5] discovered that five areas of teacher behavior were the most significant determinants as far as students were concerned.

The single strongest determinant was *teacher openness.* Teachers who rated high on this scale were those who encouraged comments on how the class could be improved and were open to criticism. The second strongest credibility area was that of teacher qualification—student perceptions of *teacher knowledge and expertise* within their subject area. The other three important areas were teacher *communication effectiveness,* teacher ability to *define expectations* clearly for students, and *teacher objectivity*—the ability to treat students fairly and with an even hand.

Lapan has developed a form called the Teacher Credibility Questionnaire. This questionnaire is appropriate for use with all secondary school students (see pages 512–515).

In Perspective

All of the professional activities described thus far—pre-service and in-service programs, graduate work, membership and participation in professional organizations, science-related jobs, travel, and leisure-time activities—can contribute to a person becoming a master teacher of science. But no one of these is more important than the opportunities for professional development that are present daily in every science classroom.

Each lesson presents many opportunities to operate in the ways of the scientist. Do you observe carefully student behavior and the results obtained from using a particular teaching approach? Are you willing to experiment with new strategies and materials? Do you incorporate recent

---

[5]Stephen D. Lapan, "The Development and Validation of an Instrument That Measures Student Perceptions of Teacher Credibility." Unpublished Doctoral Dissertation, University of Connecticut, 1972; paper presented at The American Educational Research Association Convention, San Francisco, April 1976.

advances and current events in your teaching? These are but a few of the many things that can be done in the spirit of science to make each lesson a learning experience for the teacher as well as for the students.

Interaction with students who are working independently on research projects has many benefits for the teacher. In addition to learning about lasers, cloning, "wonder water," and other topics in science, the teacher in these situations can better grasp the nature and level of student interests, attitudes, and values. Understanding students and knowing how to work with them effectively is an important part of science teaching.

Advances in science are built on the contributions made by many generations of earlier scientists. The teaching of science also has this cumulative quality. Each of us who teachers science is partially a product of many science teachers with whom we have studied or in whose classrooms we served as student aides or student teachers. It can be argued that each of us, because of our debts, has a professional obligation to help those who aspire to be science teachers or beginning teachers in need of assistance. Such an argument, however, is shortsighted and overlooks the opportunities for professional development associated with serving as a cooperating teacher or as a "big brother" or "big sister" to a beginning teacher.

Science teaching, like any demanding profession, takes a lot out of a person. This is largely because of the need to give of one's self—to put the needs of others before those of your own. To do so continuously means we need sources of renewal. The professional development activities described in this chapter are one such source, and none is more important than operating in the classroom in consistent ways with the nature of science. A willingness to experiment is a prescription for eternal youth— the hallmark of the master teacher of science.

Review Questions

1. Briefly describe the general education, teaching specialty, and professional education components of a typical undergraduate program for the preparation of science teachers for secondary schools. Include in your description the major reasons for including each component in a teacher education program.

2. List ways, in addition to taking courses, that prospective science teachers can develop academic and professional competencies.

3. Summarize the major reasons why student teachers may make errors such as those listed in Figure 12.3.

4. What are some of the ways that a profession such as teaching differs from an occupation or a job?

5. What must be done to obtain a teaching certificate?

6. Name several approaches that can be used to obtain a teaching position.

7. Give as many examples as possible of the in-service opportunities that exist in most parts of the country for science teachers. What other ways exist for science teachers to continue their professional development?

For Application and Analysis

Readers of this chapter may wish to administer the Teacher Credibility Questionnaire to students with whom they are or will be working. The following directions are supplied by the author of the questionnaire. In the final section the author presents data that have come from actual use of the questionnaire that can be used for comparative purposes.

These directions are intended as a guide for giving the Teacher Credibility Questionnaire. Once you have mastered the basic principles and necessary direction steps there is no need for you to quote from it verbatim.

Introduction. It is recommended that someone other than you administer the Teacher Credibility Questionnaire (TCQ) to your class. In this way your students are assured of a higher degree of anonymity, which is of the utmost importance in using such a student feedback tool.

If you cannot find anyone to administer the TCQ, then select a student to do it for you. *In any case, under no circumstances should you, the teacher, be in the room while the students are completing the instrument.*

1. Make sure the teacher has left the room. If necessary, let him or her select a student to retrieve him or her after everything is completed.

2. Say to the students, "I'm going to hand out a questionnaire for you to fill out. It gives you a chance to react to how you feel about your teacher for this class. (Teacher's name) wants this information so that he (or she) can improve the way he (or she) teaches. So—be honest in your reactions. This is not a test, so it is your personal opinion that counts. Don't put your name on the questionnaire or on the answer sheet. This way, no one will know who answered the questions in what way.

3. Hand out the TCQ questionnaires, telling the students once again not to put their names on them. Also tell them not to write on the forms at all.

4. Read the directions printed on the questionnaire.

5. Hand out the answer sheets. Say to the students: "You don't mark on the questionnaire because we want to use them over. Instead, you answer each question by circling the number you have chosen on the answer sheet. Please

---

*The teacher interested in getting feedback on credibility with kindergarten to fifth-grade youngsters is encouraged to modify the questionnaire, using a simpler format, fewer questions, and words that are more at the level of these students.

make sure that you circle only one number for each question. If you circle more than one, your answer cannot be counted."

6. Hold up the sheet and show them how you might answer the first question on the questionnaire.

7. Students may begin. Tell them it should take them only about ten to fifteen minutes to finish.

8. Have one student collect all of the answer sheets and another collect all the questionnaires when everyone has finished.

9. After stacking the answer sheets in a pile with a paper clip holding them together, label the stack with the teacher's name, and the identity of the class that completed the TCQ.

10. Ask one of the students to inform the teacher that she or he may return to the room.

Note: You may answer procedural questions for the students, but do not interpret statements or suggest answers for them. Encourage them to answer each question.

The Teacher Credibility Questionnaire

This *Teacher Credibility Questionnaire* (TCQ)* was developed for use by the classroom teacher in order that he or she might gather information regarding his or her credibility as a teacher. It is *not* intended to be used as an evaluation tool by supervisors or administrators, nor should it be. Collecting feedback for self-improvement should be the sole purpose in utilizing the TCQ.

*Formerly called the Source Credibility Measure, Lapan, Copyright, 1973.

THE TEACHER CREDIBILITY QUESTIONNAIRE

Read Each Statement Below

On the sheet provided circle the number that best describes your teacher for each of these statements. Be sure to answer every statement. Also, be sure not to circle more than one answer for each statement.

Begin each statement with: The teacher for this class . . .	Almost never true	Seldom true	True about ½ the time	True most of the time	Almost always true
1. . . .listens to criticisms about the class.	1	2	3	4	5
2. . . .lets you know how well you are doing in the class.	1	2	3	4	5
3. . . .is skilled in the subject of the class.	1	2	3	4	5
4. . . .makes presentations that are not generally understood.	1	2	3	4	5

THE TEACHER CREDIBILITY QUESTIONNAIRE (*Continued*)

Begin each statement with: The teacher for this class...	Almost never true	Seldom true	True about ½ the time	True most of the time	Almost always true
5. ...makes sure that everyone understands the material before going on.	1	2	3	4	5
6. ...gives good grades only to students he or she likes.	1	2	3	4	5
7. ...knows his or her stuff.	1	2	3	4	5
8. ...encourages your comments on how the class could be improved.	1	2	3	4	5
9. ...doesn't give reasons for why the class is run the way it is.	1	2	3	4	5
10. ...doesn't let you know how you are doing until grades come out.	1	2	3	4	5
11. ...is well trained in the subject area of the class.	1	2	3	4	5
12. ...makes material difficult to understand because it is not well organized.	1	2	3	4	5
13. ...gives you good grades if you do good work.	1	2	3	4	5
14. ...wants to know what your opinions are.	1	2	3	4	5
15. ...knows little about the information taught in class.	1	2	3	4	5
16. ...makes material easy to understand.	1	2	3	4	5
17. ...grades class members according to grades they have received in the past.	1	2	3	4	5
18. ...is not experienced with the subject of the class.	1	2	3	4	5
19. ...encourages you to tell how the class is going.	1	2	3	4	5
20. ...grades class members according to how popular they are.	1	2	3	4	5
21. ...cannot take criticism from others.	1	2	3	4	5
22. ...is knowledgeable in the subject area he or she teaches.	1	2	3	4	5
23. ...listens to what you have to say.	1	2	3	4	5
24. ...presents material in a way that makes it hard to understand.	1	2	3	4	5
25. ...is fair in giving grades.	1	2	3	4	5
26. ...does not like you to explain what is going wrong with the way the class is taught.	1	2	3	4	5
27. ...tells you how well you are doing in class.	1	2	3	4	5
28. ...considers what students say with an open mind.	1	2	3	4	5
29. ...is not an expert in the subject that is being taught.	1	2	3	4	5

Sample Answer Sheet

Please do not put your name on this sheet. Be sure to circle only one number for each statement.

	Almost Never True	Seldom True	True About ½ the Time	True Most of the Time	Almost Always True		Almost Never True	Seldom True	True About ½ the Time	True Most of the Time	Almost Always True
1.	1	2	3	4	5	16.	1	2	3	4	5
2.	1	2	3	4	5	17.	1	2	3	4	5
3.	1	2	3	4	5	18.	1	2	3	4	5
4.	1	2	3	4	5	19.	1	2	3	4	5
5.	1	2	3	4	5	20.	1	2	3	4	5
6.	1	2	3	4	5	21.	1	2	3	4	5
7.	1	2	3	4	5	22.	1	2	3	4	5
8.	1	2	3	4	5	23.	1	2	3	4	5
9.	1	2	3	4	5	24.	1	2	3	4	5
10.	1	2	3	4	5	25.	1	2	3	4	5
11.	1	2	3	4	5	26.	1	2	3	4	5
12.	1	2	3	4	5	27.	1	2	3	4	5
13.	1	2	3	4	5	28.	1	2	3	4	5
14.	1	2	3	4	5	29.	1	2	3	4	5
15.	1	2	3	4	5						

What Your Results Mean

After you have obtained completed questionnaires from your students you may either calculate an average score on each item (adding up all of your ones through fives then dividing by the number of students) or you may choose to put together the average scores for all items that represent each credibility dimension to see how you rate on areas like openness or qualification. If you select the second approach you will be able to see what specific areas you need to work on in order to improve your credibility in the eyes of the students. In so doing, you might consider fours or fives good for positively stated items and ones or twos good for negatively stated ones.

Another way to judge how well you did on each item is to compare your score with the scores of sixty-eight teachers whose students (1,477 of them) filled out Teacher Credibility Questionnaires on them (see page 516).

A third way to decide how well you did according to each item on the Teacher Credibility Questionnaire is to sit down before the students complete it and mark how you want to score on each of the items. In this way you can compare your student averages with how you wanted to do and decide where improvements are needed.

In any event, be sure to discuss the questionnaire findings with your students to get ideas from them on how you can improve or change the way you do things in the class. This also lets the students know that you change from month to month as well as from class to class. If you get some fairly good

Average Scores for Sixty-eight Teachers

Item #	Score	Item #	Score	Item #	Score
1.	3.38	11.	4.43	21.	2.31
2.	3.40	12.	1.99	22.	4.46
3.	4.45	13.	4.35	23.	3.93
4.	2.34	14.	3.46	24.	2.25
5.	3.65	15.	1.54	25.	3.95
6.	1.76	16.	3.46	26.	2.49
7.	4.36	17.	1.89	27.	3.30
8.	2.98	18.	1.56	28.	3.65
9.	2.68	19.	2.57	29.	1.88
10.	2.54	20.	1.52		

scores from one class at one time, don't get smug or overconfident, but do find out how you did it and work on keeping your credibility at that level.[6]

References

Carleton, Robert H. *The NSTA Story: A History of Ideas, Commitments and Actions, 1944–1974.* Washington, D.C.: National Science Teachers Association, 1976.

This is an interesting account of the activities of a major professional organization for science teachers during a thirty-year period.

Combs, Arthur W. *Myths in Education: Beliefs That Hinder Progress and Their Alternatives.* Boston: Allyn and Bacon, Inc., 1979.

This provocative book explores false beliefs that cripple growth at all levels of educational practice. Recommended for those with some experience in education.

House, Ernest R., and Stephen D. Lapan. *Survival in the Classroom: Negotiating with Kids, Colleagues, and Bosses.* Boston: Allyn and Bacon, Inc., 1978.

This is an excellent treatment of "real world" problems associated with being a teacher. The authors, who are experienced teachers themselves, portray most candidly day-to-day situations faced by teachers and offer interesting suggestions for coping with students, principals, parents, and other members of the school community. Particularly appropriate for teachers who have already gained some teaching experience.

---

[6]From Ernest R. House and Stephen D. Lapan, *Survival in The Classroom: Negotiating with Kids, Colleagues, and Bosses.* Copyright © 1978 by Allyn & Bacon, Inc., Boston. Reprinted with permission.

Richardson, John S., Stanley E. Williamson, and Donald W. Stotler. *The Education of Science Teachers.* •Columbus, Ohio: Charles E. Merrill Publishing Company, 1968.

This book describes the various components of undergraduate and graduate teacher education programs and relates to the larger concerns of elementary and secondary education and society in general.

Stewart, Jesse. *To Teach, To Love.* Baltimore, Md.: Penguin Books, 1973.

This touching book, first published in 1936, describes what teaching means to the famous American teacher and writer, Jesse Stuart.

APPENDIX A

Professional
Bibliography
for Secondary
School Science

**General
Professional
Books for Science
Teachers**

Anderson, Hans O. *Readings in Science Education for the Secondary School.* New York: The Macmillan Company, 1969.

Anderson, Hans O., and Paul G. Koutnik. *Toward More Effective Science Instruction in Science Education.* New York: The Macmillan Company, 1972.

Aylesworth, Thomas G. *Planning for Effective Science Teaching.* Middletown, Conn.: Wesleyan University, 1963.

Barnard, J. Darrell (Ed.). *Ideas for Teaching Science in the Junior High School.* Washington, D.C.: National Science Teachers Association, 1963.

Butts, David P. (Ed.). *Designs for Progress in Science Education.* Washington, D.C.: National Science Teachers Association, 1969.

Bybee, Rodger W. *Personalizing Science Teaching.* Washington, D.C.: National Science Teachers Association, 1974.

Carin, Arthur, and Robert B. Sund. *Teaching Science Through Discovery.* Columbus, Ohio: Charles E. Merrill Publishing Company, 1970.

Coble, Charles R., Paul B. Hounshell, and Anne H. Adams. *Mainstreaming Science and Mathematics: Special Ideas and Activities for the Whole Class.* Santa Monica. Calif.: Goodyear Publishing Company, Inc., 1977.

Collette, Alfred T. *Science Teaching in the Secondary School.* Boston: Allyn and Bacon, Inc., 1973.

Educational Policies Commission. *The Spirit of Science.* Washington, D.C.: National Education Association, 1966.

Falk, Doris, *Biology Teaching Methods.* New York: John Wiley and Sons, Inc., 1971.

Farmer, Walter, A., and Margaret A. Farrell. *Systematic Instruction in Science for the Middle and High School Years.* Reading, Mass.: Addison-Wesley Publishing Company, 1980.

Hedges, William D. *Testing and Evaluation in the Sciences for the Secondary Schools.* Belmont, Calif.: Wadsworth Publishing Company, Inc., 1966.

Hoffman, Helen Marie, and Kenneth S. Ricker. *Sourcebook: Science Education for the Physically Handicapped.* Washington, D.C.: National Science Teachers Association, 1979.

Hurd, Paul De Hart. *New Curriculum Perspectives for Junior High School Science.* Belmont, Calif.: Wadsworth Publishing Company, Inc., 1970.

Hurd, Paul De Hart. *New Directions in Secondary School Science Teaching.* Chicago: Rand McNally & Company, 1969.

Kahle, Jane Butler, *Teaching Science in the Secondary School.* New York: D. Van Nostrand Company, 1979.

Lee, Eugene C. *New Developments in Science Teaching.* Belmont, Calif.: Wadsworth Publishing Company, Inc., 1967.

Mayer, William V. (Ed.). *The Biology Teachers' Handbook.* Third Edition. New York: John Wiley and Sons, 1978.

National Society for the Study of Education. *Rethinking Science Education.* Fifty-ninth Yearbook, Part 1, Chicago: University of Chicago Press, 1960.

Nedelsky, Leo. *Science Teaching and Testing.* New York: Harcourt, Brace and World, Inc. 1965.

Nelson, Clarence H. *Improving Objectives Tests in Science.* Washington, D.C.: National Science Teachers Association, 1967.

Novak, Joseph D. *Facilities for Secondary School Science Teaching.* Washington, D.C.: National Science Teachers Association, 1972.

Novak, Joseph D. *The Improvement of Biology Teaching.* Indianapolis, Inc.: The Bobbs-Merrill Company, Inc., 1970.

Oxenhorn, Joseph M. *Teaching Science to Underachievers in Secondary Schools.* New York: Globe Book Company, Inc., 1972.

Renner, John W., and Don G. Stafford. *Teaching Science in the Secondary School.* New York: Harper and Row, Publishers, Inc., 1972.

Romey, William D. *Inquiry Techniques for Teaching Science.* Englewood Cliffs, N.J.: Prentice-Hall, Inc., 1968.

Sund, Robert B., and Leslie W. Trowbridge. *Teaching Science by Inquiry in the Secondary School.* Columbus, Ohio: Charles E. Merrill Publishing Company, 1967.

Triezenberg, Henry J. (Ed.). *Individualized Science—Like It Is.* Washington, D.C.: National Science Teachers Association, 1972.

Voss, Burton E., and Stanley B. Brown. *Biology As Inquiry.* St. Louis: C. V. Mosby Company, 1968.

Washton, Nathan S. *Teaching Science Creatively in the Secondary Schools.* Philadelphia: W. B. Saunders Company, 1967.

Woodburn, John H., and E. S. Obourn. *Teaching the Pursuit of Science.* New York: The Macmillan Company, 1965.

Resource Books for Science Teachers

Bartholomew, Rolland B., and Frank E. Crawley. *Science Laboratory Techniques: A Handbook for Teachers and Students.* Menlo Park, Calif.: Addison-Wesley Publishing Company, 1980.

Council of Chief State School Officers. *Purchase Guide for Programs in Science, Mathematics.* New York: Ginn and Company, 1965.

Earth Science Curriculum Pamphlet Series. New York: Houghton Mifflin Company, 1971.

  Color of Minerals, by George Rapp, Jr.
  Field Guide to Astronomy Without a Telescope, by William A. Dexter
  Field Guide to Beaches, by John H. Hoyt
  Field Guide to Fossils, by James R. Beerbower
  Field Guide to Lakes, by Jacob Verduin
  Field Guide to Layered Rocks, by Tom Freeman
  Field Guide to Plutonic and Metamorphic Rocks, by William D. Romey
  Field Guide to Rock Weathering, by Robert E. Boyer
  Field Guide to Soils, by Henry Foth and Hyde S. Jacobs
  Meteorites, by Carleton B. Moore

Exline, Joseph D. *Individualized Techniques for Teaching Earth Science.* West Nyack, N.Y.: Parker Publishing Company, Inc., 1975.

Fowler, John M. *Energy-Environment Source Book.* Washington, D.C.: National Science Teachers Association, 1978.

Heller, Robert L. (Ed.). *Geology and Earth Sciences Source Book for Elementary and Secondary Schools.* New York: Holt, Rinehart & Winston, Inc., 1962.

Hittle, David R., Frank D. Stekel, Shirley L. Stekel, and Hans O. Anderson. *Soucrcebook for Chemistry and Physics.* New York: The Macmillan Company, 1972.

Joseph, Alexander, and others. *Teaching High School Science: A Source Book for the Physical Sciences.* New York: Harcourt Brace Jovanovich, Inc., 1961.

Miller, David F., and Glen W. Blaydes. *Methods and Materials for Teaching the Biological Sciences.* Second Edition. New York: McGraw-Hill Book Company, 1962.

Morholt, Evelyn, Paul F. Brandwein, and Alexander Joseph. *A Sourcebook for the Biological Sciences.* Second Edition. New York: Harcourt, Brace and World, Inc., 1966.

Neuberger, Hans, and George Nicholas. *Manual of Lecture Demonstrations, Laboratory Experiments, and Observational Equipment for Teaching Elementary Meteorology in Schools and Colleges.* University Park, Penn., College of Mineral Industries, The Pennsylvania State University, 1962.

NSTA How To Series. Washington, D.C.: National Science Teachers Association.

  Ask the Right Questions
  Care for Living Things
  Handle Radioisotopes
  How to Activities in Meteorology
  How to Activities in Physical Oceanography
  Plan . . . Minicourses
  Present Multi-Imagery
  Record and Use Data
  Teach Map & Compass
  Teach Measurements
  Tell What's Underground
  Use an Oscilloscope
  Use Chromatography

Qutub, Musa Y. *Secondary Evnironmental Science Methods.* Columbus, Ohio: Charles E. Merrill Publishing Company, 1973.

Richardson, John S., and G. P. Cahoon. *Methods and Materials for Teaching General and Physical Science.* New York: McGraw-Hill, Inc., 1951.

Saterstrom, Mary H. (Ed.). *Educators Guide to Free Science Materials.* Randolph, Wis.: Educators Progress Service (yearly).

Troost, Cornelius J., and Harold Altman. *Environmental Education: A Sourcebook.* New York: John Wiley and Sons, Inc., 1972.

Troyer, Donald L., Maurice G. Kellogg, and Hans O. Anderson. *Sourcebook for Biological Sciences.* New York: The Macmillan Company, 1972.

UNESCO. *700 Science Experiments for Everyone.* Garden City, N.Y.: Doubleday & Company, Inc., 1958.

Utgard, Russell, George Ladd, and Hans O. Andersen. *Source Book of Earth Science and Astronomy.* New York: The Macmillan Company, 1972.

Vivian, V. Eugene. *Sourcebook for Environmental Education.* St. Louis: C. V. Mosby Company, 1973.

APPENDIX

B

Professional
Organizations
and Journals
for Science
Teachers

Listed below are the national organizations of most interest to secondary school science teachers. Many states and local areas also have organizations; names and addresses of these local groups can usually be obtained from the science supervisor in the state's educational agency.

AAAS   American Association for the Advancement of Science
1515 Massachusetts Avenue, N.W.
Washington, D.C.   20005
Publications: *Science*
            Science Books and Films
            Science Education News
            Science 80

AAPT   American Association of Physics Teachers
% American Institute of Physics
335 East 45th Street
New York, New York   10017
Journal: *The Physics Teacher*

ACS   American Chemical Society
1115 Sixteen Street, N.W.
Washington, D.C.   20036
Publications: *Chemical and Engineering News*
            Journal of Chemical Education

AETS   Association For the Education of Teachers of Science
(primarily for those involved in the education of teachers)
Dr. William R. Brown
AETS Executive Secretary
Dept. of Curriculum and Instruction
Old Dominion University
Norfolk, Virginia   23508
Journal: *Science Education*

NABT   National Association of Biology Teachers
11250 Roger Bacon Drive
Reston, Virginia   22090
Journal: *The American Biology Teacher*

NARST   National Association for Research in Science Teaching
206 Memorial Hall
Drake University
Des Moines, Iowa   50311
Journal: *Journal of Research in Science Teaching*

NAGT   National Association of Geology Teachers
(also for secondary school earth science teachers)
P.O. Box 368
Lawrence, Kansas   66044
Journal: *Journal of Geological Education*

NSTA   National Science Teachers Association
1742 Connecticut Ave., N.W.
Washington, D.C.   20009

Journals: *Journal of College Science Teaching*
The Science Teacher
Science and Children

SSMA   School Science and Mathematics Association
P.O. Box 1614
Indiana University of Pennsylvania
Indiana, Pennsylvania   15704

Journal: *School Science and Mathematics*

APPENDIX C

Periodicals for
Science Teachers
and Students

Chemistry. American Chemical Society, 1155 16th Street, N.W., Washington, D.C. 20036.

Creative Computing. Creative Computing, Box 789–M, Morristown, New Jersey 07960.

Current Science. Xerox Education Publications, 1250 Fairwood Avenue, Columbus, Ohio 43216.

Gems and Minerals. P.O. Box 687, 1797 Capri Avenue, Metone, California 92359.

General Science and Biology Digest. Free upon request from Sargent-Welch Scientific Company, 7300 North Linder Avenue, Skokie, Illinois 60076.

Modern Photography. ABC Leisure Magazines, 130 East 59th Street, New York, New York 10022.

National Geographic Magazine. National Geographic Society, 1146 Sixteenth Street, N.W., Washington, D.C. 20036.

Natural History. American Museum of Natural History, Central Park West at 79th Street, New York, New York 10024.

Physics Today. American Institute of Physics, 335 East 45th Street, New York, New York 10017.

Popular Electronics. Ziff-Davis Publishing Company, One Park Avenue, New York, New York 10016.

Popular Photography. Ziff-Davis Publications, One Park Avenue, New York, New York 10016.

Popular Science. Times Mirror Magazine, Inc., 380 Madison Avenue, New York, New York 10017.

Psychology Today, Psychology Today Magazine, One Park Avenue, New York, New York 10016.

Science Digest. Science Digest, 224 West 57th Street, New York 10019.

Science News. Science Service, Inc., 1719 N Street, N.W., Washington, D.C. 20036.

Science World. Scholastic Magazine, Inc., 50 West 44th Street, New York, New York 10036.

Scientific American. Scientific American, Inc., 415 Madison Avenue, New York, New York 10017.

Turtox News. Free upon request from General Biological Supply House, Inc., 8200 South Hoyne Avenue, Chicago, Illinois 60620.

Ward's Bulletin. Free from Ward's Natural Science Establishment, Inc., P.O. Box 1712, Rochester, New York 14603.

Sky and Telescope. Sky Publishing Corporation, 49 Bay State Road, Cambridge, Massachusetts 02138.

Smithsonian. Smithsonian Institution, 900 Jefferson Drive, Washington, D.C. 20560.

Weatherwise. American Meteorological Society, 45 Beacon Street, Boston, Massachusetts 02108.

APPENDIX

D

Major Publishers of Secondary School Science Textbooks

Addison Wesley Publishing Company
2725 Sand Hill Road
Menlo Park, California   94025

Allyn and Bacon, Inc.
Pond Road
Rockleigh, New Jersey   07647

Cambridge Book Company
488 Madison Avenue
New York, New York   10022

Cebco Standard Publishing
9 Kulick Road
Fairfield, New Jersey   07006

Ginn and Company
191 Spring Street
Lexington, Maine   02173

Globe Book Company, Inc.
50 West 23rd Street
New York, New York   10010

Harcourt Brace Jovanovich
757 Third Avenue
New York, New York   10017

Harper & Row
10 East 53rd Street
New York, New York   10022

D. C. Heath and Company
122 Spring Street
Lexington, Maine   02173

Holt, Rinehart & Winston
383 Madison Avenue
New York, New York   10017

Houghton Mifflin Company
1 Beacon Street
Boston, Maine   02107

Laidlaw Brothers, A Division of
    Doubleday & Company, Inc.
Thatcher and Madison
River Forest, Illinois   60305

J. B. Lippincott Company/Harper &
Row
10 East 53rd Street
New York, New York   10022

Macmillan Science Co.
8200 South Hoyne Avenue
Chicago, Illinois   60620

McGraw-Hill, Inc.
1221 Avenue of the Americas
New York, New York   10020

Charles E. Merrill Publishing Company
1300 Alum Creek Drive
Columbus, Ohio   43216

Prentice-Hall, Inc.
P.O. Box 900
Englewood   Cliffs.   New   Jersey   07632

Rand McNally & Company
Box 7600
Chicago, Illinois   60680

Silver Burdett Company
250 James Street
Morristown, New Jersey   07960

John Wiley and Sons, Inc.
605 Third Avenue
New York, New York   10016

APPENDIX

E

Directory
of Companies
Selling Scientific
Equipment

(For a more comprehensive list of companies, see the *Guide to Scientific Instruments* published annually by the American Association for the Advancement of Science.)

Ace Scientific Supply Company, Inc.
1420 East Linden Avenue
Linden, New Jersey   07036

Allied Chemical Corporation
42 Rector Street
New York, New York   10006

American Optical Corporation
Eggert and Sugar Roads
Buffalo, New York   14215

American Type-Culture Collection
12301 Parklawn Drive
Rockville, Maryland   20852

Bausch & Lomb Inc.
1400 North Goodman Street
Rochester, New York   14602

Bel-Arts Products
Industrial Road
Pequannock, New Jersey   07440

Bioscope Manufacturing Company
P.O. Box 1492
Tulsa, Oklahoma   74101

Broadhead-Garrett Company
4560 East 71 Street
Cleveland, Ohio   44105

Carolina Biological Supply Company
2700 York Road
Burlington, North Carolina   27215

Celestron Pacific
2835 Columbia Street
Torrance, California   90593

Central Scientific Company
2600 South Kostner Avenue
Chicago, Illinois   60623

Charles Beseler Company
11th Avenue South 18th Street
East Orange, New Jersey   07018

Clay-Adams, Inc.
299 Weboro Road
Parsippany, New Jersey   07054

Colorado Geological Industries, Inc.
1244 East Colfax Avenue
Denver, Colorado   80218

Connecticut Valley Biological Supply Company, Inc.
Valley Road
Southhampton, Massachusetts   01073

Corning Glass Works
80 Houghton Park
Corning, New York   14830

Criterion Manufacturing Company
620 Oakwood Avenue
West Hartford, Connecticut   06110

Damon Corporation
80 Wilson Way
Westwood, Massachusetts   02090

Dayno Sales Company
678 Washington Street
Lynn, Massachusetts   01901

Denoyer-Geppert Company
5235 Ravenwood Avenue
Chicago, Illinois   60640

Difco Laboratories, Inc.
P.O. Box 1058A
Detroit, Michigan   48232

Dow Chemical Corporation
P.O. Box 1592
Midland, Michigan   48640

Ealing Corporation
22 Pleasant Street
Southnatick, Massachusetts   10760

Eastman Kodak Company
343 State Street
Rochester, New York   14650

Edmund Scientific Company
101 East Gloucester Pike
Barrington, New Jersey   08033

Educational Materials and Equipment Company
46 Lafayette
New Rochelle, New York   10801

Estes Industries
P.O. Box 227
Penrose, Colorado   81240

Farguhar Transparent Globes
5007 Warrington Avenue
Philadelphia, Pennsylvania   19143

Fisher Scientific Company
4901 West Lemoyne
Chicago, Illinois   60651

Hampden Engineering Corporation
99 Shaker Road
East Longmeadow, Massachusetts   01028

Harshaw Scientific Division
Harshaw Chemical Company
6801 Cochran Road
Solon, Ohio   44139

Harvard Apparatus Company, Inc.
150 Dover Road
Millis, Massachusetts   02054

Heath Company
Benton Harbor, Michigan   49022

Hubbard Scientific Company
1946 Raymond Drive
Northbrook, Illinois   60062

Jewel Aquarium Company
5005 West Armitage Avenue
Chicago, Illinois   60639

Ken-A-Vision Manufacturing Company, Inc.
5615 Raytown Road
Raytown, Maryland   64133

Kewaunee Scientific Equipment Corporation
P.O. Box 648
Adrian, Michigan   49221

Kimble Products Division, Owens-Illinois Inc.
P.O. Box 1035
Toledo, Ohio   43666

Lab Safety Supply Company
P.O. Box 1368
Janeville, Wisconsin   53545

La Motte Chemical Products Corporation
P.O. Box 329
Chestertown, Maryland   28620

E. Leitz, Inc.
Link Drive
Rockleigh, New Jersey   07647

Merck & Company, Inc.
1935 Lincoln Avenue
Rahway, New Jersey   07065

Monsanto Chemical Corporation
800 North Lindbergh Road
St. Louis, Missouri   63166

Nalgene Labware Division
Nalge/Sybron Corporation
75 Panorama Creek Drive
Rochester, New York   14602

NASCO Company
901 Janesville Avenue
Fort Atkinson, Wisconsin   53538

A. J. Nystrom & Company
3333 North Elston Avenue
Chicago, Illinois   60618

Ohaus Scale Corporation
29 Hanover Road
Florham Park, New Jersey   07932

PARCO Scientific Corporation
P.O. Box 595
Vienna, Ohio   4473

PASCO Scientific
1933 Republic Avenue
San Leandro, California   94577

Reagents, Inc.
P.O. Box 270746
Charlotte, North Carolina   28210

Sargent-Welch Scientific Company
7300 North Linder Avenue
Skokie, Illinois   60076

Science Related Materials
P.O. Box 1368
Janeville, Wisconsin   53545

Swift Instruments, Inc.
P.O. Box 95106
San Jose, California   95106

Taylor Instrument Company
Consumer Products Division
Glen Bridge Road
Arden, North Carolina   28704

Turtox/Cambosco-McMillian Science Company
8200 South Hayne Avenue
Chicago, Illinois   60620

Unitron Instrument, Inc.
101 Crossways Park West
Woodbury, New York   11797

Ward's Natural Science Establishment, Inc.
3000 Ridge Road East
Rochester, New York   14622

Wilkens-Andersen Corporation
4225 West Division Street
Chicago, Illinois   60651

PHOTO CREDITS

INDEX